Dr. Gaye Johnston

What the New Labour Heresy Did to a Democratic Socialist Party and
how that impacts on Corbyn's Labour Party today

This book is dedicated to Terry Johnston
With thanks for all his tolerance and support whilst it was being written

About Gaye Johnston

Dr. Gaye Johnston has been passionate about democratic socialist politics all her adult life. She has been actively involved in the Labour Party since student days.

Gaye was selected as a Parliamentary candidate in marginal constituencies three times during the 1970s and 80s. She was re-selected unopposed in the Cleveland and Whitby /Langbaurgh constituency. She also stood in Swindon in 1987.

She is a former Darlington Labour Councillor, Vice-Chair of Housing Committee and Labour Group Secretary. Gaye has numerous contacts in the Labour Party and movement. These were built up over many years and helped her to secure valuable information and interviews for this book.

Gaye has campaigned for Labour over a long period. She has also has been a volunteer: active in Party administration and policy making. She has attended numerous Party conferences: local and national. Her special interest is political education. Until recently she was Political Education Officer for her constituency Labour Party. Her partner worked for ten years as a full time Labour Party and MP's organiser. This gave her numerous additional opportunities to learning more about Parliamentary politics and Labour Party organisation.

She has twice spoken on platforms alongside then Prime Minister Harold Wilson. Gaye made speeches at meetings in tandem with other eminent Labour politicians including: Barbara Castle, Tony Benn, Tam Dalyell and Michael Meacher. Late Tory Home Secretary Leon Brittan described Gaye as "the most capable Parliamentary opponent I have ever faced". Gaye is a member of the Executive of the Campaign for Labour Party Democracy and was its national Chair in 2009·10 and 2014·15 and currently.

Gaye holds a Ph.D in politics/public services policy development and a research MA in social policy. She taught political subjects (including social policy and NHS policy and management) at the University of Cumbria. Previously Gaye worked as Head of Department in a College of Further Education and a Principal Officer in several local authority social services departments.

Publications: In 2005 Gaye wrote a pamphlet published by Save the Labour Party entitled *Can the Labour Party survive without the Party on the Ground?* This was favourably reviewed in *Tribune* by Kevin Maguire. Since then she has had numerous letters published in the *Guardian*. One of these appeared in the book *Letters to the Editor 2008* Gaye also contributes regularly to the political Journals *Chartist* and (the original) *Labour Briefing*. In addition she occasionally writes on the blog *Left Futures*.

ACKNOWLEDGEMENTS

Many people have contributed to this book. Their assistance has been provided mainly through interviews (and a few questionnaires) given to the stakeholders whose opinions were sought. However others have given a great deal of helpful advice and information. The book's originality lies in the quality and quantity of direct personal testimony given to the author directly by these interviewees. In addition to the interview material; these notes refer mainly to publicly available sources. These comprise of books, articles in journals, newspapers, speeches and broadcasts. Numerous references present and discuss opinion polls.

In addition to the above, the author has received advice and support from the following friends and former colleagues: Francis Beckett, Ann Black, Colette Booth, Professor Martin Bulmer, Roy Chetham, Tom Davidson, Barrister, Peter G. Kenyon, the late Michael McIlroy, Dr. John Pottinger, Anne-Marie Simpson, Professor Robin Talbot, Kevin Thorne and Peter Willsman. A special debt of gratitude is owed to the late Michael Meacher MP. Michael gave me enormous support and encouragement and plentiful advice on the writing of the book. He was able to read the late draft and very kindly wrote the Foreword shortly before his sad passing.

Thanks are also due to Liam Usher who did the layout for the book and to Alan Slingsby and colleagues who did the production.

Gaye Johnston
October 2016

Contents

FOREWORD
By The Late Rt. Hon. Michael Meacher MP — 6

INTRODUCTION
The Aims, Content and Context of this Book — 8

CHAPTER 1:
What should the Labour Party be for? — 16

CHAPTER 2
What was New Labour? — 41

CHAPTER 3
Winning and loosing elections under traditional ('Old') Labour and New labour — 74

CHAPTER 4
New Labour and the Trades Unions — 108

CHAPTER 5
Evaluations of New Labour's Policy Record — 130

CHAPTER 6
Comparison of New Labour's Policy Record compared with that of earlier Labour Governments and with the Australian Labor Government's contemporary record — 184

CHAPTER 7
What New Labour did to Internal Party Democracy — 219

CHAPTER 8
'Fixing' the Parliamentary candidate selections — 255

CHAPTER 9
Downsizing Parliamentary Democracy — 281

CHAPTER 10
Old and New Labour: Records on Party and Parliamentary democracy compared — 318

CHAPTER 11
Summary, Conclusions and Labour's Ways Forward — 347

CHAPTER 12
2011 and what followed — 397

Appendix 1
List of main participants interviewed in the research for this book — 418

Appendix 2
New Labour's New Clause 4 — 425

Glossary — 426

Select Bibliography — 429

Notes to chapters — 432

Index — 457

FOREWORD
By The Late Rt. Hon. Michael Meacher MP

This is a systematic analysis of the biggest internal coup d'etat in the history of the Labour Party. It exposes in unrivalled detail the mechanisms behind the takeover as well as the impact on the structures, role and effectiveness of the party. Unlike previous accounts of the period, mainly autobiographical self-justification, this book gets behind the personalities and focuses on the real sinews of power and how they were perverted to maximise control within the leadership for its own purposes.

The fundamental underlying principles of the Labour Party have always been its democratic structures, its support for the disadvantaged, and its opposition to capital accumulation as the controlling force within the economy. Blair, aided primarily by Mandelson, overturned all these principles. All the channels of democratic decision-making were closed down or taken over, the trade unions were suppressed and inequality let rip, and every support and assistance was given to big business and the City of London financial system. The Labour Party was utterly neutered as an instrument of reform and converted into an adjunct of the prevailing neo-liberal capitalism. They called it modernisation.

This book provides an original database of how this was done. Written by an insider – Gaye Johnston was four times a Parliamentary candidate – and painstakingly assembled from interviews with eighty leading personnel drawn from across the party spectrum, it catalogues the systematic suborning of the party's procedures at every level in order to achieve a British version of command and control democratic centralism. It is a textbook analysis of how the proud tenets of democracy can be warped and usurped from the inside if the coup-makers are wily and ruthless enough.

Blair was lucky, and luck is often an essential ingredient to succeed in politics. He had wanted to stand in 1992, but was unexpectedly given his chance by the premature death of John Smith in 1994. Assiduously promoted by Mandelson, he leapfrogged Brown to the leadership. The party, desperate to win on almost any terms after four successive electoral defeats, accepted him as their best chance even though he had already shown signs of his quasi-tory leanings. Once in office, with an overall majority of 180 which gave him unprecedented power to transform the State in a manner which the Establishment initially at least could not resist, he chose instead to do the opposite – to continue unhindered the Thatcherite imperium.

He could not however have upended Labour principles and traditions so comprehensively without one essential condition. He needed an absolutely rock-solid majority within the Parliamentary party so that with that as an impregnable base he could pursue his forays on to the world stage, which is where his real interest lay, without fear of being overturned. The coup de grace delivered by the Blairite political machine against Labour's internal democracy, which provided him with the fundamental condition he required, was the rigging of the selection process for parliamentary candidates. This transformed the PLP from a body in the 1970-80s broadly class-representative of Labour's electoral base and roughly balanced between Left and Right to one where Blairite loyalists formed a dominant majority and the Left was whittled down to a pale shadow of its former self.

On this key point Gaye Johnston's book contains a wealth of hitherto unreported material of how this was achieved. The Blairite machine gathered and fostered its own panel of ultra-reliable potential candidates (often special advisers of existing MPs) and helped to train and prepare them for the day when winnable seats might become available, exactly as the Blairite "Progress" faction continues to do within the party to this very day. When such openings emerged, especially in bulk with retirements just before a general election, a preferred Blairite candidate was chosen by the machine and offered to the constituency, quite often "parachuted in" from afar. The party's regional offices had been packed with Blairite placemen/ women, and the regional officer would be told to do everything possible to make sure the preferred person was selected. This might involve lobbying the constituency chair or secretary, or letting the candidate know who were the key influential people to talk to. It usually also involved giving the candidate the list of party members several weeks, or even months, before other candidates were allowed access, thus giving the former a crucial head start in canvassing. As a last resort it has been known for the final ballot box to be tampered with.

This is a simple outline of some of the shenanigans regularly perpetrated in the Blairite era. But it does not remotely do justice to the detailed manoeuvring which Gaye Johnston documents, which is riveting and makes the book a fascinating read on this count alone.

What makes this book so important is that it is an honest, detailed, highly readable account of what went so badly wrong, and hence what safeguards need to be put in place so that it cannot happen again. Arguably the Labour Party, together with the trade unions, is the only power in Britain which can contain and defeat the forces of neo-liberal capitalism and reverse its prime instruments of deregulated finance and uncontrolled market fundamentalism. If that power is fettered, neutralised or squandered, at least half the electorate is left unprotected at the mercy of the capitalist onslaught. That is why this book is essential reading for all who want now to build the foundations of a very different hegemony that genuinely serves the national interest and all its peoples, not the oppressing few.

Michael Meacher

Sadly Michael Meacher died as this book was due to be published. He is greatly missed: especially in the Parliamentary Labour Party and the democratic socialist left of the Party as a whole.

INTRODUCTION
The Aims, Content and Context of this Book

"Things can only get better"
Pop song used in Labour's general election campaign 1997
"Through the night of doubt and sorrow onward goes the pilgrim band singing songs of expectation marching to the Promised Land!?"
Hymn

On the morning of the first Thursday in May 1997 a group of senior local government officers, including the author, sat in a meeting in their Town Hall discussing Thatcherite policies relating to privatisation of local services. We believed that happily these might now be changed. The sun streamed into the room as the Chief Officer, who was chairing the meeting, said: "Well I feel this morning that a cloud has lifted from us. Please don't repeat that as I am not supposed to make political remarks." Everyone round the room nodded in agreement. We all felt as though the Thatcherite night of doubt and sorrow was over at last. Were we being too optimistic?

In December 2009 the author held a Party to celebrate a "big" birthday. Speeches were made by her friends that included mention of her work for the Labour Party. Taking his cue; the disc jockey started to play *Things Can Only Get Better*: the Party's 1997 theme song. At which point the author leapt to her feet and asked him to stop playing the tune as she could no longer bear to hear it.

Overview of the aims, objectives and content of the book

The overall aim of the book is to discover what New Labour (NL) did to the Labour Party, its governments and governance: how, when and with what outcomes? One of these outcomes is the ways in which New Labour (NL) ideas and followers continued to influence Party policy and internal democracy up to the present time. What were their mistakes as compared with their achievements and what are the remaining issues for Labour? As the Independent Labour Commission on Accountability, Party and Parliamentary Democracy (2007) found: New Labour (NL) was an elitist organisation managed on a top down basis[INT-1]. How far are the major changes that NL made to the Party currently helping or hindering in its contemporary transition to being a democratic socialist party under the Corbyn leadership? Investigations for this book explored *non-elite* Party stakeholder's evaluations of the performance of NL in policy making and implementation.

Following Jeremy Corbyn's 2015 resounding victory in the Labour Leadership election the time has come for a hard look at how little New Labour achieved (apart from winning elections). We need to examine what damage they did to democratic socialism and to many of the interests of working class people; with a view to learning from these mistakes. We are now in the midst of a Party Leadership election due to the opposition of right wing backbench MPs to Jeremy Corbyn's leadership. This is currently a fast changing situation. A high proportion of NL MPs remain in Parliament: mainly as the beneficiaries of manipulated selection processes discussed in Chapter 8. It is important to be able to challenge them when they hark back to the supposed halcyon days of NL and call for NL's return. This book provides evidence which will enable Party members, supporters and the electorate to do so.

The 81 Party stakeholders interviewed were drawn predominantly from the following groups: Backbench MPs, Constituency Labour Party (CLP) Secretaries and Trade Union Leaders. These formed the main constellation of interviewees who were involved in all aspects of this evaluation. Former party staff, people prevented by the party machine from being selected for Parliamentary candidatures, Annual Conference delegates and other grass-roots Party members (who had relevant experience) were interviewed during investigation into the state of Party democracy under NL.

This assessment is based evaluations of people working within the Labour Party, below the exclusive elite and during the NL era. Their personal testimonies are given almost entirely in their own words. These were individuals who were actively involved in the Party and a stake in its plans and performance. Unlike this book; most works about NL have sought only the views of its privileged elite of NL supporters. These were individuals with an active involvement within the Party and a stake in its plans and performance.

Interviews for this book were conducted during 2009-10 prior to the 2010 general election. A few interviews were held slightly later, due to personal circumstances of interviewees, for example, maternity leave.

NL's achievements, and failures, are related to the length of time in office, and to the records, of earlier Labour Governments. These evaluations of NL focus mainly on the period of government between 1997 and 2010. They also refer to policy planning and Party changes ahead of 1997. There was investigation of changes that NL made to the Party as an organisation, in order to win and retain power. Assessments are made of the effects of these changes on Party and Parliamentary democracy.

Comparisons are made with the contemporary performance of the Australian Labor Party (ALP). This is done because the ALP has long been a sister Party of UK Labour. The Parties have a similar history, traditional aims and values and were both founded in the late nineteenth century. Australia may be 10,000 miles away but its culture and society are very similar to those of Britain. The author has spent much time in Australia during the last few years and has worked with the Australian Labor Party (ALP). Federal Labor Minister Gary Gray was interviewed to help assess the ALP's performance.

Did the sum of policy achievements and failures, and the upheaval in the Labour Party that was caused by the NL revolution (which led to the loss of 62% of the Party's members between 1994 and 2010), provide justification for the NL experiment? Was winning three successive elections sufficient justification for the relatively meagre legacy of NL? What was the totality of the benefits given by NL to the world, to UK society and the Labour Party: compared with the costs?

Evaluations were undertaken during extended interviews (except in the case of CLP Secretaries who were given an internet-based questionnaire because they were scattered across England, Scotland and Wales). All interviews were conducted in person by the author who is an experienced researcher. Information from interviews was supplemented by library research. This was used to support, or refute, claims made in interviews. It also provided evidence for the comparative examination of NL's records and those of the Labour Party's historic governments and Party governance and records of the ALP.

Labour Party Literature has frequently emphasised the aims and values of the Party. Aims and values are also a baseline which has been used in many evaluations of organisational effectiveness[INT-2].

In Chapter 1 the baseline for evaluations is set by examining the aims and values of the Labour Party taken from three sources. The first source is the Party's original constitution of 1918. The second is the Party's NL (New Clause 4) constitution agreed by Annual Conference in 1995 (Appendix 2). The third is a desirable set of contemporary Party aims and values as identified by the three principal sets of interviewees (MPs, Constituency Labour Party (CLP) Secretaries and Trade Union Leaders). These are set out in rank order reflecting the number of interviewees who supported each. The key interviewees were asked to use their personally preferred set of Party aims and values to measure the performance of NL. All sets of aims and values identified by Backbench MPs and CLP Secretaries are set out and discussed in Chapter 1, those of Trade Union Leaders are debated in Chapter 4.

Assessments were conducted in respect of a number of areas. First the NL phenomenon is analysed (Chapter 2). Questions are asked there as to what NL was, what it achieved for the Labour Party and what it did to the Party's detriment? What were its aims and what were its methods of operating? How far did NL change, if not distort, Labour's traditional aims and values? Did it turn the Party into a totally different type of organisation? Was this a so-called called "Market Orientated Party" in which winning elections was more important than achievements in government? Did satisfying middle class voters living in marginal constituencies come to take priority over looking after Labour's traditional working class supporters? How did NL revolutionise the Party's public and media relations and with what consequences?

Chapter 3 examines and discusses the pre-NL record of the Labour Party in elections, Party organisation and public relations. These are assessed on a comparative basis. This compares the area of performance where NL was popularly considered to be successful: winning elections and public and media relations and that of earlier "Old Labour". The latter won more elections than did New Labour and had a longer total period in office: albeit interrupted by opposition governments.

Chapter 4 investigates, and appraises, the relationship between New Labour and the Trade Unions. It charts the increasing disillusion on both sides and growing disenchantment of Union leaders and rank and file members with NL's performance. From the outset of his leadership TB made clear that there would no longer be the same favours or consultation rights given to the unions as were granted by his predecessors[INT-3]. The NL constitutional reforms of 1997 put the *unions on the same level as business interests and voluntary bodies* at the apex of the NL policy making machinery. Despite repeated Party Leadership threats the unions managed to hold on to their share of the votes at Party Conference and seats on the National Executive Committee (NEC) until 2014. However despite Blair's attempts to secure substantial funding, from private donors, the unions continued to provide most of NL's income and especially to fund election campaigns.

NL's policy record is evaluated in Chapter 5. This relates mainly to policy making and implementation in government between 1997 and 2010. Was the good that was achieved through massive investment in public services, especially health and education, diminished by the large scale privatisation that accompanied these developments? What was the cost of virtually total neglect of social rented home building? Was the benefit of partially successful initiatives to end child poverty reduced by the widening gulf between the very rich and the rest in the UK? Did NL foreign policy (especially the Iraq war) turn Labour from a peace seeking Party to into a warmongering Party? Did NL governments perform better than their predecessors in assisting poor developing countries? Was their record better than that of previous Labour Governments in handling Northern Ireland? Policies were evaluated according to the frequency with which they were given favourable or unfavourable valuations by interviewees.

Chapter 6 reviews the policy achievements of "Old" or "Real" Labour Governments (between 1945 and 1979).Policies were evaluated by the same yardsticks as those used in Chapter 5. This chapter investigates how far the policy records of post 1945 Labour Governments, compared with that of NL governments.

Chapter 7 investigates how NL damaged internal Party democracy. This democratic diminution was NL's means to achieving authoritarian (top down) control of the Party. Party democracy was radically changed under NL's stewardship through alterations in rules, policy making machinery, management methods and Party administration. Annual Conference became a televised party political broadcast in which dissidents were precluded from speaking and virtually no real policy was made.

Chapter 8 describes NL's methods of curtailing Party member's rights and preventing "Old" Labour members from becoming Parliamentary candidates. Evidence of internal rule manipulation and alleged selection fixing was uncovered by the author's investigations. In reality: candidates were hand picked by the Party hierarchy rather than democratically by Constituency Party (CLP) members. NL's desired outcome was a supine and compliant Parliamentary Labour Party (PLP). However after 2003 some MPs became rebellious. The ideological composition of the contemporary PLP reflects the outcomes of these manipulated selections (see Chapter 12).

The number of interviewees was increased by 23 for the investigations into Party democracy (Chapters 7 and 8). It then included former Party staff, aspiring Parliamentary candidates and delegates to Annual Labour Conference and other bodies, mentioned above, in addition to MPs, trade union leaders and CLP Secretaries.

Chapter 9 focuses on management of, and democracy within, the Parliamentary Labour Party (PLP). It asks: what power and influence was permitted to Backbench MPs under NL? How far were they able to make, or affect, policy and to hold the government to account? Why did rebellions occur – especially after 2003? How did whipping: "sofa government", the select committee system and patronage operate?

In Chapter 10 there is a comparison of the states of Party and Parliamentary democracy under NL with the situation in the PLP between 1918 and 1994. This Chapter compares NL's record on Party and Parliamentary democracy with that of earlier "Old" or "Real" Labour.

In Chapter 11 the 57 principal interviewees (MPs, CLP Secretaries and trades union leaders) describe their vision and, where appropriate, their fears for the future of the Labour Party. The majority wanted Labour to return to being a democratic socialist Party which is also democratically run. There were also calls for Labour to re-adopt its traditional aims and values. As Jon Cruddas MP declared: "We have to retrieve the essence of what it is to be the Labour Party. We've lost our language and our mission." He, and other stakeholders, believed that if the Party, and its governments, continued to operate in the same outworn NL mode the Party could well divide or simply fade away for lack of activist support.

Constituency Secretaries proposed that the Party continue to court middle class people in marginal seats in order to win elections but *also* that Labour should sustain and develop policies to help the poor and working class people generally. Union leaders advocated a return to the values of working class fraternity and solidarity. Some MPs called for the radical reform of the Labour Party and of Parliament. Constituency Secretaries, and others, also wanted the Party to retain and develop the quality of public and media relations which characterised NL. Some demanded an inquiry as to how NL lost so many votes between 1997 and 2010 and research to indicate how electors, alienated over that period, could be persuaded to come back.

The strongest message, from interviewees, was that Labour should take measures to establish a more equal society in the UK. Proposals were put forward for the greening of our economy and for effective policies to counter global warming. There was a desire to continue to develop high quality, and mainly publicly owned, public services. This was an area where NL was considered to be successful; with the serious reservation that service expansion was accompanied by too much privatisation. There were calls for a significant improvement in trade union rights and protection for people at work. There was an aspiration for Labour to promote peace and good international relations and to avoid wars.

There was also support for continuing NL's commitment to assist developing countries. A lesser priority was: competent economic management and use of the proceeds to provide more rewarding jobs and funding to grow public services. Some priority was also given to winning elections. The author's own study, and the responses of many interviewees, indicated that previous Labour Governments had achieved far more, in policy terms and over interrupted terms of office, than did NL Governments in a 13 year continuous term.

The author concluded that NL turned Labour into a "Market Orientated Party" in which market research was conducted with electors and the findings were used to determine polices: irrespective of the Party's true or traditional aims and values. The author considers that the best way forward for Labour is to become a "Sales Oriented Party" promoting policies in line with its true aims and values[INT-4]. If the future Labour Party is to remain true to its basic principles and priorities: it will need to find effective ways of selling itself and its *own* characteristic policies to the public in ways that secure their votes. Policies will need to be developed in the context of contemporary social, political, economic and demographic conditions. Principled policies must be presented in a way which makes them attractive to the public and the public must be persuaded of their value. There must be an end to policy making driven by opinion polls and focus groups.

Chapter 12 is a short account of what has happened to, and within, the Labour Party between the general elections of 2010 and 2015. Its purpose is to put the book's (earlier) findings into a contemporary perspective.

Background to the rise of New Labour

There follows a brief history of the Labour Party between the 1979 general election and the election of TB as Party Leader in 1994. It analyses the background to, and causes of, the rise of the New Labour phenomenon.

In the aftermath of Labour's 1979 general election defeat the electorate became progressively more dissatisfied with the Thatcher government. Unemployment rose and expenditure on welfare benefits soared[INT-5]. Value added tax was increased and this added four points to the Retail Price Index. The recession deepened. Mrs. Thatcher introduced a set of controversial trade union reforms which sent trade unionists, previously disillusioned by Callaghan's government, back into the Labour camp. By the early 1980s Labour, led by Michael Foot, was doing well in opinion polls. In 1981 the "Gang of Four", who disliked the leftward turn the Party was taking under Foot, broke away and formed the Social Democratic Party (SDP). The advent of the SDP led to a split in Labour's vote and increased its likelihood of electoral defeat in some constituencies.

In March 1982 the Falklands war broke out. After Britain evicted Argentine forces: the political landscape changed, the Tories gained enormous popularity and Labour lost the 1983 General Election. This was Labour's worst post war election result to date. Michael Foot's outdated approach to his, and the Party's, image was blamed by many. Party General Secretary Jim Mortimer told the NEC that "disunity within the Party" was the main handicap[INT-6]. The principal reason for defeat probably lay in the South Atlantic.

Foot was replaced as leader by Neil Kinnock later in 1983. He was the first Labour Leader to be chosen by the new Electoral College, agreed by Party Conference in 1981, rather than by Labour's MPs. The mid 1980s saw the continued rise of Militant within the Labour Party. Kinnock opposed them[6]. Their most prominent members were expelled at Party Conference in 1986. At every Party Conference during the 1980s there was acrimonious televised debate which undoubtedly alienated the public. Kinnock and his colleagues decided to modernise the image and presentation of the Party: to make it more electable.

Lilleker and Lees Marshment[7] reported:

"While in the 1980s Labour utilised elements of political marketing, re-designing the Party's communication system, creating a new logo and smartening appearances, marketing was confined to *presentation* rather than the product itself – more of a sales oriented approach." In 1987 the Conservatives won the general election with an overall majority of 144[INT-7]."

During the mid 1980s and early 1990s concern grew about Labour's continuing failure to win power. In reaction, changes were made within the Party which paved the way for NL. There was also a further effort to improve the Party's self presentation, image and electoral organisation. Under Kinnock, the Leadership gradually developed tighter control of the NEC[INT-8]. The Party's "Shadow Communications Agency" was set up in 1987 to improve public relations.

A system of local electoral colleges to select Parliamentary candidates was dropped and was replaced at the 1993 Conference by One Member One Vote (OMOV) for future Parliamentary candidate selections.

Labour continued to polish its image in the lead up to the 1992 election. Meanwhile the Conservatives had privatised many state controlled utilities and industries. The outcome was that 600,000 people were no longer employed by government, they and many others owned shares in former public enterprises. These people were less likely to vote Labour than previously. In 1991, when Thatcher was toppled in a coup led by Tory minsters, she was replaced by the milder mannered John Major. Some contemporary opinion surveys reported that many electors saw this as being a different and new government. Simon Jenkins reported[INT-9]: "Major rendered a sound service to Thatcherism, entrenching it over seven years when the lady herself would possibly have blown it by losing the 1992 election." Labour lost the

1992 election. One factor was the clever and well funded Tory advertising campaign. This dishonest campaign managed to persuade even voters on the lowest incomes that, under Labour, they would pay more tax. There were memorable, but mendacious: "Labour's tax bomb" and "double tax whammy" adverts. The Party and its leaders faced increased vilification from much of the media during the Foot and Kinnock leaderships: especially from News International and the *Daily Mail*.

However, McSmith[INT-10] pointed out: the 1992 election surprised the experts. For many years no party had won four consecutive general elections, or ruled continuously (without coalition) for more than 13 years. The exceptional nature of the 1992 loss contributes to the explanation as to why the Labour Party was so desperate that it was prepared to surrender to NL in 1994.

Kinnock resigned as Leader. The ensuing leadership election was contested between John Smith and Bryan Gould. Gould advocated more attention being given by the Party to voters in marginal seats in the South of England. This foreshadowed NL's preoccupations. Smith won 90.9 % of the vote compared to Gould's 9.1%.

At the 1993 Party Conference Smith put his leadership on the line to win One Member One Vote (OMOV) for the selection of Parliamentary candidates. Many unions opposed this change: believing it would diminish their influence.

Sadly John Smith died in 1994. Tony Blair (TB) rapidly became front runner to succeed him. Gordon Brown (GB) also wanted to run. Peter Mandelson acted as kingmaker. There followed the "Granita dinner" and the rest is history. Opinion polls showed that TB would be likely to win a general election for Labour. He seemed charming, fresh and personable – but the author believes that he was not a democratic socialist.

The Labour Party was punch drunk, and desperate to win a general election and to end what (by 1997) would be 18 years of Conservative rule. It fell for Blair hook, line and sinker. What TB, and GB, did next is the focus of most of the remainder of this book.

Enter New Labour

There is no mention of "New Labour" in the current Party constitution, nor has there ever been. The term was long used in adverts and Head Office's headed notepaper. It is used less frequently today. The Party never officially changed its name. However the leadership promoted fiction was that NL was a different entity from the (old) Labour Party. The proponents of NL wanted electors to see it as a very different organisation from the Party as they previously knew it.

There was an overwhelming desire among Labour members and supporters to win a general election after the Thatcher years and another defeat in 1992. There was a chronic lack of confidence in the Party's capacity to win. This was accompanied by willingness to adopt draconian remedies to try to ensure electoral success. There was also realistic recognition that the Party's publicity, media relations and electoral organisation were no longer fit for purpose.

Austin Mitchell MP argued: "NL was the product of a situation in which the Party had given up hope. It had hoped that in the 1980s Mrs Thatcher would discredit herself and people would return to the old norms of social democracy. That didn't happen because it is easier to sell right wing populism than a left wing one."

He continued: "But by 1992, when we thought that we were going to win the general election – but didn't, we began to lose confidence. John Smith would have been able to rebuild this collapse of confidence in the Party had he lived. Under the Tories, the lot of the well off had improved. But the standard of living of ordinary people, whose quality of life depends largely on public spending, had declined. Had we had patience we would have won in 1997 whoever had been leader. The Tory experiment in liberalisation had been seen to fail. *But we gave up on our real selves*."

Jeremy Corbyn said: "There was a huge thirst to win the 1997 general election. Blair used this as a means to change party rules and devalue Conference, the NEC, and even the Parliamentary Labour Party (PLP), in favour of leadership control and policy forums.

Dr. Lynne Jones MP proposed: "Going back to 1997 the Party was desperate to win and willing to do anything to get elected. In 1997 people had a lot of hope; but how can you have much hope when what you are promising is so little? I think we would have got elected whoever was leader. We lost John Smith who would probably have got as large a majority as Blair. Then I think things would have been very different. We should have argued our case but we capitulated." Some internal issues, within the Labour Party, which led to the NL take over, are discussed and analysed, in more depth, in Chapter 2.

CHAPTER 1:
What should the Labour Party be for?

"Philip Gould suggested that Blair was a very pragmatic political leader to the extent that he lacked purpose at times. He said: "This was a failure – leadership depends on purpose ... politics depend on purpose ... in this world which is so chaotic and disordered, without purpose, you are lost. It's an essential part of leadership now."
Patrick Wintour, *Guardian*, 19.9.11, p.8

"The duty of the Labour Movement is to provide a light on the hill."
Ben Chiffley, late Labor Prime Minister of Australia

Q. "Inequality of Income has been greatly exaggerated in the past 25 years. Is it going to take a huge political change to shift that back?
A. Economic historian Robert Sidelsky: "Isn't that what the Labour Party is for?"
***Observer, The New Review*, 25.08.13 p.5**

Chapter contents
Introduction: The overall aim of the book:
What are aims and values and why they should matter to the
Labour Party as a political organisation?
Original purpose, values and aims of the Labour Party as set out in the 1918 constitution How the
1995 Constitution (New Clause 4) changed the original
constitution and the Party's purpose, aims and values
Participants identify their ideal contemporary purpose, values and aims for Labour which they
subsequently used to assess New Labour's(NL's) performa

When the author was a young Parliamentary candidate in the, then unwinnable, seat of Scarborough and Whitby, in 1970, she had to face more public meetings than is common in 21st Century campaigns. On such occasions she was often faced with the questions: "What is the Labour Party trying to achieve and what are its values? Like death this question, fired off in public, concentrates the mind. Therefore she soon found answers: some informed by helpful leaflets from Labour's National HQ.

Introduction: the overall aim of the book

The purpose of this book is to conduct an evaluation of the performance of New Labour between 1994 and 2010 (especially whilst in government) and of the continuing outcomes of its methods of operation and its work.

The Labour Party was justifiably proud of many achievements between its foundation and 1979 and especially valued its attainments in government during that period. Most of those achievements reflected its traditional aims and values. However between 1979 and 1997, despite intermittent popularity, it failed to win a general election. Whilst it was in opposition, successive governments, especially those led by Margaret Thatcher, had done incalculable damage to rights at work, to the welfare state and to the living standards of working class people, especially the poorest. After four successive general election defeats, the Party, and its leaders, were desperate to find a way of winning back power. This consideration became paramount above all others: including planning policies to benefit Labour's supporters and others in need. The Party then resorted to New Labour (NL) whose paramount, and almost only, aim was to win elections and to hold on to power (see Chapter 2). Members, and the Party hierarchy, overlooked the fact that many of NL's aims, values and projected policies were more akin to those typical of the Conservatives. Being in office became the end in itself rather than the means to more important and significant ends.

By the late 1990s, when the implications of these changes became widely recognised. many grass roots members left the Party. MPs from the left and centre left were increasingly marginalised and some retired early. The Party became hollowed out. The relationship with the trade unions, which NL leaderships seemed to regard as an unfortunate necessity, required to secure the Party's finances when other methods failed. The public relations fanfare for NL was all about image and promoting alien policies. Policy came to be made by focus group and opinion poll rather than by a democratic process largely internal to the Party and reflecting its aims and values (see Chapter 2).

The policy making machinery of the Party was drastically changed in order to disempower the Annual Conference and replace it with the toothless National Policy Forum and by appointed (rather than elected) policy commissions. The National Executive Committee was given less influence in policy making and more in controlling the Party, and its members, in a top down fashion (see Chapter 7). NL Governments could boast of some significant policy achievements. There was a huge increase in spending on health and education. This was largely focused on building projects. However it was accompanied by large scale privatisation of these services. There was minimal spending on new social housing. There were effective measures to address child poverty, low wages and deprivation in developing countries. However NL's policy achievements were relatively paltry when compared with the attainments of earlier Labour Governments (see Chapters 6 and 10).

In order to endow the Party with a more right wing image; the constitution of the Party was radically altered by New Clause 4 (See this Chapter and Appendix 2). The objective was to change its aims and values Whilst this gave a cursory nod to "democratic socialism" it was really about turning Labour into a semi Conservative Party which would hopefully appeal to the floating voter.

In anticipation of the NL requirement to change the ideological complexion of the Party and to secure tame and compliant MPs, the Party secretariat was "reformed". Older and experienced party staff, traditionally those who had previous political or trade union Organising experience, were encouraged to retire. Instead young people with little, or no, relevant experience and no commitment to democratic socialism, replaced them. These became the agents of NL's clandestine priority project: namely to replace sitting MPs with New Labour sycophants by stealth. These would be unquestioningly loyal the NL Leadership and do what they were instructed by them (see Chapter 7). The selection processes were regularly changed, and policed by Party staff, to ensure this outcome (see Chapter 8). Remaining dissident MPs were controlled by pager and totalitarian management (see Chapter 9).

In anticipation of the NL requirement to change the ideological complexion of the Party and to secure tame and compliant MPs, the Party secretariat was "reformed". Older and experienced party staff, traditionally those who had previous political or trade union Organising experience, were encouraged to retire. Instead young people with little, or no, relevant experience and no commitment to democratic socialism, replaced them. These became the agents of NL's clandestine priority project: namely to replace sitting MPs with New Labour sycophants by stealth. These would be unquestioningly loyal the NL Leadership and do what they were instructed by them (see Chapter 7). The selection processes were regularly changed, and policed by Party staff, to ensure this outcome (see Chapter 8). Remaining dissident MPs were controlled by pager and totalitarian management (see Chapter 9).

The loss of the 2010 general election did not herald the end of New Labour: although it was now discredited with the electors. As a result of measures described above the Parliamentary Labour Party and the Party secretariat were still stuffed with New Labour disciples (see Chapter 12). This created serious problems for Ed Miliband and contributed significantly to Labour's 2015 general election defeat. Despite Jeremy Corbyn having received overwhelming support for his leadership from Labour's grass roots and the trades unions: he still faces an uphill struggle: due to the continuing large majority cohort of New Labour supporters in the Parliamentary Labour Party and the Party secretariat.

The story of New Labour, as presented in this book, is told mainly in their own words, by more than 80 contemporary Labour MPs, Constituency Party officers, trade union leaders, retired party staff, Parliamentary hopefuls, conference delegates and local Party activists.

The performance of an organisation can be assessed by judging how far its values, aims and objectives have been achieved over a specified period. Values should ideally be of a durable nature, as John Prescott[C1-1] spoke of "traditional values in a modern setting". That is: values should be adaptable and able to be applied appropriately in changed social, political, economic and technological environments with which they must interact in order to survive and develop[C1-2].

This environment will affect how they should formulate their aims and objectives (in accordance with their pre-determined values) in order to survive, thrive and grow. Assessment of the degree of achievement of aims and detailed objectives allows organisations to assess their own performance at both strategic and operational levels. This book examines that operation in respect of the British Labour Party during the NL regime.

Organisational gurus Peters and Waterman[C1-3] pointed out that excellent organisations: "… have a basic philosophy and set of values" … "The philosophy must be established and maintained from the top to the bottom of the organisation … this explicit understanding of a commitment to a system of values is probably the single most important key to excellence."

The theory of management by objectives was developed by Drucker, 1957,[C1-4] in the context of industrial management. Objectives are more detailed than aims and represent specific elements of aims, usually to be achieved within a defined time span. Sometimes the concepts of aim and objective are (wrongly) used interchangeably.

Drucker defined the concept of objective: Objectives must be *derived from our aims which are:* "what our business is, what it will be and what it should be … Objectives are the action commitments through which the mission (purpose) of a business is to be carried out[C1-5]".

Handy said: "(organisational) overarching goals (aims) have to matter to the people involved"[6]. Handy argued that goals influence organisational cultures, and are, in turn affected by them. Organisational cultures can be changed to push organisations to change.[C1-6] This is what NL attempted to engineer within the Labour Party. That planned cultural change was a purpose of Labour's New Clause 4 (NC4) of 1995 (see Appendix 2).

However the coming of NL led to complications in identifying the Party's aims and objectives. The original aims and objectives were set out in the Party's first constitution of 1918 (Old Clause 4). This was limited in scope and its language had become somewhat antiquated but up until 1994 it was universally valued in the Party because it committed the party to ensuring fairly paid work for all employees, redistribution of wealth and public ownership of manufacturing and service industries.[C1-9] Between 1918 and 1995 the Party's aims were developed in accord with old Clause 4 and these developments were often incorporated into general election manifestos.

For example, in his introduction to Labour's 1964 general election manifesto, Leader Harold Wilson described Labour's aims as:

"A New Britain – mobilising the resources of technology under a national plan; harnessing our national wealth in brains our genius for scientific invention and medical discovery; reversing the decline of thirteen wasted years; affording a new opportunity to equal, and if possible surpass, the roaring progress of other western powers. The country needs fresh and virile leadership. Labour is ready[C1-7]"

With the coming to power of New Labour its leadership decided to change the Party's values and aims by writing the New Clause 4 (Appendix 2) and setting up the vote of Party members on NC4 so that it was likely to be accepted although many sections of the Party such as its European MPs and most members of CLP General Committees did not want this (see below). By the time that research for this book was done from 2008-11 many Party members were disenchanted with NC4 and did not regard it as reflecting he Party's legitimate contemporary aims and values.

Therefore the 57 main stakeholders interviewed here were requested to articulate their own favoured contemporary aims and values for the Labour Party and subsequently to assess how far these had been achieved during the New Labour years.

The author interviewed these 57 about NL's record in the 1994-97 period, in government (1997-2010) and about NL's governance of the Party in Parliament and the Party on the ground. These stakeholders were: 27 Backbench MPs, 27 Constituency Labour Party (CLP) Secretaries and three national trade union leaders. Other stakeholders – aspiring Parliamentary candidates, retired party staff, conference delegates and key activists – were interviewed about specific aspects of New Labour's rule, primarily relating to party democracy.

The greatest test of a political organisation's effectiveness will be how far it has achieved its aims and objectives and lived out its values over a term of office. NL seems to have presumed that so long as it won elections it was achieving its aims and objectives. However electoral dividends reduced after 2001, and no notice was taken by the Party Leadership of failure to achieve other, more progressive, goals long held by the Party (for example, improved rights in the workplace).

Later in the book (Chapters 7, 8 and 9) there is assessment as to how far the organisational management of NL contributed, or otherwise, to it changing the Party and achieving appropriate objectives.

In this Chapter stakeholders are asked: *"What should the Labour Party be for?" Aims, reflecting the established purpose and values, set out to answer this question.* Former Leader Neil Kinnock was reported to have flown into a temper and asked "What is the Labour Party For?"[C1-8] when critically questioning some of TB's actions shortly after the latter became leader.

Labour's values, aims and objectives need to be understood *and shared* throughout the whole organisation. That is in Government, Parliament, political operations of affiliated bodies and the Party on the ground – if they are to be consistently achieved. During the NL era the Labour Party should have developed wide ranging feedback loops throughout the organisation (as well as those emanating from the public) in order to continuously assess how MPs, grass-roots members and other stakeholders were judging its performance and to make improvements in response. NL became dysfunctional because it destroyed internal feedback loops and managed the Party in a top down manner. Examples were ending free speech at Conference (see Chapter 7) and excluding potential dissidents from the Parliamentary Labour Party (see Chapter 8). Research exercises, such as that undertaken for this book, and for the LabOUR Commission 2007[C1-9], became essential to provide alternative feedback loops. These internal feedback loops were unwanted by the Blairite elite. They could have been used to avoid making mistakes in future and to enable NL to learn from those successes that were congruent with stakeholder aims and values identified here.

It has never been easy to establish a single, and consistent, set of values for the Labour Party. Aims need to be updated in line with the contemporary political and social environment. Jon Cruddas MP pointed out, in interview, that there *"have always been tensions in the party between a democratic socialist approach and a Liberal one but in the last 20 years these tensions have been played out in terms of the history of NL. Tony Blair (TB) said he wanted to reconcile these two traditions: it is the contested terrain of modern Labour."* There is little evidence of any efforts by TB to effect this reconciliation. *This book contrasts the actual liberal approach of New Labour with the democratic socialist one that most stakeholders interviewed here would have preferred.*

Labour can learn from the Australian Labor Party (ALP) in this context. The ALP is a sister Party to UK's Labour, has comparable history, values aims and objectives and operates in a country with a similar cultural environment. This is the rationale for comparisons made in this book. These have been facilitated by the author's recent extensive experience of living part time in Australia. Australian Federal Minister Gary Gray said in interview: "In the global context we are the oldest of the world's social democratic parties with parliamentary representation. We are 30-40 years older than the British Labour Party. We formed a government before many other Labour parties were formed. Our Labour and trades union leadership in the late 19th century sought influence through Parliamentary methods rather than through external methods."

Relevant advice was provided by the ALP's Hawke Wran Report (2002) about the future of the Australian Labor Party[C1-10]: "The way we (live and work) … have changed dramatically and are still changing. When all around us, individuals and organisations have had to make adjustments to cope with these new realities" … "The keys to making that adjustment most effectively are *first, to identify the essential, unchanging and unchangeable elements of Labor philosophy that distinguish us from our conservative opponents*; second, having done that, to amend our practices and procedures in a way which will best equip the Party to attract genuinely committed members and to win government with policies co-operatively developed on the basis of those fundamental Labor principles." NL should have acted on *the same* precept.

The most important of its aims and values are usually set out in a body's constitution and rules. There have only been two comprehensive Labour Party constitutions: the first of 1918[C1-11] and that of NL in 1995 (Appendix 2). The Party revises individual constitutional rules at Annual Conference. General election manifestos usually set out a contemporary version of the aims which the Party promises to adopt if Labour is elected.

Like this writer, Hawke Wran argued that a Party's aims and values are derived from the ever changing social and political environment in which it exists[C1-12]. Therefore Labour's aims cannot be static and must change in response to environmental changes; but not so drastically that the change creates an unrecognisably different organisation which ditches its overall purposes and values. Some have argued that the changes introduced by NL were so considerable that they created a totally different type of Party from the pre 1995 Labour Party[C1-13].

In the UK Labour Party new single aims, and sometimes specific objectives, have always been set, in theory, by its Annual Conference. In recent reality they usually originate in Leadership and/or National Executive Committee (NEC) decisions. NL redefined the Party's aims at Conference in 1995 in a formal new constitution (New Clause 4 (NC4)). In the past the Leadership did not always get their way in these matters: for example when Conference declined to allow Gaitskell to replace old Clause 4 in 1959[C1-14]. Within the Party, aims/objectives can be interpreted, and changed during use, by the perceptions of key individuals and in the process of communication and implementation of those aims.

What emerged from research for this book was the existence of three different sets of Labour Party aims and values (1918/traditional Labour, New Labour and those shared by current non-elite stakeholders interviewed). The conclusion is that, between 1994 and 2010, the Labour Party was being run on conflicting sets of values and aims. In the knowledge of this conflict, NL's top down managers attempted to stamp out more radical aims and values derived from the 1918 Constitution and those frequently adopted by contemporary grass-roots Party members, dissident MPs and union leaders. TB could be compared to Disraeli who, according to Lord Salisbury's daughter Gwendolen Cecil: "was always pursuing objects which he could not own, manoeuvring his Party into alliances which, though unobjectionable from his own standpoint, were discreditable and indefensible from theirs."[C1-15]

Nevertheless, as research for the Independent LabOUR Commission[C1-16] and for this book demonstrated, many stakeholders, within Parliament and the Party on the ground, cleaved to a set of aims and values more closely identified with "Old Labour". Even some of the policies of NL governments retained features derived from "Old Labour" aims and values, as Frank Dobson MP pointed out when interviewed.

The question must be asked as to whether the fundamental core purpose (including values and aims) of the Labour Party was so radically changed, under NL, as to destroy the whole purpose of the organisation as originally established? [C1-17][C1-18]. NL could be compared with a hermit crab which occupies the shell of a dead mollusc. The crab is not the same type of creature as the dead shell fish but another species imitating it by assuming the late mollusc's habitat. Perhaps John Prescott had this image in mind when he compared one of NL's architects, Peter Mandelson, to a crab that he inspected?

The stakeholder's identification of aims and values outlined below led into discussion and analysis of desirable contemporary aims and values for the Party. This assessment was made in the areas of public relations and electoral success (Chapter 2) and in policy planning and policy outcomes in government (Chapter 5). It also informed judgements about NL's effectiveness in promoting and delivering Party and Parliamentary democracy (Chapters 7, 8 and 9).

The historic overall mission and aims of the Labour Party

This is a vital topic: because it enables the origins and development of the Party's values and aims to be examined in historical context; as well as an assessment of their durability. Despite the introduction of NC4 these earlier aims (derived from the 1918 constitution) were likely to continue to influence stakeholders in the Party. NL tried to bury the old aims and present the 'New Labour Party' as a novel and different type of organisation (see Chapter 2). However an NHS management study[18] and interview evidence have shown, along with former Party officer Malcolm's testimony (see Chapter 7), it does not pay organisations to abandon their collective memory because they will then cease to learn from their past. They may then lose their way so that their effectiveness is reduced.

From the outset the infant Labour Party or "Labour Representation Committee" (LRC) was a restless coalition of uneasy bedfellows. From its beginning it was formally joined to the majority of trades unions. It frequently maintained connections with the Liberal Party and had a secret pact with the latter not to oppose them in the first two general elections of the twentieth century.

Initially the LRC was a coalition of organisations sharing minimal common goals and values. Trade union initiatives to organise political and parliamentary representation for working people became intertwined with democratic socialist interests.

In 1917 Labour Leader Arthur Henderson and Fabian Sidney Webb then drew up a first draft constitution for the Party [C1-19]. This was of a democratic socialist character. Another first was that the new constitution explicitly committed the Party to a democratic socialist value base and political position. This was encapsulated in what is now popularly known as "Old Clause 4". It read:

"To secure for the producers by hand and brain the full fruits of their industry, and the most equitable distribution thereof that may be possible, upon the basis of the common ownership of the means of production and the best obtainable system of popular administration and control of each industry or service."

This remained the Labour Party's official mission statement until it was repealed, under NL, in 1995.

The Party Conference of June 1918 accepted a policy statement drafted by Sidney Webb: *"Labour and the New Social Order".*[C1-20] This set out policy aims for the Party and formed the underpinning for Labour Party (and government) policy up to the 1950 general election. It was comprised of four principles:

1. Establishment of a National Minimum: a comprehensive policy of full employment with a minimum wage and minimum standard of working conditions together with a maximum working week of 48 hours.

2. Democratic control of industry: the imperative to nationalise industry (in line with 'Old Clause 4') and to encourage trades union membership in the workplace.

3. The revolution of national finance: i.e. the subsidisation of socially useful services by heavy taxation of the incomes of the wealthy and an immediate capital levy to pay off part of the cost of the war.

4 The Surplus for the common good: the balance of the country's wealth should, as far as possible, be committed to expanding educational and cultural opportunities for the population as whole.

The Labour Party was now a unitary organisation with a clear mission statement and set of policy aims. It had formal alliances with its trade union and Co-operative partners. Its aims would continue to be developed, especially through its plans set out in Party policy statements and election manifestos.

There were few developments in explicit Party aims and values during the 1930s and the Attlee years: but there was extensive action converting existing values and aims into democratic socialist policies. The 1959 election defeat was followed by internal Party reviews about where they were going wrong. At a post election special conference, Leader Hugh Gaitskell called for a revision of the Party's mission and objectives: that had not been changed since 1918. He advocated the abandonment of Clause 4 of the party Constitution, as TB did successfully in 1995. This led to much argument within the Party. Gaitskell was forced to accept a compromise in which the NEC recommended the retention of Clause 4 to Conference (this was carried). That was agreed with the proviso that the Party publish a new statement of principles[Cl-21].

The Party's survival, with a relatively unchanged overall mission and set of values, from the 1918 constitution to the NL introduced changes in 1995, provides testimony to its consistency and durability during that period. It also bears witness to the worth and utility of the original mission and values which addressed the needs of UK society for much of that period. This was evidenced by election successes and the "Butskellite" settlement whereby the post 1945 welfare state was accepted, and highly valued, by most of the population and by both major parties.

During intervening periods the Party's aims and values were set out more informally, and in part, in successive general election manifestos[Cl-22].

Comparisons with the record of The Australian Labor Party are made throughout the book. The relevance of these is that both parties have similar origins and values and operate in similar cultural environments,

What New Labour did to established Labour Party aims and values

The NL leadership was determined to change the aims, and even values, of the Party drastically. This appears to have been perceived as a means of changing its image, trying to make it more electable and pushing the Party away from its democratic socialist traditions. The NL aim *was to replace democratic socialist precepts with Gladstonian Liberal and neoconservative ideologies instead.* NL guru Philip Gould, preached that the Party needed: *"New foundations; a reason for its existence as a political party; a new structure, a central message to help change the political map; a new superstructure ..."*[C1_23]. Gould believed that Labour could only win elections if it completely rebuilt the Party from scratch.

The history of New Clause 4 was chequered. TB announced to the 1994 Conference, his first as leader, that he wanted to change old Clause 4. Gould[C1_24] reported that he considered this to be a risky move. *TB discussed his proposal with neither the NEC nor the shadow cabinet before he announced it.* This suggests TB's negative attitude to, and even contempt for, both bodies. Its docile acceptance shows how desperate the Party was to secure his leadership. Meg Russell argued this demonstrated that the NEC had already lost much of its power. Kinnock's then recently developed control of the NEC may have moved it towards submissiveness. Gould argued that TB's aim was to demonstrate clearly that the Party had changed[C1_25].

Within three months 20 Labour MEPs launched a campaign opposing the new NC4. A contemporary survey suggested that most Constituency General Committee (GC) delegates opposed it . Surmising that this would produce a result more favourable to them; the Party hierarchy then urged CLPs to postal ballot all their members about the NC4 proposal. The result was that 467 out of 470 CLPs that ran this ballot, voted in favour of a change[C1_26]. The form of balloting was allegedly changed to produce TB's desired result. Inactive members were correctly supposed to be less radical than active ones. This tactic was carried over into NL's use of OMOV (One Member One Vote) in Parliamentary Candidate selections (Chapter 8). The only union that supported NC4 was the Communication Workers Union (CWU).

NC4 was brought to a Special Party Conference in 1995. Only 54.6 % of union votes were cast for the change but 90% of CLP votes were in favour. The desire to bolster the image of the new leader and to win the forthcoming general election probably concentrated the minds of those who voted to accept[C1_27]. Since 1995 the official aims and values of the Labour Party have been set out in the NC4 of the Party's Constitutional Rules (Appendix 2).

The author considers that NC4 is a "feel good", but almost meaningless, concoction of words capable of several interpretations. Its purposes were probably twofold: the first was to give TB and the NL Project carte blanche to do what they wanted with the Party; this was facilitated because they now had a vague and flexible mandate. The second purpose was possibly to convince floating voter that this was not the actual Labour Party but a watered down Conservative Party that they could trust when they had grown weary of the genuine article. The gentle reader may consider this an unduly cynical analysis of NC4(i). That clause is imprecisely worded and ambiguous. It is therefore an inaccurate yardstick to measure the purpose, direction and ultimately performance of NL Governments. It incorporates a much diluted version of traditional Labour values. Its adoption was likely to impair the functioning of the organisation, in the long term, because many of these values ran contrary to Labour's long established value system. This was evidenced by the subsequent hollowing out of the Party, through the loss of nearly two thirds of the individual membership between 1996 and 2010, a massive loss of votes in 2005 and the 2010 election defeat.

The more specific objectives of In NC4 (ii) were presumably intended to be the means of working towards achieving the general aim heading NC4 (i). NC4 aims are compared, immediately below, with Party aims and values as perceived by contemporary stakeholders interviewed.

Party stakeholders' views of ideal contemporary values for the Labour Party

The aim of this investigation was an evaluation of the overall performance of NL: from the perspectives of key stakeholders outside the senior party elite. The identities, roles and offices of the fifty-seven stakeholders who were interviewed for the core research for this book (Backbench MPs, Trade Union Leaders and CLP Secretaries) appear in Appendix 1. Additional categories of Party member (mentioned above p.1), were surveyed in less depth for studies of internal Party democracy discussed in Chapters 7 and 8. Detailed questionnaires were used for the three principal groups of interviewees.

The first question asked of the fifty-seven main stakeholders was: "What should be the Labour Party's enduring values?" Secondly they were asked what the main contemporary aims of the Labour Party should ideally be? Their responses were collected under themed headings. The number of interviewees who chose each theme indicates its relative significance. There was also an opinion poll survey applied to CLP Secretaries. This became a straw poll because the eventual sample was not large enough to be statistically representative.

Predictably similar themes appeared in values and aims statements. Sometimes participants were uncertain initially as to which was an aim and which a value. Clarification by the author followed. Values underpin and determine aims. The aims identified by stakeholders we re used as yardsticks by them to judge out how successful Labour Government policies had been (see Chapter 5).

Their answers were categorised, summarised and aggregated, by the author, into a short statement of each value (or aim) which appears in italics. Further detail is supplied through examples of participant's supporting statements. It was appropriate to present their views in this collective way because there was much agreement between interviewees.

Values are discussed in the order of frequency of being stated and the importance attributed to each by interviewees. Values supported by the three categories of principal stakeholder were:

The most important value was regarded as being: *We support equality of opportunity (where possible also equality of outcome) and social justice for all. We believe in creating a much more equal society in the UK, in facilitating redistribution of wealth and resources and in ending poverty in Britain.*

This value was favoured by the great majority of stakeholders; as was the similar Party aim. It was identified by 20 of the 27 MPs, all three trade union leaders and by 26 out of 27 CLP secretaries.

MPs' statements included: Jon Cruddas, who said: "Many people have said this before, but the values of the Labour Party involve working for greater equality. That is the Party's purpose domestically". Michael Meacher offered: "The world is changing and we have to change with it. We have to look to see how we can get a modern, progressive and left party that reflects our ideals in each changing generation that we live through. The key values are equality and social justice."

Louise Ellman argued: "The Labour Party's values are about more equality, more social justice, about prosperity for all and about caring for the underdog." Roger Berry affirmed: "Labour's values are about creating a fairer and more just society, in which everyone is treated with equal respect. We should create the greatest redistribution of income and wealth that is possible. Historically the Party was created as an opposition to those who did not share these values."

Gordon Prentice named the enduring values as: "Fairness and equality: a relentless drive for a more equal society where money is put into social good (social capital)." Backbencher B. suggested: "Caring about the ordinary people of this country: the mass of the people (who are) still entitled to a decent life and to good opportunities. That's crucial to me and as relevant as it ever has been". Peter Kilfoyle responded: 'Fairness and justice: equal opportunities for all. Every so often the Leadership talks the talk but doesn't walk the walk. The values and principles in Labour's original constitution are as valid now as they were then. Give working people a fair go." John McDonnell said simply: "That we are all equal."

Union leaders' proposals included that of Billy Hayes (Communication Workers) who said: "I see the Party's traditional and enduring values as being essentially: a commitment to equality. *Labour Party values include social transformation of society. Working for a better, and fairer, world.* The Labour Party is the only instrument able to improve the lot of ordinary working people now and in the last 100 years. The trades unions are the vehicle that I'm currently using as a means of getting social justice.*" Hayes had started: "In doing this interview "I don't accept the pigeon hole of a trades union viewpoint because I think that surrenders a bit to the idea that trades unions only have one role. I don't see myself primarily as a 'trade unionist'. I just believe *that I've got a commitment to social justice that finds expression mainly in the trade union movement.* I don't see a distinction here between trade unionists and others."

Unite's Len McCluskey proposed Labour's mission statement should be: "To bring justice, equality and fairness into society. All working people should be given a fair crack of the whip. It's about having a society which is civilised because of the and way it deals with 99% of its citizens … to make things better for ordinary working people." In an *Observer* interview, McCluskey also advocated the principles of "fairness, equality and justice*"*[C1_28].

McCluskey continued: *"The "I'm all right Jack": "No such thing as society" concept started by Thatcherism was also cultivated under Blairism. The culture of collectivism, community spirit has taken a battering for ages. Of course I voted Labour, although I was never a supporter of Blairism."*[C1_29]

All three union leaders interviewed sought a more equal society in which the interests of working class people are advanced, and improved, and in which all are guaranteed a good quality of life and in which there is social justice for all. In a recent opinion study of life satisfaction in European countries, conducted in the UK by the Office for National Statistics, (July 2013), average life satisfaction scores were highest in the most equal countries of Denmark, Sweden and Finland (average over 80%) but only 73% in the less equal UK[C1_30].

CLP Secretaries' views follow. Fred summarised: "Inclusiveness, fairness, always on the side of the poorest people, radical in its aspirations and redistributive in its actions." Colin said: "The transfer of wealth from the rich to the poor and creating a more egalitarian society." Diane suggested: "To create a national community that looks after those in our society least able to look after themselves".

Gary proposed: "To tackle inequalities through socialism." Vince said: "The Party should champion the unheard voices in our society." Una suggested: "To promote … equality of outcome – not just of opportunity. To defend and speak for those who cannot speak for themselves and to persuade enough of those who are comfortably off that this is the right thing to do, either morally, or because 'There but for the grace of God go I'." Key words "fairness": "equality" and "social justice" appeared repeatedly in accounts of what the majority of interviewees deemed Labour's most important values.

The second best supported value was: *We believe in having first class publicly owned and run, public services and (some) publicly owned enterprises which are managed within our mixed economy.*

This value was favoured by nine MPs, two TU leaders and five Secretaries. MP's Views: Frank Dobson, Roger Berry, Gordon Prentice, Austin Mitchell and Alice Mahon all emphasised that the only way in which good, comprehensive and universal public services (particularly health, education, social housing and police) can be provided effectively is collectively, through state funding and in the public sector. They believed this must be reflected in our values.

Clare Short and Linda Riordan spoke about the value of commitment to public ownership of enterprises. Short said: "On the question of (Old) Clause 4, I don't think that Labour's commitment to public ownership was because of public ownership per se. It was a means to the end of creating a mutually respectful, inclusive and egalitarian society." Linda Riordan wanted: "Re-nationalisation of public transport privatised by the Conservatives."

CLP secretaries, Quentin, Roland and Simon mentioned valuing public services and called for "outstanding education and health care": "defending and extending public services" and "a review of public services to make them more diverse, accountable and responsive to individual needs". Helen wanted "essential services to be free (at the point of use)".

The value ranked third was: *We uphold the principle of solidarity, fraternity and collectivism amongst working people and believe in working collectively to improve the rights, conditions and rewards at work for all employees.*

This was cited by 14 stakeholders: all three trade union leaders, seven MPs. and four Secretaries.

MP John Cryer said: "There's got to be an element of a belief in collectivism – but not in the way that the Soviet Union saw it. During the last 30 years our society has been moving in the direction of uber individualism. Our belief should be the reverse of that. We should believe in collective action. Society can only function successfully through collective action." Lynne Jones MP asserted Labour's main value is: "To achieve more together than we can achieve on our own: that applies at local, national and international levels."

Other MPs' views: Frank Dobson argued: "We've got to act together if we want (public) services, for example: education and health." John McDonnell believed: "We are all in this together: it's about solidarity."

Alan Simpson mentioned the need for a: "return to notions of collective interdependence". He asked rhetorically whether the Party "still values collective solutions and mutual dependency or whether we have become a Party that is much more concerned with individuals and opportunities for private and personal aspirations? – As though they could deliver the same societal outcomes." Katy Clark proposed: "What distinguishes the Labour Party from other parties is a belief in collectivism with orientation towards working class communities. Parties like the Liberal Democrats, at times, have had policies that may seem more left wing than those of Labour. *However their orientation is very different in terms of the class issue. I think that's very significant in a class ridden society such as the UK's."*

Liz Snape, Assistant General Secretary of Unison, suggested that the Party's purpose is: "To stand up for, and advance, the situation of ordinary hard working people." She saw these values as being: "to make things better for ordinary working people. To defend what working people have won over decades." Billy Hayes (CWU) claimed: *"The Labour Party is the only instrument able to improve the lot of ordinary working people now and in the last 100 years."*

CLP Secretary's opinions included that of Irene, who cited "solidarity" as one of the Party's four main values. Vince also mentioned the importance of "solidarity". Una referred to "Community collaboration based on a mutual respect for difference, creativity and innovation".

The fourth value, in rank order, was: *We believe in internationalism and in promoting peace and justice throughout the world as well as in reducing poverty worldwide.* This value was identified by only seven MPs and four CLP secretaries.

Examples of MPs' views follow. Clare Short stated: "The Labour Party has a moral purpose that includes building an international system that extends respect, care, and the principle of fair shares for everyone, to all human beings in the world". Similarly Jon Cruddas said: "We believe in working for greater equality internationally." Jeremy Corbyn mentioned: "Internationalism in world affairs, support for the principles of the United Nations Charter and all the UN's agencies and declarations … Commitment to working for peace and disarmament." Kelvin Hopkins argued: "… I have always felt that inequality leads to conflict and eventually to war. We need equality both within and between nations".

CLP Secretary Oliver described a key value as being "Internationalism (so that the principles that we support in the UK we should also support worldwide). Labour values should be linked strongly to European and global values (including) democracy, participation and human rights."

The value ranked fifth was: *The Party believes in strong democratic values and the democratic practice of politics within institutions; in Britain and throughout the world. It also believes in robust internal democracy within the Party.* This was favoured by eight stakeholders: the majority of whom were MPs.

John Grogan MP envisioned one Labour value as being: "Democracy in the economy and democracy in all spheres of life." MP Michael Meacher said: "values should include avoidance of top-down government, democratic accountability (relating to the public and Party) and granting civil liberties."

Graham Stringer MP believed: "We must ensure that people have access to democratic institutions. If people don't like either the policies or the politicians then they must be able to get them to change the policies or throw the rascals out." John McDonnell said: "One of our values is democracy. We have a right to have a say and to be heard."

The value ranked sixth was: *We value good economic management in the UK (as it will facilitate a strong economy which can, in turn, underpin public services, job creation and greater economic equality.)*

This was favoured by seven respondents, most of whom were CLP secretaries.

Supporting MPs included Kelvin Hopkins, who called for "effective management of the economy in order to secure full employment and make more resources available to benefit the less well off". Colin Challen said: "We cannot be intensely relaxed about the filthy rich because the only way people get to be filthy rich is by behaving in a rather self-serving fashion – whether legal or illegal. After the "prawn cocktail offensive" in the City we became too enamored with the idea that simply making money was … an end in itself. (This was) despite knowing the effect of the city on our industries: short term investment rather than long term vision. These attitudes to money and to the City should not be part of our values in future."

Examples of CLP Secretaries' opinions follow. Eric said: "We need a (Labour) government to lead in the development of human capital. Everybody must be given the chance to develop their true potential." Mike called for the achievement of "economic well-being". Simon wanted: "The nations' resources to be managed for the benefit of the majority of the people not just the few". Una argued: "The British economy will never return to the days of mass employment in heavy, unskilled industry (therefore) the Labour Party has to empower people to be innovative and creative in our technology focused knowledge economy … and to be aligned to the aspirations of the new layer of independent entrepreneurs and community activists. The Labour Party must re-configure our understanding of the economy so that small businesses can compete against large businesses."

The seventh most favoured value was: *We believe that everyone has a right to equality of opportunity and outcome through not being discriminated against, on grounds of gender, age, racial or ethnic origin, religious belief, sexual orientation or disability.* This was proposed only by 5 MPs and a Peer.

MP Christine McCafferty said: "I think this has to be the basis of national and local government and is fundamental to the purpose of the Labour Party". Roger Berry argued: "We need to tackle every kind of discrimination. Our value is fairness, equal rights and equal opportunities – that's what the Labour Party was created for."

Senior backbencher M. pointed out: "There is now a very welcome value, accepted across the Party, that we should address the issue of non-economic inequalities – particularly those for gay people. This value was not seen as a high priority until the latter half of the twentieth century because social attitudes, and even the law, were different previously. He continued: "Things change with the times. For example: in the earlier twentieth century many in the Party held pacifist values but this is not so common now. Colin Challen advocated: "Equality for people in terms of ethnic mix". Lord S. said: "I'm very encouraged by young people being more liberal (small L) than previous generations. I think that's important as part of the philosophy of the Labour Party: allowing people to be themselves. I think that the whole point of society is to ensure that people have a better life living inside society rather than outside it".

Ranked eighth was: *"We believe in the principle of saving our planet for its current population and for future generations by adopting environmentally friendly principles ('green ideas') to inform our practice".* This was supported by 4 respondents (equally divided between MPs and CLP officers).

Senior backbencher A. said: "This cannot be described as: 'a traditional Labour value' because it is one that has come to prominence relatively recently but it's consistent with the approach we ought to have". He continued: "… our relationship to the planet, sustainability, humanity's dominion over the planet seems highly questionable to me." Alice Mahon MP offered: "We should provide a safe environment for the working class people of this country to live in".

Examples of Secretary's views: Eric said: "We need to be protecting our planet Earth". Oliver contended: "Being environmentally responsible should be one of our values."

It is interesting to examine how the values included in NC4 of the Labour party's current constitution (1995) compare with those articulated by stakeholders interviewed here. The first section of NC4 focuses on Party values. Surprisingly it describes the Party as a "democratic socialist party". This phrase was not used, in public, by TB after the 1997 election. Stakeholder's responses indicated that this is how many of them still see the Party. However there was some coyness about the use of the 'S' (socialist) word. Surprisingly the NC4 values include a positive affirmation of the value of fraternity and collective action that was strongly supported by stakeholders. However some of the impact of this is weakened by an individualist emphasis on everyone achieving their individual full potential. This could be seen as a legitimate aspect of giving equality of opportunity, but not of that of outcome.

The celebrated phrase about the value of: "Power, wealth and opportunity being in the hands of the many not the few" takes ambiguity to its ultimate. Party members are clearly intended to draw the meaning that the word "many" relates to the working class and possibly also the less affluent middle classes. However it could literally mean that "the many" is the two thirds of the population who do *not* live below the poverty line, so excluding the poorest. That might "justify" the failure of NL, under GB, to control bankers' obscene level of bonuses. There is also a mention of citizens' duties (unspecified) which was not reflected in respondent's value systems. That requirement echoes the Conservative policies of John Major.

Values of the Australian Labor Party (ALP): The author investigated the values of the Australian Labor Party so that these could be compared with British traditional (post 1918) Labour values and those of NC4. Hopefully UK Labour can be encouraged to emulate them. The Hawke-Wran Report, which was the most recent review of the ALP available in 2010, identified the following as Labor's core philosophy (combining aims and values) as being[C1_31]:

"The right of individuals to use their talents for self advancement balanced by the collective responsibility of society to provide reasonable standards for those unable to fend adequately for themselves; the creation of equal opportunities for individuals to develop those talents through education, training and re – training; and an unqualified opposition to discrimination based on race, colour, creed or gender.

"Belief in, and commitment to, a growing economy as a basis for improved standards and quality of life and as a source of revenue to finance services relevant to those standards and qualities that only governments can provide;

"Commitment to the defence and security of our country;

"The pursuit of an independent foreign policy calculated to advance our country's best interests within the framework of respect for the aspirations of other nations and our responsibility as a developed economy to play, with other such economies, a constructive role in assisting the tragically large proportion of the world's population living in poverty; Protection of the natural environment, including the improvement and more efficient use of our water resources; and the right of workers to organise and bargain collectively."

Thus there was emphasis on equality of opportunity, provision of structures to support that value, opposition to discrimination on grounds of race, ethnicity or gender and a commitment to worker's and trades union rights. Despite modern Australia sometimes claiming to have been established as an ideal society for the emigrant working classes, equality was not strongly emphasised. However workers' and trade union rights were upheld. So was provision of a safety net for the poorest nationally and internationally as Megalagenis[C1-32] reported. Many of these values overlap with the traditional values of the UK Labour Party.

Stakeholder's judgements of ideal Labour Party aims

Views of Backbench MPs, Trade Union leaders and Constituency Secretaries on *Party aims* follow:

Preferred aims were identified by asking interviewees to state what they thought should be the main aims of the contemporary Labour Party. These aims were to be identified within the framework of the values that they had already described. As with these values, their answers were categorised, summarised and then aggregated by the author. This produced a brief statement of each aim which appears in italics. Further detail is supplied through examples of their supporting statements. The degree of attainment of electoral aims is discussed in Chapter 3, of policy aims in Chapter 5 and of Party and Parliamentary democracy aims in Chapters 7and 9. Aims are discussed in the order of frequency and importance as selected by stakeholders:

The most popular, almost universally favoured, aim was the theme of *Promoting a more equal society which redistributes wealth, power, opportunities and privilege: a society characterised by greater social mobility and social justice.*

Most respondents emphasised equality of opportunity. Only a minority called for equality of outcome. This theme was identified by all 27 Backbench MPs interviewed, by 21 of the 27 constituency secretaries and all three trade union leaders. Typical examples were:

From MPs' suggestions: "To ensure social justice, fairness and equality in society" (Lynne Jones). "To advance the cause of social justice in Britain (and the world) and to create a fairer, more equal society where everyone's talents can be fulfilled." (John Grogan) and "The Labour Party's mission is about encouraging and developing more prosperity for all, promoting equal opportunities and fighting for social justice." (Louise Ellman).

John McDonnell believed it was: "achieving equality through the mechanism of democracy." This related to an extract from his book: "How is it possible that ten years of Labour Government has created a society that is more unequal now than at any time since the second World War? It shouldn't be that (currently) three million of our children and two million of our pensioners still live in poverty[C1-33]."

Graham Stringer said: "My short answer is Social Justice, giving people control over their own lives, making sure people live in a just society where those who need it are looked after." Jeremy Corbyn asserted: "Our Party's history shows that our whole purpose ought to be about the elimination of poverty and sharing the riches of our society. In his context he praised the achievements of Labour governments including the national minimum wage (enabled by NL), the Equal Pay Act and various pension acts. Michael Meacher said: "The purpose of the Labour Party is what it has always been: to support those with less advantage, less opportunity and less income against those who have power, wealth and position. We must ensure that *our* people (at least two thirds of the population) get a fair and decent deal. We will never get pure equality – but there should be no more than reasonable inequality".

Austin Mitchell MP declared: "(It's) a case of every valley shall be exalted: supporting the bottom dock, improving the lives of what used to be referred to as the working class but now they're described as the 'underprivileged'." Katy Clark suggested: "To achieve genuine equality and fairness. Individuals must genuinely have an equal share of the power and wealth in society. The Labour Party's mission should be about making that a reality. It's about eradicating the huge gap that we have between rich and poor and bringing about a civilised society where everybody gets a reasonable chance in life. These are words that every Labour politician could speak; but not all are willing to do what is necessary to deliver that radical dream."

Some MPs, including John Cryer, called for the "redistribution of wealth and power" ... "(we need) exactly the opposite of the sort of casino economics that we saw over many years that resulted in the credit crunch which (in turn) resulted from abuses in the city and in boardrooms all over the world." Likewise Gordon Prentice called for a more equal society and added: "It's a matter of regret that the gap between the richest and poorest has widened during the rule of this Labour Government. They have followed a neo-liberal model that the rich should get richer. I recall Mandelson saying that he was 'intensely relaxed about people getting filthy rich' and that there would be a trickle down effect. *That distorted Labour's politics over the last 10-12 years.* It led to complete immobility at the suggestion that Labour's top income tax rate might be increased. Only at the end of our period in government will it be raised and then after the (2010) general election." Frank Dobson and Colin Challen also criticised the Mandelson "filthy rich speech" in this context.

Roger Berry believed that an aspect of Labour's current aims: "Ought to be to increase taxation, as it is only fair that those with the largest incomes should pay more. Labour now has to go in a more progressive direction by force of circumstances." The last word, on this topic, went to Jon Cruddas who said: "To my mind the Labour Party is the most appropriate vehicle to engage in a progressive search for equality on the basis of our interdependence. The Labour Party is a vehicle to ensure greater equality which is an ethic (that underpins) what we are here to do. To go back to fundamental issues; it's about how you view the human condition."

From among CLP Secretaries, Alison recalled a Marxist precept: "I like the old phrase 'From each according to their ability, to each according to their need'." She related this particularly to asylum seekers and to people in prison. Keith shared this view. A more typical response, from Fred, was: "To address inequality and create opportunity". Zach said the aim should be: "To minimise the differences between the weak and the strong, between the able and less able; between the 'haves' and 'have nots'. Furthermore to minimise the implications those differences have on the lives of the disadvantaged." Eric, echoing Cruddas, said: "As I am an egalitarian I think the Labour Party is the best home for me."

Most interviewees prioritised promoting and securing equality as one of Labour's most important aims and the one which best reflects its enduring values. Virtually all shades of socialist thought have subscribed to these views: from Karl Marx to old Clause 4 (1918) Labour Party constitution. Both this, and seeking equality of *outcomes,* involve not only redistribution of wealth but also that those who are able should work and contribute to the common wealth.

A special 2007 report from *The Economist*[C1-34] noted: "Income in Britain is distributed more unequally than in any big rich country except America. Switzerland excepted, the UK is far less equitable than all other European countries. The top 10% gets 27.3% of the cake the bottom 10% get 2.6%." The report continued: "Over the past decade the move to even greater inequality has been slowed by policies such as the minimum wage and benefits to the poor. Even so the pay of the top earners has rocketed whereas the disposable income of average households has risen only modestly."

On the left of the Labour Party there has always been ideological support for promoting economic equality. However right wing Labour thinkers from Anthony Crosland through to TB and GB have argued that distribution of wealth to the disadvantaged should be funded from the proceeds of new economic growth and "trickle down" from the wealthy to the poor rather than though systematic redistribution of existing wealth; for example through direct taxation. The present crisis of global warming and need for green policies makes this reactionary reliance on economic growth to fund redistribution no longer viable.

There is a newer, evidenced, line of argument that more equal societies are happier and better functioning societies for all who belong to them: even the most privileged. This is cogently advanced by Wilkinson and Pickett[C1-35]. In *The Sprit Level: why equality is better for everyone* (2009) they examined inequality of various kinds in the 20 richest developed countries in the world. Using official statistics from each country, they compared the ratio of income received by the top 20% to that of the bottom 20% whenever they assessed inequality between countries. Of the 20 countries studied; the UK had the third greatest inequality in income levels. Only Portugal and the USA were more unequal. Finland, Norway, Sweden, and especially Japan, had much greater equality[C1-36].

The second most popular aim was: *To provide and maintain high quality, mainly publicly provided, public services especially in: health, education and social housing. To increase public ownership and to cease privatising services and enterprises generally.* This was supported by 12 MPs, all three trade union leaders and six CLP Secretaries.

Public Services: Parliamentarians' views included those of Lord S., who believed we need: "A proper health service and an important education service". He added: "What differentiates me from NL these days is that I still believe in the need for the state to actually intervene and, therefore, I don't agree with this idea that we don't need big government – it's as critical now as it was in the past." Kelvin Hopkins called for: "A good welfare state with a substantial public sector." Jeremy Corbyn wanted Labour to take forward its "incredible achievements of the post-war welfare state". Austin Mitchell said: "Most working class people need a platform of publicly provided health, education and social housing to support themselves and to launch themselves into a more successful life than they otherwise would have done."

CLP secretaries offered: "The Labour Party is in existence to ensure that there is a social infrastructure and fabric that supports people and communities when they need help." (Fred) and: "To ensure that all citizens have access to the best possible health care, education and social services."(Helen). Quentin called for "promotion of outstanding health care and education". None of these statements explicitly say they should be publicly owned and run. Eric directly praised the government's provision of NHS services and Roland advocated a Party aim of "defending and extending public services".

Public Ownership of Enterprises: Among Backbenchers interviewed, there was debate about the common ownership of industrial and business enterprises. This was *blatantly omitted* from NC4. Alan Simpson MP wanted re-instatement of the part of Old Clause 4 about common ownership which he said was "not only about a shift in power but also a way to move from the individual to the collective". Alice Mahon argued: "Labour should be the Party of public ownership … I think that some of the privatisation policies undertaken by Thatcher, Major, Blair and Brown have been disastrous."

Kelvin Hopkins suggested that, in the recent past, Labour should have used, and in future should utilise, public ownership to regulate the major financial institutions. Jeremy Corbyn observed that the change in Clause 4 signalled a move, that was then already in progress, away from (Labour's belief in) a planned economy to reliance on market economics. John Cryer asserted: "Part of the emancipation of working people is public ownership".

Conversely senior backbencher M. said: "Historically, the Labour Party has had wonderful battles of left and right about tactics necessary for achievement – arguments about nationalisation. Nationalisation is not an objective per se, it is a tactic to achieve other objectives (for example, creating a more equal society). Early nationalisations, for instance of the coal industry, were not done because nationalisation was the objective but because they were the means for miners, and their families, to achieve greater economic prosperity."

CLP secretaries did not mention any aims relating to public enterprise.

The third greatest degree of support was given to the theme of *promoting fraternity and solidarity among working people, and within the Labour movement, taking a collectivist approach to social and other policies and enhancing trades union rights and rights at work*. This was favoured by 11 MPs, all three trade union leaders and four CLP secretaries. Attainment of this aim will be assessed in Chapter 4.

Examples of MP's viewpoints were: Jon Cruddas suggested that "the governing framework for the Labour Party" should be: "solidarity, fraternity and interdependence at the expense of those who emphasise atomised exchange and individualism." It should also be to reject the views of "those who believe that self interest is the only governing framework for the world".

Austin Mitchell believed a purpose of the Labour Party is: "to restore unity in society". Alan Simpson added that the Party "needs to move from the individual to the collective, not as an ideological standpoint, but because we believe that society is much better when we affirm that what we hold in common is a great deal better than what we hold individually."

Frank Dobson thought Labour needs to believe that: "If we are going to improve things we are all in this together." He continued: "The public got this point in 1997 and so voted Labour." Backbencher *B*. considered the Labour Party should work for: "Full and decent employment with fair working conditions". Peter Kilfoyle said: "The aim of the Labour Party is to represent the interests of the working people of Britain. That's as pertinent as it ever was."

Len McCluskey of Unite and Liz Snape of Unison also called for the repeal of most, if not all, of the Thatcher era's anti trade union laws.

CLP Secretary's views included Eric's. He stated: "I believe in mutualism. It gives access to otherwise unavailable services such as those provided by the NHS. I see the trades unions as an embodiment of mutualism. I used to like the mutual building societies. They are now missed."

The fourth most favoured aim was: *to promote peace, good international relations and third world development*. This was supported by 10 Backbenchers and five CLP secretaries.

MPs' views included: Senior Backbencher A, who proposed: "Internationalism is at the core of what we believe in". Clare Short said: "A Labour Britain should use its influence to secure world peace and international justice."

Frank Dobson wanted the Party to "work to improve prospects for peace and for peaceful societies abroad". Alice Mahon argued: "The Labour Party should be the Party of Peace". Jeremy Corbyn added: "One of the main aims of the Labour Party ought to be about securing international peace and the rule of international law." Colin Challen stated the Labour Party's "agenda of fairness can no longer be delivered on a socialism in one country type model."

In the sphere of helping developing countries the following aims were suggested: "We should focus, as we have already done, on the poorest people in the poorest countries." (Chris Mullin) and "We need a positive agenda for the world as a whole to deal with poverty and illiteracy." "Because I think third world countries need help to tackle those problems" (Backbencher B). Labour should promote" equitable international development" (Clare Short).

Secretaries made judgements about foreign policy: Bob believed the Labour Party should "work with others across the whole world to make it a better and fairer place". Quentin said that the Party should "promote the cause of peace and justice throughout the world". William had professional expertise in this field. He proposed that the Party should pursue the following more detailed objectives: "Work for a Middle East two state solution, really be at the heart of Europe, agree to Turkish EU membership (once they pass all the tests) and give practical and financial support to the United Nations."

Oliver wanted Labour "to work for a world where the benefits of modern technology are put to use in a fair way and people are enabled to develop their creativity and talents." He added that: "The Labour Party should work with others across the whole world to make it a better and fairer place."

The Labour Party has long advocated working for peace and good international relations. Many members, including Neil Kinnock and TB, once belonged to the Campaign for Nuclear Disarmament but later dropped their memberships. Like their predecessors, NL governments were handicapped by inheriting the legacy of Empire, the "Special Relationship" with the US and large, expensive armed forces.

The next aim (5th in ranked order) was supported by a sixth of all stakeholders. It was: *To manage the country's economy effectively, to secure economic growth and thus to increase the incomes of the population, secure full employment, generate wealth and levy direct taxes to redistribute wealth to fund public services.*

MPs' statements included Kelvin Hopkins', who said: "(A Labour) Government needs to provide much more for the less well off and (to secure) a society of full employment with the government managing the economy to make sure that that happens." Roger Berry argued: "in dealing with the global economic crisis and the public sector deficit, it is not good enough for a Labour government to contemplate *only* cutting spending. The other side of the coin is increasing taxation and it's only fair that those with the biggest pockets should pay". Colin Challen contended: "We are dependent on our competitiveness in a global market so we should re-calibrate our policies to recognise that".

From among CLP Secretaries: Oliver thought that Labour Governments should aim to run a "regulated economy". Fred said that Labour "should run the economy in such a way that people are rewarded for success". Diane called for Labour Governments "to increase the country's wealth and distribute it so that the whole population benefits." Simon wanted "the prioritisation of full, or a high level of, employment".

Although not always articulated clearly, good economic management and a healthy economy have usually been regarded as essential by Labour Governments eager to underpin and grow public and social services[C1-37].

The next most popular aim, 6th in ranked order, (supported by six CLP secretaries and only two MPs) was: *To win elections nationally and locally and to keep the Conservatives out of power.* Attainment of this aim is a focus of Chapter 2.

Chris Mullin MP said: "You have to take the centre ground with you. There's no point in being ideologically pure but powerless".

Particularly noteworthy was that three of the CLP secretaries presented winning elections as their *one and only aim* for the Party. They described it as an end in itself not as a means to any end. This view of power as an end in itself is disconcerting. However it was probably held by TB and GB; as was evidenced by Lilleker and Lees-Marshment[C1-38]. Two thoughtful contributions came from Irene who proposed: "To be in government locally and nationally so as to be able to take action to build a fairer and more equal Britain and to tackle disadvantage in all its forms"; and Tom, who said: "The Labour Party needs to keep out the Tories so reducing the damage that can be done … in government Labour is now doing damage to the interests of the working class – but the Tories would be worse."

7th equal was: *To deal with the environmental crisis, carbon emissions and the environmental threats of urban development; these are major issues of our times".* This was chosen by only five respondents, almost all MPs.

Clare Short said: "This is *the* big issue of our times. We must deal with the environmental crisis, carbon emissions and environmental threats of urban development." Chris Mullin stated: "The big issue, that I think will become the biggest, as the years pass, is the future of the planet. There I would expect us to become rather more engaged."

Colin Challen argued: "Tackling climate change is the overriding priority in this, and any other, developed country. NL, going along with global liberalisation market agendas, has accelerated carbon dioxide emissions and made tackling climate change worse. We could instead use global institutions to tackle climate change effectively."

Secretary William claimed: (Labour should) "make bold moves to combat climate change and introduce a green economy and society. The opportunity provided by the current economic and environmental crisis is too good to waste but it won't last long."

The relative lack of urgency to develop green policies and address global warming seems to reflect the indifference of Western society in general. However Linden[C1-39] pointed out that the last decades of the twentieth century saw "an unmistakable and extraordinary warming". This started in 1980 and the record warmest years in the USA started in 1995 with virtually every successive year beating the temperature record of the previous one. During the same period there were record droughts and floods across the world and the strongest El Niño in 150,000 years. Joyce argued: "When ocean waters rise above 82.4 degrees Fahrenheit, evaporation increases dramatically, providing an enormous reservoir of potential energy for storms[41]."

Also 7th (equal) was: *To promote democracy and democratic institutions within the UK and throughout the world and to develop, and improve, democracy and democratic practice within the Labour Party.* Attainment of this aim is discussed in Chapters 3, 7 and 10. This goal was identified by five interviewees: a mixture of CLP secretaries and backbenchers.

Some MPs' views: Michael Meacher believed that "NL was weak on democratic accountability both to the public and within the Party itself." John Grogan called for "more democracy in running the economy".

Several CLP secretaries identified this theme. Fred said: "The Labour Party was formed to change the social system, so that it is more representative of the needs of ordinary people, so that entrenched interest is challenged and so that people are enabled to speak for themselves." Quentin considered a major aim of the Party should be: "To encourage a fair, open and transparent system of government". William called for the Party to commit to: "Electoral and democratic reform (including Proportional Representation or Alternative Vote) and much greater devolution of power and resources."

The remaining significant theme indicated by a few MPs, but by fewer CLP secretaries, was:

7th equal: *Promoting equalities (of opportunity and outcome) and countering discrimination for frequently disadvantaged groups of people: women, racial and ethnic minorities, gay people and lesbians, minority religious groups, young people and people with disabilities. i.e. equalities other than those relating to wealth and social class.* This was favoured by four MPs and two CLP secretaries.

MP's comments included: Clare Short's. She said: "Everyone should have the opportunity to be a fulfilled person." She clarified that this was not only about distribution of wealth and power but also about countering other disadvantages. Jeremy Corbyn spoke of the "importance of past and future race relations legislation". Michael Meacher argued: "It's the Party's job to oppose barriers of gender and disability as well as those of social class." Senior backbencher M. proposed that Labour should "oppose sexism and promote the rights of gay, lesbian and disabled people".

Both CLP secretaries wrote in terms of helping disadvantaged people of all kinds and arising from all causes.

A pessimistic general postscript came from Secretary Vince who offered: "*It is unclear to me now what the purpose of the Labour Party is. Ever since the creation of NL it seems to have lost its identity and merely tried to appeal to the section of society that will ensure that it attains power.*" This topic is addressed in Chapter 2.

It is vital to include a discussion of the use of the word "socialism" in any debate about the Labour Party's values and aims. It was virtually unspoken in the latter days of NL. One could surmise that the Leadership thought, as Peter Pan did in respect of not believing in fairies, that if anyone mentioned "socialism" (even when prefaced by the word "democratic") another 2,000 votes would die in every marginal seat. Only three MPs and three secretaries ventured to mention it when defining the Party's aims. Examples were: "To recreate the democratic socialist world that we were on our way to before it all crashed under Thatcher" (Kelvin Hopkins) and "To implement democratic socialist principles in government" (Secretary Colin). More details of trade union leaders' opinions about Party aims and values appear in Chapter 4.

Most interviewees proposed promoting social equality as the paramount Labour Party aim. This was underpinned by a related value. There is much justification for these aspirations for the Party. They come from the Party's democratic socialist traditions, working class roots and enduring values. However, as Wilkinson and Pickett[C1-41] pointed out: greater equality is also required in order to make our society more successful and cohesive. NC4 did not advocate promoting social or economic equality; only the oversight of all included in TB's voluminous big tent: whether rich or poor. Interviewees and NC4 agreed about the importance of good public services but the former were more inclined to suggest that they should be publicly owned and that some business enterprises/public utilities should also be publicly owned.

The above groups of interviewees advocated maintaining peace as a major priority in international relations but NC4 did not (in the author's opinion, TB might well have found it difficult to be Prime Minister without engaging in war). Both viewpoints prioritised assistance to poor countries. These respondents, outside the NL elite, sometimes advocated fraternity and working class solidarity but NL's 1995 constitution rejected this in favour of amorphous duties to everyone in their magnum size marquee.

Interviewees' 5th and 6th priorities of good economic management and winning elections were much higher in NL's order of priorities.

How do these stakeholder aims relate to New Clause 4?

It is now relevant to review the aims in NC4 sections 2, 3, 4 and 5 (Appendix 2) in the context of aims identified by stakeholders. Many of the same elements are included in both sets of aims but, in NC4, they are frequently fudged and not clearly expressed. Their emphasis often differs significantly from that given by interviewed stakeholders. NC4's wording was so ambiguous that it could well have been a ploy to convince Party members that it meant one thing and floating voters that it meant the opposite.

In order of presentation NC4 gives first place (in section 2A) to effective management of a dynamic economy based on the (unfettered) free market and on competition. It also mentions "a thriving private sector". These factors were seldom raised by interviewees. However there was frequent stakeholder acknowledgement that we need a successful economy, but mainly as a means to provide jobs and fund public services. Some interviewees suggested that the financial institutions should be regulated more effectively. Most acknowledged that we have to survive in global markets.

In NC4 there is no mention of publicly owned enterprise. The latter was dear to the hearts of many respondents. The clause refers to partnership and co-operation to produce wealth. At best this can only be interpreted as being through public – private partnership or, possibly, some form of encouragement of mutual organisations (mentioned by one CLP secretary) and advocated subsequently in Lord Glasman's "Blue Labour"[C1-42]. Many respondents, together with this NC4 aim, argued that a strong economy should underpin the "opportunity for all to work and prosper".

The clause's section about the economy (NC4 2A) related to the second most popular aim identified by respondents. It called for high quality public services. However these were only required where they were thought to be essential to the common good (by whom?). Would they be owned by the public or accountable to them? Accountability for care of the vulnerable, for education (e.g. at Academies) and for managing social rented housing is difficult to enforce in respect of private profit making providers and even in respect of not for profit organisations. The 2011 collapse of Southern Cross private care homes illustrated this problem. Private providers often have to be managed through virtually meaningless and vaguely worded contracts, enforced at arms length. Residential and domiciliary care of vulnerable older people is essential to the common good but its private sector management and accountability systems are commonly ineffective, as many contemporary Care Quality Commission reports and the Southern Cross debacle demonstrated. What many interviewees called for was publicly owned public services.

The second section of NC4, to some extent, reflected the most popular category of Party aims chosen by interviewees. Headed "A just society", it indicated that Labour should support the weak – but (only) as much as the strong. Like many respondents, it aspires to eradicate poverty in Britain and promises to provide security against fear (of something unspecified). Hopefully that something might be Beveridge's giant of "want"[C1-43]? This section of NC4 calls for equality of opportunity but not of outcome – unlike some respondents. It promises the nurturing of families but not specifically of those who are disadvantaged. It is a half-hearted, mealy mouthed, attempt at articulating the drive to combat class and economic inequality which stakeholder interviewees considered should be the Party's top priority aim. Section of NC4 2B is at one with many respondents in calling for the Party to deliver people from "the tyranny of prejudice". It also calls for the protection from the "abuse of power". Section 2C promises an open and accountable democracy. This aim was supported by a relatively small number of respondents. Most of these believed that NL might have conducted public or Party democracy in a more transparent and accountable manner (see Chapters 7, 8 and 9). As in NC4 section 2D; a minority of respondents identified a Party aim as being "to secure a healthy environment which is to be protected for future generations."

Section 3 of NC4 deals with foreign policy. Its first sub-section deals with strong defence and security. That aim was not highlighted by any Party stakeholder interviewed. However significant numbers of interviewees mentioned securing "peace, freedom, economic security and environmental protection for all". Many participants complained about the ways in which TB engaged in military intervention. The Chilcot Report on the War in Iraq was published in early July 2016. It was very critical of the UK's conduct of the war, and of Tony Blair's actions in that context. However the report did not give an opinion as to the war's legality or otherwise. This was claimed to be outside Chilcot's terms of reference. A number of respondents, as this clause, wanted the Party's government, to work in co-operation with the United Nations, the European Union and the Commonwealth. Section 4 of NC4 relates to the collectivism and fraternity aspects of interviewees' chosen aims by calling for working with trades unions and co-operative societies to achieve our aims – as is the Party's tradition. However Blair's all inclusive Party was created to include working equally with voluntary organisations, consumer groups and other unspecified representative bodies. This addition also featured in the specifications for Party policy-making machinery that appeared in the Partnership in Power constitutional changes (1997) CI-44. These latter priorities did not feature strongly in stakeholder's identifications.

Chapter Conclusion

With the coming of New Labour the Party's aims and values were embodied in the new constitution (New Clause 4). This abandoned all commitment to public ownership of enterprises and of many public services. The prior commitment became to help the strong virtually as much as the weak. The only pre-existing Party aims that were retained, in full, were winning elections and good management of the economy. However as responses from MPs, CLP secretaries and TU leaders, in this Chapter and in Chapter 11, have demonstrated you can take the Party out of Labour but you can't take Labour out of the Party. It is no accident that CLPs have recently started to call for the restoration of the Old Clause 4, in terms of content if not verbatim. The remainder of the book examines how far NL Governments between 1997 and 2010 met both their own NC4 aims and those traditional aims adopted by significant, but non – elite, party stakeholders interviewed here.

CHAPTER 2
What was New Labour?

Was it merely a project about public relations, concessions to
neo-liberalism and frequent electoral success?

"In matters of style swim with the current, in matters of principle stand like a rock"
Thomas Jefferson

"I regard New Labour as an unfortunate interregnum"
Michael Meacher MP (Labour Leadership Candidate 2007)

*"Fundamentally New Labour was anti-democratic: a centralised
monolith incorporated more like a large corporation than a political party.
What's the brand and how do we sell it? What's the market? How do we
make sure that we have a disciplined sales force?"*
John McDonnell MP (Labour Leadership candidate, 2007)

Chapter Contents
Overview of the New Labour phenomenon Main
characteristics of New Labour:
Winning elections the greatest, if not sole, priority Preoccupation
with public/media relations and spin
Focus groups, opinion polls and press barons determine policy Light
on ideology (neo-liberalism) aside
Blair's 'big tent' was too big Party
organisation
Emasculating the Real Labour Party
Doing good by excessive stealth
Could Labour have won elections after 1994 without turning 'New'?

Around the time that NL took over the Party, there was a popular TV series, based in Ireland, in which a young, and officially celibate, priest fell in love with a local young woman (Ballykissangel). When he came to confess this to her, he told the story of a young polar bear who complained to his mother that he did not feel like a bear any more. Mother bear retorted that "Of course he was a bear, because he walked like a bear, grunted like a bear, and looked like a bear." The young bear sadly replied: "But I'm freezing". It occurred to the author that many in the Labour Party, including herself, shared the juvenile bear's predicament: we looked and behaved like traditional Labour Party members, but felt excluded and stigmatised by our, now almost unrecognisable, Party. We were freezing and being frozen out.

Introduction: What was the New Labour phenomenon?

This Chapter gives backbencher, trade union leader and constituency secretary interviewees the opportunity to assess New Labour's changes to the Party, as a political organisation. Subjects identified by them as being significant included: communications, populism, media relations, organisational management, policy strategy, the narrow focus on winning elections and fundamental changes to the ideology of the Party itself. They were asked to state their opinions of NL, this included defining it and assessing its tactics and strategy. Their views are grouped under theme headings that reflect the pattern of their responses. These interviewees also considered the changes in organisational culture and methods of operating (such as top down control) that NL adopted as a means to winning and retaining power. They then analysed the related political implications.

Some respondents raised the question as to *what* NL *really was?* Was it a mere publicity machine with little ideological substance? Did it have effective tactics but no strategy? Did NL have the overriding objective of developing neo-liberal economic policies? Alternatively was NL a fantasy creation because it was not officially recognised, as a distinct entity, within the Party rules and constitution? Arguably it was a cuckoo in the Labour Party's nest that evicted many genuine Labour offspring: in terms of people, policies and ideas.

Development of the New Labour approach:

Early development of NL began under Neil Kinnock's leadership in the late 1980s but it did not reach maturity until after Tony Blair (TB) became Party leader in 1994.

Peter Mandelson (then newly appointed Party Head of Communications) told Party Guru Philip Gould[C2-1], as early as 1985, that the Party needed to develop: "one or two key thoughts, statements and messages that we want to ram home by constant repetition." Mandelson continued – "and we have to present an image of the Party, or messages or use language or whatever, that chimes with what people want to think".

During the 1987 election campaign Gould warned Kinnock to change speeches that suggested that Labour tax policies would make the middle classes worse off[C2-2]. In the early 1990s Gould submitted a report to the Party. It included ten principles around which the communications and outputs of the party should be based[C2-3]. These were:

• An agreed early strategy.

• Selectivity of target audience.

• A simple message often repeated.

• Orchestrated, cohesive presentation of that message.

• Clear allocation of responsibility for tasks, clear lines of authority and accountability and adequate structures of co-ordination.

• Positive, proactive press relations.

• A shift in campaigning emphasis from grass roots/opinion forming to influencing electoral opinion through the mass media (which implied fewer campaign workers on the ground).

• Proper use of outside expertise.

• Less publicity material but used more often.

• Highest-level political authority and support for these principles.

The NL new model public relations machine, designed by Gould and Mandelson, initially proved very effective; but it subsequently developed flaws.

Between 1997 and 2007 NL's hallmark was winning all general elections. NL governments boasted the longest continuous period in power in the Party's history. It exceeded that of the combined Wilson/Callaghan governments by a tiny margin. The most significant factors in these victories were the Party's media and public relations, populist policies aimed at voters in key marginals and turning the Party into what Lilleker and Lees-Marshment termed a "Market Oriented Party" (MOP)[C2-4]. Between 1979 and 1992 the Party's public and media relations were frequently unproductive. Labour failed to win every general election during that period. Action was required to market the party more effectively.

NL viewed Party relations with the media as a suitable case for treatment. Gould reported: "Mandelson was infuriated by his lack of control over the media – our communications vehicles are TV, radio and newspapers[C2-5]".

When asked to identify the Labour Party's main aims, backbenchers, union leaders and Constituency Labour Party (CLP) secretaries collectively rated the aim of 'winning elections" as only the sixth equal priority out of nine (See Chapter 1). Only two MPs gave it priority but six out of 27 CLP secretaries prioritised it. Half of those secretaries identified this as *the sole aim* for the Labour Party rather than seeing it as a means to more important ends. This total orientation to power, as the end in itself, is a measure of the success of the NL message 14 years after the Party was captured by NL.

Winning elections is vital and little can be achieved politically without it. In the words of Leader Ed Miliband in at Labour's National Policy Forum on 20th November 2010[C2-6]: "Opposition is crap!" However sight should never be lost of what elections are being won *for*. If they are being won only for the goals and values of a Party to be confounded, as the Party severely trims its aims and policies to please floating voters and the right wing media, then those victories are hollow and almost purposeless. Winning elections should not be achieved at a destructively high price for the Party itself and those whose interests the Party should be serving.

As Roy Hattersley observed: *"Sometimes politicians have to moderate their principles to win power. But abandoning them altogether makes winning pointless*[C2-7]*."* NL Governments achieved some of, what can be regarded as, the Party's traditional ideological aims. However it sold out on many others (see Chapters 5 and 6).

New Labour: a market oriented party

Lilleker and Lees-Marshment (L and LM)[C2-8] advocated the concept of a "Market Oriented Party": largely based on their study of NL. This offers a model which helps to explain the NL phenomenon. They examined the use of political marketing in the UK (and in similar Western Liberal Democracies) over an extended period. They researched the nature of NL Government and Conservative Opposition between 1997 and 2003 and reviewed relevant research of others. They concluded that the "*dominant goal* of the major parties is to obtain control of government through long term electoral success." Other contemporary research[C2-9, C2-10 C2-11] provides supporting evidence. On the basis of Lilleker and Lees-Marshment's own research, they judged UK Labour and Conservative Parties to have adopted electoral success as their most important goal during much of the previous 40 year period. The author considers (see Chapter 5) that this trend was less pronounced in respect of Labour before the mid 1980s. L and LM[C2-12] argued that: "Smaller parties, which do not aim to win control of the national government, can be inclined to exert influence over the political agenda on behalf of one (or more) sections of society".

It appears that the tightly knit group of creators of the NL Project had a carefully constructed game plan which was covertly and skilfully implemented. Theories explaining NL's tactics and strategy for political marketing were put forward by L and LM[C2-13]. They defined political marketing as: "the use of marketing concepts and techniques in politics." …parties … "increasingly conduct market intelligence to identify citizen concerns, change their behaviour to meet those demands and communicate their 'product offering' more effectively."

L and LM defined a Party's "product" as including: the people, characteristics and methods of operation involving its leadership, MPs (including candidates), grass-roots members, staff, constitution, symbols, activities and policies. They then proposed a three part typology (classification system)[C2-14] which classified parties according to their attitude to, and practices of, marketing.

A "Product Oriented Party" (POP) is a conviction-based party which develops its "product" to match its established ideologies and values. The paradigm is "Eat it and like it". This type of Party argues its case to try to persuade electors of the value of this "product", which it does not change to win their support. This category sometimes described the Labour Party prior to the NL era. However between 1945 and 1994, the Labour Party sometimes changed its policies, or relied on presentation, to sell its message. For example, during the Kinnock leadership there was a major effort to improve the Party's image through election literature and adoption of the red rose symbol.[C2-15]

Lilleker and Lees-Marshment's[C2-16] second category is the "Sales Oriented Party" (SOP). This type of Party tries to persuade voters to 'buy' their product through extensive use of market research followed by marketing communications. It uses knowledge of ways in which the market can be manipulated. Research is done about how to construct messages and communicate them. *This type of Party does not radically change its values and policies to suit what people want but it tries, through presentation and persuasion, to make people want what it offers.*

Their third category was the "Market Oriented Party" (MOP). L and LM argued that the MOP adopts the principle that: "to win an election a party needs to identify and understand public priorities, concerns and demands *beforehand*; then it must design an *entire new* 'product' that reflects them." There is no effort made to change elector's opinions. The Party delivers what voters say they need, want and ask for. The organisation is driven not by any ideology or by its Leader's opinion: it delivers policies and structures solely to satisfy its market. Some MPs, for example: Alan Simpson and Kelvin Hopkins, complain bitterly about this approach later in this chapter.

L and LM, believed that the expertise of *all* Party members from the leadership downwards is then used *to develop responses to elector's demands rather than to dictate, or even suggest, policy to them. The total membership, they argue, will design a model product (policy programme) on the basis of market research findings.* This is not what NL did. Ordinary Party members, trade unionists and even Backbench MPs, had little influence on which government policies were prioritised. The Leadership, and Party machine, developed responses to electors' demands: designed to meet their requirements. Electors are then told that the Party is offering the product that they say they want.

When the market oriented "product" has been provisionally designed it is tested for durability according to set criteria and further adjusted. These criteria include: achievability – if it is not achievable, *and* subsequently achieved, the Party will lose voter support. Therefore they must make realistic policy promises *and be able to deliver them effectively.* L and LM argued that failing to deliver on promises adversely affected NL's election results: especially after the 2001 election. They attributed this to TB,
like Thatcher before him, having become less focused on the delivery agenda. They asserted that: after 2001 NL often acted on TB's personal convictions rather than on findings of its market research. This requirement for delivery underpinned the 1997 Prescott pledge card: whose simple promises were thought to be achievable[C2-17].

In a MOP, competition analysis should follow. This analysis aims to identify strengths and weaknesses of the Opposition and of the Party itself. It searches for gaps in the market for the Party to fill: just as a business would do for its goods. This may have led to triangulation in respect of policies: that is conflating them with Tory measures. L and LM added[C2-18] that acting on the results of competition analysis could involve making changes to *any* aspect of the Party (not only policies):NL did this extensively. Following competition analysis; a Party attempts to build on its strengths and reduce its weaknesses. It attacks the opposition publicly for their perceived weaknesses[C2-19].

In the MOP model the Party *redesigns itself* to satisfy voter demand. This can involve drastic changes to the Party for example:in leadership, member's rights, constitution and behaviour. L and LM warned[C2-20]: "This can *generate internal opposition* and is *unlikely to be effectively implemented without some adjustment and internal management.*" That explains NL's replacement of long serving Party staff by new employees who lacked democratic socialist principles. This facilitated the drastic change of culture among Party staff that permitted a top down management style. Staff were required to impose the new ideology and culture on the membership: marginalising those who did not comply (see Chapter 7). However many of Labour's members were, and remain, ideologically motivated along democratic socialist lines (YouGov poll for LabOUR Commission, 2007)[C2-21].

Core voters became disillusioned. Research by Seyd and Whiteley in 2002[C2-22] discovered that NL disengaged class and ideological loyalties. This led to low turnouts of electors in 'heartland' constituencies. Many MPs felt marginalised and dissent among them grew.[C2-23]

A MOP has to engage in "support analysis". This identifies which sectors of the electorate's support are crucial to winning elections and then targets them. Currently in the UK, with its first-past-the-post electoral system for Westminster, floating voters in marginal constituencies are targeted. This has led to a narrow focus on meeting their needs and demands. This orientation is unlikely to address either the needs of the most disadvantaged people or Labour's longstanding political priorities. These marginal voter's priorities are certainly not 'the religion of socialism' of which Nye Bevan spoke. This pragmatic choice of priorities, by NL, led to numerous complaints from stakeholders interviewed. Their grievances were heightened because insufficient priority was given to policies to assist the least affluent. Even worse: NL's pro-poor policies were often concealed, or played down, so as not to upset Middle England (see section "Doing Good by Excessive Stealth" below).

Lynne Jones MP said: "I've always favoured proportional representation. I liked the recent Jenkins Commission[C2-24] recommendations which kept proportionality with party top-ups. Any system in which a few marginal constituencies decide which way the total vote goes means the leadership of a party will just go with their flow."

The final stage of this marketing process is unifying the Party around the "proposed product" before it is marketed to voters. L and LM[C2-25] pointed out that, if the majority of party members, candidates and MPs, are not in sympathy with 'the proposed product' then they will not be able (or willing) to promote it convincingly and effectively. Probably this view was shared by NL's hierarchy and partly explains their alleged fixing of the Parliamentary candidate selection process (see Chapter 8). The NL Leadership apparently disregarded the damage that much grass-roots defection and disillusion might do to doorstep campaigning. They relied on the mass media for campaigning instead.

A critical question posed by L and L·M, at the conclusion of their research, was: "*Whether any MOP can achieve a market orientation, win a general election, and still have the support of the majority of the Party's MPs, Candidates and members?* "[C2-26] The outcome of NL was that it achieved a market orientation nationally and externally but was reduced to an elite Parliamentary organisation with withered grass roots. The author's opinion is that this is what the NL Leadership set out to achieve, or at least was willing to countenance. L and LM believed that destruction of a Party's grass roots would be fatal in the UK. This was because British parties (especially Labour) were already poorly funded and could ill afford to run constituency-based campaigns without numerous volunteers. The desire to reduce financial dependence on ordinary (and trades union affiliated) members, according to Oborne, explains why NL was keen to recruit wealthy private donors who were not 'genuinely' Labour[C2-27] and why it sought state funding which it had hoped, in vain, that the Hayden Philips Committee would recommend and secure[C2-28].

Mair[C2-29] argued, as did the author in her *Save the Labour Party* pamphlet[C2-30], that political parties heavily depend on ordinary members for support, campaigning and fundraising related to national and local politics. Grass-roots members are needed to give public credibility and democratic legitimacy to a Party.

'Winning elections matters above all else'

L and LM's research led them to conclude that, from 1994 onwards, winning general elections was the most important, and virtually *only*, aim adopted by *both* major UK parties. When examining NL's conduct they found that Labour Leaders used the results of market research to change *every* aspect of what they termed the Labour Party's "Product".

Exclusion of grass roots members from internal decision making processes helped to lose NL 62% of its individual members between 1997 and 2010[C2-31]. Some trades unions gave up their Labour Party affiliation during the NL era (see Chapter 4). This further reduced campaign funds and workers. These trends substantiate the views of some MPs interviewed such as Roger Berry and Graham Stringer. They argued that usually, when Labour goes into government, many members evaluate its performance and are dissatisfied. Possibly when a Party is in opposition, and there is no 'own' government performance to appraise, disappointment is less likely to arise among the grass roots. After their study of NL's progress; L and LM concluded that perhaps the MOP model was not as useful to a government in office as it is to an opposition seeking election. They also asserted: "Being seen as a strong leader but one who is also responsive is not an easy task."[C2-32]

This dilemma undermined the popularity of TB and Gordon Brown (GB).

L and LM[C2-33] also discovered that NL (and the Conservatives) sometimes suffered electorally at *local* level, because their message was standardised centrally and delivered *nationally*. In accordance with findings of research done for Ed Miliband about the 2010 general election results, it was shown that MPs and parties who ran a good, locally oriented, campaign did better than average[C2-34]. All this suggested that candidates who marketed themselves as "the local representative, fighting for the concerns of local people" and who got themselves a strong local media profile received an improvement in their share of the vote and a concomitant increase in turnout.

Lynne Jones MP said: "I'm a great believer in asking people what they think about local issues, in local action and in building trust within the community. That's how I came into politics: understanding local issues and campaigning on them." The centralised approach of the MOP party, based on national market research, has difficulty in meeting this localised demand. Political market research tends to highlight short term demands and national trends. It is doubtful whether it can accurately identify longer term, or local, political requirements.

The political and social environments, in which a Party operates, are constantly changing. A political organisation wanting to survive, and prosper, must constantly survey these environments and make changes to accommodate their demands. However it should not lose its fundamental values and direction in the process. The core of NL's strategy was to change its 'product' by denying the Party's past; including its traditional aims and values.[C2-35] Roy Hattersley believed: "Labour will not succeed, and may not even survive, if it fears that its future depends on apologising for its beliefs."[C2-36]

Was just winning NL's only significant goal? Almost all MPs, union leaders and CLP secretaries interviewed believed that winning, and retaining, power was an essential prerequisite for Labour to implement its priorities and policies. However few considered that winning should be its sole, or even paramount, aim. Philip Gould[C2-37] set a different benchmark: "New Labour should be obsessed with winning. Winning has to be the central aim of politics, because only with power can genuine politics start."

MPs' opinions follow: Jon Cruddas argued: "To my mind retaining power became an end in itself. This increased as the (NL) coalition splintered and fractured when the Party became about positioning. 2008 saw the end of NL. This was shown in terms of the last election results (in June 2008 for local authorities and the European Assembly) being the worst since 1910. It was also demonstrated in terms of the collapse of our (Party) membership."

Backbencher B. asserted: "*Obviously we have to win an election to do anything*. It's getting the balance as to whether, and when, you are seen to be standing for something." Michael Meacher described NL as being: "... very largely a power project which is mainly about winning elections".

John Grogan said: "To be brutally honest; I've had a career as MP for Selby for 13 years and I wouldn't have had that if we hadn't won elections. In Blair and Brown we had two winners when they were at their best. Grogan continued: "I suppose, because TB and GB won elections, they centralised power. I might have been tempted to do the same. Blair must have thought 'I won: so now everything will go through Downing St.' ... Without that sort of leadership I would never have won Selby as there are lots of Tories there." Such views, and the gratitude they engendered, probably contributed to keeping most Backbench MPs quiescent, during the early Blair years. However they were not the only reasons for Backbench compliance. This issue will be discussed, in the context of Parliamentary selections and discipline, in Chapters 8 and 9.

Alice Mahon suggested: "In a sense winning elections has become an end in itself not a means to an end. It's a dilemma: if you want to change things you've got to have power". Conversely Chris Mullin argued: "I don't think that winning elections became an end in itself."

In response to the question of whether winning became almost the sole aim for NL, Roy Hattersley said: "The constant criticism of NL both from the Conservatives and from within the Party, that Blair leads, is that priority of place that is always given to electoral advantage and the consequent downgrading of principle."[C2_38] TB said, soon after he became Labour leader: "Past Labour leaders lost (elections) because they compromised ... I will never compromise ... *I would rather be beaten and leave politics than bend to the Party.*"[C2_39]

Katy Clark MP said: "I believe that NL probably genuinely started as a wish from some people to change the Party in a way that they honestly thought would make it more electable. Many started to believe in the brand. However, actually, it had been created not because it was the right thing to do, in terms of policy content, but because it was the view of some people, that it was the only way that Labour was going to win power again. Some people, who were willing to go down the NL line when TB was elected, never dreamed it would have gone as far as it did."

Peter Kilfoyle MP asserted: "The *whole point for the NL leadership was being at the top: not what they did there. Their ambition was just to stay in post irrespective of what they achieved.* They would do *anything* to stay in power."

CLP Secretary Vince contended: "We should learn that a political party should have principles and an ideology that can win arguments and not just target specific areas of the electorate simply in order to win power."

Simon Jenkins, 2007 argued: "Blair treated the Labour Party as had none of his predecessors. He simply tore it apart. When the re-construction was more or less complete in 1996 Labour was no longer a 'labour movement 'but an electoral machine for the advancement of Blair himself, in effect, his court ... an electable Labour Party, was liberated from past ideological content – everything that stood in the way of winning votes must be discarded. Blair camouflaged this shift to the right in a fog of abstraction."[C2_40]

In 2000 Alastair Campbell reported that TB had rejected any idea that the Labour Party should stand for the interest of any specific social class because this would be an excluding message. Above all Labour must not give the impression that it is talking only about the working class.[C2_41]

Thus the Labour Party became a different type of organisation from the one that TB inherited. The overriding need to win elections subsumed principle, ideology and the Party's traditional aims and values. In 2001 a retired national Party officer, who continued to do voluntary work at the Millbank Headquarters, told the author: "The Party is a completely different type of organisation to what it was when I last worked there in the early 1990s."

Public relations and spin

At the core of NL's activity were public relations and political marketing: improving the Party's relationship with electors in order to enhance its appeal to them and to secure electoral victory. Spin, the main instrument of NL public relations, can be defined as talking up the policies or actions of a Government – mainly to secure favourable media coverage – by using press conferences and the like. This is usually done by public relations staff; or by senior politicians on the advice of the latter. The NL Project devoted time and attention obsessively to building up relationships and currying favour with the media's proprietors. One indicator of this was TB's visit to Australia to address the senior staff of Murdoch's Newscorp before the 1997 election. Journalist John Harris wrote: "Self-evidently, powerful people tend to cluster together. Those who control the media are a particularly strong magnet for the rich and influential, there is a long history of people from all sides of politics sharing their company."[C2_42]

Alongside spin there was extensive use of "rebuttal". During the NL era the Party ran a Rebuttal Unit whose sole task was to rebut damaging or hostile stories in the media. The author encountered Mandelson aide Benjamin Wegg-Prosser in the mid-1990s. He informed her that he then worked full-time in the Party's "important rebuttal unit". He explained that the function of this unit was to instantly deny the truth of *every* developing media story hostile to NL. However, unlike spin doctoring, rebuttal scarcely featured in interviewees' responses. It was mentioned only once, by one constituency secretary. During Ed Miliband's leadership the Party still ran a rebuttal unit. However it could have been used more effectively than it actually was then, especially during the 2015 general election campaign.

Public relations methods used by NL were described by Clare Short: "NL was a public relations machine built around advertising techniques, focus groups, soundbites and a massive emphasis on spin. It was centralised to cope with the twenty-four hour media. Their regime was absolutely obsessed with keeping Mr Murdoch and managers of his regime happy."

In her book *An Honourable Deception* Clare Short remembered that John Smith "disliked Mandelson's divisive style of spinning the tough qualities of the leader at the expense of the treasured values of the party[C2_43]." Many backbenchers had serious reservations about the style, content and frequent use of spin by the NL Leadership. It was seen as a device to win and retain power rather than a set of values, aims and an ideology within the traditions of the Labour Party.

MP Alan Simpson said: "I think *it's a mistake to see NL as a political party. It's a marketing device. In the same way that product brands have a shelf life – exactly the same applies to NL.*"

Backbencher A. said: "In the end NL was largely a matter of presentation rather than policy. It was a way of getting elected. The first thing was the strategic re-positioning of the Party which was partly about the way we sold ourselves and partly about policy changes. The first big achievement was to be elected on such a large mandate."

NL was undoubtedly developed as a well-oiled public relations machine focussed on maximising electoral popularity. The question of whether it had more substance than that is discussed later in this Chapter.

Roger Berry argued: "It was inevitable, and right, that Labour had to deal with public relations, in opposition. It faced a remarkably hostile media. NL had to be mindful of the need to use the media to put across a message that was going to be more sympathetic to Labour. Politicians have been spinning since the Garden of Eden: there's nothing new about politicians trying to put a good front on what they're doing". Perhaps 'spinning' should have come more naturally to the old Labour Party which more evidently embraced Peasant's Revolt Leader John Ball's observation: 'When Adam delved and Eve span who was then the gentleman'?!"

Berry continued: "Labour had to address that problem. Campbell, and others, deserve enormous credit for what they did. By far the biggest spinning machine is not Number 10. It's all the private companies in public relations. We had to respond to outrageous misrepresentations and to be clear and be more disciplined about our messages."

John Cryer claimed: "We *should* spin. Spin has always existed. The Tudors, Gladstone, Churchill and Wilson all used spin. Under Blair and Alastair Campbell, our performance at operating media relations was superb. Spin always was and will be there *but I'm more interested in politics.*"

Journalist Nick Cohen contended: "Hearteningly the public saw through the swindle. Spin became a dirty word … the politicians who wasted their days searching for 'eye-catching initiatives', to use Blair's language, looked paltry and ridiculous figures even in the good times of the 1990s."**C1_44**

MP Colin Challen remembered: "Until early November 2006 it appeared that nothing could go wrong with our public relations. Then Peter Kilfoyle spoke about the reality of the Party's poor performance in the 2005 election."

Kilfoyle believed: "There was nothing wrong with the argument that we had to improve our way of communicating with people. I worked on setting up the Party's Strategic Communications Unit. However we lost coherence in our message when it became a substitute for policy and debates on policy. It became just presentation. I found that unacceptable and antithetical to what the Party is supposed to be about. The Labour Party should be honest and transparent in practice. *You can't massage the truth to mislead people and then be a Party of high moral principle.*"

Backbencher B. said: "After Kinnock's defeat in 1992 we *had* to get elected. So NL did various things, some of which I agreed with. There was a determination at times to be too popular. MP Louise Ellman referred back to the 1990s saying: "We'd been in the doldrums since 1979 and it seemed we were incapable of getting into a position to introduce policies to benefit the people we should be helping. However we seemed to become obsessed with public relations."

These contributions, and those of MPs that follow, illustrate how, although there were earlier public relations problems that needed rectifying, the Party became saddled with the indiscriminate use of spin.

Lynne Jones argued: "All the stuff (about policy that's put out by the Party centrally) is leading questions and manipulating people to give the answers that you want: rather than going out and finding out what they think. Now the expenses issue has led to general disillusion with politics. It was unfair that we were all tarred with the same brush. 'Politics is the art of the possible' and while we can't charge ahead of public opinion we should be leading it. *We should engage with the public and persuade people of what we believe in.*"

Alice Mahon claimed she was "not against modernisation as such. I recognise that, with the demon press in the UK, something had to be done to tackle our image. We needed to attract a wider spectrum of voters. They had to get rid of old Clause 4 in order to bring in their 'Project'. It was Project like no other, the planning was meticulous." Christine McCafferty MP said: "I am a pragmatist and was never in the 'hate Blair' camp. I thought that he and Gordon did a good job transforming the image of the Party at a time when it probably needed it: a kick up the jacksie to put it bluntly. The 24 hour media is a problem – especially now (2009). In the 90s the media were more sympathetic and wanted a change of government."

Katy Clark said: "There were positive things about NL's spin. NL had huge skill, drive and energy. It was an exceptionally slick operation. Perhaps we needed that. We needed more professionalism about the way we presented ourselves as a party. We need to relate to where people are and to speak in a language that they understand. I consider that NL did that: perhaps in a way that the left didn't. The Labour Party often speaks to itself, and speaks its own language. This is quite old fashioned and doesn't necessarily relate to where people are now. I think that NL understood that and that was one of the reasons it was successful." She regretted: "NL spin is not based on principle, or belief or morality, it's all based on opinion polls and basically on what those who have power in the world want us to do. It adopts the view that it's OK to lie, or maybe not be fully truthful, to sell a political message."

The above opinions highlight some of the disadvantages that accompanied NL spin. These included generating cynicism among electors by manipulating them, tightening the grip of the NL project on the Party and the acceptance of mendacity as a propaganda tool.

Two other interviewees regretted the way in which the imperative to spin distorted policy making and took Labour away from its democratic socialist roots. Alastair Campbell's excuse was that; life at the top of politics was blighted by the ruthless 24-hour rolling media. He suggested that NL did things both well and badly when dealing with it.[C2-45]

Lord S. said: "*The public relations that got the Party elected has, to a certain extent, altered the way we run government, which troubles me.* Ministers were badgered to have "an initiative a day" (what a way to make policy!). "We concentrated on process, which the civil service loves. Now there's a process for everything but it's quite difficult to come across people capable of taking decisions (in the civil service). So we had consultants and made change after change – some of which were not necessary."

However Simon Jenkins argued: "The most revealing documents on Blair's style of government … were the Hutton and Butler Inquiries of 2004 and 2005. Both formally cleared the government but in terms that only deepened suspicion that something improper had indeed occurred."[C2-46] The Chilcot Report[C2-47] concerning UK entry into, and participation in, the Iraq had recently been published, but key material about what passed between TB and George W. Bush was suppressed.[C2-48]

Linda Riordan spoke of how spin and aspects of NL Policies "came to grief in the lead up to the 2010 general election. We are so low in the polls at present (August 2009) because nobody sees much difference between us and the Tories. We are not looking after the people we need to look after as true socialists should."

Constituency Secretaries' views included Irene's, she demanded: "Less reliance on slickness and special advisers." Oliver complained: "The Party's spinning and smearing has been disgraceful."

Campbell was unrepentant. In his diaries he argued that the media is more to blame for disillusion with politics than are politicians. He believed that whether media staff appeared friendly or not, all of them were trying to trip politicians up.[C2-49]

Prostration before the media: permitting its right wing tails to wag the policy dog

Who could forget the humiliating 'assassination' of Neil Kinnock by the *Sun* on polling day 1992? The arrival of 24-hour television and internet rolling news presented new challenges, as Christine McCafferty and Campbell confirmed. Few would deny that radical change in Labour's media relations was required.

There were Leadership concerns about how right wing papers would present proposed policies. Further, the Tory press often nudged policies away from Labours' traditional priorities and egalitarian approach. Imperatives for favourable coverage were not the only distorting factor in respect of the policy agenda. Many members of the leadership elite, especially TB, probably believed in them or sought to please reactionary friends like George W. Bush who did!

TB was criticised for pandering to readers of the *Daily Mail* and similar papers. For example, he wrote an article for the *Daily Mail* (30/06/1995) promising "a health service that would be neither private nor centralised … but locally based … patient led … a sensible third way."[C2_50] Alastair Campbell reported that in February 1998 editor David English reassured TB that, because he had just made "a brilliant patriotic speech at the Dome", the *Mail* would find it much harder to criticise effectively.[C2_51]

Backbenchers' views follow: Lynne Jones believed: "A constant feeling with NL is that they've always got one eye over their shoulder for what the *Daily Mail* or the Murdoch press will be thinking. It means that we produce policies to please the likes of the *Mail*. These are consistently outside our fundamental values." She suggested the Party Leadership's view was: "There are no core principles: it's just what we can get away with".

Chris Mullin argued: "We've put far too much effort into trying to appease institutions that we thought we ought to appease, for instance, the Murdoch press. I accept that in the run-up to our first election victory in 1997 it was right to try to neutralise them. Piers Morgan's Diary said that he counted up the number of times that he's had dinner with Tony Blair whilst he was Prime Minister and it came to an astonishing number. No doubt the Murdoch editors got more. But entertaining Morgan did us no good as the *Mirror* turned against us over the Iraq War. I would have slapped Murdoch on the back and laughed at his jokes prior to the 1997 election, but would have struck with force after we'd won. The Murdoch press plays a role in opinion forming. I don't think that we should have tried to get them on our side; they never really were." He continued: "Further courting … would have involved us in a certain amount of humiliation."

CLP Secretaries were asked to give a view about what the Party could learn from NL about presentation and management of its public image.

Keith believed: "The principal lesson that we can learn from NL is media management. Despite the allegations of spin and such humour as was used in the TV programme *In the Thick of It*, it is vital that we tap into the people's needs and aspirations and *then carry the people with us in the implementation of our policies.* Bob highlighted "a need for clear presentation of policies".

Fred drew Party manager's attention to: "The fact that the world has changed. Young people do not have the same alliances as previous generations. New technology means that information swings round at a much faster rate and individual issues become far more prominent."

Zach regretted: "In the 1990s we had the ear of the media; now the Tories have it. This is where we are losing the fight. Our policies are by far the best of all the political parties, but the public are being given a different message."

Leading up to the 2010 election these CLP officers recognised the need to communicate policies effectively to the public – using the media and keeping abreast of modern communication techniques: thus emulating the best practices of NL. *According to Vince, rebuttal was an NL practice that should continue to be used.* He contended: "We *should re-discover the NL attitude to rebuttal* and a positive media profile. Too many ministers are now 'not available' (for media interviews). *At the moment (October 2009) too many Tory and Lib Dem. media claims are going unchallenged.* Are ministers too lazy, too tired or too insecure to respond?"

Developing relationships with unsympathetically disposed media was never going to be easy. Neil Kinnock was reported as having said to Alastair Campbell: "You imagine what it's like to have your f··ing head stuck inside an f··ing light bulb … Then you tell me how I'm supposed to feel when I see you set off halfway round the world to grease him (Murdoch) up."[C2_51]

Jonathan Powell, TB's Chief of Staff from 1997-2007, refused to apologise for the efforts of NL to cultivate Rupert Murdoch and Lord Rothermere from 1994. He contended that: this is because politicians can only survive if they can get themselves heard by the public, and the only way they can do that is through the media.[C2_52]

The price of improved NL media relations, in terms of the surrender of values and policies was high. The grovelling to right wing media magnates was difficult for many in the Party to stomach. However NL media tactics and strategy got messages over to the public which helped to deliver three general election victories and, by extension, NL's limited positive policy achievements.

Gould commented: "This is a world of exploding media opportunity, where news is constant, news outlets proliferate almost exponentially, where television is fragmented from two channels to 200."[C2_53]

An editorial in the *Observer* of 24.07.2011[C2_54] claimed: "… it has looked dangerously as if, under successive governments, Labour and Conservative, News Corp has viewed Number 10 as the political outer office of its commercial empire." In the wake of the Leveson Report it is possible that new methods of media regulation will prevent the Party from having to prostrate itself to such a great extent before hostile media in the future.

TB and GB held monthly press conferences. There was rumoured leaders' fortnightly dining with one or more of the Murdoch paper editors and regular dinners with Piers Morgan of the Mirror Group.

A practice was adopted whereby new policies were no longer announced first in Parliament according to constitutional custom. Instead they were frequently presented at press conferences timed to meet deadlines for the weekend papers. The British constitutional expert Bagehot argued that House of Commons' debates reflected that Britain was a free nation and "The newspapers only repeat the side their purchasers like – the favourable arguments are set out, elaborated, illustrated, the adverse arguments maimed, misstated, confused." He continued: "The annual legislation of Parliament is a result of singular importance; were it not so, it could not be … the main result of its annual assembling."[C2_55]

Arguments in favour of learning from, and replicating, NL's quality of media relations (shorn of their worst excesses) seem unanswerable. However grovelling to right wing press barons is wrong and, as Chris Mullin asserted, should not occur unless there is no viable alternative.

Focus groups and opinion polls determine policy

Gould, NL's focus group guru declared: "Focus groups are – simply – eight people in a room talking. Their importance in modern politics is that they enable politicians directly to hear the voters' voices."[C2_56] The author asks: "What: the voices of only eight of them?" Perhaps this may not have been the best way of going about the task nor one likely to produce the most accurate results?

By comparison: focus group academics Barbour and Kitzinger[C2_57] argued that the conduct of focus groups needs to draw on recognised group work and communication theories. The groups need to have a diversity of members and to provide a structured rather than a random sample. They should be carefully constructed to enable groups to answer viable research questions and allow qualitative sampling. Groups should meet at least ten times and have consistent membership. They should observe the research ethics: principles of informed consent and confidentiality. It is possible that Gould adhered to some of these, and other recognised guidelines, but there is no mention of this in his book. Unhappily it was the conclusions from these groups that shaped policy advice given by Gould to the NL leadership and frequently taken by them.

Opinion polling has an extensive and respectable history in terms of producing valid data. Sampling techniques are widely accepted and respected by most professional polling organisations. These also conduct most private polls commissioned by UK parties. NL used respected American pollster Stanley Greenberg during the 1990s. Of course the electorate should be heeded but, however accurate and well analysed the poll results, the question arises as to whether policy should mainly be determined by their present (probably transient) demands: as it frequently was under NL governments. Was there not also a case for using polling and focus group data to inform political education and persuasion of the public?

Clare Short argued: "Obviously all governments have to try to get their public relations right but, as John Smith said, 'People selling beans ask how they can best sell beans, they don't go to the advertising company and ask what shall we sell?' 'I think NL was so keen to be popular with the powers that be, and the media, that it was willing to bend over backwards to please them: and it lost its way."

Constituency Secretaries' opinions varied. Una proposed: "In policy terms it's no good having a manifesto that appeals only to *Guardian* readers because there aren't enough of them to elect us. So policy needs to be adjusted towards the centre sufficiently to win a working majority but *no further than necessary.*"

Lewis said: "We need more responsiveness to public opinion. Quentin considered "we should listen to those not on our side". Nigel believed: "British voters won't accept a left wing government. Blair proved that a centre left government is the only one acceptable to voters. Government has been very London (and urban) based. Therefore rural communities suffer."

Advice from American Democrat's adviser Joe Napolitano, seconded to Kinnock's office in the lead up to the 1987 general election, was: "Deliberate adoption of a policy that puts a policy or candidate at serious liability, even before the campaign begins, raises doubts about the ability of that party or candidate to accept serious strategy recommendations that might overcome the self-inflicted wound[C2_58]."

Whilst swimming against a strong tide of public opinion is electoral suicide, there is no justification for grovelling before the prejudices of Labour's political opponents and abandoning core values and principles.

Party electoral organisation

The above developments were combined with improved electoral organisation and some effective use of the internet. There were past shortcomings in the effectiveness of electoral organisation. For example: Pelling[C2-59] reported poor electoral organisation during many periods in the Party's history but added that there were improvements leading to successes in 1945 and during the Wilson era. Pimlott[C2-60] concurred. The Party's pre NL record on electoral organisation is reviewed in Chapter 3.

In the Partnership in Power (1997)[C2-61] constitutional changes, responsibility for election organisation was retained by the NEC Organisation Sub-Committee which was now given virtual autonomy from the NEC. Numbers of potential campaign workers were greatly increased in 1996 when the Party's individual membership reached 400,000. Before the 1997 election the practice of recruiting temporary, paid election organisers for the lead up to general elections was introduced. They were given training and supervision by Party Staff. This practice continued after the millennium although shortage of money, especially after 2005, forced cut backs in the size of the scheme. One such organiser was Ben, whose views are discussed in Chapter 7. That Chapter also relates how, during the late 1990s, older and experienced, Party organisational staff were replaced by new young and temporary staff with little relevant experience. Chapters 7 and 8 relate how these new staff were allegedly proactive in delivering candidate selection outcomes required by the Leadership/Party machine and in controlling local parties generally. They also managed election organisation in the constituencies and in local election campaigns. As former senior organisers pointed out (Chapters 7 and 8) the lack of knowledge, skill and experience of these greenhorn staff frequently reduced the quality and effectiveness of campaigning.

Jeremy Corbyn MP said: "NL always pretended that the party was totally disorganised and totally divided before they came along. It wasn't exactly true. For example: Party membership had been growing steadily ever since Thatcher became prime minister" (in 1994, before John Smith's death, it reached 300,000).Corbyn continued: "They (the Leadership) raised a huge amount of money from private sources prior to the 1997 election. They used this for organisational work and recruiting members. In the 1997 campaign Labour probably had better organisation than any other party and probably as much money to spend on the election campaign as the Tories".

New Labour ideology and related policy development

Some respondents thought that there was so little policy, philosophical or ideological substance in NL' s programme that the Party was, in effect, a hollow battle winning machine like the Trojan Horse. There was some justification in their claim; but there was always a neo-liberal ideological element underlying NL's approach. Conversely, Simon Jenkins, claimed that, in the early 1990s: "The word modernisation was kept content free. It was all about image."[C2_62]

NL's approach was about inclusivity in the sense of trying to please most of the people for most of the time along the lines of a pragmatic, neo-Thatcherite agenda. Gould declared: "NL seeks to build big inclusive coalitions; it understands the central importance of the middle class; it wants ideas that work; not ideologies that don't."[C2_63]

Chris Mullin MP believed: "The Party became excessively dependent on the favours of rich men (e.g. to fund election campaigns). *We tried to take too may people into our 'big tent'. We only need about 60% not 99% (*of the electorate*)*".

The NL Leadership managed to commandeer the monopoly of policy making and communication. TB's presidential style of sofa government is well known (see Chapter 9). Simon Jenkins reported 2007 that: "He (Blair) was not naturally collegial' except within his close circle, treating ministers, not constitutionally, as sovereign over their departments under statutes, but as might a president."[C2_64] In the autumn of 1995 TB stated in an *Observer* interview: ''Those who fail to fall in (with his modernising project) need their heads examined."[C2_65]

According to Leo Abse, their unfettered scope for policy making permitted a right wing leadership to devise policies in accordance with their own political agenda. He believed that: "Blair is the populist who … panders to a widespread mood by seeking to depoliticise the Labour Party,"[C2_66]

Blairism was light on ideology, and on profound precepts and on values. The author believes that TB's convictions had minimal connections with democratic socialism. Blairism was a bland populist philosophy designed to appeal to all. The wording of NC4 is a prime example (Appendix 2). Another example came from Giddens in *The Third Way and its Critics*. Giddens stated that the Third Way places emphasis on personal responsibility, and on reform and transparency of state institutions.[C2_67] In 2012 TB announced: "I'm still an unashamed Third Wayer."[C2_68]

Simon Jenkins said: "From (TB) emerged the mélange of third way phraseology that was to become known as Blairism. Apart from a commitment to religion … Blair seems to have believed deeply in nothing to which anyone could take exception. He read few books."[C2_69]

GB's agenda was slightly different. Tom Bower contended that GB was different from TB and was genuinely searching for a central idea to unite both Labour and Britain.[C2_70] The success of GB's plans depended upon concealing the redistribution of wealth while placating and deceiving the middle classes. The problem was that Brown's "secret Santa" strategy so effectively camouflaged the nature of his policies that Labour members and supporters, as well as core voters, frequently failed to recognise them.

Len McCluskey, Leader of Unite, argued: "The 'I'm all right Jack', 'no such thing as society' concept started by Thatcherism was also cultivated under Blairism. The culture of collectivism and community spirit has taken a battering for ages. Of course I voted Labour, although I was never a supporter of Blairism. They treated the union movement with disdain: happy to take our money but not to attempt to understand our values, which are about collectivism, working for one another and with one another."[C2_71]

In interview for this book McCluskey said: *"TB's own life, his career and friends, were influenced by merit. This is probably why he was so comfortable with the captains of industry. TB appeared to dislike trade unions: possibly he didn't understand us. The NL leadership wanted the Party to have money given by wealthy people rath*er than relying on money from the trade unions. GB was much warmer towards the unions than TB. We were more comfortable with him. He understood us better and had closer links with unions in Scotland."

McCluskey continued: "NL did have a good image. TB won three landslide victories; that's why he was so popular in the Party. No other Labour leader has done anything like that. He had a very good media image and was a huge success. It's pointless being churlish. At the start he had this very powerful message that 'things can only get better'. Later things fractured slowly. The Iraq war tarnished and exposed NL. In the first place TB and GB were able to present the image of a bright new dawn. People tend to blame GB for loss of votes latterly but four million votes vanished under TB's leadership. Spin doctors' (reputations) were then stripped bare and the Project failed. It is interesting to wonder how things would have gone in the 1990s if John Smith had not died?"

Liz Snape, Assistant General Secretary of Unison, said: "I appreciated what NL did before the 1997 election in rebranding and re-positioning the Party and introducing clever marketing. I was unhappy with their position in which they proposed policies which did not challenge the rich. But, at the time, I felt that this was a price worth paying to get elected. Their early marketing campaigns were very effective. They worked well until about two years after the election. But later they began to lose their way: particularly when they refused to acknowledge or advocate policies to help the poor. Then they began to base policies on relying on the market and private sector. They supported a limited future role for the state in providing public services with reliance on the private sector to deliver. Recently Dave Prentis, our General Secretary, said: *'New Labour built the bridge over which the Tories now march to dismantle the National Health Service'.* This turned out to be prophetic."

However the Party and some unions remained joined at the hip. This was probably due to history, tradition and the phenomenon which Billy Hayes, CWU General Secretary, quoted as having been identified by Marxist academic Tariq Ali: "There may only be 6% of difference between the Labour and Tory policies but we can, and have to, live within that 6%."

On the subject of NL, its ideology and Party presentation: Billy Hayes said: "NL got 43.7% of the vote in 1997. It's now May 2010 and we're on 29% of the vote. So, as a Project, it's ending its natural life. It did improve media relations, well Campbell did, and it continued to do so on its own later. Campbell was a terrier for the Labour Party. Yes, there was a need for improvement. But I think that NL as an idea, as a new party – I think that's nonsense. Fundamentally the core of the Labour Party, the people who joined the Party in recent years, are obviously different from the people who were in it prior to NL. What there was, in the run up to 1997, was a thirst to have a Labour Government."

Hayes continued: "In many ways I wasn't surprised or disappointed with the NL project. I knew it was a particular thing they wanted to do and it served its purpose." … "Tony Blair famously said that the biggest mistake was the break between the Liberals and the newly emerging Labour Party at the beginning of the last century."

NL's policy programmes (see Chapter 5) were a rag bag of bids to secure short term electoral and ideological gains and not part of a considered, or coherent, long term strategy with a principled purpose. On the whole they were crafted to woo the floating voter and avoided clear ideological direction. Exceptions were: wholesale espousal of American foreign policy and unfettered market economics: neither of which chimed with traditional Labour values.

Backbench MPs observations: Jon Cruddas contended: "Empirically NL was a vibrant policy coalition and was electorally successful. *It was appropriate for a specific time and place. But later it offered diminishing returns."*

Colin Challen complained: "There were repeats and re-packages of the same policies which made me wince. The message was 'everything turns to gold when NL touches it.' Backbencher B. remembered: "I worked with other MPs to try to modify some policies. Obviously we have to move with changing times. Some of Labour's early history is not helpful and policies must adjust to new situations."

Lynne Jones argued: "We have not really used the last 12 years of government to educate the public. There is no consistent philosophy running through our policies; for example as between the NHS and social care." Had the Government done what L J recommended, it could have turned Labour into the Sales Oriented type of Party discussed earlier in this Chapter (and in Chapter 12). It would also have given Labour governments a coherent strategic direction and purpose. In areas like health and social care policy, cited by Lynne Jones, it would have facilitated provision of joined up and more effective services.

Graham Stringer said: "While Blair had a lot of confidence in his communication with the electorate, he never had enough confidence in knowing how to achieve what he wanted to. His policy changes created confusion with the electorate and the civil service." Stringer proposed that Labour victories in the last three general elections "were based partly on Blair's personality and partly on shutting off some policy options because they were seen to be electorally damaging. We *appealed to the centre ground and that became the driver of the policies.* In the long term this probably did some damage but in the short term it stopped Labour from frightening the electorate. There's been much success, but some failures in areas where you would have expected success. One problem in 1997 was that the manifesto was very muddled. It boiled down to six commitments on a pledge card which it was thought could be carried out."

Lord S. accentuated the positive when assessing NL's policy record. He contended: "The Blair, Mandelson and Brown project was well worked out. They planned in advance what policies they would implement after 1997. These were reasons for the great victories in 1997 and 2001. Credit must be given to TB and Mandelson for the way they went about getting middle England: because unless we got them we were never going to win an election … so I applaud them."

A major focus of the NL Project *was* winning middle class votes and much of the policy programme was slanted to contribute to this effort.

Austin Mitchell complained: "Tony Blair was adamant that it was only by building this wider coalition that we could win power." Mitchell believed the result (of the coming of NL) was that: "The dilution of everything we sold as Labour was too total – so that we didn't frighten people. The abandonment of progressive beliefs was all about winning power. We allowed ourselves to keep the Tory spending limits for more than three years."

One example of a worthy, but concealed, policy was given by Christine McCafferty MP. She reported that even she, a campaigner for the removal of VAT from women's sanitary protection, did not realise that GB had agreed for this to be implemented. This was because he refused to announce it publicly (presumably to avoid personal embarrassment!). However this measure was found to be in breach of EU regulations and was dropped. Nevertheless it was mainly redistributive policies that were hidden from affluent voters.

There *were* needs to reform the operation of public services used by the majority. From a democratic socialist viewpoint, NL tended to seek inappropriate ways of doing this (for example: through privatisation and the private finance initiative (PFI). This approach came from NL's neoconservative aims and values.

Senior backbencher A. recalled: "We arrived at a position strategically where it was difficult to win middle class votes, particularly in the South. Therefore we re-positioned ourselves In policy terms. Strategically the problem was to make the middle classes vote Labour *and to make sure that their children, their parents and they themselves used state schools and hospitals.* I shared with NL the perception that the public services were unresponsive to their users. They were very hierarchical and run on the (Herbert) Morrison model. In many ways they were wonderful but the structures, hierarchies and unresponsiveness had to be changed."

A. continued: "What was important about public services funded by the taxpayer was their ethos: that you're there to serve people. It's a fantastic ethic where it's properly established. There is nothing at variance with traditional Labour principles of equality, social justice and equal access to health and related opportunities. *NL's blind spot was to draw the unsubstantiated conclusion that to do this you had to privatise.* The answer was better recruitment and training for public sector staff (including managers). They already had the public sector ethos. That public sector ethos may be abandoned when the profit motive becomes an organisation's main objective." (see Alice Mahon's views about privatised hospital cleaning in Chapter 5).

Roger Berry observed: *"There are those who pretend we can run Scandinavian levels of welfare on American levels of taxation.* Leading up to 1997, people who said that were regarded as being 'unhelpful' and rocking the boat. There have also been ministers (including TB) that have gone along with the *Daily Mail* on issues like incapacity benefit (suggesting that claimants are 'scroungers')."

Elliott and Atkinson[C2-72] caricatured opinions about the Blair era: "To leftist critics, the Prime Minister is a war criminal who enjoys rubbing the noses of the poor into the dirt whilst he hangs out with the super rich, a class he patently admires. To those on the right he is a supine incompetent who has allowed violent louts out of prison and who has taken the economy to the brink of the abyss."

Len McCluskey of Unite said: "Clearly the old alliance based on values and principles held in common between the unions and Labour was breaking down during the NL years. It had become an exploitative relationship in which the unions paid and Labour took; giving little to benefit union members in return. NL tried to switch to raising money from rich donors who also wanted something in return whether it was gongs for gifts or government contracts or goodies derived from privatisation. He added: "I recently criticised NL publicly because there is still a strong feeling among trade unionists that NL Governments let us down. It was a betrayal and a deep disappointment. It explains why, in the end, NL lost the support of so many people."

The late Bob Crow, General Secretary of the RMT union, which was not affiliated to the Labour Party from the early 2000s onwards, believed: "New Labour under Tony Blair … squandered a massive landslide from an electorate hungry for change, poured billions of pounds into private pockets and accelerated the growing gap between rich and poor."[C2-73].

Gordon Prentice MP argued: "Values adopted by TB undermined Labour's traditional value of working for a more equal society. The government has been reluctant to create a less deferential and unequal society. We've had 12 years to change the consciousness of people though our actions and argue that collective goods are worth going for – that it is not all about tax rates. We haven't persuaded people. We've been locked in consumerist arguments about politics. When I hear my colleagues on the front bench talk about the "offer" that the government will make to the electorate: it makes me squirm." According to Prentice, here was an opportunity for Labour to be a more sales oriented Party that was lost. He continued: *"The NL leadership have probably learnt nothing from the successes of 'Old' Labour."*

Prentice declared: *"Winning elections is important but the Party and its MPs have been cut out of policy making. The architecture of the Labour Party became ceremonial rather than functional. There was no way that the Party membership could influence the leadership.* The leadership tells MPs various things about the dividing lines between Labour and the Tories – for instance 'they want cuts we want investment'. This is so juvenile. It doesn't engage in debate and infantilises MPs". His views were probably valued by MPs because they elected Prentice to be their representative on the Parliamentary Committee where he advocated their views to the Leadership.

In his introduction to B*lair* Seldon[C2-74] said: "Most premiers have been rooted in a party or body of thought. Blair … has travelled lightly in terms of ideology and tribe, but has been influenced … by a series of powerful people." Perhaps power was all and principle valueless in TB's lexicon. Many of the people who influenced him for example: his father Leo and Professor John Macmurray could not remotely be described as democratic socialists. However Macmurray did once show sound judgement by admiring the author when a baby in her pram!

Michael Meacher said: "I do not believe that there is an NL ideology; it is largely inseparable from that of the Tories. They have adopted a very few small concessions in the direction of what most of us would regard as Labour policy. Under TB and GB we have had virtually a one party state in which both parties are struggling to find red or blue water between them and their opposition. But they found that very difficult. In some respects the Tories are actually to the left of NL. NL's success is that it has won three general elections· – NL has a strong affinity with the Tories. After the first 2·3 months of government the *Daily Telegraph* carried an article about TB headed "To Thatcher a Son". This epitomised the situation.

Peter Kilfoyle declared: "NL was an advertising slogan: that's all. Blair and his cronies were hunting around to find something peculiar to them such as communitarianism and the Third Way but they didn't really find anything. I was once speaking *at a fringe meeting debate at Conference with Ben Bradshaw MP. I asked him what NL was and he didn't, or couldn't, respond clearly. He said: 'You either feel New Labour or you don't'. It's like a religion or a philosophy*."

As interviewed MPs saw it, NL was a way of conducting media and public relations and, initially, of securing resounding election victories. Discussion of what passed for ideology and popular policy making were seen only as a means to the latter end. Perhaps a pubic relations machine was almost all that NL was (if its Old Labour style measures and other minor achievements are overlooked). If so: it was a classic case of Marshall McLuhan's phenomenon that "The Medium is the Message."[C2-75]

Kelvin Hopkins contended: "NL drove through a neo·liberal agenda in terms of economics and a neoconservative agenda in terms of international power. Most Labour MPs have no sense of history and don't understand what's happened in respect of the growth of the gap between rich and poor."

Graham Stringer believed that: "From around 2001 TB took his eye off the domestic policy agenda. A government needs 2·3 years to play itself in. The delivery period should have been from 2000 to the present – but it wasn't. I don't think that either TB or GB had a theoretical model of the state, either local or national, or about what they wanted to do. In crude terms they didn't know who to support and who to put down." He continued: "I've been publicly critical in expressing my opinion of GB. I don't think he knows what he's doing. He wanted to be Prime Minister and now (2009) has no idea what to do with the job. People don't like him, he doesn't like himself. I can't think of anything he's achieved since he's been Prime Minister. He doesn't know whether he's running a *Daily Mail* agenda or a long term strategy. I never understood where he got his intellectual reputation from."

Michael Meacher summed up: "NL was predominantly a public relations and election winning machine *but it also* had the fundamental underlying aim of developing Britain's economic and social policies according to a neoconservative agenda."

Because virtually its whole focus was on winning elections, NL was stuck with policy·light manifestos which it had to deliver 100% in order to survive in the longer term. To achieve this it abandoned Labour's long·standing ideological and moral compass. This led to inconsistent short term policy programmes which could be presented in a simplistic way and be acceptable to the right wing media, as well as to floating voters. Therefore it ran a muddled, right wing and populist programme. The author considers that because TB and GB arrogated so much power to themselves in policy making: there was a vacuum which they knowingly filled in accordance with their own precepts. These precepts favoured running an unfettered free market economy and following a neoconservative foreign policy in the wake of a right wing US president. GB declared that the father of market economics, Adam Smith, was his hero. Suggestions have been made that Blair's fondness for going to war was another aspect of his populism. His judgement in this respect was possibly based on what the Falklands war had achieved for Mrs. Thatcher's popularity. Lilleker and Lees-Marshment[C2-76] suggested that NL lost electoral popularity when controversial military intervention dominated its policies after 2001: in the form of the Iraq and Afghan wars. Overall they attributed the post-millennium loss of popularity to policies based on NL's ideology rather than its previous pragmatism. Further loss of public support was engendered by the ultimate failure of some of Brown's economic policies related to the 2008 world financial crisis and credit crunch. However the UK would probably have emerged from that world crisis more damaged but for other measures that GB took.

As will be argued in Chapter 6, the lack of appropriate political direction, and early reliance on opportunism, resulted in far less of value and substance being achieved by NL administrations than was secured by earlier majority Labour Governments over shorter time periods.

Emasculating the real Labour Party

In order to get away with imposing this alien philosophy, set of priorities and policies upon a previously independent minded Party on the ground, drastic internal changes were virtually imposed on the Party. Hunger for victory and subsequent gratitude for success in the mid-nineties induced the Party to sell itself into the bondage of Partnership in Power and New Clause 4 (see Chapter 1 and Appendix 2). The overarching organisational and cultural changes are discussed immediately below. Smaller operational changes are explored in Chapters 7, 8 and 9. TB craved an internal revolution. Gould[C2-77] recalled that when he suggested to TB that they should rebrand the Party as 'New Labour,' the latter retorted: "This is all very well but as far as I can see Labour will only win when it is changed from top to bottom."

GB was also ruthless in his attitude to Party management. Andrew Turnbull, Cabinet Secretary from 2001-2005, even broke convention by calling Gordon Brown a Stalinist.

Top Down Management (Democratic Centralism as a way of life)

NL's key task, as Philip Gould identified it, was to establish a chain of command from the Leadership in which orders were carried downwards but through which it was difficult for critical messages to rise. As an anonymous management expert once put it: "a hierarchical organisation is one in which communication goes down through a series of loudspeakers and comes up through a series of filters." Intermittent local policy forums (see Chapter 7) were one example of this phenomenon. Many participants believed that their local forum's policy recommendations were binned rather than being taken upwards to the Leadership or National Executive Committee (NEC). Furthermore: feedback from the top, about what had happened to local policy forum's recommendations, was never communicated back to the grassroots.[C2_78]

Some respondents, notably former adherents to the Marxist-Leninist left, perceived NL as being a "democratic centralist" phenomenon. There were a striking number of NL ministers (including Alan Milburn, John Reid and Peter Mandelson) who had previously belonged to revolutionary socialist organisations (Communist and Trotskyite). A right wing, control freak, NL leadership found techniques used in democratic centralism and continuous revolution invaluable. This method of operation is often a feature of a top down controlled Party (like the NL Party) as was evidenced in the *Independent LabOUR Commission on Accountability, Party and Parliamentary Democracy* 2007. Party members were expected to accept and obey commands of the Party Leadership and even the Policy Commissions and National Policy Forum (see Chapter 7).

MP's reactions were typified by the ostrich-like perceptions of those NL MPs who jeered Peter Kilfoyle, at a Parliamentary Labour Party (PLP) meeting, when he pointed out how badly Labour had done in the 2005 general election, and how ill this boded for the next election. Surely any MP, with an ounce of competence, studies and learns from general election results? If they knew the facts, and were in deliberate denial, this was sheer folly. They refused to learn from NL'S past mistakes. The denial of a respectful hearing for Kilfoyle illustrated democratic centralist control of the PLP (see Chapter 9). Kilfoyle himself claimed: "NL thought that everything could be done from the centre. Beyond that; all you needed was to project the right image on TV and you were home. *The idea that you need a network of people across the country to work and campaign for you was immaterial to them.*"

Gordon Prentice MP argued: "TB's leadership marked the year zero for the NL project which is essentially Leninist. They exaggerated for effect. It was a kind of vanguardism whereby the people at the centre of the Party spoke for it. This approach led to the hollowing out of the Party." … "No one was in a position to challenge the views of the leadership: it was a democratic centralist model."

A definition of democratic centralism (*Penguin Dictionary of Politics*) [C2_79] is "a Leninist doctrine which lays down that conflicting opinions and views should be freely expressed and widely discussed at all levels of the Party hierarchy, and that the central committee should take them into account when making any decision, but *once a decision has been made, the policy must be unquestioningly accepted and carried out by all party members.*" NL's method of managing the Party and its policy making machinery appeared to be derived from this model.

Michael Meacher said: "NL was a well orchestrated machine and highly disciplinarian. They made an enormous effort at communication, projecting their own image and attempting to control the story. Democratic centralism was also applied to implementation of national policy. Kelvin Hopkins alleged that: "Blair went out of his way to reduce power at every level outside Downing St. He introduced a 'consultocracy': consultants at every level. This approach is Leninist and democratic centralist: everything controlled from the centre. There were consultants acting like commissars making sure that the government's will was carried out at every level of the health service."

Lynne Jones stated: "I've tried to consistently scrutinise government actions, not just to do as I'm told by the whips. It's very hard work for MPs if they don't take what's handed down from on high. We've lost many of our idealists because the Government lost its principles." John McDonnell contended: "NL had a ruthlessness that brooked no opposition – a brutality such as we've never seen before in the Party. They suppressed dissent and brutally discarded people, even some who supported NL but were no longer of any use to them."

The LabOUR Commission Report (2007)[C2_80] claimed: "The extent of the challenge facing Labour should not be underestimated. Underlying the loss of votes, seats and members is a profound cultural crisis arising from the side-lining of Party democracy by centralised command and control."

Clare Short summed up NL as being: "A coup by a very small number of people that manipulated the Labour Party and the loyalty of its people for them to take things over as they wished. The democratic structures of the Party were gradually eroded and crushed. It destroyed the integrity of the Party Comprehensively NL has failed and is now falling apart. The great tragedy is the wasted opportunity and the enormous damage done to the Labour Party and to Labour's record and reputation. As we sit here (in October 2009) it isn't clear to me whether that will ever be rescued."

The LabOUR Commission Report recommended: "We call for recognition on the part of the Leadership and Party HQ that command and control is finished. The Party should seize the opportunity now offered by new technology to provide a clear audit trail of all consultations –whether on policy or Party issues – in which all views are shared and debated."[C2_81]

CLP Secretaries said much on this subject: Irene pleaded "… above all (we must) return to being a real political party that can act in a bottom-up fashion and not be told from above what our policies are: *so that people can feel that there are advantages in joining the Party.*" Yvonne advocated: "trying to use the policy forum system to reflect what the membership want." Philip made a similar comment.

Tom lamented: "Unfortunately, having won a landslide victory, the right was able to push home its programme by finishing off Party democracy and, as they knew would happen, disaffected members simply exited from the Party so that little opposition remained. The party is now supine and possibly beyond saving." He continued: "We need to jettison NL. Neil Kinnock is credited with defeating 'entryism' but, in fact, it was only entryism by some left-wingers (with whom I disagreed but could work along side). *The right wing learned from Militant and won control of the party by entryism, causing the unnecessary despair of many members.*"

Peter Oborne[C2_82] argued: "… the political class is not merely separated from ordinary people and common modes of life: it is actively hostile. It sets the rules of conduct which everybody else must obey."

One example of top down party management was all women shortlists (AWS) in candidate selections as enforced by the NEC. This was mentioned by only one secretary (John) who said the Party "should ditch all women shortlists in the interest of better public relations" (he apologised for making the point). These AWS selections were not run on a fair and transparent basis because only NL women were allowed to benefit in winnable seats (see Chapter 8).

The last word about NL Party management should go to Una: a prominent Party member. She said: "*The leadership has assumed that the activists are always wrong, following the internal wars of the 1980s. In fact they are only sometimes wrong – they were right to oppose the 75p pension rise and the 10% tax band.*"

The damage to the Party on the ground, caused by top down dictatorship, was so great that the LabOUR Commission[C2-83] recommended: a Charter of Party members' rights. This had become necessary to allow democratic rights of participation for ordinary members again. It is still necessary to guarantee members' full participation in: Selecting candidates for public office and in local Party meetings; to seek selection to public office; to have regular leadership and deputy leadership elections; to have transparency and accountability about Party finances; to participate in Party policy making and to been given full information about all policy making processes; and to complain about unethical and unconstitutional behaviour by people acting on behalf of the Party. This proposal was repeatedly knocked back at Party Conference by the Conference Arrangements committee from 2008 onwards. The damage done to the Party on the ground by NL, which these rights would have helped to redress, is discussed in Chapters 7 and 8. There was a contemporary move to introduce a Charter of Member's Rights into the Australian Labor Party led by Senator John Faulkner.

High-handed, presidential leadership style

TB and GB were often accused of aspiring to be UK presidents and of operating in an autocratic presidential mode. The former relied on his personal charisma which undoubtedly contributed to his electoral success. Simon Jenkins claimed: "Blair was mesmerised by Clinton. He was intrigued – by his technique of personal projection, by his manipulation of the media and ability to bring a leader's personality into the homes of millions."[C2-84] Clinton often said that contemporary politics was about charismatic leadership.

MPs' opinions included: Graham Stringer who recalled: "As soon as Blair walked into Downing St. he created huge expectations of 'NL' and 'New Britain': a young society and wanting to lead Britain and the world." Linda Riordan said: "I think that things will change after the (2010) general election. Then they will have to listen to the left, the Campaign Group for instance. We do not have true Labour policies that we want to get through (to people) and become the Labour Party again. I've always supported GB – I think he's a good man; but he gets bogged down in the nitty gritty of things. Whoever takes over from GB as Party leader has got to listen. Let's hope that when the majority is reduced (after 2010) they will listen."

The NL Leadership secured much power for themselves. They then quarrelled about whose wishes would predominate in decision making.[C2-85] Backbench MPs, trade union leaders and grass-roots party members were comprehensively disempowered in the Leadership's collective favour. Through alleged cronyism and fixing (see Chapters 7, 8 and 9) they hand picked everyone given any significant power. The outcome was something more akin to Henry V111's court than a democratically run political Party.

Concern was expressed by CLP secretaries about presidential pretensions: For example: Oliver complained: "Presidential style government is not viable nor is celebrity-style politics". Simon Jenkins[C2-86] alleged: "The image left by Hutton and Butler Inquiries (2004 and 2005) was of a regime that had cast form, decorum and constitutional convention to the winds."

Jenkins, reflecting on the Labour election victory of 1997, said: "The purpose of Blair's project had come to fruition. He had achieved power and had done so largely through the endeavours of himself and a small group of associates … the Labour party as such was not in evidence." Jenkins claimed that Blair's style of leadership was dangerous because *it used democratic means to legitimise not a programme, or set of interests, but a person rather than a policy programme or group of interests.* "[C2-87]

Colin Crouch described Blair as a "post-democratic leader seeking authority in the vaguest of terms. 'We have a covenant – Give me your faith – I give you my word – trust me."[C2-88] TB's presidential attitude to the Parliamentary Labour Party (PLP) is discussed further in Chapters 8 and 9.

Doing good by excessive stealth

This was the strategy by which TB and GB concealed their policies that were designed to help the poorest in society. Traditionally governments do not hide their lights under bushels. This is especially true when illumination will probably reveal achievements likely to appeal to their most loyal supporters and those who they are supposed to be in primarily in existence to support.

MPs' views: Frank Dobson diagnosed the problem as being "that we have not emphasised the fact that the least well off are much better off (under NL) because ultra Blairites thought that emphasising that would alienate our comfortably-off middle class voters. I don't accept that at all. I think that it might upset unpleasant Tories. I consider that anyone who thinks of voting Labour, however well off they are, likes the idea that nobody is on poverty wages any longer and is willing to make, at least minor, sacrifices to bring that about."

Senior backbencher A. recalled: "The refinancing of the public services was not declared. This 'our crowning achievement' was a limited ambition. We didn't start by saying it would be our achievement but that's what we *have* achieved. It might have been that we did not explain clearly enough what we were doing for people to understand."

In a letter to the *Guardian* in March 2014; Labour Peer Jeremy Beecham praised the achievements of NL governments in health, education and the minimum wage but criticised "its failure to make enough of these achievements" and added "Doing good by stealth is not a recipe for political success."[C2-89]

Louise Ellman said: "I have a lot of very poor people in my constituency but few connect the family and educational policies, which are benefiting them, with the present Labour government!" Chris Mullin contended: "We've probably achieved more than we ourselves acknowledge; certainly more than our enemies acknowledge. We've kept rather quiet about our measures to help poor people for fear of upsetting the southern middle classes. We proceeded with unnecessary stealth."

TB and GB appear to have considered that a party of the left must, in Seldon's words: "discard the old images of … being obsessed with the poor, the unions, minorities and special interests. Instead it should forge a populism of the centre."[C2-90] To that end NL tried to hide, or disguise, their pro-poor and pro disadvantaged minority policies.

Ellman continued: "I remember the 1992 election campaign when we sought to increase some of the higher rates of tax to increase old age pensions and child benefit. But as the election campaign developed people, who would have benefited, thought they would end up the losers. I asked pensioners who said that they could not afford to vote Labour 'Why?' They replied: ' because we would have to pay more taxes.' In the interests of public relations we did not talk about the ways we were helping poor families and pensioners (even in 1992). We only spoke about how we were helping people who were better off." Analysis of the 2010 election results done by Ed Miliband's office[C2-91] also showed that many beneficiaries of such measures appreciated them but did not attribute them to the NL government.

Robin Cook criticised TB for concealment of NL's pro-poor initiatives, complaining that Party grass roots never heard TB speaking to them about how his government had greatly reduced child poverty. [C2-92] He probably kept his popularity with Party members because of the popularity that he had won for Labour.

Senior backbencher M. suggested: "Post 1997 Labour Governments were cautious in what they tried to do, and in proclaiming what they were trying to achieve. If they had been franker, especially about policies for the poor, they were afraid that there would have been trouble in the marginals and had middle class revolts. That was a mistake *because it meant that we blurred our identity. It made it difficult to maintain our sense of vision that is needed to inform a radical party. In a sense it weakened our moral compass as a Party and as a movement. That was a mistake because it weakened our future and future achievements. It demoralised our own supporters who hadn't been given much reason to believe and to re-commit to the Party."*

Although this accusation of hiding policies to benefit the disadvantaged was made by numerous MPs, not one CLP secretary identified it. It is possible that some of them were also unaware of progressive policies that were so ill publicised: surmising that these did not exist.

Toynbee and Walker believed: "Labour convinced themselves that progressive policies could only be pursued by stealth and must be offset by populist Tory gestures on choice or 'reform'. In their second term the camouflage became the purpose."[C2_93]

Could Labour have won in 1997 without turning 'new'?

Alastair Campbell, wrote in the *Sunday Telegraph* in 1993:[C2_94] "I see the real divide as between 'frantics' and 'long gamers'. The long gamers (in which he included John Smith, Margaret Beckett, and Robin Cook) all believe that Labour has time on its side. What makes the 'frantics' (including TB and GB) frantic is that the Party does not know what it is for other than opposing the Government." This latter charge could viably have been made against NL Governments in later years.

Andy McSmith believed: "John Smith had deliberately delayed giving answers to specific questions, because in 1992, he had seen his shadow budget run into difficulties over conclusions reached in 1989 at a time of economic boom, but which were problematic in a recession." McSmith described this as "masterly inactivity."[C2_95]

Writing shortly after John Smith's death; McSmith said: "... Smith had always believed that Labour could win from the moment he put himself forward to be party leader. For months opinion polls had been telling him he was right. Now (nine days before his death) he had confirmation from a nationwide poll[96]." Repeated at a general election that would have taken Smith into Downing St with a majority similar to those Thatcher achieved in the 1980s. Probably the Party did not need TB, GB and the NL apostasy to win the next election.

NL claimed that without their leadership and approach Labour would not have won the general elections of 1997, 2001 and 2005. However some interviewees believed that, because of the swing of the electoral pendulum and other factors, Labour would have won in 1997 and 2001 anyway. Some also believed that, without NL, Labour might have done better in 2005 because there would probably have been no involvement in an Iraq war.

Backbenchers' views included Alan Simpson's assertion: "When we first came to power in 1997, NL, and the machine that sold NL, presented itself to the Party, and the public, in terms that this was the victory of NL. But Professor John Curtis of Strathclyde University did longitudinal studies on electors' attitudes over many general elections. In 1997 he gave a presentation to MPs about this. He suggested that we might find it difficult to hear this, but his research findings showed that: "The feeling among voters was that those who had shifted to Labour voted for 'Blair the person'. They liked the youthfulness and freshness. They appreciated the sense that he was going to take government away from the state that the Tories had left behind and into a new, bright and open era. So the image they voted for was 'Blair the person'."[C2_97]

Simpson continued: "Voters surveyed were then asked to consider the policies of Blair. However the researchers actually presented them with a menu that was a mixture of the policies of the NL agenda and policies of the John Smith era. Participants were asked to indicate which policies they had voted for in supporting Blair. They still felt that they had voted for Blair the image but, by a massive margin, they wanted to vote for the policies from the John Smith manifesto and not NL's." Simpson summed up: "I think that the electorate assumed that it was still Labour that was elected – but with a new image."

Alan Simpson continued: "I believe that NL won because the Tories lost popularity after the economic crash of 1992 when thousands in my constituency lost their homes and tens of thousands were in negative equity. People were terrified of that and many swore they would never vote Tory again. People voted in 1997 to get rid of the Tories. If Labour had been led by Margaret Beckett or Bryan Gould we'd have won by the same majority without NL. If John Smith had survived, we would have won just as easily. NL tried to brainwash the Party that it was because of NL; but that wasn't so. Turnout has fallen since then because electors see all three main parties as having the same economic philosophy: privatisation and markets. If the Labour Party had a genuine democratic socialist programme we'd get much more support and could win next time (2010). But NL won't do that because of fear of losing face."

Austin Mitchell MP said: "A Party that was upset and had given up hope believed him (TB). Had we had sufficient confidence in ourselves, we would have seen that this was cynical and that the Tories would disgrace themselves."

Michael Meacher contended: "Had John Smith survived he would have won easily in 1997; possibly not with such a big majority; but with well over 100. John Smith was on the right of the Party but all sections of the Party, including the left, felt that they could do business with him. I don't think it's true that NL won the 1997 election: the Tories lost it. We won the 2001 election because the country was still fed up with the Tories and didn't want them back." He summed up: "Really none of the three election victories was down to NL."

Kelvin Hopkins argued: "NL created an untrue mythology about spin." Echoing arguments of Meacher and Mitchell about NL's take on past election results he continued: "We didn't lose in 1979 because our policies were 'too left wing' we lost because we imposed a pay policy which was grotesquely unfair. In 1978 they imposed a pay rise that was half the level of inflation. The poor couldn't live with that. In 1983 we lost because of the Falklands War, not because of our manifesto. Foot had a massive lead over Thatcher in the opinion polls before that war. Then Labour had the largest poll lead on record of any opposition in peace time. This lead was recorded before the SDP breakaway. Labour didn't win in1997 because of NL, or Tony Blair, or because they got rid of dissent (within the Party).

There seems to be much evidence that Labour could have won the 1997 election without turning 'New' with the top down control and right wing policies that that becoming NL entailed. The Labour majority might not have been as large as it turned out; but that outcome would also have exerted some restraint over the behaviour of the NL Leadership.

Conclusion

It is clear that, through adopting a "market oriented" approach to running the Party, NL radically changed the whole nature of Labour as an organisation and all its characteristics (its 'product' as defined by Lilleker and Lees Marshment, 2005 p.6).[C2-98] These changes probably helped to secure election victories with   large majorities in 1997 and 2001. This revolution was secured at a very high price. That price was the alienation and de motivation of many party members and core voters (Chapter 7). This upheaval also led to the transformation of the PLP by allegedly corrupt means (Chapter 8) and the disempowerment of the Parliamentary Labour Party (Chapter 9). Most significant of all: it changed the aims and values of the Labour Party and confounded its long established purpose. Furthermore the longer New Labour was in office, the smaller the electoral dividends which this marketing led approach paid. That was demonstrated by general election results in 2005 and 2010.

This development of Labour as a "Market Oriented Party" can be examined from two perspectives: the first is the election victories and policy record of NL. The second is the price that the Party paid as an organisation. The policy record is discussed in detail in Chapter 5. Winning elections is discussed above and in Chapter 3. Organisational costs to the Party and its members are assessed in Chapters, 7, 8, and 9.

CHAPTER 3
Winning and loosing elections under traditional ('Old') Labour and New labour

An assessment of key factors

An assessment of key factors

Clem Attlee "... wanted the Labour Party to say exactly what it believed, rather than what it thought the electorate wanted to hear"

Francis Beckett, 2000

*"... there is a tide in the affairs of men,
Which, taken at the flood, leads on to
fortune; Omitted all the fortunes of their life
Is bound in shallows and in miseries."*

Shakespeare, *Julius Caesar*

The electorate looked "onwards and upwards"; they work hard; they want to do better for themselves and their families ... Labour must become the Party of achievement and aspiration for ordinary working people."

Philip Gould, *The Unfinished Revolution*, 1998

Chapter Contents

Introduction

Application of the Lilleker and Lees-Marshment model to the original Pre-New Labour Party Electoral record of the original Pre-New Labour Party:

The role of electoral organisation   The contributions of Party members and supporters The use of media and public relations Leadership issues Internal Squabbling: the role of intruding and quitting factions The role of changing social and political attitudes External events, timing of elections and the tennis phenomenon

Winning and losing elections: the influence of policies and their outcomes on opinions and voting

Brief Overview of New Labour's Election successes

Conclusions

When the author stood as Labour Parliamentary candidate in Swindon in 1987, she was hopeful of victory. Last minute opinion polls and local bookmakers predicted this. Her result was not due until the early hours of the morning. Having put on her elegant red suit and her enormous red rosette, for what turned out to be the last time, she switched on the television and heard the declaration of a Conservative victory in Basildon. When she heard this her heart sank; she knew that victory in this weathervane seat signified that all was probably lost for her.

Introduction

Chapter 2 argued that New Labour (NL) was primarily about a focus on winning elections through using tactics and strategies which changed the whole nature of the Labour Party as an organisation. An attempt as made to turn NL into a "Market Orientated Party" (MOP)[C3-1]. In such a Party, priority was given to enhanced public and media relations and power was concentrated in the Leadership and their close associates and the whole organisation was managed in a top down and authoritarian fashion.[C3-2] Policy was determined by a pragmatic orientation to what the most influential groups of voters told pollsters and focus groups that they wanted. In their denigration of the pre-New Labour Party, NL played down achievements and two general election victories under Attlee's leadership and four when the Party was led by Harold Wilson. Most of these historic elections delivered small, and in February 1994 virtually unworkable, majorities. However, as is demonstrated in Chapter 6, the Labour governments they produced delivered policy achievements far superior to those of NL governments between 1997 and 2010.

This Chapter examines the "Old" Labour Party's history in winning and losing elections in order to compare the Party's performance in earlier years with that under NL and to learn lessons for future use. It was the desire to win elections with large majorities that drove revolutionary changes within the Party. These changes were made in order to transform the Labour Party into New Labour: a market oriented Party.[C3-3] This "reform" revolutionised contemporary Party governance and internal democracy. This Chapter presents, and discusses, examples of how the "Old "Labour Party addressed the need to win elections before 1994.

Application of the Lilleker and Lees-Marshment model to the pre New Labour Party

Lilleker and Lees-Marshment's three category model: Product Oriented Party (POP), Sales Oriented Party (SOP) and Market Oriented Party (MOP) (previously discussed in Chapter 2) is used to assess "Old Labour's" performance. It can be demonstrated that the Labour Representation Committee and Labour Party was mainly a "Product Oriented Party" (POP)[C3-4] up to 1940. That is: It adhered to the fundamental principles that it already stood for and asked voters to support those. The Labour Party was originally founded to create a democratic socialist party which supported the interests of organised labour. It supplemented what was offered by the contemporary Liberal Party on the radical wing of UK politics. Together they formed a number of coalitions prior to 1940. Labour did not form a majority government until 1945.

As is discussed below, and in the Ken Loach Film *The Spirit of '45* (2013).[C3-5] there is evidence that, by 1945, voters had been radicalised by wartime experiences and had adopted most of the Labour Party's positions (product). However the Party had started to act like a Sales Oriented Party (SOP) through promoting the Beveridge Report (1942)[C3-6] by creating the Welfare State and by building public acceptance on people's positive experiences of public ownership during the war.

The SOP tries to persuade voters to support what it offers. By and large Harold Wilson sought to build, and lead, an "SOP" and did so successfully. The Labour image makeover of the late 1980s (see below) was central to Kinnock's, and later John Smith's, attempts to run Labour as an "SOP" (see Chapter 2), McSmith[C3-7] demonstrated that John Smith would probably have won a general election using this Sales Oriented (SOP) approach, had he lived. The SOP does not change its values, aims and political programme (radically) to match what key voters want. Like Attlee, the SOP remains true to its established identity and values but tries to persuade electors of their worth.

It is widely recognised that elections can be lost due to redistribution of voters and size of constituencies. In the 1951 general election Labour won the most votes but secured fewer seats than the Conservatives because votes piled up in safe Labour seats. However the need to "sell" policies to voters in marginals effectively was not yet appreciated.

Labour under Wilson and Callaghan operated primarily as an SOP. Marketing techniques were sometimes adopted to promote the Party's values and policies but these were not consistently applied[C3-8]. Some of Wilson's election campaigning bowed to opinion poll results. Market research was occasionally used in presenting the Party. However much government action remained true to the Party's principles and established methods of operating. The exception was some aspects of the "special relationship" with the USA. This alliance sometimes also influenced Attlee's governments and led to British involvement in the (legal) Korean War.

NL turned the Party into an undiluted "MOP"[C3-9]. Labour was already creeping in this direction in the latter days of Kinnock's leadership (under Mandelson's and Gould's guidance). As noted in Chapter 2, an "MOP" makes no attempt to persuade voters of its own pre-existing values or aspirations. A "MOP" is virtually devoid of ideology. "Its aim is to develop and deliver a set of realistic policies that will meet the needs (i.e. wishes) of its market."[C3-10] NL's adherence to the MOP model is discussed in Chapter 2.

In discussing the records of "Old" and New Labour in winning elections (including the probability of a Smith-led Party having won in 1997) account is taken of whether they were operating as POP, SOP, or MOP. Chapters 7 and 9 examine the costs to the Party as an organisation and to the Parliamentary Labour Party (PLP) of its having become an "MOP".

Electoral Record of the Pre New Labour Party

The Role of Electoral organisation

Pelling[10] linked electoral success to effective campaign organisation. He pointed out that Conservative organisation was frequently superior to that of Labour.

To win an election, a political party needs effective organisation on the ground. Since the 1950s the mass media has played an increasingly significant role; subsuming some of the "doorstep" and other electoral activity that used to be undertaken locally. The Party's electoral and campaigning organisation was both criticised and praised between its foundation and 1994. Before 1994 the Party machine was sometimes inefficient and often underfunded, especially as compared with the wealthier Conservatives. For example, Pelling[C3-11] linked electoral success with effective campaign organisation. Both he and Pimlott[C3-12] pointed out that the Conservatives' organisation was frequently superior to that of the Labour Party. This was often due to the Tories having more money to spend on their campaigns.

The historical assessment in this Chapter begins in 1917 when the Labour Party's constitution turned it into a unitary party (rather than being a looser alliance of constituent bodies. It had by, then, acquired the realistic prospect of winning elections in its own right and not in coalition with the Liberals). In 1917 a disagreement with the Liberals (about forming alliances with European socialists) catalysed significant changes in the organisational character, objectives and values of the Labour Party. Thence forward, Arthur Henderson (Party Secretary) began to focus more closely on the way that the Party was run. He devised a major re-structuring of the Party and made other changes designed to give it a better chance of winning the next general election. The US Ambassador wrote to President Wilson in early 1918: "The Labour Party is already playing for supremacy."[C3-13] After this the Party was able win extra seats and to enter into coalitions with the Liberals. This was followed by the Ramsay MacDonald defection. After that Labour was in the political wilderness until 1940 when the Party joined the National Government.

The 1945 General Election campaign was atypical. It was conducted on an out of date register. However all members of the forces were given postal votes.[C3-14] Subsequent experience has shown that Labour is often more successful with a high postal vote. Political education of the forces during the war, determination to secure further improvements of living standards for working people that had failed to materialise after World War 1 and the and desire for a fairer society, rather than electoral organisation, probably clinched this contest for Labour.[C3-15]

In the 1950 general election campaign Labour's organisation was poor and that of the Tories was superior. Labour was handicapped by the crowding of its supporters into safe seats and having fewer supporters in marginals. After the unfair 1951 election result, Labour's fortunes went into a downward spiral. That Labour had narrowly won a majority of votes in 1951, lulled them into misplaced complacency. They failed to heed the imperative to review and improve Party organisation. The need to focus on winning votes in marginals continued to be periodically neglected. This issue was probably over-emphasised under NL; it came to seriously bias policies.

In the 1955 election, yet again, the Party's organisation was found wanting.[C3-16] The Party had lost 25% of its full time agents since the last general election. Tory organisation was as effective as ever. Key organisational factors that lost Labour the 1955 general election were to recur intermittently up until 1997. In 1955 the Labour National Executive Committee (NEC) set up a special Sub-Committee to review election organisation. This was chaired by Harold Wilson. They found that there had been a shortage of volunteers in the election campaign, as there was in 2005 and 2010 under NL.

Wilson's Committee revealed shortcomings in the work of Party staff and use of Party funds. In response the Party set up the Organisation Sub-Committee of the NEC and Regional Party Offices. NL made questionable use of these later (see Chapters 7 and 8). In the mid fifties the Party also established a special scheme for organisers to assist marginal constituencies. Labour won general elections in 1964 and 1966.

Pelling[C3-17] reported that again the Conservatives had more money and superior organisation to that of Labour at the 1970 general election – Labour lost. During the early seventies, and out of government (1970-1974), the Party improved its organisation again. Previously the number of full-time organisers had been reduced. The author was a first time Parliamentary candidate in 1970. In her constituency there were sufficient volunteers. A few of the Party were initially reluctant to help – but proved persuadable. Elsewhere Pelling reported[C3-18] that "there was a shortage of volunteers to campaign .There were wounds that could only heal with time and reaction to the unfriendly policies of a Conservative Government."

Many organisers were ineffective because they were based in rural Tory-voting areas where their salary was supported by profitable tote schemes. Most agents were now enrolled in a new "National Agency Scheme" and placed in marginal seats. Training videos about canvassing (starring John Cleese) were produced. Members' training and publicity were improved. Parliamentary candidates in marginal seats were given coaching. The author shared hers with, among others Robert Kilroy-Silk who, during the course, announced his intention of becoming Labour Prime Minister in the near future! A new, more dynamic, General Secretary, Ron Hayward, was appointed. A committed democratic socialist, along with his successor Jim Mortimer, he was more overtly political and left wing than other General Secretaries were before or since. These improvements led to two election victories in 1974 (the first by a whisker).

Labour's organisation in the 1983 general election was less impressive. Its election literature was verbose and difficult to read. However organisation was probably a minor factor in Labour's defeat (see below). In looking to the coming general election, Larry Whitty was appointed to be General Secretary in 1985. He believed that major reorganisation and cultural change were vital to enable Labour to win. He asserted that *"there need be no contradiction between socialism and professionalism"*. He told the 1985 Conference that Labour should be the Party to bring *"fun and style into people's lives."*[C3-19] Whitty's head office re-organisation soon followed. Then there was the successful Fulham by-election campaign of 1986 where telephone canvassing was first used. Further *there was a sustained effort to improve Party organisation during the period 1983-1992*. More use was made of telephone canvassing and information technology to keep track of electors. Labour introduced targeted, often personalised, mail aimed at young and floating voters in marginal seats. Use of these tactics was increased under NL, which continued and developed them. When the internet arrived NL used this for campaigning but also for sending top down messages to grass-roots Party members to which they were prevented from replying![C3-20]

NL initially benefitted from increased membership of the Party. This provided more campaign workers. However as disillusion set in; the Party membership decreased, particularly after the Iraq war began in 2003. During the later 1990s the Party staff was drastically changed. The machine replaced older experienced, politically committed workers with younger, inexperienced, apolitical ones (see Chapter 7). This process of stripping the Party staff of ideology was a crucial aspect of creating the MOP. The Party secretariat was denuded of campaigning knowledge and experience by the same means. These staff changes led to greater inefficiency in election campaigning (see interviews with former Party staff 'Malcolm' and Peter Kilfoyle MP in Chapter 7). Henceforward the Party had fewer permanent employees and took on temporary organisers to run general election campaigns (for example, Ben interviewed for this book). Longer term NL Party staff, especially at regional level, allegedly spent time manipulating candidate selections rather than organising for elections (see Chapter 8). These developments probably contributed to the disappointing election result in 2005 and loss of power in 2010.

Whilst the "Old" Labour Party's election organisation over the years was of varying effectiveness, there is little evidence that NL's was consistently better: especially as the 21st century progressed.

The Contributions of grass-roots Labour Party Members

As noted immediately above, a larger Party membership brings more voters, campaign workers and funds. [C3_21] Individual membership of the Party doubled between 1928 (214,970) and 1937 (447,150) despite the MacDonald defection and consequent loss of power. In order to empower Constituency Labour Parties (CLPs) the number of their representatives on the NEC was increased from five to seven at the 1937 Party Conference (significantly, it was reduced to six in 1997).[C3_22]

With the exception of the World War 2 years, when it declined due to the war effort, individual Party membership rose steadily to its peak in 1952 (1,014,524) following the brilliant Attlee administrations. Membership then fluctuated, or fell, by around 100,000 each year. There was a gradual overall decline. In 1974 membership was 691,889.[C2_23] Shortly before the 1997 general election, membership rose to just over 400,000. This was then seen as being spectacular.[C3_24]

After the euphoria of the 1997 election result subsided, and as NL ratcheted up its control of the Party (see Chapters 2 and 7) and pursued policies which offended the principles and values of many Party members, the membership declined to about 160,000 in 2010.[C3_25] After its "honeymoon" NL's membership recruitment and retention record was inferior to that of most preceding periods.

Public and Media Relations

By 1931 the TUC and the Labour Party had long owned and controlled the *Daily Herald*, which gave them a press organ to use for their respective benefits. Since the demise of the *Herald*, there has not been an absolutely loyal Labour supporting national newspaper. However the *Guardian*, *Daily Mirror* and *Observer* support Labour much of the time. Particularly vicious attacks on Labour, by the right wing press and media generally, commenced during the Foot leadership. The Murdoch press supported NL from 1994 until after 2007 but subject to Labour leadership obeisance. Simon Jenkins observed: "Both (TB and Cameron) "used the media as their mirrors and flew too close to Rupert Murdoch."[C3_26]

Labour campaigns suffered increasingly when the Party attracted diminishing press support after the demise of its own newspaper. From the 1980s the media became more all embracing and influential. The right wing press became more viciously hostile to Labour and more devious in its methods of operation. One more recent example was phone hacking. Reasonably successful press and public relations had been conducted under the leaderships of Attlee and Wilson and, some of the time, also under Gaitskell and Callaghan.

It would be wrong to allege that spin was the sole property of NL and its immediate predecessors. During the 1940s, 1960s and 1970s Labour spokespeople could still "tell a good tale" as Roger Berry MP contended (see Chapter 2). Under Kinnock and Smith leaderships there were strenuous attempts to improve media and public relations but they were not always successful. Much learned from these experiences was used to improve media and public relations during the NL period.

One aspect of Labour's public relations, over a long time, was the use of opinion polling to inform their publicity. In the pre NL era, opinion polling was more commonly used to check how the then Sales Oriented Party (SOP) was performing.

Under NL polling was used to guide policy making and public relations. Polling was also then deployed in "segmentation" techniques to identify and target those voters who had the greatest power: swing voters living in marginal constituencies. This was not "government by the people, for the people or on behalf of the people". It was "Government for and on behalf of the minority of people to whom the electoral system gave the greatest power". It could be termed not democracy but "marginalocracy". Policy was determined not by the Party policy making machinery or by the Party's own established aims and values, but by the outputs of opinion polls and focus groups. This was one of the hallmarks of a Market Oriented Party (MOP).

In 1985 Peter Mandelson was appointed Labour's Director of Communications. Philip Gould, an associate of Mandelson, suggested that Labour should adopt slick Tory communication methods. The latter commissioned him to do a communications audit for the Party. Gould's verdict was that the public had a mainly negative view of the Party and particularly disliked what they regarded as extreme policies and politicians. He found that Labour had no co-ordinated communications strategy, that it used over-complicated language in its propaganda and its campaigns were directed more at Party members than at the voting public.[C3_27] This fits the model of the POP identified by Lilleker and Lees-Marshment (see Chapter 2).

Gould proposed improvements to remedy these problems. He then convened focus groups (see Chapter 2) and subsequently addressed the NEC informing them Labour was seen as disunited quarrelling and full of militants and without recent government experience. The Party was associated with the poor, the unemployed, the elderly, the sick, people with disabilities, pacifists, immigrants, minorities and the unions. Kinnock reportedly saw this as confirmation of what he had long suspected.[C3_28] Modern style publicity was used in the Fulham by-election campaign of 1986. Labour won this Tory seat on a swing of 10.9%. Increasingly Kinnock's main aim became making Labour electable through improved public relations.

In 1986 Kinnock argued that Labour should change its logo to the red rose. He decided to use Conference 1986 to launch this project and to use that Conference to provide Labour with a new image. Kinnock correctly surmised that this might be the last Conference before a general election. Conference had a striking contemporary set and Mandelson instructed that only smartly dressed delegates should be called to speak! Did the medium become the message?

In 1987 relationships between the Labour Leader's office and the press deteriorated.[C3-29] During the 1987 election campaign Kinnock conducted half his press conferences outside London in the hope of getting his message through without being attacked by hostile London journalists. Problems were caused by conflicting messages from Kinnock and Deputy Leader Hattersley about the levels of income tax that a Labour government would levy.

The 1987 election publicity was modern in appearance, glossy and overgrown with red roses. Labour decided to attack the Tories, more than defending their own policies, and to play for SDP/Liberal Alliance votes. Campaign meetings and press briefings were better organised than in 1983. There was a new style election broadcast which *made no mention of policies, Labour or the election.* After this Labour's campaign seemed to take off. Kinnock avoided visiting Militant strongholds for fear of hostile receptions being reported in the media. He only accepted questions at press conferences on the Party's designated theme of the day. Despite this publicity revolution Labour lost decisively.[C3-30]

By 1992 much pre-election planning had been done by the Party and daily press conferences were run competently from its new HQ in Millbank. Kinnock seemed to create a positive impression with his grasp of subjects. Labour made much use of celebrity supporters during the campaign. They had to cope with a hostile right wing press aggravated by the "M" factors: Murdoch and (the *Daily*) *Mail*. In the 1992 general election Labour gained 42 seats (making a total of 271), polled 34.4% of the votes and obtained a positive swing of 3.4%. However the Conservatives obtained 41.9% of the total vote, won 336 seats and retained power.

David Hill's (Party head of organisation) election report for the Leader's Committee was leaked to the *Guardian* in January 1993. He claimed that it had been wrong for the Party to have believed that opinion polls before the 1992 election had been correct in assessing how people *would actually* vote. Of course this happened again at the 2015 election. The Party's private qualitative polling showed that nothing had changed in 1992 since the 1987 election. People told pollsters that they would vote Labour because they wanted to register dissatisfaction with the Tories, but they had not genuinely changed their loyalty. They said that Labour had "no clear identity, had not made any significant progress since 1987, was still a party of the past, untrustworthy, inexperienced, and more in favour of minorities than the ordinary man and woman". Hill argued that there must be a clear set of messages for voters by the 1993 Party Conference. He also said: "Our major long term problem appears to be that we carry too much baggage from the late 70s and early 80s to persuade people that they can fully trust us."[C2-31]. Shadow Minister Jack Cunningham, from the "old right" of the Party, believed the election result was due to "the damage that Labour did to its reputation and its credibility, way back in the early 80s; surprisingly perhaps, it is still a major problem for us."[C3-32]

With the advent of NL, the Party's public and media relations resembled those of a "MOP". This entailed departure from Labour's traditional aims and values (see Chapter 2). This was reflected in policies and campaigns. Some MPs alleged that policies were shaped to please readers of the reactionary press. (Chapters 2 and 9).

The difference between marketing and public relations, as between NL and earlier Labour, can be seen as a modernisation exercise that made operations slicker and more effective. However, principles, values and political strategic direction were lost in the process. Tony Blair (TB) was accused of having no strategic direction, favouring opportunism instead. The ideal ways forward would have been a slicker and more modern Labour approach to the electors and to have paid some attention to opinion polls and focus groups but to have retained the Party's core principles and values and maintained a strategic policy direction that chimed with those.

Leadership Issues

It is clear that one of the most crucial determinants of whether or not a party wins elections is the quality of its leadership. Leaders must be able to present themselves well and give account of their actions effectively to the public and within the Party. Labour lost under Gaitskell partly because he appeared weak, compared with Macmillan, *and there was little difference between their policy platforms*. As mentioned below, in respect of Major and Kinnock, when rival Parties' policies are similar, then the focus of electors is often on which leader's personality they prefer. A popular leader will be able to retain power for a period subject to not making crucial policy mistakes, such as Callaghan made with industrial relations and Thatcher with the poll tax. It also appears, from the Wilson and Major experiences, that a new Leader can be attractive to voters by virtue of their novelty. Much of NL's entire approach, with TB prominently at the helm of its ship, was modelled on the novelty premise.

Clem Attlee was once described as "having all the charisma of a building society manager". A viewing of old newsreel clips, and Loach's film[C3_33] suggest some validity in this observation. But, as Beckett asserted, this superficial impression "does the man a huge disservice and reflects ill on the values of our own age"[34]. Currently good looks and charm are often seen to be the most important qualities for a political leader. They certainly assisted TB but not GB, who apparently lacked them. Media feedback on the TV leader's election debates from 1997 onwards demonstrated this. However Attlee's policy prospectus, publicised in election literature, chimed with contemporary public aspirations.[C3_35] Churchill's campaign attempt to smear Attlee as Laski's (Chair of the NEC) puppet was rebutted by Attlee but did not convince the public.[C3_36]

The 1959 election defeat was followed by more internal heart-searching about where the Party was going wrong. Was it out of touch and/or out of date in the eyes of the public? At a post-election special conference Gaitskell called for a revision of the Party's mission and objectives, which had not been changed since 1918. He advocated the abandonment of Clause 4 of the Party Constitution as Blair did in 1995. This led to contention within the Party and Gaitskell was forced to accept a compromise.

Following Gaitskell's unexpected death, new Leader Harold Wilson, was welcomed by the public as a refreshing newcomer. This coincided with the Tory government losing popularity. In personality, style and cultivated image Wilson seemed to fit the electorate's requirements. This was reflected in contemporary results of opinion polls and by-election results[C3_37]. During the successful 1964 election campaign, Wilson led from the front and made a positive impression in the media. He was little known to, and therefore not feared by, the Establishment. Wilson demonstrated effective and pragmatic leadership. Labour again won the 1966 election with a strong emphasis on housing policy to benefit less advantaged people. The 1966 Labour Government's public relations were initially unsuccessful. Then it postponed manifesto promises but agreed a substantial rise in MPs' salaries and lost support as a consequence.

The core of Labour's 1970 election campaign, led by Wilson, was designed to appeal to the floating voter. It played down ideological and policy differences between the major parties (a precursor of NL triangulation). The campaign boasted Labour's recent successful economic management – usually a sure fire winner but Labour unexpectedly lost the election.

Public relations for the two 1974 elections were skilfully managed by a rejuvenated Wilson. He presented himself as peacemaker following industrial disputes and strikes during the Heath government. Labour went into these elections with a left manifesto that included repeal of Tory industrial relations legislation, a wealth tax and an extension of nationalisation in the engineering industry. [C3_38] Labour did not attempt to hide the political complexion of this programme which was carefully sold to the public. Its core contents were used to fight both 1974 elections.[C3_39] Labour was becoming a successful SOP.

Wilson retired in 1976 and was replaced as Prime Minister by James Callaghan. Callaghan had a pleasant and down to earth manner and was generally liked and respected. He could also be tough and obstinate, but did not seem dour.

"Jolly Jim" inherited a minute Labour majority that rapidly dwindled as ageing MPs died. The government managed to cling on to, what became, minority government through the skills of the whips. Particularly noteworthy was the skill of Deputy Chief Whip Walter Harrison whose acquaintance with the author showed him to be exceptionally insightful and energetic. Eventually the Lib Lab Pact (which was not a formal coalition) was concocted. At length this broke down which led to the 1979 general election. The late seventies were marked by severe inflation, pressure from the trade unions for higher pay settlements and the avoidance of pay restraint policies that Callaghan wanted. In the face of economic difficulties a loan was sought from the International Monetary Fund. This came with a requirement for unpopular "draconian spending cuts".[C3_40] It later emerged that this loan had been unnecessary. Callaghan chose to defer the election from Autumn 1978, when the economic outlook was slightly better and he might have won, until the spring of 1979. By then he had no room for manoeuvre and had suffered the "Winter of Discontent" involving widespread and publicly unpopular industrial action.

Michael Foot, who became Leader after the 1979 election, was reported to be a highly principled man who was committed to the Labour Party's mission (unlike TB and, to some extent, GB). He was a persuasive orator and widely recognised as a man of integrity. Foot was a skilled negotiator who listened carefully to everyone whose opinions should be considered.[C3_41] This last description could also be applied to John Smith but not to Kinnock, in his latter days, nor to TB or GB. Collegiality was the trait which enabled both Foot and Smith to preside over the Party in a democratic and diplomatic manner.

Foot was an intelligent and fair minded leader. However there were issues with his image which did not improve Labour's prospects of electoral success. He presented Labour's case in a verbose and intellectual manner which was disliked by many voters. His age (late sixties), and to some extent ill health, were used against him by the Tories and Conservative media.[C3_42] The most flagrant example was the televised 1983 Young Conservative election rally. There comedian Kenny Everett urged the audience to "kick away Michael Foot's stick." Adversaries attacked Foot for his dress sense. The most celebrated example was his attire at the Cenotaph one Remembrance Sunday. For the record: he wore a new green jacket (not a duffle coat as the press reported) and the Queen Mother congratulated him on his smart appearance. Alas what should have been regarded as superficial factors, some of which would have damned even an Attlee in the 1980s, became significant: in terms of their electoral impact. GB also had an image and self presentation that was not media friendly (for example in his YouTube speech fiasco in 2009). Barbara Castle once said: "It is absolutely essential for a leader in politics to master the television arts. They should work at it—take pride in it; they shouldn't be ashamed of it. The more left wing they are, the more important it is that they should learn the art of presentation."[C3_43]

When Foot became Labour leader, he took on problems to which Wilson and Callaghan had turned a blind eye. They did this in the interests of avoiding publicised strife within the Party. In 1982, Foot turned his attention to Militant (see below).

Graham Stringer MP (and the author's personal recollections of the 1983 Darlington by election and general election campaigns) indicated that, during the Foot leadership, Labour had plentiful voluntary workers available during campaigns. This may well have reflected opposition to Thatcherism *and* enthusiasm for the Foot led Party's policies and internal democracy.

At the outset the Kinnock/Hattersley Leadership was widely welcomed in the Party because it was seen to provide two credible leaders (one from the left and the other from the right): a so called "Dream ticket". Both were more adept than Foot at self presentation. Upon election Kinnock did a BBC TV interview in which he emphasised the need for Party unity and advocated minimal change.[C2_43] He said: "There are organisational changes that need to be made and different deployments of our strength in Parliament—there are questions of *presentation* (author's italics) in our policies that need to be looked at. "[C3_44]

Kinnock was aged 41, and in rude health, when he became leader. Like Foot, and his hero Aneurin Bevan, he was a fine orator, as he demonstrated at public meetings and in Parliament. However he sometimes lapsed into boring and long-winded waffle. This frequently happened in Parliament when he was confronted with a hostile, largely Tory, audience.[C3_45] It led to his being dubbed, by the opposition and media, as a "Welsh Windbag". It is probable that there was some populist anti-Welsh prejudice around. It may also be that there is some irrational hostility to people with red hair. Both recently impacted on former Australian Prime Minister Julia Gillard (born in Wales). Kinnock acquired a reputation for frivolity by sometimes lapsing into humour, during a serious speech. This public persona was used by the Tory press to discredit him. In early 1987 Clare Short was convinced that there was a long-standing conspiracy in the media to underestimate NK's intelligence. Barbara Castle complained that the press were accentuating the negative with their boyo jokes and anti-Welsh remarks. During the 1987 election campaign, derogatory remarks were frequently made to the author (as parliamentary candidate) about Kinnock. These were to the effect that they did not like, or trust, him and considered him unsuitable to be PM.

In the 1988 leadership election Kinnock was challenged by Tony Benn. However Kinnock won with 88.6% of the votes.[C3_46] Ron Todd, then TGWU leader, claimed "The last dregs of socialism are being drained out of the Party".[C3_47] In November 1988 Labour lost a "safe" seat at Glasgow Govan to the Scottish National Party by a 38% swing. Thatcher then had a massive 33% opinion poll lead over Kinnock for "leadership competence". A few months later MORI put Kinnock's personal poll rating, as leader, at 27 % – his lowest yet.[C3_48] Inflation was rising and stood at 7.5%. Soon public support for the Tories, and the market economy, began to diminish. In the spring of 1989 a Party and Trades Union delegation, led by Gerald Kaufman MP, visited Moscow. They returned with the news that the Russians were no longer interested in a unilateral agreement with the UK but wanted to pursue multi-lateral nuclear disarmament. Kinnock wanted to change the Party's defence policies. In May he persuaded the NEC. This change was incorporated in the new Policy Programme: "Meet the Challenge, Make the Change: a new agenda for Britain."

During 1988 Kinnock took advice and improved his speech making technique.[C3_49] The new policy programme, was given a "trendy" media launch. Within two weeks a MORI poll gave Labour 43% of the votes compared to the Tories' 41%. This was followed by "Meet the Challenge" meetings across the country. In 1989 the Party organised a drive to smarten up the appearance of ministers, MPs, candidates and conference delegates. This included recruiting style guru Barbara Follett as advisor.

From 1990 Mandelson campaigned to have Kinnock portrayed as an international statesman. He made favourable media presentations about Kinnock's overseas visits. In April 1991 Labour launched a sequel to "Meet the Challenge" called "Opportunity Britain". This was the final stage of the policy review which was attractively presented as a draft manifesto.

Polls in the *Sunday Express* and *Observer*[C3_50, C3_51] showed that 25% of respondents would be more likely to vote Labour if "the Party got rid of Kinnock" and 38% of potential supporters would not vote Labour because they "don't like Mr. Kinnock". The following day the Murdoch-owned *Times* alleged: "Mr Kinnock's perceived defects can be summarised as a lack of brains and gravitas".[C3_52] A September MORI poll indicated that if John Smith were Labour Leader the Party would gain 10% more support. Addressing the CBI, a week later, Kinnock asserted he was "in charge" and Labour recovered a small lead in a MORI poll.

It was claimed that latterly (Kinnock) ran the Party in a tyrannical way. During his leadership Labour moved from being a democratic socialist party to being a Leader's Party.[C3_53] Clare Short, an old friend of Kinnock, lamented that he "needed to play the big, tough leader and kick everyone around."[C3_54]

From November 1990 Prime Minister's question time was televised. Kinnock did well from his exposure. His MORI poll rating rose to 42% praising his performance compared with 36% liking that of Mrs T. Later that month Thatcher left office after doing badly in the Tory leadership election. She was succeeded by John Major, whose political style was different from hers. The following month MORI found that only 37% were satisfied with Kinnock's performance as Leader. Kinnock's own verdict was: "All that mattered was that Major wasn't Mrs Thatcher".[C3-55] The public seemed to react as though there had been a general election and to perceive Major's as being a new government. They apparently overlooked the fact that Major had been Chancellor and bore much responsibility for unpopular Tory economic and fiscal policies.

On 16.9.91 the *Independent* reported a survey of voters in marginal constituencies. Their majority view was that Kinnock should express himself more intelligibly and succinctly and demonstrate that he could think clearly. *They also considered that he had made his career on the left and had cynically ditched most of his earlier beliefs.*[C2-56] Simultaneously, Gould discovered (through private polling for the SCA) that 73% of voters believed the Tories would privatise the NHS. The Party campaigned on this theme led by Kinnock's speeches. Conference 1991 was a stage-managed showcase. Following Conference Labour regained an average two point lead in the polls. The Party then ran a poster campaign about Tory plans for the NHS and a rogue MORI poll gave it a 16% lead.[C3-57] *The Party promoted Kinnock's changed position on many policy issues. During the election campaign the Tories represented him as lacking in principles and consistency. On 14.3.92 a poll for ITV's "Special Inquiry" indicated that the most significant reason for elector's doubts about voting Labour was that 47% were unhappy with Kinnock.*

During the 1992 election campaign the Murdoch press indulged in an orgy of hostility towards Kinnock. In the final week the *Daily Express* asked: "Dare we really trust this man continuing that he had been wrong on Europe, privatisation, nuclear deterrence and the cold war?" On election eve the *Sun* ran an article headed "Lest we forget" with a picture of streets full of rubbish in 1978-9. On polling day they famously featured a photo of Kinnock in a light bulb shaped frame with the caption "If Kinnock wins today will the last person to leave Britain switch out the lights." The *Sun* estimated that this edition was seen by 22% of the population. This must have been one of the worst campaigns of personal vilification run against a Party leader in a UK general election. At this point in the campaign, Major cast aside the status symbols of PM and "adopted" a soap box which he took round the country and used as a podium. The aim was probably to make Kinnock, with his confident, and sometimes ostentatious, presentation, appear pretentious. Even so on 1/4/91 a *Guardian* /ICM poll[C3-58] gave Labour a 6% lead and a Times/ MORI poll put Labour's lead at 7%. Then followed the Sheffield Rally, a grandiose event for Party workers from surrounding regions. It featured videos of celebrities supporting Labour. In his excitement Kinnock punched his fist and shouted "Well, all right" resembling Welsh comedian Max Boyce at a rugby match. Probably the prime ministerial image he had been cultivating was shattered. The stage was decked with National flags. Some perceived similarity to a Nazi rally. It also appeared Labour was taking victory for granted. After this rally, Labour began to fall back in the opinion polls.

The campaign seemed to have peaked a week too early; little new was presented towards its end. The next day Kinnock mentioned proportional representation but only to say that Labour would convert the sitting Plant Commission into a government inquiry. This announcement was planned as a sop to wavering Liberal voters but its effect was to raise the issue of a possible hung Parliament and a Lib Lab coalition. Kinnock was then interviewed on *This Week* by Sir Robin Day and was unwise enough to confess past policy mistakes on air. Next he launched a shadow Queen's Speech which canvassers were told was "arrogant".

By contrast TB was the golden boy with the public and media from the outset of his leadership. He was chosen as being a sure fire winner. Mandelson correctly divined that the public would not have warmed to GB in the same way. After a short honeymoon period in 2007, GB was not so well received by the public, as polls demonstrated. This factor contributed to the election defeat of 2010.

Kinnock was succeeded by John Smith. In a recent tribute John Prescott said of John Smith's Leadership that he was "amiable and ferociously intelligent … he didn't worry about image, focus groups and newspaper headlines. He cared about policies, priorities and, above all, people".[C3_59]

Smith supporters even included "hard" left-winger Dennis Canavan[C3_60] who valued his democratic leadership style. Smith's popularity was probably bolstered by his reputation for fair-mindedness. He attracted widespread support from the left as well as the right, from which he came. Unlike TB and GB, Smith would probably have retained Party members and electoral support over time. The hostile right wing media focuses on leadership calibre, seeking to expose and magnify every wart. This became a serious public relations issue for Labour during the 1980s and early 1990s and is so again from 2010 to the present.

By the time Kinnock triangulated he was neither new nor credible to the public. Major was treated as a totally new politician leading a fresh government. Like many of what TV's *Spitting Image* once described as "The Vegetables" (Thatcher Cabinet), Major seemed to be a relatively low profile and uncontroversial figure while Mrs Thatcher ruled. The early 80s dislike of Labour did not appear to attach to John Smith once he became leader.

This section shows *that the quality and presentation of the Party's leadership is a vital factor in winning elections*. The Kinnock experience demonstrated that a long-standing leader who radically changes their policy positions may not remain credible. A Leader, unacceptable to public opinion, is a heavy, if not fatal, vote looser. The same phenomenon seems to have affected Ed Miliband between 2010 and 2015.

To promote party democracy and retain widespread support within the Party, the Leader should ideally listen to all shades of opinion and promote people across a wide spectrum of viewpoints. The autocratic alternative is to exterminate politically those who do not slavishly follow their own ideology. This what many in the Party think that TB and GB did (see Chapters 8 and 9).

From the principled, but ageing and uncool, Michael Foot to the fickleness of Neil Kinnock, who was seen eventually to abandon almost all his beliefs and principles in the interests of electoral expediency, neither of Labour's leaders of the 1980s seemed to have the personality or presence that the public expected of a Prime Minister. Sadly TB, who many believed, possessed those attributes, lacked the ideals and principles which the former two had held. However the Party subjected itself to TB's arguably alien yoke in an effort to win elections.

What can be learnt from the NL era is that when a Leader (for instance allegedly TB over the Iraq weapons of mass destruction affair) conceals his alleged lack of personal integrity from the media and wider public then it may not be an election looser – in the short run. That people, within his Party, and the political classes, have their suspicions becomes temporarily immaterial. When Leaders are subsequently exposed, as TB was over the Weapons of Mass Destruction affair, then their credibility and popularity plummet.

GB had a fleeting political honeymoon. In 2009 Gordon Prentice MP reflected: "I've nothing against Brown personally but I believe that he doesn't have all the tools to be Party leader. He is surrounded by a small coterie of people into which he's brought people that he's known for years (such as Ed Balls). He doesn't consult other people. Brown is there and we're not going to be able to dislodge him. He has his people around him but many are not very close to him: Purnell, Flint and Hazel Blears. I believe that he'll take us all down with the ship. We missed a trick by not asking him to go earlier." The same year Alice Mahon said: "There's no doubt we need a change of leader. I am really disappointed with Brown's leadership. I accept that he probably rescued our finances but the way he acted has done nothing to push the bankers into being more responsible since." These views turned out to be accurate forecasts.

Internal squabbling: Intruders and Quitters – the Militant Tendency and Social Democratic Party (SDP)

The *Militant Tendency* received increasing publicity which was damaging the Party and its electoral prospects. Under old Clause 2 of the Party constitution, an organisation with its own programme, principles, policy, members and local branches was not permitted to affiliate to the Party, nor could its members join Labour. Militant would not admit to meeting these criteria. They claimed they were simply "readers of *Militant* Newspaper". That this claim was false was evidenced when General Secretary Ron Hayward spoke to Ted Grant, a Militant leader. Grant, when charged with sexist attitudes of Militant supporters replied: "That's not true, we'd have expelled them!"[C3_61]

By late 1981 the membership of Militant was about 4,000. It was believed to have more staff than the Labour Party. Foot, and his general secretaries, decided to take action. The NEC set up an inquiry into Militant. A crackdown was agreed at the 1982 Conference and a scheme was agreed whereby groups wishing to operate within the Party had to register and prove acceptability. Militant refused to apply. The NEC then proscribed Militant and expelled its leaders. By then there were eight members of Militant endorsed as Parliamentary candidates for the 1983 election. There was then no constitutional means of de-selecting them until afterwards.

Faced with the prospect of councillors being personally liable to pay council debts in virtually all large authorities, Labour councillors agreed to set a rate within Government defined limits. However Liverpool City council was controlled by "Militant" councillors. On an election promise of "No cuts in jobs and services" that council introduced an urban regeneration scheme costing in excess of Tory Government spending norms. Six moderate Labour councillors voted against the Militant's budget, preventing its approval. At the 1985 Conference Kinnock made a speech that condemned Militant. It received a standing ovation. He declared: "You can't play politics with people's jobs."[C3_62]

In July 1991 Kinnock declined to attend the Durham Miners' Gala for the first time. This was probably a means of disassociating himself from Labour's traditional image. At the Liverpool Walton by-election afterwards Labour fielded Peter Kilfoyle, who had played a major role in exposing and controlling Militants locally. Militant had its own candidate which enabled Labour to expel Militants who worked for her. However Tory MPs still made capital out of the supposed extent of Militant's presence in the Party (interview with P. Kilfoyle).

The ***Social Democratic Party (SDP)*** was another source of trouble for the Labour leadership. The first move was the departure from the Labour Party of the "Gang of Four" (MPs Shirley Williams, Roy Jenkins, Bill Rogers and David Owen). They then founded the SDP in March 1981. Only ten Labour MPs left with them, but others departed later. In her media-released resignation letter, Shirley Williams gave her reasons for leaving: "The Party was no longer a democratic socialist party and she disagreed with Conference decisions about the Electoral College to choose the Leader, reselection of MPs and Europe."[C3_63] Many of the old right such as Denis Healey and Roy Hattersley remained loyal.

SDP leaders gave mixed messages about the ideology of their new Party. Owen claimed: "We are going to have a socialist Party, seen to be on the left, with strong links with the trades unions."[C3_64] However Roy Jenkins was quoted in the *Sunday Times* saying: "I haven't used that word (socialism) for years".[C3_65] The SDP's electoral success and in opinion polls may have been due to its lack of frankness about its political agenda. It certainly took more Labour votes than had been anticipated.[C3_66] However a relatively small number of grass-roots Party members departed with "the Gang". This limited damage to local campaign teams.

'Squabbling among themselves': the effects of publicised internecine strife

In western countries public squabbling within a Party seems inevitably to lead to disaffection from the electorate. In September 1931 Leader Ramsay MacDonald, and other Labour MPs, joined the Tory-led coalition. A general election followed in October. A bitter campaign was conducted against the Party by coalition candidates: especially the MacDonald "Labour" faction which smeared the Labour rump as "bolsheviks". Labour lost 2 million votes and the PLP was decimated to 51 members. Five of these were ILP MPs who fought the election on a different manifesto. These events severely weakened the PLP's influence, within the Party. After the defection of MacDonald and associates the Party was largely run by a new Council of Labour dominated by the unions until 1940. The Party re-united around Attlee during the war and in the post war years.[C3_67]

The loss of an election has frequently been followed by recrimination and splits in the Labour Party. After the 1951 Labour election loss, ideological conflicts, that were already simmering quietly whilst Labour was in Government, burst into the open and escalated. However conflict did not break out in the Party after the 1970 election defeat because many considered that Wilson deserved another chance. In 1979, as in 1951; when the Labour Party lost power, there was a thorough, and bitter, review of the faults of the last government.[C3_68] Specific criticisms were made of indifference to – or defiance of – the opinions of the Party rank and file and Party Conference resolutions.[C3_69] *Organisational learning from mistakes is vital to the future success of a Party. However publicised dissent within the Party, that can accompany a review of mistakes, undermines credibility with the public.* The difficulties that Labour encountered with Militant and the nascent SDP (discussed above) also gave rise to public perceptions of "squabbling among themselves".

Opinion poll after poll, and innumerable pundits, have informed Labour, and other parties worldwide, that they forfeit public support when they are seen to be quarrelling among themselves. Democratic debate is one of the media through which politics is conducted. However if it ceases to be amicable and is linked to personal animosity or naked power-seeking then it can drive voters to support the opposition or refuse to vote. The situation will be exacerbated if the quarrels are about abstruse political or procedural points not understood, or regarded as important, by the public.

The Labour Party, prior to NL, had an admirable tradition of public debate in the exercise of public and party democracy and general transparency. However, acrimonious airing of disputes in view of the media lost votes. For example, when, after the 1979 election, Foot became Leader, publicised wrangling broke out about re-selection of MPs and electing the Party Leader and Deputy. This was followed by a high profile Deputy Leadership election (Benn vs. Healey – narrowly won by Healey). These events undoubtedly reduced the Party's popularity with the public.

After the 1987 election defeat, the Party's Shadow Communications Agency (SCA) produced a diagnostic report. This showed private polls indicating that "extremism and conflict" were the main reasons for not voting Labour. Labour had lost most support among women. Women were reported, by pollsters, as perceiving Labour as "too aggressive" and its leadership as "untrustworthy".

Democratic debate was rudely ended by the NL regime. They pulled the plug, sometimes literally, on Conference and public debate of Party governance and policy. Debate of policy at Conference was increasingly restricted by TB then GB. This is discussed in detail in Chapter 7. In the short run, the NL gag probably served to conserve votes. In the long run democracy requires a form of debate which avoids losing votes (for example by holding some debates in private session without live media coverage).

Similarly a classic Australian Labor case of unpopular internal squabbling arose in 2010. Kevin Rudd led Labor into the winning election campaign in 2007. Thereafter he headed a popular government. Notably he successfully steered Australia through the Global Economic Crisis. He subsequently incurred unpopularity over climate change policies and a mining tax that were reflected in opinion polls. The Australian Labor Party (ALP) constitution allows the Caucus (Parliamentary Labour Party) to change the Party leader on a majority vote, even when they are in government. This they did in June 2010, installing Julia Gillard to replace Rudd as prime minister. *No official explanation was given to the public at the time. Unsurprisingly the ALP lost more support, was unable to win the August 2010 general election outright, and had to form a rainbow coalitio*n.

After Foreign Secretary Rudd unsuccessfully challenged for the Leadership in 2012, Gillard and her supporters admitted that they made a major error by not explaining to the public why they replaced Rudd in the first place (because he was allegedly very difficult to work with). They revealed intra-party conflict in both 2010 (losing votes) and in 2012. In 2013 as Gillard became progressively more unpopular there was an aborted attempt to re-install Rudd followed by a successful one. Whilst the ALP's popularity has increased since Rudd was re-installed the squabbling that led to that harmed Labor in the September 2013 general election. If the electors can understand and identify with a political disagreement then perhaps it is less likely to alienate them.

The role of changing social and political attitudes on UK electoral trends

Shakespeare referred to a *"tide in the affairs of men"* or opportunity that must be seized (quotation in Chapter head). From time to time there are undoubtedly widespread surges of public attitude and feeling which affect the public and their voting behaviour. These attitudes will be influenced by relevant experience from the recent past. One such trend was the widespread view, held in Britain after World War 2, that it was time to improve social justice and quality of life of people in the UK as a whole through the foundation of the welfare state. These attitudes were probably affected by the privations and struggles of that conflict and its focus on standing up to Nazism and fascism. They also reflected a determination not to allow the repetition of broken World War 1 assurances, made by Lloyd George, whose promised land "fit for heroes" failed to materialise.

Another theory was put forward by a retired Labour constituency organiser Harry Tout, on active service throughout the Second World War. He believed that people became politically radicalised in the forces where the Labour Party was very popular.[C3-70] Similarly Francis Beckett reported that a friend who was ill in a military hospital in India told him that when the 1945 Labour Government was confirmed on radio news "men confined to bed got up and danced in the wards".[C3-71]

Another example was contemporary UK public support for the Falklands war. Perhaps this developed because Argentina had, without recent provocation, invaded a British colony whose inhabitants clearly found that invasion unacceptable. Public sentiment will usually fluctuate. What Parties have to do to win elections is to catch the tide at the right time and to ride it in. That is what Labour did in 1945 and the Conservatives achieved in 1983. Likewise In 1997 there was a public thirst for something different to replace 18 years of Thatcherite Conservative rule.

Sometimes such issues are of a social rather than a political nature. They often reflect undesirable contemporary social attitudes. On occasion they are whipped up by the popular media. During the 1980s and up to 1992, the Conservatives, and their cheerleading press, waged a ferocious campaign against "Labour's Loony Left". The examples given were almost entirely about local authorities in Greater London and Liverpool. A related target was the promotion of gay and lesbian rights: particularly that by the GLC and some London Boroughs. Gay rights also became significant during the Bermondsey by-election campaign where both Peter Tatchell and Simon Hughes (who had not yet "come out") were candidates. Homophobia and related discrimination were then more publicly acceptable. By the late 1990s this was no longer a factor because social attitudes had changed; thanks partly to earlier campaigning by the same Labour local councils. In recent years, championing gay rights has been seen as a vote winner for Labour and even the Conservatives after 2010 (see views of senior backbencher M, Chapter 5). That public attitudes have since become more progressive on gay rights was evidenced by widespread support for Gay marriage in 2013. The NL Government introduced Civil Partnerships. Political parties can sometimes find themselves in tune with current opinion trends and able to develop policies that were not electorally popular in the past.

A Sales Oriented Party ('SOP') adheres, by and large, to its values and aims. However in formulating policies it still has to take into account changes in political conditions, in society, in economic conditions and in technological and scientific progress. It has to try to hone policies, in accordance with its aims and values, which fit these conditions and meet the priority needs that they generate. This is what the phrase "Traditional Values in a Modern Setting"[C3-72] was intended to convey. However NL was actually a Market Oriented Party (MOP) which modelled its policies mainly on what the most powerful voters told focus groups that they wanted. The Party's traditional aims and values were usually ignored by NL (see Chapter 1).

Sometimes elections are won mainly because voters are weary of the incumbents. NL prospered in the early years by becoming a MOP but they also profited from dislike of the Tories after their 18 years in power and from the public desire for a change to something apparently new and different (John Smith would also have benefitted here).

External events, timing of elections and the tennis phenomenon

The second, policy related factor, in winning and losing elections is what Harold Macmillan described as "events, dear boy". That is unplanned, or unforeseen, national or international events or even so-called "Acts of God". These can enhance, or damage, a government's reputation by its handing of them or by the effects of past government decisions. A classic contrasting example was Prime Minister Anthony Eden's handling of the Suez crisis. Conclusions can be drawn from Thatcher's management of the Falklands invasion.

If a government can foresee the possibility of an event, some form of robust planning should be possible. Ironically Callaghan anticipated an Argentine invasion of the Falklands in 1978·9. He successfully took evasive action by increasing British naval presence there. However while appropriate action can prevent a catastrophe it may not gain electoral popularity once a disaster has been averted. The public may not then believe in the reality of a former threat when they experienced no crisis. Consequently they will not show gratitude to the averter: as they did not to Callaghan in 1979. An "Act of God" example was the English floods soon after GB became Labour leader. He gained temporary popularity through his competent handing of this crisis.

A related issue is the timing of general elections. Callaghan (in 1979) and Brown (GB) (in 2010) delayed calling elections after only one term in office. Perhaps they sought to prolong their tenure of Number 10? Had Callaghan called the election in the Autumn of 1978, when the economy was doing well, he might have won. By hinting at an early election and then postponing it he lost support and also faced the "Winter of Discontent" in the intervening period. Perhaps JC and GB sought to prolong their tenure of Number 10? In both cases the election was lost by Labour.

NL initially benefitted from the "Black Wednesday" financial debacle and extended weariness of the Conservatives after the "new", initially attractive, image of John Major had lost its shine. GB experienced a "honeymoon" period for a few months after he became leader. However he failed to capitalise on this popularity by not calling a general election in the autumn of 2007. In 2010 NL suffered from the aftermath of the (apparently unanticipated) 2008 international financial crisis, subsequent failure to regulate the financial institutions and the 2009 Parliamentary expenses scandal.

Linked to all the above factors is the phenomenon whereby politics resembles tennis: players win "points" (support) as the consequence of their opponent's mistakes. Political players, like tennis competitors, can deliberately precipitate, and/or capitalise on, opponent's mistakes. It is prudent for governments, and parties, to try to avoid mistakes and media publicity that may highlight errors, especially when an election is in the offing. Even trivial mistakes can spell disaster – as when Neil Kinnock fell over on Brighton beach immediately after being elected as Leader. As the cliché says: "You don't get a second chance to make a first impression".

Winning and Losing Elections: the effects of policies and related events:

This section focuses on the role of policy prospectuses (election manifestos) in winning elections before the advent of the NL phenomenon. The actual policy record of earlier Labour governments is reviewed in Chapter 6. However some *specific policies and related political events appear to have influenced particular election results in a significant way.*

A significant factor in winning and losing elections is the policy prospectus (manifesto) put forward by a Party. Lilleker and Lees-Marshment[C3-73] proposed that, in order for it to be credible, such a policy programme needs to be brief, clear and apparently deliverable within a reasonable time. As they asserted, failure to deliver on election promises usually loses votes at the subsequent election (as Wilson discovered in 1970). Policy messages must be given clearly, consistently and unambiguously. This was illustrated by some Labour electoral mistakes in the 80s and early 90s. Experience at that time suggested that Party spokespeople should not give conflicting statements about the same topic within a short time of each other. This may seem obvious, but it occurred repeatedly during the eighties and early nineties. Nor should they make announcements that conflict with other recent policy proposals emanating from their party, themselves or other senior colleagues. One example was that, in the early 1990s, Smith (as Shadow Chancellor) and Kinnock fell into this trap concerning personal taxation policy.

A chronological account appears below. This section reviews the link between the policy prospectus, policy record and actual election results in the pre NL period. It can be compared with the record of NL in winning elections.

In the 1945 general election 393 Labour MPs were elected – a 146 overall majority. In these pre-opinion poll days it was difficult to accurately ascertain reasons for electoral success. One possibility was unpopularity of the Liberals and Conservatives over the Munich Agreement, failure to re-arm and to curb massive unemployment and wage cuts during the 1930s. During the 1945 Labour government the public seemed content until latter years. This Government lost *no* seats in by-elections. By the general election of 1950 Labour's prospects had deteriorated. *The public were weary of austerity and rationing.* Labour won 315 seats compared with 298 for the Conservatives, nine for the Liberals and two Irish Nationalists – which gave it a precarious hold on power. Electors were probably upset by *price rises* due to the economic impact of the Korean War which put up the cost of transport and raw materials. The retail price index was 113 in February 1950, but by the next general election (October 1951) it had risen to 129.[C3-74]

After the 1950 election, which Labour narrowly won, the first *divisive policy* issue to arise was German re-armament. Attlee wanted to support the Tories in agreeing policy with the USA. The PLP voted on the issue and the pro-re-armers won by a majority of only nine. Disagreement arose across the Labour party about Britain's nuclear weapons; many in the Party supported unilateral nuclear disarmament. Labour lost the 1952 election.

In 1955 Churchill unexpectedly retired as PM and was succeeded by Eden. Problems arose from internal Labour Party conflict in respect of the British Hydrogen bomb. Eden swiftly called a general election at what was opportune timing for the Tories. Industrial disputes can also spell trouble for the Labour Party. There had been industrial action in the early summer of 1955: a month-long newspaper strike, a dock strike (during the election campaign) and the threat of a rail strike. A disaffected public turned anti-Labour because of their union links. Further, the economy was doing well at the time and the Tories had recently made tax cuts. The Conservative's share of the vote in 1955 was 3% more than Labour's.

Nye Bevan did a "U turn" on the H bomb declaring that "Britain must not go naked into the conference chamber". However a consumer spending boom led to a pro-Tory feel-good factor. The Iron and Steel Federation, who wanted to avoid re-nationalisation, funded a major advertising campaign on the Tories' behalf.

Halfway through the 1959 campaign the major parties were running neck and neck. *Labour then made pledges not to increase taxation: which seemed to go down badly with the electorate!* Public aversion to tax and spend had not yet developed! The Tories won the election with an increased majority. Labour's share of the vote went down to 43.8%.

The Suez crisis led to Eden's resignation but not to a general election. His successor Macmillan was a moderate Tory whose domestic policy was not very different from Labour's – a so-called "Butskellite" position. Despite his effete manner: "Super Mac" was able to gain strong public support for his government because of the contemporary economic boom. Incoming Premier Lord Douglas-Home was not as popular as Macmillan, who retired in autumn 1963. During the winter of 1962-3 the economy was in difficulty and unemployment rose. However later in 1963 there was an economic and consumer boom and Conservative popularity improved.

When the 1964 general election was called the two main parties were running neck and neck in the polls. Labour could capitalise on the Tory government's failings and on Chancellor Selwyn Lloyd's policy of restricting economic expansion. The economic situation appeared to have deteriorated so badly that Lloyd was regularly observed taking the collection at the Methodist church attended by the author's mother! The Tories boasted about recent full employment and rising living standards.[C3-75] Labour gained 56 seats: but an overall majority of only four.

The 1964 Manifesto included a set of aims: a statement of what the Labour Government was for.[C3-76]

Despite a having majority of three in 1964 this Labour government pressed ahead with a bold programme. The 1965 budget introduced capital gains tax and corporation tax.[C3-77] The government managed to bring inflation under control. They were doing well in opinion polls and by-elections. Wilson called an election in 1966 because he needed a larger majority. The 1966 election campaign was said to be a dull one with no new policies proposed and "several of the old ones were abandoned or modified". Wilson presented himself as a moderate and pragmatic leader. The campaign was effective and there was a 2.7% swing to Labour.[C3-78] Labour won 47.9% of the total poll and an overall majority of 96 – sufficient to underpin a normal parliamentary term.

The 1966 Government did badly in by-elections, local government elections and opinion polls throughout the first three years. It was recently argued that this indicated a strong, and slowly building, body of hostile opinion which was still present in 1969 thus accounting for the "surprise" election defeat in 1970.[C3_79] This phenomenon was partly due to unpopular economic and industrial policies and measures such as the introduction of prescription charges for the first time (1968). This policy was clumsily announced just before the local elections. Contemporary Health Minister Richard Crossman personally admitted this to the author (in conversation at a 1970 Labour Party School). Towards the end of 1969 economic prospects improved and the balance of payments went into surplus (Spring 1970). Opinion polls improved and Labour did well in local elections. Wilson called a general election for June 1970.

Labour went into the 1970 campaign with the slogan: "Now Britain's strong again let's make it great to live in". This referred to the ending of the balance of payments deficit and thus the promised availability of money for social and other public spending. Principal messages in the manifesto were: continuation of prudent economic management; development of industry; creation and preservation of jobs; and a promised increase in aid to poor countries. The core of the 1970 campaign was designed to appeal to the floating voter and played down ideological and policy differences between the major parties. There was a last minute 4.7% swing to Conservative. Heath secured an overall majority of 31 seats.

Labour was well prepared to contest the February 1974 election. Wilson still commanded much respect within the Party. In June 1973 he was re-elected unopposed to the Leadership. The Party went into this election with arguably its most left wing manifesto to date. This was launched at a large meeting in Middlesbrough Town Hall at which both Harold Wilson and the author, who was then a local Parliamentary candidate, spoke from the platform. Although he always conveyed the impression of being laid back and confident when speaking, she was surprised to notice that Wilson's hands trembled as he spoke.

In February 1974 the manifesto contained the now celebrated promise of: "A fundamental and irreversible shift in the balance of power and wealth in favour of working people and their families". [C3_80] This shift would involve wealth tax and capital transfer tax. There was to be nationalisation of development land, mineral rights and parts of the engineering industry. A new National Enterprise Board was to oversee the public industrial sector. There were also plans for a voluntary social contract between government and unions to regulate wage increases and prices. The February 1974 manifesto also included repeal of the Tory Industrial Relations Act and re-negotiation of the terms of entry into the EEC. Labour's win was a narrow triumph for a democratic socialist prospectus.

Industrial action intervened: campaigning was impeded by the three day week – the government response to a miner's strike. Opinion polls were volatile and (according to Harris Polls) voters were more likely to abandon their habitual Party allegiance. Labour polled only 37.1 % of the vote, this gave them 301 seats, four more than the Conservatives. There were 23 MPs elected from minor parties and no overall Labour majority.

Because of the difficulties of minority government, Labour was defeated on numerous major bills. Wilson called another general election for October 1974. The manifesto was entitled "Britain will win with Labour" re-iterated the pledges of its February predecessor. It also emphasised the social contract with the unions and promised new employment protection legislation. This included new rights for unions to recruit and organise, rights to strike and to engage in collective bargaining. There was also to be health and safety at work legislation and provision for "union shops" (where all employees must join a union) in their workplace. For the first time there was promise of a referendum on devolution for Scotland and Wales. The population was promised a referendum on our EEC membership within a year: following upon British re-negotiation of the original terms of entry. The main promises of the February manifesto were also repeated. Labour won an overall majority of three on a swing of 2.2%. Eventually this precarious situation led to the negotiation of the Lib-Lab Pact. The Labour percentage of the poll rose to 39.2%. Most election promises were kept.

During the 1970s there was also much Labour legislation that established services to benefit people at work, to improve health and safety in the workplace and public transport.[C3_81] A comprehensive policy programme was developed to assist people with mental health and learning disability issues.

Wilson retired unexpectedly in 1976 and was replaced by James Callaghan. Soon afterwards Britain's nuclear warheads (Chevaline) were updated without the agreement of the full Cabinet. Following the demise of the Lib-Lab pact in the summer of 1978 a general election became inevitable. At Callaghan's instigation the contemporary wage norm was set at 5%. This was below the inflation rate and therefore involved a cut in real wages. It prompted adverse reaction from the unions. Chancellor Healey subsequently pronounced this norm to have been a mistake. Between December 1978 and February 1979 there was the wave of, mainly public sector, strikes. They included a strike of Liverpool gravediggers which caused widespread outrage. Disastrous lost referenda on devolution for Scotland and Wales followed in March 1979. These further undermined government credibility. Economic improvements of autumn 1978 were not sustained and fuelled the 1979 Saatchi and Saatchi Tory advertising campaign based around the slogan "Labour isn't working". The Labour manifesto for the 1979 election included the first proposal for a wealth tax; planning agreements with large companies; and some nationalisation of banking and insurance. Labour lost heavily and the public was subjected to the sickening view of a hypocritical Mrs. Thatcher quoting St. Francis of Assisi on the steps of 10 Downing St. Far worse was to follow.

In the months after the 1979 election defeat, Labour appeared to have a good chance of winning the next general election. The economy was fast going into recession: unemployment and inflation were growing rapidly. Opinion polls showed Thatcher to be unpopular personally.[C3_82] In 1981 Labour organised a major campaign for jobs including a mass rally in Liverpool and a march of unemployed people across the country. In both these Labour Leader Michael Foot played a prominent part.[C3_83]

President Reagan and Mrs. Thatcher refused to hold disarmament talks with the Soviet Union in 1981. Then contacts between Foot, the Opposition and the Russians developed into peace talks in Moscow. Because of protocol, it was a Party-to-Party session but included a meeting with Russian President Brezhnev. The outcome was that Brezhnev made an important announcement that he was ready to reduce the number of SS20 missiles if the USA would suspend the use of Cruise and Pershing missiles. The Western and Russian media were impressed. They reported that Foot "had been taken very seriously" and he was able to claim that he had taken the initiative whilst Thatcher was tied to negative US policies.[C3_84]

After that came the Falklands war and subsequent UK victory. It was celebrated at a triumphal Tory rally July 1981. In Thatcher's speech there she used the phrase the "Falklands Factor" for the first time. Quoting it repeatedly became the Tory mantra for the 1983 general election. Leading up to the campaign there was a wide gap in the polls between the main parties. The difference between their leader's popularity was even wider.

In March 1983 came the Darlington by-election. Labour produced its best by-election campaign and result for many years. The seat was held and its modest Labour majority doubled. There was a slick and efficient campaign managed by the author's partner Terry Johnston. The author escorted the actor Bill Owen (Compo), to meet voters and drum up support for Labour. He proved very popular with women voters who dropped their shopping and flocked to the market hall to glad hand him. Legions of campaign workers volunteered from the North East, many from the nearby Langbaurgh constituency, where the author was then parliamentary candidate.

A disastrous general election followed six weeks later. Mervyn Jones[C3_85] believed that owing to public relations disasters in the previous two years the election was lost in advance. However another important reason for Labour's defeat was probably its failure to convince the electors of the viability of its manifesto commitments relating to disarmament, the economy and jobs. Callaghan made a damaging intervention. Speaking mid-campaign: he praised rejection of unilateralism by British governments. Two days later, Wilson gave an interview to the *Daily Mail* published under the headline "Where my party has gone wrong" in which he criticised Foot for tolerating Militant (about which he himself had taken no action) and making Labour subservient to the unions. The election voting was Conservatives 43.5%, Labour 28.3% and the SDP Liberal Alliance 26% (at the 2010 general election Labour only polled 29%: two thirds of a per cent more). Foot resigned as Leader immediately afterwards. In 1983 Conference carried two contradictory resolutions favouring multi-lateral and unilateral nuclear disarmament respectively.

Under the new Leader, Neil Kinnock, Labour initially did well. By February 1984 Marplan reported Labour on 40% and Conservatives on 39%: the first time Labour had been in the lead since the Falklands war. Labour polled well in European elections that year, increasing its seats in the European Parliament from 17 to 32. Most of its extra votes were gained at the expense of the SDP/Liberal Alliance.

Labour even won public support for opposing the Government's anti-trades union policies such as the union membership ban at the UK spy headquarters GCHQ. In 1984 came another miner's strike. Kinnock supported the right for miners to strike, although he disagreed with miners' leader Arthur Scargill's tactics. When Thatcher described miners as "the enemy within", Kinnock protested at the 1985 TUC Congress saying: "A government that wants to treat British trade unionists as the enemy within is a government at war with itself." Nevertheless many miners believed he was giving them too little support. [C3_86] *When the strike ended it was Labour, not the Conservatives, who benefitted in the polls, moving 6% ahead of the Tories in April 1985.*

The next policy problem came from high spending Labour Councils whom the Government threatened to penalise with a system of rate-capping. Kinnock argued that the Labour campaign should focus on defence of public services. When the Westland Helicopters crisis occurred, Kinnock, and the PLP, were able to inflict wounds on the Tories and radically undermine Thatcher's credibility.

The Labour Party had adopted the policy of unilateral nuclear disarmament over many years. Neil and Glenys Kinnock were long-standing members of the Campaign for Nuclear Disarmament (CND). They made a high profile visit to the Greenham Peace camp in the early 1980s. Kinnock had several meetings with senior US and NATO Officials during 1986 where he supported a non-nuclear defence system for Britain but received hostile receptions. The Party then published its defence policy "Modern Britain in the Modern World". This pledged Labour's commitment to NATO but with a non-nuclear defence policy. In February 1987 Kinnock had a meeting with Reagan but the White House set it up so that it received minimal media publicity. At this meeting, White House advisors attacked Labour's defence policy. Kinnock and Healey announced to the media that it had been a successful meeting but the White House press office publicly contradicted this. They reported that the meeting had been acrimonious and lasted only 17 minutes (it actually lasted half an hour).

In spring 1986 Labour launched a "Freedom and Fairness" campaign.[C3_87] This centred on policy pledges recommended by the Party's new Shadow Communications Agency (SCA) *based on their opinion survey findings*. This was an early move towards becoming a MOP. These pledges covered under-5s' services, cervical cancer screening, unleaded petrol, improved street lighting and help for first time home buyers. This campaign was accompanied by a flamboyant televised launch and trendy presentation packs. The colour scheme and design was changed from the customary predominant red with red flags to red roses on a cream background. Under attack for Labour's defence policy: Kinnock gave an acclaimed speech to Conference. He said: "I would die for my country, but I would never let it die for me."[C3_88].

Since spring 1986 Labour had continuously scored between two and five per cent above the Conservatives in opinion polls. They now believed they could win the coming general election. At Conference 1986 Kinnock spoke, affirming his belief in unilateral nuclear disarmament . It was said that Labour had undergone a cosmetic facelift; but its unpopular policies were almost the same.[C3_89]

By the mid 1980s Kinnock was accused of failing to mention "socialism". However the preface to Kinnock's book *Making our Way*[C3_90] starts by defining his concept of a socialist.

His priorities were: obtaining long term, stable economic growth, large scale development of British manufacturing industry and development of the infrastructure for vocational training and technology He also called for an end to monetarism being used as our principal economic theory. He also demanded the abandonment of Thatcher's "free-market mania". Adding that: "The market is a good servant – but a bad master". Like his Labour predecessors he called for a planned economy.

By September 1986 the Tories were 5% behind Labour in opinion polls. However immediately after the Conservative Conference, Tory popularity increased and Thatcher's personal popularity rating rose by 5%. In 1987 Tory central office concentrated its fire on Kinnock portraying him as unpatriotic, ready to leave the country defenceless and unfit to lead it. They assembled a dirt file on him and distributed it to Tory candidates and MPs. Hostilities at Westminster increased – for example, a vitriolic speech made by Edwina Currie MP in February 1987.[C3_91] Then the respective whips met and agreed that hostilities had gone too far and become too personal. Meanwhile Labour recovered in the polls. The Conservatives were only 1.5% ahead in early February 1987.

The next problem for Labour was the Greenwich by-election in February 1987. Labour fielded a local councillor (an allegedly "hard left" candidate). The SDP and Tories waged a campaign of personal vilification against her. It was said that she proved unable to withstand the pressure. On polling day there was a massive swing against Labour and the SDP won. After the by-election a BBC *Newsnight* Gallup poll put the Tories on 37.7%, Labour on 33.7% and Alliance on 26.6%.

Labour's hopes of general election victory were waning. It did badly in the 1987 local elections losing 220 seats and control of six councils. The SDP/ Liberal Alliance gained 448 seats. The draft general election manifesto realised Kinnock's wishes. It enabled him to fight the general election as an ethical campaign against Thatcherism and promote Labour as the Party of fairness and decency.[C3_92] The Labour manifesto was less than half the length of its 1983 predecessor and allowed council tenants the right to buy their homes.

The Conservatives concentrated their fire on Labour's policies attacking their "Iceberg Manifesto" – "one tenth of its socialism visible, nine tenths below the surface". (Thatcher launching the Tory campaign). Labour overtook the SDP in the polls in late May. These recorded support at: Conservatives 41%, Labour 33% and SDP 21%. The Tory campaign was unimpressive and Thatcher made blunders. Kinnock made a mistake on defence policy in a TV interview with David Frost. He implied that Labour would not put up armed resistance to a Soviet nuclear attack. This gave the Conservatives ammunition for attacks on Labour's defence policy and Reagan condemned it.[C3_93]

In 1987 the author was Labour's Parliamentary candidate in the marginal seat of Swindon. The local Labour council had an excellent record much praised by residents. A common response on the doorstep was "we'll vote for you locally but not nationally". They frequently added: "We're frightened by what 'loony left' councils in London are doing". Thus voters were apparently more influenced by national Tory propaganda about someone else's local issues than by their own local experience. When canvassing the author was sometimes told "there's no need for you to call we're watching it all on TV." This was clearly a media led campaign. The other main theme on doorsteps was Conservative Leadership. Many said to canvassers: "We're not voting for you, we're voting for *her*" (i.e. Margaret Thatcher).

During the latter part of the campaign Labour seemed to be gaining support. Defence policy was not alarming voters as much as had been feared, but Tory policies on education and housing were scaring voters.[93] Mrs. Thatcher foolishly revealed her personal use of private healthcare. After a rogue poll in the *Daily Telegraph* showing the Tories on 40.55% and Labour on 36.5% the Conservatives stepped up hostilities. They hyped up their poster campaign particularly focusing on defence policy (there was a poster showing a soldier waving a white flag of surrender: captioned "Labour's Defence policy"). Meanwhile the Labour campaign ran out of momentum. Then came a Conservative "Labour's Tax grab campaign" highlighting inconsistencies in Labour's fiscal policies. Editorials appeared in the hostile press examining discrepancies between the content of Labour's glossy manifesto and policy and spending commitments made by opposition spokespeople since 1983. Labour held a flamboyant eve of election rally at which Kinnock proclaimed that the end of Thatcherism was nigh. The Conservatives were returned with a 102 majority. Labour, who gained only 20 seats and received 30.8% of the vote. The Conservatives polled 42.3% and the SDP 22.6%. The Tory share of the vote was similar to that of 1983.

Labour Conference 1987 supported a major policy review by the Party, championed by Kinnock. There was widespread recognition that the Party needed to understand the aspirations of voters, who had deserted Labour, and to change policies to meet these. The National Union of Public Employees' Tom Sawyer told Conference: "Listen to what Labour's missing millions have to say and make some real connection between our ideas and their aspirations."[C3_94] That contrasted with the forthcoming change that went to the opposite extreme i.e. giving key voters what they desired under NL.

The Shadow Communications Agency (SCA) post election study found that many considered the Party to be poor at economic management, old fashioned and keen to set up a nanny state.[C3_95] There was widespread rejection of unilateral nuclear disarmament. A "Labour Listens" exercise was set up and questionnaires sent out. This provided limited information. However as a public relations exercise, showing willingness to listen, it probably did some good. The next policy review's duration was two years and to be followed by *gaining support* for policies in the next two. It was to focus on economic and industrial policy. Defence was included – despite Kinnock's reluctance.

Labour focused on domestic policies for the European elections in 1989. The Tory poll tax was the bone of contention. Support for Alliance Parties collapsed and Labour ended up with 44% of the votes and won 45 seats in the European Parliament. Kinnock's personal poll rating overtook Thatcher's for the first time since the 1987 election (Kinnock 41%, Thatcher 34% for "doing a good job".

In mid March 1990 Labour overturned a 14,000 Tory majority in the Mid Staffordshire by election; having fought a high profile campaign. On 31 March 1990, in London, there was a mass rally of 40,000 people against the poll tax. This was accompanied by violence and looting which was condemned by Kinnock.

In early 1991 the Government abolished the poll tax. Tory policy initiatives, such as Citizens' Charters, proved underwhelming for the public. At the Monmouth by election (May 1991) Labour captured this Tory seat on a 12.6% swing following a showy campaign. After this result, and poor Tory performance in contemporary local elections, there was no prospect of an imminent general election.

Labour next abandoned all its spending commitments – other than raising pensions and child benefits. In September 1991 inflation fell to 4.7% and the base interest rate to 10.5%, The Tories reaped the electoral benefit. Labour had been 6% ahead in opinion polls, over the summer but this now turned to a Tory lead of 3%. Conference 1991 was heavily stage managed. Following it Labour regained an average two point lead in the polls. Afterwards they ran a poster campaign on Tory plans for the NHS and a MORI poll gave it a 16% lead. An economic downturn, and splits in the Government over Europe, hit Tory popularity. Kinnock failed to speak well in the Commons on the Maastricht Treaty (late November) but redeemed himself by launching an effective attack on Major in a December Commons debate on Europe.[C3_96] An allocation of an extra £11 billion for government Departments of Health and "care" was announced in the Chancellor's Autumn Statement (November 1991). This virtually wiped out Labour's poll lead.

As the 1992 election approached Margaret Beckett, then Shadow Financial Secretary to the Treasury, approached the City to give reassurance about the prospect of a Labour Government. Commitments were made to introduce a national minimum wage of £3.40 per hour and to work towards full employment.

As they had done before the 1987 general election, Conservative Central Office costed all Labour's spending pledges and published their calculations. They focused on Labour's tax plans. Conservatives alleged that most people would be £20 a week worse off under Labour. This was untrue, as the detriment applied only to basic rate taxpayers. However the *Labour publicity machine proved unable to refute their allegation effectively.* This was partly because Kinnock and John Smith gave conflicting messages about phasing in tax plans. The false allegation was replicated in the infamous "Labour's Tax bombshell" and "Labour's Double Whammy" posters used during the 1992 election campaign.

Kinnock predicted in the *Financial Times*[C3_97] that Labour would win the election with an overall majority of 20. The March Conservative budget did not change the standard rate of income tax but brought in a new rate of 20% for the low paid. When the 1992 election campaign commenced Labour had a poll lead of 3% over the Tories. Inflation and house prices were falling.

Early in the campaign John Smith, then Shadow Chancellor, announced detailed budget figures showing that everyone with an annual income less than £22,000 would be better off (eight out of ten taxpayers). However salaries in the South were higher than in the North. £22,000 pa there was relatively average. The *Sun* and *Daily Mail* produced hostile headlines falsely implying many more would be caught by increased taxation. Louise Ellman MP recalled that communication problems, arising from these tactics, lost votes: "I remember in the 1992 election campaign we sought to increase some of the higher rates of tax to fund increases in old age pensions and child benefit. But as the election campaign developed people, who would have benefited, thought they would end up losers. I asked pensioners who said that they could not afford to vote Labour: "Why?" They replied: "Because we would pay more taxes". In the interests of public relations we did not talk about the ways we were helping poor families and pensioners (even in 1992). We only spoke about how we were helping the better off."

The 1992 Labour manifesto was launched with a fanfare. Apart from financial information, there was little significant content. One controversial issue was the "Jennifer's ear case". A young girl, who had been waiting a year for a minor ear operation, was the focus of a Labour broadcast about Tory neglect of the NHS. The feature claimed her family could not afford private treatment. A Kinnock aide let slip information about the girl which enabled the media to identify her. Press digging revealed that her grandfather had been a Conservative mayor and her father had other children at a private school. The SCA had failed to discover these embarrassments when they recruited her family. Now the *Sun*, and other hostile papers, accused Labour of lying. Soon afterwards a MORI poll indicated Labour's lead over the Conservatives on health policy had plummeted from 27% to 18%.

During the last days of the campaign Labour gave the impression that they were drifting to victory. Labour's private polls suggested they were losing support among key voters.

Polls during the campaign gave a misleading impression: all but seven of 50 national polls showed Labour ahead. The end result was Labour 271 seats, Conservatives 336 and Liberal Democrats 20. *Labour did relatively better in many marginals than elsewhere and so reduced the Tory majority by 80%.* Labour's total percentage of the vote was 34.4%; however its 11.5 million votes represented no improvement on its result when it lost in 1979.

Kinnock resigned the leadership immediately after the 1992 election. From the outset John Smith was clear favourite to take over. As leader, Smith developed his proposals for Party policy in broad brush, strategic mode. This was possibly a reaction to him having been caught out, as Shadow Chancellor, when his shadow budget for the 1992 election was seen to lack credibility. This problem occurred because this budget had been largely formulated in 1989 and became inappropriate for 1992. It was a boom time budget unsuitable for the subsequent recessionary conditions. Later Smith resolved to promote outline policies that could not be so readily out dated or necessitate transformation as conditions changed. Under Smith the strategic policy commitments of the Party were: fair taxation, full employment, a national minimum wage, universal state benefits and a new approach to the welfare state. Little was settled about defence policy.

In a speech to the TUC (7.09.93) Smith said: "The goal of full employment remains at the heart of Labour's vision for Britain. Labour's economic strategy will ensure that all instruments of macro economic management, whether it concerns interest rates, the exchange rate, or the levels of borrowing will be geared to sustained growth and rising employment."[98] Smith asserted earlier: "I don't believe that you should rush forward and put everything in your shop window next Wednesday … You've got to do the patient and careful work of taking some original thoughts, working them through in practical ways, and when you're ready to do so, presenting them to the public in a way which commands and maximises not only the support for the policies but for the Party."[C3_99] There Smith sought to convince the public of what the Party believed to be right rather than simply doing what opinion polls suggested. John Prescott supported him, broadly arguing that the Party should campaign on its traditional issues of health, employment, housing and education with more conviction. Labour remained a principled Sales Oriented Party.

Unlike his NL successors, Smith did not believe in the unbridled free market. In the R.H. Tawney Lecture (1993) he attacked the Thatcher Government claiming that it had operated from a "seriously flawed explanation of human behaviour and of markets". It had "had caused economic and social ruin". [C3_100] In Smith's 1993 Conference speech he said: "Our commitment to full employment is central to our economic approach. It means using not just interest rates – but all of the instruments of economic policy to go for growth, jobs and investment."[C3_101]

In the autumn of 1993 the Conservative government generated an economic crisis. The pound's parity with the Deutschmark became unsustainable. The government lost an estimated £1.8 billion of taxpayer's money. They raised interest rates from 10% to 15% in one day (Black Wednesday) in a failed attempt to control currency markets. The Tory Chancellor had to confess that the basis of the Government's economic policy had failed. Smith called for the realignment of European currencies and publicly continued to oppose devaluation.

There were divisions of opinion within the PLP about signing the social protocol attached to the Maastricht Treaty. However, when Major threatened to resign over the issue, John Smith cleverly turned it into a vote of "no confidence" in the Prime Minister, which all Labour MPs supported. This reduced the government majority to three.

Nevertheless Smith continued to play the long game and did not behave as though he expected an early general election. He had planned to spend the next two years attacking the government. During 1994 and 1995 Labour's alternative programme was to be established. It was to be founded on a strong sense of personal morality.[C3_102]

Smith had long favoured reform of the House of Lords. He advocated making a start by abolishing the voting rights of hereditary peers (which occurred later under TB). He was careful not to commit himself on the issue of proportional representation. He seemed to be keeping that in reserve for possible negotiations with the Liberal Democrats in the event of a hung Parliament. Smith favoured a system of proportional representation similar to that subsequently adopted in Britain for elections to the European Parliament. He also set up the Social Justice Commission which was independent of the Party and included Liberal Democrat members. Its task was to examine policies to promote social justice and to reform the welfare state (including benefits). Smith announced that he personally favoured universal benefits.

Smith died suddenly in 1994, whilst still working hard and being widely respected. There were mutterings, after he became Leader, to the effect that "No one any longer knew what Labour stood for". Nick Raynsford MP wrote: "If we go on like this, are we not at risk of sleepwalking into electoral oblivion?"[C3_103]. McSmith's verdict was: "Never a man for self doubt Smith, had always believed that Labour could win from the moment he put himself forward to be Party leader. (When he died) for months opinion polls had been telling him he was right."[C3_104] *The Thursday before John Smith's death Labour took 42% of the poll in the 1994 nationwide local elections. In a general election; that result would have returned a Labour government with a good working majority.*

Brief account of New Labour's electoral successes

As Senior Backbencher M. asserted, (quoting Tory Francis Pym) a large majority gives the Leadership the opportunity to rule in a dictatorial fashion and to ignore the views of the Party as a whole and even of the Cabinet. Winning by large majorities, as happened during the NL era, can present a problem for the Party. It can make adherence to long held aims and values difficult. It does not guarantee a more productive or satisfactory legislative programme. As is demonstrated in Chapter 6; earlier Labour governments – those of Attlee and Wilson/Callaghan – achieved much more in policy terms and in shorter periods than NL did. Nevertheless, as followed in 1997, having a large majority at one election carries the advantage of making it logistically easier to retain power at the following one. This benefitted NL in 2001 and, to a lesser extent, in 2005 (see tables immediately below).

As tables below demonstrate, in the New Labour landslide of 1997, there was an 8.8% swing to Labour from the 1992 General election result. Labour won 43.2% of the total vote and 418 seats in the House of Commons. In 2001 New Labour did almost as well, winning 413 seats, sustaining a negative swing of 2.5% and obtaining 40.7% of the total vote. However their result was much worse in 2005, after the Iraq war and a longer period in office, when New Labour lost 47 Commons seats, winning a total of 355 seats on only 35.2% of the vote. In 2007 Gordon Brown became Prime Minister and Party Leader without a contest. After a short honeymoon period he became unpopular. Then came the international financial crisis (which Brown partly staved of for the UK) but for which he got little public acknowledgement. In the 2010 general election Labour got one of its worst ever results securing only 29.0% of the total vote, losing a further 91 seats and suffering an adverse swing of 6.2%. The post 2011 situation is discussed in more detail in Chapter 12. Ed Miliband became Leader in 2010 and at the 2015 election Labour actually obtained positive swing of 1.5% but lost a further 26 seats and won 30.4% of the vote (1.4% more than in 2011). The most significant factor in the outcome was the run away success of the Scottish National Party which took all but one of Labour's 41 seats in Scotland.

United Kingdom general election, 1992

Leader	John Major	Neil Kinnock	Paddy Ashdown
Party	Conservative	Labou	Liberal Democrat
Leader since	28 November 1990	2 October 1983	16 July 1988
Leader's seat	Huntingdon	Islwyn	Yeovil
Last election	376 seats, 42.2%	229 seats, 30.8%	22 seats, 22.6%
Seats won	336	271	20
Seat change	▼40	▲42	▼2
Popular vote	14,093,007	11,560,484	5,999,384
Percentage	41.9%	34.4%	17.8%
Swing	▼0.3%	▲3.6%	▼4.8%

United Kingdom general election, 1997

Leader	Tony Blair	John Major	Paddy Ashdown
Party	Labou	Conservative	Liberal Democrat
Leader since	21 July 1994	28 November 1990	16 July 1988
Leader's seat	Sedgefield	Huntingdon	Yeovil
Last election	271 seats, 34.4%	336 seats, 41.9%	20 seats, 17.8%
Seats before	273	343	18
Seats won	418	165	46
Seat change	▲145*	▼178*	▲28*
Popular vote	13,518,167	9,600,943	5,242,947
Percentage	43.2%	30.7%	16.8%
Swing	▲8.8	▼11.2	▼1.0

United Kingdom general election, 2001

Leader	Tony Blair	William Hague	Charles Kennedy
Party	Labou	Conservative	Liberal Democrat
Leader since	21 July 1994	19 June 1997	9 August 1999
Leader's seat	Sedgefield	Richmond (Yorks)	Ross, Skye and Inverness
Last election	418 seats, 43.2%	165 seats, 30.7%	46 seats, 16.8%
Seats won	413	166	52
Seat change	▼5	▲1	▲6
Popular vote	10,724,953	8,357,615	4,814,321
Percentage	40.7%	31.7%	18.3%
Swing	▼2.5%	▲1%	▲1.5%

United Kingdom general election, 2005

Leader	Tony Blair	Michael Howard	Charles Kennedy
Party	Labou	Conservative	Liberal Democrat
Leader since	21 July 1994	6 November 2003	9 August 1999
Leader's seat	Sedgefield	Folkestone and Hythe	Ross, Skye and Lochaber
Last election	413 seats, 40.7%	166 seats, 31.7%	52 seats, 18.3%
Seats before	403	165	52
Seats won	355	198	62
Seat change	▼47^	▲33*	▲11*
Popular vote	9,552,436	8,784,915	5,985,454
Percentage	35.2%	32.4%	22.0%
Swing	▼5.5%	▲0.7%	▲3.7%

United Kingdom general election, 2010

Leader	David Cameron	Gordon Brown	Nick Clegg
Party	Conservative	Labou	Liberal Democrat
Leader since	6 December 2005	24 June 2007	18 December 2007
Leader's seat	Witney	Kirkcaldy and	Sheffield Hallam
Last election	198, 32.4%	355, 35.2%	62, 22.0%
Seats before	210	349	62
Seats won	306	258	57
Seat change	▲97*	▼91*	▼5*
Popular vote	10,703,654	8,606,517	6,836,248
Percentage	36.1%	29.0%	23.0%
Swing	▲3.7%	▼6.2%	▲1.0%

United Kingdom general election, 2015

Leader	David Cameron	Ed Miliband
Party	**Conservative**	**Labou**
Leader since	6 December 2005	25 September 2010
Leader's seat	Witney	Doncaster North
Last election	306 seats, 36.1%	258 seats, 29.0%
Seats before	302	256
Seats won	330	232
Seat change	▲ 24	▼ 26
Popular vote	11,334,576	9,347,304
Percentage	36.9%	30.4%
Swing	▲ 0.8%	▲ 1.5%

Leader	Nicola Sturgeon	Nick Clegg
Party	SNP	Liberal Democrat
Leader since	14 November 2014	18 December 2007
Leader's seat	Did not stand (n 1)	Sheffield Hallam
Last election	6 seats, 1.7%	57 seats, 23.0%
Seats before	6	56
Seats won	56	8
Seat change	▲ 50	▼ 49
Popular vote	1,454,436	2,415,862
Percentage	4.7%	7.9%
Swing	▲ 3.1%	▼ 15.2%

Summary

The Labour Party showed itself able to win general elections, or receive the majority of votes, during periods from 1945 to 1952 and 1964-1974. Labour actually won six general elections during that period. Only one of these (February 1974) produced a minority government. After 1945 Labour majorities were sometimes small, unlike NL's in 1997 and 2001, but much of the time they proved workable. In some cases, notably in 1979, Labour was gradually ousted by losing by-elections. In earlier periods Labour MPs tended to be older on average and more infirm. During NL's "Children's Crusade" resulting in the selection of many young candidates (see Chapter 8) there were far more younger and healthier MPs. Consequently by-elections were fewer and resulting loss of power less problematic. However, much potential wisdom and life experience was lost to the PLP as a consequence.

The period from 1979 to 1994 was an unhappy one for the Labour Party. It was sometimes at the mercy of events, most notably the Falklands war. The electorate obstinately dwelt on all of Labour's failures from the Winter of Discontent to Militant for an unprecedentedly long time. Conversely, they seemed to overlook the shortcomings of Thatcher governments and initially accepted John Major's leadership as being "new" and "separate". Labour's genuine periods of popularity in opposition never seemed to last until the next election. There is little doubt that incompetent public and media relations were also to blame.

Lessons provided by the electoral performance of Labour during the Foot and Kinnock eras demonstrate that there must always be caution exercised before drawing over-optimistic conclusions in the mid-term period. This is especially true of non-Westminster election results, by-election outcomes and opinion polls (above). These results may represent protests and registration only of current dissatisfaction with the incumbent Government. They may be designed to change its current policies but may not represent a firm intention to evict it at the next general election. On the other hand they may mark the start of a gradual mounting of dissatisfaction which will manifest itself in later elections as they did in respect of Wilson Governments in the late 1960s. The sort of in-depth private polling done by the Party during the late 80s and early 90s provided the type of information which should be sought and acted on by Labour in the run up to future general elections.

Conclusions

During the period from its foundation to 1994 the Labour sometimes acted as a Product Oriented Party (POP) but more frequently as a "Sales Oriented Party" (SOP).[C3_105] Therefore the Party usually decided on its values and objectives, developed policies in line with these, then tried to persuade the voters of their desirability. During the Wilson/Callaghan years there was also triangulation at election times incorporating a few policies favoured by the Opposition. This did not preclude having a predominantly democratic socialist programme which the public was to be persuaded to accept. Triangulation started in earnest during the later Kinnock years but was little used by Smith. It was taken on as a main policy strategy, along with policies proposed by focus groups and media moguls under TB's and GB's leaderships after 1994.

By the late 1980s there was little difference between the policies of the two major parties. As demonstrated above, a triangulation strategy did not work for Kinnock in his latter days as Leader because polls showed that the public recalled his earlier policy positions, especially on defence. They doubted the sincerity of his conversion. TB had a questionable history as a democratic socialist and therefore his triangulation proved to be more credible to voters.

This Chapter reviews Labour's frequently successful efforts to win elections prior to the advent of NL. It also shows that Labour *could win without* being a predominantly Market Oriented Party. [C3_106] It was able to win power as a "Sales Oriented Party". The chapter demonstrates that, in this respect, the campaigns of TB, GB and their followers to discredit everything before NL were unjust and mistaken. During the 1945-79 democratic socialist era that preceded NL general elections were won six times (compared with NL's three in a row). Power was lost by Labour governments twice during the earlier period. Although Labour Parliamentary majorities were smaller they were usually still large enough to permit the effective use of power in implementing democratic socialist policies (see Chapter 6). It is arguable that smaller majorities led to Labour governments that were more accountable to the PLP, the Party membership and the general public than were those headed by TB and GB.

CHAPTER 4
New Labour and the Trades Unions

"Blair forged a new fairness not favours relationship with the trades unions, which he felt had not fully understood or faced up to change."
Alastair Campbell, *The Blair Years*

"I think that there's a danger that when you say 'trades unionist' it sets up the argument about producer interest as opposed to (service and product) users. For example John Reid said in the past: "Trades unions are a producer interest.' This is a very narrow focus. People who are in trade unions have got much wider social issues than just simply the workplace. But that's obviously a very important part of what we do.
Billy Hayes, General Secretary, Communication Workers Union. In interview with the author 2012

Introduction

The Historical Relationship between the Labour Party and the Trades Unions New Labour's Relationships with the Unions: Union Leaders' Views

Union Leaders' Appraisal of New Labour's Policy Record in Government How New Labour failed to meet Trade Union Needs and Expectations Trades Unions and Funding of the Labour Party

On continuing Union Affiliation to the Labour Party? Towards a More Ideal Partnership?

What can UK Labour learn from the Australian Labor Party about relationships with Trades Unions?

Conclusion

To start: a story of a cold day in February 1973. The author perched precariously on a scaffolding platform outside a Teesside steel works and told a cheering crowd of steel workers that, unlike the Tories, an incoming Labour government would save steel making on Teesside. After the 1974 elections they did just that and, to her great joy, they rescued the small special steel works at Skinningrove in the constituency where she had recently been Labour candidate. This works remains open (under the name British Steel at the time of publication).

Introduction

The three trade union leaders interviewed for this book are still working, two served in these posts during the NL era and the remaining interviewee, Len McCluskey of Unite, launched a campaign to prevent NL from taking over the Party further in the future so it seemed appropriate to interview him. Two were the heads of large and influential unions and the third (a very impressive woman) is Assistant General Secretary of another. Numerous other union leaders are quoted from a variety of sources. Two of the union leaders interviewed were still in office in 2016.

Billy Hayes regarded working through trade unions as the best way to create a more equal and just society in Britain – as his statement at the head of this Chapter shows. He has always endeavoured to do this in tandem with the Labour Party. However he had been disappointed when the Party failed to share the union's democratic socialist objectives as it frequently did in respect of Post Office Privatisation.

There were many reasons why the Labour Party-trades union relationship might have deteriorated under New Labour (NL). They included regular sabre-rattling from Tony Blair (TB) about wanting to weaken, if not destroy, the union link with the Labour Party. Thus he probably sought to turn the Labour Party into something resembling the late 19th Century Liberal Party. This was reflected in aspects of the 1997 Partnership in Power[C4-1] constitutional settlement and NL's failure to repeal any of the anti-trades union laws of late 20th century Tory Governments (unlike their contemporary Australian counterparts). John Prescott's diary reported a meeting over dinner in 1995 between himself, Tony Blair and eight of the of the then most powerful trades union general secretaries. He reported that TB made it absolutely clear to them: "… that the old days were gone, that he wouldn't be following any union diktat and that they should not expect any deals".[C4-2]

Then there was the "cash for honours scandal". The associated search for wealthy donors, together coupled with attempts to induce Sir Hayden Phillips, and his inquiry team[C4-3], to press for state funding of political parties. These were thinly veiled attempts to reduce the Labour Party's resource dependence upon trades unions for funding. However, on the whole, the fraternal glue stuck. Around the time of the 1997 election, union delegates voted for controversial constitutional reforms (New Clause 4 (NC4) (Appendix 2) and "Partnership into Power"[C4-4] which would partly disempower them. In 2007 Brown's (GB's) initiative "Renewing and Extending Party Democracy"[C4-5] further neutered Labour's Annual Conference where the unions still had 50% of the votes. The relationship was radically changed in 2014 consequent upon the Party's Collins Report[C4-6] (see Chapter 12).

Some ordinary members of trades unions, who paid the political levy, came to resent the dearth of political support forthcoming from the NL Government to unions, despite the fact that they were its principal bankrollers. Some unions disaffiliated from the Labour Party. These included the Rail, Maritime and Transport Union (RMT) and the Fire Brigades Union (FBU). The Communication Workers Union (CWU) threatened to disaffiliate in the face of proposed Post Office part privatisation. Unison's Conference threatened to "divorce" several times in response to various aspects of NL's public service policies. Many grass-roots trades unionists ceased to be active in the Labour Party.

In 2009, senior backbencher A. argued: "We need to encourage the trade union rank and file to come back into the Party. I joined the Party in 1969 at the end of a Wilson government. It was pretty hollowed out then. But trades unionists played an active role in Labour Party branches. They bring a different perspective and they're more grounded in a culture of work. Numbers attending branch meetings now are about the same as when I joined but fewer are trades unionists."

The historic relationship between the Labour Party and the trades unions

In order to appreciate the nature of this relationship in recent times, it is necessary to trace its history. This will assist an appreciation of the nature of this symbiotic and fractious relationship.

The Party's conception resulted from the growth and power of trade unions for all types of manual workers from the 1880s onwards. A politically active Employer's Parliamentary Council was founded in 1898. This aimed to promote the interests of employers at Westminster. This development called for opposition from organised labour. Trades union initiatives to organise political and parliamentary representation for working people became intertwined with democratic socialist interests. The associated federal body became the Labour Representation Committee (LRC).

Socialist interests in the LRC were championed by the Fabian Society, Independent Labour Party (ILP) and the Social Democratic Federation (a Marxist group). The latter bodies initially had a predominantly middle class leadership.[C4-7] Many early members of the Labour Representation Committee (LRC) came from strong non-conformist backgrounds. This is probably the origin of the claim that the Labour Party owed as much to Methodism as it did to Marxism.[C4-8]

In 1899 the Trades Union Congress (TUC) carried a resolution to establish the LRC to promote the election of working men to Parliament independent of the Liberal Party. Prior to this numerous trades union aspirants had sought to be selected as Liberal Candidates but, except in mining areas, middle class candidates who could fund themselves, had been chosen. In mining areas the numbers of miner's union members in the Liberal Party were sufficient to ensure selection of one of their own number. These became known as "Lib-Labs".

Keir Hardie, and other ILP leaders, were keen to form a Labour Party separate from existing political organisations. Newer unions, representing unskilled workers, were hopeful that the new party would ensure their continuing viability. Nevertheless a secret electoral pact was made between Keir Hardie and Gladstone shortly after the founding conference: Liberal and Labour candidates did not oppose each other in the next two general elections. Up until 1910, ten Miners' union MPs were sponsored by the Liberal Party.

In 1909 a court case, the Osborne Judgement, deprived the LRC of income from Trades unions when this type of funding was outlawed. This judgement forbade trades unions to use their funds to support political parties. *The impecunious LRC could not have continued to contest Parliamentary elections for long without these funds.* They therefore had to continue to work in informal coalitions with the Liberals in the 1910 general election and, afterwards, on a promise of a change to the statute law which would reverse the Osborne ruling. This change was enacted in 1913. Because the Liberals had their own policies, which they insisted be given priority, Labour had to put the realisation of its own, already limited, political objectives on the back burner during the 1909-1913 period.

LRC membership had grown considerably by 1914. There was then no individual membership of the Party but only of its constituent organisations. Membership of the socialist societies had grown to 33,000. Trade union individual membership, which diminished after the Osborne judgement, stood at one and a half million. There were now 85 affiliated trades councils and 73 local Labour Parties.[C4-9]

From 1918 NEC members were elected by a vote of the whole conference. However this change broke up the original federal structure of the LRC, one feature of which was that socialist societies and trade unions elected their own representatives to the Labour National Executive Committee (NEC). Continuation of the previous system which gave unions larger representation would have led to major union domination of the NEC.

By 1917 the rift between the Independent Labour Party (ILP) (many of whose younger members had refused conscription) and the rest of the LRC (who supported the war effort) had deepened. At the 1917 Annual Conference[C4_10] a move was made to exclude the socialist societies from the NEC. It was proposed by trade union delegates and carried by a narrow majority. The following year it was agreed that trade union delegates elect their own fixed number of representatives on the NEC, an arrangement that arrangement is still current.

In 1921 liaison with the trades unions was strengthened by the establishment of a National Joint Council between the newly formed Trades Union Congress, the Parliamentary Labour Party (PLP) and the NEC.

During the 1920s the proportion of Labour MPs who were union sponsored was reduced. Trade union leaders tended to concentrate more on the industrial side of their work than on the political side.[C4_11]

The 1924 general election was won by the Conservatives. This Tory Government agreed to allow miners' wages to be cut. In 1926 the TUC General Council supported a general strike to enforce an embargo on the movement of coal. Labour Leader Ramsay MacDonald was unhappy because of this use of industrial pressure for general political ends, but he and the PLP remained quietly on the sidelines. When the strike action failed to bring the country to a standstill, the TUC had to admit defeat. Following this failure, union leaders decided that it was preferable not to bypass the constitutional processes of government. This recognition arguably prevented a damaging general strike against a Labour government in future.[C4_12]

In August 1931 MacDonald resigned and agreed to form a coalition government with the Conservatives and Liberals. No internal Labour Party consultation had taken place. Only seven Labour ministers left to join the coalition. MacDonald's cowardice was neatly portrayed by Winston Churchill who described him in Parliament during 1931 as "the Boneless Wonder sitting on the Treasury Bench".[C4_13]

The rump of the Labour Cabinet and the TUC called a "Council of War", as Hugh Dalton named it. All but a small proportion of the Parliamentary Labour Party (PLP) and all the affiliated trades unions were now in a Party opposed to the coalition. As Pelling reported: the MacDonald era was over: control of the Party was passing to extra Parliamentary organisations again and to the TUC.[C4_14]

This meant that some of the pre-1918 federal aspects of the Party were being revived. Resulting ambiguity developed again, in respect of the Party's mission and values. In August 1931 the TUC and Party on the ground took control of the PLP in an unprecedented act. Transport House, completed in 1928, became the headquarters of the Transport and General Workers Union (who built and owned it), the TUC *and* the Labour Party. This sharing of head office accommodation clearly illustrates the close inter-relationships and characteristics of the three organisations.

In 1927 the Tory government, using the Trade Disputes Act, disaffiliated public sector trades unions from the Labour Party. In 1948 this law was changed (by the Attlee Government) and then the CWU, and civil service unions, were re-affiliated.

After the 1931 election the majority of the PLP were trade union sponsored MPs. Half of these were miners – the majority from South Wales. These changes in the PLP weakened its influence within the Party because they limited its representativeness.

From 1932, Ernest Bevin and Lord Citrine took actual control of the Party on behalf of the TUC. Citrine demanded that the TUC General Council had "the right to initiate and participate in any political matter which it deemed to be of direct concern to its constituents" (see the report of a contemporary TUC General Council meeting by V. L. Allen).[C4_15]

The National Council of Labour (NCL) (consisting of PLP, TUC and NEC) met frequently throughout the 1930s and often issued collective statements on Labour Party policy. Bevin regarded these decisions as binding even on the leader of the PLP. However the Leader, George Lansbury, did not always accept its authority.[C4_16]

112

From 1932 the TUC General Council virtually ruled the Party for more than eight years. The dominant Party hierarchy of parliamentary politicians, which has characterised the rest of the Labour Party's history, was sidelined.

Differences arose between the Parliamentary Leader (Lansbury) and the NCL. Lansbury was a left-wing pacifist who was opposed to all use of armaments and even to the existence of the League of Nations (LoN). He regarded the LoN as a self-seeking alliance of wealthy countries. The TUC saw the LoN as a forum for international collective bargaining which could offer countries collective security. The NCL committed the Party to the Coalition Government's re-armament programme, bypassing the leader.

During the early years of the 1940 wartime National Coalition Government power was restored to the Parliamentary leadership of the Party. Less authority remained in the hands of the trade unions and the party on the ground than had been the case during the 1930s.[C4-17] Ernest Bevin, the most senior trade union leader, was brought into the Government.

Bevin did not wish to take powers to compel civilian war work so he advocated and developed "voluntaryism" based on co-operation and the conviction that people would make greater sacrifices willingly than they would under compulsion. The trade unions were to be partners in this venture. There was, however, an Emergency Powers Act to allow people to be compelled to take specified jobs but this was to be used but only if "voluntaryism" failed.

During Attlee Governments the party on the ground was very loyal to the leadership. So were most trade unions who were kept "on board" by Bevin. This showed that many individual members and trade unionists appreciated the public ownership and welfare state policies of their Labour government.

From 1947 the British Communist Party started to denounce Attlee and Bevin as "loyal supporters of the imperialists".[C4-18] Labour trade unionists voiced concerns that Communists might gain sufficient presence and influence in UK unions to be able to change the outcomes of policy votes at Labour's Conference. Two of the larger unions: the Transport and General Worker's Union (TGWU) and the General and Municipal Worker's Union (GMWU) banned Communists from holding office.

Gaitskell, from the right of the Party, succeeded Attlee as Leader. However, in general, he worked closely with the trades unions. During the famous 1950s debates on the Party constitution and defence policy Gaitskell formed the Campaign for Democratic Socialism on the right of the Party. He was joined in this by many affiliated unions.

Gaitskell died suddenly in January 1963. This precipitated an unexpected leadership election. At this time the TUC was focused on wages and unemployment and was relatively disengaged from the Party. Contemporary union leaders could not agree on their choice for the next Labour leader (Harold Wilson, from the left, was victorious).

During Wilson and Callaghan governments there was regular informal consultation between the Labour Premier and trade union leaders. This came to be popularly known as "beer and sandwiches at Number 10". The most unpopular measure proposed during Wilson's 1964-70 governments, as far as the unions were concerned, was a wages and prices freeze scheduled to last six months. It was then to be followed by six months "severe restraint". This was intended to be a voluntary scheme based on the hope that the unions would co-operate, but as a backstop statutory provision for compulsion was introduced (Prices and Incomes Act). Union leader Frank Cousins resigned from the Cabinet in protest. There was much criticism from union delegates at the 1966 Party Conference. Wilson indicated that he would not climb down but he was not defeated at Conference. Higher unemployment followed (2–2.5% instead of the 1–1.5% that had been the average in recent years).

In January 1969 the Government published the infamous White Paper *In Place of Strife*[C4-19] which proposed a month-long conciliation period before a strike could take place. The government could also insist on a ballot of the membership before a strike could begin. These recommendations were stronger than those of the government commissioned Donovan Report[C4-20]. This White Paper was favoured by UK public opinion and probably also by overseas creditors. The larger unions, under the new, and more left wing, leadership of Jack Jones and Hugh Scanlon were strongly opposed. A special TUC congress condemned the proposals by a massive majority and an overwhelming PLP revolt was threatened. Wilson and Barbara Castle agreed with the TUC to drop the penal clauses in the bill in return for a promise that the TUC would try to prevent unofficial strikes. There was also legislation agreed which ended casual labour on the docks.

In 1971 the new Conservative government passed an Industrial Relations Act. This was similar to Labour's withdrawn legislation and there was vehement opposition from the PLP and the unions. The latter held several one-day strikes in protest. The unions had to register in a more formal way than previously. Certain activities were outlawed: unofficial and sympathy strikes; breaches of legally binding contracts; and refusal of employers to recognise registered unions. The closed shop was prohibited but a more limited "agency shop" was allowed, permitting a union to represent all employees in a specified workplace, subject to agreement with employers or a member's ballot. The government could also order pre-strike ballots and there was a special court to hear disputes under the Act. The aim of this Act was to reduce the number of strikes; but in its immediate aftermath it had the opposite effect. The number of working days lost through industrial action in 1972 (24 million) was the highest since 1926, the year of the General Strike.[C4-21] The miners' strike for higher wages, underpinned by picketing of power stations, led to a Government surrender. Following this the Tory Government developed a pay policy and price controls.

The TUC fought the implementation of the 1971 Industrial Relations Act. Their campaign brought the TUC and the Labour Party closer together than they had been for many years. The 1971 Labour Conference voted for "the complete repeal of the act in the first session of a new Labour Government".[C4-22] In 1972 an enduring institution was created – the TUC-Labour Party Liaison Committee was established. This type of body has continued to function until the present day under various names.

In January 1974 the mineworkers balloted for another strike. This was supported by an overwhelming majority of their members. However Tory Prime Minister Heath called a general election on the issue of "Who rules? The Government or the unions?" The government then announced a three-day week accompanied by power shutdowns. The first Labour 1974 election manifesto promised to repeal all recent Tory industrial relations legislation. Campaigning was impeded by the three-day week – a Government response to the miners' strike – and a cold and wet February. This election was won by Labour with no overall majority but it elected to govern on its own.

The miners' strike was then settled instantly and the three-day week ended. Bills were introduced to repeal the Tory Industrial Relations Act and Pay Board as promised. Because of the lack of a majority the Bills were much amended during their passage through Parliament. However they accomplished their basic objectives.

After much proposed legislation had been defeated, Wilson called another election for October 1974 which Labour won with a working majority. The manifesto emphasised the social contract with the unions and promised new employment protection legislation.

As a result of the following EEC membership (post re-negotiation) referendum, the left was weakened. In this climate some left trade union leaders softened their stance on incomes policy. Jack Jones (TGWU), proposed a flat-rate wage increase policy for 1975-6. This was promptly adopted by the Government and was then approved by the TU Congress. The scheme was underpinned by a prices freeze and legal action against private sector employers who disobeyed. By the end of 1976 inflation seemed to be better controlled.[C4_23]

However when, in the late 1970s, Prime Minister James Callaghan pressed for further wage restraint policies which the unions were reluctant to accept, then relationships deteriorated. Unemployment was also rising. This led to the so called "winter of discontent" of widespread industrial action in early 1979 during which the right wing media stirred up public hatred of the unions.

The Conservatives won the general election of May 1979 which ushered in the Thatcher era. Among her draconian union "reforms", secondary picketing was made illegal and closed shops were destroyed. Union-only Labour agreements were prohibited. Immunities for trades unions, relating to the actions of their members, were curtailed.[C4_24, C4_25] The governance of trades unions was strictly controlled and the periodic re-election of their general secretaries and regular opting in of members to permit political contributions were enforced. These ballots were to be conducted by post (to facilitate secrecy) but they cost the unions dear in administrative and postal charges (see interview with Liz Snape of Unison below).

Jenkins[C4_26] and Thatcher[C4_27] reported that, by the late 1980s, more regulatory trade union laws were passed almost "annually". Each one "tidied up" the law. The requirement for strike ballots was extended. Unions were made vulnerable to civil legal actions for damages. Jenkins recalled:[C4_28] "Each union reform was opposed across the political spectrum and Labour pledged itself to repeal every one."

TB, when newly elected as an MP in 1983, raged that it was: "unacceptable in a democratic society" for a Government to interfere in the affairs of unions, even with their enforcement of closed shops.[C4_29] *This implied that a Labour Government led by TB would repeal the Tory anti-union legislation* and, once again, treat the unions as junior partners in Government with the Labour Party. However that turned out to be an empty promise.

Under Mrs. Thatcher, there were also privatisations of the electricity and gas industries, much to the dismay of the trades unions. As Prime Minister John Major presided over the privatisations of the remains of the coal industry and the railways. At an earlier time these would have provoked major industrial action. However the unions had already been so bowed by the Thatcherite yoke that there was little organised resistance.

Therefore when it came to the Blair leadership most unions supported TB in the hope, and anticipation of a better relationship to come. The subsequent development of that relationship is discussed in interviews reported below.

New Labour's relationships with the trade unions

Key interviews took place between 2010-12 with Billy Hayes, General Secretary, Communication Workers' Union (affiliated to the Labour Party), Liz Snape, Assistant General Secretary, Unison (Political Fund affiliated to the Labour Party) and Len McCluskey, General Secretary, Unite (affiliated to the Labour Party). They were augmented with contemporary published commentary made by other senior union leaders. Although the last two interviews took place after the 2010 election, interviewees were asked to focus on the periods of NL government when all of them worked in senior trade union positions if not in their current post.

Billy Hayes said: "The Labour/union relationship has always been an uneasy one – the 'Contentious Alliance' as Lewis Minkin described it.[C4-30] There were a number of aspects to it. *I'm sure that there were those in the Party, at that time, who would now like to see a severing of the link"*.

How prophetic Hayes proved to be. By 2013 it appeared that many NL supporters, in the PLP and in the Progress group, emerged from the post NL shadows and worked hard to secure severance of the TU link with the Labour Party. That year the Collins Commission was set up by the Party to examine the Link. Its report recommended a loosening of the ties. Some of the Collins Commission's report[C4-31] recommendations were adopted at a special Party Conference in 2014 (see Chapter 12). There now needs to be a widespread recognition that if the Labour Party is to have any credibility in differing from the Conservatives and Liberal Democrats, and with organised workers it should recognise that NL was a pragmatic experiment which has now turned to baggage that the Party cannot afford.

Liz Snape was Assistant General Secretary of Unison. She had worked for the union for many years, in less senior positions.

Her views echoed a press interview given by Dave Prentis in 2011. Prentis, then said that he felt very much let down by NL – "In 1997 there was a real feeling of movement and being in this together to improve society. But as time went on they just kept espousing principles of markets and privatisation which didn't appeal to a single voter. They brought in private companies but without looking at their *effectiveness*. Also, after a time, no one felt excited: it wasn't working".[C4-32] Prentis proved to be prophetic because the Tory and Liberal Coalition marched over NL's bridge to fragment the NHS. Snape also highlighted the issues (discussed in Chapter 2) whereby NL abandoned principles and values to offer the public policies that marketing researchers said key voters desired.

Also speaking to Euan Ferguson for the same *Observer* interviews as did Prentis, in 2011, Len McCluskey, General Secretary of Unite the Union said: *"Clearly the old alliance based on values and principles held in common between the unions and Labour was breaking down during the NL era. It had become an exploitative relationship in which the unions paid and Labour took; giving little to benefit union members in return. NL tried to switch to raising money from rich donors who also wanted something in return whether it was gongs for gifts or government contracts or goodies derived from privatisation."*[33]

In an interview with the author in the same year, McCluskey added: *"I recently criticised NL publicly because there is still a strong feeling among trade unionists that NL Governments let us down. It was a betrayal and a deep disappointment. It explains why, in the end, NL lost the support of so many people. They must now learn how to reconnect. We must make sure that trade union values, replaced by the NL leadership, are now restored by Labour. NL supported individualism and meritocracy to replace collectivism".*

He continued: "Thatcherism, and the Blairite version of it, rejected the importance of fraternity and collectivism – the methods of operating used by trade unions and their members. Everything was a matter for the individual who was left in charge of finding their own economic and social salvation in however weak a position in society they might find themselves."

In a contemporary *Observer* interview Mary Boustead, General Secretary of the Association of Teachers and Lecturers, (not affiliated to the Labour Party) regretted: "We've gone through a period where the emphasis has been on individualism, on petty, mean-minded selfishness. There's now a growing realisation that to get anything done you don't have much power as an individual but you do it collectively."[C4-34]

Trade Union Leaders' Appraisals of New Labour's Policy Record in Government

In May 2010 Billy Hayes said: "You asked which the best policies of NL Governments were from a trade union perspective?

"The first one was peace in Ireland, then the minimum wage (NMW), followed by devolution with the new administrations. They *began* to redress some of the ravages caused by the inequality brought in during the Thatcher/Major years. Obviously employment rights could have been improved. In 2005 and 2009 we (our union) defeated attempts to privatise Royal Mail by a Party (Labour) which, on paper, was opposed to the privatisation of Royal Mail. We opposed that privatisation and we were successful. In 2009 we were able to head off privatisation led by Peter Mandelson. This was a great victory but it may be more difficult with a Tory government." This last forecast proved to be all too accurate in 2013.

Hayes continued: "NL's main policy failures, those I disliked, were the war in Iraq and their infatuation with the market. CWU members disliked Labour Government privatisation policies and its public expenditure cuts since 1997. Royal Mail, like the BBC, is a public corporation, so it funds itself. This did make a difference, especially to the pension fund. One of the biggest problems was that the pension fund wasn't funded. Of course we've got members in the private sector (in BT and other telecoms businesses). The biggest problem overall has been the privatisation of Royal Mail."

Clearly this threatened privatisation overshadowed the CWU's relationship with NL government. There was also unhappiness that almost all the Thatcher /Major anti-union legislation remained in place. However where the union did spot the odd jewels in NL's crown these were: the NMW and Northern Ireland on the peace-making front.

When asked about NL's best policies: Liz Snape said that "the NMW was a critically important and fundamental policy. Much of the equalities legislation was very important such as: maternal and parental leave and rights to work flexible hours. There was recognition that the world was changing and women's needs should be recognised. I was impressed with the huge expenditure on expansion of public services. I also recognise their adventurousness in creating the radical Sure Start scheme. This was so important in creating opportunities in the early years. It was set up in a way which has made it difficult for the Tories to close down because it's run alongside social work, child psychology and maternal advice services." However the 2010-2015 Coalition Government closed down about 25% of Sure Start schemes, unit by unit.

Snape continued: "Turning to policies that I disapproved of, I was unhappy with the initial flirtation with the market and later total embrace of the market model. I've criticised creeping Tory privatisation of public services. I disapproved of most of the wars; especially Iraq but wonder whether we should have intervened in Rwanda on humanitarian grounds."

Dave Prentis, General Secretary of Unison, said: "If there's one thing I could have stopped, with hindsight, it would be the invasion of Iraq. It changed completely the nature of the Labour government and we never recovered from it. He suggested that the contemporary Coalition government came about: "because the starting point was that Labour lost the 2010 election because it lost its way."[C4_35]

Brendan Barber, then General Secretary of the Trades Union Congress, believed: "The economy has doubled in size but the earnings of ordinary people have not kept pace. As wealth is increasingly sucked up by the elite, there are major dysfunctions we have to deal with".[C4_36]

Liz Snapes' acclaim for the NMW echoed that of Hayes and some backbench MPs. She was also at one with the backbenchers in welcoming the expansion of public services including policies to benefit women and young children. In addition: Snape agreed with many MPs in her criticisms of NL's unfettered market approach and the Iraq war. These two latter concerns were shared by Prentis and Barber.

Len McCluskey contended: "All new trade union legislation introduced by NL was about individual workers' rights. Collective rights were dismissed off the agenda by the NL Project. British trade unionists now have the worst conditions in Western Europe. That's why TB boasted that *'Britain's trades union laws are the most restrictive in Western Europe.' It's no good having a Labour Government if that's so.* How can we be right to support NL when British trade union laws and union rights have been made worse and the UK has worse rights at work than the rest of Europe? We want to give workers their freedom. We only want a level playing field on which trade union freedoms for the brothers and sisters are the basis for industrial relations. We think that's what ordinary working people want. We want a society like the one we've seen in the Olympic Torch events and even the Jubilee (although I'm not a believer in the Monarchy) where ordinary working people socialise happily together – all belonging to the same community."

He continued: "NL did nothing to get rid of Thatcher's anti-union laws. They only changed one piece of legislation – NL made it illegal for workers to be sacked when taking legal industrial action. All the rest of the Thatcher industrial legislation is the same. Now we have a right-wing Tory government and insufficient protection. We are currently working with all trades unions to try to influence Ed (Miliband). *We get ideas and advice from Australian trades unions who were in a similar situation."*

Here is further criticism for NL's rejection of collectivism and for its failure to repeal Thatcher's anti-union laws. An individualised approach, which has since been adopted by Ed Miliband and Sadiq Khan, is inimical to workers having any strength in the workplace to secure fair pay and working conditions and to protect their jobs.

McCluskey continued" "I disliked NL's neo-liberal economic policies. The free market was disastrously wrong. Margaret Thatcher's statement was very significant when she was asked what was her greatest achievement? She replied: "Tony Blair and New Labour." Thatcher destroyed our manufacturing industry and *a million manufacturing jobs were lost during the years of NL Government.* The UK was up for sale and factories were closed on NL's watch. NL's failure was the widening gap between rich and poor. Those comments from NL ministers about not being bothered if people were filthy rich were terrible. TB's (personal) fortune is now enormous. There were some good policies from NL such as family friendly policies and the NMW. Of course that was, and is, far too low. The Fairness at Work legislation was helpful but was spoiled by Thatcher's trade union legislation still being on the statute book. Her philosophy was to stand in the way of organised labour. We need to make it more difficult for future governments to do that. We need a strong and vibrant manufacturing industry. Towards the end GB and Mandelson saw that they had got that wrong. We also need strong public services."

In this context; Brendan Barber pointed out that there used to be over 7 million people in manufacturing (before 1979) but that in 2011 there were only 3 million: this had had its effects on trade unions and trade unionism.[C4_37] The late Bob Crow, then General Secretary of the RMT (not affiliated to the Labour Party), stated that only about 33% of the workforce was currently in a union, which is down from 67% in 1977. This is a problem for trades unions and trades unionism.[C4_38]

Owen Jones[C4_39] reported that, under NL: "Britain did not suffer the same ruinous level of unemployment as in the 1980s and early 1990s, even as the economy went into free fall following the 2008 financial crash." He continued by arguing that frequently part-time and low paid service sector jobs were provided instead. These could not revive communities worst hit by the Thatcherism in the 1980s. Jones continued: "It is not surprising that so many working class people felt alienated from Labour. They felt it was no longer fighting on their side." This alienation was to increase and continue up to, and including, the 2015 general election.

Len McCluskey continued: "Unite has one and a half million members. Most work in the private sector so they have not been affected directly by privatisation of public services. But they have been badly affected by contracting out, casualisation of labour and zero hours contracts. Wages have been driven down by the actions of Thatcher, Major and NL who made it easy to use agency workers. Recent lack of economic growth has also depressed incomes of these workers."

Here McCluskey was at one with Hayes and Snape on public sector and other issues. He also pointed out how workers in the private sector had been disadvantaged by NL's policies affecting remuneration and job security.

He continued: "I object to the way NL clones are now trying to revive and restore NL and go back to the Third Way. *The Progress Group are now swimming against the tide. But we must be vigilant and protect different attitudes from the progressive left.* But these are only minor problems. We need to go back to basics and say what kind of society we really want. *We need to improve candidate selections and get a progressive Parliamentary Labour Party.* The Unions and the Party must unite and work together to get activists to re-join the Party."

There is now a covert, but strong counter-left movement in the Party fronted and funded by Peter Mandelson, Lord Sainsbury (the main Progress bankroller)[C4-40] and Progress, as McCluskey identified. It is more important than ever that the Party recognises, and does not return to, the follies and problems of the NL period. The activities of Progress partly explain why so many Blairites have continued to be selected as Parliamentary candidates. The other explanation is the continuing presence at Westminster of numerous beneficiaries of New Labour's suspect selection processes (see Chapter 8).

Discussing benefits received by his members, through being affiliated to the Labour Party since 1997, Billy Hayes asserted: "We have exerted quite a lot of influence in policy making. Alistair Darling and the Government were tempted to privatise Royal Mail. It was stopped through pressure from the PLP and decision making forums in the Party. We were also able to get a commitment to universal access to broadband as part of the Party election manifesto. So we had influence in terms of policies formally adopted. These were useful springboards. Once you get a 'springboard' you can establish and develop a policy, but it is harder to get the Party to carry it through. So we've been successful in that regard; but it's been a huge strain and tremendously difficult to do."

How New Labour failed to meet the Trade Unions' needs and expectations

Billy Hayes recalled: "In 1948 the law was changed and the CWU, and other civil service unions, were re-affiliated to the Labour Party. It was not until 1966 that the Post Office Engineering Union (POEU), as it then was, re-affiliated. Only in 1990 did the clerical side of our union, which worked primarily for BT, re-affiliate. So the federal structure has always been a bone of contention.

Hayes continued: "I would say that the attitude of post 1997 Labour Governments to the trade unions is something like: 'Trade unions do good things e.g. health and safety – as they would see it *but the proportion of interest they represent is only a narrow section of society.* With some justification, they now think that trade unions only represent an increasingly smaller part of the workforce. In terms of all trades unions: we now (2010) probably represent 28% of the British workforce. The unions affiliated to the Labour Party probably represent about 14% of all workers in Britain. So in terms of input from working people, I suppose they would say that affiliated unions don't represent the majority. They would probably say that the TUC (which includes all the unions in the UK) represents a much larger section of society." This appears to be an accurate and significant observation.

BH believed: "The other thing is that NL regard us as old fashioned, conservative and not up to speed in terms of the new world order – so to speak. My answer to that would be: 'That's true –and it's factual in terms of the arithmetic. But *what comes out of trades unions – what Lenin once called 'the schools of socialism' – is what they do even now –* albeit with reduced numbers. *They become schools for educating activists – for lots of people. The professional classes have their professions to be schools to educate them in self confidence and the ability to challenge and to govern and to manage. Whereas trades unionists and working class people only have their trades unions'."*

Hayes continued: "My life experience and watching the lives of others tells me that *trades unions are an important part of citizenship in the UK today. By that means the trades unions are very important to the Labour Party.* Yes they now represent a smaller minority of the workforce but *they are still an activist base.* All the evidence is that some of the best activists have exclusively had their training in the trade union movement."

The need for improved and more widespread political education was also recognised by senior backbencher A. The he saw educating the public, especially the working class public, as being a potentially significant role for Labour MPs. If Labour is to govern according to its traditional values and principles, albeit in a modern setting, it will need to develop widely available political education to support its struggle to become a Sales Oriented Party (see Chapter 13).

Hayes continued "My feel is that it's not like it was in the 1970s and 1980s. This is because:

1. Trades unions don't have as much clout in society as they did years ago, particularly in terms of representation of the workforce.

2. As I said earlier, while trades unions are regarded as doing good things, a lot of people in the Party hierarchy are not very fond of collectivism. It seems to them old fashioned and not in keeping with the world of work. We now live in a very individualistic society. So they have less empathy with trades unions, as institutions, than they did 20 years ago. There's less sympathy for trades unions and, I think, a certain degree of patronisation of unions.

3. *The bigger problem has been having a Labour government and not being able to see how it was making a difference.* There *is* a difference but some people say 'not much'. But that's what it's been like with NL. But our members don't see the benefit of a Labour Government in terms of the way that they (NL) worked."

The difficulty of demonstrating to Union members that the NL government had been on their side and working for them was also mentioned by Liz Snape. She instanced desirable measures, that would not have been high profile, but that would have made the union's administrative operations easier.

She said: "It would have been politically difficult for NL Governments to '"go big" on trades union rights and freedoms or to legalise secondary picketing for example. But there are many less high profile things they could have done to make the union's lives less difficult. In the context of Thatcher's anti-union laws we are forced to run enormous, and regular, postal ballots of all our members on issues including political affiliation to the Labour Party and on who holds the General Secretaryship of the union. These involve an enormous amount of administrative work for union staff and are very expensive to run. Our last ballot on political affiliation cost the Union £1 million in postage alone. The financial burden is even greater for smaller unions. There is no reason why these ballots could not be held more cheaply and easily in workplaces. I think that Thatcher took these measures to try to cripple the unions financially."

She added "Minister Stephen Byers was approached to allow email voting in union ballots (which the Labour Party itself does in elections, for the NEC for example). But he refused. The Labour government could have reformed union ballot procedures without attracting criticism. I believe that union strength comes from union democracy."

Snape continued: *"TB was always diplomatic and charming in face to face dealings with unions. He approached us in a managerial manner. However when I read the Alastair Campbell Diaries, he included a number of quotations from TB in which he expressed great hostility to the unions along the lines of "Not the f---ing trades unions again!"* This illustrated what John Monks, former TUC General Secretary, said about TB regarding the unions as being like "embarrassing elderly relations". She asserted: "TB had no political affinity with the unions but he had to put up with us. GB had a better understanding of the unions and a more positive attitude towards us. Of course he was more grounded in the Labour movement."

The alienation of TB from the trade unions initially seemed remarkable. He was the first Labour Leader, apart from possibly Ramsay MacDonald, to be hostile and rejecting towards this crucial element of the British Labour movement. Even the early 20th century Liberals were not so hostile, despite the unions having formed a rival Party.

Len McCluskey believed "Partnership in Power[C4-41] was based on the idea of a more equal society. *When NL left power we had a less equal society. Partnership in power didn't give sufficient recognition to the trades unions' role in the Party.* Ordinary working people are less worried about the exercise of Party democracy than they are about the policies. We need radical policies. Working people want homes and jobs first."

LMcL continued: "Our union got no benefits from sticking with NL; or at any rate not enough. *This is why we say that our experiences with NL must not be repeated. Ed (Miliband) (as at 2012) has to regain the trust lost by NL and TB. We need Labour to demonstrate that they are still our Party.* We are now navigating in waters that we haven't been through before. Labour has to look after trade unionists and organised Labour. If they don't organised Labour will have to review the situation. Hopefully things will go in the right direction and we will support Ed in the new approach. He must be bold and courageous. I think he is sensitive enough to understand that minor changes won't do."

Here are warnings that in 2015 (after the Falkirk Parliamentary selection debacle and its aftermath) need to be heeded more than ever before. If Labour sheds its trade union partners it may well lose many members, much income and a multitude of voters. It is far from certain that state funding of political parties can be secured as a substitute and Labour's membership was still declining until the Leadership election campaign of 2015 (see Chapter 13).

Trades Unions and funding the Labour Party

Billy Hayes declared: "Thinking *about the financial relationship between the trades unions and the Labour Party, during the NL period,* I would guess that the trade unions paid a large proportion of the Party's costs at the 2010 general election. Because the Party's former wealthy backers will have declined. The Hayden Phillips proposals (for state funding) were intended to weaken the financial relationship between the Party and the Unions. *The trade unions founded the Labour Party but the Labour Party is not the trades unions in government.* CWU members got restive around the privatisation of Royal Mail and also the dispute in 2009. They weren't very happy that we were affiliated to a party that was in government and that was attacking, or was seen to be attacking, our members. And they couldn't understand why, after us working for the return of a Labour Government, from 1997 onwards they wanted to privatise Royal Mail. That led to a tremendous strain of course. But our members don't recognise the benefit of a Labour Government in terms of the way that they worked: Sure Start; the education building programme; improvements in the railways."

Liz Snape said: "Of course there is a very historic relationship between the unions and the Party. The unions kept the Party going through difficult years. *Under NL union money almost became regarded as second class money. Private donors were the most highly regarded.* Unions should be able to fund the Party openly. Before 1994 all donors to Labour were regarded as equal. Predictably later *private donors put in money for their own gain.* Later this was cleared up. Unions have always contributed for the right reasons. I am ambivalent about state funding for parties. The union financial link with the Labour Party is a proud link and should continue. She added: "Money given by Unison to the Labour Party is *not* given in order to exert undue influence. What we wanted was a fair say and for our voice to be heard. –and we *did* once have a fair say."

If union funding were to end it would be difficult to replace its quantity and provenance. However many union members will not willingly continue to donate while they consider they are being treated with contempt (see Chapter 13 for subsequent developments)

Len McCluskey stated: "The financial support given by the unions to the Party, under NL, was dramatic. When I ran for General Secretary of Unite at every meeting I attended I was asked why Unite was giving so much money to the Party when we get nothing out of it? In future our financial support, other than affiliation fees, will be based on whether we get a new approach from the Labour leadership that appreciates our values. We get so many queries from the members about why we give so much money to the Party that if we had an all-member ballot now it would say 'disaffiliate'. The activists would be less keen to do so."

In 2007 the LabOUR Commission[C4-42] reported: "Party accounts show that although the income received from trade union affiliations has declined as a percentage, it continues to be its consistent and major source of income. There are many political reasons to maintain the mutually beneficial link. There is also a powerful financial argument for doing so. It remains the most transparent and effective method of financing a political party by individual citizens." Several senior trade unionists sat on this Commission. They were: Barry Camfield, Assistant General Secretary TGWU, John O'Regan, National Political Officer Amicus, Keith Sonnett, Deputy General Secretary Unison and Mary Turner, President, GMB.

On continuing affiliation to the Labour Party

Billy Hayes said: "At this year's CWU Conference – now there's a Tory led coalition government – there was no suggestion that we could disaffiliate from the Labour Party. I think that, in respect of those who want to disaffiliate from the Party, it's a debate about 'red unionism'. This is the argument that we should treat unions that are more left wing differently. To me to get a just society would be enough. I think you've got to work within the institutions of the British working class and that still is the Labour Party and the British trade union movement."

Unison (founded 1996) was an amalgamation of three public service unions; NALGO, NUPE and COHSE. NALGO was never affiliated to the Labour Party. This has led to Unison having different arrangements about affiliation to the Labour Party from other trade unions. After amalgamation it was democratically agreed that the Union would have three funding sections. One in which members paid no political levy, a second where they paid into a fund for general political purposes not linked to any Party or to: "The Affiliated Political Fund" whose members were affiliated to the Labour Party.

Liz Snape reported: "There were two moves to disaffiliate the Union from the Labour Party altogether during the NL era. The first was started after then Minister Stephen Byers spoke at the Unison Conference in 1999. He announced that he strongly believed in the use of the private sector in running public services and added: "You lot need to live in the real world". This was not a flip comment; it was an integral part of his speech. It produced a gasp of horror and a very hostile reaction from the members. Members began to ask, 'Why do we put so much money into the Labour Party?' The following year there were the first motions sent to Unison Conference proposing that the Union disaffiliate from the Labour Party altogether. The Executive had to agree to review the situation over the next two years.

Four years later another motion came to the union's Conference proposing total disaffiliation. This was in response to increasing NL Government privatisation of public services. Again the motion was watered down to having another review. *After 1999 no Labour minister was invited to speak at Unison Conference:it was thought that it would lead to more potential unrest. GB sought an invitation but was turned down.*"

Ms. Snape added: "Privatisation and public expenditure cuts radically affected Unison members' political views. *In 1997 polls showed that 86% of public service workers voted Labour. By 2010 this was reduced to 20%.* This was also evidenced by analysis of general election results. In the big Labour abstention of 2010 many public service workers didn't vote."

Len McCluskey reported: "There is currently no pressure to disaffiliate from the Party in Unite. Some smaller unions did disaffiliate during NL's time and I can understand why. *They must come back if we get the Party to adopt our values.*

The late Bob Crow described himself as a "communist stroke socialist". He said: "Labour is all over the shop because it wants to represent both big business and workers. You can't. It's got to make up its mind. *Or the trade union movement has to cut ties with Labour and form a new party of labour. Yes, we might be approaching that time.*" In the context of Labour leadership behaviour he added: "When it comes to a strike you're either on the side of the bosses or the side of the workers. There's no in between."[C4_43]

At an interview in September 2011, Crow criticised Labour Leader Ed Miliband for refusing to attend the Durham Miners' Gala that year (however Miliband rectified this omission by attending the Gala in 2012).[C4_44] Greater criticism can be extended to TB and GB neither of whom attended the Gala whilst Party Leader.

Matt Wrack, General Secretary of the Fire Brigades Union (no longer affiliated to the Labour Party since the NL Government's refusal to respond favourably to their last major strike), was asked in September 2011 whether the contemporary Coalition's public service staff related cuts were ideologically driven. He replied: "One of my concerns is the ideological consensus – that a Labour Government would have done something similar. *We don't care who is doing it; we just protect our members*".[C4-45] This is a significant statement about the contemporary lack of any special relationship between NL and the unions.

Attitudes were rather different when it came to the Labor Party Down Under. Wayne Swan, Labor Treasurer (Chancellor of the Exchequer) of Australia said in a speech to the Australian National Press Club on 5.03.12 that "the union movement donates to the ALP and seeks to shape the policies of the Labor government. I'm really proud of our links to the trade union movement – The unions are made up of working Australians who seek to lobby collectively for their rights. They're just doing what normal lobby groups do, or interest groups do in our society. I believe in a pluralistic society. I believe in the rights of trades unions to organise".[C4-46] With apologies to BBC TV's' *Mock the Week*, this fits into a category of "Unlikely things to hear in a speech by an NL minister".

Towards a more ideal partnership?

What should have been the contemporary role of the trade unions in the wider Labour movement as the situation was before 2010 and what in the post NL era? Billy Hayes said: *"The unions are still an important conduit for the experience of working class people in work. I think that some trades unions do have to stay in the Labour Party but there are moves to break the link.* I believe that the Tories (in government) will attack union funding of parties and *I don't think it's just the Tory Party.* We're obviously resisting this." How prophetic Hayes proved to be!

He continued: "I was recently watching a programme with Christopher Hitchens talking about his Oxford Days. He was there with people like Clinton. Hitchens said that he realised, seeing all these people close up that they had a different idea about what was going on from most people. *This goes back to my point about trades unions and their training activity. That gives people the confidence to be able to challenge debate and discuss with people in power in this country.*

Dave Prentis claimed: "One jewel in our crown is our learning agenda. We've taken people who've left school, who can't read or write back into learning among their peers so they don't feel inferior and taken some all the way to a Ph.D. It's about having faith in the best in people and a moral compass."[C4-47]

Thus two influential union leaders flagged up the vital role that trades unions can, and do, play in political and social education of their members. In turn education builds up self confidence and the ability to contribute effectively in democratic politics and in the workplace.

Billy Hayes asserted: "Since the franchise the reasons why there are such problems on trades union rights is that the middle class in this country have just about got used to the idea of the franchise – just! But they've never really got used to democracy per se, i.e. the country still believes in the hereditary principle. They never really had the confidence: so it's got to be democracy because equality is essentially about democracy. Democracy is a modern idea although it started long ago in Greece. But in terms of its introduction: it is still a very modern idea that has a long way to run."

Hayes continued: *"The Labour Party is the only vehicle that I can see in this country, to get to get progressive social change.* We've experienced that through our sectorial achievements in postal and telecoms."

Liz Snape said: "The problem is in getting union activists to join the Party and help transform it. That's going to be a bit easier, paradoxically, now that there's a Tory government. I understand that, (since the 2010 general election), there's been 14,000–20,000 new Party members joined. It's always easier to get progress, in terms of the Party itself, when the Party's out of power. But *we need to make sure that commitments made when the Party's out of power are taken into power with it.*"

Union leaders suggested that *Labour Party democracy* was generally of less interest to their members than were policies relating to their jobs, standard of living and rights at work. This is understandable: people will tend to be most concerned with issues that affect their own daily lives and those of their families. However the Leaders also admitted that violations of Party democracy, which permitted the NL leadership to adopt policies that disadvantaged people at work, were of concern to them.

This concern sometimes led to action. Relating to New Clause 4 (1995) (Appendix 2) and *Partnership in Power* (PiP) (1997)[C4-48], Billy Hayes said: "I wasn't involved at my present level when PiP came in. I attended my first National Policy Forum (NPF) meeting in 2003-4. I went with some scepticism. *I was encouraged that the unions were beginning to get their act together in terms of the NPF.* This happened again more recently. We played a part in getting the most recent changes so that the NPF delegates will be voted for by all Party members."

Hayes continued: "The problem is not so much one about structures: *it's about the self-confidence of the Party and being able to trust its activist base.* Whatever structures you've got, it's a problem that bedevils all activist organisations. Your activist base is always going to be more radical. It isn't just the Labour Party. It's true of any organisation whether it's the Tory Party or trades unions. Activists are a bit like the football supporters' clubs. They tend to be a bit more to the fore. That said, I think you've got to have a bit more faith in the Party institutions. So, for example, the Party's policy on votes at 16 was changed at the NPF and was part of our 2010 election manifesto. They listened more on (working conditions of) agency workers and so on."

BH continued: "I have to be honest; in one way I think that (Party) structures are neither here nor there. The problem is *it got to the point where the Party leadership were more worried about the impact of any particular decision on the media.* Strangely enough *for NL, the Leadership had an obsession with the past. It was: 'No return to the 80s and no return to all the internal strife'.* I don't think that's going to happen. I think we've seen, even with the leadership election that's currently on (2010), it's going to get more strident but it's not going to be at the same level of acrimony that there once was back in the 80s and previously. So I think that the Leadership should have more faith in party democracy. *If you undermine your activist base you also undermine yourself: that's the problem."*

BH identified a key issue here. This NL distrust and marginalisation of the Party grass roots membership, including its trade union members, has undoubtedly contributed to the massive loss of members. For many this is because they consider they can no longer participate meaningfully in policy making (see Chapter 7). For the Party to be viable and vibrant, trust of the membership must be restored.

Hayes asserted: "I personally haven't experienced either the influence of Party staff on Conference (Constituency) delegates or undue influence of the Party hierarchy in internal selections and elections. But that said, I think you can have rules and guidelines and protocols separated out. But that is true of any organisation. In a way you're talking about governance structures. If you look, for example, at the UK government there are (powerful) civil servants and hence the introduction of Special Political Advisors (SPADs). They are quasi civil servants but they are also people who are deeply committed to the policies. *The dilemma of the Party staff is that, on the one hand they work for the Party, but, on the other, if the Prime Minister wants a particular thing to happen he's going to expect the Party machinery to support him as Leader of the Party. With all the problems that creates you can have protocols: I think that's necessary.* But to imagine that anyone, as soon as they become a party staffer, doesn't have any personal views is a difficult one to deal with. What is true is that when you approach Conference, or have decision making, there is an imbalance – particularly when we're in government."

BH continued: "How the imbalance affects trades unions is that, if you are elected, as I am, as General Secretary of an affiliated union you've got institutional support behind you (for example at the NPF). You also have a degree of status and self-confidence based on the job that you do. Whereas if you're the *delegate from say Cleethorpes CLP it's quite awe inspiring to be asked to come and meet the Home Secretary or for that matter the Prime Minister. I've had instances of that (pressure), on particular policy points, and I find that intimidating. So someone who's a new delegate to Conference is going to find that even more intimidating,* unless they've been round the block a while and been seasoned (see Chapter 7). So, in some ways, you're not going to be able to overcome authority, status and even experience. *What I'm coming to is saying that there should be ways of equalising and making things much easier for new conference delegates and people involved in the NPF and even for less experienced trades union leaders at Conference.* I can only go on my own experience. I've experienced great pressure from the Prime Minister downwards."

One example of such heavy pressure being put on a senior trade unionist was of persistent, and overbearing pressure, applied to then General Secretary of Unison, Rodney Bickerstaffe, by the Leadership, over his decision to support an increase in pensions, against the Conference Platform in 2001.

C4_49

Hayes continued: *"All this talk about open primaries and almost virtual membership; I think are deeply damaging for the Party, for CWU members and for the Labour Link.* But autocracy top downism definitely doesn't work. There is a kind of elite political class (all the clever clogs) who are much more aware of what's going on."

In 2012 Len McCluskey said: "The National Policy Forum and Policy Commissions are now discredited (Liz Snape shared this view – see Chapter 7). Any attempt to secure greater democracy in the Party is welcome. I am glad that Jon Cruddas has now been made responsible for policy development instead of Liam Byrne so hopefully things will continue to become more democratic. More radical policies are likely to be developed, therefore more people will want to get involved. *TB couldn't involve more people in policy making: he knew that his neo-liberal policies wouldn't get through Conference."*

Both these union leaders were calling for improved and genuine Party democracy rather than gimmicks designed to give yet more power to an unaccountable Labour political elite.

What can UK Labour learn from Australian Labor about relationships with the trades unions?

Both parties have similar relationship histories in this context. Both were founded in the 19th century (the ALP before the UK Labour Party) under the wing of the trades unions. Labour Parties in both countries had a mission to secure the election for more working class people to national and local government and to represent the interests of working class people generally.

The Hawke Wran Report[C4_50] on the future of the Australian Labor Party demonstrates a commitment to a strong and continuing partnership between the ALP and the Australian Trade Union Movement. The Report points out that contemporary Australian Liberal and National (i.e. conservative) Party leaders have publicly reviled their trade union movement. It recognises that the wages and conditions of the large majority of Australians have been established by the work and financial input of the organised trade union movement. The Report stated[C4_51]: "Far from recommending that our Party should walk away from the trade unions, we acknowledge both their historical contribution and the way in which they are themselves currently undertaking significant adaptation to a changing environment." They continued: "*It is possible to have a party of social democracy without the unions but it is not possible to have a Labor/our Party without the unions.* The way ahead is not to sever the union connection but to renew and reinvigorate the partnership."[C4_52] TB and GB did not appear to get this point.

The Report adds that changes in economic and work patterns have, in Australia as in similar countries (like the UK), also led to a smaller proportion and numbers of the workforce being in union membership. But in the previous two years more had joined unions "as a result of the union's own restructuring, education and recruitment programmes." Almost two million Australians were then in trades unions. They welcomed that, on average, Australian union members earned about 15% more than non unionists and that public attitudes to unions had become more positive. Labor claimed that this level of union participation made it "appropriate that through their organisations and (hopefully) individually, their voices be heard in the councils of our Party." In justification they pointed out[C4_53] that the Australian Labor Party and trades union movement had "represented the same core constituency" i.e. workers and their families. It had fought for a better standard of living for them for more than 100 years. This was despite the fact that the ALP now represented 'a broader constituency' as well.

Further, they argued, both the ALP and the trades union movement drew on a common set of principles to which the union movement continued to make a significant contribution. They also keep the Party 'directly and structurally engaged with the concerns and aspirations of working families.' "*We have a shared purpose and set of goals for which we strive for the benefit of our shared constituency. This is our fundamental task*".[C4_54]

The Australian report proposed that Labor MPs should be more responsive to local trade unionists in and near their constituencies. This work should extend to adjacent areas where there was no ALP MP or Senator. This was both to deal with the trade unionist's concerns and enable them to contribute to policy making. *They should run joint local meetings and policy forums for union and individual Party members.*

The report urges[C4_55] that those enrolling Party members should try to make sure that these are also union members. They suggest discounted Party subscriptions for union members possibly including lower membership fee on first joining the Party (This was introduced by the UK Labour Party in 2014). In addition they seek ways of encouraging ALP members, who are employers, to hire union labour. Many points are made here which highlight the shortcomings of NL but also point to the ideal nature of a more positive relationship between the British trades unions and the Labour Party in the future (see Chapter 13 for discussion of post 2013 developments).

Conclusion

There is no doubt that, as Trades Union leaders quoted above indicated there was real disappointment, in union circles, with the record of NL government and their relationship with it. NL Government produced a few policies including the NMW (albeit at too low a level), increased parental leave and improved statutory holiday entitlements. These did benefit people at work. However there was a failure to repeal the great mass of constraining anti-union legislation introduced by Thatcher Governments or to enact new union friendly laws. For example, no attempt was made to enact measures that would make it easier for unions to recruit members in the new service sectors where an increasing proportion of the workforce is employed. Nor were attempts made to ease Thatcher's obligatory and expensive bureaucracy for unions trying to persuade members to affiliate to the Labour Party.

One consequence of these disappointments was the disaffiliation of several unions (e.g. the Fire Brigades Union) from the Labour Party and campaigns in which other unions threatened to do so. Furthermore, up to the 2010 general election, and since, some trade unions have been pouring money into the Labour Party. They paid for about 90% of the 2010 election campaign expenses. As Len McCluskey indicated, unions are getting weary of playing the cash cow in exchange for minimal political returns for their members. Further they will not continue to pay up indefinitely. Unions have also been alienated by some of the pronouncements from the Labour leadership since NL's last government e.g.in 2013 emanating from the Falkirk Westminster Parliamentary selection debacle.

There was also recognition by TU leaders that TB wanted to downgrade the relationship between the Party and the trade unions. Before the 1997 election TB boasted to the *Sun:* "We will not be held to ransom by the unions. We will stand up to strikes. We will not cave in to unrealistic pay demands." As Len McCluskey noted (above) GB was more amenable to co-operation with the unions; his political background differed from TB's and he was more firmly rooted in the Labour movement.

Some union leaders mentioned that unions affiliated to the Labour Party now represent only about 14% of the UK workforce and that even TUC affiliated trade unions represent just under one third of British employees. Therefore they could only speak on behalf of a minority of workers. This is bound to limit their influence. Some also realised that a hostile climate of public opinion in this country, which has been carefully nurtured by the right wing media, is reluctant to tolerate a Labour Party or Government which is thought to be too close, or too favourable, to trade unions. This is an issue that the Labour Party needs to address through public political education as it becomes a Sales Oriented Party (see Chapter 2 and Chapter 12). The answer is not to become estranged, this would be a tragedy for working people, for the unions and for the Labour Party. It would spell the end of Labour democratic socialism in Britain: unless a viable alternative Party could be founded.

CHAPTER 5
Evaluations of New Labour's Policy Record

"The Indian owners of Corus ... decided in 2009 to close most of its Teesside steel production site: with the loss of 1,700 jobs. Redcar's unemployment rate, already 9.6%, could only increase. Why did market collapse in the City demand relief from the state when a dubious decision by a foreign company brought forth no government action?"
Reported in Toynbee and Walker, *The Verdict*, 2010

"Rather than question whether huge salaries are morally justified, we should celebrate the fact that people can be enormously successful in this country."
John Hutton, Business Secretary, March 2008
Reported in Toynbee and Walker, *Unjust Rewards*, 2008

"As I looked out of my window that February afternoon, I was catching a glimpse of the largest demonstration in British history. Greater than the Chartist marches – greater than the suffragette demonstrations – they were ordinary people in their everyday clothes, from every walk of life and every age group in Britain."
Robin Cook, *The Point of Departure*, 2003

Chapter Contents
Introduction

Part 1
MPs' Evaluations

Economic Policy and Management, Fiscal Policy, Social Rented Housing, National Minimum Wage, Poverty in the UK, Trade Union and Worker's Rights (MPs' perspective), Crime and Civil Liberties, Other Human Rights and Equalities, Investment in Public Services, Private Sector Investment in Public Services and Enterprises, Foreign and Defence Policy, Devolution and Constitutional Reform, Representative Democracy and Loss of Public Trust, Summary of MPs' views

Part 2
Constituency Labour Party Secretaries' Evaluations

Economic and Fiscal Policies, Housing and Tackling UK Poverty, Work(lace and Trades Union Rights, Civil Rights and Law and Order, Investment in Public Services, Privatisation of Public Services and Enterprises, Public Democracy, Loss of Public Trust Responses to surveys of CLP Secretaries' opinions
Conclusion

When the author first met her future partner, during the 1970 general election campaign, he showed her photos of himself with MPs Nye Bevan and Bessie Braddock taken during the latter's visits to Party Conference at Scarborough during the 1960s. Although the author joined the Party in 1965, and was then active locally in South London, sadly she was unable to get to Conference until 1970 after both Bevan and Braddock had died. Therefore: she was unable to hear or meet them. She believes that one of Bevan's most important observations was that politics is the language of priorities which should be the religion of socialism. Labour governments have a limited time in office which should be used to promote and implement as many priority policies as possible. These should reflect democratic socialist principles. Governmental time spent promoting policies which favour the rich and privileged are a wrongful use of that precious time.

Introduction

This Chapter examines the policy records of New Labour Governments. Here stakeholders assess how far NL government time was effectively spent in developing and implementing policies in line with the aims and values of the Party (which they identified in Chapter1).

This Chapter also sets out and discusses the views of the Backbench MPs and Constituency Party (CLP) Secretaries and union leaders who were interviewed. In respect of CLP Secretaries' assessments, some comparisons are drawn with the results of a YouGov quantitative survey undertaken with a representative sample of Labour Party members for the LabOUR Commission (2007).[C5-1] Both surveys covered similar topics. Some discussions with union leaders about policies affecting their members were reported in Chapter 4.

Backbench MPs were asked to evaluate New Labour's (NL's) policies: to identify those they thought to be most successful and those they considered failures. Some policies were seen to have had positive *and* negative outcomes. In some cases their effects had improved or diminished over time. Interviewees were questioned directly about any policies on which they personally had voted against the government. When answering questions MPs were requested to bear in mind aims for the Labour Party which they had previously nominated (see Chapter 1). As a reminder: "Promoting equality and social justice" was their top priority aim followed by "developing and promoting public services", next came "promoting peace and good international relations" and equally promoting "solidarity and a collectivist approach". This reflected their proposals for of Party values. Aims are usually devised to reflect these values. MPs were asked to relate principally to actual policies and priorities during the NL period of government 1997-2010. Some policies introduced after 1997 were shaped earlier. Policies are classified under theme headings but some themes are inevitably intertwined.

Economic Policy and Management

It is a truth universally acknowledged that effective *economic policy and financial performance* are crucial to underpin most other policies. This is particularly true for a government, such as NL's, that aimed to build good public services and ensure prosperity for the majority of the population. See Clause 4 of the New Labour Party constitution, 1995, (Appendix 2). The performance of an economy is considered to be the main deciding factor in many national elections. This has long been evidenced by UK opinion surveys. It was famously supported by US President Clinton who claimed "It's the economy, stupid" (that determines election results). Economic management cannot simply be viewed in terms of technical competence, overall economic growth and employment levels – the performance criteria are more complex.

However well the economy is managed there are still major issues of the distribution of wealth and the occurrence of inequality in our society. Of course redistribution is politically easier when the economy is doing well, as the late Tony Crosland and his Fabian colleagues pointed out. Several economic measures increased inequality. One was a failure to increase the availability of social rented housing. Access to housing was also made more difficult by the increased availability of credit. This increased demand and therefore raised the price of private owner occupied housing .Another factor that exacerbated inequality was the generous taxation levels permitted to the rich until the latter stage of Brown's premiership. Examination of the effectiveness of economic policy, in terms of meeting a spectrum of Party objectives, is a complex exercise. It calls for analysis of interwoven themes. Toynbee and Walker (2010) [C5_2] argued: "Labour's trick was to detach living standards from incomes. During stable, low inflationary growth, people readily took on more debt while running down their savings. When nearly seven out of ten households owned their own homes, property inflation created a widespread sense of being better off, with added ease of borrowing."

Another major indictment of NL Government, following in the footsteps of its Tory predecessors, was the ever growing gap between rich and poor. Between 1979 and 2010 the Gini Co-efficient (which measures levels of inequality in a society) rocketed from .25 to .40. In the *Guardian* Radeep Ramesh reported that in 2010 the richest 10% of the UK population were worth 273 times more than the poorest 10%.[C5_3]

Backbenchers praised what, initially, seemed to be competent overall management of the UK economy between 1997 and 2008. One aspect of this was *growth in jobs and many more being in employment.* John Cryer remembered that, when he was first selected in his Essex seat in 1994: "I used to knock on doors during the daytime and many people were at home due to unemployment, but by the millennium and up to late 2008, a much higher proportion of them were out at work." Government statistics bear this out: 2.2 million new jobs were created in Britain between 1998 and 2007.[C5_4] Over half of these were public sector jobs or in voluntary organisations and firms dependent on public sector contracts. Senior backbencher M. said: "There was a transformation of the centre of my city which created more jobs."

However, few skilled and well paid manufacturing jobs were created to replace those lost in the shutdown of manufacturing industries which Thatcherite Tory governments initiated and that NL failed to replace. These lost jobs were mainly sited North of Watford. Lower paid, less secure service jobs replaced them. This trend is illustrated by Owen Jones' research in Ashington, Northumberland.[C5_5]

Louise Ellman MP contended: "Economic growth was particularly important in areas like Liverpool." She added: "Liverpool has changed dramatically since 1997 – more investment and prosperity. Significant numbers of people have benefited … The Regional Development agencies led investment in businesses and secured major projects, for example research laboratories at Daresbury (nearby in Cheshire) and the Liverpool Convention Centre, which has been a great success. It's a pity that the Government gave up plans for the regional authorities that they promised."

Graham Stringer MP believed: "Full employment was a real success. The 2001 and 2005 elections saw the government going to the electors with more people employed than there were in 1997." In Manchester, where he had led the council, unemployment dropped from 8.4% in June 1997 to 3.8% in January 2007. GS pointed out that this was a better record than that of any previous Labour Government (including that of Attlee). Roger Berry added: "… this meant that a major source of inequality was being removed. Creating more jobs was an impressive Labour achievement."

One of the real benefits of this growth in jobs was that much of it took place in the regions and notably in the run-down former industrial areas. This contrasts with the meagre contemporary economic growth under the Conservative led government which is concentrated in the relatively prosperous South East and London regions.

Senior backbencher A., who represented a former mining area, said: "There were still people on their knees for a along time after the strike. The general state of the (local) economy was poor. All the shops were closed and smashed up. There was very high unemployment, particularly youth unemployment. All this was put right. For a significant number of years we maintained high employment. This is very important for Labour voters." He added: "We ran a successful and profitable economy prior to the crisis. That successful economy effectively refinanced the public services. It would be reprehensible not to mention the economy as a major achievement of this Labour Government." Owen Jones also reported that Britain's pit villages had been devastated by the collapse of industry.[C5_6]

However welcome the benefits of the early NL economic boom, they had lulled Labour politicians, and the Party, into a false sense of security. They believed that the current wave of prosperity would last indefinitely. Therefore such flaws as might exist in contemporary economic policy should be overlooked. Most seemed to be beguiled by GB's claim that he had brought an end to boom and bust.

Jon Cruddas also welcomed earlier prosperity, but said: "My comments have to be seen in the context of the 2008 recession to which economic policies during this more buoyant period contributed." Colin Challen MP was pleased that "people overall were materially better off than they had been 15 years previously".

John Grogan MP claimed: "Most Labour backbenchers took little interest in economic policy, and certainly did not appraise it prior to 2008. This was because there seemed to be evidence that Gordon Brown's assertion that boom and bust were over was true. So they let him get on with his economic management without their surveillance. We did not have a Vince Cable (contemporary Liberal Democrat Economic spokesperson) on the Labour backbenches with economic competence and expertise. Everyone trusted us on the economy. We left the economic critique to Cable!" What an admission! Toynbee and Walker claimed[C5_7] that the City and business were to expected to grow jobs and government income while Labour looked after the poor. Averaged over the NL years, annual growth in GDP per capita was 1.6%. The 1948-1998 figure had been 2.2%.

Senior backbencher A. added: "The division of the economic spoils between capital and Labour has significantly shifted in favour of capital. That's been achieved in a number of ways. Work has become more insecure. We've faced huge numbers of people coming into the UK who will work for less money than indigenous workers. In almost every work place you've got people coming in from Eastern Europe and elsewhere. NL embraced this" (this claim was also supported by Lanchester[C5_8]). A. continued: "We created a large financial sector in the City of London which paid taxes and provided capital that helped to refinance the public services. But the price of labour went down and work became insecure. People borrowed on the value of their homes. There was a massive explosion of credit which eventually became a balloon bound to burst. Then people said: 'What am I left with? A bloody insecure job, for which New Labour is saying 'you've got to retrain every 5-6 years.' They are thinking: 'My job's insecure, it's poorly paid, I'm stuck with all this debt and my house is worth much less than it was six months ago." Mrs. Parry of Ashington told Owen Jones that her father and husband were both miners and that when the pit closed her father retired and quickly died and that her marriage broke up.[C5_9]

Backbencher A. continued: "We've pulled off a fantastic trick. It goes back to Anthony Crosland's book *The Future of Socialism*[C5-10] about using capitalism to pay for the poor. I think that the people behind NL's economic strategy saw that they could use finance and the City of London to work for the poor and for a time this worked."

Austin Mitchell MP asserted: "*We had the best years of economic growth that we've ever had (during a Labour government) but didn't use them to improve the lot of the people we represented.* Gains were minimal for them. Brown trots out a list of minor measures brought in to benefit them". Kelvin Hopkins MP said: "They established laissez-faire capitalism instead of social democracy. Blair was about the corporate world. The big corporations wanted the UK to be an off-shore Las Vegas but there was much resistance. Allegedly the gambling corporations were very disappointed as their boy Tony didn't manage it (GB curtailed TB's Casino plans in 2007 shortly after becoming Prime Minister). In general the rich have got richer."

Whatever the short and medium term benefits of the 1997-2008 economic strategy it was riddled with problems. The opportunity was lost to rebuild parts of the economy that had broken down and our economy remained tied long term to the City and Banks and to service industries. The chance was missed to rebuild public and not for profit housing. Through the private housing market people were encouraged to get into debt which would be unsustainable long term. Meanwhile the City was given unfettered power that it used to benefit itself, regardless of the wider national interest and of the probability of adverse long term consequences for the national economy. It was bound to end in tears. As Toynbee and Walker proposed: "Cosset the golden goose and she will still keep laying" (NL hoped).[C5-11]

Alan Simpson MP regretted: "The City of London was enabled to create limitless amounts of credit that could go in pursuit of ever rising home prices. *You can only get an ever rising spiral of house prices if there's under supply.* So you have a competitive market developed with considerable money chasing a limited supply … another dimension of profiteering is to allow big housing developers to go into their own gold rush in terms of speculative land acquisitions and upward bidding of land prices to ludicrous amounts."

Thus opinions on this overall theme largely welcomed prosperity achieved earlier and increased employment, with the caveat that some of NL's economic policies paved the way for the ensuing recession and led to even greater inequality. Some more radical respondents thought that more effective use could have been made of the wealth created. In fact it was used as a sticking plaster to give temporary protection to the poor from the growing inequality in the distribution of wealth and while the boom lasted.

Katy Clark MP believed: "We accepted a neo-liberal analysis of what was going on in the world. If we had taken a different course we might not have had such serious problems when the crisis came. *Of course it was an international crisis and it is nonsense to suggest that it was the Labour Government's fault that we got into that situation.*"

John McDonnell believed: "NL became imbued with the neo-liberalism of Thatcherism and managed the economy according to those principles. They accepted Thatcherism's unfettered market economics." He continued: "So far as NL's economic record is concerned, when we came into government in 1997 large scale investment in public services was needed. To some extent New Labour delivered this. They brought us back to the level of the best years of previous Tory governments, but no more. The scale of what they did has been exaggerated .Much of their public investment was turned into profits for the private sector. One example was the London Underground development."

NL let the market rip in pursuing its neo-liberal economic philosophy. Had they not done so, or better still, had they resorted to Keynesian policies (such as funding public works and grants to people on lower incomes as the Australian (Rudd) Labour government did when the crisis broke) Britain might have avoided the worst of the contemporary world economic crisis. However; as both Gordon Brown (GB) and Katy Clark pointed out: much of the crisis was internationally generated. During the boom years, instead of having an effective strategy to redistribute the extra wealth, concentrated on the needy. They relied on the notoriously ineffective mechanism of "indirect trickle down" to try to benefit the poor.

Roger Berry lamented: "Sadly it's taken the financial crisis for some in the Labour Party to realise that you can't just rely on the market and that government public spending and taxation policies have to be progressive to maintain a level of demand in the economy. GB now subscribes to that very strongly but he didn't feel so strongly when Peter Hain and I wrote a paper about it in 1997".[C5_12]

Peter Kilfoyle contended: "All the economic policies of NL government were obsessed with middle England and benefitting the filthy rich. They were regarded with equanimity by GB, Blair and Mandelson who were unconcerned with the growing gap between rich and poor."

Jon Cruddas proposed that NL's economic management reflected that their politics "was driven by growth that enabled them to swerve round some distributional conflicts because they thought that 15 years of growth would continue inexorably. So a trickle down approach to the economy would suffice because they believed it was a positive sum environment that would continue. In the middle of 2008, the music stopped. Now different policies are needed covering some of the big distributional issues: poverty and inequality. In effect, issues that NL swerved round because it thought that it could just use the process of growth to distribute resources. Last year (2008) marked, not just the end of NL, but also of a specific, growth-based approach to social democracy."

There was really no viable mechanism for coping with resulting poverty when the bubble burst because the escalating benefits bill, especially that for working family's tax credits and job seekers allowance, became increasingly difficult to cover; let alone cover increased demand.

Many MPs discussed issues in ways which linked policy relating the financial institutions with the 2008 economic crisis. Those institutions had clearly been major players in precipitating the meltdown. Factors, identified by MPs as contributing to that crisis included excessive reliance on the market economy and deregulation of the banks and city financial institutions. There was concern about NL economic policy's pernicious effects on inequality in the UK as exacerbated by the government's fiscal and housing policies.

Colin Challen argued: "We didn't build enough into the economy to take the shocks – prior to the recession. That was down to Gordon. Our (current) level of public debt is worrying. Are we about to fulfil the old adage that Labour Governments always finish with an economic crisis? It may be said that we were economically incompetent (I don't think this is true) despite glowing testimonials that Gordon had in his first 10 years (as Chancellor)". Challen added: "With the benign economic climate that they inherited in 1997; *the New Labour Government was able to pay off their friends in the City with deregulation."*

Clare Short believed: "The credit crunch was a disaster – the current claim that GB has helped to get us out of the crisis leaves out of the picture that he was Chancellor in the period leading up to that crisis." Everyone now says that deregulation went too far. Brown never acknowledged what was wrong with the regulatory system and just went on calling for more 'light touch regulation".

Austin Mitchell's verdict was: "When the bubble burst and the recession came we floundered. We didn't know what to do in a recession … *we needed regulation and intervention – all of which we had neglected.* Brown responded better than I had expected, but it was a total reversal of policy. Now (after October 2009) it will be very difficult for us to win an election."

Mervyn King, contemporary Governor of the Bank of England, believed that markets should always be unconstrained by government. Like GB, he considered that the state could, and should, not be an active controller of markets. He thought that markets should determine a state's economic policy. King told the *Guardian*:[C5_13] "The origins of the financial crisis lay in our inability to cope with the consequences of the entry into the world trading system of countries such as China, India and the former Soviet Empire in a word globalisation."

Graham Stringer said: "One of the early policies was giving independence to the Bank of England and slacker financial regulation. That was a way of assuring the City that a Labour Chancellor and Government would not be messing about with things that weren't in the Country's, or City's, economic and financial interests. It looks different now and will look even stranger in five to six years time. Now we've nationalised a great chunk of the banking sector and the problems facing our economy are more than just inflation."

He continued: "If inflation is perceived as the major threat to the economy, then setting up an independent Bank of England and separate financial controls through the Financial Services Authority (FSA) looks acceptable. If you're faced with rogue banks intervening in international trade relations and you have to nationalise banks then the whole situation is different: giving away democratic control of a major influence on the economy looks less good."

Toynbee and Walker declared: "Labour made the Bank of England independent in the belief that only central banks can be trusted to ensure strict monetary discipline and keep inflation down."[C5_14]

Giving independence to the Bank of England in 1997 was controversial. It was a huge and dubious surrender of economic power by the Executive. Senior Government economist Kate Barker severely criticised the grant of independence to the Bank of England in 2012 in a BBC Radio 4 interview.[C5_15]

Lord S. said: *"One of the reasons we got out of the recent recession, the worst for decades, faster was that the government intervened. Banks went bust, but in order to save the depositors, as the man the street put their money into building societies, we had to nationalise Northern Rock and Royal Bank of Scotland."*

Jeremy Corbyn suggested the effects of NL's deregulation policies were "not much noticed in the late 1990s but became very obvious when the banking crisis finally hit in 2008. Problems arose because of the ridiculous levels of credit given to people here (and in the USA). Because we had such a deregulated system and had encouraged the privatisation of building societies: we were in a poor position to defend against it."

Michael Meacher asserted: "Both before, and after, he became Chancellor, Brown used to go regularly to the Mansion House to 'hose them down' with adulation. Industry regarded NL as a friendly political machine – as much as the Tories – that's why they (including the CBI) started contributing money. This was not because they believed in NL or its ideology. It was because NL supported a neo liberal economy; deregulated, organised flexible labour markets. Wealth was allowed to go rip." He offered the infamous Mandelson "filthy rich" quote and added: "He doesn't like to be reminded of this now but it *is an aspect of NL*. The banks have been utterly out of control. All aspects of that model are now uncontrolled and breaking down."

From his interviews with Treasury officials Rawnsley reported that officers at the Treasury and the Bank of England met each other far less frequently than they had done before 1997.[C5_16]

Chris Mullin MP regretted: "We've become excessively dependent on rich men". Kelvin Hopkins contended: "Blair was also about the corporate world. They have been trying to liberalise as much as possible." Alice Mahon agreed: "The neo-conservative economic policy was very unfortunate. We deregulated *and* refused trades unions more freedoms. I objected to the Thatcherite/Reagan agenda adopted for economics: that the market could do everything. It was significant that they had to get rid of Clause 4. *New Labour is wedded to the bankers and big business. I remember Michael Meacher, as a really good minister, dealing with climate change, complaining that their first consideration was for big business.* There are over 30 former ministers who've now taken appointments with businesses working in areas over which they've had oversight in office."

John Grogan said: "In some of the things we've done we've forgotten our progressive attitudes. For example: we probably cosied up a bit too much to the City and have been a bit too much in love with rich people. So we've probably forgotten that progressive approach that goes beyond the social democracy that we've shared with Democrats in the States – we sympathise with the small guy and are rather suspicious of monopolies and oligarchies."

Austin Mitchell argued: "Our letting the market rip was particularly true of finance. We deregulated banks as part of concentrating on housing ownership. This gave us ten prosperous years until the housing boom ended. That policy carried its own nemesis. But the rich were getting better off faster and the poor were coming up only slowly. The advantage was that the Tories had no policy that was more attractive. We set up the Financial Services Authority but then extracted its teeth."

In 2020 John Lanchester[C5_17] complained that UK banks were both too large and too interconnected. Lanchester,[C5_18] writing later in the same year, reported that no legislation had yet been passed across the developed world to prevent a repetition of the 2008 financial crash.

Lanchester believed that, from Mrs Thatcher's administration onwards, British Governments had indulged the City. He considered that, after 1986, all the historic barriers, separations and rules separating different areas of banking, finance and the operation of the stock market were abolished. The outcome was the City's increasing dominance of UK economic life. When NL came to power in 1997 they introduced "light touch" financial regulation.[C5_19]

John McDonnell wrote: "Government economic policies are tailored and shaped by market economic forces and practices. They have re-fashioned the state so that its interests coincide more and more with those of the corporate sector." In an interview he regretted: "They deregulated the City and failed to introduce a planned economy which we needed."[C5_20]

Katy Clark suggested: "We allowed money to run riot and weren't willing to take on the financial institutions of the city. I think that we should have been bolder in regulating the banks and financial sector and controlling the speculators."

Journalist William Keegan summed up: "Having given us the debt crisis, and passed the financial and private sector's debts over to the public sector's balance sheet, the financial sector now has the audacity to complain about the public sector debt crisis it created." [C5_21]

As Polly Toynbee pointed out in the in the *Guardian*:[C5_22] "Boardroom pay rose 30% per annum and bankers' bonuses soared." Jeremy Corbyn concluded: "NL enshrined the idea that the market comes first; that wealth comes first above equality."

NL's indulgence of the City, flowing in Thatcher's footsteps, led directly to the severity of the UK's suffering during the world economic crisis. What is even more perturbing is that NL did virtually nothing to tighten up the regulation of UK financial institutions and markets whilst still in office.

Fiscal Policy

The disadvantaged, were battered not only by laissez faire economic policies, but throughout NL's reign, also by most of its *fiscal policies*. There was a deplorable failure to develop a seriously redistributive taxation system. Heavy reliance continued to be placed on Value Added Tax (VAT), a regressive indirect tax that hits the poorest, and those on fixed incomes, hardest because everyone pays the same price for vatted goods irrespective of their income. While food and children's clothes are VAT free, this tax is levied on most other essentials and at the same rate on these as on luxury goods. The long forgotten purchase tax fell more heavily on non essential luxuries than on basic necessities. Direct taxation can be made more equitable and redistributive.

Roger Berry argued: "What Labour failed to do was to tackle inequality by dealing with those on high incomes. I've long advocated that people with £100,000 per year or more should pay a higher marginal rate of tax than 40%. Until recently this was regarded as completely unacceptable as it would "scare the horses". Subsequently a higher rate was agreed for those earning more than £100,000 per year. However this did not take effect until 2010 as Labour left office.

Conversely, Gordon Brown (GB) decided to hit the lowest earners when, in 2007, he abolished the 10p tax rate that he previously introduced to benefit them. From 2009 even the lowest earners had to pay tax at 20p in the pound. The NL government's ill gotten gains were used to fund a 20p basic rate of tax for all but the highest earners in the run up to the 2010 general election. There was a widespread public outcry when the change was implemented. NL was good at promoting equality but less effective on tackling inequality.

There *was* a need for more progressive taxation. Taking all age groups of UK households together, the average income for a two adult, childless household in 2008 (adjusted for housing costs and after tax and benefits were counted) was £18,824 per year. The OECD then defined poverty as being 60% of average income which was currently £11,924 per year for the same type of household In 2008 nearly 13 million people, about 20% of the British population, had incomes below that official poverty line. Poverty was not evenly spread: for example: in 2000 38% of the population of Blackburn, Lancashire were classified as poor.[C5_23]

Kelvin Hopkins argued, that despite growing UK prosperity: "We have gone to extremes of inequality, largely due to tax changes introduced by Thatcher. We should have had a really redistributive taxation system with higher taxes on the rich and more attempts to stop tax avoidance and tax evasion. At the end of Callaghan's premiership the top marginal rate of taxation was 83%, it's now (2009) 40%. There's been a massive move of wealth to the rich through the taxation system."

Gordon Prentice MP deplored "The gap between the richest and poorest has widened after 12 years of a Labour Government which has followed a neo liberal model. It believes that the rich should get richer and that there would be a trickle down effect. That has distorted Labour's politics since 1997. There has been complete immobility at any suggestion that the top rate of income tax should be raised. It's only at the end of this period that the has been any proposal to raise it and now it will be increased *after the (2010) general election"*.

The Conservative led Coalition government subsequently reduced the higher rate of income tax introduced in the Brown government's dying days and re instated the over generous 40% rate for higher income earners.

Senior backbencher M. believed: "There is still huge inequality. Labour's eternal mission is not finished yet … now we have a situation where the majority are better off but we can't abandon the most dispossessed in our society. These are mainly the people I represent. We've narrowed the equality gap in some areas but not enough, or in a consistent fashion, in those areas where class and social disadvantage is such a determinant of children's futures."

Michael Meacher argued: "The rich will always get on by themselves, they have the Tory Party to help them. But between one half and two thirds of the population need political representation ... Therefore *Blair has disenfranchised more than half of the population who feel that there is no one in Westminster arguing forcefully and cogently for them*. This, together with the Iraq war, will be NL's legacy."

Austin Mitchell contended that, due to permissive market policies: "We now have a vast, alienated working class. This working class believes that it has not got much out of an NL Government. We abandoned our belief in progressive taxation and public spending to win power. *We gave up our real selves and our real mission and subjected (ourselves) to the rigour of market deregulation.* We made minimal advances that didn't alienate high taxpayers, or the city, or the great financial interests expected to generate new wealth for the UK."

Regressive fiscal policies were fuelling the fires of growing class inequality in the UK and leading to widespread resentment among Labour's so-called core voters. The BBC conducted an opinion poll of the White British Working Class in 2008.[C5_24] This indicated that 58% of the white working class thought that no UK political Party spoke up for them. *At this time NL's leaders disregarded this discontent boasting publicly that working class voters had "nowhere else to go". The subsequent dramatic rise in support for UKIP and the Scottish National Party showed that this assumption would not be valid indefinitely.*

Robert Peston reported that in 2006 the typical FTSE 100 boss earned 72.5 times what the average earning employee was paid. "The high earning elite is, to a large extent found in the financial sector, where a combination of globalisation and a technological revolution has allowed a talent for making money to be rewarded in ways that are breaking all known barriers. Vast sums "are accruing to brainy individuals who create and trade in almost incomprehensible (and often very risky) new financial products."[C5_25]

A minority of individuals generated vast wealth for themselves as virtually sole traders in the business of buying and selling entire companies. For example: Sir Philip Green, owner of BHS, Top Shop and other chain stores, paid himself a tax-free dividend of £1.2 billion in 2005. Through a technicality the dividend went to his wife (who was not a UK resident), to avoid payment of any tax.

Alan Simpson's diagnosis was: "As private debt was branded as 'good debt' people were encouraged to take out vast amounts of personal credit debt on extortionate terms. At the same time public debt (but not Private Finance Initiative (PFI)) was the area not to be engaged with. This confused me. Government is the biggest borrower, so when it goes to borrow it can command lower interest rates than you or I could. If it borrows in the form of government bonds: these are the safest deal for private investors". Interest rates for PFI loans were much higher.[C5_26]

AS continued: "The City of London could privatise the ever rising spiral of wealth and well-being so long as they could provide limitless amounts of credit ... The package of economic shifts, that was NL, involved a move from the collective to the personal ... a shift from an economic strategy that saw itself as interventionist and directing pace and shape of change to one that was entirely market driven, arms length, deregulatory and permissive. *It was little different historically from what Liberal and Conservative administrations have done.*"

Social Rented Housing

The policy of easy availability of credit had knock-on effects in respect of a significant area of public services – social rented housing. Here NL's performance was very poor. They inherited a situation in which the stock of council housing had been greatly diminished by the Tory instigated "right to buy". They largely failed to rebuild homes in the public rented sector. A very limited amount of new rented housing was provided for management by voluntary sector Housing Associations. NL continued with this policy of public no build – until its dying days. It also largely divested councils of their social landlord function by passing their stock to housing associations or arms length management arrangements.

Alan Simpson MP stated: "The public sector home building programme was curtailed to create an under supply and drive up demand for owner occupied housing and thence house prices for which the banks would provide credit, often to those who could not afford it. Austin Mitchell, who is a social housing expert, and a prominent supporter of the Defend Council Housing interest group, pointed out: "the percentage of GDP spent on social housing fell from just over 6% in the late 1970s to just over 1.6% today (October 2009)."

Economist Kate Barker wrote a housing report for the Treasury in 2004. She contended that credit for house purchase was too readily available. Supply was not meeting demand and speculative builders were purchasing housing land and then not developing it. She calculated that to keep house price inflation at 1.8%, it was necessary to build 70,000 extra homes each year. This was in addition to homes already planned. Housing starts had fallen after 1997 then they rose to a pre-recession peak but halved from that peak in 2005-6 and went down by 42% in 2006-9.[C5_27] The NL record on building social homes for rent was poor.

Backbencher A. reported that dilapidated former National Coal Board rented housing in his constituency had been greatly improved since 1997. Another MP reported that there had been much new social housing stock built in central Manchester. The government offered to subsidise the demolition of crumbling older houses in the North, Scotland and Wales. After five years this "housing renewal programme" had demolished 10,200 sub-standard homes, refurbished 40,000 and built a meagre 1,100 new ones.

Jeremy Corbyn welcomed some commendable special social housing initiatives for severely disadvantaged homeless people; including former service people and ex-offenders. There was also a praiseworthy NL initiative for modernising existing social housing. By 2010 they had invested £37 billion in a "Decent Homes" programme, installing central heating, new kitchens and bathrooms. In 2001 39% of social housing stock was classified as sub-standard; but by 2009 only 8% of homes were still regarded as unfit.[C5_28]

National Minimum Wage

One of the most popular measures enacted by NL government was aimed at tackling poverty among those in work. This was the National Minimum Wage (NMW). This measure had been Party policy long before 1997 and was strongly advocated by the trades unions over many years.

John Cryer designated the NMW as the government's "best measure" and Jeremy Corbyn said that it was: "one of the good things that the Labour government has done since 1997". Jon Cruddas described it as: "One of the more enduring social democratic measures that occurred in the early years". A similar assessment was made by John Grogan. Graham Stringer said it was: "… a huge success, one not achieved by previous Labour governments although it was always seen as desirable."

The NMW was promised by earlier Labour Governments but never implemented. It was introduced in 1997 and regularly uprated after that. It enabled about 2 million people, mainly women, to have an improved wage. The machinery to secure compliance by employers was weak and underfunded. There were issues of immigrant workers, often organised by gangmasters, who covertly and illegally undercut the NMW. Enforcement of the NMW was patchy overall. Nevertheless the view of Labour MPs was favourable.

Roger Berry called it: "A very impressive thing. I remember that the Conservatives fought us night after night in the House of Commons" (to oppose the NMW). Lord S. described it as:" a great policy". Frank Dobson claimed that: "The NMW (together with other benefit changes) has meant that people in work have seen the biggest increases ever in their living standards." Chris Mullin said: "It has certainly made a difference to the lives of poor people in Sunderland" (his constituency).

The minimum wage was not the same thing as a living wage. Even families drawing tax credits for children, frequently fell below the poverty line.[C5-29] Subsequently the demand for a real living wage has escalated and sometimes been met.

Kelvin Hopkins assessed the NMW as being: "… a success but it was forced on 'them' by the trade union movement and the Labour movement as a whole. TB, GB and Mandelson would have loved not to implement it. The alternative would have been a massive Backbench rebellion." Clare Short echoed this view: "The Minimum Wage was one of the early positive achievements of the Government. It came from a commitment made way back before the growth of NL. It was such a strong commitment that it had to be carried out." Michael Meacher added that the NMW: "was one of the few concessions the NL Government made in the direction of what we regard as true Labour policy."

Katy Clark thought that: "The NMW has transformed the lives of millions of people. When I was Parliamentary candidate in rural Scotland in 1997, I knew many people who were earning around, or less than, a pound an hour. Many people forget that and what a significant policy the NMW was. At the time, we were told by the Conservatives that it would cause an economic crisis and huge job losses. But in reality it's been very successful. I'd like to see a higher minimum wage but its achievement alone was a very significant one for Labour."

Responses showed this to be a hugely popular, and mainly uncontroversial, policy. It was cited positively by 18 out of 27 backbenchers interviewed. Alan Simpson was the only (partial) critic of this measure. He judged that it was "A good thing but the level is not high enough". The inadequacy of the NMW's level has been demonstrated by a subsequent Campaign for a Living Wage. This is particularly vital in parts of the UK such as London and the South East where the cost of living is exceptionally high.

Tacking Poverty in the UK

Linked to the NMW is the broader issue of tackling poverty in the UK generally. Poverty had increased under the Tories due to high unemployment and the disappearance of well paid blue collar jobs. Wages became depressed by Thatcher's statutory weakening of the trades unions and the transition to low paid service jobs in poorly unionised work places. NL's response was not to re-empower unions or help to generate high value well paid jobs but to subsidise the employers of low paid workers by paying their staff tax credits. Child benefit was also increased. As Simon Jenkins noted: "TB had no time for unions and believed strongly that government's role in the economy was primarily to promote business."[C5_30]

Austin Mitchell named Working Families Tax Credit (WFTC) as being "another of the few measures to support the people that Labour should help. Others are child tax credits and better maternity benefits. Although these measures shifted money to the less well off, they also supported the low wage economy. In 2000 Blair promised to abolish child poverty in 20 years, reaching the half way mark by 2010. However instead of halving the number of poor children, NL only managed to cut the number of poor children by one sixth by 2010."

Louise Ellman also spoke of addressing child poverty. "There's been more support for people on low incomes. WFTC was opposed by the Tories but is now established and accepted. It is complicated to administer but is beneficial never the less."

Echoing Mitchell's last remark, others considered that NL did not do enough to help people in poverty, despite the articulation of modest good intentions. In 2000 TB made a speech at Toynbee Hall, the famous East End Settlement where Clement Attlee worked before entering Parliament. It was in this speech that he promised to abolish child poverty in the UK within 20 years. This target was formalised by a Child Poverty Act of 2009.

Michael Meacher argued: "The point of the Labour Party is to challenge the existing power structure on behalf of those who have been disadvantaged by factors in the economy, social policy and access to housing, pensions and jobs. In these terms the lower half of the population, in respect of income, are always disadvantaged. NL does not accept this." Alice Mahon said: "NL thought that it would be popular if they bashed the poor; carrying on the Peter Lilley (former Conservative Minister's) approach. We are here to solve the problems of the poor not to humiliate them. NL thought it would be popular with middle England if they attacked single parents."

Katy Clark believed: "We tried to do a lot about child poverty and poverty generally and some of that was successful. At least Labour was *trying* to move in that direction which meant that we had *some* achievements and brought many children out of relative poverty. I think some of the anti-poverty initiatives were important, but I wish we'd done better."

In a report for the post 2010 Coalition Government, Frank Field MP wrote: "The government transferred £134 billion to families since 1999 and the money was producing only modest results, a fall from 3.4 million to 2.8 million children in poverty. But that is still a lot of children spared the misery of poverty."[C5_31] NL regressed back to reliance on the system of means testing.

Means testing has long been controversial in Labour circles. Evidence from research by anti-poverty interest groups has long demonstrated that many people eligible for any means tested benefit fail to apply for it. Estimates of the percentage who neglect to do so range between 25% and 33% of those entitled. Reasons given for failure to claim ranged from pride and unwillingness to be seen as objects of charity, to a lack of knowledge of their rights which may be compounded by inadequate publicity, or complex application forms and information, and by fear of being humiliated during the application process.

Alan Simpson regretted: "We have seen a shift away from universalism in favour of means testing. This is somewhat perverse in the light of Labour's history. For the whole of my lifetime elections have been fought on the basis of Labour supporting universalism and the Tories favouring means testing. Suddenly we became the Party of means testing. The initial rebellion was over one parent benefits. It was presented that somehow people would be better off. Thirty-eight of us (Backbench MPs) felt that was an absolute lie. A heresy that we could not sign up to – so massive pressure was put on us."

Lynne Jones said: "There's been more and more means testing inside the social security system. They've failed to restore the link between state pensions and earnings. It was only due to Adair Turner's report, outside his terms of reference (actually private pensions), that secured an agreement. Restoring the link (between pensions and earnings levels in 2011) is still too far away. A non means tested welfare state encourages people to do more for themselves. Means tested benefits mean disincentives built into the system."

Kelvin Hopkins took up her argument: "Instead of adopting the principle of universality put forward by Beveridge[C5-32] and Titmuss[C5-33]; they took the opposite direction and provided means tested benefits whenever possible. We need higher universal benefits. During the Thatcher era there was a massive increase in poverty and the gap between rich and poor widened greatly. NL hardly changed that. We are miles from where we were in 1979. In terms of child poverty we are the fourth worst in the EU; similar to countries like Poland and Romania. I was astonished that a Labour Government would abolish the 10p tax rate." Linda Riordan criticised the one parent family benefit cut together with other welfare reform bills.

Toynbee and Walker[C5-34] praised the non means tested tax credits as "the great dam holding back inequality, channelling money to lower income families and pensioners".

Roger Berry, a long term campaigner for people with disabilities, said: "In debates on so-called welfare reform the government has been less than totally progressive. They have put a lot of money into disabled people to enable them to stay at work or to secure employment. There have been occasions when some members of the government have not been able to resist playing to the *Daily Mail* – especially in relation to incapacity benefit (in 1999). There was a letter from 'Tony Blair' sent to the *Mail* playing into its argument that people on incapacity benefit are 'scroungers'. This is complete tosh! But organisations representing disabled people believe that NL delivered more equal opportunities than the Tories ever did." He added: "Labour has significantly reduced the numbers of children and pensioners in poverty – that's factual. Overall working families' tax credits brought very significant benefits to those on the lowest incomes. I have many constituents who value it highly but there have been real issues about the administration of the system which come from means testing through the tax system.

Graham Stringer praised: "Free bus passes for the elderly and disabled which were a huge success. These were not brought in by any previous Labour Government, although always seen as desirable. GB did get the credit for this." Jon Cruddas asserted: "Much was achieved around tackling child poverty. The early years agenda is a quite radical and extremely durable one." Colin Challen said: "Despite the equality gap, we have done a great deal to address absolute poverty and child poverty. But as the higher paid have got richer the gap has increased and it's made the situation look worse."

There remained the vexed issue of incapacity benefit (IB) mentioned by Roger Berry. In 1963 there were fewer than half a million people claiming incapacity benefit. By 2009 it was 2.6 million. However there was no evidence of a parallel increase in incapacity for work. That was only a 2.1% increase. Under Tory governments, from 1979 to 1997 there was a massive increase in IB claimants. This included about 800,000 during the recession of the early 1990s. Incapacity benefit was undoubtedly used to mask actual unemployment statistics.[C5-35]

Chris Mullin stated: "There has been a modest redistribution of wealth: particularly through tax credits and the NMW." Senior backbencher M, who represents an inner city seat, pointed out: "The greatest issue for my constituents is poverty. There is gross inequality in our society. A child born there will inevitably lead a life that is more truncated, in terms of years, and in their scope to aspire and to achieve those aspirations. A child born there will live an average of eight years less than one born in an affluent area. That child will not get full access to the education system or the opportunities that society offers generally. Labour has done a lot more for people while in government, through pro-poor policies, than it gets credit for. Because of the complexities of the benefit system: these have not always had the desired effect. But the desire to implement them has been there".

In summary, NL's considerable efforts to redress the gross inequality and poverty created by Thatcher and Major Governments were only partly effective.

Trades Union and workers' rights

Trades Union and workers' rights (from Labour MPs' perspectives) have been a fundamental focus of the Labour Party since the foundation of the Labour Representation Committee. This topic is discussed, from a trade union perspective, in Chapter 4. The foundation of the Labour Party was at the instigation of the trades unions. They are still affiliated and are linked, in theory, by the long established radical values of solidarity and fraternity.

Katy Clark applauded "the increases in public holidays and holiday entitlements for all employees given by the Labour Government, but we should have done more to develop individual worker's rights in this country."

John Cryer praised the first trades union legislation that NL produced. This included the "50% recognition rule" which provided extra individual workplace rights and offered improved rights for unions to be recognised in a workplace, more maternity and paternity leave and better compensation for unfair dismissal. But, apart from that, they were not able to negotiate any special bilateral deals to union's advantage at the expense of capital". Jon Cruddas believed: "Labour market reforms are enduring social democratic reforms from the early NL years". Senior backbencher A. said: "The legacy of the miners' strike in my constituency was very difficult – but the way in which the compensation package for miners' diseases worked – it put huge amounts of money into the hands of people who were living in extreme poverty."

After these early reforms, NL's performance in this area was disappointing. They failed to repeal the majority of restrictive trades union "reforms" introduced by Thatcher and Major governments. This cramped the style and effectiveness of Britain's unions (see Chapter 4).

Alice Mahon complained: "We refused the trades unions more freedoms ... it almost became unpopular to talk about trades unions. We lagged behind France and Germany when it came to basic rights for working people." Michael Meacher berated NL for having: "ignored the trades unions and organised a flexible Labour market". Austin Mitchell claimed: "Rebranding as 'NL' meant dissociation from the trades unions. We curtailed the powers of the unions who became less and less relevant and decreasingly listened to by us. We alienated ourselves from them."

John McDonnell wrote about "the Government's denial of trades union rights. The neo-liberal dominance of the markets promoted by NL meant that they refused the re-establishment of rights for trade unionists." He added: "Wages and salaries as a share of gross national income have fallen from 50% in 1992 to 46% in 2005, a trend reinforced by NL's decision to retain most of the Tory anti-union laws."[C5_36]

Only six backbenchers commented on this theme which suggests that they did not credit it with much importance. TB sought radical change in the relationship between Labour and the trades unions. In a speech to the Transport and General Worker's Union (TGWU) in July 1995, he said:"*We would listen to the unions but make clear that there would be no special relationship and certainly no favours*".[C5_37] Soon after this, TB had an informal meeting with eight of the most senior trade union leaders. According to John Prescott: "Over the meal Tony made it absolutely clear that the old days were gone and that he wouldn't be following any union diktat and they should not expect any deals ... he was challenging them, expecting them to complain or argue but the response was muted.[C5_38]

Over the 13 years TB was Labour Leader, he never attended that great annual trade union rally, the Durham Miners' Gala. That is held less than 10 miles from his former Sedgefield constituency. This rally was regularly visited by every previous Labour Party leader and virtually every other North East Labour MP before him. TB and Lord Levy apparently agreed that the Party needed to limit its dependence on money from the trades unions. The union contribution fell from two thirds of funding, when Blair became leader, to a low of less than a quarter.[C5-39] As Labour Party Treasurers reported back to Conference the Party continued to be heavily financially dependent on the unions especially for general election funding. This situation largely continued up to the 2010 general election.

Crime and Civil Liberties

NL government's record on *civil liberties* was considered dubious by a number of respondents. It was linked to TB's pledge to be "tough on crime, tough on the causes of crime" which led to the introduction of such measures as Anti-Social Behaviour Orders (ASBOs). It also reflected growing reactions to radical Islamist attacks after the Twin Towers Bombing of 9/11. The *fewest positive comments* were made about these policies by MPs interviewed.

Chris Mullin reported: "I was Chair of the Home Affairs Select Committee and was very reluctant to extend detention without trial, certainly to the length that was proposed (90 days). I was happy *not* to vote for this; it resulted in a defeat for the government in the Commons."

Christine McCafferty stated that she had "been unhappy about the Government's (original) policy on detention without trial (28 days). But I've supported them as there have been at least some checks and balances and some judicial oversight (introduced). We had to work very hard to ensure that the 90 day detention became completely unacceptable. It distressed me that this policy came from a Labour government; but the Government's first duty has to be to protect its citizens."

Clare Short argued: "Our policy on the criminal justice system is bad. There are masses of new offences. These are criminalising a higher proportion of the population and increasing the prison population. This doesn't curb crime; but it is enormously expensive and destructive. The whole 90 days detention thing was wrong." Michael Meacher criticised "increasing surveillance at home and the police increasingly out of control; as we saw at the 2009 G10 Meeting riots. The powers of the state have increased under NL. The existing power structure has been strengthened."

Other Human Rights and Equalities

When it came to other human rights and equalities, stakeholder's evaluations were more favourable. Chris Mullin positively mentioned the Human Rights Act (HRA) as being the "jewel in the crown" in this context; he added praise for the ban on smoking in public places which, he predicted: "will endure". TB later publicly lamented that he had supported the HRA.

Promoting greater social class equality (as distinct from equal opportunities) scarcely featured on the NL radar. As Owen Jones lamented,[C5-40] "the expulsion of class from the nation's vocabulary by Thatcherism and NL has ensured minimal scrutiny of the manifestly unjust distribution of wealth and power in modern Britain." However there was a stronger NL commitment to promote other equalities of gender, disability, race, ethnicity, religion and sexual orientation.

Christine McCafferty said: "the government has brought in quite a lot of equalities legislation; some of it causing controversy". Katy Clark praised "some of the work done around equalities including rights to parental leave". The equalities theme was taken forward by senior backbencher M. who said:"My constituency is a very diverse one. It is ethnically diverse but also diverse in terms of lifestyle. It
houses one of the most active gay communities in the country. I'm very proud of our record on policies for diversity. Policies specifically around discrimination have been commendable. Gay and lesbian people have benefited especially – after Tory discrimination, for example Thatcher's section 28. One gay constituent told me that the right for him to have a civil partner was, alone, 'enough to make him vote Labour for ever'. The rights given have, he said 'transformed his life'. These rights are one of our progressive achievements."

Lynne Jones welcomed that: "There are areas in society that are much better notably in relation to discrimination against gay and lesbian people. I'm also involved with people who are trans-gender. They have benefited. *There's been a sea change in people's attitudes to people with mental health problems, the last great area of stigma.* Many changes have been brought about by the people (involved) themselves but the government has been dragged screaming to support them. NL is afraid of standing up to the types of opinion frequently seen in the *Daily Mail*."

John Grogan applauded: "Some of our equality measures. The idea of having a gay cabinet minister was just not dreamed of in the early 1990s; but who would bat an eyelid about that now? This advance will endure." Jeremy Corbyn also welcomed "the government's contribution to increasing rights and opportunities for gay and lesbian people".

Roger Berry summed up: "Social policy has been remarkably progressive in relation to the equal rights agenda. We have moved on from the days when, as a Labour candidate, I was criticised by my Tory MP opponent for supporting gay rights. There has been a lot of public support for this equal rights agenda. NL can count it as a major achievement."

NL boasted of setting up the Equalities and Human Rights Commission: an amalgamation of earlier quangos. However Toynbee and Walker[C5-41] claimed: "The Equalities and Human Rights Commission's purposes were vaguely specified, disappointing those who had hoped for more enlightenment over the balance between competing rights".

Another type of right, the right to ramble, was successfully championed by Gordon Prentice who said: "My constituency, Pendle, is surrounded by (rural) land which is out of bounds to the public. When I won in the private member's bill ballot, I decided to cover the right to ramble. I drew up a draft bill with the help of the Ramblers' Association. There was then two years delay. TB appeared terrified of the Countryside Alliance and wealthy people from the countryside. There was endless consultation. Michael Meacher was the Minister and was supportive. The government drew up its own 'Rights of Way in the Countryside Bill'. I was on the bill's committee which was led by Meacher." Prentice then tried to amend the bill to include prohibition of hunting with dogs. The bill went ahead without this addition. However he, and others, managed to "push Jack Straw into allowing a separate bill which banned hunting".

Massive investment in public services

One of NL's undoubted policy triumphs was its provision for increased investment in the public services: especially after 2000 when it abandoned adherence to the spending plans of its predecessor Conservative government. However this investment had its down side because much of the relevant capital development was funded by the controversial Private Finance Initiative (PFI). The effects of this investment were widely seen by MPs as a victory. Even some radical MPs welcomed these developments, especially where they benefitted their own constituents, despite them having been funded through privatisation of funding. After the financial crisis and the 2010 election the Conservatives were able to stigmatise this expenditure as profligate because it was not underpinned by increased taxation to cover the cost.

Frank Dobson said that his "proudest achievement as Secretary of State for Health (in the 1990s) was *investment in the NHS*. Although controversial, and related to PFI, we started the biggest hospital building programme in UK history. All over the country there are now magnificent hospital buildings, the equipment is up to date and the staff excellent. The most expensive new hospital is in my constituency (Holborn and St. Pancras).I used to go there when it was run down and the equipment was faulty. The National Service Frameworks spelt out what services should be available in every part of the country and in all service areas. These put in place a basic structure that enabled staff. My job was to help NHS staff to do their jobs as they would like to do them. If you want something done better the best people to ask advice of are the people you want to keep on doing it. We introduced measures to spread good practice: which we didn't have prior to 1997."

Dobson continued: "Quality and speed of treatment was massively improved. NHS Direct was very successful .People moan about the National Institute for Clinical Excellence (NICE) but it is so effective that its decisions are used by private health companies in the UK and USA. We introduced the world's first Meningitis C vaccinations." He also considered that his social services policy was successful, particularly in improving the lot of children in care with the 'Quality Protects' framework.

The author, who was a University teacher of health and social services management during this period, agrees with FD's self assessment – except in respect of the effectiveness of NICE and scepticism about PFI (on grounds of excessive long term costs[C5-42]). Lord S. agreed with Dobson: "There is no doubt that the Health Service is infinitely better now and getting the benefit of the extra money going in."

Two MPs had recent positive personal experience of the improved NHS. Most Labour MPs do lead by example by using the NHS personally. This they should do in terms of socialist principles and also to learn from their experiences and use this in Parliamentary and constituency work.

Lynne Jones said: "A lot of money has been put into the Health Services. My husband is going into hospital for a major operation next week and this has brought home to me how much the NHS has improved. It was dying on its knees before this Labour government. We have been inconsistent because we fight hard to fund the NHS though the tax system, to provide free care for all (even the wealthy) but we have means testing for social care services. Before 1997 you would visit schools and head teachers were despairing and feeling that they were not being given funding to do their job properly now things have improved."

Linda Riordan reported: "We have a brand new hospital in Halifax. I see it every month when I visit it with my husband. The Tories had promised one for years. As soon as Labour got in they gave us our new hospital. I think that money ploughed into our NHS has had a positive effect." She also applauded government expenditure on education.

The above comments on the NHS and schools indicate how vital it is that MPs use both the NHS for themselves and their families. That way they gain direct personal experience of its operation and lead by example. Likewise MPs, who are parents, should be users of state education.

In 2001 the Labour government took a decision agreed with the PLP to ask everyone to pay 1% extra on their National Insurance. The money was to go direct to the NHS. That resulted in an increase of £31 billion. In 2009 this sum was in the region of £93 billion annually. Labour tripled the money going into the NHS by that single hike. The Tories voted against this.

NHS staff increased by 26% from 1997. That increase provided 272,000 more employees in the next 10 years. The Health Service employed 89,000 more nurses and 44,000 more doctors, recruiting them through greatly improved salaries. NHS capital spending rose from £1.1 billion to £5.5 billion over the decade to 2007·8. That built 100 new hospitals. These replaced many old and outdated hospitals. By 2010 only one fifth were (built) before 1948.[C5_43] Toynbee and Walker reported that staff productivity in the NHS fell during this period.[C5_44] The author believes that this was possibly due to the introduction of the lax implementation of the "Agenda for Change" job evaluation scheme.

Frank Dobson was ambivalent about the quality of *educational investment* saying: "There have been improvements in school buildings and equipment and most children are getting a better schooling than they were. Some initiatives have benefited children from badly off backgrounds but there has not been enough effort to make things more equal. If something isn't good enough for your own children then it's not good enough for anyone else's."

Graham Stringer argued: "One success has been more money for education in poor areas, for instance for our local College of Further Education. Getting more 16·year·olds into further education and a higher percentage of young people into universities has been a huge success. But if you look at standards in schools it's a more complicated and less successful story – s the official data on school achievement show. Looking at GCSE results suggests that things have gone backwards." Katy Clark declared: "A significant achievement was the amount of money spent in the public sector on health and education and the hospital and school building programmes. We've seen a huge investment in many public services that were drained of money before that: a lasting legacy."

It was argued that NL did not increase spending on education as greatly as it did on health. Total education spending went up by 1% of GDP to 5.8% in 2008. But it was probably sufficient to make a difference to children from poor homes.[C5_45]

Christine McCafferty said: "Education was in a bad state by 1997. Many schools had old buildings with outside WCs. One local high school (in Calder Valley) had 17 portakabins. This now has a wonderful new building. There were too many children per teacher. All our local schools (but one) have improved dramatically in terms of buildings, teacher·pupil ratios and results." She continued: "Our local hospital was in Victorian buildings. We tried for 30 years to get a new hospital and by 1999 we had one – admittedly through PFI. We had one of the highest neo·natal mortality rates in the UK – which has improved. Our new hospital has excellent services and can attract good staff."

Senior backbencher M commented: "There's been a transformation of inner city schools and the Central Hospital Trust in my constituency has the second biggest capital expenditure programme in the country. This spending is not waste or profligate. It's repairing the under·spending of Tory years. What spending went on then was politically driven and put into the more affluent areas. Poor areas were denied access to public spending." Alice Mahon affirmed: "Some of the educational projects were excellent, for example the literacy programme. Some are being back·tracked on now (2009). Sure Start was very good; they recognised that you need to target children when they are very young."

The number of university teachers rose by 10% from 2003. Four fifths of the students who enrolled obtained degrees. This was a low drop·out rate by international standards. However the abolition of student maintenance grants was abolished and replaced by student loans – except for the very poorest – controversially introduced in 1998. Annual tuition fees of £1,000 per year were introduced in 2010. Peter Kilfoyle, a former mature student, stated that the NL government should not have introduced tuition fees for university students.

There were strong plaudits for increased expenditure on education, especially on capital projects for schools where new building had been long neglected. As in the case of hospitals, the sting in the tail was the frequent use of PFI. The initiatives to try to improve educational standards in schools and to enable more working class young people to enter Universities were of more mixed benefit.

During its first term the NL government famously adhered to the spending plans of its Tory predecessor. The big increase in spending on public services in 2002 was partly funded by an increase in National Insurance contributions.[C5-46]

Senior backbencher A argued: "This Government's key action was to *refinance the public services*, which has been an overwhelming success. The public services had fallen into complete ruin during the previous 18 years. In former coalfields a gap was left by the collapse of the Coal Industry Social Welfare Organisation. In my constituency the financing of public services was very poor. There almost all the public services, (schools, doctors and dentists surgeries, hospitals and local government) have been refinanced and refitted. This was our crowning achievement. The objective of the Tories was to have a public realm so impoverished that the middle classes would opt out and private health and education services would expand. The Tories would then use this to justify further tax cuts on the grounds that increasing numbers were not using the public services. The consequence would have been that those left behind were the most deprived and needy."

John Grogan agreed: "We succeeded in regenerating and renewing our public services in terms of education, schools and other services. Some were near collapse when we took over. We've done a good job in investing in those services: the NHS in particular." John Cryer valued them as "a real triumph". Jon Cruddas proposed: "The refinancing of public services should not be underestimated in terms of the sheer fiscal investment in those services." Michael Meacher observed," Much of the new expenditure on the NHS and education was in the form of PFI."

Clare Short was the only MP to give a wholly negative assessment of public services investment. She contended: "Expenditure on the NHS hasn't been well spent due to centralised targets and a Stalinist approach. This has demoralised staff in the public sector rather than getting everyone excited about building a better service." As a contemporary tutor of NHS managers, the author considered that this Stalinist approach was real and was a trade mark of the Milburn, Hutton and Johnson health regimes.

One survey also demonstrated[C5-47] that: "Public satisfaction with health and education improved dramatically over the same period. Satisfaction with the NHS is at an all time high. When Labour gained power in 1997: 34% were satisfied with the NHS, the lowest level since this survey began in 1983. In 2009 satisfaction ... stood at 64%. Reduced waiting times, after the introduction of targets, are a crucial factor in this." In 1996 56% thought that schools taught basic skills well; this rose to 73% by 2008. It is interesting that these public service areas, from which a larger proportion of the population experience benefit and into which money was poured, received great public acceptance and acclaim.

It is also significant that adequate taxes to fund these health and educational developments were never levied.[C5-48] Thus the myth of the feasibility of combining low taxes and high spending was perpetuated by NL. This had serious economic consequences. The NL government purported to deliver good services despite low taxes. The annual average increase in total investment in public services *between 1999-2000 and 2007-8 was just over 16% compared with minus 5% between 1979-80 and 1996-7.*[C5-49] *NL was too afraid to inform the public of this or to come clean with them that taxes had not ben increased sufficiently to cover this increased spending.*

When he quit government in May 2010 Chief Secretary to the Treasury Liam Byrne left a note for this Conservative successor saying there was no money left. The Tory Party has dined out on this indiscretion ever since and milked it heavily during their victorious 2015 general election campaign (see Chapter 12).

Private sector involvement in public services and enterprises

Another aspect of public services policy was privatisation (including PFI). MPs' overviews included: "The NL Government has done much privatisation and in the case of the NHS it has made it worse." (Michael Meacher). "Privatisation has been one of the government's less praiseworthy initiatives, especially the problems that it has created with public transport." (Louise Ellman) and "Thatcher privatised, and used, the receipts (from privatisation) to give tax relief to the well off .We should have reversed this" (Austin Mitchell). Jeremy Corbyn condemned the government's "refusal to take back into public ownership any of the utilities de-nationalised by the Conservatives and pouring money into the privatised train companies."

Frank Dobson asserted: "Experience of private health services throughout the world shows that they tend to carry out a simple menu of treatments on healthy people, leaving the public health services to treat people who were unhealthy. Here (under "patient choice") the private sector got paid 11% more per operation (on NHS patients) than did the NHS. Under contracts they were guaranteed a supply of patients, which the NHS were not – so the private services got paid whether they did the work or not. If they lost a contract at the end of the contract period they were compensated. There was no justification for that.

Toynbee and Walker wrote: "The NHS improved from 1997 on most indicators – as waiting times fell, so use of the private sector shrank – even allowing for the rise in private cosmetic operations … ministers wasted time, political energy and money on non stop re-organisation."[C5-50] Popular appraisal was confirmed by the public adulation for the Opening Ceremony of the 2012 London Olympic Games.

Alice Mahon used her personal experience to evidence her comments: "I dislike creeping privatisation for the health service. I think that Primary Care Trusts (PCTs) were set up to assist this process. I was hit with this when I started the eye treatment campaign" (after she developed a serious progressive eye disease). "The PCT decided there was a 50/50 chance as to whether they were willing to treat me. A special committee looked at whether you were worth giving money to or not. I had to wait a month for consideration and then they turned me down on the grounds it might not work. Finally we did get NICE (National Institute for Clinical Excellence) to change their policy on that. They have a policy that if you get this disease in your second eye they'll treat you. So 'go blind in one eye and we'll treat the other!' It's a national system that these small PCT committees can override the consultant. (Another outcome of NHS privatisation) is hospital based infection which I think is due to poor cleaning. I trained as a nurse and then everything had to be spotless to satisfy matrons. But that's gone and conditions are deteriorating rapidly, particularly when cleaning is contracted out. Also private clinics don't train people; they poach staff from the NHS. This Labour government should hang its head in shame about NHS privatisation."

Lynne Jones alleged: "We are laying the foundations for the break-up of the welfare state. In health and education we are moving to foundation hospitals and academy schools. These are essentially funded by the state and yet independent: as accountability is to a board that is not accountable to the community or elected by them. I think that an incoming Tory Government would say 'thanks very much ' and start to introduce more competition and the fragmentation of health and education. The kind of legacy we will leave will actually make it easier for an incoming Tory Government to break up the welfare state. In mental health services some specialist services are already provided by the private or voluntary sector. It is free at the point of use and contractors are ostensibly accountable. That's only acceptable if they are providing something innovative that is then mainstreamed by the public sector. It is dangerous if decision making is privatised as well. I am not sure that PCTs are sufficiently accountable".

One element of NL's NHS reforms was Foundation Hospital Trusts. This policy never appeared in an election manifesto, nor was it discussed by Labour's National Policy Forum or the Labour Conference. Health Secretary Alan Milburn saw these hospitals as "the battering ram for reform of the Health Service". Milburn believed in giving choice about their own care and treatment to everyone and his answer was to break with the "overly centralised paternalistic model" and "allow choice and diversity of provision".[C5_51] GB, on the other hand, argued: "The consumer can't be sovereign in public services because they don't have sufficient information to make sensible choices."[C5_52] In 2006 the Department of Health did focus group research with NHS patients and found that what most wanted was not choice of hospital so much as a good hospital near their own home with a high standard of personal care and attention.[C5_53]

Another form of NHS privatisation was the Government developing a new private health sector. They established Independent Sector Treatment Centres (ISTCs), new small private hospitals doing less complicated surgery. These were set up through government commissioning. They were paid 15% more than NHS hospitals for the same operations. The centres were guaranteed payment for a fixed number of operations *regardless of how many they actually did!* By 2010 private hospitals undertook only 10% of all elective surgery and their productivity was poorer than that of the NHS.[C5_54]

Turning to education, Linda Riordan believed: "The Churches should not be involved in education; even if they think their beliefs are best for children. One half of my constituency (the poorest end) has a grammar school, so local children get a poor service. Parents can attend church in order to get their children into a church school (a custom) known locally as the "Trinity Trots". I disagree with academies, although I am glad that the children are getting new schools. In the southern part of the constituency we have a good comprehensive and children get a better deal." She added: "I do not want to privatise the NHS. We are chipping bits off now. Doctors' surgeries are already being run by private companies locally and across the country. That's not what a Labour government should be about."

Kelvin Hopkins asserted: "(NL) has been trying to unpick the welfare state, local government and public provision at every level. They have been following the agenda of the neo-cons and neo-liberals, to the right of Thatcher, who wanted local authorities to meet once a year to hand out contracts to private contractors."

Privatised faith schools and academies were not universally welcomed by the communities that they served. As John Harris[C5_55] found that in 2005 academies were being run by private patrons for a down payment of £2 million (an estimated 10% of their true set-up costs.). These patrons could appoint school governors, and through them the staff, and ignore the national curriculum. They were not bound by national pay and conditions for teachers. Patrons could teach their own religious beliefs in these schools. For example: some patrons had creationism taught instead of evolution.

Graham Stringer asserted: "If you look at Blair's policies on privatisation of education and health he changed his views at least twice." Senior backbencher A. said: "We needed to get the higher tax paying middle classes to use the public services which meant that we had to engage in a process of reform which had to be done to get public support. But I think that the way that public services reform was driven and the direction of reform were mistaken. In the end, it hasn't delivered. I mobilised and voted against it. I think we could have built consensus in the community about refinancing public services without the excesses of reform. Some of these views came from my (earlier) experience as leader of a large Labour local authority. The hierarchies and unresponsiveness within health and education had to be deconstructed. In care services for the elderly, nurseries, schools and throughout the NHS there was a strong public service ethos. It seemed that we were moving towards jettisoning that ethos in favour of an ethos of competition and market testing. I believe that this is anathema to an ethos of care."

John McDonnell complained: "The delivery of public services followed a neo-liberal agenda. This was in terms of privatisation. Under NL we privatised more public sector jobs than did Thatcher and Major put together."

Alan Simpson regretted that: "There has been a massive shift from the public to the private sector – even by deceit. Privatisation of public services has played well into Brown's obsession with deregulating markets and having arms-length government. The package that was New Labour involved a shift from the collective to the personal, from the public sector to the private. A shift from an economic strategy that saw itself as interventionist and directing the pace and shape of change to one that was entirely market driven, arms-length, deregulatory and permissive. It was little different from what more Liberal and Conservative administrations have done."

Frank Dobson thought that TB considered that his desired health reforms were going too slowly.

Although the major preoccupation of MPs, relating to privatisation, was with health and education services; there was also concern about public transport and the proposed privatisation of the Post Office.

Senior Backbencher B. said: "Some services: such as transport, ought to remain in the public sector as they are so crucial. I disagreed with some of our privatisation, for instance of air traffic control. I worked to change the detail of legislation on this. I am very much opposed to selling off any part of the Post Office, there is no reason for it." Gordon Prentice added: "Many MPs, including myself, have resisted privatisation of the Post Office in response to outside pressure, for example the threat of the Communication Workers Union to disaffiliate from the Labour Party". He deplored the government's policy on faith schools which, he pointed out: "never went through Party conference". Prentice also raised the issue of increasing University tuition fees in a PLP meeting to object to it."

Linda Riordan asked: "Why did Gordon Brown not stop Post Office Privatisation earlier? He could have been a hero! Who is advising our Prime Minister? Some of my researchers could do better."

She added: "Why did GB wait till MPs resisted before he dropped the privatisation of the Post Office? When he became leader he should have stopped privatisation of the Post Office immediately." She added: "They should have re-nationalised public transport. Local bus services are a nightmare. They *had* to re-nationalise the North East main railway line."

Katy Clark thought that: "Privatisation of public services was a huge mistake." John Cryer claimed: "There have always been relationships between the public and private sector right back into the 1950s and 60s. But, under NL, we went a long way down the path of allowing the private sector far too great a role in running the public sector. We also extended privatisation, for instance QinetiQ was previously a successful company but (when privatised) became a money-making machine for those at the top.

Simon Jenkins argued: "Revolution, reform, change was all. Thatcher said so and Blair agreed. His continued quest for competition and choice … left his party angry and the country baffled.[C5_56]

Jeremy Corbyn contended: "NL paid off their friends in the City with deregulation and privatisation because the money was there to do it. Continuing privatisation of public services damaged the workers through threatening jobs, prospects and pensions." He added: "The government encouraged the privatisation of the building societies which caused problems during the financial crisis from 2008 onwards." John Grogan believed: "We've too often seen the market and the private sector as the only solution – even downgraded the public service ethos. That ethos is many people's motivation for getting up in the morning."

John McDonnell wrote in 2007: "Previously state funded and accountable public services are now subject to competition, private finance initiatives, privatisation, internal markets, cost cutting 'efficiencies' and relentless, ever-changing targets. People who use and depend on services are now known as 'consumers' compelled to exercise 'choice' as if they were in a supermarket. The state is increasingly reduced to funding and commissioning services delivered by the private sector."[C5_57]

However this approach was not even popular with the public. A YouGov survey for the *Guardian* on 25/08/2006 found that only 19% of the public favoured choice in public services but 43% wanted "an end to continuing reforms".

The Private Finance Initiative (PFI) was a device introduced by the previous Conservative government. Its use was increased by NL governments. Instead of government borrowing to fund capital (usually building) developments, public authorities contracted with private financiers to build the required buildings and then rented them back from them. Professor Allyson Pollock (commissioned by Unison) calculated that, on average, PFI projects cost three times as much in interest repayments as direct public borrowing would have done. Public/private partnership was a scheme that was partly financed by PFI and partly by public borrowing.

Senior backbencher A argued: "We should have financed public services investment in a different way. Once you have PFI there is a danger that the staff and other running costs bear the burden of funding the new facility. If there is a squeeze on recurrent non-capital expenditure, that can cause difficulties for existing staff and running costs. I personally have resisted PFI and there's not been much in my constituency." Katy Clark said: "I didn't agree with PFI. I thought it didn't make economic sense."

Colin Challen commented: "Some of the PFI will possibly unravel, as chickens come home to roost". Christine McCafferty stated: "In principle I don't favour schools or hospitals being funded privately. I am against academies. But I am pragmatic about it being used for new hospitals and schools. For example, our new local hospital surpassed government targets on waiting lists last year. It has state of the art technology and therefore attracts top professionals and gives high quality services. Its neo-natal unit is the best in the country and we have a new IVF unit. What matters most is people's health and education. Whether we would have got this quality of services in the old hospital I doubt."

Simon Jenkins[C5-58] believed that GB (as Chancellor) needed to increase public investment without destroying the Government's annual budget. Therefore GB instituted borrowing in such a way that it did not appear in the public accounts. His chosen method was through PFI projects.

Frank Dobson said that he had "no objection to giving private contractors the contract to design, build and maintain a hospital. Such a contract gives the contractor an incentive to build properly as they have to maintain it afterwards. But doubts creep in when contracts include other services: cleaning, telecommunications etc. The Treasury insisted on this. PFI was supposed to transfer risks. But there were no risks in these support services. *I had meetings with Tony (Blair) about the NHS when privatisation was not mentioned. Afterwards civil servants would ring me and say 'Tony Blair wants more privatisation" After I left, that's what they proceeded to bring about. I was totally unhappy about it as I believe that it breaks the concept on which the NHS was based. Secondly, it's extraordinarily expensive.*"

Jenkins[C5-59] reported that, by mid 2003, GB had announced the completion of 450 PFI projects, including 34 hospitals, 39 schools, 34 fire and police stations, 12 prisons and 12 waste projects. By 2005 the NHS had £36 billion to use for PFI schemes with a further £11 billion in the pipeline. By the mid 2000s virtually all NHS investment was being financed by PFI.

Senior backbencher M. proposed: "The kindest view is that it has cut waiting for new schools and hospitals. I've never regarded PFI as being an objective. It's a mechanism. It's given the community a historically unprecedented level of public spending. However it's a tactic that may have sown the seeds of its own future destruction. Some of the contracts were stupid and we'll live to regret them. Our new city hospital is a great specialist and teaching hospital, but it's also our district general hospital. Because it's so specialist it has high running costs. A future Tory government could close it down because it's so expensive, leaving us without a district general hospital."

Alan Simpson lamented that: "There has been a massive move away from public investment. It has taken place through PFI and Public/Private investment schemes, all of which saddled the public sector with massively expensive loans and long-term contracts. They transferred no risk to the private sector but guaranteed income streams to them. This left the public poorer and with services that became progressively less accountable. Brown was the architect of off-balance sheet accounting in government. PFI schemes could all be funded but didn't appear on the books – although they *were public sector borrowing.* Extortionate rates of interest were charged (average 16.4%). The public paid these as a result of private borrowing. Public debt was branded as 'bad debt ' and private debt as 'good debt'."

PFI was used as an accounting trick which concealed public investment from the public and also from the International Monetary Fund and allied institutions. However, it was far from cost effective; it did not provide good value for money and built up debts for the public sector stretching far into the future. The financial crisis of 2008 and after exacerbated these problems. After 2010 these debts would lead to hospital failures, closures and threats to the financial viability of other public services.

Foreign and Defence Policy

This turned out to be one of the most controversial policy areas, as it had been throughout the Labour Party's history, especially when it came to issues of war and peace.

Reducing worldwide poverty was one of NL's consistent overseas priorities. It was also probably the least controversial within the Party. The Government signed an agreement that, by 2013, it would reach the United Nations aid target of 0.7 % of GNP per year which previous Labour Governments had promised but failed to achieve, despite the target's existence during the previous 40 years . Amazingly the incoming Coalition Government of 2010 also adopted this policy.

Toynbee and Walker[C5-60] were positive in their assessment: "The UK proved to be one of the most pro‑poor and least protectionist OECD (Organization for Economic Co‑operation and Development) donors. By 2005, Labour claimed to have lifted 2 million people permanently out of poverty each year, around the world." UK Aid spending rose from 2000 onwards to levels comparable with those of France and Germany and by 2005 it exceeded them.

The Make Poverty History campaign pushed the G8 leaders (at the Gleneagles summit in 2015) to make commitments on and to write off debts for Africa. The debts of the world's 15 poorest states were paid off.

Katy Clark suggested: "The big issue was foreign policy and our orientation. Labour was at the forefront of some of the right arguments in terms of international development; but nobody remembers that because of Iraq and our other foreign policy interventions." Jon Cruddas mentioned "setting up the Department for International Development (DFID) and working to combat poverty in developing countries," as being one of NL's positive achievements. It was surprising that relatively few MPs interviewed highlighted this area of policy as a success.

Toynbee and Walker[C5-61] praised the work of Clare Short (and other ministers) in overseas development.

Short herself said: "The old Colonial Office became the Ministry of Overseas Development, but the Tories later took it back into the Foreign Office. In 1997 it became a separate department again and we became a world leader. We influenced the World Bank, getting it more focussed on systematically reducing poverty, changing the terms of trade, ending conflict and environmental agreements including developing countries and assisting them. If you then gang up with Bush, declare wars, behave in a deeply reactionary way in the UN and have a sort of tokenistic development policy where you spend some money on the poor, that isn't consistent development."

She continued: "If you really intend development you've got to change the way you operate on the international stage. For a time we did well and then, post Iraq, it became almost a piece of triangulation.

"Perhaps the overall verdict has to be 'two stars for achievement' – tis pity that warmongering undid the good will which should have accompanied this impressive legacy for the Third World."

B*lair's Wars:* This was the area of overseas policy, about which many MPs were intensely critical. The greatest source of resentment was the war in Iraq. MPs reflected first on the causation of Britain's proactive involvement in that and other conflicts.

Jeremy Corbyn recalled" "British troops have been in action somewhere ever since we (NL) were elected. We might debate (the legitimacy of) Yugoslavia and Sierra Leone. The reality is that we sold our foreign policy to the neo‑cons in the USA. In his own defence, Blair said (at a PLP meeting) that he was the first Labour Prime Minister that had to deal with a Republican US President throughout most of his term of office (compared to Attlee/ Truman, Wilson/Johnson, Callaghan/Carter)." However "a veteran Liberal Democrat MP" recently told *Guardian* journalist Michael White that: "*When asked why he didn't get more concessions out of George Bush, Blair said: 'I actually agreed with him'.*"

Corbyn continued: "Of course the UK were number one in the world in supporting Bush without ever challenging him. The profundity of the (resulting) damage to the Labour Party cannot be underestimated. We have lost probably 100,000 members through these wars. They disillusioned many Labour voters and, while many turned out and vote for us in 2005, it was a very reluctant Labour vote." He continued: "In international terms, the worst policy failure was the lies told over Iraq. *I never had much faith in New Labour but I did not imagine that they would be so keen on wars.* Foreign policy was sold out to the neo-cons in the US." Lord S. argued: "The Iraq war did not have the same United Nations sanction as did the Afghanistan war and therefore was less legitimate."

Robin Cook went to Beaconsfield, in 1983, to support TB as their by-election candidate. This was immediately after the UK victory in the Falklands war. He surmised: "I have often wondered in recent years whether that formative experience of being turned over at the polls by a governing party led by a war hero has not left Tony Blair too inclined to associate military victory with political popularity."[C5_62] Unfortunately TB's possible tendency could have been reinforced by the apparent relative success and legitimacy of his first military ventures in Bosnia and Sierra Leone. When it came to Iraq, circumstances differed and the war was very unpopular and allegedly a breach of international law.

Kelvin Hopkins claimed: "There was clearly a deal done privately with the US neo-cons prior to 1997 and that deal was that the USA would go easy on the UK and allow us to have our Labour government provided that Blair supported US aspirations and interventions internationally … The first time the U.S. neo-cons got their way with Blair was after 9/11. Then Rumsfeld probably said: 'We've now got our chance to attack Iraq and build bases there'. Blair went along with that and used every trick to drag the PLP through the lobbies to make sure he got that decision."

Chris Mullin argued: "Blair's biggest mistake was to link us umbilically to the worst American president of my lifetime – with bad consequences. It led us into a quagmire: Guantanamo Bay and Abu Ghraib. Because of (those mistakes) it's now difficult for us to take a credible stance on human rights abroad as these are quoted back to us."

John McDonnell deplored that: "NL transformed us from being a party with a commitment to peace and conflict prevention and resolution into a party committed to military adventures in alliance with the most reactionary US president since Reagan." He wrote: "New Labour's anything but ethical foreign policy is a series of disaster zones, which have left Britain increasingly isolated internationally. The British and U.S. governments have taken on the role of self-appointed enforcers of the new world order (or rather: disorder) that has emerged since the end of the cold war."[C5_63]

Peter Kilfoyle described the Labour Government's position on the Iraq war as being "part of a wider genuflection to the US superpower. It was worse than that done by any previous UK government. The extent to which this was done was an exercise in self-abasement."

The war in Iraq came to dominate TB's political legacy and to affect the Labour Party's electability in the long and short term. It destroyed Britain's credibility in the developing and Muslim worlds.

Katy Clark believed: "The Labour government's big policy mistake was Iraq. Unfortunately it's going to be our lasting legacy. We've lost a huge amount of support because of Iraq. Everything else pales into insignificance."

Michael Meacher claimed: "We did worse in the 2005 election because of the Iraq war, the most important of the five wars into which Blair took us. One of the two biggest criticisms of Blair is that he took us into an (possibly) illegal war." Christine McCafferty said she was "unhappy about the Iraq war. I personally don't link Iraq to Palestine but people in Iraq see a link." Gordon Prentice had raised the Iraq war in the Parliamentary Committee and PLP meetings to object to it. John Cryer asserted: "The biggest downside (of NL Governments) was the Iraq war which undermined trust in the government."

Senior backbencher M. said: "Any achievements of Tony Blair must be measured against his Iraq policy. Many people originally came to the conclusion that it was justified but later came to the view that they had been misled. In retrospect the war was seen to be a mistake and never achieved what they wanted. This is the block to a better evaluation of Tony Blair's government. It's prevented the generation that's only known this Labour government from accepting us, and ourselves from taking the moral high ground. The good things that we've done have been obscured."

Linda Riordan believed: "The Iraq war was our biggest failure. I voted against the war and for the public inquiry. I consider it was TB's biggest error and his legacy." Backbencher P recalled he had "voted against the government on the Iraq war. It was the first time I had voted against them since 1997. I raised questions in the house both to TB and the Foreign Secretary. I could not support the Government on this but voted for the amendment, then abstained". Alan Simpson voted against the war in Parliament and was prominent in the "Labour against the War" movement.

Clare Short resigned as a cabinet minister over the war but, some thought, belatedly. On March 18 2003 a total of 139 Labour MPs voted against Britain joining the Iraq war. It was the largest Backbench rebellion in modern British politics, as Cowley, reported.[C5_64]

The war in Iraq was allegedly a breach of international law: it was not sanctioned by an appropriate United Nations resolution. Allegedly the Attorney General was leant up on by TB to change his initial judgement and declare it legal.

Robin Cook, believed that during the summer of 2002 TB succeeded in convincing President Bush that they would secure more international and domestic support for an attack on Iraq if the President put the issue before the UN.[C5_65] Cook reported (2003) that in late September 2002, TB presented the infamous dossier, justifying the war, to Parliament. Cook thought that "the bulk of the document was derived from what we knew about Saddam's arsenal of chemical and biological weapons as it had been in 1991: chemical and biological agents that Saddam had retained for a decade would long ago have degenerated to the point where they were of no operational use. Half the text relating to Iraq's weapons capacity is drawn from the period before 1998."[C5_66] In the aftermath of war this claim (that Saddam Hussain could deploy weapons of mass destruction in 45 minutes) was proved false. Not only were chemical and biological weapons never fired by Saddam's forces but, none could be found anywhere, never mind within a 45 minute radius of the artillery emplacements from the Hutton Inquiry. Cook continued: "We have now discovered not only that the intelligence was uncorroborated and came from a single source but that he, in turn, was reporting hearsay from another uncorroborated single source." Many of Cook's surmises were cofirmed in the Chilcot Report(published 2016).[C5_67]

Roger Berry concluded: "Iraq was a policy disaster. There was no moral justification for it. I believe there was no doubt it was contrary to international law. There was no UN mandate. Iraq was not threatening other countries. It turned out that the weapons (of mass destruction) weren't there. It exacerbated the situation in the Middle East. Al Quaeda was not in Iraq (when the war broke out) but they are there now. The war created terrorism. It was a wrong decision, one of the government's worst."

John McDonnell wrote: "The 2003 invasion of Iraq, which broke international law and defied the United Nations, has resulted in untold harm and misery. Launched on the basis of doctored intelligence, the occupation unleashed a bloody civil war and resulted in the deaths of up to 655,000 civilians."[C5_68]

Cowley reported that, since President Bush's famous "axis of evil" speech in January 2002, there had been much concern amongst Labour MPs about the possibility of an invasion of Iraq, especially an invasion without a UN resolution authorising it.[C5_69]

An Early Day Motion (EDM) put forward by Alice Mahon in March 2002 expressed "deep unease at the prospect that HM Government might support US military action against Iraq." The motion was signed by 133 Labour MPs, the same number as had rebelled during the whole 1997 parliament. A contemporary slogan of Labour whips was reported by Cowley, to be: "Do you support regime change in Baghdad or Downing St?"[C5-70] Alice Mahon recalled: "It was difficult being approached by the whips … sometimes not very nicely. Another example was when I took a different view from most on the Bosnian war. About two dozen of us said it was illegal and a settlement could be made. (Some called it 'the war of Clinton's penis' because he needed a distraction from the Lewinsky affair at the time). Some of us thought it was the beginning of Blair's war policies which he adopted when he made his Chicago speech about intervention."

The British public largely resented the UK Government's involvement in the war but remained supportive of UK troops who were involved in it. Two million people marched through London to protest against the war shortly before Britain and the USA invaded. One reason for the unpopularity of the Iraq war was that people in the UK did not support it.

Robin Cook considered that "Number 10's belief that it could get away with ignoring public opposition to the war was based on two calculations. The first was that when the war started a majority would swing behind our troops." The polls did reflect this support, but it was for the troops not the government. Secondly that the war would be short and so would be the political fall out." Cook continued: "I believe Tony genuinely expected that delivering victory in Baghdad would wipe the slate clean on the political controversy over whether the war was justified."[C5-71] This hope proved vain.

John Keegan believed: "The (Iraq) war was mysterious in almost every respect. Mystery surrounded the justification for going to war. The war was launched because Saddam Hussein refused to co-operate with United Nations inspectors in their search for his forbidden weapons of mass destruction. Yet even after his defeat—such weapons eluded discovery."[C5-72]

The Government also pressurised the media to spin the progress of the war in way favourable to themselves. There was certainly much press manipulation. John Pilger reported that Rageh Omaar confessed to him concerning his reports for the BBC on the victorious entry into Baghdad: "I hold my hand up and say that one didn't press the most uncomfortable buttons hard enough". Pilger asserted: "The sheer magnitude of Iraqi suffering in the onslaught had little place in the news." Dan Rather (of CBS news) told Pilger that had journalists questioned the deceptions that led to the Iraq war, instead of amplifying them, the invasion would never have happened."[C5-73]

Moving on to the war in Afghanistan which commenced in 2001, Lord S. said: "The Afghan War has been much criticised but it is a completely mandated and UN supported policy. The General Assembly called for this war. Obviously it's tragic that we are losing troops in Afghanistan; but I don't blame the government; they were right in going in."

Conversely Alice Mahon protested: "I have a strong objection to the war in Afghanistan and will not re-join the Labour Party until we end our participation in it." Jeremy Corbyn objected to "lies told about the Afghan war under both TB and GB." He continued: "As we speak now, in 2009, the debate is about helicopters and equipment for Afghanistan. This is nonsense; the issue is not about that but about whether troops should be there at all."

Rawnsley[C5-74] suggested that TB was more forthcoming in the original justifications for military intervention in Afghanistan than was Bush. TB argued in Parliament that the West helped to create the monster of Al Quaeda by allowing Afghanistan to become a failed state after the Soviet Union retreated. In talks with Afghan President Karzai, Blair pledged that the West would not betray Afghanistan again.

The question of the *affordability of UK defence policy* was raised by some MPs (in the context of Afghanistan). Toynbee and Walker reported that troop numbers in Afghanistan rose immediately after the exit from Iraq. They suggested that the 2009 defence cuts were made purely because the budget could not support both helicopters and fighters.[C5-75]

NL's peace-making success was in *Northern Ireland.* The Good Friday Agreement was hard won and proved to be reasonably durable although rogue terrorist elements such as the Real IRA continued to cause occasional trouble for some years afterwards.

Chris Mullin proposed that: "One of Blair's biggest achievements was peace in Northern Ireland. This had eluded all previous British Prime Ministers. Blair put a great deal of personal effort into this." Clare Short also hailed "Peace in Northern Ireland as a great achievement … but the work for it started well before 1997. Whitelaw started talks with Sinn Fein and SDLP leaders. He put in an enormous amount of effort. Major and Blair (as opposition Leader) did their own bits. NL spoke as though they had done it all: but that's not true."

Without the humane and sensitive approach of the late Mo Mowlam it is doubtful whether the Good Friday agreement would have been reached. She recalled: (Mowlam, 2002) "I decided to split my time between the talks and talking to the folk outside so that people didn't feel cut out of what was going on in the talks – not to say anything about what was being said, but just to be engaging with others I thought was important. I think it is very important in any negotiations to be as inclusive as possible. People like to know in broad terms what is going on, particularly if they have been involved in earlier negotiations."[C5_76]

Shamefully the *Daily Telegraph* mooted the idea of keeping Mo out of negotiations with David Trimble because Blair had had to take over from her at one point. But they also admitted, correctly, that Sinn Fein and the SDLP would be very unhappy if this happened.

Of the successful outcome Mo reported in 2002: "Bertie Ahern (Irish PM) said the agreement marked 'a new beginning for us all'; it was 'a day we should all treasure'. I finally went round to the delegation rooms to thank everyone for their efforts. I found a number of people who were very emotional. Many in the building had worked for years to get where we had got."[C5_77]

Alastair Campbell reported that Bill Clinton played a key role in bringing the negotiations to a successful conclusion and that TB thanked his staff, which was a rare event![C5_78]

Christine McCafferty was the only MP to raise Middle East issues. She said: "We've failed in *Palestine* and failed to secure peace in the Middle East. There will be no peace in the region unless we have a final settlement. The problem is that the USA has the money and clout and we don't have the same leverage in Israel. My constituents are very interested in the Middle East; I get many letters about foreign policy. We failed to follow the right policies in Palestine. We could have punched above our weight."

Nuclear weapons and nuclear power have long figured in the concerns of Labour MPs and members of the Labour Party at all levels. However an alleged Party machine conspiracy (nobbling the Conference Arrangements Committee) prevented the topic being discussed at Labour's Annual Conference from the millennium. This embargo on discussion was lifted at Conference 2015. This embargo partly explains why Labour was unwilling to discuss the renewal of the Trident Missile system with the Scottish National Party during the 2015 general election campaign

Senior Backbencher B. was the only MP to mention the UK's nuclear arsenal. He said: "The world has changed and we now have to deal with nuclear weapons and even accidents from nuclear power. We have to have effective policies to deal with the threat of nuclear accidents."

According to Toynbee and Walker, the defence budget was stretched to cover Trident and the Eurofighter (the new aircraft intended to replace the Tornado). They contended that the NL Government did not make a good case, or indeed any case, to justify Trident renewal.[C5_79]

In respect of *Supporting international organisations*, both Jon Cruddas and Jeremy Corbyn praised the government for being a party to establishing the International Criminal Court. Corbyn applauded Britain re-joining UNESCO. Austin Mitchell criticised NL for favouring the UK's membership of, and participation in, the European Union "without understanding what that really meant". He was the only MP interviewed who mentioned the EU. This was despite a Blair presidency of the EU, the rejected constitution and the Lisbon Treaty signing occurring during NL's term and the growth of support for UKIP.

The UK's relations with the EU were undoubtedly affected by the differing attitudes of TB and GB to the EC. TB was strongly and outwardly pro-European whereas GB was lukewarm and reluctant to be assertive in his relations with Europe. When it came to dealing with the European treaty, following GB's obtaining the premiership, he became inactive when confronted with difficulties. Labour's refusal keep its manifesto promise of a referendum on the European treaty was causing hostility in the right wing press. GB metaphorically stuck his head in the sand. The Europe Minister was forced to take the legislation for ratifying the treaty through Parliament by making the debates as boring as possible (a tactic also mentioned by backbencher B see Chapter 9).

Devolution and Constitutional Reform were rated by most interviewees who mentioned them as positive achievements of NL. The big issues in this area were: devolution to Scotland, Wales, Northern Ireland and a new governing body for Greater London. The latter initiative came in the wake of Thatcher's abolition of the Greater London Council (GLC). Its replacement had been continuously promised by the Labour Party and Labour Governments since. The last Labour Government, led by James Callaghan, attempted to introduce devolution for Scotland but it had been thwarted by a wrecking amendment tabled by a Scottish backbencher which required an unrealistically high percentage of all Scots to agree in a ballot (see Chapter 6).

Tentative steps were taken towards House of Lords reform and the creation of a reformed second chamber of Parliament However the options to be voted on were so arranged that it was statistically impossible for any one option to win.

Devolution was the personal project of former Labour Leader John Smith and Donald Dewar who became Scotland's first First Minister. Under NL government there were referenda on devolution in Scotland and Wales. In Scotland 74% of the 62% who voted were in favour. In Wales only 50% of those eligible to vote turned out and only just over half of them voted for a Welsh Assembly. Devolution both shifted power away from Westminster and created new and effective Parliaments in Scotland and Wales. As Toynbee and Walker stated, this made "the edifice by the Thames look even more antique."[79] The voting systems for elections to the new Parliaments used proportional representation. This was NL's tacit acknowledgement of Westminster's backwardness in adhering to the first past the post system.

Clare Short cited devolution as being "One of the early achievements of the Government. This came out of commitments that were made well before the NL era. It was such a strong commitment in the 1997 manifesto that it had to be carried out." Kelvin Hopkins concurred: "The NL government was committed to devolution. It was known that Blair loathed it because it gave power away to alternative institutions. He wanted power centralised with Downing St. in control. Blair went to great lengths to ensure that devolution did not produce majority Labour governments that would have produced more socialist programmes and challenged the government."

John Grogan suggested: "Devolution will be an enduring legacy in Scotland, Wales and Northern Ireland." Jon Cruddas argued that: "devolution was one of the government's greatest achievements".

Chris Mullin welcomed the Freedom of Information Act as a "Government achievement".

Shortly after the 2001 general election, Robin Cook described the reform of the House of Lords as a major item of unfinished business. He recounted the Commons debate on options on reforming the Lords on 4/02/03. The Commons was required to vote separately on a number of conflicting options. However the majority against the wholly elected option was, to Cook's surprise only 17 votes. However the next vote on an 80% elected chamber was also lost; but by only three votes. In the end every option for change had been defeated. Only the Commons can change the composition of the Lords. Cook believed that many MPs preferred the status quo because "They relish the fact that the Commons enjoys undisputed primacy and that so long as the Lords has no legitimacy it will have no real powers."[C5_80]

Representative Democracy and Loss of Public Trust

Another policy area identified as being significant, by interviewed MPs, *was representative democracy; sometimes linked with loss of public trust.* Distrust of politicians seemed to rise to an all-time high under NL. Posters on many types of demonstration featured the slogan 'BLIAR'. MPs John Cryer and Christine McCafferty identified two causes that were not new. NL's addiction to spin and related campaigning techniques had, according to Lynne Jones, also spawned distrust which she attributed additionally to the First Past the Post electoral system having fallen into disrepute. Public concerns grew after the Parliamentary expenses scandal of Summer 2009.

John Cryer lamented: "People say that they don't trust you. You ask why and eventually you come back to Iraq: the biggest down side of NL's record". Christine McCafferty had a different interpretation saying: "I think that public trust was a problem prior to NL. I would compare the job done by GB and TB favourably to that once done by the Tories. They have succeeded in making people believe that they are trustworthy and electable although I believe that's an illusion."

Lynne Jones said: "The type of methods for local campaigning put forward by NL mean that you don't build up trust. The lack of trust is not just with the Labour Party; it's with politics in general. When TB came in people thought that they could trust him. He was 'new and straight'; they thought 'he'll be open and honest with us'. They now realise that was never the case. They were manipulated. Now Cameron has come along he can't do the same. People have been bitten once; they are cynical. She continued: "The general public is very cynical especially after the MPs' expenses issue. But that's our fault. We talked about transparency but didn't do it. It will take a long time to rebuild trust in politics. The problem now is that we don't have the members on the ground." (ie in 2009).

LJ was joined by six other MPs in citing the then recent MPs' expenses scandal as having generated distrust and disillusion. Katy Clark thought: "One of the reasons we lost the 2010 election was that people no longer trusted the government to tell the truth. That's one of the reasons why the MPs' expenses crisis related to where the British public were. There's a belief that politicians don't tell the truth and that it's all spin." Kelvin Hopkins, Chris Mullin, Clare Short and Graham Stringer all mentioned the anger and hostility they encountered on electors' doorsteps in respect of the MPs' expenses issue.

The issue of MPs' wrongful expenses claims became public when GB's Government was already unpopular. Stephen Glover in the *Independent* (quoted in Winnett and Rayner)[C5-81] contended: "The expenses story will be written about by historians in 100 years. It will become part of journalistic lore … the day to day presentation of often complicated facts was a challenge which the paper brilliantly met."

Private Eye (also quoted in Winnett and Rayner)[C5-82] summarised the way the expenses system worked:

"Those expense claims rules in full:

1. All claims made by MPs are within the rules.

2. All rules are made by MPs

3. Er …

4. That's it."

The intervention of Speaker Michael Martin to try to prevent the full disclosure of MPs' expense claims was disgraceful and led to his unprecedented dismissal. He shrugged off criticism by Labour's Kate Hoey who suggested that "it would be best simply to publish MPs' expenses as quickly as possible". The expenses scandal led to a major loss of public confidence in Labour (and politicians generally). This included abysmal results and doorstep responses in EU and local elections in 2009 and arguably also in the general election of 2010. The whole issue, and its fallout, are discussed further in Chapter 9.

There is no doubt that the public's respect for, and valuation of, MPs took a nosedive after the expenses revelations. This is evidenced by responses to the author from Constituency Labour Party secretaries (see below in this Chapter).

Lynne Jones said she favoured "proportional representation for Westminster general elections. I regret that the recommendations of the Jenkins report on Proportional Representation have not been implemented".

Toynbee and Walker[C5_83] agreed with her. They attributed the decision to TB's reluctance to opt for a system which entailed that the numbers of MPs elected reflected the percentage of votes obtained because, on the basis of recent past results, that would disadvantage Labour.

NL's attitude to the civil service

Lord S. voiced concern about the role of the civil service in our democracy. He said: "They are good at giving advice to ministers but are weak at running things. In a sense Mrs Thatcher was right to set up agencies and about having to set targets and push people. Public services should be as good as private services." Frank Dobson echoed the latter view.

Paving the way to realise a Conservative Government's aspirations?

An issue, raised by three MPs (in 2009) was the question as to whether some NL policies would pave the way for an incoming (then presumed to be Tory) government to develop these policies further.

John Grogan foresaw: "We've shifted the public and political centre of gravity in relation to a whole range of public services. So it will be difficult for the Tories to dismantle them if they get into government. Just as Mrs Thatcher shifted Labour on the market, we've shifted the centre of gravity of the Tories on public services." Events after the 2010 election did not bear out his optimism.

In a similar vein, Colin Challen proposed: "The country's mood has changed and, *due to NL policies, we are now locked into a pink version of Thatcherism rather than a true blue version.*" More pessimistically, Linda Riordan thought: "We're now in a situation where the Tories are likely to come into government and privatise our precious NHS – and we've made it easy for them to do that through our privatisations and the creation of foundation hospitals which are ripe for privatisation." How right she turned out to be in respect of the incoming Coalition Government, even though this threat did not appear in the 2010 Conservative manifesto.

Summary of MPs' views on NL Governments' Policy Record

Examples were given of policies delivered since 1997, which previous Labour governments had promised, but never implemented. These included the NMW, increased statutory holidays, free bus passes for pensioners and devolution for Scotland and Wales. The record on economic management, as assessed by MP respondents, apparently contained the seeds of its own destruction through the financial crisis of 2008. It also increased economic inequality as highly paid blue collar jobs disappeared. These economic trends were only partly mitigated by the NL government's well intentioned policies to combat child and family poverty.

Public investment in public services was seen as a triumph and the quality of the NHS and state education were improved. However that was attended by increasing use of private finance to fund developments (especially capital projects). That strategy contained its own cost time bomb which has yet to explode fully. It was also accompanied by a failure to tax sufficiently to fund the developments without large scale long term public borrowing. Provision of social rented housing was allowed to wither on the vine.

Northern Ireland's peace settlement was regarded as one of NL's major successes. The government's record on waging war was much criticised, especially in respect of the war in Iraq, and the government tactics that preceded it. Overall there were 13 years of mixed policy achievements. There were some triumphs but also significant tragedies involving the abandonment of many of Labour's original core principles.

Part 2 Constituency Labour Party Secretaries' Policy Evaluations

The judgements made about NL government policies by Backbench MPs are discussed in the context of judgements of some contemporary political writers about them. Unless an issue was *not* discussed in the context of political commentaries above, other writers' commentaries are not included here. Hence the relative brevity of Part 2.

The 27 Constituency Labour Party (CLP) secretaries surveyed were volunteers living throughout England, Scotland and Wales. To facilitate comparison with MPs' views, when assessing NL's policy record, the first set of questions were the same as those put to MP respondents. These were designed to identify which they considered were NL's most successful and unsuccessful policies? They were asked what should we learn, positive and negative, from the prioritisation and implementation of these. They were then asked direct questions about NL's policy record in a survey type questionnaire. All their responses are discussed below.

Economic and fiscal policy

CLP Secretaries regarded economic and fiscal policies as being of paramount importance. Here they anticipated the apparent priorities of the electorate in the 2015 general election. Their main preoccupation was with the lack of sufficiently strong regulation of key financial institutions. Secretary Oliver believed: "Deregulation of the markets brought on the financial crisis." Mike added: "They should have taken a fairer line on tax, the city and bankers." William suggested: "They should have had more progressive taxation and tighter financial regulation but should have rewarded real wealth creation, that is, where it creates rewarding jobs … they should have rewarded strong long-term investment in green jobs and lifestyles."

Bob made a general comment about economic policy: "You need to take hard decisions earlier or they come back to haunt you." He continued: "On the whole the government had quite a good record on regulation but there are areas, such as banking, where regulation has been lamentably poor."

Fred proposed: "The government should have been a champion of free and innovative enterprise but should also have challenged the growth of monopolies such as supermarkets, banks and the media conglomerates. They should have placed more emphasis on the role of science and technology, engineering and design in the economy." Colin summed up: "They should not have adopted neo-liberal economic policies."

Other secretaries were also preoccupied with the non-egalitarian aspect of economic policies and the way in which NL allowed the market to work along neo-liberal lines without appropriate government controls.

Eric asserted: "Orwell (in *Animal Farm*) gave us the idea of four legs good, two legs bad. NL has been a bit like that with the public and private sectors. The UK needs a healthy mixed economy; that was not fully recognised." He continued: "NL needs to understand that we don't owe the rich a living. We have entrepreneurs who would run a mile from risk taking. They run enterprises designed to tap into government expenditure. You are only guaranteed two things from consultants: the first is their invoices and the second is that they will put everything into growing those invoices." Simon claimed: "There has been too much reliance on big business."

Fred proposed: "The government should have been a champion of free and innovative enterprise but should have challenged the growth of monopolies such as supermarkets, banks and the media conglomerates. They should have placed more emphasis on the role of science and technology, engineering and design in the economy." Colin summed up: "They should *not* have adopted neo-liberal economic policies."

Housing and tackling UK Poverty

This policy area was mentioned by a handful of secretaries. William argued that there "has not been enough investment in social housing". Surprisingly little was said about this topic by secretaries overall. John criticised the disempowerment of local government (which included giving them, for the most part, only an arms length role in managing social housing). Little was said spontaneously about the national minimum wage, which was welcomed by William. However responses to a direct question showed that it was appreciated by the majority of secretaries.

Yvonne praised "the strong support given to families." William welcomed "support for poor families and the Sure Start programme." Diane praised "The great social reforms which benefit the many." Sure Start and helping poor families were widely welcomed in secretaries' responses to direct questions.

Workplace and trades union rights:

Mike believed *"NL neglected the consensus with the trades unions that now needs rebuilding.* William thought: "Family friendly working arrangements need improving." Irene considered: "There should have been more influence given to trades unions in policy making." Secretaries said relatively little about this policy area (it was discussed in detail in Chapter 4.)

Civil rights and law and order

These were subjects about which TB had waxed eloquent before, and after, becoming Prime Minister. William said: "I approve of the policing and crime policies of the government although the police have been bogged down with too much paperwork." Eric alleged: "Too many police complain about their paperwork burden, but it's a cover. What they are actually doing is hiding in offices where they feel safe away from the action of policing." Fred thought: "The emphasis on crime and policing has been a great help." Simon said that (in general) "there has been too much control." Bob wanted a change to "genuinely progressive policies in the Ministry of Justice/Home Office areas." Policing policy featured in only one backbencher's policy evaluations.

Home Office Quarterly Reports indicated that around 15,000 extra police officers were recruited – taking police numbers to record levels. The new ancillary role of community support officer was created. Overall crime levels fell, but some types of violent crime, particularly gun and knife crime, increased.

William "strongly supported the Human Rights Act." Implying criticism of the NL government, he proposed "opening up and democratising our public institutions". Irene considered that "more influence in decision-making should have been given to the voluntary sector."

None of the secretaries mentioned NL's agenda for non social class equalities. These related to gender, race, ethnicity, disability and sexual orientation. However this was a marked preoccupation of Parliamentary respondents. As Owen Jones contended: "The left continues to champion the most marginalised groups in society – as indeed it should – but all to often this has been in search of something to replace the working class with."[83]

Investment in public services

For CLP secretaries, as well as MPs, investment in public services (notably the NHS and state education) was a very positive development. William applauded "strong investment in public services", but added the reservation that: "We should have moved to service entitlements, rather than targets, and put these into law. This would have been good in itself and would have confounded a future Tory government." He continued: "There have been too many targets, although these did play a positive role for some years." He also highlighted the need for: "further expansion of the Universities and of education generally". Mike valued "NL government focus on education."

Yvonne welcomed: "Past increased financial support of the government for health and education, but I would like to see more in future." Likewise, Adele appreciated investment in the NHS but regretted: "The Government's focus on patient choice when people would prefer good and close services rather than so-called 'choice'."

As mentioned earlier in this Chapter, Government polls demonstrated that the public was more interested in having a good public hospital situated near their home than in patient choice.

Diane criticised "the way in which some of the reforms in health and education have been implemented". She continued: "We should discard the tick box mentality that seems to be running the NHS at present … and is in danger of taking over the education system too. Proper reforms of these services should be done with a view to providing services to people. There should be not so much emphasis on 'efficiency' (with regard to the NHS) or 'league tables' (which are destroying the education of our children)."

Privatisation of public services and enterprises

In respect of privatisation, NL's policies were even more strongly disliked among CLP secretaries than they were by many MPs.

Keith resented the reluctance of NL governments "to contemplate re-nationalisation or public ownership. All public services have become an extension of the fiefdom of the private sector. The government, and Party, must become aware that there is a contradiction in providing services for the public and making a profit. Thatcher blurred the edges of that contradiction and Blair blithely carried it on. I fear that we have become dependent on the injection of private capital as a quick fix to public sector problems without considering why private capitalists would want to inject their funds."

Eric indicated that public sector enforcement of private sector contracts had been less than rigorous: "When people, or organisations, are paid for providing a service to the government, there need to be very strict controls in place to ensure that they provide value for money". He also suggested that the government had undervalued the public sector, saying: "I feel the record of the public sector needs to be re-evaluated upwards". William said: "PFI projects have been too loosely controlled." Adele called for "the railways to be re-nationalised".

Foreign Policy

Like the MPs, Secretaries had much to say about foreign policy. William, who is professionally involved in foreign affairs, applauded the government for "its adoption and retention of the Millennium Development goals, for aid to poor countries and its overseas aid policy generally." He praised "the government's support for the UN – most of the time". He called for "Free and fair trade" and advocated "stronger environmental policies" in this context.

In respect of Blair's wars, John disliked "the government's 'liberal interventionism" (abroad)" and called for it to end – "They should start reducing the armed forces to a realistic level." William said: "I objected to military intervention where it was not legal, but added: "I supported it where *it was legal and* it was clearly needed to avert catastrophe, for example in Sierra Leone."

William also deplored the retention, and renewal, of the Trident nuclear missile system. Adele rejected the government's policy on nuclear arms. She called for total UK nuclear disarmament.

One CLP secretary expressed concern about UK polices supportive to Israel; as did one MP. William sought: "a trade boycott of Israel unless they reverse the illegal settlements." He asked: "Why do we castigate other countries for flouting United Nations resolutions but let Israel continue to do so?"

Only one MP mentioned the EU and only secretary William did so. He wanted a more pro-European foreign policy and EU enlargement under the Community's rules.

None of the secretaries mentioned peace in Northern Ireland, an achievement highly rated by some MPs.

Public democracy

Oliver made a serious criticism when he declared that: "Presidential-style government is not viable, nor is celebrity-style politics. Our government must get back to probity, transparency and cabinet government." William called for: "necessary constitutional reform" and, in response to NL's performance, for "a reversal of the centralisation of power and decision making".

Secretaries shared with some MPs a view that the time has come to re-empower local government and Parliamentary democracy both of which had been severely weakened by Thatcherite style Government – Conservative and Labour.

Irene saw the need for "an increase in the influence of Labour councils in Government decision and policy-making." John said: "Local government has been run down and needs rebuilding". He implied criticism of NL's affection for the first past the post system for Westminster elections. William and Adele called for "reform of the voting system to include some form of proportional representation for all elections".

Loss of public trust

MPs raised the issue of loss of public trust in the NL Government. CLP Secretaries were asked a specific question about this in their straw poll. This straw poll was set up as an opinion poll questionnaire to CLP Secretaries participating in research for the book. However because 27 was not a representative sample of 540 CLP secretaries, the results are treated as those of straw poll. This specific question was drafted after negative experiences campaigning in 2009 in the author's constituency and media reports about the problem. The question related to respondent's recent personal experience. It was: "How did you find that the 2009 revelations about MP's expenses affected electors' reactions during canvassing for the local and European elections in 2009?"The responses were:

Elector's reactions were:

Very positive 0; Quite positive 0; No different 2 (7.5%); Quite hostile 16 (59.3%); Very hostile 5 (18.5%); Don't know/didn't say 4 (14.8 %).

These worrying figures about public reactions demonstrate the folly of the NL government in not tackling the expenses issue firmly and much earlier. The scepticism about MPs and their expenses probably adversely affected general election results for the main parties in 2010 and 2015.

Responses to Questionnaire Survey of the CLP Secretaries.

The additional direct questionnaire survey of the CLP Secretaries was designed to assist them in focusing on potentially significant topics and also to produce data which could viably be compared with information obtained from research done with a representative sample of volunteer grass-roots Party members (in 2006) by YouGov for the LabOUR Commission 2007.[C5_84]

As noted in Chapter 1, the low percentage of CLP secretaries (27 out of a possible total of 638) who participated in the direct questionnaire means that, taken on its own, the poll of their opinions cannot be regarded as a statistically representative survey and must be classified as a straw poll. The policy questions were similar to those asked to the 2007 representative sample of party members. However questions put to CLP secretaries here were updated to cover subsequent developments and events.

Secretaries were asked to rank the NL government's most important policy achievements from a list of 18. Each could choose up to seven. Responses are set out in: Tables 1, 2 and 3 for Chapter 5.

CLP Secretaries' most favoured policy was: "Helping poor families through the national minimum wage and tax credits" – 22 (81.5% of respondents). "Improvements to NHS services" came second, supported by 20 (74.1%). Third came: "Good economic management up to the 2008 financial crisis" which 19 (70.4%) supported. Fourth came: "Setting up and running Sure Start centres", chosen by 18 (66.6%) and fifth was: "Increasing the overseas aid budget and leading world efforts to help Africa' 16 (59.3%). Number 6 was: "Improving standards of education in state schools" – 13 (48.2%) and seventh equal were: "Reducing the average waiting times for hospital operations" and "Devolution for Scotland, Wales and London" – 11 (40.7%) each.

Far less popular policies: supported by only two (7.5%) secretaries – were" "Introducing the new deal for school leavers"; "Building more hospitals" (some through PFI) and "Increasing school building (mainly through PFI and the Academy Programme)". Their apparent dislike of PFI is unremarkable but, unlike the MPs, they did not equate the provision of better buildings with an improved service which those could have facilitated (e.g. by attracting more skilled staff). Least popular of all were: "Being instrumental in removing Saddam Hussein from power in Iraq" and "Giving military aid to the Afghan government". Both of which were supported by *no* respondents.

Consigned to a metaphorical Room 101 were seven policies regarded by secretaries (from a list of 19) as being the least successful. Most *un*popular was: "Taking part in the invasion of Iraq" chosen by 19 respondents (70.4%). Next came "Keeping and updating Britain's nuclear weapons" (selected by two thirds of secretaries). Thirdly followed: "Imposing badly thought out reforms on state schools – 16 secretaries (59.3%). Next came: "Relying too heavily on the privatisation of public services" – 15 (55.6%). Fifth equal were: "Being subservient to a right wing American President" and "Imposing a stealth tax on private pensions", each chosen by 14 secretaries (51.9%). Sixth was: "Using the terrorist threat to curb our civil liberties" – 13 respondents (48.2%). Seventh was: "Not raising income taxes on the rich or reducing them enough for the poor" – 11 respondents (40.7%).

Other unsuccessful policies (equally) were: "Failure to control immigration" and "Failure to administer the National Minimum Wage and working family tax credits effectively". These were chosen by only one respondent (3.7%) each. No respondent chose "Failure to reduce violent crime" as being an issue.

The responses to two separate questions put to secretaries about UK and USA participation in the wars in Afghanistan and Iraq follow. In respect of Iraq, 22 secretaries (81.5%) said that UK involvement was wrong. Five agreed (18.5%) with our participation and none "Did not know". On the question of the Afghan war, opinion was slightly more divided. Just over one third (10) were in favour of UK participation and slightly under two thirds (16) were opposed – with one "Don't know". Clearly the Afghan war was less controversial – perhaps, as Lord S. pointed out, because it was legal in international law and had UN approval. Secretaries may also have perceived a closer link to preventing terrorism in the UK.

A 2006 survey was undertaken by YouGov for the LabOUR Commission with a representative sample of 670 Labour Party members (also drawn from all regions of England, Scotland and Wales).[C5_85] This was a statistically valid quantitative survey. The Commission survey asked policy questions in a similar format on similar, but not identical, topics. Exact comparisons cannot be made with the 2009 straw poll undertaken for this book. However the results of the much larger, and statistically representative, study of 2006 shed light on, and offer some corroboration for, the results of the later, much smaller scale, survey of 2009.

The Commission survey asked respondents to identify the six most important policy achievements of the Government since 1997 and the six most undesirable policies, each to be selected from a list of 18 options. Considered most successful was: "Running a strong economy with low unemployment, inflation and interest rates" (as at June 2006). This was given top rating by 78% of members surveyed. Second came "Helping poor families through the minimum wage and tax credits" (77%). A much lower third came "Reducing average waiting times for hospital operations" (50%). Fourth was "Improving standards in state schools" (43%). The fifth choice was: "Increasing the overseas aid budget and leading international efforts to help Africa", favoured by 38%. Sixth equal were "Setting up Sure Start Centres" and "Expelling most hereditary peers from the House of Lords" (30% each). Polices least favoured in equal measure (15% each) were "Reducing crime levels" and 'Helping to remove Saddam Hussein from power in Iraq" and "None of these" (one respondent).

The earlier members survey gave "top marks" to good economic management and the CLP secretaries only rated this third most important. Good economic management was supported by over 70% of these Party members. This judgement related to the period *before* the economic crisis of 2007·8. (The YouGov poll dates from June 2006). However the CLP secretaries were able to use hindsight as they answered the questionnaire *after* the credit crunch.

The first choice of the CLP secretaries (see above) (81%): "Helping poorer families through the National Minimum Wage and Tax Credits" was the marginal second choice of the larger sample of Party members (and was supported by 77%). YouGov respondents were not asked the general question about improving the standards of the NHS (favoured by 20 secretaries (74%), but their third best rating went to "Reducing average waiting times for hospital operations" (50%). The larger members survey included "Improving standards of education in state schools": "Increasing the overseas aid budget", as its fourth and fifth most successful policies respectively and at sixth equal were rated: "Setting up Sure Start Centres" and "Expelling *most* hereditary peers from the House of Lords" (only 30% for each). Apart from "The expulsion of hereditary peers", which came low down the CLP secretaries' rankings, the YouGov rankings were very similar to those of the former – so far as the best policies were concerned. Perhaps differences reflect the Commission survey being taken sooner after the expulsion of some peers and by 2009 there was more cynicism because it was, by then, certain that House of Lords reform was in a state of stalemate. Also the timing of the expenses scandal, which came to light between the YouGov survey and the CLP secretaries' survey undertaken for this book will probably account for some differences in the results of each survey.

The Labour Commission survey proceeded to ask members responding for their judgement of the six *least* desirable policies. Participation in the Iraq invasion came top (but was only mentioned by 52%). Second came "Being subservient to a right wing US president" (still then in office) (49%). Third was "Relying too heavily on privatisation in public provision" (46%). Fourth, in order of unpopularity, was "Refusing to increase the rates of income tax paid by people earning more than £100,000 per year". Fifth was "Introducing, then increasing, fees for higher education" (32%). Sixth came "Using the terrorist threat to curb civil liberties" (29%).

Seen as being *least objectionable* were "Banning fox hunting" (5%), banning tobacco advertising, and passing a law to ban smoking in offices, bars and restaurants (each 3%). Looking at the 2009 responses, the menace of the "Right wing American President" appeared to have diminished because he (Bush) had left office and been replaced by the Democrat Obama. Keeping Britain's nuclear weapons was seen as a policy failure by only 12% of the 2006 members sample as compared with two thirds of the CLP secretaries who gave it second place in their list of most undesirable policies. This may have reflected more serious proposals to scrap Trident which were being widely canvassed by 2009 in the context of a proposed Defence spending review. Otherwise *the rankings were fairly similar as between the party members of 2006 and the CLP secretaries of 2009.* This gives credibility to the results of the secretaries' straw poll which was probably fairly representative of the opinions of that respondent group.

When the 2006 members sample were asked, separately, whether they thought that British and American participation in the Iraq war was right, 37% answered in the affirmative, 53% in the negative with 10% uncertain. They were not posed the same question about Afghanistan. The figures were very different in respect of the constituency secretaries, 81.5% of whom were opposed to participation in the Iraq war and only 18.5% in favour. Critical opinions may have intensified as the media coverage of various public inquiries emerged.

The Constituency Secretaries had similar priorities for the aims of the Labour Party to those favoured by MPs interviewed. Broadly these policy priorities informed their selection of the Labour government's best policies such as the national minimum wage, Sure Start and substantial aid for poor countries. Less positive responses were given on foreign and defence policy. These reflected the respondents' earlier identified Party aims in these spheres. They were generally not the highest priorities of the NL hierarchy.

Conclusion

Domestic policies that were welcomed by Labour Party stakeholders interviewed tended to have, as Frank Dobson suggested: "an 'Old Labour' tinge about them". Some policies, such as massive investment in public services, notably health and education, were widely welcomed, but the privatisation – that the NL Leadership insisted should accompany them – was not. The NMW and measures to help poor families were also widely acclaimed. When it came to defence and overseas policies, there was approval for the peace settlement in Northern Ireland and particularly for the generous overseas aid programme. Condemnation of the Iraq war was almost universal but a significant minority approved of the intervention in Afghanistan.

However, in order to win power for a sustained period, and thus to be able to introduce the policies discussed here, NL had to focus on tactics to facilitate winning elections and holding on to power. These were discussed, analysed and evaluated in Chapter 2. As that chapter demonstrates; electoral considerations, as reflected by the media, often played an excessively large role in determining policies and policy priorities. TB and GB tended to consult market research results and other opinion polls and then, allegedly, to shape their policies to match favoured responses appearing in these results – especially where these came from swing voters in marginal constituencies.

CHAPTER 6
Comparison of New Labour's Policy Record compared with that of earlier Labour Governments and with the Australian Labor Government's contemporary record

Among Labour Prime Ministers only one made real, tangible, lasting changes to the way people live in Britain; Attlee, Prime Minister from 1945-1951
Francis Beckett, *Clem Attlee*, 2000

The principal achievement of New Labour was to stay in government for 13 years. The Attlee governments achieved very much more in less than half that time. What matters is the quality of what you do, not how long you're in office
Peter Kilfoyle MP, 2010

The Labour Party is a moral crusade or it is nothing
Harold Wilson
(In 2015 it is accepted that a Wilson's language is no longer acceptable in multicultural Britain – but his sentiment was right)

If the Party is only a vehicle for ambition then you've no need to worry about history
Colin Challen, MP

Both Labour prime ministers (TB and GB) were, like John Major before them, prisoners of a revolution effected by Margaret Thatcher in the 1980s. They had abandoned traditional Labour policies and espoused the revolution to gain office in 1997 and found that, in her phrase, there 'was no alternative'
Simon Jenkins, *Thatcher and Sons*, 2007

Contents
Introduction
Labour values and policy aspirations in the period before majority Labour Governments Labour's planned and actual policies during earlier periods of majority
government 1945-52 followed by 1964-79 (not continuous)
New Labour government 1993-2010 How it dealt with contemporary policy issues How does its record compare with that of mid twentieth century Labour governments?
Evaluation of policy developments, newly developed or radically changed, by NL governments
Controversial and failed policies, developed or radically changed, by NL governments
Record of the contemporary Australian Labour Government compare with that of NL

Conclusion: Old Labour vs New Labour governments: comparative assessment of their total policy achievements

A well known writer addressed the pupils of the author's school. She likened the values and achievements of the school, over the years, to a continuing chain. She then urged us to live our lives so that we "Keep bright the chain". Some of we adolescents were inappropriately amused, at the time, partly because the diminutive writer repeated her motto several times in a voice like a foghorn. One of the boys (the son of a late Labour MP) brought in a WC chain and hung it up in the sixth form common room with a notice attached saying: "See how they keep bright the chain". On reflection, this motto seems very appropriate for the Labour Party. We are part of a long chain comprised of aims, values and political achievements stretching back to Keir Hardie and beyond that to the Chartists and the Tolpuddle Martyrs. One of the contemporary big issues for the Labour Party is how far has New Labour kept bright the chain?

Introduction

New Labour (NL) governments achieved many objectives that were commendable. There was competent economic management until the 2008 crash and then within the constraints of a global economic disaster; although their earlier economic policy planted the seeds of that disaster. They also invested massively in UK public services – albeit accompanied by much privatisation. Further, they instituted measures to counter poverty in Britain, and in developing countries, but they failed to halt the widening gap between rich and poor at home. *The key question in this Chapter is did they achieve sufficient worthwhile policy outcomes during their reign in government, relative to its length?*

There is a charge to be answered that NL, with 13 years in power and a sometimes large, and always workable, majority in Parliament, did not attain sufficient valuable policy outputs in relation to the time and power at their disposal. As evidence in this debate, NL's policy performance is compared with that of previous Labour governments. Their policy feats are discussed in Chapter 5 where it appears that the policy successes of the Brown government were even fewer than those of Blair administrations.

The overall verdict of four senior MPs: Clare Short said: "Labour's big chance in 1997 was to get a large country to go down the social democrat route and become that kind of attractive and equal society. A less unequal society would have less crime, fewer drop outs, less teenage pregnancy and vandalism the evidence is clear".[C6-1] "Social democracy works. I disagree with all this talk about Labour's ideas being old fashioned and being stuck in the past. The argument that we had to have NL because the Party was dying was all nonsense. The NL view was a stereotype of Labour's history that wasn't true. As though everything Labour had done in the past was worth nothing."

Short continued: "The government's achievements have been very disappointing across the piste. The Labour Party is no longer a 'moral crusade' as Harold Wilson once described it … But look at the great achievements of the post war Labour government. If you look at the records of Wilson and Callaghan they were left with tiny majorities in very difficult times but they still kept to their principles – more than NL ever managed to."

Jon Cruddas claimed: "A few years ago we had the opportunity to change tack. GB came in with a change agenda in terms of re-establishing an ethic of public service and changing the direction of failed policies, for instance public housing and employment insecurity. Unfortunately there was the election that never happened, after which he seemed to lose his nerve. Then there was the economic crisis where he did a lot of effective firefighting. But there's not really been any work done in terms of alternative systems that are needed as we move from one era to another. The problem is that we've missed that opportunity."

Senior Backbencher M. said: "We've often done good by stealth. We haven't actually achieved as much as we could have in the time. We've never been in office as long and I suppose that previous generations would have thought that in 13 years of uninterrupted power we could have made far greater changes. We've narrowed the equality gap in some areas. The more equal society (with a narrower gap in social and economic terms between rich and poor) wasn't the society that TB wanted to achieve. His achievements were considerable as Prime Minister, although this may not be appreciated in poor areas, like my constituency, as much as it is in better off ones.

Graham Stringer said: "*The manifesto commitments were limited, so that left a policy vacuum.* As a result, given two governments with huge majorities and one with a working majority, the (policy) achievement has been limited."

The most significant records must be those of achievements and failures of Labour governments. Time spent in government is a crucial yardstick of performance here. Attlee's consecutive majority governments lasted a total of seven years (1945-52) and the Wilson/Callaghan governments two periods of six years (1964-70) and five years (1974-79) respectively: eleven years in all. Collectively these administrations covered 18 years with interruptions; compared with NL's continuous total of 13. Because these earlier Labour governments were not continuously in power: Conservative governments that "interrupted' them "undid" some of their attainments. Returning Labour administrations therefore had to spend time re-making undone policies. This was especially true in respect of public ownership of enterprises and industrial relations law.

NL should have spent far more time counteracting the policies of 18 years of Thatcherite rule. However in most areas, particularly in respect of rights at work and industrial relations, NL failed to do this.

As Clare Short asserted (above), earlier Labour governments often had miniscule majorities. This was bound to inhibit their progress: yet they achieved so much despite these handicaps.

Labour Values and planned Policies in the period before majority Labour Governments

Some early background on Labour's policy development out of power, and in coalition, before there were majority Labour Governments and during the World War 2 National Government is given below:

The Labour Representation Committed (LRC) started with the basic aim of getting more working men elected to Parliament and, by implication, promoting the interests of working class people generally. After 1918 Labour became a unitary democratic socialist party, rather than a looser federation, and adopted aims concerning public ownership of industry, fair pay for work and educational and social opportunity for all. In the mid twentieth century its aims extended to providing a welfare state and effective public services for all, including health services.

Opposition to war, and sometimes pacifism, featured regularly the Party's history. When the 1914-18 war was declared, the socialists in the LRC were opposed to it. Ramsay MacDonald called for Britain to remain neutral[C6-2]. The majority of other Labour MPs (those not in the ILP) became prepared to support the war effort once hostilities broke out. This situation was a significant pointer to much of the war and peace debate which has taken place within the Labour Party up to modern times.[C6-3]

Ten years after the LRC was founded some of its candidates were elected to Parliament. Then the Osborne Judgement (1909) deprived the nascent Labour Party of all income from trades unions. This legal judgement prohibited unions from using their funds to support political parties. The impecunious LRC could not have continued to contest Parliamentary elections without this funding.[C6-4] Nor could they have continued to support (then otherwise unsalaried) MPs. Labour therefore had to continue to work in *de facto* coalitions with the Liberals in the 1910 general election, and beyond, on the promise of a change to the statute law which would reverse the Osborne ruling. This change was enacted in 1913. The PLP also supported the Liberals in 1911 when they introduced a contributory National Insurance scheme for working men. Some in the Party, who had been members of the Poor Law Commission, wanted a non-contributory scheme but the trade unions disagreed.[C6-5]

Labour was founded on the basis of promoting equality between social and economic classes. However it was slower to recognise that other types of equalities were as important. Labour had usually supported women's and racial equality since its foundation. However Keir Hardie, and his fellow Labour MPs, once refused to support a bill to allow women's suffrage for the plausible reason that this particular bill linked voting to property ownership. Socialist and feminist principles were in conflict.

Labour formed coalition governments with the Liberals during the First World War. In 1924-26 there was a minority Labour Government with some Liberal support. Its Wheatley Housing Act provided for government financial assistance for building council homes. MacDonald played a key role in negotiating the Dawes Plan whereby the US underwrote post-war German reparations payments to the UK. These reparations could not otherwise have been paid. The government supported the inauguration of the League of Nations in the Versailles Treaty and improved Anglo-Russian relations by recognising the Soviet Russian Government.[C6-6]

The Conservatives won general elections in 1926 and 1931. In 1931 Labour leader Ramsay MacDonald took Labour into coalition with the Tories without consulting his Party. Only seven Labour MPs went with him and the remainder of the PLP went into opposition.

The Labour Party was founded by the trades unions and has maintained a link with them since. The unions also had long-standing and continuing direct involvement in party governance (see Chapter 4). After MacDonald and his meagre band of colleagues were expelled from the Party they joined the Tories in coalition. The Labour Party (then in opposition) was run for the next 10 years by the National Council of Labour which was, in effect, an enlarged TUC general council.

Prelude to 1945: Labour participated in a National coalition government during the Second World War. This was largely focussed on the war effort but enacted, or prepared the way for some progressive measures. Labour formed its first majority government in 1945. This turned out to be a great reforming administration dedicated, by and large, to principles of democratic socialism.

Paving Labour's way, in 1944, the National Government published a white paper which adopted the policy of securing full employment through government intervention. As Attlee acknowledged, this was in line with Labour policy priorities.[C6-7] Early in the 1940-45 National Government, Ernest Bevin was able to present a complete programme of action to the war cabinet. As a committed trades unionist he did not want to take compulsory powers so he developed and advocated "voluntaryism" based on co-operation and the conviction that people would make greater sacrifices willingly than under compulsion. The trades unions were to be partners in this venture. Bevin, a far sighted Minster of Labour, demanded that all decisions concerning personnel and labour questions should rest with him.[C6-8] He set up a production council consisting of himself, three junior ministers and the president of the Board of Trade to turn all strategic decisions into production programmes.

Most of the National Government's home affairs policy making was delegated to Attlee. The monumental Beveridge Report on social security, health and welfare was published in 1942. However, despite media acclaim, it was never adopted by the National government but was put on hold until after the war. Labour made an impact on domestic policy through a number of measures: the Catering Wages Act, a Hydro Electricity Scheme for Scotland and the Location of Industry Act. The 1944 Education Act was a "Con-Lab" measure drafted by Rab Butler and Chuter Ede. It turned the former Board of Education into a fully fledged ministry with power to impose duties on local education authorities. Most importantly, it decreed that education should be free and universally available. The act created the 11+ examination and a three tier system of grammar schools, technical schools and secondary moderns. This system contravened a Labour Party policy which supported universal comprehensive education. That policy was adopted at the 1942 Conference.[C6-9]

Labour's planned and actual policies during periods of majority government

The record of Majority Labour Governments 1945-52: The party fought the 1945 election on a manifesto called *Let us Face the Future*[C6_10] drawn up by Herbert Morrison. Its main promises were the nationalisation of the Bank of England and of a number of industries. There was a major programme of social legislation largely based on the recommendations of the Beveridge Report.[C6_11] Effect was given to "old clause 4" through an extensive programme of nationalisation.

Economic Policy: In 1944 the Government published a white paper which adopted the policy of securing full employment through government intervention, as Attlee acknowledged, this was very much in line with Labour policy priorities.[C6_12] The cost of establishing the welfare state was enormous. Economic rescue came in 1947 in the form of the Marshall Plan for US aid to Britain and other European countries. However the escalating cost of repayments caught up with the Labour government and in September 1949 the pound had to be devalued. Despite shaky financial underpinning Labour went ahead with the establishment of the welfare state and increasing public ownership.

Public Ownership of Business and Industry: After the Labour government was elected in 1945; effect was given to "old clause 4". This was achieved through an extensive programme of nationalisation in which Herbert Morrison took the lead. First nationalisations were the Bank of England; the National Coal Board; the British Transport Commission (railways, canals and road haulage); cable and wireless companies; and civil airlines (BEA and BOAC). Electricity, gas, iron and steel followed. Parts of civil aviation, gas, electricity and telecommunications were already state owned by the end of the war. Many of these moves to state ownership were not widely opposed because the organisations and industries involved were not being managed effectively at that time. Coal was particularly neglected and especially vital to the economy. Professor Peter Hennessey wrote: "Coal never lost its symbolic, almost romantic place in the Labour movement the industry where the excesses of capitalism had left blood in the seams."[C6_13]

There was greater controversy surrounding nationalisation of the road haulage and iron and steel industries, which were more efficient and profitable. All other enterprises nationalised fitted the test that Attlee had promised to the American Senate: which lent a great deal of money to his Government. Attlee's test question was: *"Is this industry a natural monopoly and, if so, is it safe to leave it in private hands?"* There were currently 3,800 private road haulage companies which made the task of nationalisation daunting. Nationalising iron and steel met with fierce resistance. However there was a strong desire in Cabinet and Parliament to succeed. *All the Labour Party's existing proposals for nationalisation were implemented during this first majority government.* In this respect, the Party's mission and objectives were being well attained. *By 1950 20% of the economy was in public ownership.*

The 1950·2 Labour government had a tiny overall majority (13) but it enabled the nationalisation of iron and steel to go forward in 1951. This was permitted under legislation already passed in 1949. The Conservatives made much political capital from this. The miniscule government majority rendered it impossible to pass new controversial legislation.

Health and Welfare Services and Social Security: The 1946 National Insurance Act insured everyone for sickness, unemployment and retirement. It also provided non-means tested widow's pensions, maternity grants and death grants with allowances for dependents. There was also a Disability Employment Act which gave some guarantees of work to people with disabilities. The National Assistance Act provided for those in need, but not eligible for National Insurance benefits. This Act created a "safety net" that ensured that no one fell below the subsistence level. The 1946 Industrial Injuries Act included the whole workforce in a compensation scheme for workplace injuries and increased levels of payments. Attlee ignored warnings that the system might be open to abuse or benefit the "undeserving poor". He said that it was more important to have a system that prevented the misery that he had seen as a social worker in East London than to establish one that was completely proof against abuse.[C6-14] Aneurin Bevan was implacably opposed to means testing. He made an impassioned speech about it when the National Assistance Act came into effect. He related his deep, burning hatred of the Tory Party that his personal experiences of the means test had generated. Bevan continued: "So far as I am concerned they are lower than vermin"[C6-15]. Perhaps he also had a premonition of the present social security policies of Ian Duncan Smith? Following Bevan's declaration Attlee requested him to speak more carefully in future!

In 1946 the National Health Service (NHS) was announced. Its development was delegated to Bevan. Well to the left of Attlee, he always worked within the framework of Party policy. The new service found little already established to build on. The British medical establishment was already sharpening its sword to oppose the development. The founding principles were of the health service were that it should be universally available; able to meet every medical need; offer the same standards of care throughout the UK; and free at the point of use. Bevan decided to nationalise all existing hospitals that were run by local authorities and charities in order provide uniformity and a standard quality of service. He believed that hospitals should not be beholden to charitable contributions or private benefactors but should be funded out of progressive taxation.

Collectively the doctors were hostile to the NHS; many did not wish to be public employees. At one stage every item in Bevan's plan for the NHS was rejected by the British Medical Association (BMA) Assembly. In November 1946 the NHS plans became law but were not due to be implemented until July 1948 (NHS Act, 1946).[C6-16] At first, the BMA urged all doctors to boycott the service but the government did not capitulate. It made a few concessions to allow the BMA to climb down without loss of face. One of these was to allow GPs to work as independent contractors. This this led to difficulties with planning and coordinating community health services for many years. The NHS began, as it continued, by being very expensive: it was courageous of the Government to go ahead in view of its own dire financial situation. However the NHS became so popular that even the Conservatives eventually accepted it and Mrs. Thatcher postponed meddling with it until her later years as PM. By September 1948: 93% of the population were registered as NHS patients.[C6-17]

The achievement of the 1945 Labour government in setting up the NHS, in very difficult circumstances, is without parallel in Britain. However, the lack of finance available for capital projects and the contemporary state of the building industry meant that the infant NHS often had to make do with adapting existing local authority and voluntary sector hospital and clinic buildings: many of which were up to 100 years old (too many of these continued in use until NL's Private Finance Initiative (PFI) building spree after the millennium). Although pay beds were not abolished there was no additional privatisation. Further, the founding principles of the NHS – to be universally available and able to meet all health needs – were adhered to. Later there were compromises on the principle of "free at the point of use" allegedly due to economic constraints.

The perennial question asked about the welfare state in the 1940s, and to the present, is: "Can we afford it?" Attlee answered this eloquently in a speech to the House of Commons during the debate on the National Insurance Bill in 1946.[C6_18] For the first time this insured everyone for sickness, unemployment and retirement and provided widow's benefits, maternity allowances and death grants. Attlee declared: "I cannot believe that our productivity is so low, that our willingness to work is so feeble … that we can submit to the world. Supposing the answer is 'no': what does that mean? It really means that the sum total of goods produced and the services rendered by the people of this country is not sufficient to provide for all our people at all times in sickness and in health, in youth and in age the very modest standard of life set out (in the National Insurance Bill). I cannot believe that … the masses of our people must be condemned to penury."[C6_19]

Beckett[C6_20] reported: "The welfare state and a better life for ordinary people were the major achievements of Clem Attlee's government." Peter Hennessy (quoted in Beckett[C6_21]) believed: "The transformation in life chances for those at the bottom of the heap was quite dramatic". In York in 1936, 31% of households lived in poverty. In 1950 the figure was under 3%."

In 1951 Gaitskell breached the founding principles of the NHS that services would be free at the point of delivery by introducing charges for teeth and spectacles. Bevan and Wilson resigned from the cabinet in protest.[C6_22]

Education: Labour (in the National Government) was a party to the 1944 Education Act which made free education universally available and set up a state school system. Many Labour Party members hoped that Education Minister Ellen Wilkinson would repeal the 1944 Education Act by abolishing the 11+ and the three tier secondary education system.[C6_23] However, Wilkinson prioritised raising the school leaving age to 15 and increasing the number of university state scholarships. These measures involved a major school and university building programme and rapid training of 35,000 extra teachers. The number of university places was increased from about 50,000 in 1938·9 to almost 77,000 in 1947·8. These places were needed not only by state scholars but also by people who had deferred their higher education for war service. The school meals system was improved and free school milk was provided for the first time.

Social Housing: A Housing Act which encouraged local authorities to build affordable homes for rent was less successful. Despite good intentions, this programme did not reach the Government's target of providing 200,000 new homes annually.[C6_24] Bevan gave a central government subsidy of 75% to local councils to build social housing. Nearly one third of Britain's homes had been destroyed, or damaged, during the war. No housing repairs had been done for six years. The government instructed local authorities to give priority to repairing damaged housing. Virtually no social rented housing had been built during the mainly Tory 1930s. There was also a severe shortage of building material and skilled labour and the aftermath of the war, which hindered the policy's implementation.

*Foreign Policy and Defence: A*ttlee's governments began to end British imperialism. They started with the Indian Subcontinent. Attlee fixed a time limit for the withdrawal of British troops and sent Lord Mountbatten as Viceroy to oversee the transfer of power. Two new nations: India and Pakistan were created in 1948. The former was predominantly Hindu and the latter largely Muslim. Despite the best efforts of the British forces the division was accompanied by much inter faith bloodshed. Burma and Ceylon also became independent at around the same time. Only Burma left the Commonwealth. The independence of Palestine in 1948 also led to violent conflict between local Arab and Jewish people. This ended with the creation of the state of Israel. Here the situation was not very effectively handled and a strife torn Israel/Palestine state has continued ever since without an effective peace settlement.[C6_25, C6_25]

Bevin found the Russians unwilling to co-operate effectively with the Labour Government, despite his efforts to improve relations. However he worked co-operatively with the USA and helped to create the Marshall Plan which underpinned the economic recovery in the UK and the rest of Europe. Bevin also played a major role in establishing NATO which supported re-armament in order to resist Russia. The subservient trans Atlantic Special Relationship began. This last move was very unpopular within in the Labour Party whose members wanted the UK to take a more neutral position (or even to ally with Russia). Members also wanted the adoption of a socialist foreign policy.[C6_27, C6_28]

In June 1950 North Korea invaded the South. President Truman sent in US Forces and the UN Security Council demanded the withdrawal of South Korean forces (which legalised this war). Attlee took British forces into Korea to support them, but used his position covertly to try to restrain Truman from escalating the conflict. The British defence budget was increased and existing post war conscription was lengthened from 18 months to two years. This also generated controversy within the PLP and the wider Party.[C6_29]

Beckett summed up Attlee's career as Prime Minister: "Far from the modest little man with plenty to be modest about (as Churchill once described him), Attlee was a subtle and skilful political operator – swift, decisive, ruthless and cunning. Inspired by a hatred of the living conditions he had seen in the East End of London (as a social worker), he determined to put an end to poverty – with the result that between 1945 and 1951 his government revolutionised British society."[C6_30]

These Labour governments sought to eliminate Beveridge's "Five Giants: disease, ignorance, squalor and idleness" and, above all, to narrow the vast contemporary gap between the very rich and the most impoverished in society. They regarded the task of establishing the welfare state as being so vital that The Government gave itself, and met, the deadline of July 1948 to have all the legislation in force. This was timely because Labour lost office in 1951 and did not regain it until 1964.

The Record of Wilson and Callaghan Governments 1964–1979

Gaitskell died in 1963 and was succeeded by the more left wing Harold Wilson.[C6_31] When Wilson became Labour leader, Richard Crossman wrote in the *Sunday Pictorial*[C6_32] that Wilson was: "A man who might become the most successful prime minister in Labour's history". A record of the 1964 and 1966 Wilson governments follows:

After the 1966 election the government soon became unpopular and remained so up until shortly before the 1970 general election. This was largely due to its economic and industrial policies. Many of these impacted severely on working class people in general and trades unionists in particular.

The Economy, Fiscal Policy and the effects of contemporary foreign policy: In 1964 Labour inherited a balance of trade deficit of £800 million and its tiny majority again made governing very difficult. Wilson, a competent economist, imposed a substantial and temporary import surcharge, negotiated large loans from foreign banks and guided Chancellor James Callaghan in skilful economic management. The latter recalled: "Harold gave me unfailing support and encouragement, helping me through a most trying experience"[C6_33] An example of Callaghan's trials follows. "His frustration is illustrated: Nothing could equal in frustration sitting at the Chancellor's desk watching our currency reserves gurgle down the plug hole day by day."[C6_34]

The bank rate rose to 7%. The government initiated long term strategies to improve the balance of trade. Economic planning was adopted. There was a five year plan for national economic development (the National Plan).[C6_35] This government showpiece was overseen by George Brown. However, because of its novelty, the plan had to be "sold", which Brown tried hard to do. It was lauded by the media but, in the end, fell victim to sceptical ministers and civil servants.[C6_36] In 1966, Minsters had to abandon plans for economic growth in order to avoid devaluation. There was also criticism, from some trades union quarters, of aspects of the incomes policy – especially the early warning provisions relating to wage claims. The government's main aim was to avoid devaluation of the pound.

To head off inflation, the government cut defence expenditure through a gradual recall of troops from East of Suez (with the exception of Hong Kong). Economic problems prevented this government from having an extensive programme of social expenditure.

There were economic set backs due to the Israel-Arab war and the civil war in Nigeria. These led to import surcharges on oil and other goods. Harold the cautious refused to repeal reserve powers to delay pay increases.[36] Devaluation of the pound became inevitable in November 1967. This measure improved exports but raised the price of imported goods. By the 1970 general election Labour Britain had transformed its inherited balance of payments deficit into a healthy surplus. However Labour lost the election and Heath became Tory Premier.

In February 1974 the Labour manifesto contained the now celebrated promise of "a fundamental and irreversible shift in the balance of power and wealth in favour of working people and their families" (Labour Manifesto *Let Us Work Together*).[C6_37] This shift would involve a wealth tax and capital transfer tax. There was to be nationalisation of development land, mineral rights and parts of the engineering industry. A new National Enterprise Board was to manage the public industrial sector. There were also plans for a voluntary social contract between government and unions to regulate wage increases and prices. Labour won with a tiny majority, went to the electorate again the following October and increased its majority to being slightly more viable.

After the first election Denis Healey became chancellor. His first budget was neutral but a second, in the summer, was mildly reflationary and included a reduction in Value Added Tax from 10% to 8% which brought down prices. Subsequently economic problems loomed. In 1975 Healey produced a severely deflationary budget. This included cuts in housing and food subsidies. The budget broke several 1974 election promises. Unemployment was rising and there was a "double dip" recession. A Temporary Employment Subsidy was introduced and delayed some redundancies. The Manpower Services Commission was established to create jobs and oversee job training. This Commission developed, and ran, large scale work training schemes for young people. In July 1975 the value of the pound fell below what was then regarded as the minimum acceptable rate of U.S. $2.20. Thereafter business confidence diminished. The voluntary incomes policy appeared to be under threat, so did the compulsory wages policy. When these arrangements broke down; the "Winter of Discontent" followed.

Wilson retired suddenly in 1976 and Callaghan took over as Premier. In 1977 the government obtained a loan from the Bank of International Settlements to protect the precarious pound. Six months later the pound was "in free fall" and down in value to $1.63. Callaghan told Party Conference: "We used to think you could spend your way out of a recession and increase employment by cutting taxes and boosting government spending ... that option no longer exists."[C6_38] Soon afterwards, Chancellor Healey negotiated the infamous International Monetary Fund (IMF) loan. He agreed to make expenditure cuts of £ 1 billion, on top of the £1 billion cuts made three months earlier. There were to be cuts of a further £1 billion in 1977–8, if the British economy did not revive. This agreement was attacked in Cabinet from both left and right. Eventually it was decided to accept the IMF terms, subject to detailed discussion of where the cuts were to be made. From autumn 1977 the economy was improving. The IMF loan (which allegedly had not been needed) was repaid and the balance of payments deficit had been transformed into a healthy surplus. North Sea Oil was beginning to flow and inflation was down to 7%. However unemployment was still rising.

Public Ownership of Business and Industry: An early White Paper on the "Re-nationalisation of steel" was issued and greeted by rebellion from two right wing MPs: Woodrow Wyatt and Desmond Donnelly. [C6_39] In the end, as the vote could not have been won, steel nationalisation had to be postponed until after the 1966 election, which Labour won. Steel was eventually re-nationalised in 1967 and the National Freight Corporation was set up to integrate road and rail services. A Transport Act provided for subsidies for uneconomic public transport which met social need. There was increased expenditure on roads and more road safety measures were introduced. These included the rudely named "Barbara's bags" (Mrs Castle's breathalysers).

The 1974 election manifestos contained a commitment to extend public ownership, but they did not go as far as left inclined Ministers desired. The 1974 Labour government increased public ownership of development land and mineral rights. They also set up the National Enterprise Board to manage the public industrial sector at a strategic level and to increase public ownership as much as possible.[C6_40] In the mid 1970s there were bills to nationalise the aerospace and shipbuilding industries and to extend the working regulations that covered ports and container depots.

Trades Union and Industrial Relations: A new prices and incomes policy was planned in partnership with employers and unions. This area was to be policed by the new National Board for Prices and Incomes. The government's popularity was undermined by a seaman's strike (May 1966) and continuing the stop-go economy initiated by previous Tory Governments. There were balance of payments problems looming.

The most unpopular measure was a wages and prices freeze scheduled to last six months and then be followed by six months of "severe restraint". This was to be a voluntary scheme based on the hope that the unions would co-operate. It was actually a backstop before compulsion was introduced. Higher unemployment followed. Its level was 2.5% instead of the 1.5% that had been the average in recent years. The economy improved early in 1967 because the balance of payments was coming into surplus.

There was then welcome legislation to end casual labour on the docks.

Later Wilson decided to use trades union reform as, he hoped, a means to improve economic management and please the electorate. This led to the white paper *In Place of Strife* (1969).[C6-41] As Pimlott reported, what followed was serious conflict with the unions.[C6-42] This White Paper proposed a month-long conciliation period before a strike could take place. The government could also insist on a ballot of the membership before a strike started. The White Paper was favoured by UK public opinion and was designed to impress overseas creditors. Larger unions, under the new, and more left wing, leadership of Jack Jones and Hugh Scanlon were strongly opposed. A special TUC congress condemned the proposals by a massive majority. An overwhelming Parliamentary Labour Party (PLP) revolt was threatened. Wilson and Barbara Castle agreed, with the TUC, to drop penal clauses in the bill. This was in return for a promise that the TUC would try to prevent unofficial strikes Labour lost the 1970 election to the Conservatives; possibly this was partly as a consequence of adverse publicity about industrial relations and having upset the unions.

The next General Election was in February 1974 during a miner's strike and three day week. Labour won the majority of seats but not an overall majority. Pimlott recalled: "After the February 1974 election Wilson bravely opted to govern as a minority government after the Liberals put forward unacceptable terms for forming a coalition."[C6-43] The miners' strike was settled instantly and the three day week ended. Bills were introduced to repeal the Tory Industrial Relations Act and Pay Board. For the want of a majority, these bills were considerably amended during their passage through Parliament, but did accomplish their basic objectives.

In the summer of 1974 a Trades Union and Labour Relations Act and a Health and Safety at Work Act became law. This was despite the Government's minority situation. Both acts were formulated in co-operation with the TUC. They were designed to improve rights and safety at work and rights of trades unions to organise, recruit and strike. These were an integral part of Labour's designated "Social Contract". Some left wing union leaders softened their stance on incomes policy.

After the minority Labour government had been defeated on 20 major bills, Wilson called another general election in October 1974 which he won with a small majority.

After the October 1974 election victory, Jack Jones, TGWU General Secretary, proposed a flat rate wage increase policy for 1975-6. This was adopted by the Government and was approved by the TU Congress. Such co-operative working with the unions proved alien to NL. The 1974 scheme was underpinned by a prices freeze and threat of legal action against private sector employers who disobeyed. By the end of 1976 inflation was better controlled. The Government froze rents. The Government introduced a Trades Union and Labour Relations Act which greatly improved union rights (see above).[C6-44]

A new prices and incomes policy was underpinned by a prices freeze and legal action against private sector employers who disobeyed. By late 1976 inflation was more effectively controlled. There was a second Trades Union and Labour Relations Act and an Employment Protection Act.[C6_45, C6_46] The latter Acts compelled employers to recognise and bargain with the unions. Employers were obliged to provide any information that unions needed and to permit meetings in working time. Jack Jones called it "A shop stewards' charter". There was also an Equal Pay Act to secure equal pay for women for work of equal value (sometimes difficult to demonstrate which led to issues with implementation). ACAS (the government's arbitration and conciliation service) was established as an independent body with its own resources. There was great media hostility to these developments. *All this was achieved despite a small Parliamentary majority.*

During the 1970s there was much Labour legislation to create services to benefit people at work, to improve health and safety in the workplace and public transport.[C6_47] The Labour manifesto for the 1979 election included the first proposal for a wealth tax and instituted planning agreements with large companies and some nationalisation of banking and insurance.[C6_48]

When James Callaghan took over as Labour Leader and Premier in 1976, plans for a second year of wage restraint were developed and agreed for the next 12 months. This followed difficult negotiations with the unions. This restraint was opposed by the Tribune Group: many of whom abstained in the Commons vote. The Government only retained power on a confidence vote. By 1977 the unions decided it was safe to challenge the incomes policy so the social contract ended. Henceforward the Government dictated incomes policy unilaterally. Neil Kinnock complained to Michael Foot that "in the 1974 election manifestos Labour had promised "a fundamental and irreversible shift of power and wealth in favour of working people."[C6_49]

Measures to promote fairness and equality: In line with their aims, Wilson-led Labour governments enacted a number of equalities measures. These were mainly the product of private members' bills, not government legislation. The Sexual Offences Act of 1967 legalised gay sex between consenting adults over 21.[C6_50] David Steele's 1967 Abortion Act[C5_51] (supported mainly by Labour MPs), legalised abortion in some circumstances. Divorce was made simpler to obtain and settlements were made fairer for women. In 1970 Alf Morris MP secured improvements to the rights of people with disabilities through his Chronically Sick and Disabled Person's Act.[C6_52] Wilson governments subsequently enacted Equal Opportunities, Equal Pay Act and Race Relations Acts years.[C6_53] During the mid 1970s there were also measures to abolish employees' tied housing and to require all local authorities to introduce comprehensive schools.

Health, Welfare and Benefits: During the 1960s, Labour governments adopted commendable housing, education and health policies. NHS expenditure increased by 0.8 % of GNP and the hospital building programme was doubled. Their NHS building programme was not as extensive as NL's but was still significant. The programme was funded by direct public borrowing (at lower interest rates) rather than by a Private Finance Initiative (PFI) as was subsequently used by NL administrations.

Family allowances were more than doubled by the 1960s and 1970s Labour Governments and a redundancy payments scheme was introduced. The social security system was reorganised to make it more user-friendly. The Labour Government's final budget removed the poorest taxpayer's liability for income tax. This compares favourably with GB's 2009 decision to rescind the 10p tax rate, which he had previously introduced, for lower earners. Nevertheless, Professor Peter Townsend declared that the relative gap between the poor and better off was no narrower in 1970 than it had been in 1964.[C6_54]

The 1966 Labour Government unwisely postponed rises in state pensions, sickness and unemployment benefits which had been promised in their election manifesto (this was for "administrative reasons"). There were also cuts in the housing and road building programmes. Controversially NHS prescription charges were introduced for the first time and dental charges increased. Labour's unanticipated loss of the 1970 election was blamed, in part, on these.

In the two Labour Governments elected in 1974, Barbara Castle served as the Secretary of State for Health and Social Security. On the left, she fought hard to increase health and social services expenditure and levels of social security benefits. However Labour increased prescription and dental charges twice.

Education: Public expenditure on education rose from 4.8% of GNP in 1964 to 5.9% in 1968.[C6_55] Teacher training places and the numbers of pupils staying at school voluntarily to the age of 16 increased significantly. University places grew by 10%. The Open University, seen by some as one of Labour's greatest achievements since 1950, and championed by Harold Wilson personally, was founded in 1966 and was developed by Labour governments of the 1960s and 1970s.

New school building also increased. The nationwide Comprehensive school system was established but some grammar schools survived and the 11+ examination continued in some areas. In the mid 1970s there was legislation to require all local authorities to introduce comprehensive schools. All Wilson governments attempted to increase equality in education and to end the social divisiveness of the 11 plus exam. As Secretary of State for Education Anthony Crosland pledged "to destroy every f···ing grammar school in England, Wales and Northern Ireland." Because implementation was then the legal responsibility of local authorities, he did not succeed completely. However, by 1970 the proportion of pupils in Comprehensive Schools had increased from 10% to 32%.[C6_56] Nothing was done to challenge private school education.

By 1967, Labour had established 29 Polytechnics which would extend and develop access to higher and further education. These were developed and extended during the 1970s. In 1974 Education Minister Reg Prentice took action to accelerate the comprehensive schools programme.[C6_57] However, free school milk was ended for secondary school pupils and raising the school leaving age to 16 was postponed from 1971 to1973. There were Government resignations in protest.

Social Housing: Between 1966 and 1969 an average of over 400,000 new council homes was built every year. This contrasts with New Labour's abysmal record of providing scarcely any additional social rented housing (see Chapter 5). Tony Crosland took action to discourage council house sales.[C6_58] A Leasehold Reform Act (promised in the 1966 election manifesto) was passed to enable holders of long leases on their homes to buy the freehold. In the mid 1970s there was legislation to give security to the tenants of tied housing.

More about Fiscal Policies: The 1965 budget introduced capital gains tax and corporation tax. [C6_59] Between 1964 and 1970 there was no reduction in personal taxation. The Selective Employment Tax (SET) was introduced in an effort to shift jobs from the service sector to exporting industries.

Healey's first 1974 budget was neutral but a second, in the summer, was mildly reflationary and included a reduction in VAT from 10% to 8%. This reduced prices. There was also a freeze on rents. Both 1966 Wilson and 1976 Callaghan governments managed to improve the country's economic situation. Wilson by eliminating balance of payments deficit in early 1970 and Callaghan by repaying the IMF loan before the 1979 election. However in neither case did Labour get electoral dividends sufficient to win the respective imminent general elections.[C6_60]

Foreign Affairs and related issues: Further controls on immigration were opposed by the left of the PLP. The 1966 Labour manifesto had promised not to restrict immigration further. There was also legislation to counter discrimination against immigrants already settled in the UK. Immigration policy subsequently came under review again. There were ethical objections, from within the Party, to the over hasty change in the law to exclude Kenyan Asians with British passports who faced expulsion. Consciences were mollified by the passing of another race relations act to prevent discrimination in housing and employment.

Meanwhile the Vietnam War was escalating. Much to the disquiet of the left, the Government gave diplomatic and moral support to the Americans in their war against North Vietnam. Pimlott reported: "As the war became more ferocious and intractable, Wilson himself was increasingly blamed, not just by political activists, but by normally apolitical people for Britain's apparent inaction (tacit support). A *Private Eye* cover by Gerald Scarfe, which showed Wilson applying his tongue to Johnson's naked rump, summed up the way that many had come to see the relationship". Had these critics been able to foresee the relationship between Tony Blair and George W. Bush, in the context of the Iraq war, they would have considered that they had "seen nothing yet".[C6_61] With hindsight, many on the contemporary Labour left, who, like the author, were originally critical of the Wilson Government over Vietnam, have since changed their attitude. They now think that, whilst the Government stance on Vietnam was not ideal, Harold Wilson is to be praised because, unlike TB, he did not tamely follow the Americans into allegedly illegal neo-colonial wars.

Wilson was unwilling to weaken ties with the USA significantly because of the cold war (which was over when TB and GB came to office). He repeatedly tried, in vain, to find a formula for a peace settlement. This compares with NL's atlanticist sycophancy and slavish joining of US instigated wars. Even Australia, unlike the UK, followed America into Vietnam.

Wilson, whilst refusing to condemn US involvement in the Vietnam War commendably declined to send British troops.[C6_62]

Harold Wilson had a personal commitment to addressing international debt and deprivation. In 1953 he wrote two publications on the subject.[C6_63, C6_64] How refreshingly different from the publication record of TB! The 1970 Labour manifesto[C6_65] promised to enable the UK to meet the United Nations Aid target for developed nations of 1.7 % of GNP per year. However, due to subsequent economic crises, this was not achieved by Labour Governments of the 1970s and the 1980s, who adopted these commitments in principle and put them into general election manifestos. GB's government did agree to meet this target by 2013.

In autumn 1965 unilateral independence was declared in Rhodesia. This occurred despite a diplomatic visit made by Wilson to Rhodesia beforehand to seek a settlement. The Government decided against military intervention but in favour of economic sanctions. They gained the support of the UN for these. Such support was more than TB obtained before joining the Iraq invasion. Much to the annoyance of African Commonwealth countries, a settlement with the white Rhodesian rebels continued to elude the Government and the UN. The rebels declared a republic in 1968. There was a Government ban on selling arms to apartheid South Africa; but not to the Nigerian Government which was facing a controversial civil war. One of the questionable decisions of this Wilson government was to reduce aid to developing countries when under financial pressure. In this respect, the record of NL, even following the 2008 financial crisis, was superior.

In 1966 there was the enforced, and unethical, re-settlement of the Chagos Islanders to Mauritius, without proper compensation. The objective was to make way for a US military base on Diego Garcia.

Civil unrest in Northern Ireland intensified during the late sixties and British troops were sent there for "peacekeeping" operations. A review of defence spending resulted in the scrapping of several costly aircraft projects even though this caused some loss of British jobs. After the Conservatives won the 1970 election, on what became known as "Bloody Sunday" in 1973, British troops killed 12 unarmed civilian demonstrators and injured many more. The Saville Inquiry into "Bloody Sunday" published its findings in 2010. Its conclusions exonerated all the protesters, many of whom had been accused of violent behaviour. Subsequently civil violence escalated in Northern Ireland and continued unabated until the Good Friday agreement negotiated by Mo Mowlam and Tony Blair in 1999.

In 1974, following a coup in Chile and the murder of its President Allende, the Labour Government delivered only one of four commissioned frigates to the incoming fascist dictatorship. The Chileans had previously paid for all of these. NL governments would probably have delivered the whole order. This was a small step towards developing an ethical foreign policy.

Arguments continued, within the Cabinet and PLP, about the terms of the UK's EEC membership which Heath had negotiated. Wilson re-negotiated minor improvements to the terms of Britain's entry to the EEC; then persuaded the Cabinet to recommend a "Yes" vote in the referendum in June 1975. However, Minsters were permitted to campaign either way as individuals. Most on the left opted for the "No" campaign. The campaign was grossly unequal. In the 'Yes' corner was the European Movement which was well financed, mainly by big business. It could afford spectacular publicity. The media was almost exclusively pro-market. In the "No' corner, the campaign had little money or organisation. It relied mainly "on modest individual donations". The campaign was cross-Party and the author had her one and only surreal experience of canvassing (in Oxford) alongside Tories including Tim Bell. Unsurprisingly the "Yes" campaign won the referendum. They secured 67.2% of the vote to 32.8% against.

Callaghan's government secretly authorised the updating of Polaris missiles behind the backs of the public, Parliament and even some members of the Cabinet. This was an undemocratic act and atypical of Labour prior to 1997. Chalmers[C6-66] reported: "As a result of the high priority attached to nuclear weapons over several decades, Britain now has a wide range of these. Estimates vary from 577 to 1,500. Callaghan also refused to recall the protection vessel from the Falklands area because he correctly surmised that Argentina was seeking an opportunity to invade.

Jenkins[C6-67] recalled that towards the end of the Falklands war, he had asked James Callaghan how he thought that it was going. Callaghan answered with a sigh. "If only I had had a war". Jenkins continued: "the war was critical to Thatcher's future as Prime Minister. Had it been lost she would have been finished".

The First Attempt to secure Devolution: The first bill to establish devolution in Scotland and Wales was published in late 1976. It was contentious inside, and outside, the Labour Party. There was dispute about whether there should be public referenda. The Tories tabled a "No confidence vote" relating to procedure for the debate. This vote seemed likely to be lost, so it was reluctantly decided to do a deal with the Liberals and form the "Lib-Lab Pact". This entailed the formation of a two-Party consultative Committee to meet regularly and discuss all policy issues. This Pact was disliked by the Labour left. However, it facilitated the defeat of the "No Confidence" motion. Nevertheless, the bill seemed unlikely to pass the Commons, so it was dropped in favour of separate bills for Scotland and Wales. These began to progress through Parliament. Then, in 1978, a Scottish Labour MP successfully moved an amendment to enact that devolution would require a "Yes" vote from 40% *of the whole electorate* of Scotland (not just of those voting). This made a positive outcome improbable.

The referenda were held in March 1979. The Welsh referendum was lost by a massive majority. In Scotland there was a narrow majority in favour but it fell short of the required 40% of the electorate. Consequently the prospects of devolution died until after the 1997 election.

In early 1979 the Lib Lab pact broke down over the issue of proportional representation and the Liberals abstained in a vote of confidence. An election seemed imminent. However it was postponed until forced by joint opposition action in March 1979.

A summative assessment of the Wilson/Callaghan Governments

Wilson made the shock announcement of his resignation in 1976. He was barely 60, apparently in good health and had given no prior hint of this intention. However, he had led the Party for 13 years, as did Blair, but only eight of Wilson's were in periods of government. James Callaghan was elected as his successor and served as Prime Minister until Labour lost the 1979 general election.

Arguably 1974-1979 Labour governments had many positive achievements to their credit. Until the final "winter of discontent" there was no significant industrial action industrial, inflation had been reduced and there had been a successful programme of industrial investment.[C6_68]

In May 2012 Ken Livingstone asserted that: "Britain's GDP and level of economic and industrial investment were much better over the whole 30 year 1945-1979 periods than they were under New Labour."[C6_69]

From this section of the Chapter it can be seen that, in policy terms, the productivity of earlier Labour governments was considerable. These achievements were frequently made in the face of considerable economic difficulties and small Parliamentary majorities. The following section will demonstrate that the NL years were far less fruitful judged by the same yardsticks.

New Labour Government: how it dealt with contemporary core policy areas. How does this compare to the records of mid twentieth century Labour Governments discussed in previous section?

Overview

Overall, stakeholders interviewed were of the opinion that NL governments had positive policy achievements to their credit. Frank Dobson MP suggested that most of the popular policies "had an Old Labour tinge about them". *The key question is whether or not NL outshone the policy achievements of previous Labour governments in number and quality?* This assessment must be done in the context of the number of years each had in office and whether their government was continuous or not. Intermissions of Tory government are likely to lead to reparation work for an incoming Labour Government. However, this did not apply to NL governments in respect of industrial relations law, for example. Expectations of a continuous period of government must be higher than those of interrupted government of the same or similar total length. This section provides some answers to the question of whether "New" or "Old" (traditional/real) Labour made more effective use of their time in power.

New Labour's Development of long-standing core policy areas

This section deals with core policy areas in which pre-NL Labour Governments had a predominantly positive record. It examines how NL developed policies in these areas and how such policies compared and contrasted with the record of those earlier Labour governments in the same policy fields. More detailed discussion and evaluation of NL governments' policies appeared in Chapter 5.

Attack on UK Poverty: Austin Mitchell reported (see Chapter 5) that NL promised to halve the number of UK children in poverty by 2010 and abolish it by 2020. However, only one sixth of children had been taken out of poverty by 2010. In 2010 Frank Field MP told the *Guardian*[C6-70] that the Government had transferred £134 billion to families since 1999 but the number of British children in poverty had only fallen from 3.4 million to 2.8 million. There were serious problems with the administration of working families' tax credit which diminished its benefits as mentioned by Louise Ellman MP.

Under NL many benefits for families and older people (e.g. pension credit) were still conditional on the means tests which were scorned by Nye Bevan. These usually led to about a third of those eligible not receiving the benefits to which they were entitled. Of the CLP Secretaries surveyed, 81.5 % rated the National Minimum Wage (NMW), together with tax credits for poor families, as NL's greatest policy achievement and the establishment of Sure Start as its fourth best policy. These latter schemes for disadvantaged pre-schoolers were praised by Alice Mahon MP. In addition to miserable levels of state pension rises for older people, the Government played a mean trick by imposing a stealth tax on private pensions in the mid-1990s. They also refused to implement the excellent recommendations of the Royal Commission on Long Term Care of the Elderly for a comprehensive national care service.[C6-71] This neglect was criticised by more than half the CLP secretaries interviewed (see Chapter 5).

Improving Health and Education Services: One NL success story was real improvements to the NHS and Education service[C6-72] (also see Chapter 5). These received considerable (mainly capital) investment from 2000 onwards. Earlier there had been tangible improvements in mental health, cancer and coronary care services, as Frank Dobson pointed out when he referred accurately to his tenure as Secretary of State for Health. There were massive school and hospital building programmes. These were welcomed by virtually all respondents. However many had mixed feelings about them due to the fact that most of these projects were facilitated by the Private Finance Initiative (PFI) and often involved privatisation of services.

NL's increased university tuition fees were criticised as being unfair and likely to deter potential students from poorer homes. Previous Labour Governments' assistance for University students, including the payment of fees, was generous. However parents of younger students, and mature students themselves, were means tested. This earlier system benefitted NL ministers such as Jack Straw and David Blunkett during their student years.

Serious investment in public services did not start until 1999 because of a pledge to adhere to the spending plans of the previous Conservative government until then. Frank Dobson described "the biggest hospital building plan in UK history" which he praised although he had some reservations about its heavy use of PFI finance. He also believed, along with the author, that service standards were improved and upheld through the creation of NHS Service Frameworks applying uniform care standards to every health service in the UK. Some standards were introduced for social services e.g. "Quality Protects" in children's services. Unfortunately there was extensive privatisation of care services for older people and the issue of sound and fair funding for these services in England and Wales was never tackled. The wise recommendations of the Royal Commission on the Long Term Care of Older People (1999)[C6-73] which planned for adequate funding, were rejected out of hand. 74.1% of CLP Secretaries surveyed considered that the improvement of NHS services was NL's second greatest policy achievement. 40.7% of them also applauded "Reducing average waiting times for hospital operations". However some criticised "patient choice" and "too many targets".

After 1997, Labour kept their election promise to adhere to their Tory predecessors' level of spending for three years. Then, as they had also pledged, they increased spending on the NHS by 7% more per year between 2000 and 2010. This led to considerable improvements in the effectiveness and efficiency of the Health Service.[C6_74]

There was much new school building, again usually by means of PFI. Many MPs interviewed praised the massive health and education capital building programmes. Praise was heaped on these programmes by Jeremy Corbyn, Jon Cruddas, Senior backbenchers A and M, Christine McCafferty and John Cryer who described them as "a real triumph". MPs Lynne Jones and Linda Riordan had had personal first rate experience of the new hospitals. There was less positive appraisal of the quality of education and some resentment of Academies. CLP Secretaries were equally divided about whether NL reforms had improved standards in state schools or not.

Toynbee and Walker claimed that Labour were educational idealists. A previous Labour Government had castigated itself over failure to increase the school leaving age to 16 in 1964 and left a Conservative government to do this in 1972. NL doubled public spending on education between 1997 and 2009 – an increase in real terms of 75%.[C6_75]

Economic and Fiscal management: Past UK Governments, especially Labour ones, have often relentlessly pursued the goal of economic growth. In the era of environmental threats the wisdom of this will be questioned in future as it was by Alan Simpson. Britain's GDP increased by one third between 1997 and 2007.[C6_76]

Although interviewees praised NL's economic management between 1997 and 2008, many interviewees pointed out that the seeds of economic failure occurring after 2008 were sown during the earlier period of government. There was widespread criticism of excessive reliance on the market economy, too close an affinity with the banks and financial institutions and failing to control them adequately. In this respect adverse comparison can be made with all previous Labour governments. The latter accepted a more regulated mixed economy, a system of economic planning and government managed investment in enterprises. Running a successful economy always proved challenging for earlier Labour Governments. They usually inherited economic problems – Attlee from the cost of World War 2 and Wilson from twice inheriting an economic mess left by outgoing Conservative Governments. However *both Attlee and Wilson/Callaghan managed to keep afloat economically and to keep unemployment very low (until the mid 1970s). This was achieved through a mixture of international borrowing and economic restraint coupled with a Keynesian approach and the skilful use of economic planning. They also presided over high levels of Gross Domestic Product (GDP) and industrial investment. By contrast NL adopted the Thatcherite neo-liberal model of an uncontrolled and unplanned market economy. This was combined with a deregulated Labour market that was swelled latterly by mass migration of workers from the EU. NL governments also let the markets rip.*

Initially this NL economic strategy proved successful in terms of generating a prosperous economy and growing the City of London as a leading financial centre. During the first ten years the creation of many more jobs significantly reduced UK unemployment. This was acknowledged by MPs Graham Stringer and John Cryer. Deregulation and labour mobility drove down wages despite the introduction of the National Minimum Wage. NL economic policies sowed the seeds of their own destruction from 2008 onwards. This came about through failure to regulate financial institutions and their products effectively. Contrary to GB's prophesy: "Boom and Bust" did not end. As Clare Short complained, laissez-faire market capitalism ruled. Roger Berry MP lamented that "it has taken the financial crisis for many in the Party to realise that the market could not be relied on. Government public spending and taxation policies need to be progressive to maintain a level of demand in the economy". The majority of Constituency Secretaries (70.4%) praised the effective economic management of the NL government *up to 2008* but two criticised their deregulation of the markets overall.

Austin Mitchell MP regretted that *the best ever years of economic growth, under a Labour government, did not see the proceeds used to improve the lives of Britain's working people. This contrasts with the positive measures for the benefit of working people and welfare provision enacted by Attlee, Wilson and Callaghan Governments who had less cash to splash.* Jeremy Corbyn contended that NL believed that the market came first and that wealth was more important than equality. This is the converse priority to that given by most interviewees when articulating Labour's ideal values and objectives.

NL fiscal policies were, in the main, not redistributive. They thus increased economic inequality. The lie was also promoted that it was possible to expand public services without sufficiently increasing taxation to fund this. This led to a massive funding gap in the latter NL years.

International Organisations: NL had a reasonably good record of supporting international organisations. Jon Cruddas and Jeremy Corbyn praised them for helping to establish the International Criminal Court and for re-joining UNESCO. As early as 1917 the Labour Party publicly called for a League of Nations to be set up, but various elements of the Party took differing views of it during the 1920s and 1930s once it had come into being.[C6_77] The Attlee Government was involved in establishing and running the United Nations, where Britain then became a permanent member of the Security Council.

European Union: Despite the UK's presidency and the controversial Lisbon Treaty, only one MP (Austin Mitchell) mentioned the EU in his appraisal of NL policies. His view offered extensive criticism of the NL government's handling of relations with Europe. Commonly heard complaints such as breach of promise to hold a referendum on the Lisbon Treaty or praise for what, with hindsight, was GB's wisdom in preventing the UK from joining the Euro Zone, were not voiced by MPs. One constituency Secretary called for "a more proactive policy for our participation in the European Union". By contrast, the Wilson governments of 1974 prioritised holding a public referendum on Britain's continued membership of the EU after they had re-negotiated the accession treaty. This was done despite the fact that the predecessor Heath Government had already legally joined the UK to the EU – but without consulting the public.

Evaluation of policies which were newly developed, or radically changed, by New Labour governments.

This section discusses policies that were not developed or brought to fruition by previous Labour Governments (or not to any great extent). Some are policies which were not adopted by these Governments because they were regarded as being alien to the Party's traditional aims and values e.g. privatisation of public services. In other cases, policies were introduced because of pressure or rule changes from international federations to which the UK belonged. such as the United Nations. and the European Union. In the case of devolution, a previous Labour Government had not been able to secure its achievement because of lack of contemporary public support. Other policies were progressive innovations: such as the NMW.

The following policy developments were praised by many interviewees:

National Minimum Wage (NMW): The implementation of the NMW, during the 1990s, was to NL's credit. Graham Stringer MP pointed out that this measure had been promised by Labour, in and out of Government, for many years past but was never introduced. Its introduction was the result of a sustained campaign from the trade unions over many years prior to 1997. The level of the NMW has never been high enough and its enforcement has been patchy. Nevertheless MPs Chris Mullin and Katy Clark both claimed that it had made a significant difference to many poor people in their constituencies.

Non Economic Equalities: There was a widespread welcome for such equalities measures. Katy Clark praised increased rights for parental leave and Lynne Jones welcomed more support for people with mental health problems. Under Wilson there were measures to improve mental health services in the White Paper *Better Services for the Mentally Ill* (1975).[C6_78] The late 1990s Mental Health Service Frameworks[C6_79] were praised by Frank Dobson who had introduced them.

Improved rights for gay, lesbian and transgender people were widely praised. Approval came from John Grogan, Jeremy Corbyn, Senior Backbencher M. and Lynne Jones. None of the CLP secretaries registered views about NL policies for non economic equalities. Christine McCafferty and Roger Berry expressed satisfaction that the Labour Government had put its values into effect by introducing a significant quantity of equalities legislation: especially improved parental leave following births (not enacted by earlier Labour governments).

Gordon Prentice successfully, and almost singlehandedly, promoted the right to roam in the countryside. The right to roam was not enacted by earlier Labour administrations.

A Wilson government legalised gay sex between consenting adults. Gay and Lesbian rights were not strongly developed by other Labour governments although the GLC, under Ken Livingstone's leadership, led the way in promoting these equalities. More progressive measures awaited changes in public opinion and an NL government whose commitment to improved rights for gay and lesbian people were widely praised.

Respondents welcomed the Human Rights Act. This stemmed from the European convention on the subject. Such legislation had not been enacted by a previous Labour Government.

Freedom of Information: MP Chris Mullin praised the enactment of the Freedom of Information Act. It greatly expanded the public's capacity for finding out about actions and policies that had been undertaken covertly by local and national government. *With hindsight TB expressed regrets that he had agreed to the measure.* No previous Government had introduced similar legislation.

Peace Settlement in Northern Ireland: Major praise was given by MPs interviewed to the Peace Settlement in Northern Ireland. The conflicts and problems of Ulster proved intractable to Wilson and Callaghan led Governments. NL's second successful, and special: "foreign policy" achievement was the Good Friday peace settlement in the North of Ireland. Chris Mullin applauded this peace agreement as being "unique" and one of TB's greatest achievements. This attainment was also praised by Clare Short. However the latter added: "but the work for it started well before 1997". Previous Labour governments made little progress in this quest, as Mullin recalled.

Commitment to tackle poverty in developing countries: One respect in which NL outshone previous Labour Governments was in its commitment to combat Third World poverty. The international aid budget was significantly increased *and the increase was maintained.* They were helped by a UK public opinion whose sympathy towards the world's poor had been increased by campaigns such as Make Poverty History, Jubilee 2000 and Live Aid. Once adherence to Tory spending plans had ended, after 2000, aid spending levels rose to and overtook those of France and Germany.

It was decided to choose more than 20 of the most under-developed countries and to write off their debt. Towards the end of GB's reign the Government committed to raise aid to the long-standing UN target of 0.7% of GNP by 2013. Jon Cruddas praised the establishment of the Department for International Development (DFID). However several MPs, including former Secretary of State for International Development Clare Short, considered that while NL's development policies had created goodwill for the government in the Third World, much of that gratitude had been eclipsed by the Iraq war.

The record of previous Labour Governments on overseas development aid was more disappointing. During the 1940s the first priority was to assist post war economic recovery in Europe. Bevin was instrumental in working with the USA to develop the Marshall Plan for that purpose. The 1970 Labour general election manifesto mentioned the same UN target as was current in 2010 (0.7 % of GNP) for aid to developing countries, only to say that the UK meeting it was a distant aspiration. In the context of the economic problems and other priorities affecting Wilson and Callaghan governments it remained distant.

Actual Devolution: Securing devolved Parliaments in Scotland, Wales and Northern Ireland was a significant NL achievement. John Grogan MP believed devolution would be a 'lasting legacy". Scottish MP Katy Clark stated that devolution was important but not as important as the NMW or increased spending on public services. She also criticised failure to reform the House of Lords adequately. Kelvin Hopkins MP recalled that the NL Government was committed to devolution (by the 1997 election manifesto). However, he claimed, TB loathed devolution because it gave power to institutions other than Westminster and thus out of his direct control. Of the CLP secretaries interviewed, 40.7% praised devolution for Scotland, Wales and London.

Controversial policies and policy failures introduced by NL Governments

Suggested policy failures of NL administrations included: failure to increase *the quantity of social housing and to address overall concerns of the working class – particularly the white working class.* This was highlighted by Jon Cruddas and Senior backbenchers A. and B. It contrasts with better performances in these fields by earlier Labour Governments (see above).

Austin Mitchell MP stated that the percentage of UK GDP spent on social housing fell drastically in the late 1970s (Callaghan government). The Attlee government aspired to build 200,000 new council homes per year but fell short due to post war practical constraints. However *Wilson governments of the 1960s built an average of 400,000 council homes per year.*

To give NL its due, whilst its record on the provision of additional social rented homes was abysmal, they had a commendable record on the modernisation and improvement of social housing. In 2001 39% of UK social housing was deemed sub·standard but this applied to only 8% by 2009. Most CLP Secretaries had little to say about NL housing policies but one said: "There has not been enough investment in social housing".

Affordable housing (usually rented) for those in need had long been one of Labour's priorities. Providing it had became more daunting after Thatcher governments introduced the right for council tenants to buy their own homes. During Mrs. Thatcher's premiership; one quarter of the council housing stock (mainly that in better condition) was sold off.[C6_80] Very little was replaced because the Conservatives cut, and eventually withdrew, funds for building public social rented housing. Limited funds for rented home building continued to be given to the not for profit sector (mainly housing associations). *NL made no significant effort to replace social housing that had been purchased by tenants under Thatcher's Right to Buy policy. Council home sales continued apace. The shortage was exacerbated by councils being heavily pressurised by NL Governments to sell off their remaining housing stock to the non-statutory sector who could sell it on and might not keep it in good order.*

Meanwhile, under NL, the price of private housing rocketed and credit for purchase became much more readily available. This was sometimes given without adequate checks on income being made. [C6_81] Toynbee and Walker claimed: "Housing was one of Labour's weakest links ... The government resisted the logic of state intervention, *partly because social rented housing sounded Old Labour".* There was also the issue of the expense of building new homes.[C6_82]

Nuclear Weapons: After the sound and fury about Labour's policy on nuclear weapons in earlier years; there was little debate on this issue during the NL period. This was largely because Labour's Conference Arrangements Committee (CAC) prevented it being debated at Conference year after year. The ending of the cold war may have made this debate seem less urgent. NL involved the UK in Bush's Star Wars project. Backbencher B. said we still have to deal with nuclear weapons and nuclear power accidents. The issue was still exercising CLP secretaries, two thirds of whom considered "keeping and updating Britain's nuclear weapons" to be the NL government's second worst policy mistake. Two of them made demands: one called for immediate UK nuclear disarmament, and another for scrapping, rather than renewing, the Trident system.

Trades unions and rights at work: Past Labour governments did much to empower the trade unions. However both Wilson and Callaghan Governments also enacted measures to contain and control them. Many of these were developed with an element of mutual consent. There was always regular consultation at the highest level (see Chapter 4).

NL took away the unions' high level consultation rights, retained the vast majority of their Tory predecessors' anti union legislation and enacted a few measures to benefit people at work. These included the 50% recognition rule which improved a union's right to be recognised in a workplace, improved compensation for unfair dismissal and increased maternity and paternity leave.

Solidarity and fraternity within the Party are important. At the time of the 1997 general election the Labour Party had 400,000 individual members. By the time of the 2010 general election it had lost nearly two thirds of them (see Chapters 2 and 5). Before the NL era the Party membership were accustomed to meeting regularly for political and social events, and debating and participating fully in Party policy making. A speaker at the Save the Labour Party seminar in July 2005 said: "Above all, we valued opportunities for fellowship within the Party". One aspect of the co-operative working of party members was fund raising to help fund elections and thus secure shared national and local political objectives. This was often achieved through organising social events.

Public Ownership: Public ownership always featured in Labour's aims, as incorporated into its constitution, until New Clause 4 was enacted in 1995. Thatcher and Major governments implemented the privatisation of gas, water, electricity, telecoms, public road transport and the railways. In order to avoid monopolies, and possibly also to make re-nationalisation more difficult, the old publicly owned monopoly industries were broken up into private businesses such as the train operating companies. There was also some deregulation. Jenkins, reported that, by 1990, about 600,000 people were *former* government employees as a consequence of Thatcher's privatisations.[C6_83] Prior to 1997 there was frequent advocacy, supported by some Labour shadow ministers (e.g. Clare Short), for the re-nationalisation of the railways which were sold off by the Tories very shortly before the election.

Loss of public trust: As time went on there were numerous reasons for the loss of public confidence in NL. This was probably greater than that suffered by any previous Labour government, as the 2010 and 2015 general election results demonstrated. Lynne Jones thought that it was due to NL's methods of campaigning. John Cryer, and others, believed it was caused by dishonesty concerning the Iraq War. There was also widespread resentment about the Parliamentary expenses scandal of 2009. Two CLP secretaries criticised TB and GB's "presidential style of government" and two more disliked over-centralised decision making by NL governments.

One of the most serious losses of public trust resulted from the Parliamentary expenses scandal of 2009. Such abuses were not evident during previous Labour Governments. The rot began during the early 1980s when Mrs Thatcher covertly advised laxity in overseeing MPs' expenses rather than grant an electorally unpopular rise in their salaries. Lynne Jones thought that the expenses scandal had diminished public confidence in NL and in politicians generally. MPs Hopkins, Mullin, Short and Stringer all commented along the same lines. So did Christine McCafferty who added "TB and GB are no longer seen as trustworthy". Katy Clark said: (as a result) "The public no longer trust politicians". Of the 27 Party Secretaries surveyed, 16 reported that most electors were either "hostile" or "very hostile" because of the expenses scandal (when being canvassed by Labour for the 2009 European and local elections). These elections took place within a few weeks of the scandal becoming public. No secretary received positive reactions and only two said that "it made no difference".

Promoting democracy. Lynne Jones regretted that NL had not introduced the fairer system of proportional representation (PR) for general elections. She recalled that, in 2001, NL received only 25% of the votes cast and in 2005 only 21%. But they were still able to form majority governments. Before the 2010 election NL committed the Government committed to holding referendum on the Alternative Vote (AV) system of Proportional Representation (PR) if elected. The Coalition Government held such a referendum (see Chapter 12). Two CLP secretaries criticised NL's neglect of reform for our voting system and failure to introduce PR for all elections.

Centralism and continued disempowerment of local government: NL failed to reverse the relentless disempowerment of local government enacted by predecessor Tory governments. This centralised control was effected by ever increasing autocratic management of local government spending (e.g. through rate capping) and other powers. Several CLP Secretaries raised this issue, which was overlooked by MPs (other than Alan Simpson). They regretted that this democratic deficit had not been rectified by NL and called for local authorities to be re-empowered.

Privatisation: This type of NL policy was never previously adopted by Labour Governments. Linda Riordan criticised NL's privatisation of public services which had created conditions that would make it easier for an incoming Conservative government to privatise NHS services, especially through establishing foundation hospitals which were set up in a way that made them easy meat for privatisers. The policies that the last Conservative-Liberal coalition enacted escalated privatisation of the NHS. In 2013 they began selling off trust after trust to such private companies as Virgin. New Labour's policies had paved the way for this.

In terms of achieving Labour's traditional social democratic aims, privatisation was clearly a backward step. Much privatisation was facilitated through the Private Finance Initiative (PFI), whereby most new public capital expenditure was funded. New schools and hospitals were built by private finance companies and leased back to the public sector at exorbitant rents reflecting the interest rates they had paid. These averaged at three times the rate that would have been paid for direct public borrowing.[C6_84] This off balance sheet accounting was favoured by GB, probably because it was a form of disguised public borrowing that was not recorded in Public Sector Borrowing Requirement (PSBR) statistics. It saddled future generations with enormous repayment debts. Lenders often insisted that ancillary services in hospitals and schools should be also handed to them to run as private contractors. This had implications for standards of service, for instance cleanliness in hospitals and for staff conditions of employment as MP, and former nurse, Alice Mahon, pointed out.

Health Service privatisation was also progressed through creation and running of Foundation Hospitals and Primary Care Trusts. These were pressured to purchase services from the private sector. This initiative was aided by the device of "Patient Choice". The NL government also worked to create an additional private sector by the creation of new private "Diagnostic and Treatment Centres" given major contracts to treat publicly funded NHS patients. Lynne Jones believed that they were starting to break up the welfare state. Alice Mahon declared: "The Labour Government should hang its head in shame about NHS privatisation".

Schools privatisation consisted of establishing academies, often in previously failing schools. These were partly funded by private proprietors who then obtained the right to hire and fire staff and to have their own religious doctrine or other interest taught in the schools whether parents liked it or not.[C6_85]

The other public service/business where privatisation was fended off (twice in response to union and other protest action) was that of the Post Office. This privatisation was desired by the contemporary Labour leadership. John McDonnell contended that NL privatised more public services than did Thatcher and Major together. Of the CLP secretaries surveyed, 55.6% criticised NL for "Relying too heavily on the privatisation of public services". They seemed even more strongly opposed to it than were backbenchers interviewed.

NL governments also privatised some commercial businesses. The most significant cases were part-privatisation the National Air Traffic Control Service (51%) in the late 1990s and manufacturing firm Kinetic. Also noteworthy was NL's failure to re-nationalise public enterprises sold off by predecessor Tory governments. These included: gas, electricity, water, railways, telecommunications and the deregulation of public transport (which NL extended). Attlee and Wilson led Labour governments virtually always took back into public ownership industries that their Tory predecessor governments had de-nationalised. CLP Secretaries wanted contemporary nationalisation of some industries and one called for re-nationalisation of the railways. After the financial crisis from 2008 onwards, NL took some banks and the East Coast Main Line railway into public ownership, but with the proviso that they would privatise them again as soon as possible (The East Coast line remained in public ownership until the Tories organised re-privatisation in 2015).

In the field of public services and key industries, the NL record contrasts starkly with the comprehensive programme of the creation of public services and nationalisation of key industries undertaken by Labour Governments of the 1940s and early 1950s. Wilson developed machinery for managing public enterprise effectively: this included the National Enterprise Board.

Warmongering foreign policies: The Iraq war was almost universally detested among stakeholders interviewed. This cost the Party thousands of members (see LabOUR Commission Report 2007)[C6_86] and precipitated the first major Parliamentary revolt.[88] Stakeholders were more divided on the legitimacy of the war in Afghanistan.

There were strong negative views about TB marching his soldiers out to war with the star-spangled banner marching on before (and other indicators of being in thrall to a right-wing American president). This was strongly criticised by both MPs and CLP secretaries. Previous Labour governments, especially those of the 1960s and 1970s were less inclined to go to war frequently. The 1914-18 and 1939-45 World Wars saw Labour in power as partners in national/coalition governments. However those legal wars were not of their making and had widespread international support. Britain joined the US in the legal Korean war. Wilson was to be congratulated for keeping Britain out of the Vietnam conflict. Wilson and Callaghan were deferential to the Americans and co-operated with them in nuclear defence policy but never joined them in war making.

Sadly the most enduring widespread memories of the NL era, particularly those of TB's premiership, relate to the wars into which he took the UK. A common view of MPs interviewed was that there was some merit in UK involvement in Sierra Leone and Bosnia. Interviewees had divided opinions about British involvement in the UN approved Afghan conflict, but believed there was no excuse for the allegedly illegal Iraq War. Peter Kilfoyle MP described the Iraq invasion as "part of a wider genuflection to the US Superpower". Roger Berry argued that, in his opinion, the Iraq War was "immoral and contrary to international law". Most CLP secretaries judged NL's worst policy to have been participating in the invasion of Iraq, which was deplored by 70.4% of them. More than half of them criticised the NL government for "Being subservient to a right wing US president".

Lord S. claimed that the Afghan war is a completely UN mandated and supported policy and therefore legal. Jeremy Corbyn believed that lies were told about the Afghan war. The current real contemporary issue, he claimed, was not helicopters and equipment, but about whether British troops should be there. One third of CLP secretaries considered that "the UK and USA were right to take military action in Afghanistan" whereas only five out of 27 supported the Iraq invasion.

There was concern about the UK having failed to play a positive role in securing a settlement for the Palestinians. Christine McCafferty complained that NL had failed to secure a peace settlement in the Middle East. One CLP secretary thought that the Government should have protested to the United Nations about Israel frequently flouting many UN resolutions.

Toynbee and Walker claimed that Blair's Iraq war was only possible militarily because the UK "kept disproportionately large armed forces and hankered after a world role, and no one queried that posture". [C6_87] Robin Cook made noble attempts, when Foreign Secretary, to reduce the UK's dealing in arms exports from 1997 onwards. These were confounded probably because the UK's arms manufacturing industry then employed 415,000 workers: many of them living in Labour held seats.

House of Lords Reform: NL achievement in this respect was paltry. Lord S. praised the Government for abolishing the judicial powers of the House of Lords and creating the new Supreme Court in its place. In his book Robin Cook criticised the "clumsy way" votes on the future structure of the Lords were taken resulting in there being no decisive outcome.[C6_88] Some MPs interviewed suggested that the Commons engineered this result because they did not want a powerful second chamber which would threaten their own authority. Previous Labour governments did not attempt Lords reform but acquiesced in the system of Life Peers (instituted by the Conservatives in 1958). That system eschewed the hereditary principle but gave the Labour leader excessive opportunities for patronage.

Unprecedented assaults on Civil Liberties: There was much criticism of NL's proposals for detention without trial: especially where it was planned to last for 90 days. The 90 day proposal was deplored and voted against by Frank Dobson, Christine McCafferty, Clare Short and Chris Mullin (who was chair of the Home Affairs Select Committee at the material time). Of the CLP secretaries surveyed, 48.2% criticised the Government for "using the terrorist threat to curb civil liberties".

Record of the contemporary Australian Labor Party compared with that of New Labour

This section examines the policies of Australian Labor Government during the period 2007-2010 when the timing of its government overlapped with that of NL. It draws brief comparisons with the record of NL Government during the same period and draws conclusions as to what NL could have learnt from Down Under.

Record of recent Australian Labor Government: August 2007 to August 2010: The Australian Liberal (i.e. Conservative) Government was in power from the mid nineties but was defeated by Labor in August 2007. When Kevin Rudd became its first Prime Minister he increased his popularity by apologising to the "stolen generations" of Australians, indigenous and immigrant, who had been taken from their birth families and brought up in institutions. A hallmark of TB and GB was that they virtually never apologised for anything. In the case of the Iraq war, and possibly for contributing to the 2008 financial crisis, apologising would have been the appropriate course of action for them to take. TB has just given a first part apology in October 2015!

In 2011:Federal Minister Gary Gray said: "Accepting that we've only been in office for two and a half years (as at February 2010) and accepting the constraints that, within a year, we hit the global financial crisis: we have to start from that point. Our response to the global financial crisis has achieved a multitude of objectives:

1. To protect the jobs and living conditions of working Australians. When you look at the performance indicators you see a performance which has seen our country weather the global financial crisis in pretty good shape. We have also provided over 70% of our economic stimulus activity into direct human infrastructure: infrastructure for communities; infrastructure for economic activities; infrastructure that will serve generations to come.

2. We also ensured that while we dealt with the global financial crisis, essential policy matters were attended to. These related to people in the work place, particularly to unfair collective provisions introduced by the former Liberal (i.e. Conservative) government. It's important to acknowledge the work that we still have to do to correct the gap in life expectancy between indigenous people and non – indigenous. We have already pushed substantial resources into that task and massive government resources into education and health."

3. (Returning to industrial relations) he continued: "The main task was to remove substantial parts of the old 'Work Choices' framework (introduced by the previous Howard Liberal Government) that did not allow for the collective. 'Work Choices' created the mechanism to allow for individual contracting arrangements under Australian Workplace Agreements. These agreements were particularly unfair for low paid, low skilled workers. So removing that framework was an essential activity right from winning the election. It was also important to have something that had sufficient flexibility to allow labour markets to continue to work but also allowing the principle of collective bargaining to have a role – where workers wish it."

4. (With reference to the use of additional public expenditure to head off the recession): "We use the language of 'investment to support employment'. So we haven't gone out and created jobs, we've supported existing industries to get across the downturn in order to keep apprentices in employment and keep businesses working while the downturn was occurring around the globe and where whole businesses and regional economies were falling apart. We were able to bridge that gap for a range of reasons:

• The essential economic conservatism of Australia.

• The fortuitous nature of our resource economy (mainly mining and minerals).

• The rapid bounce back of our principal regional markets: Korea, India and China."

Unlike NL, the Australian Labor Government repealed virtually the whole raft of right wing industrial relations legislation enacted by the previous Howard government and replaced it with a new, more worker – friendly system for the mediation of industrial disputes. They staved off the global recession in Australia by instigating massive public works in Keynesian mode; thus keeping people in work and developing public infrastructure to support future economic development.

During the early 21st century the Australian Labor Party (ALP) indulged in triangulation, as NL had done. The Hawke Rann Report (2002)[C6-89] used findings of opinion surveys of grass-roots ALP members undertaken after that Party's loss of the 2001 general election. There only 37.8% of voters cast a first preference vote for Labor (AV system). It said: "A perceived lack of policy differentiation from our conservative opponents is second on their list of concerns ... Some suggested Labor had lost touch with its traditional blue-collar base, while others argued not." There was also a call for serious consideration of the best strategies to maintain a support base from which to reach out to swing voters."

In an article published in *Chartist* in 2009 July/ August 2009[C6-90] the author wrote: "Kevin Rudd's Australian Labor Government has been in office for a slightly shorter period than has Gordon Brown's administration. In that time it has achieved much more for working people and a better record of economic management during worldwide recession. This government promptly repealed all the anti-trades union legislation of its Liberal predecessor. That was replaced with extensive statutory rights for workers. Back in the UK we still wait for a New Labour Government to abolish any worthwhile quantity of Mrs Thatcher's draconian anti-union laws, even after twelve years in office."

She continued: "There is an active Australian Government policy to increase investment in social rented housing (which the Brown government agreed belatedly to start). In a flash of inspiration a first homebuyer's grant of £11,000 has been offered to all such buyers during a period of nine months. Most first time home buyers tend to be at the less affluent end of the purchaser spectrum. Crucially this measure has kept the Australian housing market from grinding to a halt and house prices from plummeting as rapidly as they did in Britain (during the same period)."

It continued: "In the UK pensioners have had a raw deal under Blair and Brown governments. The value of the state pension continues to wither away. Brown has promised that the state pension will again rise in line with wages from 2010 "if it can be afforded" (and, as it turned out: "if we are still in office") ... Rudd recently announced that, although some public expenditure cuts are inevitable, due to the economic situation, their new and more generous state pension scheme will not be adversely affected.

The Australian Government shored up the banks to a limited extent (during the world economic crisis). However most recession-easing investment went directly into electors' pockets. This was implemented mainly through cash payments to low income households. The equivalent of £400 was given to each of the 10 million least well off households in Australia (slightly over half the population). This was in the, largely justified, expectation that they would spend it soon on goods and services and so save jobs. The remainder was largely disbursed to pay off personal debts. This probably released money for future consumer spending.

The remaining significant Australian Labor government measure, designed to counter the threat of more serious recession, was large scale direct government investment in infrastructure – particularly in new school buildings and roads. All this paid off, in the last week of May 2009, it was officially announced that "Australia is no longer in recession". (following this the value of the Australian dollar rose steadily and by April 2011 it was one of the strongest currencies in the world). So what did the Australian public think of this dangerous democratic socialist government? Kevin Rudd attained an average 65% approval rating in opinion polls in the year to July 2009.

When the above article was penned: "Kevin Rudd seemed set fair to win a second term of office for Labor in 2010". Australian Labor has taken a principled stand on tackling climate change. Kevin Rudd proposed an emissions trading scheme and a mining tax which made the Labor Party, and himself, unpopular in early 2010. He then postponed implementation of these proposals but thereby further damaged his credibility. There were also later controversies about policy on asylum seekers and another publicly funded job creation policy. This scheme provided money for home insulation. The work was delegated to private contractors who were poorly managed by government and were not obliged to train their workforces effectively. The result was the accidental death of three young workers on the scheme. The government then abruptly ended the project, to avoid further accidents, but the outcome was that many insulation companies folded and shed employees. This attracted bad publicity. A positive policy development, commenced during this period, was planning for a national fibre optic cable broadband network which would make the internet available cheaply to every Australian household. It will be a public sector monopoly. This will be some achievement in a country with the land area and topography of Australia."

As Rudd's unpopularity grew so did a head of steam in the Federal Parliamentary ALP to dismiss him. In Summer 2010 he was replaced as Leader, and therefore as Prime Minister, by his deputy Julia Gillard. The back biting, and internecine strife, involved in this coup damaged Labor's popularity. The August 2010 Australian General election was a draw and eventually an unstable coalition was cobbled together.

In 2013, following more internecine warfare in the ALP, when Julia Gillard had become unpopular with the Australian electorate and Labour had taken a nosedive in the opinion polls, a Caucus (PLP) coup brought Kevin Rudd back to the premiership in time to fight the General Election Campaign in September that year.

UK New Labour could have learned much from Kevin Rudd's contemporary achievements in staving off the recession, developing public infrastructure, constructing a more progressive framework for industrial relations and repealing the right wing measures of his predecessors in this field. However Rudd's brave, but commendable, attempts to develop green policies proved to be a step too far and too fast for the Australian electorate at that time.

Conclusion: Old Labour vs. New Labour: the overall policy record assessed

The Attlee, Wilson and Wilson/Callaghan governments built up a comprehensive welfare state, particularly in respect of health, education, social housing and social security. As soon as these administrations came to power they implemented many of their election commitments to improve public services. They also created a safety net to protect the poorest financially. They launched initiatives to counter child poverty, notably during the 1960s. These Labour governments built a strong portfolio of publicly owned and run public services and industries. Later governments even re-nationalised enterprises de-nationalised by intervening Tory governments. They also devised improved structures for managing public enterprise such as the National Enterprise Board. These Governments were fortunate that, owing to the '"Butskellite" consensus during the 1950s and 1960s, the Conservatives seldom undid Labour welfare state measures but did reverse nationalisations of some industrial enterprises.

Earlier Labour governments adopted relatively progressive taxation policies that funded their welfare state. Sometimes unpopular measures had to be taken (for example: Stafford Cripp's exchange controls) or funding had to be supplemented by overseas borrowing, but this never became unmanageable. Callaghan found that the controversial IMF loan, once secured, was not needed. Some of the economic management, notably the 1964-70 Wilson Government's complete elimination of the large balance of payments deficit left by his Conservative predecessors, demonstrated competence. These Labour governments relied on the democratic socialist economic strategies of economic planning and Keynesian intervention.

NL Governments did not make haste to improve the welfare state. First they cut the level of benefits for one parent families. Next they announced they would adhere to the spending plans of the previous Conservative Government for their first three years. Because of the financial crisis of 2008 another two years of planned health and welfare improvements was scaled down. Improvement was not stopped but those years led to serious overspend. There was a massive spending increase on development of public services, particularly health and education, mainly between the millennium and 2008. Much of the funding drew on expensive private finance. It went into capital building projects for schools, hospitals and clinics. This provided much needed replacement for old and outdated buildings. There were initiatives to improve standards in health and education – some successful. Few resources were devoted to increasing social housing although there was some modernisation of existing stock. This government did much to privatise elements of public services through Foundation Hospitals, Academy Schools and pushing the provision of health care directly into the private sector (for example: through "patient choice") . This privatisation prompted interviewees' accusations that NL was paving the way for an incoming Tory Government to extend the process. These foundations have since been built upon by Tory governments. NL did not re-nationalise services and utilities privatised by Thatcher and Major Governments.

NL's other great attainment was securing peace in Northern Ireland. Previous Labour governments had been unable to achieve this. NL increased aid to developing countries well above the level of any previous Labour Government. Wilson Governments had long term plans to increase overseas aid which did not come to fruition because of economic issues.

NL economic management, the biggest issue for most interviewees, appeared to be successful until the great debacle of 2008. Some of the roots of that disaster grew during earlier NL years. The outcomes resulted from NL ditching economic planning and giving the market and the financial institutions total freedom. As a consequence: UK society became progressively more unequal.

An unprecedented 13 continuous years of majority Labour Government during the NL Period should have produced a wealth of policies in furtherance of democratic socialist aims and objectives. These would have benefitted the less privileged sectors of the population. Toynbee and Walker's final verdict was: "The charge is that they wasted the extraordinary opportunity of ten years of economic prosperity and secure parliamentary majorities under a leader of great political talent, facing only weak opposition."[C6_91] The overall conclusion must be that New Labour did too little and acted too late as compared with its authentic Labour predecessors.

There is little doubt that over a period of 30 years (18 of them in government) real ("old") Labour governments between 1945 and 1979 achieved far more pro rata in policy terms than did their NL successors. The 1945-1979 achievements were manifested in terms of policy outcomes and economic and social improvements. Most of these achievements fitted with the Party's traditional aims and values: unlike many of those of NL.

The attainments of NL governments, in 13 years of uninterrupted power, were tangible, but insufficient in view of the political and economic opportunities available to them. Many of their polices reflected adherence to market principles, promotion of privatisation of public services and a foreign policy centred on instigating military action (frequently following the USA and in unjustified circumstances). NL implemented a limited number of policies that reflected traditional Labour values and long established campaigns of the Labour movement (for example: the National Minimum Wage and devolution).

CHAPTER 7
What New Labour did to Internal Party Democracy

It's our party and we'll cry if we want to

*"I have always believed that the politics of organisation
is as important as the politics of ideas"*
John Prescott, speech to Labour Party Conference, 2000

*"John Prescott was worried we were saying to the Party, you've always
failed and we are only going to succeed if we change everything"*
Alastair Campbell's Diary, 20.9.1994

*"If we are ever again going to see a Labour Party that is worth its salt,
we are going to have to recapture our Party, our position on the NEC
and, less important, but vital, on the National Policy Forum"*
Michael Meacher MP, interview, June 2009

*"A senior member of Party staff told me that, when speaking to other
Party members, they refer to 'Old Labour' Members like myself as
'dinosaurs' and urge them to discredit and marginalise us"*
The late Councillor Kath Fry, former National Policy Forum Member

Selection, Powers and Accountability of the NL Party leadership

The NL Machinery of Party Governance and Policy making (you could skip this as it's not exciting, but would enlighten you about NL's repressive and complex rules)

Command and control through the Party Secretariat (machine)

Attacks on Party democracy and hollowing out of the Party on the Ground The diminishing role of Party members in policy making

The Malfunctioning of the larger policy making structures (Party Conference and the National Policy Forum)

Top down interference with the Party at local level

Introduction

This Chapter is the sad story of the diminution and hollowing out of a, once great, democratic and progressive institution, the UK Labour Party. The incident described below is illustrative.

Constituency Party Conference delegates, from the Region, gathered in a dark, ornate committee room at City Hall three weeks before the 2009 Annual Party Conference. They were full of eager anticipation about what this venture into Party policy making might bring. The two thirds of them, who were first timers, were full of hope and ideas. The young, fresh faced, regional organiser welcomed them with: "You will enjoy Conference – it's a marvellous opportunity for celebrity spotting!" Thus their role was reduced to being passive spectators only interested in rubbing shoulders with the famous. Conference was relegated to being an X Factor style show case for the benefit of New Labour (NL) elite politicians instead of being the Party's main policy making body.

As in previous years, some delegates would get intimidating exposure to "celebrities". In 2009, the vote to change elections for the National Policy Forum (NPF) from Conference delegates to the more democratic one member one vote (OMOV) postal vote system was on the agenda. When it was about to be debated numerous delegates from the South East, South West and Yorkshire regions were marched off, by Party staff, to meet a formidable minister. They told the author that he tried to pressurise them into voting for the status quo.

From the adoption of its first constitution in 1918, the Labour Party had been run as a democratic Party for most of the time. Research for the Independent LabOUR Commission, 2007[C7-1] found that: "Many party members felt 'frozen out' of the policy and decision making machinery of the Party. There is a widespread belief among members that elements of the Leadership actively want to see the role of members curtailed and to impose a heavily centralised, elitist model, funded by rich individuals and the state." They continued: "Only the revival and renewal of the Party as a truly democratic, broad based, mass membership movement of Trade Union, Socialist Society and individual members can ensure its continuing electoral and financial success."(LabOUR Commission Report, 2007 pp 6-7)[C7-2].

This Chapter analyses and discusses what NL did to the "Party on the Ground". This latter term is adopted to identify the non-elite Party outside the Executive and Parliament as defined by Mair.[C7-3] NL systematically introduced a set of changes to the Party's structure and organisational culture. This Chapter includes scrutiny of what NL did to Party policy making forums and structures for internal Party government. Of special concern: was the Party machine's management of Annual Conference, from increasing duress on voting delegates from the mid 1990s onwards to the violent eviction of octogenarian Walter Wolfgang (in 2005) and afterwards. It also investigates the way in which Party staff were recruited, trained and managed to ensure they delivered the Leadership's bidding and worked to change the Party's culture, to the detriment of ordinary members' rights.

A struggle for the values and aims of the Party between the Leadership and more radical members of the Parliamentary party and the Party on the Ground was not new and each successive generation had a different set of attitudes significantly different from its predecessors.[C7-4]

In earlier chapters those, whose opinions were reported, were either Backbench MPs, trade union leaders or constituency party secretaries. Here there are records of the opinions of former party staff and delegates to Party Conference. These are contextualised within the findings of the Independent LabOUR Commission (2007)[C7-5] and other relevant sources.

When the NL Project captured the Party, they changed the Party's organisational structure and culture in order to secure and entrench the "reforms" they craved and to pass virtually all power to the Leadership. Philip Gould, NL's political strategist, recommended: "Labour must replace competing existing structures with a single chain of command leading directly to the leader of the Party".[C7-6]

Between the 1997 and 2010 general elections the Labour Party lost 61.5% of its individual members. The LabOUR Commission Report 2007[C7-7] regretted that: "Underlying the loss of votes, seats and members is a profound cultural crisis arising from the sidelining of Party democracy by centralised command and control."

This Report[C7-8] continued: 'In the current climate local fund raising for spending locally will be easier than national fund raising until member's confidence in the Leadership and Party HQ has been restored". The report of Professor Stuart Weir on views of focus groups conducted for the LabOUR Commission said: "There was huge disillusion with the attitude of the Party's leaders and the Prime Minister and his government towards the Party's membership. It was not simply that the government ignored the Party's views – that was a historic reality. It was strongly felt that the party hierarchy had a condescending, and even contemptuous, attitude to the Party and its members, seeking to manipulate them rather than consult and work with them as equals."[C7-9]

Choice, Accountability and powers of the Labour Party Leadership

In order to discuss the role of party stakeholders in policy making it is necessary to examine the operation of the Party's governance and policy making machinery.

In respect of electing the Party Leader, maintaining their accountability and monitoring their use of their powers. Gould[C7-10] proposed that all power be ultimately vested in the Party Leader. Arguably both Tony Blair (TB) and Gordon Brown (GB) assumed almost absolute power. The Leadership, how it is elected, and its degree of accountability, is the first major topic discussed in this chapter.

Prior to 1981, the Leader of the Labour Party was primarily Leader of the Parliamentary Labour Party (PLP) and was elected solely by sitting Labour MPs.[C7-11] Party members, and members of affiliated organisations (trade unions and "socialist" societies), had no vote. In the mid 1970s the Campaign for Labour Party Democracy (CLPD)[C7-12] argued that the leader should no longer be selected by the PLP alone but should be elected by, and accountable to, the Party as a whole. This campaign gained traction when right winger James Callaghan was elected by MPs to succeed the leftish Harold Wilson in 1976 and consequently the left, within the wider Party, were dissatisfied.

On the right of the Party, there was a move to elect the leader by OMOV (One Member One Vote). At a special Party conference in 1981,[C7-13] a three sector electoral college: PLP, affiliated bodies, and Constituency Labour Parties (CLPs) was agreed. Conference decided the shares of votes in the college would be: 30% for the PLP, 30% for Constituency Labour Parties (CLPs) and 40% for trade unions and other affiliates. Foot held out against an electoral college until 1980. He favoured keeping greater authority with the PLP. The electoral college system was not implemented until 1983. Neil Kinnock was the first leader chosen by this electoral college. The same college was operational in the following leadership election (1992). The unions' role had become controversial because then they were not required to ballot their members before voting. Some – the GMB, NUPE and USDAW – ran ballots, but each union's vote was not split proportionally between candidates favoured. As a consequence, John Smith won with 90.9% of the vote. In 1993 Conference agreed to an electoral college of thirds: MPs, trades unions and affiliated organisations (e.g. the Fabian Society) and individual members: voting was by OMOV. There were to be compulsory ballots of union members to determine how each union would vote. [C7-14] This system, as modified, was operational until 2014 when it was changed (see Chapter 12). It was used to elect Ed Miliband in 2010. By that time each union member cast their vote for their own preferred candidate.

MPs remain the gatekeepers. They determine who can actually enter the leadership ballot because they have the sole right of nomination. A candidate had to receive nominations from 12.5% of all Labour MPs (this was increased to 15% in 2014) before they could enter the electoral college ballot. In 1994 this percentage represented 34 MPs but in 2007, when GB was crowned without an election, it represented 46 MPs. In 1994 TB won in the first round of the ballot with 57% of all votes. He had been identified as front runner, by the media, within days of John Smith's death[C7-15] which probably affected the outcome. When the leadership next came vacant (2007) no aspirant, other than GB, could secure the required 12.5 % of MPs' nominations. GB rapidly obtained nominations of the vast majority of the PLP. This may have occurred because MPs considered the result to be certain and did not want to incur GB's displeasure and forfeit his patronage. During the NL years most aspiring left-wingers were kept out of the PLP as they were removed from shortlists for candidate selections, in safe and many winnable seats, by the National Executive Committee Organisation Sub-Committee (see Chapter 8). Thus there were (and are) far fewer left and centre-left MPs available to stand or nominate for the Leadership. In 2012 and 2015 there was an initiative to ensure a that a fuller spectrum of Labour Party opinion was represented on the Leadership ballot paper when some democratically minded MPs nominated Diane Abbot (in 2010) and Jeremy Corbyn (in 2015).

GB's becoming leader, without the involvement of grass roots members, trades unionists and other affiliated organisations created anger and resentment among the disenfranchised. This is evidenced in comments from CLP Secretaries (below) and from backbenchers in Chapter 9.

The 2007 Deputy Leadership contest was run between six candidates. Jon Cruddas won the first ballot but Harriet Harman was ultimate victor on the third. There was no Deputy Leadership election after that until 2015. This despite a Party rule stating that one should have been held in 2010. An election for Deputy Leader was held in 2015 and Tom Watson was elected.

Between 1996 and 2010 Party rules were flouted *every year* in respect of leadership elections. The LabOUR Commission Report[C7-16] said: "The Party Rule book provides for the circulation of nomination papers for the Leader/Deputy Leader to Party units before *each* Annual Conference. Attempts by CLPs to reinstate this practice at the 2006 Annual Conference were ruled out of order by the Conference Arrangements Committee (CAC)".

MP Roger Berry said: "I think party members appreciate that they are now involved in the election of the Party leader" (normally but not in 2007). He continued: "The Deputy Leadership elections (in 2007) involved a lot of Party members." Gordon Prentice MP recalled: "When I told my constituency General Committee (GC) that I didn't think we could win with Brown as leader, it was a heated meeting. I put out a press release saying what I told them. There are no mechanisms in the Party to get rid of a leader who is taking it down. Some local members objected and it triggered a debate."

Views of 27 Constituency Labour Party (CLP) Secretaries about the Leadership come from responses to the author's questionnaire administered in October 2009.[C7-17]

The autocratic, and all powerful, NL leadership used methods of operating that owed nothing to the Party's democratic traditions and everything to the use of totalitarian regimes as role models. Constituency Labour Party (CLP) secretaries' views (2009) about how the Party was being led and about its Leadership follow:

John believed: "The leadership should be more accountable to the membership. This requires a strong annual conference – not just a glorified rally. Local parties cannot run their own affairs without constant bullying and interference from regional officials."

William criticised: "Blind centralisation and control, which should cease. The Party should be opened up and made more transparent and accountable." He continued: "We need strong visionary leadership (plural not just one person) – as long as the leaders are open and accountable".

Philip wanted: "Less influence from Downing St., more influence by ministers and by backbenchers on ministers. Professional politicians should be made more accountable to Party members."

Colin asserted: "Annual Conference policies carried with a two thirds majority should be implemented when Labour is in government and promoted when we are in opposition."

The LabOUR Commission recommended: "We urge candidates for the Leadership to support clearly and unequivocally the federal structure of the Party, and *the need to rebuild a mass and empowered membership to win forthcoming elections.*"[C7-18]

Fred believed the Party: "Should hold regular elections for its leaders *and Party organisers*".

Vince said: "There should be a leadership election every five years."

Keith contended: "All Party leaders must win an OMOV election before they take office. That would especially apply when the party is in power. The ballot paper should include the option of "None of the above". He continued: "Leadership contests should be held at five yearly intervals. If we had four year fixed Parliaments then no leader could ruin our election the second time around and then refuse to go until too late to fight back at the following election."

Gary thought: "The Leader (and Deputy) should be elected by the Party membership. This implies an OMOV election in which trades unionists would have to be individual party members in order to participate (this type of system was introduced in 2014) and MPs' votes would count for no more than those of grass-roots members."

Commenting on adoption of the contemporary leadership election system in 2005 Russell[19] contended: "The final package fell short of what many had wanted, Tony Blair is said to have complained that the settlement was too timid".

Eric believed: "The Party Leadership needs a strategy document. The strategy must comply with the Party constitution. Both strategy and constitution will need to be developed with the times. They would be no use if they were written in stone."

Quentin called for the Leadership to: "Listen and learn, show humility and honesty. Answer questions straightforwardly. Keep to Labour's core values when making policy (including fighting poverty and working for peace). Use the expertise within the Party, not just that of the chosen few. Don't just listen to those who say what the leadership want to hear."

Oliver emphasised that: "We need competent parliamentarians". He also wanted Leaders to: "Learn from social democratic parties abroad. When in power be open to pressure groups and academics as well as Backbench opinion."

Two LabOUR Commission YouGov polls of Party members (2007)[C7-19] showed that 64% of respondents thought that the Leadership did not trust them enough to involve them fully in Party decision and policy making. The percentage of lapsed members who shared this view was even higher at 81%.

Adele argued: "We elect our leaders to lead and manage, so they should not be asking the members, every five minutes 'Should we do this or that?' But they should take more notice of public opinion for example, demonstrations against the Iraq war. They should be more accountable to the public than to the Party."

Diane observed tartly of the leadership: "They have already (adopted) the modern setting (for Party values) but they need to start listening to ordinary members."

Irene called for the leadership to: "Restore internal party democracy and have increased accountability through a democratic and transparent annual conference. Yes we must!"

Una requested the leadership and party hierarchy to: "Develop two way communication, using email etc. Also to ensure that members without email access are not left out." She wanted the leadership to be "made to read the messages that members send in response to their top down exhortations, lines of the day and demands for money. Then make them reply."

The LabOUR Commission recommended that: "Labour Party Head Office create a transparent two-way internal process with publication of (policy) proposals, responses, subsequent analysis and next steps online to all members."[C7-20] This did not happen prior to the 2010 election.

Helen suggested: "Perhaps there should be an anonymous party members survey done annually". Bob wanted: "Much more use of questionnaires (like this one I am answering). More use should be made of the ideas of party members in universities, colleges and special local interest groups such as the Socialist Health Association."

The Machinery of Party Governance

Roles of the National Executive Committee (NEC): The management of Conference and the governance of the Party between Conferences is theoretically the responsibility of the National Executive Committee (NEC).[C7-21] NL's governance framework: "Partnership in Power" (PiP) (1997)[C7-22] downgraded the role of the NEC, particularly in policy making. The NL leadership now had the final say on virtually everything. However they expected the NEC to follow their bidding when required. For example, the NEC has acquired a major role in the selection of Parliamentary candidates (see Chapter 8).

The NEC retained virtually unaltered powers and composition from 1918 until the mid-1980s. Subject to accountability to Party Conference, it was then the Party's ruling body in matters of policy *and* party management. It had overall responsibility for Party policy between conferences. However during the late 1970s and the 1980s there developed conflicts about policy between the NEC and the Parliamentary leadership, notably concerning election manifestos (Golding,2003[C7-23], Seyd,1987[C7-24]). In 1983 Kinnock persuaded the NEC to agree to joint shadow cabinet/NEC committees to oversee policy making. After the 1987 election a new system of policy review groups (joint NEC and Shadow Cabinet) was established. After further review; the National Policy Forum (NPF) was established in 1993 (see below).

NEC membership during the 1980s consisted of seven delegates who were elected by CLPs (these were invariably MPs); trades unions nominated 12 delegates; there were five women delegates (in practice trades unionists and elected by the whole Conference), a youth delegate (elected by youth conference) and the Party Treasurer. In 1993 OMOV postal ballots were introduced for electing members of the constituency section.[C7-25] Partnership in Power (PiP) (1997)[C7-26] prohibited MPs from standing in other sections but created a new section for them. The new sections were; PLP and European Parliamentary Labour Party (EPLP)(3), Leader of EPLP (1), government (3), local government (2). The Leader, Deputy Leader and Party Treasurer were automatically members. The number of constituency delegates was reduced from seven to six and the five women's seats were abolished. At least 50% of the CLP representatives had to be women. Union seats still numbered 12.[C7-27] Between the implementation of PiP and the 2010 general election, the majority of candidates for the NEC constituency section were supported either by "Members First" (the author suggests, this should be named "Leadership's Position First") or the "Centre-Left Grass Roots Alliance" (CLGA).[C7-28]

From the outset there were allegations of partisan intervention by Party staff against CLGA candidates. There is a blatant confession in the diary of former Party Director of Communications, Lance Price. In 1998 he boasted that they had successfully labelled the Grass roots Alliance as being hard left, but had little success in promoting their own NL candidates. The outcome was that the party hierarchy's candidates won only two places in the constituency section to the CLGA's four. Price admitted to burying bad news by declaring the results on a Sunday, rather than the customary Wednesday, to prevent it from dragging on as a news story.[C7-29]

The timing of elections for the CLP section of the NEC ceased to be tied to Conference. They became a moveable fixture during the year, from one election to the next, making grass-roots organisation difficult. This probably adversely affected turnout.[C7-30]

PiP established a new relationship between the government and the NEC: "The NEC should be adequately informed and *their views taken into account* on key policy discussions and decisions. These rights should be matched by the responsibilities, clearly understood, to help sustain a Labour government". [C7-31] "PiP" left some NEC roles unchanged, for example the right to agree the general election manifesto. Many powers previously given to the NEC were now delegated to its subcommittees. Policy making was assigned to the new Joint Policy Commission (JPC) and to specific (subject) Policy Commissions.[C7-32] Parliamentary Candidate selections and disciplinary matters were delegated to the NEC Organisation Sub-Committee. Members of NEC subcommittees are carefully picked and managed. For instance, Peter Willsman was permitted to join the last named subcommittee during five years of NEC membership, but never allowed to sit on parliamentary selection panels, despite his numerous requests to do so.[C7-33] All subcommittees were given full delegated powers so there was no requirement for their decisions to be ratified by the whole NEC. This excluded some key NEC members, especially the relatively left wing, from participating in important decisions.

Unison Assistant General Secretary Liz Snape said: "In theory, PiP could have been good. But actually it delivered very little and had minimal impact. The union still had to battle at the National Policy Forum(NPF). What a process is worth depends on what happens at the end. *Since PiP no one knows what's happening in the policy making process.*"

MP Kelvin Hopkins argued: "They (the leadership) can keep control of the NEC because they always have a majority. A few people get on from the CLGA, they do a good job, but NL have the majority and can do what they like."

The National *Joint Policy Committee (JPC)* was set up at Conference 1997. This had an equal number of members appointed by the government and the NEC. A set of topic-based Policy Commissions was established to report to the JPC. Policy Commissions (PCs) were given a more representative membership including nominee members of the National Policy Forum (NPF) (see below). No members of these bodies were directly elected by, or accountable to, individual Party members in that capacity. Appropriate ministers were members of Policy Commissions (PCs) and one of these acted as joint convenor. Responsibility for drafting policy documents submitted to the NPF for approval was with the PCs, but in reality, this process appeared to be controlled by ministers and their special advisers working in collaboration with senior Party staff. Members of the PCs, who were not in the government, had the limited task of commenting on, and approving, drafts during brief and poorly attended meetings.[C7-34] Liz Snape, of Unison, asserted: "The Union has invested time and money in the Policy Commissions. However nothing was coming out of them and Ministerial contributions were usually very brief and lacked content. *In the end Unison stopped sending representatives.* No respect was shown to our union or to other representatives."

The JPC was the strategic coordinating body for the future policy development process, undertaken by the specialised PCs. It worked under strong guidance of senior Party staff and 10 Downing St staffers. Alternative views were not proposed at JPC and PC levels. However they were permitted, but infrequently agreed, at the NPF. The JPC then had the final say as to which NPF proposed amendments were acceptable and could be included in the Party's policy rolling programme for the next general election. This was a top down and barely democratic process. The author's findings during her work as Constituency Political Education Officer and on CLPD's Executive suggested that many in the Party probably neither understood, nor were fully aware of, the contemporary policy making machinery and processes.

The National Constitutional Committee (NCC) has oversight of constitutional and disciplinary matters in the Party. It reports and is accountable to the NEC. It has 11 members elected by ballot at Party Conference (i.e. by Conference delegates). No left of centre members were elected to it between 2006 and 2014. There were numerous delegates' complaints about alleged Party staff intervention in these elections during most of that period (see below).

The NCC hears, and rules, on disciplinary matters relating to Party rules referred by CLPs, officers of the Party and/or the NEC. If it finds rules have been broken it can impose specified disciplinary measures. These include: reprimand, suspension from holding office in the Party, being a delegate to any Party body, withholding or withdrawing endorsement as a Party candidate at any level or expulsion from Party membership.[C7-35]

According to Russell,[C7-36] in the early 1990s proposals were developed to: "create culture of greater consultation and deliberation over policy with a new *National Policy Forum (NPF)*". The NPF was set up and first met in 1993. The Forum received submissions about policy from the Policy Commissions. These were then considered, adopted and circulated to the party nationwide for comment. There was the potential to amend; but this could be accepted or rejected by the JPC. The policies formed a rolling programme. Each policy document would be discussed over two years. The first year saw consultation and debate across the Party. First year's debates were to be about principles and the second year's about detail. The whole policy programme had to be completed, over a three year period between general elections. It was then submitted to *Conference which had to accept or reject it as a whole; no amendments were (or are) permitted*. The NPF deals only with certain *future* policies (those destined for the next general election manifesto). Contemporary resolutions are supposed to deal with all current issues excluded from the NPF rolling programme but they actually only deal with issues relating to the immediate past six weeks.

The NPF had 175 members. Of these, 54 were from CLPs and 18 were regional representatives elected at Regional Conference. Thirty were representatives of affiliated trades unions. The remainder were representatives of the government, the PLP, European PLP, local government, socialist and co-operative bodies. The entire NEC (32 members) was in membership of the NPF.[C7-37] They meet at appropriate venues at irregular intervals. In theory, under NL, they met about twice a year but, in practice, under TB's and GB's leaderships, intervals between NPF meetings were often much longer. Elections for the NPF were originally conducted at Conference but NPF ballots were subject to alleged manipulation by party staff and in 2009 balloting was changed, by Conference vote, to the fairer system of OMOV (one member one vote) postal voting.

Unison's Liz Snape said: "If you see the NPF and Conference as public shows of Party strength and unity then they worked very well. They became US style rallies. But in terms of open and democratic policy making they were, and are, far from effective. They were useless at integrating the policy making parts of the Party. *Constituency Labour Parties were tricked into believing otherwise."*

Local Policy Forums were supposed to provide opportunities for local members to deliberate and comment on the policy recommendations of the NPF and to send feedback. They were open to all Party members. Originally they were run by regional Party staff. However they proved expensive and time consuming to run. The lack of an audit trail and useful feedback to members, about what had happened to their recommendations, led to them being regarded with considerable cynicism at the grass roots. The latter, on the whole, boycotted them. After the millennium they became almost obsolete. In "Renewing and Extending Party Democracy" (2007),[C7-38] GB promised to revive local policy forums but this never happened.

Clement Attlee described the *Labour Party Conference* as 'The Parliament of the movement". In 1975 Reg Underhill, then National Agent, proclaimed that: "The Annual Conference is the authoritative body of the Labour Party".[C7-39] The same year General Secretary Ron Hayward said at Conference: "I regard myself as being the guardian of Conference decisions".[C7-40]

Arguments about the sovereignty of conference raged interminably. Successive Party Leaders were castigated for ignoring Conference decisions. One example was Harold Wilson, who was criticised for ignoring a resolution demanding the UK to disassociate itself from American involvement in the Vietnam war.[C7-41]

Prior to PiP (1997),[C7-42] there was a Party rule that, if a resolution was passed by a two thirds majority at Conference, it would automatically be included in the next general election manifesto. Government policy did sometimes change after a Conference decision – as it did in practice after (Callaghan's) 5% pay policy was launched. CLPs, trades unions and other affiliated bodies sent resolutions to Conference that were usually "composited" (amalgamated in summary form under topic headings). They could also be subject to proposed amendments from affiliates ahead of Conference. Constituency parties sent in most of the resolutions and provided the majority of speakers. However, although constituencies had influence in setting the agenda, the trades unions actually decided which resolutions were supported.[C7-43] This was not a situation relished by ordinary party members. When surveyed in the early 1990s, 72% thought that "the block vote at Conference brings the Party into disrepute".[C7-44]

After TB became leader, the 1995 Party Conference agreed a rule change to allow 50% of Conference votes to remain with the unions and other affiliated organisations and 50% were allocated to CLPs. From 1992 CLPs were required to send a woman delegate every alternate year. Previously the majority had been men. Minkin[C7-45] found that 82% of the delegates to the 1983 Conference were male. The above rule change was right, in principle, but led to there being more novice delegates every year. These proved easier prey for Party staff to dominate and manipulate (see below).

Under PiP an alternative (minority) position (every alternate year) is allowed to go from NPF members to Conference. CLPs were allowed to send one "contemporary resolution" which must relate to an event occurring within the six weeks leading up to Conference. Alternatively they could submit a rule change to be discussed the following year. The Conference Arrangements Committee (CAC) vetted these "contemporaries" and ruled many out of order. For example, debate about the renewal of the Trident missile system was prohibited for two successive conferences before the 2005 election and every year thereafter. Delegates could ballot for four contemporary resolutions submitted by CLPs and four proposed by trades unions. These were debated and voted on at the start of Conference. Because of the complexity of the situation, delegates often also voted for union backed resolutions (already guaranteed a hearing by virtue of the number of union votes) . In practice, this always meant that only one or two CLP backed motions (out of a possible four) were debated as votes that could have backed CLP motions stacked up to support union resolutions already guaranteed a debate.

After the Millennium there were several defeats of the platform on contemporary resolutions. The first was a resolution on the link between earnings and state pensions. There were platform defeats on the Private Finance Initiative in 2002, foundation hospitals in 2003 and on increasing the provision of council housing the following three years. TB announced that he would ignore these decisions.

In 2007, leading up to the "phantom election", GB supported further restrictions on debate in "Renewing and Extending Party Democracy"[C7-47] This was approved by Conference in expectation of an imminent election. These rules prohibited resolutions altogether and replaced them with "contemporary issues". The latter were vaguely worded headings for debate. All that Conference could do was to vote to refer these topics to the National Policy Forum (NPF) for decision. This system was implemented in 2008 and 2009; then it was reviewed. There was a return to contemporary resolutions in 2010. *At the 2009 Conference a large number of contemporary issues were referred to the NPF but the NPF did not meet between Conference 2009 and Conference 2010 therefore the whole exercise was a pointless sham.* This may have occurred due to the deliberate tactics of the Leadership.

Far less Conference time was now required for debates, especially for delegates' speeches. Ministerial question and answer sessions and policy workshops were introduced instead. There were also promotional DVDs shown in the Conference hall. These focused on the Labour Government's achievements. However they were not shown to TV viewers watching Conference. This was because the BBC refused to carry "Party propaganda". Therefore their wider informational potential was not realised. Cynics might think that the purpose of these DVDs was to reduce the number of rank and file delegates' contributions.

The Report of the LabOUR Commission, 2007 criticised the running of Conference. It said: "From our direct knowledge we are aware that Party staff grade conference delegates according to loyalty to the Leadership. Despite the 4+4 rule (allowing selection of eight contemporary resolutions for debate) CLP delegates are encouraged to vote for unions' contemporary resolutions even though this will be a wasted vote. New delegates are particularly prone to misinformation, including "guidance" that it is a breach of Party rules for a CLP delegate to vote against the NEC's recommendations at Conference."

In Ann Black's (NEC member) unofficial Conference report of 2005[C7-48] she said: "Sadly, yet again, there were reports about harassment of constituency delegates. Particularly serious were those relating to the election of Party committees, e.g. Conference Arrangements Committee (CAC), where the code of conduct says that Party staff will not use or abuse their position, party resources or time in the process of an internal election or selection so as to further the interests of … their personally preferred candidates. One regional officer asked delegates how they were intending to vote in the CAC election and when I asked him why, he said: "It's part of my job".

Speakers and debates were allegedly selected on the basis of known views, and often gave speeches prepared by Party staff.[C7-49] Provisions for suppressing dissent from the floor of Conference were demonstrated by the Walter Wolfgang affair in 2005. An octogenarian was strong armed from this seat and evicted from the Conference hall by unusually large and muscular "party stewards". In extremis, the Conference microphone is turned off, as happened to Unison General Secretary Dave Prentis at Conference 2006.[C7-50]

Unite General Secretary Len McCluskey said: "Party staff, and people acting on their behalf, have certainly exerted undue influence on delegates to Conference and in internal Party elections. Many trades unionists wanted nothing to do with NL because it was rooted in controlling people and taking away our values. The Party is still there but we need to get our values back. People in Unite, at constituency and regional levels, are looking at this and working for this change."

Liz Snape, of Unison said: "The Party machine's handling of Conference delegates has been poor. Party staff locked delegates into rooms and tried to force them to toe the Party line. It was juvenile. They behaved like student union politicians. They made extravagant promises to delegates that if they supported the Leadership line they could have a Parliamentary seat, or other important position, fixed for them (see Chapter 8). NL MPs and Party staff didn't seem to realise that their efforts to control delegates were so clumsy that they were frequently observed and it was laughable. We should be treated as a mature Party that had confidence in itself instead of them playing silly, petty games. One has been to reschedule Conference debate on controversial topics to the end of the day when they expect the TV coverage to have ended – but usually the TV crew stay on. Many Unison members, who are active in the Party, complain about these tricks."

She continued: "The Unison Conference delegation invariably includes strong, feisty women. When they are asked by staff to move back to put the "beautiful people" in view of the cameras they refuse to budge or be manipulated! I think that the Union can make better use of its money than paying Conference expenses for delegates."

Much of the remainder of this Chapter records the views of former Party staff, MPs and CLP secretaries about how the Party's structures worked in practice.

Revolutionising the Party Secretariat

A major initiative of NL was to change the culture of the Party administration. A key means of operating the NL Party command and control regime was through personnel changes within the Party secretariat. This was facilitated by changing staff and their conditions of service. The hierarchy, and its machine, encouraged manipulation, or breach, of rules by staff in order to achieve their desired outcomes in internal policy votes, elections and selections. Staff interventions in Parliamentary candidate selections are discussed in Chapter 8. This Chapter analyses staff involvement in other aspects of Party governance: particularly in policy making processes, elections to Party committees, Annual Conference and party management.

By the mid 1990s the Party had many long serving and older employees. Typically these were people who started as voluntary organisers or trades union officers. Most had originally joined the Party because they believed in its traditional values and political priorities. They embraced the Party's established social democratic ideology. However the users of the NL new broom wanted ideology free staff who would not respect the tradition of member's participative democracy. Therefore experienced staff were replaced by younger, apolitical personnel.

Some thoughts of former Party Staff included those of David Gardner, Assistant General Secretary in the late 1990s. He joined the Party staff in 1982 as a Secretary/Agent in London and was previously National Constitutional Officer and Director of Party Organisation.

He regretted: "The Party organisation has become a machine for the command and control of the Party rather than for winning the hearts and minds of the people of Britain. The Party at large needs to be supported to win people over."

"Malcolm" was a regional organiser during the mid 1990s. He recalled: "Many long serving staff disappeared from HQ. There was a lot of: 'we have to change, we have to change or else you're out!' Things might be against the rules, but you're all under pressure to deliver. When people are on temporary contracts it's easier to manipulate them and get them to perform. The Party culture really changed. It meant a lot of experience being thrown out. They thought they were re-inventing the way to fight general elections. Some of it was good stuff, for example, having a strategy for getting out the vote and using more phone canvassing. Much of this was lifted from US marketing."

He continued: "But if you get rid of all the experienced people who can make well informed judgements about how to deploy people and what the message should be, then you're in difficulties. I've seen some remarkably poor judgements made about such things in by-election campaigns. When staff say: 'I'm in charge and that's what we're going to do', no one feels they can challenge it."

Peter Kilfoyle MP, a Party regional organiser until 1990, regretted: "Experienced Party organisers are now thin on the ground. They have recruited many young people who have no knowledge, or experience, of running campaigns. They are good at filling up check boxes, but can't think, innovate or sort out problems. They don't know the rule book and there's no longer anyone to monitor what they do or police what is done in the name of the Party."

Traditionally Labour Party organisers were people who had a history of loyalty to, and voluntary service in, the Labour Party. They generally had a track record of voluntary election work and were trained on dedicated courses run by the Party which focused on election law and organisation. They were also expected to embrace Labour's traditional aims and values and to have sufficient emotional maturity and life experience to enable them to recruit and manage volunteers successfully. These criteria applied when the author's partner was recruited as an organiser in 1974.

Malcolm continued: "The practice of putting Party staff on short term contracts started just before the 1997 election. The General Secretary extended the system of staff being on such contracts. This was to keep a grip on costs. It was extended to get rid of long serving staff who were on higher levels of pay and benefits. They recruited new graduates who were given fancy titles. The Party looked for people *without* strong political or democratic socialist views to work for them. It was all about ambition and careerism. If you get staff with strong political commitments they might take sides in a local dispute against the central Party line."

Malcolm claimed this system was designed "to maximise what you can get out of somebody – promising them that they would go places with NL. They would be able to work for an MP or perhaps be a special advisor. They knew they would be leaving so you didn't have to chuck them out."

Ben worked as a local Party organiser employed on temporary contracts during the 1990s and early 2000s. He recalled: "From the mid 1990s, the Party had a policy of recruiting young staff, particularly to regional offices. They had little political background, especially in the Labour Party, and few political views. They were more biddable because they were on temporary contracts which might not be renewed: especially if they failed to give satisfaction to their masters in the Party hierarchy." This changed the opinions and backgrounds of Party organisers. The new priorities of their managers, who were directly responsible to the Party leader through the General Secretary and NEC, altered their methods of operating and generated an ethically questionable approach.

Party staff should be partly accountable to individual and affiliated Party members. This is because the Party as a whole employs them. The staff also manage some of the Party's income and supervise much of its campaigning. In addition some staff have a great deal of power in respect of taking disciplinary action against members. During the New Labour era the reality was that Party staff were almost exclusively accountable to the Leadership and to the managers of the Party machine.

Malcolm suggested" "Because of the way in which *Regional Offices* interpret rules, if you are standing up against them you don't have a cat in hell's chance. People tend not to look at Regional Offices when they're examining Party democracy. Regional officials are utterly and totally loyal (to the Party hierarchy) and totally ruthless – sometimes with a hint of humanity."

He continued: "The choice of Regional Directors, and other senior staff, might be influenced by the leadership. You then became that person's man or woman e.g. "Blair's man". You were then expected to work for that person. So if the leader changes you become less secure. We used to say that we were the Party's civil servants, but that no longer applies."

Malcolm thought Regional staff frequently intervened, in a partisan way, on behalf of the leadership but: "In some areas, such as fighting between factions within a local Party, Regional staff don't have a vested interest – unless one faction is trying something major like deposing a council leader".

Even worse: during the NL era, Party staff were encouraged, and expected, to denigrate and vilify Party members to the left of NL and to discredit them in the eyes of their peers (see Kath Fry quotation above this Chapter).

Peter Killeen is a retired Assistant Regional Organiser who worked for the Party until the 2001 election. He expressed unhappiness that, *during the NL era, Party staff were instructed to "identify and marginalise members to the left of NL". This involved "ignoring them, devaluing their contributions to debate at meetings and denigrating them to other Party members who are to be urged not to associate with them."*

Malcolm reminisced: "When I was first employed by the Party, Larry Whitty was General Secretary. Staff were humoured and there was no real leaning on them. Later when it became apparent that I wasn't 100% (NL) policy wise they felt less able to rely on me. I'm not in the least surprised by anything that has happened because the idea of a party like the Greens, where you have ultra democracy, is a recipe for anarchy. There are reasons for having control. The problem comes if you become a control freak or get to the point where you think that you don't have to explain what you're doing. The Labour Party organisation is now wrecked because it lost its collective memory. People who were loyal to it through thick and thin were sacked or are now pissed off. I'm not just talking about paid staff but also about key volunteers. The Party will have to be re-built from scratch. I think we should go back to what we thought was best about the Party, which has seen success as well as failure, and see how that can be improved."

Some MPs reflected on *changes in the methods of operation of Party staff*. Michael Meacher said: "I don't think that Party officials were corrupt per se. I believe that they were leant on very hard by Headquarters and thought that it was the only way they could go. We need rules that prevent that."

Clare Short asserted: "What's left of the Party membership is increasingly few. There's more and more of regional offices fixing who become councillors. Now that some councillors get salaries, there's been increased financial motivation. Regional officers can manipulate the members to vote for who they want. Councillors try to keep in with Regional staff as they want to keep their own seats, I'm afraid."

Thus Party staff allegedly became obedient manipulators but lacked the time honoured organisational skills which NL debunked. This undoubtedly contributed to poor general election results in 2005 and particularly in 2010.

Attacks on Party Democracy and the Hollowing out of the Party on the Ground

This section explores *how and why the Party on the ground shrank and became moribund.* The Labour Party lost more than three fifths of its individual membership between the general elections of 1997 and 2010 (see note 5). Official Party figures, released immediately after the May 2010 election, showed that Party membership was only 154,000. It had decreased from 400,000 at the time of the 1997 general election. During this period the number of Constituency parties sending delegates to Annual Conference fell from 527 (approximately 100 below potential) in 2002 to 444 in 2009 and 412 in 2010.[C7-51] At the end of NL's reign, more than one third of constituencies no longer sent a delegate. 'The Party's 'Refounding Labour' (2011)[C7-52b] asked: " Are many local parties moribund? Is the reason the cost? *Or do local parties doubt the relevance of their attendance at Conference* (author's italics)?"

Many remained in the Party but became inactive. A survey of a representative sample of 670 Labour Party members was undertaken by YouGov for the LabOUR Commission in 2006.[C7-53b] It showed that, whilst 37% of respondents reported being "active/fairly active" in the Party, 63% considered themselves to be "occasionally active" or "inactive". The latter probably rarely, or never, campaigned in elections. Of these "inactive" members, 26% said they might seriously consider voting for another Party or not voting at all at the next general election.

What CLP Secretaries thought about contemporary party democracy? Secretaries questioned by the author were first asked their reactions to the following statement:

"Since 1993 the Labour Party outside Parliament has been run according to principles of member's democracy, transparency and according to its own rules." Do you:

agree strongly? – 2 secretaries

agree to some extent? – 3

neither agree nor disagree? – 1

disagree somewhat? – 8

disagree totally? – 13

don't know – 0

The total of 21 (77.8%) disagreeing, with one undecided, demonstrates widespread grass-roots criticism.

Former Assistant General Secretary David Gardner said: "I wholly endorse the report and conclusions of the LabOUR Commission about the Party's record on internal democracy and adherence to its rules."

Gardner continued: "Partnership in Power (PiP)[C7-54] was good in principle. It was meant to work bottom up, but became top down. It was intended to be a continuous dialogue between the Party and the Leadership over issues such as Iraq. It was strong on rhetoric but vague on detail. We need to have a transparent policy process. Policy documents should be allowed to be amended, in part, at Conference."

He added: "We need to put active (local) branches at the centre of policy if we are to have a party rooted in communities. The Party has done nothing about nurturing branches. So we lose locality, identity and links with other parts of the community. I encouraged piloting of new organisational methods. The Enfield Southgate CLP (MP then Stephen Twigg) did away with branches. It was a disaster and we lost the constituency in 2005. Alternative methods were tried but some were unsuccessful."

DG asserted: *"Members have just become foot soldiers expected to empty their pockets and knock on doors. They feel isolated and not trusted. Many don't feel any ownership of the Party. (DG was then both a Constituency and a Branch Chair). Some branch parties have socials and are still engaged in the community. But in other parts of the country the Party has become hollowed out. We particularly neglected the Party in parts of the country without Labour MPs (thinking that they don't count and are of no great use to the Party)."*

In reporting the views of focus groups that he ran for the Labour Commission in 2006, Professor Stuart Weir concluded: "There was huge disillusion with the attitude of the Party's leader and his government towards the party's membership. It was not simply that the government ignored the party's views. It was strongly felt that the party hierarchy had a condescending and even contemptuous attitude to the party and the members, seeking to manipulate them rather than consult and work with them as equals".[C7_55]

Gardner continued: "One of the first rows, in Autumn 1997, was over cutting lone parent family benefit. At regional meetings TB was told that this was going down badly and there was a need to discuss it with the Party, together with welfare and welfare to work issues. There were then 100 local policy forums round the country. TB wanted to drive through these policies: 'Because I have the mandate'.
Tom Sawyer, then General Secretary, said that the Party had to be taken along with the Leadership. TB appeared to understand but did not mention open dialogue after that. Soon afterwards Sawyer resigned. Henceforward the Party was to be told what to do."

Gardner asserted: "Labour *must become a mass party* of members who are there to be active – genuine Labour supporters. We must make it easier to join and engage in activities. We need to re-examine the high level of membership subscriptions." There has been no review and subscriptions have continued to rise since.

There was concern, expressed by some interviewees, that local councillors are sometimes primarily "in it for the money" and that, in small branch parties, selection meetings can be packed easily by the friends and relations of a candidate.

Gardner expanded: "During the 1990s the number of Labour councillors rose from approximately 6,000 to about 10,000. We now have less than 5,000 (July 2009). Local councillors are our ambassadors and champions – but there are fewer. Councillors' subscriptions go directly into Party funds and are no longer used to train and support them. Management (of these funds) is no longer transparent. The Party has allowed Labour groups to vote themselves large allowances. Many councillors remain in office to get allowances. Numerous branches are just populated by councillors, their friends and families, who are there to ensure their re-selection (similar comments were made by Clare Short). The result is few members and lack of a strong Party to fight elections locally or help in marginal areas. Labour has abandoned large areas of the UK in local government. We cannot just be a party of the cities and the old industrial areas."

MPs' views: Louise Ellman was positive about her constituency: "We still have a very active and constructive Party in Liverpool Riverside. People are very interested in local issues and local government. The year after Labour gained power nationally (1997) the Lib Dems won control of Liverpool City Council and have been in control continuously ever since. Labour has been fighting back. The results of the next local elections will be interesting and we may regain control.' (Labour subsequently regained control of Liverpool in 2010). We have some very able councillors. My relationship with my local councillors is very important; they keep me informed."

Roger Berry argued: "The best way for the Party to boost its membership is to lose the next election. The way for membership to decline is to win it. *Labour's membership is always higher in opposition than in government.* There are too many people who focus on areas where they disagree with a Labour government and forget the areas of agreement. A lot of members despaired over Iraq and withdrew. We have a problem (with membership numbers). In my own constituency membership is increasing slightly. People are asking themselves whether they really want a Tory government."

Graham Stringer supported this theme of a Party preference for being in Opposition: "There's something in the psyche of the Party that doesn't like Labour governments. The best general election campaign I've been involved in and where we recruited the most new members was 1983! Michael Foot was able to enthuse people. There were the Tories to hate and policies to support. If you look at 2001, we had a Labour government that had quite a lot of successes. The economy was doing well and there had been major manifesto implementation. But members are not as keen on boasting about the effectiveness of their government as they are about attacking it and proposing alternative policies. That's how we are and it's how the young people are that the Party relies on."

On the same theme, Chris Mullin recalled: "In the run-up to the 1997 election we advertised in the press for members. There was a difference between those members and the long-standing ones. Many of the new members were not fully committed and soon left. There is a tendency that six months after Labour goes into government the Party goes into opposition and the betrayal letters start to come in. In 1997 it happened after about two to three months. An example was complaints about special advisors. The Tories are always serious about power but, on the whole, Labour hasn't been serious about it."

These comments are telling observations about the comfort of self righteousness acquired through habitually taking an adversarial position. However, some Leadership betrayals may flout major principles and sometimes promises on which the Party fought an election. Flagrant examples, following Labour's 1997 victory, were the cuts in one parent benefit and GB's pledge to adhere to the Major government's public sending plans for three years.

Deficits in Party democracy were highlighted by several MPs. Stringer alleged: "The Labour Party has been run in a less democratic way under NL. Many local parties have withered away. My CLP is in relatively good fettle. But its members are not young or new. All my wards have Labour councillors: there's immense stability there. Colin Challen asserted: "We need to remind ourselves what the Party once stood for and learn from that."

Jeremy Corbyn regretted: "Party membership has gone down. My CLP (Islington North) always had a high membership. Many who joined never participated in the party, never campaigned, never attended meetings or social functions. In many areas, especially Tory ones, the Labour Party is a shadow of its former self. This is unprecedented in Party history. During the 1940s and early 1950s (individual) Party membership was over one million. By the 1970s, the Party had lost many members but was still a functioning organisation all over the country. By 1979 membership increased. Even when we lost in 1983, the Party membership was still enormous and had risen since 1979. *Now(2009) we are probably in the worst situation that the Party has had: the lowest membership, the biggest debts – and a complete lack of direction for members. When asked now what the core beliefs of the Party are I, and everyone else, is in difficulty."* This last admission, from a committed democratic socialist like Corbyn, is a serious indictment of a once principled party.

The consequent disruption to the Party on the ground was raised by Jon Cruddas. He argued: "The basic characteristics of the Labour Party currently are: disorientation, frustration and empirical decline. One of the consequences of the NL position in our area (Dagenham) is movement of the white working classes towards far right politics. The Labour Party has to step up to confront that. It's true in other parts of the country as well. In large parts of the electoral landscape there's just disintegration. I aim to lead from the front in the constituency. I don't underestimate the difficulty after 12-13 years in government. Maintaining a sense of momentum is difficult. There is a sense of inevitability about the loss of power that could become self-fulfilling" (and came to pass in 2010 and 2015).

Peter Kilfoyle believed: "Party democracy has been ruined .The Party is now a rubber stamp for the leadership. Once it mattered. The Project is now the plaything of the Leadership. It does not represent the party organisation or the people, within the Party, who need representation."

Frank Dobson claimed his Constituency Party (Holborn and St. Pancras) "has the largest membership in the country (over 900 members: three times as large as the average CLP). In fairness to other CLPs, this is partly because we have a large number of young people who join for a short time then move elsewhere. We've been fortunate, over the years in having an active party. Blairite policies are fairly unpopular, certainly with our activists and voters, so we've seen a massive reduction in the membership of the Party (nationally). The Party is in excruciating debt and we have hardly any staff compared with the way we were. We are not in a good position to fight elections or even just to operate as a political party. *The Party is undoubtedly at the weakest it has been in my political lifetime."*

John Grogan regretted: "In a lot of areas party membership is dying. Maybe this is now a feature of political life and a result of our low standing in opinion polls. There's disillusionment after 13 years. There are some areas, largely in London, where you still have much activity. How do you attract more members and make them more active? Perhaps MPs lack time. We get bogged down in the minutiae of political life."

John McDonnell claimed: *"NL had a ruthlessness that brooked no opposition: a brutality such as we've never seen before in the Party. They suppressed dissent and cruelly discarded people who supported NL but were no longer of use to them."*

In late 2009, Senior backbencher M. argued: "We are now six months before a general election and the time has come, win or lose, to look at the way we do our politics. *The Labour Party doesn't belong to any individual member but it has got to belong to its core base. If there is a feeling that members don't have access to the norms of a functioning democratic party then they will be dissatisfied.* There is a question as to what it means to be a modern party and how members should exert influence." These were stark admissions that NL was running a Party that was not democratic, not meeting the needs of its members and lacked legitimacy.

Kelvin Hopkins believed: "One major element in the Party is the intellectual socialists – those who are committed to socialism because it is part of their belief system and values. They believe in a socialist society even thought they may not be poor or working class themselves. They want a civilised society and believe in working towards it. The other is the working class. The Labour Party has always had the two components who've worked together. *NL is a new phenomenon*; *it's neither of these. They're not socialist and they're not working class."*

Michael Meacher declared: "We have got to find ways of restoring vital Party democracy. However inspiring MPs are, they don't have much influence unless they carry the support and enthusiasm of the Party rank and file. That's what gives them force and power within Parliament. It's scandalous that a great democratic social movement can be so eviscerated. We've now got a combination of the end of neo·liberalism and the maelstrom over Parliamentary expenses, which were truly awful. It gives us that opportunity if only we have the courage and enterprise to grasp it. I always think God moves in a mysterious way."

He continued: "The point of the Labour Party is to challenge the power structure on behalf of those who have previously been disadvantaged by it. There were certainly things wrong with the Party in the 1970s and 1980s which we were all aware of. They related to an era which has gone. *What we need now is a modern, progressive, centre-left Party which can attract the middle ground. That must have its base on the left – not the far left because we have got to win elections.* Some say that we'll never get a left wing government. I simply don't believe it. We've had neo·liberalism for 30 years because inflation and union power were once perceived to be getting out of control. The banks have been utterly out of control. The neo·liberal model is now totally discredited and breaking down."

The above quotations demonstrate that, under NL, the Party was no longer meeting the purposes for which it was established. It had ceased to be socialist and was not democratically run nor did it adequately represent the working class.

Senior backbencher A. argued: "The most fundamental issue relating to Party democracy is the attitude of the leadership to the Party as a whole. The Party has almost become an embarrassment to some members of the Government. Unfortunately it was natural that some people feared the radical collective instincts of the Labour Party and would seek to diminish its role. At the start of the 21st Century you need to define what a political party is. But we ought not to define Labour out of existence. That is what some of our leadership are trying to do now."

A. continued "In the context of the battle for ideas, if you don't have a mass organisation, with a central ethic and set of ideological values, then you'll never have a radical reforming government. Iraq was probably the biggest turning point for me and for numerous Party members. It was impossible to support the decision to go into Iraq. I became bitter about the whole democratic process – party and parliamentary. It was abused by the then Prime Minister to drive us into an awful war. The idea of war being the last possible resort seemed to be at the core of Labour's being. This is why the two things came together in Iraq."

Alice Mahon was angry: "The NL machine controls every part of the Party. They really don't mind about the loss of membership, but I do." Gordon Prentice claimed:"Blair was able to mould the Party in his own image after he became leader. When we were in opposition the PLP could elect the Shadow Cabinet. Interestingly Blair would bump along the bottom in the results. He was coming last – or one or two from the bottom. I put myself to the left of my CLP although generally they're pretty supportive of me. I always explain my position on the important issues of the day at our monthly meetings."

Above is affirmation that the Party was being run in accordance with a new and alien set of values. Moreover it was being managed in a top down, and dictatorial fashion, to meet the personal desires of the Leadership. The membership were being treated in a high handed and arrogant fashion. Labour was no longer the Party that long serving members had originally joined.[55]

Backbencher B. said: "Tony Blair never had an understanding of, or relationship with, traditional grass-roots Labour Party members. Our difficulty as a Labour Party seems that, in appealing to the upper and middle class mobile sections of the population to win their votes (which we need to win elections), we have come to be seen by our core voters as neglecting them. Regrettably some of them have turned to the BNP. Not everyone who voted BNP is racist. *But many of them fear that Labour no longer stands for the poor and for council house tenants.* We've given the impression that we've taken them for granted. We've got to appeal to those people again. *There's no point winning over a better-off section of the population and losing the poorer people.*"(as happened at the 2015 general election). "If you go round my former constituency to the council estates and the poorer areas, they don't think that Labour's doing anything for them." (B's former "safe" Labour seat was lost in 2010). TB famously said that the core vote would stick with Labour because they had no where else to go. Looking back from after the 2015 general election, in 2015 many of these voters have defected to UKIP or the SNP and others have abstained from voting.

B. continued: "We've lost a lot of Party members in recent years. The ability of members to influence the Party locally and nationally is diminished. People wonder why. My wife was a member of the Party for over 50 years but she has dropped out because of her concerns about the Party locally and nationally. She was a 'real Labour person'. For the Party to lose someone like her is a sad reflection on it."

In her 2007 Foreword to the LabOUR Commission Report, Angela Eagle MP wrote: "The era of Labour as an over centralised 'Command party' has now become counter productive."[C7-56] The Report[C7-57] said: "There is a widespread belief (among members) that elements of the leadership actively want to see the role of members curtailed and impose a heavy centralised, elitist model, funded by rich individuals and the state". This section examines that phenomenon.

Alan Simpson MP said: "All of us in the Party were given a script by the Leadership. Then told to take it out to the public, knock on doors and sell the product. It didn't matter that, at a local level, people wanted to sell a different product. *That wasn't allowed.* When people were being encouraged to participate in the 'Big Conversation'[C7-58] members were encouraged to have political conversations with the public. I did some work with the Campaign Group on Teesside. They took this exercise seriously, set out questions on a large range of issues and went out to ask the public their views. They hadn't been going for long when they were contacted by Regional Office screaming blue murder at them saying: 'What on earth are you doing?' They replied they were just having the Big Conversation with the electors. Regional Office responded: 'But look at your questions: Do you think that the railways would be better in public ownership rather than private? Would you favour the re-nationalisation of water? Should any re-nationalisation be with or without compensation?' Regional Office said: "You can't ask questions like that! *You can't have a conversation about these topics. It's not an area that we're willing to go into.*"

Simpson continued: "But the answers they were getting were massively in favour of bringing public services back into public ownership and people wanted to do it without compensation.

The group responded: "Why can't we have a conversation about real issues on which the public have real opinions but which differ from what NL is offering?" If what is on the menu at the centre is different from what the public is looking for, then change the bloody menu! That is the message that NL has fought tooth and claw to prevent. They were driven by a Thatcherite mind set. If you can keep all other alternatives off the table you can run round saying 'there is no alternative'. Then you restrict the legitimacy of debate to the only thing you're prepared to discuss. That doesn't necessarily put you in touch with the public, but it puts you in a position where you can manipulate them. Sooner or later that catches up with you."

MP Linda Riordan asked: "If party members have no say about the Party, then they think: 'What's the point of being in it?' That's why we've seen membership drop across the country. Changes will come after the general election when, being realistic, we're going to lose many seats."

Alan Simpson contended: "The Party has always relied on getting the vote out using its foot soldiers. That's how it got its meaning in localities where it was based. That was marginalised and undermined by the machine. So *the Party became no different from double glazing salespeople.* You got far more phone canvassing, more pressure to take up offers (a free mug with every Labour Party T shirt) and to pay your subscription by direct debit. *There was no longer any direct relationship between you and the Party – except a cash relationship. You became not a political citizen but a paying customer.* Everyone was spoon fed by the Party machine. CLPs who wanted to act in a different way found themselves marginalised."

The Party was no longer willing to tolerate members campaigning in line with its traditional aims, values and policies. It had begun to treat the public as 'customers' to be served through doing market research and meeting their whims and desires, irrespective of how reasonable or ethical these were, or how far they diverged from the Party's true purposes and ideals (see Chapter 2 on Market Oriented Parties (MOPs)).

Clare Short regretted: "The idea of passionate, ideological, determined political people joining the Labour Party for political discussion and working for the Party out of love and commitment has gone. When we had the Deputy Leadership election in 2007, ballot papers were sent out to *all* individual members. The number of ballot papers issued was 90,000. Whatever they say officially; actual membership is very small. They've told lies repeatedly about the size of the membership. It was 400,000 in 1997, if you count Councillors, MPs and their families and friends. That's Labour's core support. The main bulk of members used to put their life into the Party and saw it as part of their family and their moral commitment to society. Increasingly they've resigned."

CLP secretaries are at the centre of local parties and are familiar with what their members are thinking. A major party management issue, that upset members between 1994 and 2010, was *the attempt of the hierarchy to control, marginalise and ignore them.*

CLP Secretaries considered what can be learnt from the record of NL, Secretary Oliver asserted: "Presidential style government is not viable". He also applied this precept to Leadership of the PLP and Party governance.

Simon abhorred: "too much control within the Party". John wanted to: "Rebuild a democratic party with a meaningful annual conference." He continued by calling for Party members to be treated as intelligent human beings and not just as party workers". Lewis argued: "We need mass individual membership – currently it's being lost again (October 2009). He called for "a reversal of the centralisation in decision making".

Una asserted: "Over-control, against the members' wishes, is damaging. Examples were Ken Livingstone with the London Mayoralty and Rhodri Morgan with the leadership of the Welsh Assembly ... *They are still fixing internal candidate selections and internal elections held at Conference.*"

John objected to "the ability of Party regional offices – and the NEC – to impose (Westminster, European and Scottish Parliamentary and Welsh Assembly) candidates and interfere with their selections."

Manipulating selections involves not only a denial of Party members' democratic rights but is also unreasonable and unethical. It is deeply resented by grass-roots Party members.

Irene wanted the Party to: "Return to being a real political party that can act in a bottom up fashion and not be told, from above, what our policies are. People will then feel there are advantages in joining the Party." She continued: "We must retain the influence of local Labour parties. Returning more power to Regional Labour Parties would be positive". She also called for "a reversal of the centralisation in decision making".

Fred wanted Labour to: "Stop being a control freak party and open up the policy making process". Diane criticised the running of the Party saying: "The administrators need to be taught how to administer and power at the top needs to be limited." Tom wanted more autonomy for CLPs, abolition of the NPF and returning primacy to Conference" as the present system was not working satisfactorily. Quentin said: "Good management is coaching, not bullying".

Tom accused the Right in the Party of: "Finishing off Party democracy. As they knew would happen, disaffected members exited from the Party, so little opposition remained. The Party is now largely supine and possibly beyond saving. But, to make sure that the left in the Party can never rise again, the right is now pursuing its programme of destruction. This was started by rule changes, neutering Conference, establishing the NPF and the introduction of "Contact Creator" (a Party IT system), the march towards primaries and dismantling local party organisation."

The Diminished Role of Party Members in Policy Making

The NL policy making process was deeply disliked and resented by grass-roots members. The aim of the NL leadership seemed to be to cow Party members into submission and prevent the Party from ever returning to being a democratic socialist organisation. That return was what a majority of members still wanted in 2006/7 according to the YouGov poll for the independent LabOUR Commission.[C7-59]

CLP Secretaries' *proposals for improving party democracy:* Keith proposed: "We should extend the principle of OMOV throughout the Party. The only caveat that I have about this is that it opens the door to media barons to influence (Party) members in articles and programmes".

John asked for "Party members to be treated as intelligent human beings and not just as party workers". William called for "the encouragement of a grass-roots mass movement and the mobilisation of all the talents of members and supporters: Obama style." He continued: "We have to make the Party much more accountable. But we still need to win elections and avoid chaos. This can be done by transparency, trust, explanation and frankness. We are a mature Party and realise that compromises need to be made. But all members insist on being part of that process and that our inputs are acknowledged and respected. In that way we would accept not always getting our own way because we understand that is democracy."

John also wanted to: "Rebuild a democratic party with a meaningful annual conference." Lewis argued: "We need mass individual membership – currently it's being lost again" (October 2009).

These pleas for members to be trusted and treated as adults would not have had to be made in a reasonable and democratically run Party.

There was a widespread view among interviewees *that policy was made at the top and handed down* like the tablets of stone to Moses on Mount Sinai. For example, Philip Gould recalled that NL's first policy manifesto *New Life for Britain* was written by Robin Cook, Peter Mandelson, David Miliband and himself. From this came the five pledges constructed by TB's advisor, the unelected Peter Hyman.[C7-60]

Backbench MPs' opinions: Roger Berry believed: "In all political parties the leadership makes the policy; subject to the constraint that if enough party members and MPs are causing bother they can pull back. The proposed part-privatisation of the Post Office was a classic example. There is no doubt that the government withdrew that proposal because they realised the strength of feeling among MPs and within the Party."

Graham Stringer said: "Most of my members feel that if they attend a CLP meeting, have a policy debate or discussion and pass a resolution that it *has no influence at all on what happens nationally.* Party members felt disenfranchised during the 1980s because the policy making process was a clumsy one. But now they feel more disenfranchised because the policy making process is even more clumsy and ineffective."

Backbencher A. was more optimistic. He claimed: "CLP members, in my constituency, don't feel they have a role in policy making. But we mustn't talk down some of the opportunities that we have for policy making in the Party, mainly at the grass roots. *We have come to believe our own propaganda, that the party's over and we can no longer influence policy. There are huge opportunities to shape, change and regain control of the Labour Party.* That depends, to some extent, on trades unions being prepared to act on what they say. I usually listen to the Campaign for Labour Party Democracy (CLPD) and others who understand all the details. *The Party grass roots need to be able to speak to each other unmediated by the leadership.* It needs to change from the current exchange between 'us' and 'them' to an exchange amongst 'us' – the Party members (including myself as a grass-roots member) … We need to encourage the trades union rank and file to come back into the Party and participate in policy making there."

A's view was that, although the situation was adverse, there *are* still opportunities for grass-roots members to be involved in policy making. Both he and Stringer recognised cynicism and disillusion arising from the widespread belief among members that they were marginalised in policy development.

This MP's point about members being prevented from communicating with each other is valid. Up to 2010, Party internet-based policy consultations always prevented grass-roots members from sharing their policy proposals sent to Head Office with fellow members in other areas. Neither did they receive feedback from the top about their proposals and how these were being taken forward – or not.

Louise Ellman argued: "It is a shame that a great deal of the knowledge and commitment of Party members is not being fully used in policy making. Senior backbencher M. believed: "There's always tension because we can't have a mini referendum on every issue that confronts us whether we've a Labour Government or not. *But we do need structures whereby members can feel that they've had the opportunity to influence the policy debate.* Their voice adds value to that debate and should influence decisions made by others ... In the end what's important is to secure greater influence of members in the development of Party policy. However there are some areas where it may not be workable for members to get involved, for example complex finance policy."

It is probable that some Party members would not want to participate in making policy in complex financial or economic areas. Their demands are more modest. But what is the point of belonging to a political party if you are prevented from using your talents, knowledge and life experience in its policy making processes?

Jon Cruddas complained: "We are not stating what we stand for any more. Policy is built up out of focus groups rather than a journey. A sense of economic and social solidarity is what the Labour Party has lost. Press officers have formulated policy rather than drawing on frameworks and traditions of thought. *Ideology is the framework within which you should build policy.*"

Senior backbencher B. said: "When I was Labour Group leader in a Midlands city and when a party organiser in a Northern city, we used to have conferences and developed clear policy programmes at election times. Local government should be able to offer its electors their own policies. We took back control of the Northern city in 1971 on a local policy platform. We won 81 seats out of 99."

The *biggest issue*, for many grass-roots members, especially *CLP Secretaries*, was that of wishing to be given a more meaningful role in policy making. During the 1970s a badge was worn, by Labour women, proclaiming: "Labour Women make policy – not tea." Under NL it seems that neither Labour rank and file women (nor men) made policy.

In the author's straw poll, secretaries were asked how much influence each of the following groups *should have* on the policies of the current Labour government (as at October 2009)? Results were a):

Total	Trades	Party members (local)	Party Supporters (non	Backbench MPs	Civil	Private
A great	5	12 (44.4%)	1 (3.7%)	10 (37%)	2 (7.4%)	0
Some (22.2%	20 (74.1%)	15 (55.6%)	11 (55.6%)	15 (55.6%)	14 (51.9%)	6
Not much	2 (7.4%)	0	10 (37%)	1 (3.7%)	5 (18.5%)	6
None	14 (51.9%)	0	0	6	0	6
Don't know	1 (3.7%)	0	0	0	0	0

These members wanted themselves, and Backbench MPs, to have the greatest influence with significant influence also being allowed to trade unions.

Next CLP secretaries were asked (set b): "How much influence do you think that each of the following *actually does have on* the policies of the current Labour government (as at October 2009)?"

	Trades	Party members (local)	Party supporters (non	Backbench MPs	Civil	Wealthy
A great	6	0	0	0	0	8
Some	14 (51.9%)	20 (74.1%)	1 (3.7%)	5	12 (44.4%)	16 (59.3%)
Not much	4	7 (25.9%)	16 (59.3%)	7	12 (44.4%)	1 (3.7%)
None	1 (3.7%)	0	9	9	0	0
Don't know	2 (7.4%)	0	1 (3.7%)	6	3 (11.1%)	2 (7.4%)

Nearly 60% of Constituency Party secretaries questioned believed that local Party members had little or no influence in Party policy making and a third that they had none. 44.4% thought that Backbench MPs also had little influence.

Comments from CLP secretaries included Simon who said: "I don't mind the leadership deciding policies. I just wish that they would take the Party's traditions and principles into account!"

Bob believed: "The Party needs to get away from a philosophy where everything must be done instantly and through legislation. It should move to one where politics is more about influencing behaviour and culture and helping us to live together co-operatively and happily." Quentin lamented the marginalisation of party members in policy making. He also argued that: "*Large donors should not have any part in the policy making process except in their capacity as ordinary party members*. Money should not buy influence. We are not Tories – yet!"

William argued: "The Party should acknowledge, and encourage, members' inputs. They should remember there is always more energy, enthusiasm and knowledge among members (and the general public) than there is in the party hierarchy. He continued: "Having said that, a democratic party, like a democratic country, must compromise. The Party can't be purely bottom-up. We're unlikely to win elections, in contemporary Britain, like that."

Most secretaries took a "fairly hands off" attitude to Party policy making. However, they wanted the leadership to adhere to Labour's traditional aims and values and to use members' knowledge and talents in policy making.

Oliver expressed an elitist view: "The grass roots want incompatible policies and a decision making process that would make government impossible when Labour is in power … There are not enough grass-roots members any more and those who participate in meetings are not representative of the bulk of members. Instead we need competent parliamentarians and NEC members of integrity."

Eric was also opposed to grass-roots members having a larger role in policy making. He said: "I am reflecting on the grass-roots members that I know, but,for all their good qualities, there are not many of them that I would like to see making policies of national strategic importance. The Party needs the leadership of its most able members, that is capable MPs. He expressed concern about the current level of accountability of MPs saying: "At present MPs can do as much, or as little, as they like."

A few secretaries took a more hierarchical attitude to policy making on the grounds that most Party members are not philosopher kings and therefore not capable of weighing up relevant factors and making complex decisions.

Other opinions about *the operation of NL's policy making machinery* follow. Numerous claims were made about how Party staff are used to control constituency delegates to Annual Conference, one staff view follows:

Former regional organiser Malcolm recalled: "Originally the brief for staff that went to Conference was to keep and eye on delegates and report back any developments relating to motions etc. Regional staff might chase up delegates asking them if they would vote in a certain way. But it was fairly relaxed. You occasionally had a gentle word with a delegate but it was done in a subtle and reasonable way (during the mid and late 1990s). Then they introduced regional briefing meetings for delegates, including briefing by ministers.

He continued: "I never came across ballot rigging, or anything of that sort, at Conference, but I was never directly involved in ballots, counting etc. You *do* get regional staff promoting candidates at Conference (for internal Party elections). You always get a bit of favouritism, that will never disappear. Some staff take it too far. That depends on the personality of the Regional Director. These days they are chosen for being ultra loyalists."

Backbenchers hear the feedback of their constituency's delegates to Conference when the latter report back to their Constituency Party's General Committee (GC). Delegates frequently meet their MP at Conference. Most backbenchers attend Conference fairly regularly and some have attended the NPF. MPs' views about Conference follow:

Michael Meacher argued*: "We have to respect Conference above all. As we meet once per year the platform has to listen to debates and take notice of the decisions. They can't just walk away, as the Blairites did, and say: 'Well that's just the Party's view and not the Government's view'. That took my breath away. That is formally to disconnect the Party from the Government.* The central direction of the Party matters. So does the capacity of the Party to say: 'No we are not prepared to go down that route and we want you to think again!' or 'You neglected this and it is something of such profound importance that we want you to give greater attention to it and to carry though our reforms'."

He continued: "I remember when I first got into Parliament that Conference was like the heaving soul of the Party. Now it is flat, moribund and drained of all life. It's really just a farce, played out for the TV cameras, which no one believes in and no one cares about."

Thus Meacher provided compelling evidence that Conference had become disempowered and devalued.

Roger Berry argued: "I'm not convinced that Party Conference, or the NPF, have an enormous influence on policy. But the Party membership can exert influence through their normal lobbying and campaigning roles. *The days of a rolling manifesto that can be amended in formal ways each year should be over."* Berry continued: "Part of me would prefer a more classic policy-making structure; but that doesn't happen. I am sure that many members now feel that they are hardly involved in policy making. Members in my own CLP respond to policy consultations and feel good at the time, but are uncertain (of the outcome) later."

Jeremy Corbyn declared: "We have a Conference that is essentially a Leader's rally with an ever decreasing number of fringe events. NPF meetings are always held in an obscure place and people are never willing to go unless they are a member. Regional Conferences are now completely meaningless."

MPs deplored the misuse of Conference by the Leadership and its neutering as a policy making forum.

Graham Stringer asserted: *"The National Policy Forum (NPF) is a charade. I don't know anybody, including cabinet ministers, who doesn't think that.* However we should not go back to the resolutionary behaviour of the 1980s. There, for instance, you passed a resolution proposing taking into public ownership the top 200 UK companies thinking that it would change the world. In the old resolutionary politics you aimed to capture more and more of the party. We've not yet found a happy place where members feel that the Party supports them in policy making. We don't want to go back to the nonsense of the 1980s. However *things have changed for the worse and now we don't have an effective policy making process."*

John Cryer said: "Before PiP[C7-61] you had a Conference that was absolutely accountable. Everything was completely fair and worked in a transparent way. I doubt if we will go back to that. It's a case of making the NPF more accountable. That means opening up the franchise for the NPF (largely achieved later in 2009) so that there's more, and more immediate, accountability with regular reports back to affiliates and membership."

The performance of the NPF, as an alternative Party policy making forum (to Annual Conference), had not inspired MPs with confidence and was still a suitable case for treatment.

Cryer continued: "More resources would have to go into a more accountable NPF. The Party staff are now stretched to their absolute limits. People are doing three to four jobs each and the Party's broke. *The current problem with policy-making in the Party is that the process has become so obscure that members can't understand how it works* (see earlier sections of this Chapter). You have Conference, the NPF and various policy commissions where we had Conference policy, NPF policy, NEC policy and it was in the election manifesto. You couldn't have got a clearer statement that we were not going to introduce top up fees – but we were forced to legislate to introduce them. When that sort of thing happens people feel that they've been cut off."

Louise Ellman said: "The policy forums and the NPF, where national policy is formed, are not recognising the views of individual members. People attend Forum meetings but they have no idea what happens to decisions taken. There is a feeling that somebody at the top takes decisions without taking any notice of them. There's no feedback. It makes members despondent. We have many members with expert knowledge of subjects who feel that they cannot contribute to the policy making process."

John Grogan asserted: "It's a positive step that contemporary motions will again be debated at Conference (from 2009) rather than being linked to a rather vague policy forum. I'm not a romantic who says we should go back to the 80s. It might have been dramatic if you were there and raised the TV ratings. I don't believe that the best way of making Conference policy was compositing resolutions at the last minute. *But the NPF has got to be made more democratic and Conference must have meaningful debates – so people will be bothered to go.* Maybe there should be a move back to a more democratic style of Conference without going back to the days of vicious strife on the telly."

Some MPs lamented the means by which the NL leadership had wrested control of NL's policy making machinery and marginalised ordinary members in the Party's policy making structures :

Kelvin Hopkins contended: "They (NL) have stripped out policy making, within the Party, and established these policy forums and the NPF. They've managed to get total control of the NPF. It's very easy to get control of an organisation. The only thing the NL Leadership had to worry about was Conference and bit by bit they've eliminated policy making there. They had some big rebellions at Conference for example: on council housing policy. Gradually they've pushed things back so there's almost no power at Conference now."

Peter Kilfoyle claimed: "Conference is just a stage managed showpiece. It is concerned with organising ovations for the TV audience. The genesis of that was the 1980s conferences when it became an opportunity to kick each other. It should not be a blood letting. A situation half way between the two is ideal. There should be open and thoughtful debate but you have to trust the membership. The unions are a part, but only a part, of the problem."

Democratic Centralist methods and principles (see Chapter 2) were adopted by the Party machine and leadership in respect of policy making structures.

John McDonnell said: "Under NL the CLPs must be tightly controlled. The once democratic Party Conference has been transformed into a media event."

Lynne Jones complained: "There's no debate within the Party. Everything is stage managed at Conference. I went to Conference in 2008. It's a complete waste of time. Many CLPs wonder what is the point of sending delegates? The real problem with the NPF is that the policy documents are compiled by the secretaries of state for the relevant policy area. The policy documents are just tabled en bloc. There's no real opportunity to amend them (at Conference). If the leadership really wanted the Party to be engaged in policy development they would allow amendments to (NPF) policy documents. *I think that the concept behind the NPF, of having a rolling policy programme, is fine. It's been nobbled in practice because those in charge won't let go of control.*"

Alice Mahon asserted: "The NPF and Conference are completely stitched up. I was elected to the NPF (as an MP) but you were unable to move anything. There were things moved by union delegates about creeping privatisation etc. The Chair just summed up and said: 'We'll take your ideas back.' Well they got lost in some black hole in Downing St. There was no true input and many people were frustrated. I thought: 'I'm just wasting my time here'. I usually go to, and take part in everything."

She continued: "In the run up to the Iraq war, Conference was our last chance to make the case against. I made a nuisance of myself and eventually got called. But they then brought in MP Chris Bryant in to put me down. They can't lose gracefully."

Conference had become a meaningless charade. The dissident were humiliated or ignored mercilessly whatever their prestige and previous contributions to the Party. Broadly speaking the NPF was a waste of time.

Christine McCafferty had a cynical view of Conference, but acknowledged that the old ways of running it often led to bad public relations. She claimed: "Conference isn't what it was. I used to find it great and stimulating, but I also used to get frustrated. There was a lot going on that didn't seem particularly democratic. I think it's now gone too far along the orchestration line. Somewhere in the middle would be better. When it was all televised on the mainstream channels, on a daily basis, I'm sure that a lot of the public didn't really know what was going on. There was a lot of 'aggro' and people thought we were fighting among ourselves. Viewers watching probably couldn't understand what our policies were. It was right to bring more order into Conference but now it seems like Tory Conferences have always been. I'd love to be able to tell Conference what I think about development issues, but there isn't an opportunity. Ministers speak on these issues so they get their 'slot'. My impression is that chosen people are invited to speak. It feels as though open discussion on policy has been stopped."

She continued: "I think the NPF is boring. *The idea is that the NPF will be the place for policy debate. But it's predicated on existing documents and people just seem to acquiesce.* People are now (2009) feeling bad about where the Party is in the polls. We need to re-energise people to get them involved in policy – but we're not doing that. I wouldn't want to spend my time at the NPF. I can't see that I could change anything there."

If MPs like Christine and Alice Mahon find the NPF tedious and ineffectual, how is it supposed to engage the interest and commitment of rank and file Party members? Cynics might suppose that it is run in such a way as to be mind numbingly boring in order to dissuade Party members from wanting to participate in policy making.

The collapse of the Party's once democratic structures was also regretted by Gordon Prentice. He recalled: "My CLP used to have a GC meeting to go through resolutions for Conference fairly seriously. But that's withered on the vine now and no great effort is made to mandate the issues that are coming to Conference. We send a delegate. We have a few local policy forums but the conclusions probably go into the ether. I don't think we've ever actually changed anything through them … I suppose the trade off was that if we win elections then we have less of a say in what happens. That's how it was under NL. But that's over now with the Labour Party getting a historically low 16% of votes cast in the 2009 European elections."

Backbencher B. stated: "I am critical of what has happened to Conference and the NPF. It's a nonsense that you have to have a man and a woman CLP delegate alternate years for Conference. If you can't get a delegate of the required gender in the given year then you can't send a delegate. What annoys me about Conference is the way speakers are increasingly organised. *The chances of anyone being able to make a critical speech have become remote. Conference was OK as it was. It could be painfully embarrassing for the Party sometimes, but it was the Party's democratic voice.* I attended my first Conference in 1963. It was a passionate Conference: Harold Wilson's first as leader. We now want something in between –not quite as free as in 1963. We should be able to discuss any current issue. We shouldn't be stuck with an agenda largely fixed 2-3 months beforehand. Conference has no real teeth now."

The trends described by B. had the effect of lessening the motivation and commitment of CLPs to sending delegates to Conference (at considerable cost). By 2010 only 60% of CLPs participated.

Alan Simpson claimed: "The rules of Party Conference were changed to restrict debate and override votes. Even in Conference, delegates are now having their speeches written by party staff. It's supposed to be a random selection of speakers but often there are people in distinctive T shirts stationed behind either someone who is to be called or someone who is not to be summoned. The Chair understands that no matter how prominent someone appears – they could be the only person standing up in the hall – if they've got a certain party stooge behind them the Chair is not to call them. (Michael Meacher and Alice Mahon complained about the Chair of Conference failing to call them, even though they had previously indicated a wish to speak). "There has been distortion of the democratic process at Conference, not just to avoid embarrassing votes, but also critical arguments that would encourage people to think freely."

Devious practices at Conference are discussed below in the author's account of being a CLP Conference delegate in 2009. Additional views of backbenchers about NL's policy making machinery follow:

Linda Riordan thought: "The way in which Conference and the NPF are now run is bad for Party democracy. I hope that the left will gain strength in the Party so that we can alter Conference and the NPF. I don't know who is on the NPF from round here (West Yorkshire). Who is making the NPF policies? I'm not involved in them, nor is my CLP. We put things forward to Conference. but they're unlikely to get through. So we think: What's the point? Many local members feel powerless. The grass·roots Party is run on a top down basis, they have no say at Conference."

Clare Short lamented: "The Party Conference, and the NPF, are now about managing people and not about consulting them. That's why so many left the Party over Iraq. In the past they would have stayed in and put up resistance. In the meantime the democratic processes of Conference were progressively undermined. Policy forums were partly used to protest. When the idea of policy forums was first mooted by John Smith, he believed that it was a more consultative way of making policy. People could really have a voice rather than choose one resolution or another and vote. But John used to listen. *It's easy to manipulate a policy forum and so crush democracy. It's easy to crush democratic experience at Conference and turn it into a political rally. So people who were disgruntled with Party policy, instead of staying and fighting thinking 'we can change these policies', just left."*

Jon Cruddas recalled: "When we came into power Partnership in Power[64] offered a pluralism in internal party structures. But it didn't deliver it because of the very authoritarian culture that's been developed in terms of Party management. *There is no sense of a legitimate, deliberative function for the Party in policy-making. We never allowed ourselves that sort of maturity that can know difference and respect competing viewpoints. That reflects the fact that NL was created by a very small number of people, so it was never confident about itself as an electoral entity."*

John McDonnell said: "Now the policy machine (especially the Policy Commissions) has been taken over by organisational representatives from big business and Party members have got squeezed into a minority. In the 1980s and early 90s working groups of Party members with a burning interest, including academics and trades unionists, joined party working groups to develop policy."

NL delivered a policy making machine which, in practice, excluded ordinary members, however talented, representative or well qualified, and included NL cronies and representatives of capitalism with no commitment to the Party or to its ideology and values.

Chris Mullin contended: "The policy making machine, in so far as it has ever been listened to, has lost influence over recent time. In the old days, debates took place at Conference and the platform was (sometimes) defeated. Now debates take place on TV and the public doesn't understand. There is no doubt that the policy making apparatus has deteriorated. TB was persuaded, against his better judgement, to curtail the democratic policy making process. This was controversial and perhaps we shouldn't have accepted it. Policy is now largely made by the Government."

Regretting the hollowing out of Party policy making, Jeremy Corbyn said: "All this is very dangerous for the health of the Party. People who want political discussion go elsewhere to Compass, the Labour Representation Committee (LRC) etc. to single issue campaigns. If youngish people, with ideas and minds of their own and determination, don't feel that there is space for them in the Labour Party, then we will end up a weakened shell of an organisation." He continued: "Party members feel very disenfranchised. It has never been simple passing a resolution all through a branch to CLP and then to Conference or from union branch to Union executive and then Party conference. But if a policy had been agreed and campaigned on you could see the trajectory by which it would end up. *Policy forums negate the ability of Party and trades union members to have a direct influence in policy making. One receives these mind numbingly boring documents from the NPF that don't commit anybody to anything – they are just generalised directions. It's unclear to me how anyone now changes policy within the Party.* I've been a lifelong member, so I thought I understood this."

Graham Stringer said: "We've not yet found a happy place where members feel that the Party supports them in policy making. We don't want to go back to the nonsense of the 1980s. However things have changed for the worse and now we don't have an effective policy making process."

John Cryer believed: "*The current problem with Party policy-making is that the process has become so obscure that members can't understand how it works.* You have Conference, the NPF and various policy commissions. It's a very confused system and the line of accountability isn't clear. There are ways you could democratise the NPF without abolishing it. When I was an MP, before 2005, there was a feeling in my CLP that members did not have much ownership of Party policies and decisions. Examples were the Iraq War, university tuition fees and top-up fees."

The policy making process has become utterly opaque and there is no feedback or accountability from on high; so members have become disengaged. Virtually no one understands how it works so question the point in trying? *If it was beyond the extensive comprehension of new leader Jeremy Corbyn, how can anyone less able, or involved, engage with it?*

It seems that members' feelgood factor evaporates when their favoured policy apparently gets lost at Party HQ and there is no feedback to them!

The Malfunctioning of New Labour's Larger Policy Making Structures (Party Conference and the National Policy Forum)

CLP secretaries were asked, by the author, about the effectiveness of NL's Party policy making structures. First they were quizzed as to how well they thought that the two major grass-roots Party policy making bodies had worked since 1997?

In answer to a question as to how well Annual Conference has worked during this period, (straw) poll responses were:

Very well	1	(3.7%)
Quite well	6	(22.2%)
Neither well nor poorly	2	(7.5%)
Not so well	10	(37.0%)
Very poorly	8	(29.6%)

Therefore more than two thirds were dissatisfied.

In answer to the question as to how well the NPF has worked since 1997 (straw) poll replies were:

Very well	2	(7.5%)
Quite well	7	(25.9%)
Neither well nor poorly	3	(11.1%)
Not so well	9	(33.3%)
Very poorly	6	(22.2%)

This verdict was marginally better. Around a third of replies were favourable but more than half disapproved.

Secretaries were asked whether they knew who their current regional representatives on the NPF were. Nineteen (70.4%) said that they knew their identities but eight (29.6%) did not.

They were then asked how often their regional NPF representatives consulted with them and/or reported back to them? Straw poll responses were:

Quite often	8	(29.6 %)
Sometimes	7	(25.9%)
Seldom	4	(14.8%)
Never	8	(29.6%)

This is a reasonable result; but it is reprehensible that nearly a third of representatives never gave account of themselves or listened to views of the members they were supposed to represent.

CLP secretaries commented about Conference and the NPF: Philip wanted: "Attendance at Party Conference to be free." Presumably this was to encourage more CLPs to send delegates. Colin considered that: "Party policy making should be returned to Annual Conference." William said: "The Party should listen to, and debate with, CLP delegates at Conference."

Yvonne wanted the leadership to: "Use party regional conferences as a sounding board and to consult (the membership) about all major policies." Regional Conferences did not include policy debates and votes during the NL era.

Diane believed that: "The Party still seeks the opinion of grass roots members through encouraging CLPs to submit amendments to draft policies (agreed by the NPF) among other things." She continued "*BUT,* and it is a huge but, all this (member instigated) policy seems to disappear into a black hole and no one seems able to tell me where it goes."

Party policy is too frequently made outside Conference or the NPF. Secretaries also commented on the lack of more general Party policy consultations. In 2007 GB made a pie crust promise to set up a new comprehensive network of local policy forums. The Party was still waiting when he resigned in 2010.

Secretary Adele said: "There needs to be consultation of the membership on major policies. The Party should try to use policy forums to reflect members' views."

Gary regretted that: "CLPs can no longer send policy resolutions to Conference. I would like a return to that system." Adele asserted: "Policy forums were tried, but members felt that they were not listened to. In TB's time some policies seemed to be made on the hoof and bore little relationship to the policies that local members were supporting."

Xenia deplored the absence of policy consultation and called for "consultation of the membership on major policies. The Party should try to use policy forums to reflect members' views."

Helen said she was "not sure that the vast majority of Labour Party members want to get involved in policy making – that is half the problem. But when you *do* take time to get involved, it would be good to know that you make some difference rather than feeling as if you are rubber stamping policy."

By 2009 real involvement in Party policy making was history for grass roots members.

There was often alleged manipulation of internal Party ballots. The LabOUR Commission Report[C7_62] complained about, and evidenced, illicit intervention in, and manipulation of, internal party ballots. Party rules expressly prohibit intervention of staff in campaigns for these elections and ballots. Much alleged abuse took place in the context of ballots of delegates held at Party Conference. Evidence of such wrongful conduct is gathered below.

Former local *Party organis*er Ben recalled: "When it came to polices and rule changes being debated at Conference, Party staff were expected to deliver the results that the Leadership required on policy resolutions and proposed Party rule changes."

Views of backbenchers included John Grogan who believed: "Things are changing a bit. At Conference this year (2009) we decided that members of the NPF will now be chosen by individual members, not by Conference delegates. We'll all get a postal vote. That allows for the development of political argument and people standing on slates."

Grogan continued: "I believe that there's been abuse of the use of Party officials at Conference. Delegates come along, they're given briefings and some of the more malleable are told how to vote. If I were Leader of the Party, and you were a Party officer, I'd expect you to be loyal to the Party and the Leadership. But *manipulation by staff has gone too far.* If I were a Party official I would believe that I must have a loyalty to the Party membership as well as taking instructions from HQ."

JG continued: "Sometimes, when there's been a key Conference vote, Party staff would ask you, as MP, how your CLP delegate was likely to vote? From talking to delegates it's become clear that, at the briefings and receptions before and at the beginning of Conference, efforts are made to get people into line. In some cases people are just told how to vote. I don't object to the Leadership of the Party using these occasions to put their views. It's when it goes beyond that I object. Party staff should not be delivering slates – but they do."

Lynne Jones suggested: "The Party's now become adept at CLP delegates being got at. If they're young and inexperienced, and they don't really know what Party Conference is about, they're just manipulated and told that: 'You can't possibly do anything that the Leadership doesn't want. It would look bad on telly'. The NPF works, but the elections to the NPF were controlled (by the Party machine) when they were elected by Conference delegates."

Examples of manipulation by the Party machine at Conference follow:

Alice Mahon remembered: "When Pete Willsman and I stood for the Conference Arrangements Committee (then elected by a ballot of CLP delegates at Conference) we were on the CLGA slate. The Party machine was working for the two leadership favoured candidates. I saw one of the regional organisers going round introducing one leadership supported candidate to our delegates. I pulled her up and said: "What about me?' She replied: "No, no you've misunderstood it."

Linda Riordan claimed: "The elections for the CAC are not run fairly. Alice (Mahon) and her running mate faced all sorts of intervention from Party staff when they stood."

Teresa Pearce (an MP since 2010) served on the NCC up to 2008. Then she came up for re-election and lost her seat. She believed: "In the early years the elections to the NCC were fairly conducted. During Conference 2008, and leading up to the ballot, my CLP delegates (and others) told me that staff were lobbying for another candidate for the NCC (one supported by the hierarchy). They said to delegates: 'This is our preferred candidate: but it's up to you'. My own CLP didn't vote and the delegate gave no reason. It is supposed that she was leant upon. My CLP had requested her to vote for me."

CLP Secretaries were asked: "Have any of your CLP delegates to Conference in recent years reported back to you that they were put under pressure by Party staff, or people working for them, about voting or speaking? The results were:Yes 5; No 17; Don't know 4. However, an inexperienced delegate, in awe of her CLP secretary, might be wary of complaining.

In 2008 the author was invited to speak about party democracy at a CLP General Committee (GC) meeting in Greater Manchester. When she mentioned the possibility of staff pressure on Conference delegates, four people present indicated they *had* experienced it personally. They had been that CLP's Conference delegates for the previous four years! Una, who had held senior Party office, reported that her CLP's delegates were never approached by Party staff to influence them because they knew that those delegates would report this straight back to her. She has complained about such behaviour in the past.

Further case histories of pressure applied at Conference follow:

"Brenda" described shenanigans, involving Party staff, which occurred at the 1999 Bournemouth Conference where she was a delegate from her CLP.

She recalled: "The Air Traffic Controllers' Union (then IPMS) contacted CLPs, ahead of Conference, asking for support for their opposition to the privatisation of the National Air Traffic Control Service (NATS). My CLP mandated its delegates to oppose the privatisation at Conference. The subject was raised in conversation with an MP at the regional delegates' reception at Conference, but he was 'under orders' not to speak at Conference about it. I volunteered to speak, provided that he would brief me. I also met IPMS delegates at Conference and a group of protesters from NATS who were lobbying delegates. On the basis of this information I wrote a speech for the Transport debate. I let it be known, in the right quarters, that I wanted to speak. Otherwise I kept quiet."[C7_65]

However the regional organiser found out. She pursued me relentlessly: trying to stop me making the speech. At one point I had to hide in toilets to avoid her. The usual arguments were trotted forth. 'Don't give the press any ammunition about discord in the Party etc."

She continued: "On the day of the Transport debate, I ensured that I had a group of supporters around me who made so much noise that the Chair had to call me to the podium. The speech was well received by delegates, if not by ministers. I was asked to appear on the BBC TV Conference programme that evening with Denis MacShane MP (government representative). Not surprisingly great efforts were made by the interviewer to interpret my speech as 'splits in the Party'. But I reiterated that it was not unreasonable in a democratic party to challenge a decision if you thought it wrong."

As a postscript, Brenda, commented on the 2010 Conference saying: "I found life this year much easier as a socialist society delegate. No pre-Conference briefing telling you what you can and can't say and no regional organiser on your tail."

In 2005 a first time CLP delegate, known to the author, attended Conference in Brighton. When approached by a regional organiser he indicated that he intended to vote against the platform recommendation on a contemporary motion about the future of council housing. He was immediately frog marched off to an audience with John Prescott who tried, in vain, to persuade him to change his mind – yet another example of draconian pressure being applied to an inexperienced delegate.

OMOV postal ballots are usually fairer and less susceptible to interference by the Party machine. However when the author, and other CLGA nominees, stood for the NEC in 2006 she was shown email messages from Party staff from three regions sent to members to urge them to vote for candidates on the "Members First" (Party machine) slate.

The author's report of Party Conference 2009 where she was a Constituency delegate follows: "Conference 2009 saw a vote for a rule change to introduce OMOV postal balloting for the NPF. The party hierarchy was opposed to this as it would remove the power of party staff to pressurise Conference delegates to vote for the leadership slate. (The previous NPF ballot, taken at Conference 2007, produced only a handful of CLP delegates not supported by the party machine). In contrast the first OMOV ballot for the NPF in 2010 produced 19 non New Labour CLP delegates (out of 55).

At Regional Office pre-Conference delegates' lunches in 2009 anonymous fliers were placed on the tables (delegates were expected to attend these functions). The fliers were also distributed to delegates on the Conference floor. They read:[C7-67] "Protect your rights, protect your activists on your committees. Don't lose your rights as a CLP delegate and the right of your General Committee to choose who represents you on the National Policy Forum. Over the past few years the rights of CLP delegates have been eroded."

The irony of the wording in this message is that NL have long campaigned against the retention of CLP General Committees. In some areas (for example, as in Birmingham, as was reported by Lynne Jones MP) they were abolished at party officers' instigation. Secondly official advice of Party staff, during the NL era, has been that CLP's GCs are not allowed to mandate (bind) their Conference delegate's voting. The deceit of the flier was compounded by its use of the language of Party democracy activists. The machine lost this campaign. Afterwards CLP Secretary Una called for the Party to "publicise the change to OMOV for electing the NPF and encourage members to get involved. CLP Secretaries' contact details are not currently publicised. They should be given – on the Party website where the secretary is willing."

In 2009 there were the usual CLP delegate ballots for the CAC and the NCC. That year the author was a CLP delegate and stood as a candidate for the CAC: so she gained a worm's eye view of events. Along with all CLP delegates, the author was summoned to the regional session for briefing delegates a few weeks ahead of Conference (see p.1 of this Chapter). She was invited to a neo-compulsory briefing lunch at the start of Conference (see above). Both sessions were conducted by Party staff.

Research by the Campaign for Labour Party Democracy (CLPD)[67] showed that these initial regional meetings were used to assess the views of delegates. Regional staff gave information to the sympathetic, put pressure on the malleable and left the "hard nuts" alone. However, the latter were to be prevented from being called to speak and treated with contempt. Every CLP delegate was allegedly allocated to a member of regional staff as minder (the role of Nazi gauleiter comes to mind). Party staff openly suggested that they should write speeches for delegates and said they would like to see speeches that delegates had written themselves and make suggestions! It is probable that unless a delegate's speech was written, or approved, by an officer that delegate would not be called to speak. At a fringe meeting at the 2010 Conference the MP chairing, a former journalist, twice complained about the "dire quality" of delegate's speeches at Conference that year and recently. The cause is easy to guess.

Gary Heather (then from the Communication Workers Union) and the author, were the Centre Left Grass Roots Alliance (CLGA) nominees for the Conference Arrangements Committee (CAC) in 2009. They produced good quality literature and campaigned actively at Conference, within Party democracy organisations, and on Facebook. Although they received more votes than other CLGA candidates had done recently they were still beaten by the NL candidates.

The following alleged questionable practices were reported to the author during Conference 2009:

i. Two delegates from the same region reported that one of their Regional Officers spent most of Conference texting local delegates with requests as to who and what to vote for.

ii. A "dissident" delegate dozed off and missed voting in the CAC ballot. When she awoke and asked her regional staff why they didn't awaken and remind her. They retorted: "It's not our job". However the following day the same staffer fetched another compliant but sleeping delegate to vote in the NCC ballot.

iii. Two delegates from another region were instructed by regional staff to vote for the leadership's candidates in the CAC election. They told the staffer to "Get lost".

In addition abuses were reported to the daily delegates news sheet *Campaign Briefing* the following appeared on 29/09/09: "As a first time delegate to Conference, I had assumed that regional officials were like Caesar's wife (above reproach). Yesterday I was disabused of this belief. Out of the blue I was approached by a regional official who inquired who I would be voting for in the CAC election. 'Our advice is to vote for S and M (leadership favourites).' I had presumed this was a free ballot. He then went on to enquire as to my thoughts on the rule change on elections for the NPF on Wednesday. 'We can't afford to send out the ballot papers by post. Why change a situation that works well?' This abuse of Party democracy shocked me and should be investigated." *New, (now disillusioned) delegate.*

The same *Campaign Briefing* continued: "It has also been reported that (named) regional staff were telling delegates who to vote for in Monday's CAC election." The author rests her case.[C7_68]

Top Down Interference with the Party at local level

This was quite a common occurrence and some constituency parties were put in "special measures" i.e. direct control by the National Executive Committee (NEC). This usually occurred where rules had allegedly been broken or where there had been some suspected improper conduct (other than by Party staff) at local level. During the Militant affected period of the 1980s, local parties were sometimes put into "special measures" to curb Militant influence. Issues were often connected to PPC selections or alleged misconduct in local government. However special measures did not emerge as a major theme in interviews for this book.

Lynne Jones spoke about flagrant interference in Birmingham. She reported that: "Local Labour Parties in Birmingham are not allowed to have General Committees (GCs) any more. At West Midlands Regional level and at Birmingham City level, it was decided that GCs would be abandoned. In future we must have a CLP Executive Committee and an all-members meeting (unlike GCs all-members meetings do not have delegates, cannot make decisions and are not representative governing bodies). Now all-members meetings are no better attended than GCs used to be." (one argument advanced in favour of all-members meetings was that they would be better attended than GCs) She continued: "There is now no elected representative process. The authority to take decisions is in the hands of the CLP Executive Committee (EC). When the new ECs were first set up there were elections for places, but Regional Office ensured that their people were elected. Those who challenged that situation got demoralised and no longer bother. In the constituency, where I now live, at the AGM the Chair gets all his people to come along and ensures that he is re-elected. Then you don't see them again. They are not committed to the Party, just committed to him. The Party does nothing about it because, so long as he does as he's told, they're quite happy with that level of (alleged) corruption to take place."

The key message from the accounts given above must be that grass-roots Party members were neither valued nor trusted by the NL regime, in respect of Party Conference or policy making .Responsibility was delegated only to those approved by Party staff. They are supposed to be employees of the members as well as of the Leadership and the NEC.

Conclusion

This Chapter has demonstrated how New Labour stripped out the Party by alienating, and driving out, almost two thirds of its members. It also reorganised party structures and rules to deprive remaining members of effective, honestly and transparently conducted participation in Party governance and policy making. The methods used frequently involved alleged rule breaking or rule bending. The Party machine was also involved manipulation of ballots. The perpetrators of much of this activity were Party staff. The salaries of these staff are largely paid for by the Party's individual and trades union members' subscriptions and donations. Staff should have represented the interests and rights of those members as well as those of the Party hierarchy. The purpose of this manipulation was to empower the autocratic NL leadership: at the expense of the rights of grass-roots Party members and of party democracy.

CHAPTER 8
'Fixing' the Parliamentary candidate selections

A nail in the coffin of Party and Parliamentary democracy

"All animals are equal but some animals are more equal than others"
George Orwell, *Animal Farm*

"New Labour is a Children's Crusade led by the Early Middle Aged"
Austin Mitchell MP quoted in the *Little Red Book of Labour*

"At first I was offered chances to stand for Parliament but as I became more critical I was frozen out"
**TV actor and presenter Sir Tony Robinson,
Desert Island Discs, BBC Radio 4, 08/07/2011**

"It's not important who is voting, it is important who is counting"
Malalai Joya (woman former Afghan MP) describing Afghan elections, 9/04/2012, ABC TV *Lateline*

Contents: Overview of Selection Processes for Westminster candidates before and after the New Labour Ascendancy

Former Party staff speak out about New Labour's PPC selections

Backbench MPs comment on UK wide PPC selections

Members of the working classes not wanted in Parliament More women needed: but only if 100% New Labour

Grass-roots members discuss manipulation of selections in merging constituencies with ministers involved

Excluded Westminster hopeful's tales

European, Scottish, Welsh and London Assembly selections

At the Oldham East and Saddleworth post by-election social (in 1996), local MPs were asked to get up and dance. Candidates then shortlisted for a current local Parliamentary selection, including the author, were also included. To her surprise the author found herself in a chorus line of men next to a frowning Peter Mandelson. The dancers were then asked to do the cancan (which was performed in the style of a Greek syrtaki). Perhaps Mandelson was not amused by her participation and this could have harmed her Parliamentary prospects?

An overview of selection processes for Westminster Parliamentary candidates before and after the New Labour ascendancy

This Chapter examines selections of Prospective Parliamentary Candidates (PPCs). It discusses a narrower topic than is covered by other Chapters. It deals with very significant and allegedly corrupt practices engaged in by the New Labour (NL) hierarchy and their Party machine. Whilst a few individual cases of malpractice have been publicised in the media (e.g. ballot tampering at the Erith and Thamesmead selection (2009))[C8-1], there has been no comprehensive, evidenced attempt to examine this phenomenon in detail.

These questionable practices are still currently unknown – even to the majority of Labour Party members. They were widely used up to the 2010 general election. Very many beneficiaries of this system still populate the Commons benches and are hostile to the Corbyn leadership. This has changed the ideological composition of the Parliamentary Labour Party (PLP) radically from that of all its predecessors prior to 1994. The contemporary PLP membership is predominantly New Labour (NL) and this explains why it has proved so difficult to get sufficient first round nominations for non NL candidates in recent Party Leadership elections, as Diane Abbott and Jeremy Corbyn have discovered since 2010. Meanwhile NL claimed to run the Party in accordance with democratic rules and principles, but this claim was very dubious. This chapter uses direct testimonies from victims. They have an important story which has had little previous exposure.

The mildest realistic assertion must be that manipulations were used to guarantee the selection of the NL party hierarchy's chosen candidates in almost all winnable seats. This chapter reveals many plausible allegations of favouritism, cronyism, bending or ignoring the rules and ballot rigging. That is: alleged corruption. Principles of equal opportunities and party members' democratic right to select candidates were jettisoned to facilitate the hand picking of the Leadership's chosen candidates. It was a secret operation, conducted by the Party Machine. It was very difficult for the victims, and ordinary Party members, to uncover the truth while this operation was ongoing.

Chapter 7 discussed the way NL changed the rules, culture and staff of the Party in order to secure its objective of controlling and disempowering grass-roots Party members. This operation included restricting members' democracy relating to all significant internal selections and elections. As in preceding chapters, the story is told mainly by people directly involved. Their views are presented according to category of interviewee.

Meg Russell claimed: "Choosing candidates for public office is one of the most important functions of any political party".[C8-2] Antony King said: "One of the House of Commons' principal functions … is to provide the gene pool from which most ministers are drawn."[C8-3]

When elected to a Parliament, members should be capable of holding the Government to account and scrutinising draft legislation. As King claimed, they also provide the cohort from which ministers, and lesser government office holders, are usually selected. As Roy Hattersley pointed out, the aim of candidate selection, under NL, was to secure compliant MPs, rather than able, objective and principled representatives.[C8-4]

Inclined to authoritarianism, the NL Hierarchy exerted totalitarian control of the selection of potential MPs and Assembly members. The main aim of this practice was to "parachute" special ministerial advisers (SPADS) and other NL "trusties" into safe (and even just winnable) Labour seats. Soon after election, those so favoured were often promoted to ministerial positions. Former SPADs, who were selected for safe seats, then rapidly became ministers, include: Ed Balls, David Miliband, Ed Miliband, Andy Burnham, Yvette Cooper, Caroline Flint and Kitty Ussher.[C8-5] NL's Leaders would not tolerate backbenchers who might think independently and challenge the hierarchy.

This chapter demonstrates that, *from 1994 onwards. the Party hierarchy, allegedly and secretly, hand picked virtually all Labour candidates in winnable Westminster seats*. From 1999 control was overtly extended to European and Scottish Parliaments and to Welsh and Greater London Assemblies. The methods by which this invidious selection of candidates was achieved, sometimes included changing Party rules.[C8-6] It frequently involved breaking and manipulating existing rules. Occasionally there was alleged ballot rigging (see below).

Alan Simpson MP commented: "They wanted MPs who would be their 'Avon Ladies' relaying the undiluted the NL message and spinning it to party members and the public." NL also wanted MPs who looked good and were media friendly. The 2010 intake included personable TV personalities such as Tristram Hunt and Gloria De Piero. Parliament now includes even fewer working class people. In 2010 Mills[C8-7] found that only 9% of contemporary Labour MPs came from a manual working class background. In 1966 that proportion was 30%. A 2010 Smith Institute study found that 27% of contemporary Labour MPs "had an occupational background in politics".[C8-8] This frequently meant that they had had little or no experience of an ordinary job in the community.

After the 2010 election there were far fewer people, even marginally to the left of NL, in the Parliamentary Labour Party (PLP) as Michael Meacher pointed out. Austin Mitchell MP was justified when he described NL as a "children's crusade" because many of those parachuted into seats were very young. Louise Ellman MP believed (see Chapter 9) that MPs aged over 50 were seldom promoted by Tony Blair (TB). However Gordon Brown (GB) was not so ageist in his appointments.

In order to comprehend how PPC selections were controlled and manipulated, it is necessary to understand contemporary selection processes. Most alleged fixing related to Westminster seats. From 1999 tougher Party rules were drawn up to enable Party HQ to control selections for European, Celtic and London assemblies.[C8-9] These rules openly and severely restricted party members' democratic participation from the outset. Therefore less manipulation was used (see below).

Prior to 1992 the Westminster PPC selection process had remained virtually unchanged since 1945. [C8-10] That entailed an equal opportunities procedure that was regulated fairly by Party staff. It gave affiliated organisations (mainly local party and union branches) the right to hear and question candidates prior to nominating (at the entry gate). All members had an opportunity to assess every aspiring candidate personally. Their representative delegate structure, the Constituency General Committee (GC) had the right to agree the shortlist, hear and question the candidates and then vote for the winner. In order to vote: a delegate had to be present for the *whole* of the selection hustings and hear *all* candidates. "Hustings" are sessions where all shortlisted candidates speak and answer questions from members eligible to vote in the selection ballot.

Unlike One Member One Vote (OMOV), this system denied every individual member a vote in the final selection. However, at a local branch selection meeting, they could collectively instruct their delegate which candidate to support. There were no postal votes and no requirements about the inclusion of women or black/ethnic minority candidates on shortlists. These latter shortcomings required remedy. The winning candidate then had to be endorsed by the Party's National Executive Committee (NEC) but was rarely rejected, provided that no rules had been broken during the selection process. The author, who experienced this system from 1970 onwards, believes it was fair, relatively democratic and gave local members substantial control of selections.

Prior to the 1992 general election a new system of PPC selection, an electoral college, was introduced. This proved unsatisfactory and was discontinued from 1993. Selection on the basis of OMOV was agreed at the 1993 Party Conference, after John Smith put his leadership on the line to support it. OMOV is actually more democratic than earlier selection methods, with the *proviso that this system must be fairly administered giving equal opportunities to all applicants.*[C8-11] Eighteen out of 27 CLP secretaries, responding to the 2009 straw poll for this book, thought that in general "OMOV postal ballots are fairer and less open to partisan intervention".[C8-12]

Since OMOV was introduced for PPC selections, there have been two major devices whereby disregard and manipulation of the rules have been common. These were: illicit use of Party members' contact details and inappropriate use of postal votes. There have also been cases of suspected, or probable, tampering with postal votes once cast. As rules changed, new alleged ways of manipulating them were devised. The NL selection system for Westminster candidates was not the product of an integrated set of new rules. It evolved piecemeal to meet the emerging requirements of the Party hierarchy.

Within the post 1994 selection system, the only way that aspiring candidates could encounter selecting members was by being able to contact, and meet them, individually. This necessitated acquiring a local members contact list and visiting them at home – a time consuming and sometimes intrusive process. Until 2007 these lists were not officially made available to aspiring candidates until one to two weeks before the hustings. From 2007 they were made available to all applicants, at a slightly earlier date *during* the selection timetable.[C8_13] In practice there have long been one or two people, (invariably the hierarchy favourite(s) who possessed, and used, members contact lists during the *whole* selection timetable and sometimes long before a selection process officially started. Many favourites were able to do this up *to two years beforehand*. Local Party members reported that this occurred in two safe North West seats selecting for 2001.[C8_14] How these lists were distributed, and by whom, was long concealed. The author's research eventually revealed that frequently the favoured obtained them from the party hierarchy through Party regional offices. Union supported candidates sometimes obtained lists from Party offices or their union HQ. Premature distribution breached Party rules. These regulations were seldom enforced against the favourite(s) when complaints were made to Party staff (see below). In a case involving one hopeful, who received the members list two years in advance, local members related that the daughter of the retiring MP applied (but was not the hierarchy's choice). Both he and she were pressurised by Party HQ. The MP was warned that if he gave her a members contact list, and she used it before rules permitted, she would be disqualified. After the same selection local members reported that they only met *one* applicant during the whole selection process. This was not the daughter, but the Hierarchy's favourite who visited all their homes and was later selected. She used a contact list nearly two years before the permitted date.[C8_15]

One party activist, involved in the 2010 Stalybridge and Hyde selection, told *Tribune*: "Reynolds won because he is Purnell's (the retiring MP) best mate and he was able to launch a campaign two months before any of the other candidates *knew* there was going to be a selection process." (Reynolds denied this). [C8_16]

Once in possession of the list, a favourite visited every Party member, solicited their vote and tried to persuade them to vote by post. Postal voting had to be done *before* candidates could be heard at the hustings. The favourite then had a committed voter who subsequently had minimal contact with other applicants. As noted above, non-favoured applicants obtained the members list very shortly before the hustings. By that time postal voting had already started. The disadvantaged then had no prospect of meeting, and convincing, more than a few of the (average) CLP electorate (then around 400 members).

From 2007 initial interviewing of applicants, by wards and other affiliates, was ended and nomination was done from hopefuls' CVs alone.[C8_17] This meant that members had even fewer opportunities to interview most applicants. The Party devised "Meet and Greet", a superficial system reminiscent of "speed dating". At a mass meeting, prior to nominations, candidates were given between two and five minutes each to chat with small groups of members. This was not sufficient time to assess each candidate's character, political views, work record and competence or to question them meaningfully. The superficiality of this "meet and greet session" gave additional advantage to the favourites who had greater exposure through being enabled to visit individual members privately over long periods.

To ensure fairness, as many members as possible should hear all candidates speak and answer their questions before voting (as they did until 1987). There were inevitably some members working, ill or on holiday during hustings. Postal votes for the final selection were introduced before the 1992 election to enfranchise these. From then on rules permitted *all* members to have a postal vote *on demand*, irrespective of personal circumstances.[C8-18] Before the 2005 election Party rules were changed to state that: "Postal votes should only be used by those people who are unable to attend due to a medical condition, (unavailability of) travel arrangements, are away on holiday, have work commitments or caring responsibilities. They will not be made available to those choosing to undertake other engagements."[C8-19] This rule was theoretically sound but was usually ignored in practice. Members did not have to produce any *evidence* of their eligibility for a postal vote. As discussed below, postal votes had to be cast *before* the hustings when members had had no opportunity to hear, question and assess *all* shortlisted candidates.

During the Barrow-in Furness selection (October 2009) it was reported that several local activists accused John Woodcock, a senior aide to GB, who was later selected: "of colluding with Party staff to gain an unfair advantage over other candidates, and of breaking rules by sending postal vote applications to Party members not eligible to use them. *Tribune* has established that more than one quarter of the constituency's 200 plus party members will be voting by postal ballot."[C8-20]

Frequently *more votes* were cast by post, *before* the hustings, than were put in by members attending them. Postal voters therefore did not hear all shortlisted candidates before voting. For example: at the selection in Calder Valley in April 2009, *Tribune* reported: "There were 97 applications for postal votes, of which 90 were used, but only 57 members attended the hustings and voted there. The winning candidate lost the (hustings) ballot by 22 to 35 votes, but when the postal votes were added she won by 95 votes to 52 over the runner up. Claims were made that supporters of the winner "approached party members and helped them fill in their postal voting forms, which is against Party rules."[C8-21] In the same month "harvesting" of postal votes became a major issue in the selection at Erith and Thamesmead where NL adviser Philip Gould's daughter was allegedly supported by the machine, according to a contemporary article in the *Guardian*.[C8-22,C8-23]

Another postal vote complaint arose at the 2010 Stalybridge and Hyde selection. The runner up, Dr. Kailish Chand, told *Tribune*: "More than 100 votes had been cast for (the winner) before the hustings had taken place. Where is the democracy in a process where candidates are denied the chance even to present their own case, to speak to their peers?"[C8-24]

There is a long-standing need to make the Parliamentary Labour Party (PLP) more representative of women, black people and ethnic minorities generally. This led to the introduction of All Women Shortlists (AWS) and later to quotas for Black and Minority Ethnic (BAME) candidates on shortlists. These provisions (especially AWS) were hard fought for during the early and mid 1990s. AWS was originally adopted the by Party for the 1997 election. However two male members took the Party to an industrial tribunal, which ruled that AWS breached equal employment opportunities.[C8-24] The Leadership subsequently halted them. Later, the first Blair Government legalised AWS. However AWS was sometimes used to keep out unwanted male local favourites. For example one prominent male and local Asian candidate (who supported NL) was kept out of a constituency, where the BNP was strong, by the imposition of an AWS. He was later found a winnable constituency elsewhere.

Another way of controlling selections was to delegate them to the NEC, whenever a pretext could be found. Up to 1987 all shortlisting for PPC selections in by-elections was done by the CLP involved. In the late 1980s Labour lost a by-election in a safe seat and blamed the candidate on the grounds that she was "too left wing and not media friendly". At Conference 1988[C8-26] the relevant rules were changed. From then on candidate shortlisting for all by-elections was undertaken by the Party National Executive Committee (NEC) or one of its sub-committees (subject to full NEC endorsement).This rule currently remains in force. Between 1997 and 2010 the NEC shortlisted for all vacant candidatures during the six months between the preceding New Year and an anticipated general election. The number of vacancies was often increased by last minute retirements of MPs going to the Lords. Here again the Party hierarchy usually 'cleansed' shortlists thus restricting the choice of local members.

The partner of a Minister informed the author[C8-27] that NEC shortlisting had originally been introduced in order to ensure that by-election candidates were competent and could deal with the media effectively. However, they claimed, it had subsequently become a method of excluding candidates disliked by NL, particularly if they were to the left of it.

Prior to the 2010 election, the NEC's numerous interventions were usually biased. They even excluded prominent moderate candidates from shortlists in their zeal to ensure that Hierarchy's favourites won. *Tribune* investigated controversial selections at Stalybridge and Hyde and Stoke Central.[C8-28] At Stoke, *Tribune* reported that the selection of academic and TV historian Tristram Hunt: "followed speculation in the party and local and national media that he was the favoured candidate of Peter Mandelson whose support had helped him to secure the seat". A local Party member claimed, in *Tribune*, that the selection was "obviously rigged". The author's contacts in the Stoke Central Party informed her that there was a shortlist of three, of whom the other two "were not known locally and not impressive".[C8-29]

In Stalybridge and Hyde, Minister James Purnell announced, at the eleventh hour, that he was standing down. *Tribune* reported: "A controversy over the selection of Jonathan Reynolds following intervention on his behalf by Mr. Mandelson and James Purnell in the selection process. Purnell was outraged that his ally had not been included on the shortlist drawn up by NEC members and, following a meeting in the constituency, Lord Mandelson successfully lobbied for a special selection panel of the NEC to have Mr. Reynolds, who is embroiled in a civil war among local councillors, added to the list".[C8-30] These sources revealed that the moderate Glyn Ford, former local MEP and previous leader of the Democratic Socialist Group in the European Parliament, had been kept off this shortlist by the NEC. Discussing contemporary shortlisting methods of the NEC selection panel, Thomas Rainsborough alleged in *Red Pepper*: "Most (hopefuls) needn't waste their time as the front runner in each constituency will already have been decided at 10 Downing St. … Labour's General Secretary is then informed who Gordon wants parachuting in and where. Loyalists on the (NEC) selection panel are then told who No 10 wants. The trick that follows is to present local party members with a shortlist of four or six 'approved candidates' … All candidates, bar the favourite, are chosen on the exacting criteria of being no hopers."[C8-31]

In January 2010 *Labour Briefing* expressed concern about impending late selections: "How the NEC will draw up its shortlists is surrounded in secrecy. Will constituencies be given a full list of those who declare an interest in the seat? Will they be told the criteria used to assess which candidates will be shortlisted and who are deemed not good enough?"[C8-32]

The last minute blow to members' democracy, in the run up to general elections, was the Party machine's late *imposition of candidates*. Very late selections gave the NEC, *acting alone,* the opportunity to impose. In 2010 MP Geoff Hoon delayed announcing his retirement. The NEC then imposed Gloria De Piero as candidate in Ashfield. They also imposed former NL MP Chris Leslie on Nottingham East. According to *Tribune*, he was chosen by an NEC Subcommittee from their shortlist of nine. They excluded Byron Taylor, respected director of the Trades Union and Labour Organising committee. *Tribune* reported[C8_33, C8_34] that the NEC decided by eight votes to seven to impose a candidate, rather than allow constituency members to choose. The deciding vote was cast by Gordon Brown.

Former Party staff spoke about PPC selections

The views of Party staff were particularly relevant because they have been running selections and know "where the bodies are buried". Between 1993 and 2010 they were given a powerful new role: intervening in selections as agents of the hierarchy. NL's management of Party staff was discussed in Chapter 7.

David Gardner (former Party Assistant General Secretary) reported: "Parliamentary selections prior to the 1997 general election were an equal opportunities process. Although it was not perfect, all members had their say through OMOV ballots. I fought for All Women Shortlists. Between 1993 and 1997 selection ballots may have been too open and susceptible to manipulation. *Unfortunately there were anomalies with ballots and counting.* Party staff were often seen to play partisan roles and appeals against their bias went unheard."

DG continued: "Possibly too many postal votes were given and too easily. Some candidates got a members list, before shortlisting, from CLP officers and others. There were late selections, often when MPs stood down to make way for others, and were promoted to the Lords. These limited the capacity of the CLP to have full involvement in the selection."

He believed that, in general: "The best people were shortlisted by the NEC. There was some heavy leaning from Number 10. Some influential people were left out for example: the (named) partner of a prominent woman MP. Occasionally local favourites were kept out, sometimes due to their poor performance and sometimes due to 'pressures'."

Excluding local favourites denies democratic rights to constituency Party members. In the pre NL era, those who received a (defined) substantial number of local branch nominations were automatically shortlisted. This allowed local grass-roots members the opportunity to select people that many of them favoured.

DG continued: "In one case a sitting MP was prepared to stand down shortly before the 1997 general election in favour of a well known leadership sponsored candidate. The latter's interview went wrong, the NEC panel turned him down and he was later sent to the Lords. The successful candidate was selected at the last minute by an NEC panel sitting with CLP delegates. Number 10 did not always get its way completely. "Hamish", a candidate for a safe Scottish seat, was shortlisted by the NEC and was selected by OMOV despite "Flora" being the Number 10 favourite."

Former Regional Staffer "Malcolm" recalled being given the task of Organising a controversial selection. He said: "*H.Q. (eager to keep another candidate out) gave me the task of Organising it and making sure that 'Francis' (their favoured candidate) was selected. The thing was done sort of within the rules but slightly bending and interpreting them* (this links to Patricia's story about the same selection (see below)). The MP selected turned out to be a good one so the result was not a matter of regret. That selection coloured my understanding of what goes on. *Wherever you go in the country the leadership favourites will get the nomination because they work the rules to ensure this.* If you are a conspiracy minded person, as I became, there are always connections between the people involved." He suggested "Staff were often given promotions as a reward for these services".

The above report taken in conjunction with Patricia's account (below) is significant testimony. It evidences that there was, sometimes, interference with ballot papers. There was evidence of this around the same time in a Buckinghamshire constituency and subsequently at Erith and Thamesmead in 2009 and Stalybridge and Hyde in 2010.

Malcolm continued: "When it comes to the selection of candidates in safe Labour seats, the Party (centrally) takes a very keen interest, especially when it involves someone like a SPAD. If you're a favoured candidate then Regional Office will give you a contact list of members. But if it leaks out that they've been given these, and Regional staff think it's in their own interests to get a certain candidate into that seat, they will justify it on the grounds that it's in the Party's interest. *If you are **not** the hierarchy's favoured candidate for a particular seat then you will **not** get it.* Regional Staff typically say: 'Never mind if a few local people have a different view because they can't see the bigger picture'."

This demonstrates the sheer arrogance of the Labour Party machine, whose agents often took the view that they and the Leadership had the right to subvert democracy and hand pick candidates to suit their master's wishes. Their high handedness lay in their attitude that this devious behaviour was justified because members were supposedly so stupid and short sighted that they were unfit to participate in a democratic selection.

Former local organiser Ben was involved in Parliamentary selections during the 1990s. He considered that: "In theory lists of names and contact details of local Party members were not available to any hopefuls (before shortlisting). In practice, trades unions got hold of them and distributed them to their sponsored candidates. In very dodgy Tory marginal seats Party HQ took no interest in 'parachuting in' candidates, as they were thought unlikely to be won – even in 1997. It was obvious that, in safe Labour seats, candidates were 'parachuted in' at the behest of the Party hierarchy. Party staff with political or trades union experience and political nous, would organise politically for candidate selections. They would see no harm in bending or misinterpreting the Party rules or even disobeying them. There was a difference between what was in the Party rule book and what was actually done." A similar view was expressed by a former regional officer.

The next account is from a former regional party officer and is taken from a report of a flawed selection process sent to the NEC by the officer/former officer in question. It identifies some names and places involved but not those of people accused of malpractice. Publication is with consent of the author. It concerns the selection in *Liverpool West Derby* in 2007.

Peter Killeen (PK) is a former Assistant Labour Party Regional Organiser who retired in 2001. After retirement he was involved, as CLP Chair, in the pre-2007 election Parliamentary selection in Liverpool West Derby constituency. He was so dissatisfied with the way it was conducted that he wrote a report complaining to the Chair of the NEC. He also resigned from the position of CLP Chair in protest.

The report[C8-34] commences: "This is a tale of manipulation and malpractice by senior employees of the Labour Party. The main issue contained in this report is: involvement of Regional staff working to have the sitting left MP de-selected. The following rules were broken: first there was no list of members qualified to take part in the selection, nor was a membership check of those attending branch nomination meetings or the hustings. No list of qualified electors was available at the hustings and there was no signature check of postal voters there" (A signature slip should be sent in with the ballot paper in a separate sealed envelope).

The above are a sample of the most serious complaints. *All* these involved breaking contemporary Party rules. Among other complaints PK complained that, long before re-selection was due: "Marcus" an assistant employed by another MP: "Commenced knocking on the doors of members throughout West Derby, bad mouthing the sitting MP and calling for him to lose the re-selection (trigger) ballot." "Marcus" used a constituency membership list which was not available to him within the rules.

PK reported: "The members of the Constituency General Committee (GC) were so concerned that at their meeting they unanimously passed a resolution of condemnation of "Marcus" and informed Regional Office. Eventually Regional Office sent this to the Party General Secretary and indicated that a report to the CLP would follow – but it never did." The sitting MP, Bob Wareing, was later de-selected but had a right, within party rules, to be shortlisted in the following selection. The Regional Office allegedly failed to tell him that he had to apply for this shortlisting and he accidentally neglected to do so.

During the selection process the Regional Director allegedly decided (unilaterally) to postpone the shortlisting by a week. This gave the unfair advantage of extra canvassing time to any automatically shortlisted candidate (one with a specified high percentage of branch nominations).

Members were invited to submit a written question. It was then announced that candidates would all answer the same questions over 15 minutes. The outcome was it was impossible to ask any candidate anything about themselves. At the meeting PK queried the legality of this arrangement and was informed that it was "a decision of the NEC". After further questioning it was conceded that it was the decision of Party staff.

After the selection, it was discovered that there had been serious problems with balloting for branch nominations. No explanation was given to members as to how to use the forms for a multi round eliminating ballot, consequently members made numerous errors.

Complaints included that, in defiance of rules, three named aspiring candidates possessed membership lists before the *setting* of the selection timetable. Another candidate was never sent a list. In a breach of rules: one candidate circulated a leaflet in which he promised, if selected and elected, to donate £5,000 a year to the CLP and £1,000 per year to each ward party. This rule infringement was reported to the NEC. They warned the offender not to do this again. He then circulated another leaflet, making the same promises. Again he was mildly reprimanded.

Thirty-one Party rules were allegedly broken during this selection process (cited with supporting evidence, by ex-professional Killeen)!

Two recent cases of possible ballot tampering, connected with postal voting, were reported. A former party staffer reported that in one constituency, near his home and which selected in 2009, it was agreed officially that the postal votes were to be returned to the home of the retiring MP. This was unusual but might not have mattered but for the allegation that the favourite, who won, was a resident house guest of that MP during the whole selection process.

A senior lay Party officer expressed concern that, in another selection (in 2010), postal votes were initially sent to an independent solicitor. However, between the closing date and the count in the constituency, they were taken to Party HQ where they remained unguarded for a few nights before being transported by Party staff to the count (shades of Erith and Thamesmead). The runner up was surprised that he polled far fewer postal votes than he had been promised. He did a survey of local party members and found that far more people claimed to have voted for him than the number of postal votes counted in his favour. He suspected ballot box tampering.

Backbench MPs speak about Westminster PPC selections

MPs selected before 1992 had little direct experience of PPC selections under NL. Some MPs had information about malpractice from other sources. Some selected more recently had not experienced questionable intervention by "the machine" because their seats were not regarded as being winnable. Others were seen as a virtually unbeatable candidate locally and left alone. Some MPs, including John McDonnell and Linda Riordan, experienced vicious personal attacks orchestrated by the machine. The two recently retired MPs, Alice Mahon and Backbencher B., encountered machine interference when their successors were selected.

Alan Simpson MP declared: "What NL did was to hijack the machine of the Labour Party. In their more humorous moods the whips would sometimes say to me: 'Well at least we know that people like you will never be coming back into Parliament. *They will never be coming into the Parliament for Labour because you'd never make it through the selection process now'*. I'm afraid that's an accurate summary of how things currently work."

He continued: "Bright able people; radical, visionary minded women, who genuinely could transform the party, are all sifted out in order to ensure that we have a series of Downing Street clones who come in driven by personal and career ambitions. They are very light on politics."

Jon Cruddas believed: "The Erith and Thamesmead selection in Spring 2009 (see note 22) suggested that there is a profile of a certain type of candidate that they want selected and who produces the very type of problems that New Labour has. These are lack of creativity and language and lack of a sense of ideology. This became a very cynical manipulation of internal Party democracy which is very dangerous as it fills people with cynicism that creates rupture between the Party and the people it is supposed to represent."

Having lost his marginal Essex seat in 2005, John Cryer sought another constituency. He experienced selection procedures during 2009 (when not an MP). He contended: "I find it extraordinary that ward branches are not now allowed to invite candidates to come and speak to them prior to making a nomination. Frankly the "meet and greet" is a farce (see above). When I attended, each member got about two minutes with each candidate. That's completely meaningless. When I asked why branches couldn't invite candidates and question them I was told, by a regional organiser, that: 'Some people might find that a bit intimidating'. If you're going to find branch meetings intimidating then you won't cope in Parliament!" Unlike most competent democratic socialists seeking selection then: John was selected for the constituency of Leyton and Wanstead and returned to Parliament in 2010.

Graham Stringer was selected for his "safe" Manchester seat in 1996. He was then Leader of Manchester City Council. He said: "No, I don't believe that it was an equal opportunities process for everyone involved because I already had a reputation locally. But as a strong candidate, people knew my work. It was unlikely that anyone else would win. I believe that the selection procedures were fair."

From the perspective of the NL hierarchy, competent leaders of large local authorities were much harder to fix against in the region where they operated. This was because they were usually well known to Party and union members personally and through the local media.

Senior MP A, former Leader of a major local authority, regretted: "Too many young Ministers and MPs have no life experience. Many have been SPADs previously and increasingly they come from that background. Many have been 'parachuted in' through the selection procedures used recently."

Louise Ellman was selected to fight a safe Labour seat in Liverpool for the 1997 election. At that time she was Leader of Lancashire County Council. She said: "I had no Leadership support but someone I knew in Liverpool told me that the vacancy was coming up and asked me if I wanted to put my name forward as I'd always been connected with Liverpool through politics." Louise was strongly supported by the Co-operative Party locally (the author was personally involved in this selection and found no evidence of central Party intervention). Ms Ellman continued: "I do know people who've really wanted to become an MP and were thwarted by the powers that be."

The former local government leaders interviewed were not passionately NL, but most were not dissidents. The Machine probably tolerated their selections because they were difficult to beat on their own turf.

John Grogan was PPC for Selby in both 1987 and 1992 elections when he lost. He was selected for the same constituency for 1997 and won. He reported: "It was a hard seat to win as Labour was third at the outset. No one from Party HQ tried to intervene in the selection before 1997. *They probably thought we would not gain Selby."*

Kelvin Hopkins MP recalled: "The first thing that the NL Hierarchy did was to get control of selections for Parliamentary candidates in all winnable seats. This was done to minimise the number of people from the left getting in. In Parliamentary rebellions the rebels are nearly all MPs of a certain age who've been there a long time and have democratic socialist values." He continued: "The leadership chose not to interfere in my selection. They knew that I was older and thought Luton North a difficult seat to win. They probably considered that I would be more trouble than it was worth: active 30 years in the local Party, Chair of the CLP and a councillor. Only a few got through the net." He named another left MP, a former student colleague of the author, who told her that he was only allowed to be selected because his seat was considered by himself, and the hierarchy, to be virtually unwinnable. Cowley[36] identified the 14 most rebellious Labour MPs in respect of their number of votes against the whip between 2001 and 2005. All, except Kelvin Hopkins and Bob Marshall-Andrews, were elected prior to 1997.

It appears that candidates to the left of NL were sometimes tolerated if they were considered unlikely to win and might be able to cause real trouble if upset. In seats like Selby, which were considered virtually unwinnable, the machine did not bother to intervene.

Kelvin Hopkins recalled: "Earlier on Liz Davies, on the far left, was stopped by a Conference decision." Party staff reported that: 'Head Office did not want her – on the basis of her record as an Islington Councillor.' So HQ allegedly asked for flaws in the selection to be sought to provide a pretext for it being re-run. The NEC ordered a re-run, on an open shortlist, and the man, who had stood there previously, was selected."

Hopkins contended: "You got loyalist trades unions putting in candidates to make sure that someone else didn't get the seat. They got their delegates to attend selection meetings. The hierarchy only *needed* to secure their selections in safe seats but they also focused on key marginals. "Headquarters" probably followed the selections in all key seats on their computer system!"

Interviewees emphasised the importance of ending the shenanigans in PPC selections in the cause of integrity and having a Parliamentary Party that represents the range of opinions and values across the Labour Party spectrum and the occupational characteristics of the whole population.

Michael Meacher argued: "Most important of all: we must re-capture the PPC selections. We need Party officials who behave properly. We need much more open contests which result in a greater spectrum of Labour opinion being represented. In this both left and right, women and men, young and old would be selected. Rigged PPC selections happened on a very substantial scale. Part of the evidence for that is the sheer numbers of MPs who ended up in the Blairite camp. It is contrary to all past evidence of the typical ideological make up of the PLP." (as a 2006 YouGov opinion poll demonstrated, it was also contrary to the ideological make up of Party members who selected these Candidates).[C8_35]

MM continued: "It could only have happened that way if it was engineered and pushed through determinedly by the Party Machine. You cannot otherwise conceivably explain the numbers. From the start NL looked for ways to win power within the Labour Party, to get more PPCs of their own ilk and to brief against the left in order to remove their influence."

Senior Backbencher B. reflected on the PPC selection as he retired in 2005 and asserted: "I think that regional organisers now play a totally different role from what they used to (before becoming an MP: B. had been a full time local party organiser). There's now too much trying to fix who are going to be PPCs – rather than letting local parties make their own selection … PPC selection is now an unfair process."

B. continued: "It's not uncommon for the HQ favoured candidate to be given advantages over others. You must not allow one candidate to have the contact list of members when it's denied to others. When I was a constituency agent you would never have allowed such a thing. Party rules are now not necessarily used properly. But 20-30 years ago they would have been rigorously enforced."

Clare Short complained about "fixing of seats in Birmingham. This was a new thing in the mid-nineties. At the last minute before the election older Labour MPs in safe seats (who traditionally wouldn't have gone to the House of Lords as they hadn't shone) would announce that they were going there. Then senior staff became involved in a quick selection because it was last minute. For example: A journalist close to NL was put into one seat. No one had heard of him beforehand but he bounced through. Another MP retired and someone, who had worked at Party HQ, replaced them. This was a by-election, in which Regional Offices have always taken a major role. The new MP had some links to the West Midlands but had neither lived nor worked locally. Once in Parliament he was rapidly promoted."

In the case of Hayes and Harlington, the NL hierarchy faced the probable selection of one of their bogeymen, a former and respected candidate for the seat. John McDonnell contested the constituency in 1992. He lost by 54 votes. He remembered: "When it came to selections, before the 1997 election, the Party machine tried to impose an All Women Shortlist (AWS) to prevent me standing. However the local CLP lobbied them hard and West London Labour women's groups (who knew that I worked for policies to benefit women) lobbied the NEC because their move was so blatant. I was then able to be selected on my past record locally. But, in every selection around that time, Party staff were required to deliver votes for the preferred candidates of the hierarchy."

Members of the Working Classes not wanted in the Parliamentary Labour Party (PLP).

It will be recalled that the trade unions founded the Labour Party to assist working men in getting into Parliament, had it been founded even 21 years later, this would undoubtedly have been extended to working class women. This objective was totally abandoned by NL. Under NL, working class candidates were scorned and often sidelined in favour of middle class political advisors. Most of these had never worked in ordinary jobs outside politics – blue or white collar. Some of the class discrimination was very overt and is demonstrated by the case histories below:

Two MPs' perspectives were given about the pre 2005 selection in Halifax. Alice Mahon, MP for Halifax until 2005, lamented: "To me the PPC selection process has destroyed the Party. When I was selected, the GC chose the candidate. It was a good process. Now you get interference from Head Office and Regional Office in selections. My successor, a hard working councillor, had to go through great pain. She's now an excellent MP. *They didn't want her because she was a working class woman.* She suffered from arthritis in her thirties and then studied at university. The party hierarchy went to extraordinary lengths, working with Blairites in the constituency, to stop her getting the nomination. These Blairites planted stories in the local press saying that the NEC was probably not going to endorse Linda if she were selected, which initially they did not. They were working with our Regional Office and reportedly visiting it weekly. They had their own chosen candidate and told the local media that she would be endorsed. Staff from our regional office allegedly regularly visited No. 10 for meetings, at this time. They were feted there. Of course the Leader wants to see who is working for him. However they were allegedly also given an agenda: 'This is the kind of candidate we want and we hope that you're controlling the local parties'. Regional Offices interfered so much in local party democracy that people just got dispirited and walked away. We lost the most members *after* we'd selected Linda. Two thirds of them said: 'We've no say now'. After the NEC refused to endorse Linda, I got on to the trades union leaders I knew saying: 'Halifax CLP has chosen her why are you de-selecting her?' The NEC did endorse her in the end, after a lot of unpleasantness. It went to the full NEC and trades union members supported her there."

In this case, even the moderate Co-operative Party, which supported and sponsored Linda Riordan, was treated with contempt in NL's zeal to avoid the selection of a locally well supported working class democratic socialist.

Linda's own story about her selection follows: "My selection as PPC was horrendous. When I went for selection here I was a local councillor and had local support and knowledge. Near the end of the constituency selection they (the hierarchy) realised that their candidate wouldn't win, so they turned to another candidate that they thought could beat me and worked on second and third preference votes. Regional staff claim to support women but, in my opinion, it's only if they are their friends."

She continued: "When I went to the first NEC interview it was terrible. The other candidates told me they didn't get the same questions. They brought in a senior MEP. I was asked more about Europe than about national politics. I also had an interview with a senior whip (these are not the usual procedures). The local Party said that they'd selected me and wanted to keep me. That helped me to win. I had already passed the Parliamentary panel selection for the Co-operative Party. For that you had to make a speech, be interviewed and take a written test .That was far more difficult. I said that (according to the Party's agreements) my endorsement by the Co-op Party entitled me to stand. So they contacted that Party to try to have my endorsement cancelled: but they failed.''

A report about the flawed selection in Swindon North in 1995[38] was written by respected former Regional Director Eileen Murfin. This was addressed to the NEC and was endorsed by the Party General Secretary.

The background was that, due to recent boundary changes, two Swindon constituencies replaced a single one. Unusually, they still operated as one District Labour Party (DLP) which organised this selection process.

Jim D'Avila (JDA) stood as PPC for the former unitary Swindon constituency in 1992, but lost. He had been active in the Labour Party, and in his union, locally since the mid 1970s. He worked in the local car factory and was a senior union representative. A local borough councillor since 1976, JDA applied for the Swindon North parliamentary candidature in 1995.

A raft of problems arose; most connected with postal voting. There was initial confusion in which conflicting sets of instructions about postal voting were given to branch secretaries, one of whom was JDA. Regional Office subsequently wrote to JDA saying that the instructions about postal vote application that he circulated were "unacceptable". Further it alleged that JDA was in breach of the code of conduct for candidates and any further breach would disqualify him. Ms Murfin's report[C8-36] subsequently stated it was "wrong to allege that JDA was in breach of the code of conduct" and that "no criticism could properly be made of him (for his actions)".

JDA then contacted members in his ward, saying he was in error and they must contact the PS for official application forms. The Procedures Secretary (PS), who was responsible for running the selection then complained to Regional Office who again wrote to JDA saying that this last contact with members: "Constituted a grave breach of the code of conduct which I am reporting to the NEC". Next a story appeared in the *Swindon Advertiser* alleging that JDA was in danger of being disqualified from selection. Subsequently JDA received another letter from Regional Office saying that his "breach of the code was not serious".

The PS then wrote to local Party members. This followed a meeting of the DLP (*not* the Constituency Party). JDA was not invited to this gathering which was attended by regional staff. This meeting was handed a report subsequently described by Mirfin as "inaccurate in many respects" on the basis of which (assuming it to be correct) the meeting requested that JDA be declared ineligible for selection. The following week JDA had been invited to a ward nomination meeting (where he was well known). That invitation was withdrawn because of the PS's last (inaccurate) letter to members. JDA appealed, through Regional Office to, have his invitation restored. His request was not passed on to the branch. Its nomination went to Michael Wills (MW), an adviser to GB, who was subsequently selected as PPC.

JDA complained of serious delays in processing postal vote applications . *This allegedly resulted in 40-50 people, who applied, not receiving postal votes.* Next the PS, in consultation with the Party Chair, agreed for the postal votes to be opened (for the purpose of validation) before the count. She stated that she tried to get advice beforehand from Regional Office but "was unable to contact them". She claimed that her action was taken with the approval of all candidates. Most candidates did not corroborate this claim.

Most seriously, according to Ms Mirfin, this meant that: *"the votes, and in particular postal votes, may have been tampered with in this selection." This probably would have affected the result of the ballot (which MW won).* As in the 2010 case reported earlier in this Chapter: the loser (JDA) did a survey of members. This indicated that far more members said they had voted for him by post than there were postal votes counted in his favour. Mirfin said: *"It appeared that the number of postal votes actually counted did not tally with the number of postal votes that, allegedly, should have been counted."*

Ms Mirfin recommended that, as the DLP had become so compromised, the NEC should conduct a re-run ballot with the same shortlisted candidates. Alternatively, the NEC Organisation Sub-Committee could interview them and select the candidate. Despite massive pressure from JDA's union, the NEC took the latter course and chose MW.

Kelvin Hopkins MP alleged: "In Swindon North the 1992 candidate (who was a trades unionist but not that left wing) was set to be selected, but at the last minute they disallowed him and shooed in a friend of Gordon Brown. Probably they regarded the 1992 candidate as being too working class." Post script: JDA has since been awarded an MA degree and become a trade union regional officer. MW got a much reduced majority in 2005 and stepped down, rather than fight the 2010 general election, in Swindon North.

David Gardner recalled: "*Problems were caused by some Regional Directors moving away from overseeing fair play to seeing their role as ensuring the selection of favoured candidates.* Some older officers still act impartially and ensure fairness. However Jim D'Avila, (then a factory shop steward) was badly treated by regional staff because GB wanted this advisor to be selected. Jim's union took on the fight and *this led to a sense that not enough trades union candidates were being chosen*".

Senior Backbencher B. considered: "I believe we've moved into a more professional era. We're getting MPs who've never done a real job. A university education isn't the most crucial thing for an MP. Experience of life, and understanding of the types of people you're going to represent, is more important. The PLP needs to be a cross section of people. The Party organisation has reduced the traditional role and origins of MPs. There are now very few people from industry and not so many who've been active in trade unions – let alone shop stewards. Shop stewards are used to being criticised by management and also by their members. That would make them understanding MPs and good listeners." These were words of wisdom from a mature and experienced MP who had worked on the shop floor for many years.

Gordon Prentice MP argued: "I think that our internal party democracy is a bit of a farce. In candidate selection the thing that matters to me is not gender, I'm glad that we've got more women MPs and we need still more. However ideology, not gender, is what matters. I don't know if it's a good idea to have middle class barrister because she happens to be female – if she is taking the place of a working class man."

Prentice continued: "When I was talking about class before 1994, the BBC painted me as one of the PLP's few remaining class warriors. Years ago many people in the Party were talking about class. When Blair came in we were denounced as 'Neanderthals' because they were moving away from class to a new kind of politics. I think that new kind of politics led to a change in the profile of the Parliamentary Labour Party (PLP) which now includes very few working class people. I say that with humility because I'm university educated."

TB, son of an officer of the Durham Conservative Party, appeared to have little appreciation of the importance of solidarity and fraternity among working class people or of the value of their experience to the PLP. He seemed to follow the example of Mrs.Thatcher in pretending that class no longer existed or mattered. That stance denies the rights and needs of working class people.

A fringe meeting which hosted the *Observer* interview of Jon Cruddas with Andrew Rawnsley was held at the 2010 Labour Conference (on 28.9.10),[C8-37] During that interview Cruddas stated he did not think "that there are any longer *any* working class Labour MPs". This is a significant comment on the outcome of contemporary selection processes. An evidenced 2010 assessment assessed 9% of the PLP to be working class.[C8-38]

Only New Labour Women need apply for winnable seats.

The Party's women were abused by NL in PPC selection processes. If they were to the left of centre they were deceived into applying for selections where, unbeknown to them, there was no hope of them winning because they were probably secretly blacklisted. They spent money and effort in trying when they might as well have thrown thousands of pounds down the drain. NL women were foisted off on to constituencies where they had no local connection and where some of them did not last and left Parliament after a few years, possibly because, having had little previous political experience, they could not cope with the tough environment in which they were working. One left after one term because, as she told the local paper: "I do not think this town is a fit place for me to bring up my young children and send them to school". They would have attended the same primary school as the author's grandchildren where the latter did well. AWS were also probably used to keep out credible local men unwanted by the hierarchy – usually because
they were left wing or working class and in at least one case Asian (in a constituency where the BNP was strong).

Kelvin Hopkins reported: "in Blaenau Gwent they tried to force in an NL candidate, Maggie Jones, and lost a safe seat to Independent Labour. A pre 1997 example was Slough, where the left leaning Council Leader was favourite – so they allegedly imposed an AWS to stop him. Then the Leader's wife, also
a good socialist and credible, applied. They kept her off the shortlist. In the safer target seats they got in many women: but not left-wingers. If women who are on the left and able (he named some women interviewed here) had been allowed through they would have made that phalanx of NL women look silly. It would only have needed three or four women like them to get AWS seats, then suddenly that mass of Blair's babes would have looked fragmented. But *they were desperate to ensure that all left-leaning women were kept out*".

Senior Backbencher B. recalled: "We were told we must have an AWS. I'm not keen on these; but not against women candidates. I recognise that without positive action it's very difficult for women to get selected."

Before AWS, it was more challenging for women to get selected, as the author knows from personal experience, but at least women who got through could be confident that they deserved to do so.

Before NL there was never any suggestion that PPC selections were a beauty contest for women hopefuls, but in some cases this seemed to have become so under NL. One interviewee reported that her friend "Judith", an NL loyalist, applied for selection for a by-election. She was privately told by the Party "hierarchy that she was "too fat". They said: "You wouldn't look good on television but "Susan" (who was selected) is thin enough to look good on TV". Judith subsequently went to the red benches of the House of Lords. The 2010 intake saw glamorous TV presenter: Gloria De Piero imposed on a Constituency by the NEC (under GB's leadership). Minister Caroline Flint, shortlisted by the NEC twice for the 1997 election, once did a fashion shoot for the *Observer Magazine*.[C8_39]

When discussing selections with Barbara Follett, during the 1996 Labour Women's Conference, the latter advised the author to "give up as you are obviously being blocked." Initially the writer supposed this was a piece of homespun philosophy. Later it emerged that it was literally true. One left woman hopeful discussed her situation with the partner of a minister with whom she had worked. They told this woman, in a kindly and joking way: "Well you're just a trouble maker and they'll never have you as a PPC". The same MP's partner shared similar information with the author about herself. The author was also informed by senior trades union friends and, even by a sympathetic Party officer who asked HQ why she could not be shortlisted for a certain by-election, that she was unacceptable because she was on the (centre) left.

Sadly AWS were sometimes used to try to exclude left male applicants unwanted by the hierarchy for example: John McDonnell in Hayes and Harlington in 1997 (see above). Observations by focus groups of Party members conducted for the LabOUR Commission (2007) were reported by Professor Stuart Weir, who moderated them:

"Members wished to see more women and members of ethnic minorities become MPs and there was general, if cautious, approval for measures of positive discrimination with two caveats – one, the usual wish for merit to prevail, the other that it should not be used by the party to try to fix outcomes."[C8-40]

Local members spoke of manipulation of selections to benefit ministers already representing constituencies.

The manipulation, arguably fixing, of Parliamentary candidate selections was of great significance to ordinary members of the Party.[C8-41] It involved denial of their democratic rights as well as of equal opportunities for hopefuls. Selection practices were often so covert and clandestine that affected members did not know about them at the time and possibly even not afterwards. Alleged fixing was often particularly blatant in selections in merging constituencies.

Fraught selection issues arose on the disappearance of Labour held seats resulting from constituency boundary changes. These often entailed one, or more, MPs losing their seat. The author was approached by Party activists[C8-42], known to her, in a Labour held constituency merging with another where a minister was sitting MP. The Minister wanted the merged seat. He was marginally entitled, by the proportion of electors in the new seat that he currently represented, to automatic shortlisting. The Backbench MP in the other part of the new constituency (who represented the majority of its electors) also sought this candidature.

It is claimed that Regional Office phoned one existing Constituency office every day, before the inaugural meeting of the merged CLP, demanding a list of delegates to the new, enlarged, GC. When the list of delegates from one large union was supplied, five of their delegates were found to *live outside* the new constituency boundaries. Therefore Party rules did not permit them to be delegates there. There was also an attempt to smear the Backbench MP in the media.

At the inaugural meeting of the merged CLP, there was conflict between members of the two former CLPs. A regional staffer chaired the meeting. Objections from the floor were raised about the five union delegates who lived *outside* the new constituency. The author was shown documentary evidence. The Regional Officer ruled to accept these delegates. Next all the offices, in the merged CLP, were awarded to members from the Minister's area of the constituency. A senior Party organiser "Basil", from another region, was sent to work with members in this new constituency during the selection period. He campaigned for the Minister. After this meeting the Backbench MP decided that he was unlikely to get the nomination if the new CLP, and its selection, were to be run this way and withdrew his application.

The author was informed, by her Party contacts[C8-43b] in a different region, about another constituency merger. This involved a second Minister. During their selection period "Basil" was also seconded to the constituencies involved to undertake similar work with members. There was a different alleged breach of the rules here. Candidates were informed of a specified period during which they were permitted to canvass members. However it was ruled that they must not canvass before that time. Well before this date the Minister started to phone canvass members. These included friends of the backbencher involved in the selection. The minister left a phone mail message on the answerphone of one of these asking for their support in this selection. It was dated and timed by the message recorder as being before the permitted canvassing period. When the backbencher complained to Regional Office, mentioning this recorded evidence, he was informed that the rule in question was "unenforceable".

Excluded Westminster Parliamentary hopefuls' tales

The author's own experiences, and research for this book, had increasingly caused her to believe that there was probably a blacklist of people whom NL would not permit to be MPs. This was irrespective of their relevant experience and personal qualities. This belief evoked memories of the McCarthy blacklists during the post World War Two period in the USA. Testimonies, (of the putatively excluded) appearing immediately below were recorded in 2009.

At the time of interview "Patricia"[C8_44b] was in her fifties and held a senior executive position. A former Labour councillor in a large city which included being Chair of key committees, she was also a prominent campaigner for AWS. On the moderate left of the Party, she always acted on her belief that: "In public positions you do not vote, or speak, against the Party line. Instead you campaign, within the Party's democratic structures, for policy and organisational change".

Patricia was selected as a PPC in 1983 and applied for marginal seats in 1992 and 1997. The Labour Party actually approached her to stand for a challenging seat "because they knew I would do a good job". She recalled: "Later I was asked by local party members to apply for the PPC vacancy in my own constituency. Local women refused to stand against me so the Party went outside the region and persuaded another to stand. Regional office worked for that candidate, who won." Patricia contended: "Even in the 1992 selections there was a push to ensure that people, seen to be on the left, particularly women, were not selected. I was front runner in an AWS safe seat but the shortlisting was suspended after the industrial tribunal judgement (see above). Then the machine brought in more candidates."

Patricia applied for selections prior to the 2001 and 2005 elections. One, then a Labour seat, went to a local councillor who had not opposed the Iraq war. Patricia had condemned the war publicly. She claimed: "PPC selections seem to be regarded as a test of loyalty to the government rather than a debate about what policies the government should adopt. Within your own Party and the confines of a PPC selection, it's often been turned into *a test of loyalty to every government policy.* As a councillor, I voted against the Labour whip *once* on an issue concerning my own ward. I surmise that you are not allowed to stray without the Party machine stepping in and saying, 'In Parliament, she'd vote against us the whole time'. *There's a whispering campaign against you. You're not allowed to be an intellectual either*".

A serious incident, involving Patricia, ties in with the interview with former Party organiser Malcolm (above). That organiser said he "was ordered by HQ to deliver the result they wanted". Patricia said: "I would have won this selection if the number of postal votes, allowed to stand, had matched the number of postal ballot applications. There was a row about it with people representing me at the count. Party staff accepted more postal ballot papers than there had been applications. I appealed unsuccessfully to the NEC against their decision."

Patricia continued: "The introduction of OMOV (one member one vote) with postal voting *allowed people to say things to voters about candidates, away from their hearing, which they were unable to challenge.* Some people who get advance notice are ready with their promotional material the minute the selection is declared or are already in the constituency and campaigning. It's difficult to track where key local movers and shakers have been nobbled and had a specific candidate recommended. It appears that the central party machine does this. They know of someone who will serve their purposes on the backbenches. I was involved in a selection where I was shown an email sent to a trades union from No. 10 saying that Tony Blair was supporting a named candidate."

She asserted: "The postal vote system was greatly abused. This is because you can win on the postal vote alone. Well·organised candidates try to capture a commitment and postal vote from people early. So that part of the electorate doesn't have to listen to anyone else or turn up at meetings to assess other candidates. After a hustings people have said to me: 'that was a fantastic speech, you really answered the questions well'. Then you lose the selection, not because of the people who heard you, but because of the people who haven't heard you before voting, having had to cast their postal votes before hustings."

Patricia recalled: "Prior to the 2005 election I applied for a seat where I had lived for 15 years. At NEC panel interview, I was asked questions about: the Iraq war and what I'd done in local government ten years previously. I was kept off the final shortlist. Loyalty questions are asked by the NEC and, if you give honest answers, you're out. It's not like an equal opportunities job interview where you're asked a standard set of questions with possible follow ups. Questions are all individualised (see Linda Riordan's testimony above).They always managed to lead you into territory that implied you would be disloyal in Parliament. I've been to a few NEC shortlisting panels since 1993 but was never allowed through. Probably the NEC decides in advance who the candidate should be. Then they keep out everyone who might be a threat to that candidate."

Mark Seddon is now a speech writer for UN Secretary General Ban Ki-moon. He was formerly a nationally and internationally respected journalist, author and Editor of *Tribune*. In 2001 he stood in relatively difficult marginal. Since then he sought selection for winnable seats. In 2002 he applied for a by-election candidature in South Wales. There he was encouraged by Michael Foot. He said: "I was interviewed by the NEC panel. In answer to their questions I stated that I was opposed to the UK's involvement in the Afghan war and to the Private Finance Initiative. I also said that I would stick to party policy in public but would campaign, within the party, to change some policies. I was kept off the shortlist." Mark was privately informed by an officer in the General Secretary's office that the NEC panel chair had asked them "compile a dossier" on him.

In the lead up to the 2010 general election Mark applied for three Labour held seats and a marginal. All had NEC shortlistings. He was not interviewed by the NEC for any of them. Before the selection for a Midlands seat he met GB; for whom he had recently worked. He reported that GB said to him: "We need you in Parliament". A senior minister, known to Mark, told him: "I will make sure that your application is not lost and that you go before the selection panel". He continued: "I went to the constituency to meet members and discovered they were seeking another centre-left MP like me and their retiring Member. I got support from a junior minster on the NEC selection panel. He believed that I would counter a strong local BNP threat". On the NEC panel of three, this junior minster was outvoted. One panel member discounted Mark because he was "still working in the USA" (which he had not done for the two previous years). Mark believed that: "There were no equal opportunities in these selections".

Mark James, was also in his mid forties, and a former PPC and County Councillor. He is currently councillor in a London Borough. He works for an interest group and holds office in organisations lobbying for Party democracy. In the mid-1990s he applied for the candidatures of four Tory-held marginal seats but was not shortlisted. He complained of:"a very short selection period and not enough time to get round the members".

Next a selection came up in the area where he was formerly a county councillor. A man favoured by the Leadership became the front runner. Mark recalled: "Whilst there was no fiddling, there was much organisation on this candidate's behalf. The previous PPC, who had done a good job in 1992, was nobbled to stand down."

Mark J. believed: "Almost all selections under NL were a forgone conclusion. In the mid-1990s I worked for the Party at HQ and discovered that a few 'unofficial' candidates got through. This was despite selection processes being neither fair nor promoting equal opportunities. They were often farcical. The way that OMOV has been operated (for PPC selections) is neither fair nor open. That changed everything in the 1990s and made it easier for the hierarchy to parachute people in."

Ann Pettifor was then in her early sixties. She has a distinguished record of leadership in senior positions in international Non Governmental Organisations and think tanks specialising in economics. She is also former head of the Leader's office at the Inner London Education Authority. Ann sought selection to winnable parliamentary seats but remembered: "The first selection that I went for was just before John Smith died. The experience was ghastly. This was because I had been active in the Labour Women's Action Committee (LWAC) and the Campaign for Labour Party Democracy (CLPD). I was arguing that we should not be supporting the European Monetary System (ERM). I was accused of being disloyal to John Smith (then supporting ERM membership). I was fond of John Smith and would have liked him to continue as Party Leader. It soon became clear that the leading candidate, and person selected, was being backed by Party HQ."

She continued: *"There was a whispering campaign against me. I was being described as a 'Trot' (I am not a Trot or a Marxist but a middle of the road leftie).* Senior party officers probably remembered when, after the NEC stopped All Women Shortlists (AWS), five to six women, including myself, picketed an NEC meeting by standing outside Party HQ. We were all respectable types not revolutionaries. Before 1983 I had been employed at Party HQ, liaising with the public and members. I was a hard working party employee."

She recalled: "I was shortlisted for this seat, in 1993, on a mixed gender shortlist (without NEC involvement). I got few votes. I thought that local members had been infected with the story about what I was. I remember thinking 'I'll never do this again'. I didn't try for selection for many years afterwards. I felt that the machine was against me and that it was undignified to put myself through that again.

"In the mid 1990s I worked for a Labour cabinet minister as speech writer. I liked this minister but it became clear, to them, that I wasn't going to become acceptable to NL for selection. The minister asked me to run their ministerial office but I declined because, by that time, I knew that I couldn't work in an NL government." She concluded: "I regard myself as part of the Labour Party family. I, and others, have been booted out of the family and told by them that we're not good enough."

The ultimate victor in the Erith and Thamesmead selection (2009) was Teresa Pearce. She was neither the choice of the Leadership nor promoted by the Party machine. Teresa, in her early fifties, was a councillor in the constituency and served as an elected member of Labour's National Constitutional Committee for 12 years up to 2008. Before the 1997 election she applied for PPC selections in six seats and was shortlisted in some. She recalled: "In all these selections I had little hope because there was always a favoured candidate. I think the member contact list that non-favourites obtained was not the same as that given to the favourite. I once pointed this out to a Procedures Secretary (PS) who got 'very shirty'." Teresa did not apply for further selections until her own constituency came up in 2008-9. She recalled: "It was declared an AWS which gave me more confidence to apply as it excluded 'strong local men'."

She recalled: "There was rule breaking from the start. Despite complaints being lodged, nothing was done. One NL candidate attended all the CLP's political and social events for six months prior to the selection (this suggests unauthorised advance notice). She withdrew her application, on the first day of the selection timetable, without explanation. A prominent member of the Blairite Progress Group also suddenly withdrew. At this moment Georgia Gould (22-year-old daughter of late NL guru Philip) appeared. She was prominently supported by two high profile NL women who lobbied for her. She appeared to be well funded."

Teresa continued: "Ms Gould was nominated by the two ward parties that had fewest members and rarely met. Eight women were nominated and the Regional Office called for a shortlist of eight. The GC shortlisting meeting was cancelled so it was not possible to interview all eight candidates: which annoyed members. At this point the Regional Office took over the selection from the CLP saying that 'this is a very difficult selection and we are the experts'."

She remembered: "Then concern over postal votes arose. Members complained that people were coming to their doors with postal vote application forms – some already filled in. If these were not returned then second forms were brought to them. Some wrongly thought that those calling were officials. One elderly member complained to Regional Office. They did nothing. The contemporary rules stated that postal vote application forms should only be distributed by the PS."

She continued: "The night before the hustings were due the regional officer rang to say that the meeting next day was cancelled because someone had broken the seal on a ballot box (that contained completed postal votes). Half a dozen ballot papers had been ripped up (supposedly to contaminate and delay the process)."

A Party inquiry and a police inquiry followed. The inquiry found that, at the time of the alleged tampering, the ballot boxes were lodged overnight at national Party HQ. There were testable fingerprints on the affected ballot papers. However it was decided that the culprit(s) could only be identified through fingerprinting. Party staff, and their unions, insisted that this would breach their employment rights. Therefore, at an NEC inquiry in July 2010, the party and police inquiry were discontinued for lack of evidence.

Teresa continued: "A second hustings was arranged. Unlike the previous time, the postal ballot paper envelopes were not numbered. The first time it was possible for workers to see, from the envelopes, whether or not they were from their supporters. The second time all postal votes were sent to an independent lawyer." The second ballot selected Teresa as PPC.

"Julia"[C8_45b] is a successful human rights barrister. She has been applying for Parliamentary candidatures since the mid 1970s. In February 1974 she was PPC for a safe Conservative seat. Between then and 1987 she was shortlisted for a safe Labour seat and two marginals. In the late 80s she married, had children, and ceased seeking candidatures to concentrate on her family and legal career. She reported: "I decided to seek selection for the 2005 election and applied to be placed on the Party's Parliamentary panel. I was interviewed by the NEC panel which rejected me. I hoped that my record and qualifications would help. The Chair of the panel was very rude to me. I was given no reasons for being turned down." Julia was shortlisted for a safe Labour seat in 2009 (where there was no NEC involvement).

Christine Shawcroft is a long serving member of the Party's NEC. She is active in Labour left organisations. Then in her early fifties, she is former leader of Labour Group and senior committee Chair. She was also a teacher and former head of department. Christine started to seek PPC nominations prior to 1997. She reported: "Then I was nominated for a safe seat in Yorkshire, this went to NEC shortlisting and I was kept off. I was then shortlisted (without NEC involvement) for two Tory held marginals. In one of these I was *never* able to obtain a members list. In the safer seat there was an NL favourite who was supported by Regional Office and taken round by the CLP chair to meet members."

Christine recalled: "Prior to the 2001 election I applied for a safe Labour seat in the Midlands but the Regional Office intervened and disqualified me, because I was not on the Party's Parliamentary panel. This was against Party rules. I was selected as PPC for a Tory marginal seat for the 2001 election but did not win. Prior to the 2005 election I was shortlisted in three Labour held seats (two of them very marginal). These were all CLP shortlists. Latterly I avoided seats where NEC shortlisting was probable."

She continued: "Before the 2010 election I was shortlisted for my own constituency and came second to another local candidate, having won the first ballot. The other candidate had strong union backing and, it appeared, received the members contact list (from her union) long before other hopefuls did. When I complained that this candidate had the members list in breach of rules, Regional Office responded: 'this rule is unenforceable'." Christine found that: "The unofficial role of regional staff in selections seems to include handing out members lists to the favourite(s) before the due date and turning a blind eye to their premature canvassing". Christine highlighted partisan intervention of NL MPs in safe seats for which she applied. She stated that a senior Asian MP is alleged to have asked ethnic minority members in this last constituency to: "Vote for anyone but Christine".

Anni Marjoram was also in her fifties. She never supported NL. Prominent in the early campaign for AWS, Anni was selected as candidate for a safe Tory seat in 1987 and for a Tory marginal in 1992. She worked for a Labour MP, as office manager, and then for an NGO. She was also a senior policy advisor to the Labour Mayor of London. Anni recalled: "In the run up to the 1997 election I put in for a Tory target seat in the North (where I come from). I was told, to my face, by a regional official that I wouldn't get the selection. Local Party members were (covertly) told that the NEC would not endorse me and that I would be joining the Campaign Group in Parliament. I never stated the latter."

Anni attributes this discrimination to her "having played a controversial role in running the Labour Women's Conference during the late 1980s and after. I think I was penalised for rebellion against the hierarchy. This was despite my having received widespread support for my Labour Women's Conference work. *I believe that NL excluded all who were not NL supporters from candidatures.* They chose those they could trust to build the NL Project. The hollowing out of the Party, since John Smith's death, enabled them to do this. *Because the unions wanted a Labour government they were not prepared to stick their necks out to help to select candidates that NL didn't want.* NL was determined that all opposition would be crushed and the left ground under foot."

She continued: "Their selection tactics were very creative, especially the way they used AWS to get their own way. Everyone in the Labour Women's Advisory Committee, which was simply trying increase women's representation, was linked to the far left and kept out. NL learnt its tactics from the Trots".

"Mary"[C8_46b] was selected, then de-selected, as PPC in a Labour held marginal where the MP was retiring in 2008-9. She said: "As I wasn't on the panel I was interviewed, after selection, by the NEC Subcommittee. She continued: "I was wrongly accused of hiding the fact that I was a member of the Labour Representation Committee (LRC) and this led to: 'How could you be a candidate when you are left wing? – It will be an NL manifesto so how could you defend it on the doorstep if you are in the LRC'?" Nothing in party rules says that you cannot be a candidate if you belong to the LRC or are left wing.

The author was selected four times as a PPC between 1970 and 1987. The first seat was then unwinnable but the last three were Tory marginals (all won by Labour in 1997). The third seat was virtually co-extensive with the second so she was, in effect, *re-selected* by unanimous vote of the constituency General Committee. After each of her last two general election campaigns she received a unanimous standing ovation from her Constituency GC and numerous written testimonials from members.

During the 1970s she was twice chosen to speak on public platforms alongside Harold Wilson. Leon Brittan, former Tory Home Secretary, was her opponent in February 1974. He described her as: "the most capable political opponent that I have ever faced". She was selected as candidate for marginal Swindon for the 1987 election from a field of 70 applicants.

Like other aspiring PPCs interviewed, she never spoke against the Party or Party policy outside private Party meetings but worked within the organisation for change. She contested elections strictly adhering to the Party manifesto. She always made this approach clear at selection interviews. As a Councillor, she was Labour Group Secretary and Vice-Chair of two committees but only once voted against the whip (about a broken election promise concerning the housing renewal strategy for her ward).

When the author entered active Labour politics she followed the example of her hero Clement Attlee: she saw so much poverty and social injustice when doing social work that she decided to work politically to counter these. Attlee said: "To be a social worker should mean becoming a social agitator".[C8_47b] She became a senior manager in two local authority social services departments, Head of Department in a college of further education and a Principal University Lecturer. She obtained an MA in social policy and a research PhD in politics through part-time study.

After 1987 she sought a more winnable seat. She applied for several safe seats in South Yorkshire where she had lived and worked. Two of these CLP parties were then National Union of Mineworkers (NUM) dominated. She was twice shortlisted, in these constituencies, and both times came a good second to the NUM candidate. One of these seats is now held by Ed Miliband. The selection conferences were dominated by NUM delegates. She had to face barracking and taunts such as "How can a bloody woman represent this seat in Parliament?" and "How can you be our MP when you've never worked down the pit?" She replied that she was qualified by having lived locally and run some of their social services for several years. These scenes were incorporated in a 1995 television play *Love and Reason* by local playwright Ron Rose who witnessed them. In 1991 she applied for a by-election in another safe Yorkshire seat (in which she had also once lived). She was shortlisted by the NEC panel, chaired by Roy Hattersley, but not selected.

After the NL take over she applied for two by-elections. She obtained nominations but was not shortlisted by the NEC panel for either. In one case, as applicants waited in a side room for interview by the NEC panel, a local candidate announced that the interviews were a sham as the NEC had already decided the shortlist. He then reeled off a list of people shortlisted which turned out to be correct (and included himself).

In the run up to 1997, she applied for two winnable seats near her home. In both cases she was shortlisted but, like most other applicants, was unable to obtain a members contact list until a week before the hustings. In both cases the front runners were not strongly NL but were well connected locally. They obtained contact lists well in advance. At Heywood and Middleton postal votes heavily outnumbered those cast at the hustings. More than 20 members leaving those hustings told the author that they would have supported her had they heard her speak before voting.

Safe Labour seats came up again in Yorkshire, where MPs were retiring and the NUM hegemony had weakened. Through death of the MP, one case became a by-election with NEC shortlisting. The author obtained the most branch nominations but was axed by the NEC to make way for an NL Favourite without local connections. However the hierarchy's plan misfired as a local councillor, who had few nominations, was shortlisted and won. When a second seat came up in the same area the NEC arbitrarily decided to shortlist. The same favourite was brought back. Although she, and the author, jointly got the highest number of branch nominations, the author was not shortlisted by the NEC, whilst the favourite was shortlisted and won.

The author's last stand was prior to the 2001 election when: she applied for three seats. She was shortlisted for one (by the CLP) but again handicapped by receiving the members list only seven days before hustings. In another, all hopefuls gave a brief speech to a large members' meeting and many present told her that her speech was the best. Here she had no member's list but was told, by local members, that the favourite who won (a SPAD), used that list for a two-year period prior to the hustings (in breach of Party rules!).

European, Scottish, Welsh and London Assembly Selections

The extensive rule manipulation around Westminster selections was developed gradually from 1994 onwards. Selection regulations devised for candidates for other Parliaments and Assemblies were so discriminatory that the Party hierarchy had little need to bend the rules.[C8-48b] As a consequence, there was less alleged illicit intervention to investigate.

The government announced that it would change to a proportional representation system for the 1999 European elections. NL devised a selection system in which grass-roots members could participate only in the first stage. As research by Wring and others[C8-49b] discovered, this system proved very unpopular with Party members.

Former Assistant General Secretary David Gardner recalled: "Other problems arose around selections for the European Parliament. I wanted to have OMOV for the regional lists and said so: putting options forward. Neither sitting MEPs, the NEC nor the Leadership wanted OMOV. I tried to implement a consultation with the regions fairly. All responses were published openly. The majority of individual members wanted OMOV. *The NEC decided that regional panels should interview candidates and decide who went forward and in what order (which determined probability of election). This was very thorough and was a triumph for professional interviewing but not a triumph for Party democracy.*" He continued: "Sitting MEP Christine Oddy, was placed low in the ballot paper order, not re-elected and lodged an objection. In general members did not feel involved and did not work hard in the ensuing European campaign."

The NEC established joint Scottish and Welsh selection task forces for devolved Parliaments (with relevant Party Executives). Each task force chose closed panels of approved candidates from which local parties were forced to select. Relatively few hopefuls were approved in proportion to the number of candidates required. There was an appeal process but only one appeal (in Scotland) succeeded. In both nations the "added member" assembly seats were filled without any grass-roots input.[C8-50b] Bradbury and colleagues[C8-50] found that 80% of their sample of Scottish and Welsh Party members considered the process of selecting list candidates was "undemocratic and unfair". A similar system was subsequently established to select candidates for the Greater London Assembly.

Kelvin Hopkins MP commented: "They had some setbacks. When Dennis Canavan was refused permission to stand to be MSP, in his own Westminster constituency (Falkirk), the whole local Party revolted. He then stood as an Independent Socialist for the Scottish Parliament (and won). After that virtually the whole CLP membership broke away from the Labour Party and worked for him."

Significant problems arose with the selections of Party leaders for Scotland and Wales and London Mayoral candidate. The controversies all involved the determination of the Leadership to personally choose these office holders and manipulate the relevant electoral systems to obtain their desired result. There is a detailed and well-evidenced discussion of this in Russell.[C8-51]

In conclusion – up to the 2010 general election, pliable Party rules that permitted the misapplication of the OMOV system and unfair and invidious treatment for aspiring candidates remained for most selections. They were not sufficiently modified between 2010 and 2015. Many of the offending rules remain in the Party rule book. However the selection rules for PPCs are under review by the Party at the time of publication.

During the NL era there was unfairness and deceit originating from the Party hierarchy and staff. Equal opportunities were withheld from loyal and long-standing Party members who were, unknown to themselves, probably blacklisted and certainly denied selection. These spent fruitless effort and approximately £1,000 out of their own pockets (per constituency) to enter a contest they could never win. If they discovered their predicament, it was through the unofficial kindness of insider friends. *Mark Seddon, who was a victim of this unfair system, has publicly proposed that the Labour Party establish a "Truth and Reconciliation Commission", on the South African model, to investigate and apologise for these injustices. The author considers that this should still be established.*

Simultaneously the NL hierarchy deprived rank and file Party members of their long-standing right to choose a set of Labour MPs who represented the *actual* spectrum of political opinion across the Party. A representative YouGov poll of party members was undertaken for the independent LabOUR Commission (2007).[C8-52] This showed that whilst only 6% described themselves as being "very left wing", 32 % saw themselves as "fairly left wing" and 42% as "slightly left of centre". Virtually no one, who would have described themselves as even "fairly left wing", was permitted to be selected for a winnable Parliamentary seat under NL. Therefore around 48% of Party members were excluded from selection under NL. Even some of the "slightly left of centre" were excluded: especially if they were seen as being "working class". This conclusion is supported by the responses of 49% of the party members, polled by YouGov in 2006. As one of their main reasons for having joined the Labour Party they gave: "I am a socialist and I wanted to join a party that would put my aspirations into practice". This proportion is similar to the average 46.8 % of party members who regularly voted for the Centre-Left Grass Roots Alliance candidates for the CLP section of the NEC in OMOV postal ballots between 1998 and 2008.[C8-53] *The NL Leadership forcibly prevented the PLP from representing the political views of virtually half the Party's members.*

The New Labour culture of deviance and cronyism must be challenged especially now that 2015 Leadership election results show that only about 40 % of Party members and supporters are likely to support New Labour. Further: the contemporary leadership must facilitate the reform of Party governance to create a transparent, fair and constitutional candidate selection process. This is discussed in Chapter 11.

CHAPTER 9
Downsizing Parliamentary Democracy

The Road to Disnaeland

"I call Parliament 'Disnaeland' because it dis'nae matter what goes on there"
**John Reid, Secretary of State for Health, quoted by
Patrick Wintour in the *Guardian*, 2008**

"MPs must be ambassadors for the Labour Party, not shop stewards for every grievance"
**Tony Blair in a 'pep talk' at the Parliamentary Labour Party meeting on
02.02.2000, Reported by Chris Mullin MP in *A View from the Foothills*, 2010**

*"When in that House MPs divide, if they've a brain and cerebellum, too
They've got to leave that brain outside
And vote as their leaders tell 'em to"*
W. S. Gilbert (from *Iolanthe*)

Chapter contents:
Introduction
Long standing issues relating to the British Parliamentary System
New Labour (NL) top down control of the Parliamentary Labour Party (PLP) On
squandering the talents of Labour MPs
Division of the PLP into gangs based on personalities not principles Sofa
government and a marginalised cabinet
Lefties excluded from Parliamentary select committees
Restricted power of backbenchers in policy making and related revolts House of Lords issues MPs'
work in their constituencies and involvement of local members in policy making
The toxic Parliamentary expenses scandal of 2009 onwards Overview of
NL's use and abuse of the Parliamentary Labour Party

One day in 1982 the author, then a senior local government officer, was heading towards the Newcastle Civic Centre dining room. On hearing a cheerful "hello" she looked round and saw a pleasant young councillor whom she knew from Social Services Committee meetings and Labour Regional Conferences. He invited her to lunch at his table. This was the first of a number of shared lunches which always started with him asking "and how are you lefties getting on?" It was followed by an amicable discussion of Labour Politics, national and regional. This was later the MP who surprised Jeremy Corbyn by accepting the position of he and his colleagues when they voted against the cut in single parent benefits in 1997 (see below). This anecdote did not surprise the author who long believed in the fair-mindedness and reasonableness of future Chief Whip Nick Brown.

Introduction

Oliver Cromwell engineered the execution of Charles I in an effort to empower Parliament. There is a story that, when contemplating the King's lifeless body, he murmured "cruel necessity". "Cruel necessity" appears to have been Tony Blair's (TB) and Gordon Brown's (GB) view of having to have a functioning Parliamentary Labour Party (PLP) at all. As discussed in Chapter 8, from 1994 onwards virtually all new MPs were, in effect, hand picked by the New Labour (NL) Leadership. They seemed to be chosen for their sycophancy, docility and lack of ideology. As Backbench MPs they were told what to think and say and how to vote (frequently by directions on their pagers). The, initially small, number of dissidents were ridiculed and threatened but threats were seldom carried out.

The Leadership's aspiration to tame backbenchers is illustrated by the above quotation from Chris Mullin MP: backbenchers were expected to be public relations officers for the NL Government. In interview Gordon Prentice MP recalled: "After the 1997 victory I remember Tony Blair, jacket off and in a white shirt, addressing the PLP. He told us he wanted us to remember that we weren't the Labour Government's shop stewards but its ambassadors. I thought him completely wrong but that's how they saw it at the centre. Labour MPs were given message pagers and it was their job to go out and sell the message received to the Party (and the Party's duty to pass it on to electors)."

Senior backbencher A. claimed that: *"Parliament has been regarded by NL as an obstacle to the achievement of its objectives"*. Katy Clark MP believed*: "This Labour Government sees Parliament and MPs as a nuisance! The government wants to run the show and has its own ideas and agenda. MPs aren't part of that."*

TB and GB had to tolerate having a pool of MPs from which to select ministers! After the millennium ministers were increasingly chosen from among former special Advisors (SPADS) and Labour Peers. New Labour ditched the principle of the Prime Minister being "First among equals" and replaced Cabinet Government with Sofa Government. The Leadership attempted to tame Parliamentary Select Committees whose proper function is to hold the executive to account. This Chapter relates what the NL leadership did to Parliamentary Democracy and to the Parliamentary Labour Party (PLP).

Initially most Labour MPs were compliant. However, after 2001 significant numbers of backbenchers adopted the practice of rebellion[C9-1]. Some of these had gone into Parliament in the hope of promotion, did not receive it, and then became disillusioned. Many wanted to make, or help to shape, policy despite the Leadership's wishes. Others gained courage with experience. They acquired understanding of how to use the parliamentary system. Some lost their political virginity in the "No" Lobbies during the Iraq War votes and rebelled again afterwards.[C9-2] These were in addition to the 47 "usual suspects" who voted against the freeze of one parent family benefit in December 1997.

This Chapter tells that story from the viewpoint of backbenchers interviewed during 2009·10 (the final year of NL Government). It ends with a discussion about how constituency party officers viewed these developments during the NL era.

Comments by Labour MPs included those of Michael Meacher who said: "So many Blairites came in, probably declaring when they were selected and elected, that they were going to represent their Party. But as soon as they got to Parliament the insidious exercise of patronage and the desire for careerism, which the whole Blair project was built on, meant that they succumbed entirely to the pressure from the whips. He continued: "Rebellion among MPs got so bad in 2008·9, that Nick Brown (Chief Whip) said that anyone who had voted against the government in the last year couldn't expect to be a member of a select committee. That shows how far authoritarian domination of the whips was allowed to exclude MPs from Parliamentary tasks. Instead of there being a riot, people just accepted it. For the future: I think Parliamentary democracy is absolutely key."

Senior Backbencher A. regretted: "Parliament's now in a poor state. Our Parliamentary system is quite a complex animal. There is a law of gravity relating to Parliament and however powerful a person is in Number 10 or the Cabinet, eventually they will fall back into Parliament because the numbers make that necessary. We've now introduced a system where every piece of legislation is guillotined from the start so we've a fixed number of hours set to debate it. However controversial it may be and however difficult some of the issues, the hours sometimes run out when we are on the first set of amendments. There could be another 1,000 amendments that are never discussed. That can't be right. This diminishes the ability of Parliament to act as a partnership with the Executive."

John Cryer argued: "There has been a shift of power from Westminster to Whitehall that has affected Party members. Party members see that their MP has less power than before the changes. That creates a feeling that democratic accountability is missing."

Backbench MPs felt power ebbing away from them through a combination of manipulation of the Parliamentary timetable and restriction of membership of select committees. In time, rebellion, or the threat of it, became seen as the only effective vehicle to achieve change.

Longer standing issues relating to the British Governmental system

Cowley wrote: "Backbench cohesion began to weaken in late 1960s and 1970s, at exactly the same point as those much derided career politicians began to enter Westminster in such numbers."[C9-3] Some restrictions dated from the preceding Tory regime. Backbench MPs had long been their Party's Noddy Terns when it came to most Parliamentary votes (see the quotation from *Iolanthe* above). Rebellion in the lobbies, by more than a few, was comparatively rare during the 19th and 20th centuries. Garrett alleged: "Far from being supreme, our Parliament has too often been supine." He argued that Parliament must be more than a rubber stamp for what government wants to do. It should be able to insist on hearing the justification and purposes of new laws. When examining government spending, it should do so in an effective way.[4]

It has to be concluded that Parliamentary democracy was not in perfect health during the period leading up to 1997 and before it contended with the NL regime.

It is useful to consider how backbenchers saw their own roles in the pre NL era. In 1984 Austin Mitchell conducted an opinion survey of his fellow backbenchers. They considered that their most important role was" to make a contribution to the national debate" (47%); "to act as a check on the executive" (45%); and "to act as a spokesperson for local interests." (49%). 50% considered the role of a backbencher to be "fairly satisfactory" and 13% "very satisfactory". The majority believed that constituency work was "the best part of the job" followed by "participation in law making" and "just being at the centre of things."[C9-5]

Relevant Backbenchers' views included M. who echoed Garrett's view by saying: "Last week I was in Washington DC and I'm always slightly in awe of, and embarrassed by, the power exerted by the most junior member of Congress compared to a British MP. You could argue that it's our constitutional settlement: the separation of the executive and the legislature. The greater political space in the US system makes it different. Our constitutional settlement limits MPs' powers more than is good for democracy. Francis Pym, reflecting on recent Tory governments, said that the large majorities had meant more power in the hands of the Executive:the larger the majority the more powerful the Executive. I think this has been so more generally. This has consequences for the type of democracy that Labour needs to bring into its own internal workings."

John Cryer argued: "The shift of power from Parliament to Whitehall did not, in accordance with myth, happen under TB:it happened under Major. It was part of a process that had been going on for about 30 years. Thatcher started it, but Major curtailed the rights of backbenchers more than in any Parliament in living memory. TB took it a bit further, but what he did was peripheral. Backbenchers have less power now than previously."

Even before 1997, Garrett regretted the minimal contemporary focus of Parliament on the implementation of policies that it enacted. He accused it of a style which avoided systems thinking. [C9-6] Subsequently the focus of the NL Government was mainly on policy implementation (a focus that Garrett supported), for example, meeting health and education targets. Under NL Parliament's deliberations included review of policy attainment.

The vital question is whether NL not only failed to deal with the flaws in our Parliamentary system, but also compounded them? Was the effect of large parliamentary majorities to facilitate unfettered power for the leadership or to foster rebellion on the backbenches?

Top down control and management of the Parliamentary Labour Party

The aim of the NL leadership seemed to be to tame the PLP where it could not be controlled by their authority alone and to render it subservient to, and supportive of, that leadership. This Chapter examines top down control of the PLP once elected. It identifies direct control of the work of compliant MPs by the whips' office and harassment of dissidents by some whips.

Cowley wrote: "One group of politicians who got used to being dismissed as ineffectual were the Labour MPs elected en masse in 1997. They got used to being described as timid, sycophantic, acquiescent and cowardly. They acquired a reputation for … mindless loyalty and distinct lack of backbone."[C9-7] He reported that they were also often criticised for asking sycophantic questions during Prime Minister's Question Time.

Some MPs considered the NL methods of managing Parliament to be fairer and less draconian than others did.

Michael Meacher lamented: "One thing they did successfully was to produce a Parliament that cloned Blairism. How? *By producing a selection process for PPCs that was fixed by them to ensure that there was a large, critical mass within the PLP who can be relied on when things get difficult and when the Prime Minster/Government is under challenge. I estimate that this was at least two thirds of the PLP whilst Blair was PM. I* don't think they (the new MPs) were interested in ideology. They were there because of the Blairite project and were going to stick with it. They were always in the Chamber, when things got sticky and when there were Tory attacks against the Prime Minister or other Ministers. The PLP that used to be a debating chamber, where its heart and soul was fought for, became a repository where anyone who challenged the official line from Number 10 was either given a very cold and difficult hearing or shouted down by overwhelming numbers."

MM continued: "When I first came into Parliament, the right of the PLP was about 40% and the left about 40%; with about 20% in the middle. I'm aware, having tried to get every left vote in the 2007 leadership election, the most that the left has now is about 50, 70 at the edge, out of 352 MPs. So we're about a sixth of the total whereas 20·30 years ago we were nearly a half. That's the success of the Blairite machine dominating the selection process."

He was not the only MP to identify the development of a scheme to cleanse the ideological complexion of the PLP (see Chapter 8). TB, like Mrs. Thatcher before him, probably asked about potential legislators is she/he one of us?

Kelvin Hopkins contended: "I believe that, following Leninist dictum, Blair got total control of the Party and used it as a weapon. The majority of newer MPs don't have democratic socialist values. They were told that Year Zero was 1997 when Blair became Prime Minister. TB got control of the PLP: mainly by stuffing it with NL loyalists. These don't necessarily understand the ideology of NL. Many are just loyal. "I'm loyal to NL because they won this victory for me". The rebels tend to be older MPs, like myself, who were influenced by Nye Bevan and the traditional left like Tony Benn. The leadership does not need to exert much power within the PLP because they've got an automatic majority. Whenever there's an election, the whips know they can quietly circulate a slate that always gets elected. We can occasionally get someone on to the Parliamentary Committee (which represents the views of MPs to the Leadership). It's usually people of the centre·left (for example: Gordon Prentice). This is getting more difficult now as older, traditional MPs leave Parliament. If they'd had a PLP with another 100, genuine Labour MPs, life would have been very difficult for them. In the vote not to honour the Labour promise to raise single parent benefit in December 1997, most of those who abstained, or voted against, were longer serving MPs."

Jon Cruddas said: "*I don't think that the PLP has worked well (since 1997). But there have been one or two major successes*: higher education and foundation hospitals. As (previously) dominant personalities in the PLP, like Robin Cook, Mo Mowlam and Clare Short, declined, they've not been replaced by a set of political personalities that were forged outside being in government. Instead they were replaced by a distinctive political class." This phenomenon, operating across parties, was described by Oborne in 2007. C9_8

Control of backbenchers had been ratcheted up under NL. For example, Frank Dobson MP claimed: "When I became a (government) backbencher again I found I had much less power and influence than I'd had when I was a backbencher in opposition (before 1997)."

Jeremy Corbyn observed: "The PLP is a strange place because it is separated from the Party in constitutional terms and *not bound by Party policy*. Surprisingly it never has been. Blair put through changes in the Party structure that gave the PLP direct representation on the NEC and on policy forums so increasing its influence."

Initially TB appeared to try to extend control of backbenchers through personal contact. However he seemed to lack the interpersonal skills, or perhaps the will, to do so effectively.

Corbyn added: "TB wanted to meet MPs and during his first couple of years as PM there were sessions where MPs could meet, and have discussions, with him. I attended many of these and had arguments with him but he was always very patronising. You were ushered into Number 10 and given half an hour of the great man's time. *"I once asked him about what we were doing on social housing and he replied: 'Well we're doing very well on education'. I responded: 'Well that's fine Tony, maybe we are, but that's not much help to people who come to me wanting a house.' He replied: 'Well you've just got to tell them how good the education policies are'.* I said: 'When the next homeless man comes to me I'll tell him the primary schools are doing well, Sunshine.' He said: 'You're just not taking this seriously'. I replied: 'I'm taking this very seriously, are you?'."

Corbyn continued: "Another time TB wandered round the room in silence, sometimes looking out of the window, eventually he said: 'I often look out of this window and think that every Labour Prime Minister who's been here before me has come to office in the middle of an economic crisis and yet has managed to spend on public services and change things'. That was it – the group was left hanging in the air."

There was little doubt that backbenchers felt emasculated within the NL PLP. They were not listened to by the Leadership and had limited democratic rights. PLP meetings were sometimes a daunting experience and Parliament was a strange and threatening environment for new MPs. This was especially true if they were young and politically inexperienced, which was how NL wanted them to be (see Chapter 8).

Gordon Prentice reported: "We've had no elections of any consequence in the PLP. We've had elections for MPs' places on the *National Policy Forum (NPF), which doesn't count for anything*. We have elections for who goes on the Parliamentary Committee, which doesn't decide much. But the key decisions as to who goes into Cabinet and rest of the Government are decisions of the Prime Minister."

Graham Stringer stated: "To say that Labour MPs are more subservient than they were in the past, is to distort history. What that analysis doesn't do is catch the cultural change. *Most Labour Prime Ministers, prior to Blair, were accused of presidential styles but they had a greater respect for the processes of the Commons. They probably also had less of a tin ear for what their backbenchers were saying*."

Katy Clark, who entered Parliament in 2005, thought: "MPs are usually people that have come into politics with the best of intentions. Whether it's ambition or accident, they've ended up as representatives. So they have to work out what they're going to do with that position. Many MPs, when they're elected, are quite fearful because it's an intimidating world they enter. It's very difficult to go along with anything other than what's expected from you by the machine. Therefore most MPs fit in. Just like at school You don't want to be the odd one out, ridiculed, or marginalised."

She continued: "I gather that, particularly when TB was first leader, PLP meetings were an intimidating environment. There wasn't any mutual respect. During the first PLP meeting, that I attended, one MP stood beside me shouting at the MP who was speaking: 'De-select her, de-select her'. In general, there wasn't a debate. The way you got debate was through raising issues under 'points of order' early in the meeting. Next there was a government speaker who dealt with an area of policy. Then you could ask questions but it wasn't always an environment where a healthy discussion was possible. Despite that, many colleagues were very brave and made important points. They were heard but not necessarily responded to. In the recent past Tony Lloyd has been a very fair PLP Chair."

NL developed a preferred supine role for backbenchers. There was little meaningful interchange between leadership and backbenchers during PLP meetings and the leadership stood accused of having tactical deafness and not responding to MP's questions and concerns voiced there.

Alan Simpson considered: "The sort of people that NL has allowed to become MPs tell voters, when doorstep campaigning, that they are really nice and the Tories are really horrible and 'you should vote for the nice candidate. Labour is a nice party and stands for nice things'. I'm sure we do stand for nice things but, in reality, that means making difficult policy decisions. These decisions cannot be implemented without there being a fundamental shift in wealth and resources. But these people didn't want that, so NL has been their comfort blanket. It said: 'don't worry your pretty little head backbenchers; we'll make the difficult decisions for you and issue press releases'. So there is a culture in which MPs are bottle fed by the machine."

He continued: "You haven't had to deal with difficult letters from your constituents or correspond with constituents at all because your office staff could do this directly using responses drafted by the PLP machine. A noteworthy example was when GB did a budget speech and I was sent a copy of "my" press release (that had already been sent out) welcoming GB's speech and outlining benefits it would bring to my constituents. So I then put out my own press release. It said that GB had welcomed my alternative budget that I had set out the day after his budget speech, in which I made the case for a fundamental shift in resource allocation and a return to progressive taxation. I sent a copy to the Treasury who came back to me protesting: 'You can't say that GB welcomes this, he hasn't even seen it.' I replied: 'I didn't see the press release that you sent out to my constituents saying that I welcomed his budget. Either you put your press releases back in your pockets and don't presume that you can speak for me or carry on and accept that I'm going to exercise the same freedom to claim Gordon's support for my kind of budget that I know would give him a heart attack –so make your choice'!" Few MPs took such a robust stand.

Simpson proposed: "For most, it was politics without pain. Leadership took the thinking away from difficult issues. Sadly the effect of that was to produce a house trained PLP. If the Leadership put forward a policy saying: 'We are now going to support a policy of the slaughter of the first born' it would probably go through the PLP with no one voting against it."

Sadly, like a number of other more progressive MPs interviewed, AS was planning to leave Parliament at the next general election (expected for Spring 2010 at the time of interview).

He announced: "*The basis of my decision to leave Parliament was a serious question as to whether it is fit for purpose any more.* We have reached a stage where the institutions of national and international government, created at the end of World War 2, are now probably moribund and ought to be abandoned. We have to create new institutions and frameworks that will be fit to steer us through an era of planetary crisis in order to avoid climate chaos. There is nothing in the body politic of the PLP or NL Government that seems to have a grasp of the urgency and scale of the necessary transformation."

John McDonnell wrote: "The PLP was not accountable to the Party. Your job as an MP is to be lobby fodder and to turn up and vote for the whip."[C9_9]

MPs expressed a mixture of views about the nature and powers of contemporary backbencher roles and what they should ideally be.

Colin Challen said: "I want government to actually govern. I would rather see a strong leader showing leadership, even if I don't entirely agree with them, than someone who was vacillating all the time, showed no leadership and who would probably lose the election anyway. GB is like this, partly because he takes so long making up his mind."

John Grogan contended: "I reject the view that you've had a PLP as a whole that has totally ignored the executive and just done what it was told. I don't think that we've had a supine PLP as the 1997 generation has continued in Parliament. Some people, including myself and some ministers, have carved out a role for themselves questioning things. It's not the only role, but it's worthwhile, particularly when we're in government."

Clare Short believed: "It's now managing people, not consulting them, within the PLP. The spirit of the PLP, as a bunch of independent political people who sincerely consider options, feed in their ideas and give conditional loyalty that's a two way street, has gone. *We're now a bunch to be pushed around and be rewarded if they do what they're told but marginalised if they don't. The spirit of the PLP is now broken as a body of sincere political figures who can influence what the government does.*"

The LabOUR Commission Report 2007[C9-10] drew on research to evidence its argument that both the Party in the Country and the PLP were being managed in an autocratic mode.

Linda Riordan observed: "*The PLP is managed in a top down fashion*. As a new MP I used to attend PLP meetings regularly. When anyone says something that's not popular you get desk thumping. That's not the sort of meeting I want to be in. Everyone in the PLP should always be listened to. I don't attend regularly, you just hear the same rhetoric. I went to hear GB speak and was impressed. But he needs to be leader of our Party as well as Prime Minister."

She continued: "GB doesn't seem to take much notice of us. We've had the turn around on Post Office part-privatisation, but he was forced into that. Notice was taken about concerns over the abolition of the 10p tax rate but some people are still worse off. The unfairness of this policy was raised by the Campaign Group when it was first announced. Whoever becomes the next Leader of the Party should listen more to members of the Campaign Group. We're a small group but we have got good people. They should get back on track rather than us having to leave the Party. TB did not listen to MPs either."

Alice Mahon believed: "The way the PLP was run (under NL) was shocking. They really hurt anybody on the left who raised things such as the one parent family benefit issue (in 1997). The whips played a big part in this. You were held up to ridicule and quite often shouted down. TB complained about scabs on his back; I've got a lot of scabs on mine from PLP meetings. The big one was Iraq. Whips organised intervention against you and organised barracking so sometimes it was difficult to speak. Jean Corston, the then Chair of the PLP, who was lovely, tried to control it but it still happened sometimes. You had people standing up and condemning: 'lefties who are bringing the Party into disrepute'. It was sometimes suggested that I would have the whip taken off me if I rebelled. A few of us took turns to attend PLP meetings. When Tony Benn was in Parliament he was ridiculed at PLP meetings and the whips orchestrated it."

Backbencher B. believed: "Under NL the PLP increasingly became a rubber stamp. Whenever there was a controversial issue the payroll vote was steamrollered in. When it came to Iraq, the majority of Labour MPs, not on the payroll, voted against. Only a couple of ministers resigned" (Robin Cook and Lord Philip Hunt).

There were differing views about the degree of Leadership control over and failure to listen to the PLP. It certainly did not appear to be a uniformly well organised forum for political decision making or influencing the Leadership.

Chris Mullin said: "The PLP is not as bad as some of its critics allege. It is not easily browbeaten. I was a member of the Parliamentary Committee of six backbenchers who met the Prime Minister every week and have a remit to say what's on MPs' minds. The leaders do listen."

When asked how well Parliament has worked for Labour since 1994, senior backbencher M. who had held office in the PLP, responded: "It has not worked as effectively as we would want. Has the PLP worked in a way that empowered MPs? There's no absolute answer. What matters is how it works unofficially. Individuals and groups of Backbench MPs probably think that it's varied issue by issue. There's not been a spineless, inert Labour Backbench that's never done anything at all. I think that a large majority persuades a government that they can achieve their desires without the same need for arguing and explaining their case in detail. For example: I don't think the Government has made the case as to why identity cards would be a major breakthrough in British society. It's a good example of a policy that could be right but hasn't been talked through. This leads to public concern *and* concern among Labour MPs, some of whom oppose for philosophical reasons and some because their constituents object. A large majority can lead to an arrogant government attitude to policy making. It means that ministers become prisoners of the civil service, which is then likely to get its pet projects delivered. There is some evidence that large majorities give ministers a free hand. There are also examples where government has listened and changed policy – sometimes when backbenchers have threatened to rebel."

On the subject of barracking in PLP meetings, at the instigation of whips, M. said: "I'm sure that happens, but it doesn't happen often. I've attended PLP meetings regularly since 1997 and there have been different whips. I'm sure that the present Chief Whip (Nick Brown) doesn't engage in anything like that. Things have varied at different periods. Sometimes meetings may have been more robust. I've spoken at the PLP when I've been out of harmony with the mainstream government view on a subject and I've never felt intimidated. I can't say that barracking never happened, but I can't recall an example. I disapprove of heavy pressure, but can recall a couple of cases where strong views were expressed. I've always discouraged this. What's said at the PLP can be revealed to journalists and destructive reporting is unhelpful. Secondly the PLP needs civilised, healthy debate. Even recent critics of the leadership, such as Charles Clarke, didn't get intimidation from those who disagreed. Although feelings ran high, people were generally polite."

Peter Kilfoyle had a different view. He declared: "The running of the PLP has been a fix since 1993. The whole time was spent making sure that what the leader wanted went through. People who spoke out on points of principle were vilified. The PLP meetings were fixed by NL and they were the *only* Party meetings inside Parliament. Their function was to give support to the Leadership at every turn and to make sure that the leadership got their way. It was impossible to achieve anything there. Decisions were made on unimportant issues. Debate was discouraged at the PLP and people were pressurised there. MPs didn't want to be made to feel they were traitors. They were portrayed like that, if they didn't go along with the Leadership line."

Clearly there was a variety of opinions about how the meetings of the PLP were conducted and with which outcomes. It emerged that many MPs, who did not slavishly follow the NL line, seldom attended because the meetings seemed too unproductive, and sometimes too painful for them.

Lynne Jones believed: "The PLP is not run democratically. Attendance at PLP meetings is very poor unless there's something in the news, like the suggestion that Brown is fighting for his survival, then you get packed meetings. Many there just observe. It's not about policy making. In most cases, it's about personalities."

Some considered that our unwritten constitution was not currently serving the interests of public and of Parliamentary democracy. One aspect of this was failure to radically reform the House of Lords and replace it with a more democratic second chamber.

Graham Stringer believed: "The real lesson of the last 12 years has been that if you're going to *change the constitution* you can't just mess with it. You have to deal with the relationship with the crown and the royal prerogative. The Privy Council has power that doesn't flow from the Commons but from the Throne. Unless you deal with that constitutionally then you won't deal adequately with the House of Lords. The Lords is worse – having got rid of the 'Hereditaries' – than it was before, because it has more power. The real problem is control of the Executive. I can't imagine that if you were setting up a governmental structure for this country that, on day one, you would establish a structure like ours. The civil service is not corrupt; their financial services are the best in the world, it is not too politically biased or prejudiced but it *has its own agenda*."

On Squandering the Talents of Many Parliamentarians

Chapter 8 demonstrated that, when illicitly controlling the selection of Parliamentary candidates, the NL machine sought compliance rather than ability. The leadership would seldom promote dissidents, radical thinkers or those who might ask challenging questions. In addition, they would not greatly promote MPs who had relevant extra Parliamentary management and decision making experience. Further, the over-fifties were unlikely to be promoted under TB. This meant that much potential talent and experience, which could have been put to the government's service, was left lying fallow.

This left the leaders mainly with young former special advisers (SPADs) and cronies to promote. Oborne contended that SPADs have been trained like racehorses for ministerial office and for membership of the political class. Oborne identified NL SPADs as belonging to his cross Party political class. However they could remain in that Class, if they were intellectuals, only by being conservative and conventional.[C9-11] He identified David Miliband as being an example of a typical and successful member of this political class.

Many able MPs were not promoted under NL. These included a number of able and experienced former leaders of large Labour controlled Councils. Most of them had excellent track records and had exercised responsibility for making major executive decisions. Apart from Graham Stringer, briefly a whip, few of these were promoted above the rank of Parliamentary Private Secretary – if at all. Many had valuable life and work experience outside politics. Most promoted former SPADs were very young and had experienced little, in the wider society, apart from student life and being political advisors.

The way the NL regime used junior ministers caused some MPs to consider that minor promotion was a disadvantage. In his diaries Chris Mullin reported in January 2000: "Peter Kilfoyle has resigned from his lowly post at the Ministry of Defence on the grounds that the job is not the best use of his talents. I know how he feels."[C9-12] Such resignations deprived NL administrations of potentially useful talent.

MPs' thoughts about promoting SPADs and wasting other Parliamentary talent

Clare Short regretted: "In the PLP under Blair (and I suspect also under Brown) the NL apparatchiks, who worked in Party headquarters, or who had been SPADs or friends of some of the senior figures, have been plonked into seats and then straight into ministerial positions. Look at the present cabinet (2009): Ed Balls, one of the handful of most senior ministers, was recruited as special advisor to GB. In opposition he was his Treasury advisor for many years. He was then plonked into a seat and straight into a ministerial position and the Cabinet. The same is true of David Miliband, James Purnell and others. The time they've spent in the Commons is minute. Such people may be quite clever but are completely lacking in wisdom and experience. The old system was people doing local political and public service work, earning some respect in their locality, then getting selected, climbing up the greasy pole, getting experience in Parliament and maybe in opposition, because they showed ability based on experience. Now you get kids who come straight in from University to be appointed as advisor. *Clever, arrogant, pushy juveniles can work their way through the patronage systems and get, not just into the Commons, but into Cabinet leap frogging over people who've given years of service.*"

Gordon Prentice reported: "Recent former minister Kim Howells spoke lately about the 'Assisted Places scheme of fast tracking people into Parliament then the Cabinet'. I've never heard him speak about this before. I'm trying not to personalise: but Andy Burnham, David Miliband and James Purnell were all political advisors or liaison officers to senior ministers, and were fast tracked into Parliament and the Cabinet."

One MP whose considerable talent and political experience were squandered by the NL Leadership was Louise Ellman (LE) former respected Leader of Lancashire County Council. She alleged: "The Leadership seems wary of some people. I think they don't want to put into Government people who are strong managers and might challenge them. They should look at it the other way on: people who are used to running things have developed knowledge, skills and confidence that they could use in a new context." She continued: "The difference between being leader of a large local authority and a Labour backbencher is dramatic. It involves a big loss of power. However much you can make speeches and statements, you can't make decisions, or policy, in the same way. The (Parliamentary) policy making process takes longer and is a dramatic contrast from (that in a) local authority."

LE also criticised leadership practices relating to the selection and management of ministers: "Blair wanted young MPs and almost no one over 50 was promoted under him. Brown is now willing to promote older people. *Those who were promoted had a managerial approach. They had no ideology or ideals. They seemed just like a manager in any other job.*"

Graham Stringer, former Leader of Manchester City Council, said: "When you compare national government to local government, it's about 1,000 times bigger, in terms of expenditure. Of course, National government has functions that local government doesn't have, for instance, foreign policy. There is an interface between what national and local government deliver."

Senior backbencher A, also former leader of a major local authority, argued: "There is no comparison between being leader of a large council and being a minister or even a Secretary of State. This is because, in the pre 1997 local government structure, as leader of a large authority l was an executive politician making decisions and implementing them. That was the traditional culture and structure. The reason you were able to do that was that the appointment of the local government 'civil service' was in the hands of elected members. National politicians do not appoint the levels of civil servant that local government leaders do. As a consequence there is a much clearer correlation between what the political executive in local government wants and what local government achieves, than with ministers and civil servants. This doesn't seem to be understood by people who have not been at my level in local government but have gone straight into ministerial posts."

These testimonies suggest that the NL Leadership were afraid that these proven and talented former local government leaders would become "over mighty subjects" and challenge their authority. This was apparently more important to them than harnessing proven talent in the interests of providing better government. Another area from which talented MPs, who were not Leadership favourites, were sometimes excluded was select committee appointments (see below).

According to Oborne's classification, it is only MPs who are subservient to the government or their Party machines, or those who use their position to secure money or promotion, who are genuine members of the political class. However, he believed that the majority of Westminster MPs do belong to the political class because they meet these criteria.[C9_13]

The change of Labour Leadership in 2007 created an opportunity for a wider spectrum of people to be promoted and, to a limited extent, GB used this positively. He was more favourably disposed to older MPs. However this development left disappointed and demoted Blairites free to make mischief and to undermine GB's authority.

Speculating (in 2005) about the coming Brown leadership, Cowley said: "Particularly disgruntled will be those MPs who are hoping for a bright future which then does not materialise – and which has been so cruelly denied to them under Blair – there will doubtless be some promotions among the ranks of previously overlooked or dismissed Brownites. But in Party management terms these will simply be countered by a group of disgruntled Blairites who are equally likely to find themselves newly encamped on the backbenches."[C9_14]

The NL Parliamentary machine, mainly operated by whips, used carrots and sticks to maintain compliance. *The common view of MPs interviewed seemed to be that the carrot of patronage was used more extensively than the stick of discipline.* Approximately one third of the PLP were given opportunities of holding office. Whilst machine generated threats, including de-selection or being excluded from membership of select committees, were fairly frequent, few MPs were *actually* excluded or de-selected. Only Bob Wareing and Ian Gibson were, arguably, de-selected for being dissident. The former was deselected, at the second attempt, over a six year period. This was allegedly accompanied by unpopularity among activists in his CLP (see Chapter 8). Jeremy Corbyn was the only *named* example of permanent exclusion from select committee membership. Even the frequently dissident Linda Riordan was eventually allowed to join a select Committee.

Patronage was liberally used to buy the loyalty of backbenchers to the Leadership. The incentives used included not only offices in Parliament but also general national honours such as knighthoods and newly invented posts with grandiose titles but vaguely defined duties (e.g. Special Ambassador to Iraq).

Lynne Jones complained: "If you're in power you can exert a huge amount of patronage. It's only when there's a real sense that that power is ebbing away that MPs feel that they have any power at all. At the last attempted coup (2007) there wasn't sufficient momentum behind any leadership challenge. In the end it fizzled out because patronage was still operating. *The Leadership always had some patronage. But there were always checks and balances in the Party: the power of Conference and the power within Parliament. This led to more compromises than there are now.*"

Clare Short regretted: "The PLP is kept in line through ruthless use of patronage. There are a massive number of ministers, paid whips etc. If you keep moving people through and then making them special envoy of this or that, then you've got so much patronage to go round that everyone knows they can be a minister. No one thinks any more that they want to be a parliamentarian. There are a number of older members who stuck to that position but not enough to ensure that the PLP isn't completely manipulable. Older members can be offered the House of Lords."

Roger Berry stated: "I've always been a Backbench MP since entering Parliament in 1992. I was offered a Parliamentary Private Secretary (PPS) job in the late 1990s but refused it because I would have had to abandon work I was then doing on disability benefits. I would also not have been able to chair the Parliamentary Committee on Drugs any longer. I believed that unless I could take the job and still do something significant there wasn't much point."

John Grogan reported: "There was no likelihood of my ever becoming a minister. They offered to make me a Church Commissioner. I was also offered to become PPS to Dick Caborn after the 2005 election. I refused because there was not much point becoming a PPS at that stage; it restricts you speaking." Senior backbencher A. said: "I've never been a minister; I chose not to be one. I've been offered ministerial posts and turned them down on a number of occasions."

This profligate use of incentives, including newly invented posts diverted MPs' loyalties away from the Party and their constituents into uncritical support of the government.

Michael Meacher claimed: "One third of all Labour MPs can gain promotion to offices – hence the power of patronage. The PLP wants to be loyal to its own government, but it is fundamentally there to hold its government to account on behalf of the Party and the public. Power moves through these avenues into Parliament, so the Party and public must have a form of redress and a way of influencing what goes on there. Currently we are totally disconnected."

Graham Stringer argued: "On the issue of top up fees, Blair started with about 150 votes, then MPs had their arms twisted, were given incentives and loyalties were called. I have no doubt that on a free vote the PLP would never have voted for top up fees, or ever for the Iraq war."

Jeremy Corbyn said: "The whipping system underlines the patronage of the PM. There was never any attempt to be inclusive in the PLP. It was always about patronage which was ruthlessly exploited over the membership of select committees. *The government works more on patronage and threat than it does on (other) enticements for MPs.* This has worked strongly against any Parliamentary reform. There was a free vote about who should choose members of select committees (MPs or the Government) and I have never seen so many whips working so hard on a free vote to preserve patronage."

Corbyn contended: "The behaviour of whips and the attitude to dissent in the post 1997 PLP was tough. *However they always pulled back from doing anything to anyone who actually dissented.* Now, 12 years later, we have a PLP that is the most rebellious among all PLPs since the mid 19th century. There is frequent dissent but Brown knows that, if the PLP rebels, he can get legislation through with Tory support (for example on privatisation). Nick Brown, currently chief whip, is an interesting mixture. In 1997 there was dissent over one parent family benefits. When 48 MPs went into the lobby to vote against the proposals, we found Nick in there with us. He said: 'I'm not here to be converted. I think I'm too late to persuade you but I'm here to tell you that the Labour Party will be here tomorrow and we'll all be in it'. This was an interesting statement as we had all just been told by the *Evening Standard* that we would be expelled from the Party."

Alice Mahon said: "The Chief Whip and the Party General Secretary are the ones who call MPs to the 'Star Chamber' over expenses. Why? Nick Brown is ultra loyal to GB and would do anything for him. Look at what happened to Ian Gibson – that was absolutely dreadful. I suspect there will be a few more. They're going for the people that they can pick off easily. Some people are protected at the cost of others who are thrown to the wolves."

There was a clear sense that some offending MPs were punished more heavily than others. An excuse was provided to pillory those miscreants who were on the left/opposed to NL. How different was the treatment meted out to Chris Mullin, who seemed to be liked personally by TB?

Chris Mullin recalled: "TB was unhappy that I voted against the Iraq war, especially as I was an office holder at the time. He did his best to persuade me not to vote against. But he didn't care personally if you disagreed with him. Two weeks later he phoned to offer me a job which turned out to be a wonderful position that lasted two years. TB didn't bear grudges and was happy to have members of the 'sensible left' in his government. That's an alternative view of TB to the one that's often expressed. He accepted that there was scope for another view of Iraq. However people on the left, who he does not regard as sensible, had a hard time. For example, Jeremy Corbyn has never been put on a select committee, including foreign affairs, about which he is knowledgeable, which is a pity. Jeremy is a genuine socialist and would have made a good contribution to this committee where his expertise would have been utilised. There *is* some unfairness, often perpetrated by whips."

Others accepted their medicine. Christine McCafferty declared: "If you vote against your party you don't get promoted. That's not unreasonable. I have voted against the Government occasionally". According to Cowley, 2005 CM voted against the whip 20 times between 1997 and 2005. C9_15

Some were sceptical and unhappy about the role of whips. Alan Simpson said sarcastically: "Whips are wonderful people as long as you train them properly. *They have forgotten that their traditional role should have been as shop stewards for the PLP. This means they should be the conveyors of messages into the Executive and not just be conduits for instructions from Downing St.* In the early days, MPs who were unhappy with policies, had their CLP Chair phoned up by ministers or whips who said: "Look your MP's out of line, he/she is only in this place because of NL. Just get them back into line. Make it clear to them that, if that's the way they're going to behave, don't expect them to be endorsed as candidate at the next general election. Some had their wives or partners were phoned by heavy handed whips saying: 'Are you comfortable living on an MP's salary and expenses? Well don't get used to it because it will disappear at the next general election if your partner carries on with their rebellious behaviour. So get him/her to look around for other jobs'."

All of this sounds like blackmail, the fact that the threats made were not always carried out in the face of non compliance provides no excuse. As years went on dissident MPs began to realise that the threats to their continued tenure of a Parliamentary seat were frequently idle ones.

Clare Short declared: "There was the ultimate threat not to allow you to run as a Parliamentary candidate if you did not do what you were told. That is sort of what happened to Ian Gibson but it was done through the expenses situation. I never understood why being kind to his daughter, at no cost to the taxpayer, was an offence. But they'd always wanted to stop him running because he'd been an independent minded and spirited MP."

Linda Riordan followed on: "The biggest mistake recently was what they did to Ian Gibson. He was a good MP who didn't really do anything wrong, whatever the rules say. I am convinced that it was because he was a member of the Campaign Group that he was picked out by the Star Chamber. Was that good public relations? Now we have a Tory MP in Norwich North when we could have had Ian there. He has been pilloried and that may not appear right to the public. *Fortunately no one else in the Campaign Group had done anything (*for example: relating to expenses*) that they could pick on us for."*

The whipping machine's threats were frequently not carried out, but when they were the blows fell on the repeatedly rebellious for offences that were ignored when committed by compliant MPs. Other MPs, who were NL loyalists, for example Tony McNulty, allegedly made broadly similar claims to Ian Gibson's. However they were not penalised.

As noted above, very *occasionally a de-selection was engineered by the Party machine:* the West Derby case (see Chapter 8) involved de-selection of the sitting left wing MP. Some rules were allegedly broken by Party staff during de-selection. This reduced his chances of being re-selected. In recent years de-selections have been infrequent. This was partly because the rules of 1991 (containing the "trigger mechanism", whereby local members are balloted as to whether a full re-selection shall be held) make re-selection difficult to secure. An MP was considered automatically re-selected if he/she received a majority of nominations at the first stage of that process. Before the 1997 election one male MP was de-selected in Bolton. Between 1997 and 2005 two women MPs were de-selected: one in Reading and one in Southern Scotland. In more than one of these cases the personal conduct of the MP was questioned.

In the straw poll of CLP secretaries conducted by the author,[C9-17] they were asked: *"Would you like to see a Party rule change to make it easier to de-select poorly performing, or unaccountable, Labour MPs at CLP level? Of the 27 respondents, 20 said that they would like to see such a revision of Party rules, three said that they would not and four did not know.*

Senior backbencher M believed that de-selection of MPs should be made easier. He said: "Most people are not going to de-select their MP most of the time. But, as a party activist, I want to have influence in that role. As a citizen living in my city I would feel frustrated if I were not able to influence this."

In the summer of 2011 the Party consulted members on whether de-selection should be made easier[C9-16] but the outcome was endorsement of the status quo.

The PLP divided into gangs based primarily on leadership personalities rather than political views

As discussed earlier; during the NL era most entrants to the PLP were devoid of ideology. There was only a small organised left (the Campaign Group). Centre-lefties were largely un-coordinated since the covert sabotage of the Tribune Group, allegedly by TB and GB (see below). The politics of ideology and principle were replaced by the politics of personality and related factionalism. MPs divided into gangs where they operated as lackeys to their respective gang masters – TB, GB and John Prescott (JP). These gangs became the main vehicles for the exercise of patronage. The fourth "gang" was constituted of outsiders belonging to none of the above.

What MPs thought about the "gangs": Jon Cruddas described this phenomenon: "The real hallmark of the PLP in recent years has been its retreat into gangs. These are personality based factions operating around conflict between 10 Downing St and the Treasury. That's been the prominent characteristic in terms of the functioning of the PLP – its retreat into a tribal structure of different competing frameworks. MPs have retreated into this thing of gangs with charismatic leaders: Blair or Brown. We are in the era of the charismatic leader with their corresponding gangs of courtiers; without any intermediary institutions which have checks and balances. All this is a product of 15 years of (economic) growth. Now there's a whole set of different issues of scarcity and recession that has not been worked through by the Party. We are now in transition (July 2009). No one knows how it will change, but *there can be no going back to the Party of the last 15 years."*

Gordon Prentice contended: "The NL period was a government of cliques. There were, and remain, three cliques: Blairites, Brownites and Prescottites. You can identify the members and ministers in each. I remember having tea with one minister before he got office. He despaired: 'I would like to be in the Government but I'm never going to get there because I'm not in one of those three camps'. The NL Government is a government of courtiers. Patronage is dished out by a constellation of three bright stars and is allocated according to how close you were to one of them. People who have not been close to these 'supernovas' have not been promoted."

Senior Backbencher B. analysed the demise of the Tribune Group and the decline of the Campaign Group in the Commons. He remembered: "Prior to the creation of NL there was an influx of MPs into the Tribune Group including, surprisingly, TB and GB. After that it became totally ineffective – this may have been a deliberate tactic. The Tribune Group then lost its purpose – making a constructive left contribution. Later it became used as a rubber stamp for views of the TB/GB axis whilst John Smith was leader. Although the group carried on for a while, what it could do was considerably weakened. The Campaign Group continued but lacked the positivity and flexibility of the old Tribune Group."

These entryist tactics relating to the Tribune Group were allegedly planned by GB and TB to weaken and emasculate the original group which, left in its earlier vigorous form, would have resisted the ascendancy of NL. Without the presence of a larger centre-left grouping the remaining further left Campaign Group could more easily be portrayed as a small, extreme and isolated minority.

Louise Ellman stated: "I've never been willing to curry favour with individuals. I've always wanted to be independent. I felt that I was on my own since the day that I arrived in Parliament. I gathered, from information given to me, that MPs supported other senior people in government in order to get certain positions. I would never do that."

Michael Meacher believed: "There is a substantial domination of the Blair and Brown factions in the PLP. The old right and old left have been virtually eliminated. The left survives at the margins." Clare Short said: "In the old days the Parliamentary groups: the Tribune Group, Campaign Group etc. would feed their views into the formation of policy; but that all ended (with NL)."

What remains is an amorphous, disempowered and ideologically changed PLP, many of whose members pursue personal, rather than political, gain.

Sofa Government and a marginalised Cabinet

Rawnsley[C9-18] identified NL's distinguishing features as being sofa government with minimal cabinet involvement.

The term "Sofa government" describes informal, small group based, development of policy. This phenomenon usually involved the Leader and a few *unelected* policy advisors deliberating in informal meetings. During TB's leadership there was a rival sofa government in the Treasury and, to some extent, in the Prescott camp. TB and GB also had individual meetings with ministers about their area of responsibility, sometimes in small groups. However the full cabinet met only briefly. It seldom, if ever, made policy. Opinions on this topic appear below and include those of two former Cabinet ministers.

Blair's cabinet was allegedly no longer a forum in which business was discussed. It reportedly deliberated in traditional mode only when, as on the Iraq war, Blair needed to claim support for what he had already decided. Meetings tended to be short and were mostly used to brief ministers on what the PM was doing or had already done.

Seldon[C9-19] reported that Blair's mistrust extended not only to the civil service but also to many of his own ministers and Backbench MPs. It appears that he did not want a cabinet but only an advisory policy unit.

In discussing Blair's relationship with Parliament, Simon Jenkins[C9-20] reported that it "fared little better than the Cabinet under the new regime. As he admitted – the Prime Minister disliked attending the Commons, let alone listening to its debates." TB reduced Prime Minister's question time to one session per a week (from two) but the single session lasted longer. Riddell[C9-21] contended that, apart from question time, TB only showed up at the Commons when a Minister needed his support. Parliamentary records show that TB's voting record was worse than any twentieth century prime minister since Churchill.

The phenomenon of NL Prime ministers making policy in camera, closeted with special policy and media advisors, was common to TB and GB. The concept of premier as first among equals became virtually obsolete. Backbench MPs had minimal influence in policy-making (see below). As for the Party on the ground, it was almost totally excluded from making ongoing policy (see Chapter 7).

Simon Jenkins said: "Like Blair (Brown) had always worked informally with a group of loyal friends, people who preferred soccer to symphonies. Shy in the company of strangers – Brown was inexperienced in the group dynamics of somewhere like the Treasury and was certainly unwilling to learn."[C9-22]

Jenkins continued: "Although GB also governed behind closed doors with a close circle of advisers, he extended this circle to include not just political aides but private bankers and consultants such as Baroness Vadera and James Sassoon from UBS /Warburg and Richard Abadie from Price Waterhouse Coopers. Given the dominance of the Treasury, these "newcomers" became virtual spending ministers."[C9-22]

Ministers outside the Cabinet were even more marginalised in policy making than were their senior colleagues. Chris Mullin's diary entry for 1/08/1999 said: "Awoke at 3am still worrying that I have traded my self respect and the respect of others for the lowliest rung on the political ladder – and one which has not the slightest influence over anything that matters."[C9-24]

Governance had become dependent on private friendships and affinities rather than being sanctioned, on the basis of ability, through public accountability exercised through recognised publicly established offices and structures.

Relevant views of MPs included those of Clare Short, who contended: "In the PLP under Blair (although I'm no longer in the PLP I suspect also under Brown) all policy is made at Number 10 in the media suite using information from focus groups. Then the PLP has to be kept in line."

Frank Dobson, reflecting on his time as Secretary of State for Health, said: "We had collective responsibility to pursue the manifesto on which we were elected in 1997. We said that we would stick to the Tory spending limits in our first and second years in office. Therefore I supported that publicly and privately. Being careful with public money was something we clearly needed to demonstrate. Nevertheless I managed to personally inveigle from *TB £210 million pounds extra in* the first year and *£1 billion pounds* in the second year. Although the Government stuck overall to its spending limits promise, I managed to negotiate an extra *£3 billion* for the NHS in England, followed by an extra *£6 billion* and a further *£9 billion* for three years after that: a spectacular amount of money. Even then I produced a memo for Tony Blair saying that: 'Even with that, we would not get as high a quality of health service as we needed. If we wanted to travel first class, we had to pay the first class fare so we wanted more'. This led to a further big increase. TB told me later (when I was no longer Health Secretary) that it *was* my memorandum that prompted the big increase. I found that if I could get to TB, before other people did, on a health issue, I could be fairly influential with him. But I was unable to be so influential on other matters."

Again it was personal influence and interpersonal skills that succeeded with TB rather than detailed and evidenced arguments.

Turning to TB's aversion to Cabinet government and when reflecting on the *Cabinet's role in Government,* Frank Dobson continued: "*In my experience the Cabinet did not really consider anything substantial.* This was partly because TB was happy to take part in discussions with half a dozen people but I don't think he felt comfortable discussing an issue with 20 people." Relating to the Cabinet discussion on whether to go ahead with the Millennium Dome, Dobson said: "TB did leave the Cabinet meeting part way though that debate, he then announced his decision later that day. A newspaper got the notes of that meeting (I don't know how). It reported everything that I'd said except that: 'even if the Dome succeeded, it would still be a waste of money which would have been better spent on something else'."

Linda Riordan thought: "It was supposedly Cabinet government, in Blair's Parliament, but a handful of people made all the decisions. I suspect that most of the Cabinet was not involved. I've been re-reading Robin Cook's *Point of Departure.* That points out that a lot of decisions were taken outside the Cabinet."

After mentioning *the long-standing procedure whereby there were no elections to the Cabinet once Labour got into power*, Gordon Prentice contended: "It's been the Prime Minister's government for the past 12·13 years. On *the powerlessness of ministers* he observed: "Kim Howells was a junior minister in the Foreign Office for three years and responsible for Afghanistan. After he lost his job he made a speech in the Commons saying how corrupt the Afghan political establishment was. He then felt liberated to speak freely about Afghanistan, which he did not whilst in office." Katy Clark believed: "There is a management exercise designed to try to get MPs to deliver an agenda derived from elsewhere (i.e. not from the PLP)."

Not only did the Cabinet no longer rule, but the PLP had little involvement in developing the policy agenda and the government was not bound by firm commitments in the last general election manifesto. This differs from the situation in the Australian Federal PLP (see Chapter 10).

John McDonnell said: "We now have sofa government. The cabinet meets for only about 20 minutes. There was only one vote taken in the PLP over the last 12 years. It was about disciplinary proceedings to be taken against MPs who voted against the whip. There were no votes taken on policy, in the PLP, over the whole 13 years of NL government. All power was centralised in the Leadership. You were given the whip every Friday and required to vote according to it. *All policy emerged from Number 10 and you were expected to support it. Some policies, such as the introduction of university tuition fees, were never in an election manifesto."*

Roger Berry argued: "The truth is that in all political parties the Leadership makes the policy." Alice Mahon said: "When it came to policy making: *NL Leaders saw Parliament and the Cabinet as inconvenient institutions to be circumvented whenever possible."*

Graham Stringer considered: "If you have a huge Civil Service, that is going to stay there for some time, then you need a political core at the centre that is stronger than a few wet behind the ears advisors at Number 10. *If you don't set up a strong cabinet and central government, then civil servants will run every Department because you don't have that strong central direction.* (Since 1997) there's been no real cabinet government. This leaves No 10 struggling with an agenda which pleases the electors but is not necessarily good for the country. The government has not been brutal or centrist enough. It hasn't been prepared to have debates up front. The Leadership has gone over the head of the Cabinet and said to the electorate: 'this is a good thing'."

He continued: "The Labour government culturally have been less than respectful to the House of Commons and the House of Lords has become more influential. This is bad because they're not elected and have more power than previously. I'm against an elected House of Lords. *The real problem is control of the Executive.*"

If some Labour MPs thought that TB was difficult to tolerate; many of them found GB to be worse because of his alleged lack of a collegial approach and reliance on an even closer network of apparatchiks. TB's iron hand in a velvet glove was replaced by GB's iron fist in a steel gauntlet.

Gordon Prentice recalled: "I told my local Party in June (2009) that I didn't think we could win (the general election) with Brown. I've got nothing against the guy personally, but he doesn't have all the tools to be Party leader. His problems are: his Leninist approach; being surrounded by a small coterie of people; bringing on and in people he's known for years (like Ed Balls); and not consulting other people."

Prentice continued: "Leopards can't change their spots. Unfortunately Brown is there and we're not going to be able to dislodge him. After all the people who were never very close to him have gone, e.g. Blears, Purnell and Flint, he's still there. He'll take us all down with the ship. We missed a trick by not asking GB to go earlier. Losing our 20th safest seat in the Glasgow East by-election brought me to that conclusion. I knew that if we lost a seat like that we'd be crucified in others."

Linda Riordan recalled: "GB promised frank debates on the 42 days detention without trial but tried to avoid them. That's why I've come to the conclusion he ought to stand down.

Unrepresentative Parliamentary Select Committees

Appointments to select committees and, at one period, also selection of their Chairs, were used by the NL Leadership to reward and punish MPs. NL was particularly keen to avoid having dissident voices in Committee. This practice was in contravention of the Parliamentary convention that the main purpose of select Committees is to keep the government in check. These committees also exist to improve proposed legislation. This latter process has become more necessary as time for debate on the floor of the Commons has been reduced.

From the back benches: Michael Meacher argued: "The point of select committees is to have people who are holding the Government to account. If you only put loyalists on them you destroy the purpose of the exercise."

Clare Short said: "Even membership of select committees is decided by the whips. Jeremy Corbyn once asked me if he could be on the International Development Committee. He's always devoted great deal of time to international affairs. I said: 'Yes, as far as I'm concerned.' I mentioned it to the then Chief Whip (Hilary Armstrong) who replied:'Oh no, no!' He was never allowed on by NL because those positions were seen in terms of: 'You only get anything if you do what the powers that be want'."

In other words, those MPs most likely to hold the government to account, as would be their proper function, were prevented from being in a position to do so in order to make life more comfortable for the administration. However this was in contravention of the public interest.

Jeremy Corbyn regretted: "Myself, and many others, were removed from select committees in 1997. I haven't been on one since. On one occasion I was told that I was over-qualified! I took that as a compliment!"

John McDonnell said: "No one who ever expressed dissent ever got onto select committees. They were seen as suspect. The question was asked: 'are they one of us?' They were more ruthless than Thatcher."

Gordon Prentice said: "The Chair of the Public Administration Select Committee wasn't consulted about Iraq, although we prepared a plan for that inquiry and proposed a Parliamentary Commission of Inquiry. I'm on that Committee. The Prime Minister made his statement to the House of Commons about the composition and terms of reference of the inquiry without even speaking to my friend Tony Wright, our Chair. Such things must not happen in future."

Backbencher B. reported: "Some questionable tactics are used in Committees. Recently I saw the government refuse two amendments from the Liberal Democrats on the basis of spelling mistakes in the text. So we wasted time by having an hour's debate on this. Many changes to select Committee functioning were not examined because they were not favoured by Ann Taylor who was the Chair in my day. Her predecessors, Margaret Beckett and John Reid, were not interested (in the forbidden areas) either. Robin Cook was keen on reform. The degree of modernisation depended on who was in the chair. For a few days after the 1997 election Peter Pike was Chair. Then Blair decided it was to be Ann Taylor. I think that if we'd had a better chair the committee could not have gone beyond what the government wanted. But they could have focused attention on important things and considered them." Some *backbenchers had committee based achievements to be proud of:*

Louise Ellman recalled: "One of my main areas of work has been on select committees. I've been on the same committee for a long time. Its remit has changed: originally it was 'environment, transport and the regions' but I now chair the Transport Select Committee. I had the privilege of working with Gwyneth Dunwoody (GD). She was the Chair before me. I learnt a great deal and enjoy talking about transport policy and seeing results. This committee work has been productive and satisfying."

She continued: "When GD was Chair the committee was critical of the Government's transport policy, because the government hadn't reversed rail privatisation. The Government decided to deal with us as a Committee and tried to stop GD being Chair. There was a successful, cross party, Backbench rebellion against the Government in 2000. Two things happened as a result: the Government was forced to re-instate GD. That put them in a weak position. The other consequence was that, *within the PLP, there was a change in procedure for the appointment of chairs of select committees. Until then the decision was made by the Government Whips Office. After that, appointments of Chairs were made by the PLP in association with the Government.* However, the final decision was made by vote of the PLP. I was the product of that system".

Linda Riordan reported: "I'm on the Justice Select Committee. Sometimes select committees *do* get the opportunity to shape policy. Some select committees have more power, for example, the Finance Committee. There the government has to listen."

Roger Berry thought: "You can have influence in a select committee. I chair the Select Committee on Arms Export Controls. We were able to tighten up the regulations, not in Committee, but what we said in reports, and in subsequent conversations with ministers, enabled us to shift policy. This (campaign) was a product of what was said in Committee or at PLP meetings. Backbenchers *can* do things, but I wouldn't have passed up the chance to be a minister if I had thought that I could do more there."

Select Committees managed to influence policy sometimes and to exert some independence. There was also the famous victory for Parliamentary Democracy on the appointment of their Chairs. This function was transferred to a democratic vote of MPs in 2000.

According to the conventions of the British constitution, new policy and legislation was always announced, in the first instance, in the Commons by the Prime Minister or by other ministers.[C9-25] *Under NL new policy was more frequently announced at press conferences or elsewhere and timed to catch the weekend papers.* Debating time in the Commons was increasingly limited and all bills were guillotined. This was openly admitted in the 2008 Campbell Diaries.[C9-26]

MP's comments about this change included John Cryer's. He said: "There's been too great a keenness to get policy announcements into the media first, rather than making statements on the floor of the House. The Executive should be accountable to the Commons not to the media." Graham Stringer believed: "The relationship between the Executive and the Commons is more complicated than the press often says. It's not easy to analyse."

The relationship between the NL leadership and the media, and its consequences, was discussed in more detail in Chapter 2.

Limited roles of backbenchers in policy making and the related increase in Backbench rebellions

The decisions Parliament takes about policy are not usually made by backbenchers. This is not a new phenomenon; nor even an NL one. During the NL era the scope for Backbench participation in policy making was further limited by the emasculation of the PLP and the development of sofa government (discussed above). MPs with experience as senior local councillors might become restive because many had experienced direct executive decision making. This may explain why former council leaders were seldom promoted to positions where they might have challenged the leadership.

As their interviews indicate, many entered Parliament expecting to make policy but found that they could only influence it at the margins. This was often achieved by lobbying ministers. Frequently they found it possible to change an operational decision (for instance where a new hospital or school should be located) rather than a strategic policy. A few engaged in the established practice of long haul, single issue, campaigning in concert with interest groups. The NL Leadership was noted for presenting a deaf ear to backbenchers (see above). As backbenchers became increasingly disillusioned, after the millennium, and the imperative to vote against the Iraq war broke personal taboos on rebellion, revolt became common. Realistic threat of rebellion frequently became seen as *the most effective way to secure policy change*.

On influencing policy Cowley wrote:[C9-27] "A mistake made by those who dismiss Westminster is to assume that marginal or sporadic influence on policy is the same as no influence. MPs may not *make* policy, but they do constrain (and occasionally prod) government." This section demonstrates that point.

John Cryer supported Cowley's view, saying: "As an MP you can't have an enormous effect on policy making. You never could. The idea that Backbench MPs could change policy was never true. What you could sometimes do was to persuade ministers to change specific details: you could persuade them to intervene. One example is that numerous MPs lobbied successfully to have a new school or hospital built in their constituency. That's not policy, it is operational decision-making that you can affect. I never knew a Labour minister who was anything other than helpful in that type of situation. However, sometimes they were unable to do what you wanted."

Many MPs expressed regret that they could only have a disappointingly limited role in policy making. Those with senior local government experience tended to consider that they had had more power in policy making in those positions.

Senior backbencher A. claimed: "I don't think that Backbench MPs are generally listened to by the Leadership. I don't think TB had a huge amount of time for backbenchers. *I don't think that I ever met him* but, on reflection, that may have been my choice. *I came to the conclusion that TB wasn't really interested in the Labour Party. To me that was a fundamental mistake for a Leader to make in a Parliamentary system.* When we came to power in 1997 I worked in number 10 and in the Cabinet Office with Peter Mandelson. I was part of the Government management team and we sat in on most important meetings in No 10 for the first 18 months until PM 'fell under a bus'. But we weren't listened to and from our point of view the reforms became increasingly difficult to accept."

Louise Ellman said: "You *can* be influential in Parliament, but it's a very slow process. When I was in local government, we assumed the Labour Group was an important body in deciding what happened. *The task of the PLP is somewhat different. It decides nothing – it is a forum for discussion and debate.* People use its meetings to make points. That's a great shame because it's managed at times and individual members are sometimes abused."

Senior backbencher A. said: "Relating to backbencher's roles: it took me a long time to understand that we weren't there to make decisions and have them implemented. Certainly that was not the intention of the Leadership. Eventually I concluded that it's not the appropriate role for a backbencher. To some extent, the Leadership was afraid of backbenchers. *The real issue is dialectic, the exchange of ideas, the battle for opinions within the nation as a whole. If we are to have a reforming government, first the battle has to be won in the hearts and minds of the people. There is a huge task in that struggle for ideas, for understanding where we are in contemporary Britain, how people see it and giving that expression. There's quite a significant role for backbenchers there.* They don't seem to comprehend it fully. That's a shame."

This contrasts with TB's concept of MPs as ambassadors for the Labour Party who focus on public relations (see above). The NL Leadership did not want MPs to act as political educators and stimulators of dialectic debate. That was regarded as far too dangerous – as Alan Simpson found when he took groups of young Labour supporters out on Teesside to ascertain what sort of policies voters wanted on issues like public ownership (see Chapter 7).

Alice Mahon said: "I felt that, as an MP, I did not have much influence in policy making. We had Backbench committees. I was on the Backbench committee for defence. We were never listened to."

Michael Meacher exclaimed: "You must be joking if you think that Parliament made policy under NL. Parliament is at its weakest since I have known it, certainly in the last 40 years, probably at its weakest since 1945. No substantive policy has been made in parliament, except at one point where we blocked the imposition of power over the 90 days detention without trial (in TB's time) and 42 days (in GB's time). Every other time TB got his way. Why? The answer is: because NL is a power project."

MPs with interests in mundane policy topics, in which many of their colleagues were relatively uninterested, seemed to obtain more opportunities to be involved in shaping them. Some of these were topics which tend to be of greater interest to women, still in a minority among MPs.

Christine McCafferty considered: "I am fortunate in having a good platform for influencing policy. Since 1998 I've chaired the all Party group on "Population, sexual and reproductive health". This is not a select committee but it's quite powerful. I also chair the all Party "Dignity in Dying Group" which includes members of the House of Lords. I'm former Chair of the Parliamentary Friends of Islam group. The first two have been a brilliant vehicle for changing things. I wanted to exert influence through the Department for International Development (DFID). I was on the Development Select Committee throughout one Parliament, but was then given the choice of being on that or the Council of Europe and chose the latter. I can use my interest in population issues there. These Committees produce many reports that appear on the Parliamentary website. Most of these have done quite well world wide and have affected other countries' policies."

McCafferty claimed: "I *have* also influenced policy because the Population, Sexual and Reproductive Health Committee (that I Chair) held hearings on female genital mutilation (FGM) and almost all the recommendations from the hearings and its report were adopted by the Government and led to the law being changed. It became an offence to take a child abroad for FGM. The new law was a private member's bill, but it was the direct result of our work. The bill was introduced by Ann Clwyd MP, a member of our group. The government agreed to give time to such a bill. Another of our recommendations, included in the Act, was increasing the maximum prison sentence for conducting FGM from six months to 14 years. There were issues about money being top sliced from the reproductive health budget and transferred to the HIV budget during the 1990s. Many people were then dying and it was right that money should be passed. Later people were being kept alive with retrovirals. However: the funding should not have been taken from the maternal health and reproduction budget."

She continued: "The Department for International Development (DFID) policy on overseas aid changed as a result of our representations. We also contributed to the Millennium Development Goals (MDGs) on population issues. We successfully got family planning back on the agenda. Good access to family planning is very important in the developing world. Without it you can't achieve HIV control, maternal and child health. As a direct outcome of our report, the Department for International Development (DFID) recently published its HIV strategy, which has references to sexual and reproductive health in every chapter. Their last report never mentioned it. George Bush refused to include universal access to reproductive health in the MDGs because it wasn't acceptable to him politically. However, due to our Committee's campaigning, it was eventually incorporated into MDG 5 as a target."

CM continued: "My only other achievement was getting VAT removed from sanitary products. Originally we thought that GB had broken his promise to do this but, in fact, he had refused to announce it! (presumably because he was too embarrassed to do so). What I have is influence, not power. You can influence things better because procedures have modernised. Order papers were in small print and difficult to read but print has been enlarged. You used to have to submit questions two weeks beforehand and then they might not be delivered by the unreliable electronic service. You can now do it two days beforehand and from your constituency by email. It still takes a long time to learn how you can make Parliament work for you (there is no induction training for MPs). But things have improved and the women in Parliament have pushed for changes."

Important proposed policy changes can apparently be threatened by the male chauvinism of national leaders. This is another argument for improved representation of women in Parliament. Christine McCafferty demonstrated that there were effective ways and means of influencing policy if you found your way round Parliamentary systems and facilities or obtained the ear of a sympathetic minister.

Colin Challen suggested: "The power of a Backbench MP comes in fits and starts – more fits than starts! Private members' bills are one of the key ways you can try to do something. If you can get a bill through. It will be considerably watered down as it goes through its various stages. Maybe you will find three to four years later that the Government has done nothing about it and then they'll include a phrase in the bill that means that they don't have to do anything. That's dispiriting."

Challen continued: "I think that changing government legislation can be done in my area of interest – energy and environment. Alan Simpson, all power to his elbow, led a campaign on energy tariffs with a receptive minister (Ed Miliband) who went out of his way to listen. Most ministers don't bother, in my experience, unless it's to repay favours. The role of backbencher still has some substance but it's quite limited. I doubt there was ever a golden age of Parliament when backbenchers really changed things all the time. I'm not sure I'd want that anyway."

In order to be more successful in influencing policy, backbenchers needed to find their way round Parliamentary systems and procedures and how to take full advantage of these or could develop relationships with the media and obtain publicity for their favoured cause that way (as Austin Mitchell has often done).

John Grogan believed: "The PLP is quite a strange set up. Councillors are used to going to Group meetings where they discuss policies, vote on them and then vote for group decisions in council meetings; except on issues of conscience. In the PLP we go along to the weekly meeting, listen to a Minister and get the week's agenda read out to us. This differs from the Australian Labor Party where they act more like a British local council group note (see Chapter 10). *You learn from your parliamentary experience. For instance I didn't realise, until my second term, that there are Committee Clerks who are servants of the House and not the Executive. Of course whips do not tell you that these officers will draft amendments for you. I came to understand the place better and to realise that you could have influence as a backbencher: probably as much influence as a junior minister.*" (this is also evidenced by Chris Mullin's Diary[C9-28].)

Senior backbencher M. asked: "How do systems work to achieve change? Backbencher X. (name given in confidence) has managed to achieve change for a variety of causes. He has achieved a name for himself but rarely has he been supported by anyone in the PLP." (X was bitterly criticised as a "publicity seeker" by another MP interviewed). "However, because he is liked by the media, he is sometimes cast in a leadership role when many MPs are saying to the government 'Don't do this as it won't work.' There have been other times when the credit was given to X but actually it's been the achievement of many MPs. *While overt rebellion is seen as being what changes things; it isn't always rebellion or vocal rebels who achieve change. Sometimes those who've been involved in things feel frustration when seeing others get the credit; but that's politics.* X wouldn't get more than 20 MPs to agree with him on more than two to three issues. He is a loner, as a politician, and a total maverick, but he's an example of how our political process works."

All Party Groups of MPs are not part of the formal committee structures of Parliament. However they can be used to influence policies. These groups can be set up by any small but viable group of Members. They are allocated some finance and administrative support. They are sometimes regarded with scepticism because, although some have been of a progressive and altruistic nature, others have been established as lobbying vehicles for commercial interests or devices to organise recreational foreign trips for MPs.

Some MPs specialised in a specific policy field, in which they developed expertise, and acted in partnership with voluntary interest groups to progress measures of mutual concern.

Roger Berry asserted: "I believe that backbenchers can do things. You can't use the PLP to be very 'Ra Ra' but there *is* scope for debate there. I spend a lot of time lobbying and talking with ministers. Disability is the area where I've done most work. I have no doubt that backbenchers, along with (interest) organisations, can assert effective influence. In lobbying ministers, I suggest what they should do and indicate that I will be asked questions by the public, the media and/or interest groups about this. I rarely go public with criticism, except in about 2% of cases, where I think it's for the greater good."

Katy Clark contended: "There *are* ways to make a difference. But it's difficult for an MP to have a significant impact on policy. Some MPs can do it by working tirelessly for decades on a particular issue. For example an MP may specialise in housing issues or state benefits. They usually work over years with outside (interest) organisations. Other MPs oppose the government if it's preparing to do 'undesirable' things."

As mentioned above, MPs did raise the standard of revolt in a campaign to force the government's hand. Sometimes the government relented and the rebellion did not have to be taken to the barricades at voting time.

More about rebellions and their role in policy making: Cowley reported: "At 10pm on 18th March 2003, a grand total of 139 Labour MPs took part in *the largest rebellion by government backbenchers since the beginning of modern British party politics.*" He added: "As one concerned minister put it (immediately after this rebellion) 'we're not only facing the danger that Iraq will give some MPs a rebellion habit, it's also that they are not giving us the benefit of the doubt any more'."[C9_29]

Lynne Jones said "Big numbers of Labour MPs did not support the Iraq war, but the Government managed to win the vote because of Tory backing. But for that, Labour MPs would have had a great deal of power and been able to stop it."

Katy Clark said: "There have been quite a number of rebellions against the policies of this government particularly whilst I've been an MP (since 2005). There's no doubt that the Government had to back down over some of these policies as they couldn't get the legislation through Parliament. On other occasions they relied on opposition votes. During my time in Parliament TB and GB seemed increasingly happy to do that. Sadly it didn't appear to be a political problem for them."

Backbencher B., who retired in 2005, recalled that, when he voted against the Iraq war, it was the first and only time he had voted against the Government since 1997. He recalled: "It wasn't the first time I'd tried to do everything possible to try to change government policy, for instance, on things like the privatisation of air traffic control. Having been a Party organiser (prior to NL), I strongly agree with loyalty to the Party. That should come from the top as well as the bottom. I don't easily become a rebel and would never have become a serial rebel. I know that 90% of electors who voted for me did so because I had "Labour" after my name on the ballot paper."

He continued: "It's never easy to pin things down and prove you changed policies. I always tried to meet ministers to attempt to persuade them to change rather than vote against. Hopefully, I helped to modify some policies. In the end you have to decide whether you've got as near as possible to what you want. Do you vote against the Government and troop into the lobby with the Tories? The crazy thing is that when you see the serial rebels voting against the Government you reflect that they don't agree one iota with the opposition they are voting with."

B. recalled that he voted against the Government's proposals on organ donation moving from contracting in to contracting out, but added: "I don't know why they made it a three line whip – I tried to persuade them not to, but I lost. I objected to the freeze in one parent family benefit in 1997. Some of us campaigned against it but supported it after other things to help one parent families were agreed."

John Grogan recalled: "Cowley[C9-30] said that I never rebelled before the Iraq war votes but that afterwards I developed a habit of rebellion – 14 votes. This was more than any other Iraq first time dissenter. That's statistically correct. The time of the Iraq war debates was a very emotional one. My father, who inspired me to come into politics, was dying. I told him that I was going to vote against the war before I did so. He said he agreed with me but hadn't wanted to influence me. Then I heard Robin Cook give his resignation speech. *There is a psychological barrier to voting against your own party for the first time. I then saw a niche for myself in which it would be possible to have an influence on policy from the back benches.*"

Graham Stringer asserted: "There have been more rebellions by Labour backbenchers in the last 12 years than there have been at any time in modern Parliamentary history – massively more than in the 1940s and 1950s. Then there were virtually no rebellions and those that there were involved trivial numbers." Perhaps that was because then Labour Governments were more recognisably Labour in their policies and conduct?

Chris Mullin stated: "Backbench MPs have achieved slightly more than we're some times credited for. This is not necessarily on the floor of the House and not necessarily through rebellions in the PLP. The recent attempt to privatise the Post Office was stopped because of a rebellion and I think that you *can* achieve things that way. Many Labour MPs voted against the Iraq war. I'm glad I was one of them."

The Iraq war vote marked a watershed in the voting behaviour of Labour MPs. The first, 1997, rebellion against the freeze of one parent family benefits mainly involved 58 longer established and more left wing MPs. After that NL MPs were reluctant to protest in the lobbies until the Iraq war votes in 2003. Then MPs voted for the first time against the Government on this issue. Of these 28 went on to rebel again later (some numerous times) and 17 did not rebel again before 2005 (see note 42). Apparently once they had lost their virginity in the lobbies "sinning" again came more easily.

MPs Using the threat of Rebellions

Numerous backbenchers believed that the most effective way to change policy was to threaten a revolt convincingly and be prepared to carry it out if their bluff was called. Lynne Jones thought: "The *only* time that MPs have been able to exert any power has been when there have been rebellions or threats of rebellions. Whenever the government felt that it might lose its majority, it had to buy off MPs to peel away sufficient dissenters to crush the rebellion. It started with the lone parent's benefit. In the end the government made concessions which cost it more in lone parents' benefits than the original proposals would have done. In the case of state pension levels, the cost of righting the wrong decision was higher than not making that decision in the first place would have been. *The only time when Labour MPs have any real influence is when there is a (certain) level of discontent.* One example was the proposed 40 day detention without trial. There was a huge head of steam against that. *Only by using your vote in Parliament as an individual, rather than as a member of the PLP, do you actually change anything.*"

John Grogan said: "Rebellion is almost unheard of in the Australian Labor Parliamentary Group where they have internal discussions and work things out (see Chapter 10). *In our system you have to have some rebellions to make it work.* If you dissent you have to combine with colleagues, sometimes from other parties, to make a case. I recall that Cowley's book shows that there's been more rebellion in the post 1997 Labour years than previously. As a result of an early day motion the Government stepped back from privatising Royal Mail. This issue never went to a vote but, had it done so, they (NL Government) would probably have lost."

Grogan continued: "There's been a host of issues that I've been involved in including the Gambling Bill. At one stage we were going to have a super casino on every corner. Then it went down to eight, then four, then one, then none. Without going into the detail of the rebellion, it was because Parliament wouldn't have it. Sometimes the mere threat of a rebellion will lead to ministerial concessions. It's a game of bluff and counter bluff. At one stage the Home Office wanted to create super police authorities – one for the whole of Yorkshire. Some of us threatened the Minister that if they went with this the Yorkshire MPs would vote to keep the existing police authorities and would support Welsh MPs who wanted the same thing and vice versa. It was all bluff, but the government changed its mind. *From a backbencher's viewpoint: the best type of rebellion is one where the government changes tack before there is a Commons vote.* You don't want to defeat the Government if they show signs of movement beforehand."

Frank Dobson recalled: "When I became a backbencher again we had a Labour government and I approved of most of the things that it was doing. You are reluctant to criticise your colleagues. However I was probably quite influential when I was leading the campaign to stop extension of imprisonment without trial increasing from 28 to 42 days. I played a big part in ensuring that it was defeated." *In the later NL years it became apparent to many backbencher MPs that threat of a decisive rebellion was sometimes the only way to persuade the government to change its policy. Latterly the Leadership seemed to have few scruples about winning a vote by allying with the Conservatives.*"

Senior Backbencher M. stated: "Sometimes there have been sensational revolts. At other times there was no revolt because the Government changed policy. The capacity for rebellion was pretty constant since 1997. The situation we would want is one in which we don't normally end up with revolts as things change, because there is enough capacity to influence without becoming formally and overtly antagonistic (as in the Australian Labor Party system: see Chapter 10). There's been a growing tendency towards rebellion as MPs have become time worn. Those who originally came into Parliament wanting ministerial promotion in a short time, and for whom it didn't happen, got disillusioned and developed a tendency to rebel. The question is how far you should compromise with the system in the interests of your own ambition. *It's not dishonourable to rebel. Rebellion is seen to be less costly in a period where there's a large government majority. The government can accept a small rebellion because they know they can't lose. There are circumstances in which I can rebel so that my conscience is clean.*"

House of Lords issues

The official constitutional *view of the House of Lords* is that it is the Chamber that reviews and revises legislation enacted by the Commons.[C9-31] Further, the symbolic purpose of the Lords is to support the Monarchy and its remaining vestiges of power such as the Privy Council. Its very nature lends respectability to the British class system, in particular to the aristocracy.

Under NL, the Lords revised legislation already reviewed by the Commons but drawn up by the leader and his advisers. In some cases the Lords radically changed NL policies, rubber stamped or minimally altered, in "the other place". But the Lords is not democratically elected, nor are the parties representatively balanced. Therefore it is devoid of democratic legitimacy. Life peerages were introduced by a Conservative Government in 1958. Most life peers are beneficiaries of patronage of the present, or a recent, Prime Minster. Hereditary peers are often descendants of long dead royal favourites or military leaders. That must be a dysfunctional qualification for being a legislator. It qualified their heirs to be what Dennis Skinner MP once described as "Bovver Boys in Ermine".

The number of hereditary peers was reduced to a rump of 100 chosen by their own peers by the House of Lords Act 1999. This was supposedly a first step towards securing a more effective and legitimate upper house. However, the next steps in that process failed for want of a Commons majority in favour of *any* of the proposed alternative models. This was much to the concern of the late Robin Cook when Leader of the House. He claimed: "The constitutional reality is that Britain has a unicameral parliamentary system concealed by an elaborately colourful, but pathetically irrelevant, second chamber."[C9-32]

Under NL Peerages were allegedly used as an incentive to wealthy people to give money to the Party. The hidden agenda was probably that it would make the party less financially dependent on trades unions. Many of TB's and GB's friends were elevated to the Lords and then made ministers. Examples were: Charles Faulkner, Valerie Amos and Cathy Ashton. This device became the alternative to the Commons parachute for securing compliant but, sometimes competent, ministers, but the device lacked any pretention to democracy.

However former MP and cabinet minister Lord S. considered that: "Probably you've got more influence in the House of Lords than you have in the Commons. Aside from financial legislation, every act of Parliament has to go to the Lords. We can only get legislation through with support from Liberal Democrats or Crossbenchers, or with the acquiescence of the Tories. We're quite well organised in terms of whips etc. but voting can't be imposed. Peers are not paid. Three months ago I voted against Labour, for the first time, and eventually the Government dropped that particular clause. There is a lot of expertise here for example: when we were debating the Human Fertilization and Embryology Bill, Professor Robert Winston spoke about it and this was instrumental in forming my view. You get quality in debate on something technical like that."

He continued: "When it comes to drafting legislation, we sometimes get a poor service from the civil service and it has to be re-drafted. There are numerous lawyers in the Lords who have improved drafting greatly. The main representative function of the Lords is, to me, cardinal. I would prefer a 100% elected Lords. This is because Labour Peers have only 30% of the votes and crossbenchers have approximately another 30%. I don't want to be a class warrior. But if you think of the social make up of Britain and the people who get top jobs, the Chief of Defence Staff didn't go to an inner city comprehensive and nor did senior officers of the BMA or of most British professions. I know crossbenchers bring in a lot of expertise; but, due to their backgrounds, they tend to be more inclined towards the Establishment than they do to the Labour Party. That shows in their voting patterns. If you look at the number of Lords defeats that we have had each year compared to the Tories, it's *almost ten times as many*. It's been much higher under a Labour government than a Tory administration."

In recent years there has been a system of "people's peers" introduced whereby the public can nominate people with an outstanding record of service to the public. However few people know who these peers are and it is difficult to assess whether this system has benefitted he House of Lords or not. Lord S. was asked to evaluate thatsystem.

He said: "In the case of People's Peers, one of the problems is that because it's the second chamber everything must go through the Lords. It's almost a full time job. If you don't pay people it makes it quite difficult for them to attend. Retired MPs are used to the pattern of coming to London and back during the week and tend to accept it. Many crossbenchers didn't realise how much time is needed. They dip in and dip out of the Lords to debate their own favoured topics. If you are to have a proper House of Parliament you must have a breadth of individual experience. I'm not sure that applies to the Lords."

Lord S. continued: "My time in Parliament has convinced me of the need to strengthen the powers of the legislature against the powers of the executive. Looking back after all these years I sometimes feel that Minsters are almost civil servants not politicians. That's why political advisors are important but *they* can easily become administrators as well. They should find their way through a political impasse and not just administrate".

MP's Roles in their Constituencies – including their involvement of grass-roots members in policy making

It is necessary to examine *MPs' roles in their constituencies:* which some regard as their most important role. Politically and intellectually very limited demands were made on NL's backbenchers in Parliament. Perhaps their roles in the constituency provided more job satisfaction? In the late nineties a professor of politics, who had been invited to apply for Labour Parliamentary candidatures, told the author that she had decided against applying because "the role (of Labour MP) is now too undefined and its purpose non-specific".[C9_33]

The outcome of having reduced purpose at Westminster and spending longer away from it (probably due to whips urging backbenchers to return to base in the early years of NL government; so there were fewer available to create trouble at Westminster) was that more of MPs' time could be devoted to constituency work. As mentioned earlier, MPs were sometimes able to obtain extra public services or secure additional jobs in their constituency when it proved impossible to change policies at national level.

The growing gap between rich and poor, the continuing blight of inner cities, still usually represented by Labour MPs, and the decline in the availability and quality of social housing, meant that there was plenty of casework for MPs to do on their home patch. In terms of the micro level casework (as distinct from macro level economic, social and political work) many tasks commonly done by backbenchers might have been more effectively dealt with by local government councillors or staff. One pay off for MPs, in respect of less confidential constituency work, was that it could generate helpful publicity in local media.

Louise Ellman said: "I've tried to concentrate on securing services for the constituency such as health services and universities. I've focused on fighting for justice for individuals such as Michael Shields (formerly imprisoned in Romania). It took four years to get justice for him. I've often fought for asylum seekers and other migrants – some sent to Liverpool and living in dreadful conditions."

Christine McCafferty stated: "I've never thought that I haven't been listened to or felt that I haven't been able to achieve things for my constituency. My one disappointment is that I've not been able to get a new building for Todmorden High School, but I'm not quite retired yet!"

Backbencher A. argued: "I think that backbenchers get into all kinds of activities. Nowadays they mainly act as super councillors and try to get houses repaired. They do social work when *what they should actually be doing is tackling the big ideas and major problems that face the world and trying to give expression to progressive values in a British idiom and the context of their own region. In that way they could win over our own people in the way that the BNP have done.* We have to do the same thing for progressive ideas." He continued: "I originally went into Parliament thinking my job was to regenerate my constituency, which the Tories had left in a shocking state. I would just have been a constituency MP. But after I had been a PPS the first time, *I came to the view that I couldn't do what was right to change poverty in my constituency without tackling the whole direction of the government.* Eventually I decided that you can't be a constituency MP and be honest with people when a Government is doing some of the things that NL is doing."

This harks back to Clement Attlee's opinion that doing social work was not enough – you had also to be a "political agitator", or at any rate an assertive politician to tackle problems through political means at a macro level as well as possibly through addressing personal issues at the micro level.

A. added: "It drove me to becoming a parliamentarian trying to do right for my constituency in the Commons. An example of unmet need in former mining areas is the very low level of educational attainment. That's to do with aspiration, values and your attitude to education. In the past local men could always get a job in mining areas without having to achieve much at school. If the NL policies for education were to get schools competing with each other, then some schools would win and others lose. The schools that would lose would be those without much parental aspiration – that was many schools in my constituency. We could not lift my community with those policies."

A continued: "There are industrial diseases and other health problems in mining areas that require first class treatment at local hospitals accessible by good public transport. Many don't have cars. The drift of PFI, and other NHS reforms, was away from local hospitals. The idea of consumer choice, one of the core ideas of NL, effectively worked against people who were voiceless. If you don't know what to do, don't have access to the internet, don't know how to write, how to be pushy in front of middle class people (like doctors and teachers) and don't have the sharp elbows of some better off people, then you'll be left behind. *The job of Labour, surely, is to lift the poorest not to leave them behind.*"

This was an insightful testimony to what backbenchers should have been doing in respect of meeting the needs of their disadvantaged constituents.

Views of CLP secretaries about the roles of MPs representing them

MPs were widely expected to represent the views of their local Party members in their roles in policy making and party governance this time. Therefore, as part of the straw poll of 27 CLP secretaries, they were questioned about this topic:

The first question was: "Sometimes Labour Governments introduce legislation or adopt policies that differ from the policies of the Labour Party as a whole. What do you think that Labour MPs ought to do in such circumstances? Select *one* answer.

a. To support *all* government legislation and polices with their vote. (number agreeing = 0)

b. To negotiate firmly with government ministers to secure the optimum compromise before finally voting with the Government. (Number agreeing = 18)

c. To vote for the Government's legislation or policy only if it is fully compatible with the Party's policy even if that means that the Government may be defeated. (Number agreeing = 7)

d. Don't know. (Number agreeing = 2).

The second question was: "Sometimes crucial issues arise for a Labour Government that were not foreseen in time to be considered through the Party's official policy making machinery. Which of the following factors, if any, should carry most weight with Labour MPs when they decide how to vote in Parliament on these issues? Select up to *two* answers.

a. The MP's own conscience and beliefs. (Number agreeing = 13).

b. The views of Party members in the MP's own constituency. (Number agreeing = 9).

c. The views of electors in the MP's own constituency. (Number agreeing = 10).

d. Decisions of Party Conference, the NEC and NPF. (Number agreeing = 13).

e. Minister's speeches and statements. (Number agreeing = 1).

f. Don't know. (Number agreeing = 2).

Thirdly they were asked: "How far do you think that your Labour MP (if you have one) is accountable to your CLP's General and Executive Committees and to the CLP membership in general? Select one answer.

a. Very accountable (Number agreeing = 3)

b. Quite accountable (number agreeing = 6)

c. Neither accountable nor unaccountable (number selecting = 0)

d. Not very accountable (number agreeing = 3)

e. Scarcely accountable (number agreeing = 2)

f. Don't know/ don't have a Labour MP (number agreeing = 13).

The answers to the first two questions established an expectation of accountability to the Party and its policies rather than to the Party leadership's wishes; but with a preference for negotiating policy change with ministers. Allowing for the 13 CLP secretaries from non Labour held seats etc., who responded, slightly more MPs were seen to be accountable to their CLP than were not.

The toxic Parliamentary expenses issue (summer 2009 onwards)

Many NL MPs arrived at Westminster aiming for, and expecting, promotion and therefore increased salaries. A lot of them were disappointed. The working lives of some of these became boring and aimless. They rubbed shoulders with other MPs of all parties who were considerably richer than they. Some were already abusing the expenses system. After 2005 those in marginal seats sensed that the good times might not last for them. Finally, thanks to NL selection processes (see Chapter 8), many had come into Parliament without ideology, ideals or principles. They lacked political goals to pursue. If they had had any principles they would have been less likely to take advantage of a grossly unfair selection system (see Chapter 8). These people were ripe for milking the expenses system.

After the *Daily Telegraph* started to release the expenses story, in instalments, in May 2009, Winnett and Rayner announced that the story was beginning to register with the most of the wider public to an unprecedented degree. It had become the talk of almost everyone everywhere.[C9_34]

They reported that, a London cab driver told one journalist: "It's about bleedin' time these people were taken down a peg. They lord it over us but they don't like it when people find out what they've been up to."[C9_35]

MPs' offences were compounded by their insistence on redaction (blacking out) of details of MPs' expenses when they were officially published in June 2009.

Alan Simpson MP claimed: "The absurdity of the political culture that we have created has been exemplified in the recent furore over MP's expenses. At the last PLP meeting GB spoke about the complete mess he has made over the appointment of Legg (to examine the expenses issues) and how Legg has made many retrospective rule alterations.[C9_35] People were looking to GB to continue to be their safety blanket and he has got himself into a mess where he can no longer provide that. In my opinion he has lost the will to lead."

Simpson continued: "It became clear to MPs that GB was no longer intending to defend them. He would defend himself, but they were on their own. Then, for the first time in my experience, the Prime Minister was heckled by his own traditional supporters. As leader you must have distanced yourself so much from the PLP when even the dead rise up and dispute with you! It was the contrast that made it so uncomfortable. Previously you could ask the PLP for an illegal war in Iraq and they'd stick their hands up. You could request them to scrap universal benefits in favour of means testing and they'd vote for it. You could call on them to sell off the family silver of public services to private sector speculators and they'd do that. However if you ask them to sign cheques to repay expenses to the Fees Office you have civil war on your hands."

He continued: "My conclusion is that *people with no politics only make a stand when it has become personal. This is a huge shift from the era when we had very important debates in which we were saying that: politics is the personal and the personal is the politics. Were now in a position where, to a large extent, politics has gone out of the window and all that matters is the personal.* The great tragedy is that all this comes at a time in our human evolution when it has never been more important for us to take on the big picture politically."

Other backbenchers were also very concerned about this scandal and what it indicated about the culture and morality of many in the PLP, especially those who had been nurtured by the NL project. They were also worried about the effect that it would have on public opinion. But the more idealistic of them wanted the anger unleashed to be harnessed to secure Parliamentary reform.

Michael Meacher said: "If only anger about the expenses scandal could be fed into a demand for a Parliamentary regime which again provides a system that can hold a government, including our own, to account and which provides genuine accountability. We need public democracy which makes people on the street feel they have a genuine channel to power."

Colin Challen was standing down in 2010. He believed: "The MP's re‑settlement grant (£60,000) is rather generous. I wrote in saying that we should just have some kind of redundancy pay. However some pay is needed because an MP standing down is not always entirely voluntary."

Conclusion

What NL did to the wider Labour Party was explored in Chapters 7 and 8. This Chapter has shown that, like the Party on the ground, the Party in Parliament was taken over, used and abused by the NL leadership to seize power for the hierarchy and their cronies. They then used large Parliamentary majorities to increase the power of their governments.

Jon Cruddas regretted: "The notion of the Labour Party being a pluralistic democracy with its checks and balances, with its different sites of power, are characteristics that we cannot say are now reflected in the architecture of the Party in terms of it's own policy making; in terms of the nature of the PLP; in terms of pluralism; or in terms of debate. They have all gone."

Senior backbencher M. said: "The government is less likely to take notice of the Party when they've a large majority. But when you had government with a large majority that is committed to the ethos of the Party such as in 1945, that government was able to create the NHS and nationalise steel and coal because a comfortable majority was needed to get these through."

John McDonnell quoted Ostrogorski[C9-36] who wrote about political parties in the early 1900s: "The Party replaces the people, the Committee replaces the Party, then the leader replaces the Party and the Committee." McDonnell applied this model to NL. He continued:"In my opinion: Mandelson stamped his mark on the way the Party would operate. Power was centralised around Number 10 and he developed a disciplinary process involving reward and punishment."

This Chapter has demonstrated that members of the PLP had little power under NL. Backbench MPs rarely instigated policy. As Chapter 8 shows, most recently elected MPs had allegedly been hand picked by the leadership as being NL loyalists. At the outset they seemed unlikely to prove rebellious. The leadership was disinclined to listen to *any* backbenchers. However some of their powerlessness was not new; it pre-dated NL.

There *were* effective ways of influencing policy including: lobbying ministers; parliamentary committee work (possibly combined with promotion of a private member's bill); and, when all else failed, rebellion or threat of it. The latter tactic came to be seen by many MPs as the most effective one. Had MPs had some input into policies, for instance in the PLP, before they were laid before Parliament as draft legislation (as in Australian Labor Government see Chapter 10) they would probably have been less likely to revolt in the lobbies.

The PLP was divided into groups where patronage and personality based factions flourished. Many preferred the prospect of promotion to taking a principled stand. The few dissidents who remained, after the candidate selection issues (Chapter 8), were sometimes harassed and occasionally punished. When all that was required, by unprincipled MPs, was a high standard of living then misuse of the expenses system beckoned.

In summary: interviewed CLP officers (representing Party members) did not favour policy making being concentrated solely in the hands of the Leadership. They believed that, where a Labour government ignored Party policy, negotiation with the leadership was preferable to rebellion by MPs. However around 25% of them supported MP's revolt as the first resort in these circumstances. They seemed to trust their local MPs above the leadership because, where a proposed policy was not covered by the election manifesto, the two options most favoured by local Party officers were either implementing decisions of Party Conference or the MP voting according to their own beliefs.

The PLP was relatively powerless during the NL era, but numerous backbenchers (or at any rate the NL loyalists) did not care much about political issues until their pockets and perks were threatened. Almost all power for policy making and preferment passed to the Party leadership.

CHAPTER 10
Old and New Labour: Records on Party and Parliamentary democracy compared

"Our two Scottish terriers are undergoing a month of re-education to make them behave with a bit more of the discipline that should be expected of New Labour dogs"
Robin Cook, *The Point of Departure*, 2003

"Following the ruthless implementation of the policy of ethical cleansing conducted by President Blair, there does not remain one Labour politician capable of articulating a coherent vision of a society based on values that challenge the market orthodoxy espoused by the coalition"
Ian Sharp, Letter to the *Guardian* 13.6.11.

"Far from being supreme, our Parliament has often been supine:
John Garrett MP, 1992

Contents
Introduction

Party Democracy:
A short history of Labour Party Democracy in Britain
Changes to Party Democracy arising from the advent of New Labour (NL)
Comparisons with contemporary Australian Labor Party democracy Parliamentary
Democracy: A history of Labour Party Democracy 1917-1993 Changes to
Parliamentary democracy instigated by New Labour Comparisons with
contemporary Australian Labour Party Democracy

At the 1960 Labour Party Conference Hugh Gaitskell fought his corner. During the defence debate a large nuclear disarmament banner was lowered over the balcony at Labour Conference by the author's, then young socialist, future partner and his colleague who were stewards! The Gaitskellite defence statement was narrowly defeated and a resolution in favour of nuclear disarmament was narrowly carried.

Introduction

The first part of Chapter 10 examines Labour's historic record on Party democracy. This is compared to New Labour's (NL's) record in that sphere (this links with Chapters 7 and 8 where the latter is examined in detail). A central tenet of this book is that NL severely damaged Party democracy in the process of trying to make the Party more electable, taming it and bending it to their ideology and domination.

This chapter then evaluates the state of Labour Parliamentary democracy before, and after, the advent of NL. Democracy within the Parliamentary Labour Party (PLP), especially in respect of participation in policy making, was limited even before 1994.[C10-1] This section of the chapter revisits discussions in Chapter 9. It assesses trends in the development, or retrenchment, of Parliamentary democracy during the NL era. Turning Labour into a Market Oriented Party (MOP) and one with strong autocratic leadership was bound to impact on Parliamentary democracy. Parliamentary democracy became increasingly restricted after 1994 due to the subduing of the PLP by the NL leadership and whips. The effectiveness of Parliamentary committees was also damaged because MPs likely to question the government assertively in Committees were excluded (see Chapter 9). Other MPs were informed by whips that dissidence in Parliament (such as voting against the Government) would preclude them from Select Committee membership (see Chapter 9). However, after revolting against the Iraq war, many MPs became more rebellious and adopted new democratic practices for themselves.

This chapter examines milestones of Party and Parliamentary democracy in the Party's history prior to 1994. This material is presented in chronological order and compared with NL's record. It scrutinises developments unique to NL. Comparison is also made with achievements of the contemporary Australian Labor Party in the same fields.

A Short History of Labour Party Democracy

NL mounted a sustained attack on internal Party democracy. One aim was to turn Labour into a model "Market Oriented Party"[C10_2] (see Chapter 2). As part of this model, members and other stakeholders were prevented, or discouraged, from proclaiming, retaining and sustaining the democratic and socialist values and organisational characteristics that the Party had before the NL take-over. Relatively unrestricted debate (particularly at Party Conference) was ended by NL; as was effective participation in policy making by Labour's grass roots[C10_3] (see Chapter 7). The NL strategy was to change the Party's 'product'3 (see Chapter 2) completely by altering its purposes, values, methods of operating and activities. This can be illustrated by comparing the Party aims and values put forward by respondents in interviews for this book with New Clause 4 of the Party constitution (Appendix 2). The Party was then presented to the public as a totally different organisation – one which all (especially key voters in marginal constituencies) could "safely" vote for.

Such actions were bound to lead to problems. By the late 1990s Labour was a Party in ferment. Disillusion among grass-roots members increased from the late 90s onwards. This was demonstrated by the success of the Centre Left Grass Roots Alliance (CLGA) candidates for the constituency section in elections to the National Executive Committee (NEC). In One Member One Vote (OMOV) postal ballots, the CLGA usually won four out of the six available seats. Between 1998 and 2008 they polled an average 46.8% of individual member's votes.[C10_4] These results were obtained despite campaigning by Party staff (in contravention of Party rules) which aimed to prevent their election.[C10_5] Another strong indicator of growing internal disillusion with NL's functioning was a steady decline in individual Party membership. Furthermore, 21 Labour MPs first elected in 1997 stepped down voluntarily in 2001. Virtually all lacked plausible excuses. Trade unions were in revolt over the increasing privatisation agenda to the extent that TB complained publicly that they were inflicting "scars on my back".[C10_6] Many people who still cherished "Old Labour" values and aims remained in the Party. [C10_7] Manipulation by the Party machine ensured that almost all new entrants to Parliament supported NL (see Chapter 8). Many democratic socialists remained in Party membership in the hope of returning Labour to a democratic socialist path.[C10_8]

These conflicts of aims and values took the Party back to its state in the early twentieth century when the loose federation that was then the Party had *a multiplicity of aims and values operating*.[C10_9] TB's overtures to the Liberal Democrats, prior to the 1997 election, represented a further reprise of the period of co-operation with the Liberals in the early twentieth century. His sweeteners included establishing the Jenkins Commission on Proportional Representation and premature promises to implement its recommendations. TB's strategy was possibly intended to pave the way for a Lib-Lab coalition in the event of Labour not obtaining an overall majority in 1997. Had such a coalition materialised, this would have necessitated changes in the aims and values of the two collaborating parties. The NL leadership probably wanted to attain a de facto Lib-Lab Party.

Labour Party Democracy 1918-1994: a chronological and comparative account. This section reports and discusses major significant events relating to Party democracy. It is presented in chronological order. This period runs from the establishment of the Party Constitution in 1918[C10_10], which turned Labour into a coherent unitary Party with a common set of aims and rules, and with a democratic socialist brief. It makes comparisons between the Party's earlier achievements and its record under NL.

In the early 1920s the British Communist Party, a well organised group, repeatedly demanded to be allowed to affiliate to the Labour Party. When this was refused, Communist members attempted to infiltrate, and win control of, local Labour Parties. The NEC decided to tighten discipline to counter this initiative. Party Conferences between 1922 and 1925 changed rules by banning Communists from individual membership of the Party and from becoming Parliamentary candidates. However they were still permitted to attend Annual Conference as union delegates. Communists had already gained control of a number of local Parties. The NEC disaffiliated 23 of these "captured parties" in 1927 and established new local Labour parties in their stead. The Communists then organised the expelled Parties as the 'National Left Wing Movement'[C10-11]. The Independent Labour Party (ILP) continued as an entity outside the Labour Party and attracted people who desired a more socialist Labour Party. It remained permissible to be a member of both the ILP and the Labour Party. The former continued to sponsor its own Parliamentary candidates. These were generally expected to support ILP *rather than* LP policies.[C10-12] This conflict of interests led to difficult negotiations between the Parties which lasted until after MacDonald's defection in 1931.[13] In 1932 the Labour Conference decided to disaffiliate the ILP. After this the ILP declined nationwide but continued to function on a regional basis. Similar arrangements were extended to the Co-operative Party, as a sister party, and these continued throughout the NL era. However although candidates can stand as both Co-operative and Labour to this day, the two above mentioned remain separate "sister" parties and retain their own policy platforms. Co-operative candidates always stand as "Labour and Co-op".

From this period to the present, people who belong to other Parties, that oppose Labour in elections, cannot join Labour (or become affiliated or registered supporters). They are expelled if they do so.[C10-13] However numerous former members of further left parties including Peter Mandelson, Alistair Darling, John Reid and Alan Milburn held high office in NL Governments. Some members blame them and their allies for introducing the Trotskyist method of democratic centralism as NL's favoured method of Party governance.

After the 1923 general election Labour went into a coalition government with the Liberals, led by MacDonald as Prime Minister. MacDonald appointed a controversial cabinet with many Liberals in senior positions but two ministries went to ILP MPs and a few others to trade unionists. As noted above, in the mid 1990s the NL leadership appeared to be covertly preparing to form a coalition with the Liberal Democrats had the 1997 election result been hung (see above). MacDonald formed a new Coalition Government with Liberals, Tories and a handful of Labour ministers in 1931. *This was done without internal Party consultation.* Immediately the NEC expelled them from the Labour Party. In the circumstances this seemed reasonable. The TUC then ran the Party as the "National Council of Labour". This development followed the expulsions and continued until 1940. This arrangement seems undemocratic and unprecedented.

In 1939 Stafford Cripps and others started a Campaign called the "Popular Front" which involved Labour co-operation with the Communists and the ILP. This led to their expulsion from the Labour Party. This exclusion was endorsed by a massive majority at the following Party Conference. [C10-14]. However they were re-admitted a few years later. Tolerance was not always the Party's norm in earlier days either.

In 1940 the war in Western Europe was going badly. Chamberlain approached the Labour Party to join *a coalition government.* Attlee consulted the NEC who advised that Labour should only join if the National Government was led by someone other than Chamberlain. The Conservative Cabinet chose Churchill. *Attlee then returned to the sitting Labour Party Conference to ask first the TUC General Council and the NEC to approve this agreement which they did unanimously. Attlee's proposal was then put to the whole Party Conference.* They approved the arrangements by a large majority. This was a major milestone in the history of Party Democracy. It was praised by Shadow Cabinet Minister Jon Trickett at a Compass fringe meeting at the 2012 Labour Conference. Attlee's action was made more feasible because Conference was in session at the material time. In the author's opinion, it is very unlikely that TB or GB would have taken the same course of action in similar circumstances. Attlee and colleagues had learnt from MacDonald's disastrous high-handedness in 1931 when he formed a new Coalition Government without prior discussion with Labour Ministers, MPs or anyone else in the Party. After Labour lost the 2010 General Election, Gordon Brown proposed no consultation, outside the Cabinet and special advisers, on any proposals that might be put forward for a Lib-Lab coalition. The contemporary Liberal Democrats consulted widely amongst their MPs and members on the same issue.[C10_15]

During the late 1940s British Communists became critical of the foreign and industrial relations policies of the Attlee Government. Arthur Deakin and other trades union leaders expressed alarm about "extensive Communist influence" in the unions. The TUC General Council issued a warning to unions preventing communists from holding office (and thus being able to exert influence at Labour Conference).

Attlee lapsed in his usual adherence to party democracy practice when he formed the 1945 government without the consultation required by a 1933 Conference decision. He rationalised this in his memoirs. [C10_16] "The passage of time and further experience has led to these (conference) proposals being tacitly dropped". Attlee and Bevin probably wanted to progress the appointment of a cabinet and therefore avoided consultation. At least effective Cabinet government did prevail, which it did not during NL's governments (see Chapter 9). In addition to Attlee's full Cabinet there was a small inner cabinet responsible for broad areas of policy.

Attlee's customary democratic style of leadership undoubtedly gave him the support and self-confidence to withstand repeated challenges from Laski (Chair of the National Executive Committee (NEC)). In these challenges Laski was supported by Herbert Morrison (grandfather of Peter Mandelson). The day after the wartime coalition ended, Laski wrote to Attlee calling on him to resign the Leadership in the interests of the Party. Attlee replied: "Dear Laski, Thank you for your letter the contents of which have been noted".[C10_17] During the 1945 Attlee Government the party on the ground was loyal to the leadership – as were most trade unions. The latter were kept "on board" by Bevin. Many unionists, and individual Party members, valued the public ownership and welfare state policies of the government. This probably minimised discontent within the party in Parliament and at the grass roots.[C10_18]

Gaitskell followed Attlee as leader. After Gaitskell's abortive attempt to replace Clause 4 (see Chapter 6) many in the Party saw using the defence issue as a means to replace the leader. This begs the question as to why Gaitskell fell at this fence when TB managed to clear it? The answer was probably related to timing. The vast majority in the Party in 1994 were willing to please the new leader (who they deemed to be a winner) and to do virtually anything to end 18 years of Tory government. Gaitskell was not new in the job and was a more controversial figure at the material time. He went "on the stump" up and down the country campaigning for a reversal of the Conference decision on defence. HG began to make an impact and a supportive group: the "Campaign for Democratic Socialism" was formed. This campaign coordinated activists, within the Party and unions, in an effort to reverse the Conference decision. It could be compared with the Progress Group formed to support NL. A number of unions were won over. At the following Conference (1961) the nuclear defence decision was reversed by a large majority. This restored some of Gaitskell's credibility in the Party and with the public.

Subsequently Gaitskell was seen to be leading more effectively against the Tories: whose popularity was waning. After Nye Bevan died there was unusually strong opposition from some unions, especially Frank Cousins' TGWU. At the 1960 TUC Conference Gaitskell's new defence policy was approved. However a contradictory resolution from the TGWU was also carried.

Gaitskell died suddenly in January 1963. This precipitated an unexpected leadership election. The contest was between Deputy Leader George Brown, James Callaghan (both Gaitskellites) and Harold Wilson. Wilson had been in Attlee's cabinet and was still on the shadow front bench. In the early 1960s Labour cabinet ministers were also balanced between left and right, instead of the left being largely excluded from parliament, let alone the cabinet, as under NL.[C10_19] Wilson was the candidate of the left and centre-left, who united behind him. Brown and Callaghan split the right wing vote on the first ballot. On the second ballot the result was Wilson 144, Brown 103.

Wilson was the first Labour prime minister to bring his own independent advisers into Downing Street. The most prominent were Thomas (later Lord) Balogh and Lady Marcia Williams. This practice grew slowly until it waxed, by draconian proportions, under NL. These advisors were not democratically elected, but were selected for their abilities and commitment to the Labour Party as a whole. Under NL advisers were allegedly selected for their commitment to the NL Regime and their personal loyalty to the Minister in question.[C10_20]

The incoming 1970 Conservative Government negotiated Britain's entry to the European Economic Community (EEC). The question of entry, and the specifics of the terms agreed by the Government, provoked much disagreement within the Labour Party. The Party held a one day special Conference on EEC entry in July 1972. That did not take a final vote and ensured that all viewpoints were heard. In his closing speech Wilson stated that the terms being offered would not have been acceptable to him. After the Conference the NEC voted to reject entry on the current terms and requested the PLP to do so. This NEC decision was approved by the TUC and by Annual Party Conference. At the time of this Conference the author was a Vice-President of East Leeds CLP (MP then Denis Healey). A constituency meeting debated the issue of Britain's entry into the EEC beforehand. The author spoke against it and was called a "Silly Billy" by Denis Healey. Many think that Denis never actually called anyone a "silly billy" and that it was all in the minds of *Spitting Image* TV scriptwriters. After the special Conference, Denis changed his mind and followed Conference's decision. Subsequently he became "pro-market" again.

During the late 1970s a campaign developed to widen the franchise for electing the Party leader to include individual and trades union affiliated Party members. The original proposal from the Campaign for Labour Party Democracy (CLPD) was that Conference should elect the Leader. That would have given the majority voice to the unions and diminished the influence of both MPs and individual Party members. [C10_21] CLPD then put forward a proposal for an electoral college of fixed proportions of these stakeholder groups. This was agreed and took effect in 1983 (see Chapter 7).

Demand for mandatory re-selection of MPs arose from the widespread view in the Party that MPs, especially those in safe seats, should be persuaded to be effective and hard-working – on pain of dismissal. It was also an attempt to make MPs more accountable to their Constituency Labour Party (CLP). The resolution to facilitate mandatory re-selection was carried at the 1979 Conference accompanied by much sound and fury. However it initially proved to be a "damp squib"; only eight MPs were de-selected during the 1979-83 Parliament. Following de-selection by his CLP, Dick Taverne, the pro-European MP for Lincoln, resigned and successfully fought a by-election as an independent. Michael Foot, then Leader, expressed some unease about Party members' demand for greater accountability of MPs. In September 1981 Foot wrote in the *Guardian*:[C10_22] "There have been periods in the Party's history when the Conference and the Parliamentary Party, or considerable sections of it, have been at loggerheads. Of course … Conference decisions must be respected but they cannot be regarded as absolute, that is, binding in every particular and upon every Labour MP in all circumstances. MPs have other loyalties too, and no less important to their fellow members of Parliament, to their conscience, to their own political judgement, to their country." (Foot omitted the desirable addendum: "to their constituency and constituents").

TB often announced at, or shortly after, Conference, that he would not abide by a Conference decision with which he disagreed. One example was contemporary resolutions carried on council housing in 2004 and 2005. In 2007 GB promoted his "Extending and Renewing Party Democracy".[C10_23] This introduced new Party rules through which there was to be no direct voting on "contemporary issues" resolutions until after the 2010 election. Instead, brief issue statements were to be accepted, or not, without amendment and then passed to the National Policy Forum (NPF) for consideration.

In 1991 de-selection procedure for MPs was made more difficult to activate (see Chapter 8). The first step was that local Party members were balloted on whether a full re-selection should be held. Under NL whips frequently threatened dissident MPs with de-selection. However the threat was rarely carried out until after the Parliamentary expenses scandal in 2009 (see Chapter 9). Then a few "disobedient" MPs, who were often dissident (e.g. Ian Gibson), were forced by the NEC to stand down. However others who were NL, and had allegedly committed similar offences, were left in position. A handful of MPs were de-selected *after* 1983 but before the de-selection procedure was made more difficult. Those that went were dispatched through major efforts, *within their own CLP*, where they had been found wanting.

Around 1980 Campaign for Labour Party Democracy (CLPD) started to press for a change in the development process for the election manifesto. This became a live issue following Callaghan's refusal to include the abolition of the House of Lords in the 1979 manifesto. The contemporary manifesto was then decided at a joint meeting of the NEC and the Shadow Cabinet. CLPD wanted the manifesto to be decided by the NEC alone. They also called for a rolling manifesto – one that is produced/updated every year; whether an election is imminent or not. This proposal did not come to fruition until 1993 (through the establishment of the National Policy Forum (NPF).

Foot identified a problem that was later dealt with (unsatisfactorily) by *Partnership in Power* (1997). [C10_24] This issue was that the NEC did not act effectively as the Party's executive. It was a forum for wide ranging and inconclusive debate of every aspect of the Party's affairs (organisational and political). During the 1980s Tony Benn's supporters held caucus meetings before NEC meetings at which votes were pre-arranged. This may not have been very democratic but it enabled the left to get their way some of the time.

During 1980s the NEC set up a Commission of Inquiry into outstanding constitutional proposals on Party democracy but it *could not agree any* recommendations. A related special day Conference on policy named "Peace, Jobs and Freedom" took place in May 1981. That Conference adopted a comprehensive, and left, policy programme. However there was no clarification as to whether this programme took precedence over decisions made in the normal way at Annual Conferences.

Meanwhile there were growing, active pressure groups within the Party working to improve internal Party democracy. These included CLPD, the Labour Co-ordinating Committee (LCC) (founded 1978) and the Rank and File Mobilising Committee (founded 1980). The LCC was concerned with policy objectives whereas CLPD was primarily, but not exclusively, concerned with constitutional issues. These groups worked diligently but their influence was limited because they had no official status in the Party.

When NL restricted Party democracy and introduced non-democratic socialist policies between 1997 and 2010, one outcome was that nearly two thirds of the Party's individual membership and several trades unions left. By contrast, when Shirley Williams, and others, left Labour for the Social Democratic Party (SDP), announcing they disliked the Party democracy reforms of the early 1980s, very few ordinary Party members resigned with them to join the SDP.[C10_25] That the SDP was created to provide an escape from increasing party democracy was to its enduring discredit. The great bulk of the Labour Party, including most local councillors, remained in membership. Presumably they were content with Foot's approach to Party democracy. Only five members resigned from the four constituency parties in the North East whose MPs had defected to the SDP. Apparently the SDP attracted a different kind of member to that who usually joined Labour.[C10_26] A survey showed that 57% of SDP members were professional or managerial and only 7% from working class backgrounds.[C10_27]

As noted above, after Foot became Leader, divisive issues came to the fore. In addition to pressure for mandatory re-selection of MPs there was pressure for widening the franchise for electing the Party Leader and Deputy (see Chapter 7). There followed wrangling about the proportion of votes that each electoral college section should have. New rules were enacted that required regular elections for the Party Leader and Deputy; or any rate the annual opportunity for such an election to be held. These rules were observed until 1994, but were ignored during TB's and GB's Leaderships.[C10_28] None challenged Michael Foot in 1981, as many were satisfied with his broadly democratic style of leadership. Further it was widely believed he would retire two years hence. In 1981 it emerged that Tony Benn and John Silkin would probably challenge the incumbent, Denis Healey, for the Deputy Leadership.[C10_29] At that time Robin Cook declared: "A leadership cult is unhealthy, undemocratic and profoundly unsocialist".[C10_30] Only two unions balloted their members before voting and they (National Union of Public Employees and Fire Brigades Union) opted for Healey. The election result was victory for Healey, on the second ballot by 50.426% to Benn's 49.574%.

When Peter Tatchell was selected to be candidate for the Bermondsey by-election the NEC endorsed him although some in the Party hierarchy considered him to be unsuitable. After 1994 he would have probably been struck off the shortlist by the NEC. Contemporary party rules stated that *selections could only be overruled by the NEC if there had been irregularities in their conduct*: which was not the case in this instance. Therefore Tatchell went forward as candidate. Under NL selecting *with* irregularities allegedly became the norm and the NEC allegedly set selections aside if the candidate was disliked by the Leadership (often this simply meant "not NL") (see Chapter 8). Selections in which rules were broken were allegedly often upheld if the candidate was the leadership's chosen one (see Chapter 8).

Prior to 1987, CLPs were free to select their own candidates for by-elections. In that year rules changed and all by-election candidates had to be shortlisted by the NEC Organisation Sub-Committee, and endorsed by the full NEC, before final selection by the CLP (see Chapter 8) and Russell.[C10_31] The introduction of NEC shortlisting for by-election candidates was extended under NL to cover all selections six months before a general election (also see Chapter 8).

The controversial long election manifesto of 1983 was a testament to Party democracy. This manifesto, dubbed by some as "the longest suicide note in history" was unprecedented. It included *all* the proposals contained in resolutions carried at recent Party Conferences. Michael Foot saw this as being the appropriate method of showing due respect for decisions debated and adopted by Party Conference. [C10_32] In September 1981 Foot wrote: "Let us work together to ensure that the Party Conference and the Parliamentary Party embark on a new period of partnership and understanding."[C10_33]

After the 1983 general election Neil Kinnock was elected as Leader under the new electoral college system. Party democracy has frequently been restricted because of leadership fears of publicised internal dissention which usually upsets the electorate (see Chapter 3). Both Foot and Kinnock publicly quoted Bevan's speech "Never underestimate the passion for unity in the Party, and never forget that it is the decent instinct of people who want to do something."[C10_34] Foot had the right democratic approach at the wrong turbulent time in the Party's history. Kinnock wished to enforce party discipline, latterly through authoritarian rule, but often failed. Neither persuasion by Foot nor dictatorship by Kinnock could evoke this passion for unity. Party democracy reforms were enacted and, in Foot's case, enabled, by his democratic leadership approach. Unfortunately the accompanying publicised strife harmed the Party's image. Opinion polls showed that open public debate was often construed by electors as warfare.

In the context of Party democracy Foot and Kinnock took the lead in constitutional action, through the NEC and Conference, to expel the undemocratic Militant Tendency and avoid the creation of Labour Party black sections.

During the Kinnock and Foot leaderships, the Party's policy continued to be made by Conference, in the established way. Policy was created by considering and voting on NEC Statements and debating, amending and voting on policy resolutions (sometimes composited, that is, amalgamated (see Chapter 7). One problem with this relatively democratic system was that sometimes resolutions passed over the years, or occasionally in the same year, contradicted each other. This was pointed out several times by Foot during his leadership. Before NL, when a resolution received a two thirds majority of Annual Conference votes it had the automatic right to be included in the next general election manifesto. Foot and Kinnock adhered to this rule. Other policy was made by the NEC and sometimes by the Shadow Cabinet in concert with the NEC. All NEC policy documents had to be ratified by Conference.

From the early 1980s the CLPD had called for a rolling manifesto: one produced /updated every year whether an election was imminent or not. This method of operation was adopted through the NPF (see Chapter 7). The NPF was established informally by Conference in 1990 (and was operational from 1993). In 1997 Conference agreed to set up Policy Commissions (see Chapter 7). These would manage the Party's policy documents.[C10_35] However, although the NPF met eight times before the 1997 election, it was not mentioned in the Party rule book and had no official status or policy making powers until that year. [C10_36] Meanwhile, the formal powers and procedures of annual conference remained the same.

In 1984 new leader Neil Kinnock proposed OMOV (one member one vote) for Parliamentary re-selections but this was defeated at Conference that year. The next year the NEC set up a working Party on "widening the franchise". In 1987 Conference rejected using OMOV for Parliamentary selections, but agreed a local electoral college that combined trades union votes with OMOV for individual members instead. This operated in selections up to the 1992 general election. In 1988 Conference rejected a motion to put one woman on every Parliamentary shortlist. However, between 1989 and 1991 Conferences accepted internal quotas for women delegates to Conference, NEC, NPF, CLPs and branch officers. In 1991 Conference agreed that unions must ballot their members before voting in the electoral college. Conference 1993 decided to drop local electoral colleges and to replace them with OMOV for Parliamentary selections (see Chapter 8).

In his early years as Leader, Kinnock faced much opposition on the NEC. On this Committee the Benn faction then had a majority. By the end of his tenure as leader he commanded a majority on the NEC, which invariably did his bidding.[C10_37] (and see Chapter 7). This majority had been achieved by political manoeuvring and manipulation. In his defence Kinnock (unlike his NL successors), did not allegedly allow *breach of* Party rules to achieve his own ends. However it could be argued that the Party did not explicitly sanction the initial makeover of style and presentation which was promoted by Kinnock, Mandelson and the Shadow Communications Agency (SCA). The Party did accept these changes when they were ratified by Conference. The red rose "new look" was criticised at Conference by a few including the late Eric Heffer MP.

From the mid-1980s Kinnock used some strategies that constituted threats to Party democracy. On TV AM, in May 1986, he threatened to turn the Labour movement against its own left if they thwarted a Labour Government from implementing its policies. Measures to reform the left-leaning Party Young Socialists were introduced. These reduced their maximum age from 26 to 21. This was intended to exclude older, further left, organisers.[C10_38]

In response to the 1987 policy review there were fears, expressed by Ken Livingstone at Conference, that if unilateralism were abandoned it would split the Party.[C10_39] The policy review began with a statement of "aims and values" (see Chapter 2). This policy review generated antagonism within the Party by praising free market values.[C10_40]

Sometimes, during Kinnock's Leadership, Party policy was distorted in the process of developing Labour's glossy election prospectus. This occurred during the 1987 election campaign.[C10_41] Drower reported that, immediately after the 1987 election, Kinnock "decided that somehow Labour's policies would have to be utterly transformed".[C10_42] A major policy review followed. Kinnock, and advisors such as Tom Sawyer, decided that this had to be conducted by various methods which *included* sounding out the views of Party members. There followed a "Labour Listens" exercise which sought opinions of Party members and the public. This led into a four year review process: two years to develop policies and two years to "sell" them. This scenario suggests that Labour was still operating as a "Sales Oriented Party". [C10_43] (see Chapter 3). The Party's policies still had to be agreed by Conference item by item, a system which was abolished in 1997[C10_44] (see Chapter7).

The left worried that this policy review might result in abandonment of traditional democratic socialist policies. They regretted not contesting the Leadership and Deputy Leadership at the 1987 Party Conference. This contest was then feasible and permitted in accordance with the Party constitution and practice. After 1997 such an election was precluded by refusal of the Party machine to distribute the nomination forms each year as was ordained by contemporary Party rules.[C10_45]

In January 1988 the left Campaign Group launched "Agenda for Change: a Campaign for Socialism Programme"[C10_46]. This called for wholehearted support for contemporary industrial action being conducted by nurses, seamen and teachers and reaffirmation of support for collective action. In 1988 Benn and Heffer challenged Kinnock and Hattersley for the leadership and deputy leadership but lost.

Subsequently it was revealed that, in summer 1991, Kinnock's office proposed dropping some pledges in Labour's democratically agreed policy programme. These included increased pensions and child benefits. *This proposal was abandoned for fear that Labour would be considered, by the public, to have no principles left*. During the 1992 election campaign Kinnock claimed, on BBC TV *Panorama*, that changes in the domestic and foreign policy climate since 1989 meant that the "Meet the Challenge" policy review (also agreed by the Party) was now obsolete.

Since Labour's earlier years, leadership allies, who were usually the majority on the Conference Arrangements Committee (CAC), sometimes used compositing to alter the meaning or emphasis of Conference resolutions or to omit a significant point (see Chapter 7). Frequently resolutions were ruled out of order and often Conference was asked to agree to remit them to the NEC for further consideration. Ballots for constituency representatives on the NEC were elected, quite properly, by Constituency Labour Parties (CLPs) mandating their delegate(s) to vote for the candidates of their choice at Conference. This system continued up to the death of John Smith.

As Chapter 7 indicates, during the NL era Conference Arrangements Committee (CAC) elections were allegedly manipulated by the Party Machine. This was to secure the election of members who would do the Leadership's bidding. During the NL era the CAC frequently disqualified resolutions disliked by the Leadership (e.g. concerning modernisation of Trident in 2006). It also had power to decide how many contemporary resolutions would be debated (usually as few as possible). In 1997[C10_47] a Conference decision agreed that up to eight contemporary resolutions could be debated each year, four selected by trades unions and four by constituency delegates. These had to be chosen from a CAC selected shortlist of those submitted. This practice continued until contemporary resolutions were withdrawn, subject to review, in 2007. The process was re-instated after 2009.

John Smith was mindful of the need to avoid antagonising the Party. When Neil Kinnock wanted to stand down after the 1992 election, Smith wisely declared he would have preferred Kinnock to stay on.[C10_48] Clare Short believed thought that NK was acting badly saying: "The instigator of the plan to elect a new leader with indecent haste was Neil Kinnock. He appeared to be acting alone. Many of us suspected that he just could not bear it any more and wanted to go quickly … he does not trust the Party to have a civilised election".[C10_49]

The NEC intervened to delay the election for three weeks. Many in the Party wanted to demonstrate unity by giving Smith a walkover. As in 2007 with GB, this could have caused ill feeling within the Party and country. Brian Gould was keen to stand and gave the Party a contest in which Smith triumphed. The Party rule, then in force, demanded that to enter the starting gate as a candidate for Leadership or Deputy: an MP must be nominated by at least one fifth of the PLP. This rule was introduced in 1988 following the Benn/Heffer candidature. This rule prevented a full leadership contest in 2007, with adverse consequences. The problem occurred then because no other candidate could quite attain the required number of MPs' nominations.

When the 1992 Deputy Leadership contest followed, the union block vote in the electoral college was controversial. Despite John Prescott's considerable union support, Margaret Beckett won with 57% of the vote compared to Prescott's 28%. John Smith was criticised for being the candidate of the unions. To counter this accusation, Smith hastily declared his support for the principle of One Member One Vote (OMOV). He promised: "We will have OMOV for all our key decisions, but we have to find a way in which OMOV is consistent with organisations being in the Party."[C10_50]

As had happened previously, after the 1992 election defeat, the Party and its Conference, became preoccupied with internal Party democracy questions. These included the union block vote and the selection of Prospective Parliamentary Candidates. These took priority over discussing political questions such as economic management.[C10_51] In late 1992, with Smith's support, the NEC set up a working Party to examine links with trade unions. This group was directly answerable to the NEC.[C10_52] The NL Leadership *never* emulated this course of action. They took the back door route of seeking alternative (private) sources of funding and trying to persuade Sir Hayden Phillips[C10_53] to curtail union political funding.

John Smith's greatest contribution to Party democracy was his championship of OMOV for Parliamentary selections. For the sake of this he put his leadership on the line in 1993 (see Chapter 8). The principal of OMOV in selections and elections remains important. This system is now also used to elect CLP representatives on Labour's NEC and its NPF. What Smith probably did not foresee was the way the system would be deviously implemented by the Party machine after his death (see Chapters 7 and 8). This mode of implementation institutionalised nepotism and cronyism and entailed total denial of equal opportunities. The converse device was the "Monty Python Foot" used to exclude almost all left-leaning candidates and many of those from working class occupations (see Chapter 8).

Changes in Party Democracy arising from the advent of New Labour

In order to gain total control of the Party, as well as to change its public image, there was a savage onslaught on Party democracy from the moment that TB became Leader. This is discussed fully in Chapters 7 and 8. It included the escalation of manoeuvres started by Kinnock and Mandelson from the late 1980s onwards (see above). It also consisted of innovations in Party governance of a type that had no place in the Labour Party before 1994.

After constitutional changes including the New Clause 4 of the party constitution in 1995, Tony Blair boasted at the next Labour Conference: "We have transformed our Party – our constitution rewritten, our relations with the trades unions changed and better defined for today's world, our Party organisation improved."[C10_54]

These developments marked the advent of the top-down managed, command and control party. That change was secured by means of rule changes, mainly between 1995 and 1997, but also, over time, through subversion and manipulation of these, and older, regulations. This was done by the new cadre of Party staff, allegedly on the direct orders of the leadership (see Chapter 7). The unsatisfactory nature of NL's methods of party governance was highlighted by Angela Eagle MP, then Chair of the independent LabOUR Commission[C10_55] in 2007.

The NPF was beefed up and Conference disempowered by the Partnership in Power Agreement of 1997 Russell[C10_56] (and see Chapter 7). Each policy document was debated in a loosely consultative fashion within the Party over two years and views submitted to HQ and then to the NPF. Conference had no direct control over the detail of these policy documents as they had to be accepted or rejected as a whole (see Chapter 7).

Under New Labour, more internal groups which focussed on Party democracy, were formed. The most prominent of these were: Labour Reform, Save the Labour Party (of which the author was co-founder), the further left Labour Representation Committee (LRC). The last was not restricted to Party members. In 1998 the Centre-Left Grass Roots Alliance was founded to organise centre left and left candidates for the NEC in the CLPs section. The Grass Roots Umbrella Network (also co-founded by the author) was established to co-ordinate and brief Conference delegates to help them to withstand leadership instigated interventions from party staff at Conference. Meanwhile that grand old organisation CLPD continued organising changes to Party rules to promote internal democracy. The Labour Co-ordinating Committee (LCC) was captured by the right and virtually disappeared during the 1990s. Development of these organisations, their aims and activities was a response to the savage attacks on party democracy under the NL regime. The Campaign for Labour Party Democracy (CLPD) continued to circulate model resolutions for Conference and model Party rule changes to their members and supporters.

Concerns about marginalisation of Party members in policy making were ignored by the Party hierarchy. This was demonstrated by the introduction of the "Renewing and Extending Party Democracy" regime at Conference 2007.[C10_57] This innovation terminated all voting on policy resolutions at Conference for a trial two year period (it was restored after the 2010 election). In this way the Party members surrendered their remaining rights to make policy at Conference, probably because the phantom general election seemed imminent.[C10_58] The majority of Parliamentary candidate selections were undemocratically controlled by the Leadership right up to the election in May 2010 (see Chapter 8). Further, the NPF, which was supposed to draft the 2010 election manifesto, did not meet for over a year beforehand. The election manifesto was drafted by a working group led by Ed Miliband. This number of internal pro-democracy organisations, and extent of their campaigns, was unknown during the Party's earlier history – they had not been so necessary.

A YouGov poll of Party members undertaken for the LabOUR Commission in 2007[C10-59] demonstrated their overwhelming majority verdict to be that the role of individual Party members in policy-making had been reduced to "very little or none". Only absolute loyalists were permitted to speak at Conference (unless they proposed a rule change or contemporary motion). Loyalists frequently delivered speeches written for them by Party staff. Conference had become a vacuous jamboree designed to showcase Ministers (see Chapter 7).

Many respondents, questioned by the author, deemed the NPF to be ineffectual and in thrall to the leadership. Those interviewed, after that event, welcomed the 2009 Conference decision to transfer the vote for the NPF's constituency members from Conference delegates to a secret OMOV postal ballot of all members (see Chapter 7).

Another tactic used in managing Party members was the frequent dispatch of emails purporting to be from the Leader, cabinet members and senior Party officials bearing messages containing the NL Party line. Unfortunately these emails were usually written in a format that made them technologically impossible to reply to. When occasionally e-messages were in consultative mode it was rendered technologically impossible for members to share their ideas directly with peers or their MP. The estimated 30% of Party members not online did not receive these Orwellian, Big Brother style, messages at all.

Why did individual, and trades union affiliated, members of the Labour Party give away their democratic freedoms for a mess of New Labour pottage by voting for NL's constitutional reforms between 1995 and 1997? As Billy Hayes pointed out in interview, members were desperate to return a Labour government after 18 years of Tory rule. They were persuaded that this goal required them to surrender their democratic rights and to deny Labour's history, values and traditions. In 2007 a further surrender was made in the mistaken belief that a general election was imminent. The NL revolutionary changes were supposedly made in the interest of winning elections by a Market Oriented Party (see Chapter 2). After the latter sacrifice; it is ironic that, in the 2010 general election, the Labour Party polled only 0.7% less of the vote than they did in 1983. That was during Foot's leadership, which was so despised by NL's protagonists.

At the time of the 1997 general election the Labour Party had 400,000 individual members. By the time of the 2010 general election it had 'mislaid' nearly two thirds of them.[C10-60] The Party membership were accustomed to meet for political and social events, to debate and participate fully in Party policy making". One aspect of the co-operative working of party members was fund raising to help fund elections and thus secure shared national and local political objectives. This was often achieved through organising social events which virtually ceased during the late 1990s.

As the Party shrank, and became more desperate for funds, individual subscriptions were raised to a level which people on lower incomes could scarcely afford. The consequence was that membership declined further and the least affluent often dropped out. So much for Labour being the Party of the working class!

Comparison with contemporary Australian Labor Party (ALP) Party Democracy

This discussion is by way of comparison with the record of New Labour and to ascertain what UK Labour can learn from its Australian Sister Party. It is based partly on the author's 2010 interview with Federal Minister Gary Gray and the ALP's earlier Hawke Wran Report (2002)[C10-61] on the contemporary state of their Party. That was the most recent review of the functioning of the ALP during the NL era.

Federal Minister Gary Gray reported: "The State parties elect delegates to attend national ALP Conference. At National Conference we have only delegates of individual party members (not of trades unions). We have affiliated trades unions but we don't have any other affiliated organisations. Within our Party *State* arrangements and conferences, unions generally comprise about 50% of the voting block." UK national Labour Conferences, although disempowered by NL, remain more representative. However, under NL, Regional Conferences ceased to discuss and vote on policy resolutions." At least Labour still has significant union delegations at our national conferences.

He continued: "We believe that our Party Conferences are masters of their own destiny and may choose to debate anything at all. The opportunity and capacity to speak at ALP Conferences tends to be open. I've known it to be an issue that people who wish to are not allowed to get up and speak – unless they can't convince enough people in their own State/area/faction groups that they are worth hearing. But it's not the Leadership, or their agents, that decide who can speak." (This differs from the NL model where speakers were carefully selected and their speeches frequently written for them).

Gray continued: "The ALP model of government and the authority given to the Executive is a deeply pragmatic thing. But *in our policymaking there's lots of consultation and that gives people ownership.*" NL should certainly have retained an approach to policy making which gave members a sense of ownership (see Chapter 7). Over its history UK Labour has fared better by having a constitution that spells out its values, aims and objectives in order to provide appropriate direction (even when that is in a constitution diluted by NL).

GG reported: "We don't have election manifestos, but we do have election policy. In the course of an election campaign we announce numbers (for example 40) of different policies for the election. These become mechanisms for obtaining political support, focuses for creating campaign events and mechanisms for addressing particular wants and needs as we progress our way into an election." Perhaps Labour is better off having a manifesto which clearly states our programme's case to electors and campaigners alike: a focus for our "sales orientation". This Labour approach probably has more durability than does a loose collection of variegated policies. It can be more effectively linked to our set of underpinning values and aims (see Chapter 1). The issue under NL was *how* the manifesto was constructed and the roles of major stakeholder groups in that process.

The Hawke Wran Report (HW)[C10-62] quoted a 2002 survey of Labor grass-roots members: "Many Party members view National Conference as a stage managed affair run by factional leaders, devoid of real policy debate (here they agreed with Gray). They continued: "We share *the concern of many members that vigorous debate on controversial issues is being avoided for the sake of a purely cosmetic unity.* For a Party like ours this is bound to be ultimately counter productive." This is a long-standing issue for UK Labour too.

H·W recommended that the size of national and state conferences be increased in order to maximise the numbers of grass·roots members involved and to ensure that delegates from rural areas were present; delegates from cities tended to predominate. HW also called for: "Increased participation in policy debate." Gray continued: "National Policies *are* debated at National and State ALP Conferences. But what may pass between side A and side B may sometimes not be described as a policy debate. Conferences can move amendments that differ from the established agenda." Perhaps Labour should consider this? He continued: "It is generally accepted that *a Labor Government would not breach the platform (collection of decisions/de facto manifesto) of the National Conference*. However Government may not implement *everything* in the platform. Because an item is in the Party platform it doesn't mean that it will be Labor Government policy. The ALP remains committed to giving the trades unions a major say in policy making." Whilst these arrangements were not flawless they were an improvement on those adopted by the NL Party.

The HW Report also recommended that: "The Federal ALP consult regularly with representatives of large and small business sectors, social welfare and community groups[C10_63] (about policy development). However these arrangements were not incorporated into the formal Party machinery as they were into the most senior UK Labour Joint Policy Committee and Policy Commissions structures under Partnership in Power 1997.[C10_64] More informal arrangements would have given the NL Party, greater flexibility in consulting interest groups. HW saw an enlarged National Conference as one way of opening out the policy development process (NL had no such aspirations and continued to rely on the semi· impotent NPF). After the 2001 election defeat, the ALP decided to revisit all policies. An exception was their opposition to the full privatisation of Telstra. Telstra was previously their national, publicly owned, telecommunication corporation. Shadow Ministers held extensive consultations at many levels to review policies. These included Party forums, meetings and discussions with interest groups and academics across the country. Their remit covered reviewing ALP policy making machinery including National Conference, Policy Committees, stated Platform Objectives (Manifesto) and the ALP's own think tank (Chiffley Research Centre). They expressed concern that a policy vacuum had been filled by policy resolutions passed by Parliamentary Caucus (Parliamentary Labor Party) and policy drafts from their Shadow Ministers. Here was a method of policy making which NL should have emulated.

To address the lack of grass·roots participation in policymaking, HW[C10_65] recommended having one permanent National Policy Committee (similar to Labour's Joint Policy Committee). Its task was to oversee the co·ordination of platform development in the run up to National Conference. To this end it was to conduct rolling reviews of the ALP's policies. HW[C10_66] authorised the Labor NEC to appoint members of the new committee. They were directed to include Party members with considerable experience in policy development and to work closely with State Policy Committees. They could co·opt non·voting members with expertise relevant to the policy area being considered and contribute to debates at National Conference. This resembled some exercises mounted by Kinnock and his NL successors.

HW[C10_67] called for State ALPs to run training schools to be addressed by the Leadership and Ministers for candidates, aspiring candidates and young Party members.

These were to be complemented by mentoring and skills programmes. Such programmes were especially necessary for candidates for the Senate where complex issues were generally dealt with. These were activities that NL sometimes emulated.

ALP members requested HW for periodic performance reviews and other measures to ensure accountability to selectors and electors. *Australian Parliamentarians automatically had to face pre-selection (i.e. a new selection) every general election.* Perhaps NL should have done this too, or at least made de·selection easier when for legitimate reasons. In the State of Victoria members could call for the opening of an uncontested re·selection if 20% of them were unhappy with the outcome. HW recommended the extension of this system to the whole of Australia and also a new process for local Parties to report on activities of their local MPs to Federal Electoral bodies.[C10_68]

Members were advised to give MPs and Senators details of local events in which they could participate. HW recommended:[C10-69] "Local branches and MPs should institute, and participate in, regular joint community consultation processes to raise the profile of the ALP and provide feedback on policy and Party initiatives" (for NL's dubious community consultation practices see Chapter 7).

HW[C10-70] considered that, as in the UK, party branch meetings had become procedure driven and were often difficult for new members to follow and appreciate. They called for the Party to bring imagination and flexibility to the running of branches. There *needed to be a structured orientation programme for new Party members*. They aimed to "add to the membership experience and help and *rebuild local ALP communities.* "[C10-71] This latter imperative is now vital for the Labour Party. To this end HW suggested setting up policy area based branches (instead of geographically based ones). These would focus on debating a specific area of policy. They would feed into national and state ALP policy making machinery. They also mooted online branches.[C10-72] In the UK there would have to be online feedback between members. Face to face participation is probably more satisfactory where there is no distance or transport factor: as there is in much of Australia outside the major cities. HW also suggested online policy forums – these would only be worthwhile if contributors could read and respond to what others have proposed. Which they were not been permitted to do during NL's online policy consultations.

HW proposed running occupation, workplace and employment related branches at state level. Earlier Labour and NL's experience with these was not encouraging; they seldom proved popular. To involve more young people, HW called for a rule change to permit establishment of University and FE College based ALP branches (not yet tried in UK – only those for Young and Student Labour). They also envisaged supporters' clubs. These would be clubs that met in person, raising funds and campaigning . They would not be isolated individuals passively subjected to internet based "mushroom management" (kept in the dark and fed manure) as were NL's "supporters".

Rank and file ALP members would be offered "mentoring opportunities, education forums, online civics and party courses, campaign and branch manuals and other communication strategies in order to enhance the branch member experience and quality of their contribution".[C10-73] A lesson for the UK Labour Party is that if you want something from members, including their continuation, you have to give something in return to make membership interesting and satisfying for them.

Parliamentary Democracy (UK)

Trends in Labour Parliamentary Democracy 1917-1994: this section identifies significant trends and events in the field of Labour Parliamentary democracy between 1917 and 1994 and compares these with aspects of the development of NL Parliamentary democracy between 1994 and 2010.

When, in 1931, Ramsay MacDonald formed the coalition with the Conservatives, he failed to consult the rest of the PLP or the Party on the ground. Unsurprisingly, the PLP and the wider Party went their own way.

As Leader, Attlee was a champion of independence of the Parliamentary Labour Party from the NEC. He said: "At no time and no circumstances has the NEC ever sought to give, or given, instructions to the PLP – the Chairman has not the power to give me instructions."[C10_74] The 1945 mixed intake of Labour MPs contrasted both with the all working class PLP of 1906 and with the narrow middle class/political class backgrounds of many candidates eased into Labour seats during the NL era (see Chapter 8).

Self-discipline in the PLP was so great, in June 1946, that standing orders prohibiting MPs from voting against PLP decisions were abolished. To promote Parliamentary democracy, between 1940 and 1945 the PLP set up an "administrative committee" *whose members could not be ministers.* Ministers could attend as observers from time to time. H. Lees Smith MP became Acting Chair of the PLP, which then made him unofficial Leader of the Opposition. This seems a strange arrangement now; but perhaps it acted as some guarantee of Parliamentary democracy.

In 1950 the small majority meant that Labour MPs had to be ever present at Westminster. However several of Labour's senior figures, including Attlee, fell ill. When Attlee entered hospital in 1951 public arguments broke out in the cabinet. The first salvo between the Bevanites and the Labour leadership exploded in a 1952 in the context of a Commons debate on (UK) re-armament. Attlee moved an amendment to a Conservative government motion but 57 MPs from the left opposed it. As standing orders were in abeyance, there was no formal breach of Party discipline. However the PLP immediately re-imposed standing orders in an effort to gag the rebels. Anyone who rebelled was likely to be expelled from the PLP and be forced to stand as an independent at the next general election. Some of the Bevanite leaders were prominent political journalists (e.g. Richard Crossman and Michael Foot). They could readily get their work published in *Tribune* the *New Statesman* and elsewhere without breaching PLP discipline. At the 1952 Party conference the Bevanites won six out of seven constituency party seats on the NEC (at this time and until 1997, the CLP seats were usually occupied by MPs). Shortly afterwards Bevan was elected to the Shadow Cabinet. The TUC demanded the dissolution of the Tribune Group. Attlee then *requested* the PLP to ban all sub group activity. This was agreed by a large majority. Attlee did not take a unilateral decision in these circumstances as his NL successors would probably have done.

For all their record of control, neither TB nor GB tried to have the parliamentary Tribune Group (which had been re-instated) or Campaign Group banned. They simply joined the Tribune group themselves and allegedly diluted its work. This led to its demise (see Chapter 9). Then they took action within the Party to prevent anyone who might possibly join left groups from becoming an MP (see Chapter 8).

In 1952 Bevan interrupted Attlee's Commons speech on keeping the H bomb. The Shadow Cabinet, at the instigation of Herbert Morrison, decided to withdraw the whip from Bevan. This was confirmed in the PLP by a narrow majority. Morrison then tried to persuade the NEC to expel Bevan from the Party altogether. However many felt that this would cause damage to the Party by creating a martyr. Attlee proposed a compromise whereby Bevan could stay if he apologised for interrupting and thus it was settled. Parliamentary democracy was imperfect even before NL!

From 1957 Wilson and Bevan were both in the shadow cabinet. This deprived potential rebels of leadership. This tactic was one eschewed by Blair and Brown who simply marginalised and excluded potential rebel leaders. According to Cowley the resulting frustrations eventually led to many rebellions in the PLP.[C10_75]

After Bevan's death, the majority of the PLP supported Gaitskell's defence statement, despite his defeat by Conference on defence policy. Gaitskell had defied the Conference decision and announced that he would "fight, fight and fight again to save the Party he loved" – by securing a reversal. This high handedness was in conflict with the Party's contemporary traditions and many were dissatisfied with his continuing leadership. When Parliament re-convened Gaitskell was challenged for the leadership by Harold Wilson but the PLP electorate gave Gaitskell 166 votes and Wilson only 81. Gaitskell's supporter George Brown was elected as Deputy Leader. The outcome was ill feeling and recrimination across the Party.[C10_76]

Pimlott[C10_77] reported that, as new Prime Minister, Wilson made judicious and relatively balanced cabinet appointments. These were shared out fairly evenly between left and right (unlike TB and GB's actions). Pelling reported, in Wilson's favour, that: "The old suspicion of leadership in the Party, which was a legacy of 1931, was now fading away as the PLP changed in composition."[C10_78]

During the Heath government (1970-74) Wilson reformed the PLP and gave up his own (automatic) post as Party Chair. He was respected by the contemporary, predominantly left-wing, trade union leadership, partly because of this.

After the 1974 February general election, most of the Shadow Cabinet became ministers. Tony Benn was Secretary for Industry. Left *and* right were well represented. A new entry from the left was Michael Foot at Employment. Of 54 new Labour MPs, 26 joined the Tribune Group – how different from the characteristics of new intakes of MPs under NL!

After Wilson's resignation in 1976, the leadership election (still restricted to MPs) ended up, in the third round, as a contest between James Callaghan and Michael Foot. Callaghan won by 176 votes to Foot's 137. This illustrated how the whole PLP was apportioned between left and right at this time. Roy Jenkins was eliminated at the first ballot. Callaghan's first cabinet was also appointed designed to represent left and right. Michael Foot became Lord President of the Council with responsibility for steering devolution.

The 1975 EEC referendum result weakened the influence of the left in the Government and Commons; Ian Mikardo had already lost the chair of the PLP. Eric Heffer was forced to resign from the Cabinet because he spoke against government policy in Parliament, in defiance of Wilson's guidelines. Wilson forced Tony Benn to exchange his office with that of Eric Varley and sacked Judith Hart. A new grouping was formed within the PLP called the "Manifesto Group". It organised centrist and right-wing MPs and acted in opposition to the restored Tribune Group. On the whole Wilson was a model of fairness and tactical competence in keeping all wings of the PLP, unions and the party on the ground functioning in relative co-operation and harmony.[C10_81]

Wilson believed in cabinet government. For example, when the social contract was reviewed he allowed a full two and a half hour cabinet discussion,[C10_82] despite his personal reservations. In the author's opinion, it is doubtful whether TB or GB would have even taken the matter to Cabinet in the same circumstances. When the 1975 referendum on Britain's EEC membership was run, the Government recommended a "Yes" vote. Several Cabinet Ministers (including Barbara Castle) wanted to support the "No" campaign publicly. Wilson reluctantly agreed that they could do so even though it flouted the convention of collective responsibility. Could one imagine TB or GB doing the same?

A new measure might be introduced in a private member's bill. This had long been so, but always involved a complex process. It produced some important progressive legislation such as the abolition of the death penalty in 1962 (promoted by Sidney Silverman) and the Alf Morris Chronically Sick and Disabled Persons Act, (1970). Colin Challen MP reported that, under NL, private member's bills often got deferred and became lost in the system (see Chapter 9). Under NL bills became more viable if they featured in recommendations of the report of a Select Committee or All Party Committee. Christine McCafferty MP reported that measures to prohibit female circumcision in the UK had become law by this route (see Chapter 9).

One of Foot's main objections to EEC membership was his *veneration of the Westminster Parliament*. He wrote In the *Times* (23.5.75): "The authority of our distinctive Parliament is one of the stakes in the choice now before the people ... the British Parliamentary system has been made farcical and unworkable by ... the semi-secret law making process of the (European) Council of Ministers."[80] When Callaghan became Leader and PM in 1976, he was careful not to antagonise the left of the PLP, although he was identified with the right. John Smith was later to emulate this example. This contrasts with TB and GB who generally seemed to marginalise the left in the PLP. They allegedly ignored those who remained having been elected during the period before 1994 (e.g. Jeremy Corbyn, see Chapters 8 and 9). The Leadership also appeared to encourage the whips to harass the Parliamentary left (see Chapter 9). Callaghan (JC) established "a close working relationship of trust and co-operation" with the left-leaning Foot (his Leader of the House). Nevertheless JC excluded Aldermaston veteran Foot from secret ministerial discussions about the re-arming of Chevaline warheads (see Chapter 6).

In 1976 the Government drafted a bill to establish Scottish and Welsh Parliaments. However devolution was not achieved despite their intention. After the 1979 election defeat Foot was elected Leader. This was done by the PLP although the Electoral College had already been agreed in principle by Party Conference. Foot had long championed the rights of Parliament and was a champion for parliamentary democracy. At Party Conference 1979 there were critical observations from the platform about accountability of the Leadership and PLP under Callaghan. Frank Allaun MP (Party Chair) said: "The feeling was growing up at the grass roots about the Parliamentary leaders and the PLP: 'Whatever we say they take no notice at all'." This sentiment was echoed by Party General Secretary Ron Hayward: "We didn't work and spend to send an MP to the House of Commons to forget whence he came and whom he represents."[81] In 1978-79 the Cabinet, supported by MPs, had ignored numerous Conference and Congress decisions.

In November 1979 the incoming Thatcher government commenced the practice of proposing controversial new policies in written answers to Parliamentary questions rather than announcing them in the Commons where they were open for debate (this practice was later frequently adopted by TB and GB). The Tories, in a written answer, announced massive redundancies in the then publicly owned steel industry. A 30% increase in council home rents was publicised in the same way. The latter measure was declared as MPs were due to go to the Lords to hear the Queen's speech. A number of Labour MPs formed a quasi picket line and barred Michael Heseltine's way. When the session resumed Foot demanded that the statement about council rents be withdrawn saying: "The Rights of the House of Commons have been grossly interfered with by the behaviour of the Secretary of State for the Environment – he and the government were guilty of a grave offence against the House."[82] Heseltine then withdrew the housing document and agreed to hold consultations – a victory for Parliamentary democracy.

Under NL, it also became common practice to announce policy changes to press conferences in written answers rather than on the floor of the House. They were usually timed to catch the weekend newspapers. This was arguably a change in the unwritten UK constitution.

An interesting debate arose during the Party hierarchy's unsuccessful attempt to prevent Peter Tatchell (PT) being endorsed as Labour candidate in the Bermondsey by-election in 1981. Foot unearthed an article by Tatchell in *London Labour Briefing* on the topic of extra Parliamentary action. PT wrote: "Reliance on the present token and ineffectual parliamentary opposition will advance us nowhere ... we must look to new, more militant forms of extra parliamentary opposition which involve mass popular participation and challenge the government's right to rule."[83] Similar arguments were articulated by MP Alan Simpson in his interview for this book (see Chapter 9).

Despite Foot's veneration of the supremacy of Parliament, he often participated in demonstrations, and other political action, outside Parliament. For example he was veteran of many Aldermaston CND marches. He led a mass march against unemployment in Liverpool in 1981. What Foot objected to in Tatchell's 1981 article was its implication that the House of Commons was ineffectual and that political struggles should be waged in other places instead. Foot's attack on Tatchell probably contributed to the loss of the seat in the by-election.

Shortly after Argentina invaded the Falklands in May 1981 there was a Commons debate on entering the war which had, in effect, started. The Labour whip's order was abstention, but 33 Labour MPs voted against. The three front bench spokespeople, who defied the whip, were forced by Foot to resign. However; Foot was not like an NL the type of leader who would punish the disloyal by blocking their future hopes of advancement.

Neil Kinnock started his leadership as a strong advocate and practitioner of parliamentary democracy. He initially took controversial issues to the PLP, spoke to try to convince them, and then a vote was taken. Foot had adopted this practice before him. However TB and GB seldom attended the PLP *to listen* to backbenchers. When present they tended to lecture them and never allowed them to vote after a "consultation" by the leader.

John Smith proved himself a moderniser on constitutional issues. As a minster, he favoured reforming the Lords and argued that a start should be made by removing the voting rights of hereditary peers. Smith appeared to prefer the German model of Proportional Representation (PR). This is comprised of direct elections in constituencies with added members to ensure proportionality. He is said to have intimated to Liberal Democrat Leader Paddy Ashdown, in a private conversation, that he favoured PR and would support it for the Commons, Scottish Parliament and Welsh Assembly. This would have been in return for Liberal support for a minority Labour government.[84]

In 1992, the House of Lords sat an average of seven hours a day for around 150 days a year. It spent about 60% of its time on legislation, 16 % on general debates and 10% on questions. Its debates had been televised since 1985. Between 1979 and 1991 there were 170 (Tory) government defeats in the House of Lords. They included issues such as child benefit, mobility allowances, housing benefits, community care, social security and school transport. Their purport was to water down Government legislation. Many of these Lords measures were later overturned by the Commons, but gave the beneficiaries breathing space. Garrett maintained that the Lords had become the social conscience of Parliament at a time when the Tory government lacked one.[85] During NL governments the Lords were also proactive in a positive way, most notably in respect of preserving infringements of civil liberties such as prolonged detention without trial.

Garrett, then a long serving Labour MP, believed that in all aspects of the work of Parliament, the government not only resists opposition to decisions, but also tries to avoid inquiry, scrutiny and discussion. He considered that the government drives forward, abandoning Parliament, as Austin Mitchell said, "heckling the steamroller". Garrett suggested that one of the causes of this weakness was traditional dominance of the debating chamber and the inferior status of investigatory and legislative committees.[85] Garret believed that, in 1992, the Parliamentary Labour Party was relatively free of restrictions and authoritarian control from the leadership. However, he thought that the contemporary Parliamentary Conservative Party was highly disciplined, organised and acted collectively.[86] Both TB and GB tried to run the PLP using the Conservative model described by Garrett. They largely succeeded: until major voting rebellions occurred after the start of the Iraq war.

Parliamentary 'Democracy' during the New Labour Period

General Observations: As reported by MPs Alan Simpson and Jeremy Corbyn (see Chapter 9), under NL MPs who did not toe the line were threatened by the whips with de-selection (which seldom happened) and with exclusion from office holding, including select committee membership (that often occurred). Alice Mahon and Linda Riordan (see Chapter 9) complained they were frequently harassed by the whips in and out of PLP meetings. Previously MPs had the scope to be more independent minded, although repeated rebellion sometimes still precluded them from being given office. It did not prevent them from sitting upon select and other Parliamentary Committees (author's interview with Ted Fletcher MP, 1979).

Past leaders often secured loyalty and co-operation from Labour MPs through the use of interpersonal skills. Attlee, Wilson and Callaghan reportedly had much personal interaction with their MPs and even with Parliamentary candidates, as the author can testify in respect of the last two. Two prominent backbenchers since the early 1990s, Gordon Prentice MP and Backbencher A., informed the author that they *had never met TB*. Jeremy Corbyn reported that he had once been granted a short audience with "the great man", during which there was scant meaningful communication between them and little active listening by TB (see Chapter 5)!

Between 1997 and 2001 there were 96 Backbench revolts by Labour MPs. Cowley claimed that every Parliament since the early 1960s had seen rebellions. Over time, NL backbenchers, particularly "the usual suspects", became increasingly likely to rebel in the voting lobbies 87. Rebellion was frequently perceived as a way to change government-proposed legislation and policy. According to John Grogan MP, many MPs preferred to organise a threatened putsch in the hope that this would secure a change before actual rebellion became necessary. As one Northern MP reported, it was common for an MP like himself to vote against on one reading of a bill and not on a second reading to make a point rather than "going to the barricades" by voting against every time.

M.Ps' constituency roles had long been important. This was illustrated by Austin Mitchell's 1988 survey of backbenchers (see Chapter 9). John Garrett recorded that in 1992 the main regular workload of and MP's office is mail relating to the problems and complaints of individual constituents. He also mentioned that most MPs held regular advice surgeries in their constituencies.[93] Under NL, particularly in the early years when Labour's majority was very large, the Whips often sent a proportion of backbenchers back to their constituencies whilst Parliament was sitting. One purpose was to give local service to the public in marginals in order to shore up the majority there.

Former MP John Garrett examined the way in which Parliament redressed complaints of individuals and groups as one area of contemporary success. Many constituents were helped by MPs taking up their cases. He stated that there are several ways in which an MP can address a minister with a constituent's complaint and by which attention can be drawn to an injustice.[88] This aspect of Parliamentary activity was still important during the NL era. Then whips were said to encourage constituency casework for the ulterior reason that it kept members of the then large PLP away from, or less pre-occupied with, Westminster and rebellion against the Leadership in the face of a thin legislative programme (interview with Clare Short – Chapter 9).

During the NL era, Blairite supporters were appointed to the House of Lords in significant numbers and many were quickly made ministers. TB appointed numerous new life peers. This was an undemocratic practice which greatly increased the leaders' powers of patronage. However the Lords, as a whole, often still acted as a check on the Executive. Interviewee Lord S. (Chapter 9) contended that the Lords benefitted from having numerous members who were national experts in their professional or academic field. A practice condemned by Clare Short was the ennoblement of a clutch of ageing MPs shortly before a general election, a period when Party rules permitted shortlisting by the NEC of NL favourites to replace them: facing minimal competition in the process.

The central role of Parliament in policy making was being downgraded by changes in media coverage even before the advent of NL. The new generation of Parliamentarians were encouraged to be more adept at giving sound bites and presenting themselves well on TV rather than in making detailed speeches in Parliament. The result was a focus on tomorrow's media release rather than on strategic thinking about policies for the coming year. Michael Meacher (see Chapter 9) made a point saying that our Parliament is not as effective as it should be because over 100 of the "brightest and best" of the largest Party are in government and others, together with many of the opposition, aspire to be.

*Overview of innovations in parliamentary democracy and undemocratic practices developed by New Labour (*see also Chapter 9). Under NL Most MPs interviewed believed that Government policy largely came from the Leader and his advisers by means of "Sofa Government' (see Chapter 9). This view was shared by many grass-roots constituency officers surveyed. MPs who were 1990s Cabinet ministers (e.g. Frank Dobson) indicated that few decisions were taken in Cabinet. During previous Labour Governments major policy decisions were generally taken in Cabinet. One notable exception was Callaghan's decision (with a secret sub group of the Cabinet) to re-arm Polaris (See Chapter 6).

New policy initiatives were frequently announced by policy advisers or at a Prime Ministerial or Ministerial press conference, rather than in Parliament, according to well-established constitutional practice. It is small wonder that John Reid MP felt able to describe Parliament as "Disnaeland: because it disn'ae matter what goes on there." Senior backbencher A. argued that backbenchers were not allowed to make decisions in Parliament and to have them implemented as senior local councillors were.

Parliamentary democracy took serious punishment under NL. The PLP became even more supine than Garrett perceived it as having been during the Thatcher premiership (see above). An ideology-free PLP was sought, and largely achieved, by the NL leadership (see Chapters 8 and 9). Consequently more members of the PLP lacked political convictions and were more obedient to the NL Leadership with each successive election. Cowley stated that this held true when they entered Parliament and for a significant period afterwards.[95]

In 2009 a Downing Street insider told the author that the Leadership were still very distrustful of the Party membership and seemed almost to see themselves as being "at war with them". This phenomenon had not occurred in the Party since the leadership of Ramsay MacDonald. Under NL, MPs were increasingly micro-managed. They were spoon-fed official messages on their pagers and constrained by the whips to obey them. Whips also distributed advice about the content of speeches and offered to write these. During the NL years, PLP meetings were usually poorly attended and the leaders seldom present. Some policy debates took place but no votes were taken. According to MPs Chris Mullin and Gordon Prentice, limited power was vested in the Parliamentary Committee – a small group elected by MPs to represent their views to the Leadership.

Alan Simpson MP reported that MPs were instructed that their *main role* was to sell the NL Party to the Party members and through and with them to the public. This was not seen as a major aspect of Labour MP's roles previously.

NL Governments were characterised by unprecedented, and extensive, use of patronage, rewards by the leadership for compliance and support. However, some MPs, who had excellent track records in spheres such as local government, were overlooked for promotion. This was probably because they had experience, authority and could think for themselves. That would have enabled them to offer credible challenges to the Leadership. The dissident were punished, or threatened with punishment. Most were also denied even the most minor promotion. In previous Labour Governments local government and trades union leaders who became MPs were frequently promoted, Ernest Bevin was one example. Previous Labour leaders also used patronage but not in such an extreme way: merit usually counted.

Backbenchers desiring office were advised to join one of the "gangs of Parliament". This entailed forming friendships and currying favour with one of the three demagogues. The "Supreme Leader" Blair, the "Dear Leader" Brown or the "Vox Pop. Deputy Leader" Prescott. Office for MPs was the outcome of being championed by one of these three. Promotion for favourites, at their courts, was traded between them. There was much friction involved. In his autobiography *Prezza*, Prescott reported that the leaders and their close associates: "were continually getting pissed off with each other, jealous, and furious when, in turn, they felt carved up, excluded or briefed against, working themselves into sulks and rages."[89]. From 1964 to 1994, Prime Ministers were careful to have an ideologically broad based cabinet. Before his demise John Smith seemed poised to do the same in office.

There was also life imitating art in respect of Swift's Gulliver's *Travels in Lilliput*.[90] There, politicians were satirised as having to perform complex feats of jumping and tight-rope walking in order to obtain the favour needed to win office. Gordon Prentice MP observed that if an MP sought promotion, but did not know any of the "three big beasts" personally, then their prospects for promotion were doomed. This led to an inconsistent and dubious, approach to running the Government and the PLP.

NL administrations neutered Parliamentary Select Committees whose function is officially to keep an independent watch on the government in specific policy areas. Prior to NL, MPs were generally appointed to these committees on the basis of interest and expertise in the field covered by the Committee. During the whole NL era MPs who rebelled in any way (including voting against the Government) were usually not permitted to be a member of such a committee, no matter how much expertise they had in the area of its remit. At one point the Leader tried to assume the right to appoint the Chairs of select committees but this was fiercely resisted and a system was then established whereby they were elected by all MPs.

Voting rebellions commenced, on a large scale, in respect of votes on the Iraq war. Lynne Jones MP believed: "It's only by using your vote in Parliament as an individual, rather than as a member of the PLP, that you actually get to change anything." Another way for Backbench MPs to try to influence policy was to lobby the relevant minister. Many found it easier to influence operational rather than strategic decisions. Some MPs would work with a colleague in the House of Lords to get a provision introduced there first.

Another product of many MPs' relative idleness, combined with lack of ideology and principle, was the expenses scandal which broke in spring 2009. Garrett reported that the topics of MPs' pay, allowances and working conditions were sensitive subjects, mainly because of the media's interest in them. His personal opinion then was that the remuneration of an MP was about the same as that of a junior to middle manager in industry or public administration, well below that of a journalist on a national newspaper. He considered that the hours of a conscientious MP were excessive.[98] When the expenses storm broke in 2009, MPs attended PLP meetings in unusually large numbers to seek protection. When GB refused to intervene to protect them they booed him. Alan Simpson MP observed: "People with no politics only take a stand when the issue has become personal"(see Chapter 9).

Minor Lords reform was enacted under NL – the removal of the majority of hereditary peers and the creation of a new Supreme Court to replace the judicial function of the Lords. However the attempt to replace the Lords entirely by a wholly or partly democratically elected Chamber was arguably wrecked, allegedly by the way in which TB handled it.

CLP secretaries were surveyed by the author about their views of contemporary (NL) Parliamentary democracy.

Only three out of 27 CLP secretaries thought that "Expelling most hereditary peers from the House of Lords" was one of the NL's government's seven best policies. Ten secretaries agreed that "bringing devolution to Scotland, Wales and London" was also one of the seven best policies. Eleven of them considered failure to review reform and control the Parliamentary expenses system earlier "as one of the NL government's seven worst policy mistakes".

Secretaries were asked how MPs *should* behave "If a Labour government introduces legislation or adopts policies that differ from the policy of the Labour Party as a whole?" and "Relating to circumstances in which crucial issues arise for a Labour Government that were not foreseen in time to be considered through the Party's official policy making machinery how should MPs vote?". The were also asked: "How far do you think your Labour MP (if you have one) is accountable to your CLP's General Committee and to your CLP membership in general?" Details of their responses appear in Chapter 9.

When asked whether they would like to see a Party rule change to make it easier to de-select MPs, *20 (out of 27) agreed that they would welcome this*, three did not want such a change and four did not know. When asked whether internal party elections and candidate selection (including Prospective Parliamentary Candidates) were run on an equal opportunities basis, five said "Yes"; 12 said "to some extent"; three said "No"; and four did not know.

Questioned as to whether they thought that Ministers, MPs and/or Party staff sometimes intervene in internal selections in a biased way? *18 said "Yes"*; three said "No"; and four "Didn't know"; 21 wanted votes for selection of PPCs to be cast only *after the hustings (i.e. when members had heard and questioned all shortlisted candidates)*. One did not want this and five did not know.

Questions followed about how much influence Backbench MPs should have on policies of the contemporary Labour government (2009). Ten replied: "A great deal of influence"; 15 said "some influence"; one said "Not much influence"; and None said "No influence" or "Don't know". Next, they were asked how much influence Backbench MPs *actually did have* on the policies of government. None said a great deal; 12 said "Some influence"; the same number said "Not much influence"; and three did not know. Party members were clearly aware of the contemporary disempowerment of their MPs. NL's iron control of backbenchers was a limiting factor on accountability of Backbench MPs to their CLPs and to their scope for promoting Party policies agreed by Conference and by the NPF.

Comparative Assessment of the Operation of Australian Labor Parliamentary Democracy

As in the UK Labour Party prior to 1983, the Leader of the Australian PLP (Caucus) is chosen by its members on a majority vote. The Caucus consists of all ALP Federal MPs (House of Representatives) and Senators (Upper House). The Caucus membership in April 2012 stood at 103 after a hung general election in 2010. In June 2010 Prime Minister Kevin Rudd lost public popularity (due to a proposed green policy) having previously been very popular. Following a brief, and largely covert, campaign within the Caucus, a "spill" (re-election of Leader) was called. After it became clear that he could not win, Rudd stood down in favour of Julia Gillard who immediately became Prime Minister. This was without a general election or a contest within the Party as a whole. The underlying reasons (that the caucus deplored Rudd's management style) were never properly explained to the Australian public (or even to the Labor Conference) until after Rudd's unsuccessful bid to regain the leadership in 2012. For much of the intervening period polls of electors showed Gillard to be less popular than Rudd. At the August 2010 general election, the result was a dead heat. Labor subsequently formed a coalition government with the Green Party and a handful of independents. This followed four weeks of negotiations. From the Party democracy perspective, it is regrettable that the Caucus alone chooses the leader (sometimes therefore Prime Minister). Their choice is apparently influenced by left or right factions and trades union leaders. No one else in the ALP has a vote. UK Labour is more democratic in this respect, provided that MPs permit a wide ideological range at the nomination stage. As became apparent in Gillard's Cabinet reshuffles during 2012, patronage was a major influence, as it was for GB in 2007. Then the Party, other than the PLP, was excluded from having a say. *After the 2012 "spill" pressure mounted in the ALP for the leadership electorate to be widened.*

As under NL, many ALP members were dissatisfied with the processes and outcomes of Parliamentary candidate selections. The HW survey of ALP members showed: "Frustration of the rank and file who believe that they are increasingly left out of the selection process. This, they claim, has a detrimental effect on the suitability of candidates for their local electorates."[91] This survey produced some complaints about the predominance of young political staffers among parliamentary candidates. This issue was also one for the NL Party (See Chapter 8). Some commentators among ALP members preferred candidates with "a record of Party activism, local standing and community connections." However the Hawke Wran Report argued that, whilst they needed quality candidates in all seats, "the Party must actively identify and encourage candidates from a *wide range* of occupations and life experiences",[92] NL should have done likewise.

This Australian report argued: "All quality candidates should be given opportunities". The Party needed "to present a diverse group of candidates to the electorate – that represents the broad range of opinions and experiences in our Party" (as contrasted with the ideologically homogenous NL candidates). An issue besetting the ALP at local, State and National levels was the operation of factions in the candidate selection process. Some Party members complained to the HW survey that these factions tended to dominate selections: "Effectively locking up the process by excluding non-aligned members." HW claimed: "This drastically reduces local input and creates a situation where candidates are rewarded for their service to a faction" – rather than because of more important factors. Some Labor members complained of "inter-factional deal-making, where a small group of factional leaders decide (unilaterally) which grouping within the Party will stand candidates in each seat."[93] This was undesirable, but at least it came from the grass roots. NL allegedly covertly and wrongly excluded all who would have been in a left faction from selection in winnable seats (see Chapter 8). Under NL, there was virtually no representation of left or centre left shades of opinion or of manual working experience in the Party's candidates selected in recent years (see Chapter 8). Regional factionalism has seldom been a significant issue in the UK Labour Party: except perhaps in London and Scotland.

Federal MP Gary Gray said: "When I was National ALP Secretary, we made the first attempts at trying to improve the representation of women. At that time, less than 11% of our members of Parliament were women. Now 25% are women (taking both Houses together)." Hawke Wran reported that the 1994 ALP Conference set a target of 35% women Federal MPs. Following the 2001, election 31% of the Labor members of the House of Representatives were women. Hawke Wran[94] recommended reinstatement of the 35% target; together with a new deadline and enforcement mechanism. There was a requirement that State Branches provide an annual affirmative action report about the measures they adopted to improve women's representation. Gray continued: "It's done by a range of different methods, from a weighted vote through to proportional requirements. If you look at the Federal House of Representatives, out of every four Labor MPs, two are women and two are men. So we have a clear 50% attainment although, under our rules, it need only be 40%." The ALP has been slightly more successful than British NL by obtaining a higher percentage of women MPs and senators. In view of the resistance met within the UK Party to All Women Shortlists, perhaps NL should have examined the detail of the ALP's selection procedures with a view to adopting them. Gray stated: "We have no positive promotional measures for black and ethnic minority candidates (including aboriginal people).There is currently one aboriginal Labor minister in the West Australian State government."

On the subject of Policy making within the Federal Parliament, Gary Gray claimed (in March 2010): "As in all political structures, there are formal and informal ways for MPs and Senators to seek to influence or be a part of decision making. Potential legislation must first be submitted for approval to the Caucus (PLP). All matters that go before Parliament must have been approved first by the main Caucus (Executive) Committee. All matters originating from the Executive must go before Cabinet and to Caucus but they *must* also pass through the Caucus (specialist sub) Committees who make recommendations to the Caucus (as a whole). There are several levels of interaction and engagement used. One of the hallmarks of our first two and a half years of government is that we have managed to keep the stresses, tensions and difficulties around policy and programme decisions in house. But I am not certain that we'll be able to do so in the future!"

Gray continued: "There is a variety of Caucus committees that scrutinise the whole range of different policy areas. I, for instance, am an ordinary member of the infrastructure and regional development caucus committee. I'm also an ordinary member of the climate change and environment caucus committee. There are many other caucus committees to which Caucus can nominate. The Caucus, as a whole, can vote on the membership of Caucus committees should that be necessary. But normally, if you wish to be on a caucus committee, you either nominate yourself or simply turn up. These are *not* Cabinet or Prime Ministerial appointments," (How different this was from the control of membership of Select Committees under NL).

He said: "Most policy decisions are first debated by the Cabinet and then after Cabinet by the Caucus committees. From there they go to the full caucus meeting. I've been in the Caucus for two and a half years and I've been a senior official of the ALP since 1986. I have not, in recent years, known of any (policy) votes taking place in Caucus. There can be deeply contested views. For example, there were strongly contested views on the issue of nuclear waste depositories discussed in Caucus last week. But the matter passed on 'voices' (verbal acclaim). However we *can* vote by a show of hands. One MP has one vote whether they are a senator or representative or minister or backbencher. As in Britain, members of the Cabinet are bound by Cabinet decisions. Cabinet always debates an issue before Caucus does. Ultimately it doesn't happen that backbenchers are against something that cabinet has agreed. This is because there are sufficient internal communication mechanisms to deal with difficult matters. For example, the precise format of the (recent) industrial relations changes was highly contentious. So *internal dialogue took place to ensure that what went through Cabinet could go through the Caucus Committee and Caucus could then support the Cabinet.*

"Australian Labor senators and MPs might vote against their Party, in Parliament, in future, but it has never *happened in the past. We have a deeply held position that the view of the Caucus prevails.* In the future there may be pressure to allow people to break caucus votes. But the general principle that the decision of caucus is final and you are bound by that, has been honoured in the ALP (Australian Labour Party) for 120 years. We have a provision to allow for what we call 'conscience votes'. Right to life issues have generally been defined as being in that category. Members can put forward a private member's bill. They would do this through caucus." The above resembles the system of binding majority decision making in Council Labour Groups in Britain as Senior Backbencher A described it.

This system appears to be superior to that used by the UK PLP. It probably gives Australian MPs a sense of "ownership" of policies. It arguably gives them more influence in policy making than have their UK counterparts. The system certainly heads off rebellion on the floor of Parliament. Clearly the UK PLP would benefit from adopting some of these procedures. They would probably circumvent acrimonious public dispute in view of the media. With a system like this the PLP would surely have been much happier and have run more smoothly during the NL era and previously. However, as noted earlier, Caucus has the sole power to appoint and dismiss the Party leader even if they are currently prime minister. That is an undemocratic practice which the UK Labour Party should not adopt.

Gary Gray continued: "Proportional representation, compulsory voting and Saturday elections all work well for the ALP. This because they are an acculturated part of our voting processes. Voting processes need to be stable and accepted. Governments shouldn't change voting processes unless there is overwhelming support in Parliament on both sides and in respect of both PR voting systems used in Australia (Single Transferable Vote in the Senate (Upper House) and Alternative Vote in the House of Representatives). In my view you change these rules only when the Parties on both sides agree. You don't change the rules just because you've got a simple Parliamentary majority in favour. I don't think that Proportional Representation helps the ALP. In a PR system your policies will be honed towards the wishes of minorities."

"I think that compulsory voting is accepted in Australia. There are 14 million people in Australia registered to vote; but there are another 1.4 million who are eligible to vote but not on the roll. These are a whole variety of people." These are views which should be taken into account by the UK Labour Party. In March 2013 the author worked in the West Australian Parliamentary election campaign in a very marginal constituency which Labor won. Compulsory voting seemed to work very well in that it increased the turnout, was not resented by the electors and made election organisation far less onerous than campaigning in voluntary UK elections.

Conclusion

New Labour set out to remodel the Party and change its core characteristics from those of the Party that had subsisted since the 1918 first constitution. As a means to achieving this end they undertook a number of tasks:

• To strengthen the Leadership and give it autocratic power.

• To move its ideology to the right and to facilitate it acting in a non ideological way.

• To improve public relations in the context of having to deal with a hostile right wing media.

• To create a Market Oriented Party: more likely to win elections.

NL set out to disempower both rank and file Party Members and Parliamentarians.

This disempowerment involved an internal, top-down revolution which saw both rank and file Party members and Labour MPs lose democratic rights and powers on a grand scale. Thus were Party and Parliamentary democracy greatly downgraded. This was in addition to pacification of the PLP though punishment and patronage, allegedly fixing Parliamentary selections and driving many members out of the Party.

CHAPTER 11
Summary, Conclusions and Labour's Ways Forward

"Almost all problems which are more common at the bottom of the social ladder are more common in more unequal societies"
Wilkinson and Pickett, 2009

"The idea of equality will remain and the Labour Party is the best possible vehicle for it"
Roy Hattersley, quoted by John Harris, 2005

"We need to return to the social democratic tradition and green it up. It's the most desirable political tradition and that's where Labour should be in the future"
Clare Short in interview

Part 1: Introduction, Evaluation: Attainment of Labour's Aims and underlying values as proposed by stakeholders

Part 2: Visions for the Future of the Labour Party,
a Contemporary Reflections on Labour's election defeat in 2010 b
The Future Strategic Direction of the Labour Party:
Overview of proposed future strategic direction, Overview of future strategic policies, A strategy to reform the Party as an Organisation

Part 1: Introduction: the yardstick of Labour's enduring aims and values

At the core of assessment of New Labour's (NL's) performance used in this book is the set of Party aims and values identified at the outset by the principal 57 stakeholders interviewed (see Chapter 1). These stakeholders were drawn from Backbench Labour MPs, Constituency Labour Party (CLP) Secretaries and Trade Union Leaders. That Chapter also investigated the values underpinning those aims that were identified by the major stakeholders interviewed. Chapter 1 also includes the official NL aims and values adopted by the Party's Annual Conference in 1995 (Appendix 2). Both sets of aims are compared and contrasted in that Chapter. Interviewees were asked to evaluate NL's performance using their own preferred aims and underpinning values as the yardstick. These evaluations were ranked in order of the quantity of support each received from stakeholders interviewed. This chapter starts by revisiting those *aims* and assessing how *far* interviewees considered they were achieved during the NL era. There is also comparison with the performance of earlier Labour governments in the same policy areas as appropriate.

Labour's aims and underlying values as proposed by stakeholders surveyed: how were they prioritised and how far were they achieved?

1) The most popular, almost universally favoured, aim from the stakeholders' perspectives was the theme of *"Promoting a more equal society which redistributes wealth, power, opportunities and privilege: a society characterised by greater social mobility and social justice."*

This aim was defined in social class and economic terms. Other types of non-economic equalities were included in a separate, lower priority aim ranked 7th equal. Most respondents emphasised the need for equality of opportunity. Only a minority called for equality of outcome.

There was a clear commitment to make our society more equal with much smaller distances in terms of the distribution of advantage and wealth between top, middle and bottom. This would be a fairer society offering equal opportunities. Although almost all respondents desired this, some were sceptical about the feasibility of achieving widespread equalities of outcome. However equality of opportunity alone does not create more equal society. This was pointed out by Wilkinson and Pickett.[C11_1] They found that greater social mobility helps some people to move from working to middle class but equality of outcome is also vital in order to benefit the vast majority of working people.

Social mobility is lower in more unequal countries according to Wilkinson and Pickett.[C11_2]. Only nine countries were involved in this aspect of their research (USA, UK, Canada, Portugal, Germany, Denmark, Sweden, Finland and Norway). The USA, Portugal and the UK (a close third), were by far the most unequal societies in terms of income inequality and they had the lowest rates of social mobility. All the other countries surveyed had much lower income inequality and far greater social mobility. Norway was the most equal and mobile, closely followed by Sweden, Denmark and Canada.

NL governments took positive steps to attempt to address poverty and disadvantage. These policies included the national minimum wage; working families' tax credits; increased child benefits linked to targets to end child poverty; the Sure Start programme; free bus travel; increased winter fuel allowance; and TV licence concessions for older pensioners. The problem with the national minimum wage as one of its champions, a retired union leader, recently claimed, was that it has always been too low. It was not effectively enforced with employers and neither was legislation to regulate gang masters where they operated.

A major issue arose from the decline of manufacturing industry and mining. This was the outcome of the policies of Thatcherite governments; but NL did little to remedy the damage they inflicted. The disappearance of many thousands of skilled, well paid, working class jobs followed. These jobs had been disproportionately located outside South East England. They were replaced by lower skilled and poorly remunerated work in service industries. This new employment was often in workplaces where trade union representation was inadequate and was difficult to increase. This problem was frequently due to factors such as shift patterns; multiplicity of sites; hostility of employers; and a predominantly female workforce, many of whom were not accustomed to being unionised. This trend was highlighted by Lord S. Owen Jones stated: "Successive governments have completely neglected to answer the question 'Where are the missing jobs to put people into?' Even where there are jobs available, they are often low-paid, temporary and of poor quality."[C11_3]

Working families' tax credits were bedevilled with problems because frequent accidental over-payment left poor families having to repay large sums long after mistakes were made by administrators. NL governments did take 600,000 children out of poverty. Their child poverty targets were unlikely to be met after Labour lost office in 2010. The Sure Start programme and pensioner benefits were, by and large, successful but the main state pension was not increased sufficiently and in line with income levels.

There was an almost complete failure to build social housing until the latter days of the Brown (GB) government. Tony Blair (TB) told Jeremy Corbyn to tell constituents unable to be housed that NL was doing very well on education" (Chapter 5). Access to decent, affordable housing is a significant benefit to people on below average incomes. Much council housing was sold off by previous Tory governments and continued to be sold under NL. Very little was replaced. As a result of housing shortages, private house prices rose and many working class families had to commit to unaffordable mortgages in order to have a home. NL started the system of student loans, replacing grants and followed this up with heavy university tuition fees for all but the very poorest. There was improvement in educational standards but this was insufficient to prevent the majority of children from disadvantaged homes from falling behind in their educational development thus damaging their life and career chances.

Meanwhile gaps between rich and poor and between the wealthy and the middle classes yawned wider. As well as disparities in income, this inequality was due to a non progressive tax system which relied on regressive indirect taxes like Value Added Tax (VAT). There was also failure, until the later GB days, to introduce lower rates of tax for people on low incomes (this reduction turned out to be temporary). Only latterly did GB increase the maximum rate of tax on high earners introduced by Thatcherite governments. This was only by 5%. The overall tax take was insufficient to cover NL's welcome increased social expenditure on benefits and on public services. The market economy allowed obscene levels of salaries and bonuses to be paid to the richest in society –mainly to the top 10%. Tax evasion became rife. Moreover, "trickle down" had not worked. A Resolution Foundation Report (July 2011) stated that of every £100 rise in national income since 1977, the half of the population on average or below average income received just £12. Meanwhile, the top tenth received a £14 share.[C11_4]

Toynbee and Walker concluded: "The country remains strongly defined by class, regional disparity, inequality, and individual and business under-achievement."[C11_5]

In many respects, earlier Labour Governments did much better, despite having less favourable economic situations. The core mission of Attlee governments was to tackle poverty and economic disadvantage. They used a National Assistance Act to develop a safety net for incomes of those unable to work. The National Insurance scheme was extended and made more comprehensive. More jobs were provided in the new nationalised industries and in repairing war damage. The cost was subsidised by the US Marshall Plan.

Wilson governments sought to increase welfare benefits and pensions; although implementation sometimes had to be delayed due to economic problems. Unemployment remained relatively low; it never rose above 2.5%. Between 1966 and 1969 the government oversaw the building of an average 400,000 new council homes per year. Between 1964 and 1968 public expenditure on education rose from 4.8% to 5.95% of Gross National Product (GNP). A scheme for earnings related pensions was devised and the non – means tested child benefits greatly improved.

2) The second most popular aim was: *"To provide and maintain high quality, mainly publicly provided public services especially in health, education and social housing. To increase public ownership and to cease privatising services and enterprises e.g. public transport."*

Interviewees believed that the development of new public services, especially through capital building projects providing new hospitals and schools, had been commendable. Many old, substandard schools and health buildings were replaced. These attracted new equipment and better staff. When NL came to office in 1997, spending on public services (excluding pensions and welfare benefits) was 20% of National income. At its highest, before the financial crisis bit, spending on public services rose to 25% of GDP.[C11_6]

1. In respect of public capital building (for example, schools and hospitals), there were negative stakeholder views about accompanying Private Finance Initiatives (PFI). Most capital projects were funded by PFI schemes which left the service paying an extortionate rate of interest for many years. This was likely to impact on financial viability of services in future. Evidence has recently been provided by the South London Health Care Trust which, in 2012, was placed in special measures due to a deficit of £150 million pounds. This deficit was the outcome of the Trust having to find £61 million pounds per year to repay the £ 2.5 billion pound PFI loan used to rebuild its hospitals before 2010. Often PFI schemes included privatisation of some services (e.g. hospital cleaning). There was also some privatisation of entire services including private diagnostic and treatment centres and academy schools. PFI was rightly seen as creating large, unnecessary financial burdens for future services, as in the South London hospitals case. Patient choice, excessive use of service targets and undesirable freedoms given to academy proprietors were also criticised. Of NL Governments, Toynbee and Walker, 2010, said "(They) fixed essentials in the public realm, work made urgent by earlier Tory imprudence."[C11_7]

The record on provision of new social housing (discussed in last section) was abysmal. Owen Jones contended: "New Labour was ideologically opposed to building council housing, because of its commitment to build 'a property owning democracy'.[C11_8] However, councils were banned from building their own homes for rent until 2009 when the average council's waiting list for social rented homes stood at 8,000.[C11_9]

However, as Jeremy Corbyn pointed out, NL had a better record on the improvement and modernisation of older social homes. By 2010 Labour had invested £37 billion in a "Decent Homes" Programme to install central heating, new kitchens and bathrooms in social rented homes.

By comparison with NL, the record of Attlee Governments in establishing a huge network of public services is famous. By 1948 they were able to offer a National Health Service that was available to all, covered virtually every health need and was free at the point of use. Public social care services were established. There was improvement of Butler's wartime Education Act and more school buildings and teachers were provided. However, unlike NL, they did not build many new hospitals to benefit the NHS.

Wilson governments set up the Comprehensive school system and ended the 11+ exam for most children. There was impressive achievement in council home building, as discussed above. The Open University was founded on Wilson's watch. In summary, earlier Labour Governments achieved much more over slightly longer, but interrupted, periods of government.

3) 3rd = approval rating was given to the aim of *"Promoting fraternity and solidarity among working people, and within the Labour movement, taking a collectivist approach to social and other policies and enhancing trades union rights and rights at work"*.

This aim had been crucial to the UK Labour movement and Labour Party from its beginnings. However, it was largely alien to NL. Blair openly set out to downgrade and devalue the relationship between the Party and the trades unions. Rawnsley, 2010,[C11_10] reported that both TB and Lord Levy agreed that the Party needed to reduce its dependence on money from the trades unions. The union contribution fell from two thirds of Party funding, when TB became Labour Leader, to less than a quarter at the lowest point. Owen Jones said that "TB once boasted that after NL's (and Thatcher's) changes Britain's law remains the most restrictive in the Western World: as far as unions are concerned."[C11_11]

Two examples of TB's intention to distance himself from the unions follow: John Prescott recalled a meal with senior trade union leaders in 1995 where TB "Made it absolutely clear that the old days were gone and he wouldn't be allowing any union diktat and they should not expect any deals."[C11_12] Alastair Campbell reported that Rodney Bickerstaffe visited him in May 1995. Campbell said that RB stated that TB had to realise that he would need the unions at a later stage. Campbell reported back to TB, who said: "They can just fuck off. We will never get elected if every little change produces this kind of nonsense".
[C11_13]

There was minimal legislation to improve rights at work, (see comments of John Cryer, in Chapter 5) but the great bulk of repressive anti-union laws, enacted by Thatcher and Major regimes, remained on the statute book. This contrasts with the Australian Labor government of 2007 who repealed all the anti-union legislation of their predecessor Liberals on taking office. No steps were taken by NL to help unions to recruit members in the growing, poorly paid, service sector. Thus the unions remained weakened which, in turn, led to a continuation of de-industrialisation and decline of well paid working class jobs.

The individualistic society, which NL nurtured, differed from the society that fostered collective solutions and mutual assistance as was encouraged by earlier Labour Governments. NL's method of operating, some of which threatened the future of public services and enterprises, was mainly tolerated by the public. Many people seemed not to appreciate that the less affluent sections of the population can only have a civilised quality of life if essential public services are publicly provided though a collective welfare state as Frank Dobson pointed out (Chapter5).

During the Attlee years, the trades unions and the government worked virtually as one. The unions had literally run the party during most of the 1930s. Attlee appointed several powerful former union leaders, including Ernest Bevin, as Cabinet Ministers. The unions were pleased by the extensive programmes of nationalisation and by the Welfare state. They were even persuaded to accept a policy of wage restraint designed to make British exports more competitive.

The first Wilson governments introduced wages control, limiting annual rises to 3.5 % and giving the government powers to delay increases. In 1969, the White Paper *In Place of Strife* gave the Government powers to impose conciliation periods before industrial action, to delay strikes and to insist on pre-strike ballots. This went beyond the proposals of the Government's Donovan Commission on Trade Unions. The TUC refused to accept the Government's proposals. Subsequently a meeting between the TUC and ministers agreed to drop the penal clauses in the bill in return for the TUC promising to try to prevent unofficial strikes. On returning to power, in 1974, Wilson promised to repeal the hated Tory Industrial Relations Act. He also immediately settled the miners' strike. By 1975, the Cabinet, and some union leaders and then the TUC agreed to a flat sum wage increase to control inflation. During earlier Labour governments, the Quaker slogan "Co-operation is better than conflict" often characterised relations between Labour Government and unions. Sadly that did not hold true the late 1970s under Callaghan's leadership.

3)=. One of the third most strongly supported aims was: *"To promote peace, good international relations and third world development"*.

Owen Jones considered that Labour Party members, especially those on the left, frequently prized this aim above all others and that this sometimes put them at variance with most working class Labour supporters. Jones thought that although working class people sometimes opposed wars, they were often more concerned about issues like housing and employment.[C11-14] The moderate degree of priority given by Party stakeholders to international issues here suggests that they did not give it topmost priority either.

There was universal praise for NL's priority for a major effort to massively increase aid and trade with poor countries. They planned to meet the UN target by giving 0.7% of gross national product (GNP) in aid to poor countries annually. NL claimed to have already taken two million people in the Third World permanently out of poverty each year between 2000 and 2005. They also published the first white paper on aid to poor countries. Toynbee and Walker recognised this achievement.[C11-15] This policy was seen, by interviewees, as being one of NL's best achievements. So was the achievement of peace in Northern Ireland.

MPs interviewed were full of praise for the settlement of the troubles in Northern Ireland as were contemporary senior American politicians (including President Bill Clinton who mediated in person).

However, there was strong stakeholder condemnation of Blair's wars, particularly of the allegedly illegal war in Iraq and, to a lesser extent, of the conflict in Afghanistan. Before entering the Iraq war Blair simply said to the public: "Trust me". Simon Jenkins, 2007,[C11_16] argued that knowing that his Cabinet and Party would be sceptical, he found himself sucked into a web of deception which undermined his credibility as a leader. Nothing caused Blair more trouble or weakened trust in his leadership than did Iraq. Jenkins said: "Blair ... was never in control of events. He had involved British troops in a shooting war, whose course; conduct and outcome were in the hands of the Americans. *No British interest was at stake in Afghanistan or Iraq"*.[C11_17]

Stakeholders expressed intense negativity about TB's subservience to the ultra right wing George W. Bush. Some criticised the Government's failure to engage in any form of nuclear disarmament. There was widespread stakeholder view that Labour should always try to promote peace and good international relations.

Apart from joining the UN backed Korean war in the wake of receipt of massive financial aid from the USA, Attlee governments kept clear of foreign military adventures. However they also facilitated the foundation of NATO and joined Britain to it. Labour maintained post-war conscription but cut its duration. They presided over the granting of independence to the countries of the Indian Sub Continent and Burma as smoothly as they could in view of local ethnic and political tensions. They participated in the establishment of the state of Israel which was less successful.

By the time Wilson became PM, Britain had its own nuclear weapons, linked to those of the USA. These had long been controversial within the Party. Wilson avoided a military commitment abroad by answering Unilateral Independence in Rhodesia with economic sanctions. He also declined to join the USA in the Vietnam war.

The next aim, (5th in ranked order) was supported by a sixth of all stakeholders. It was: *"To manage the country's economy effectively, to secure economic growth and thus to increase the incomes of the population, provide jobs and generate wealth to fund public services".*

The overall view of stakeholders was that, on the whole, the economy had been well managed between 1997 and 2007-8. There was good economic growth and it then appeared that GB's boast that he had ended boom and bust was realistic. It was thought that the decision to adhere to Tory spending plans until 2000, although not in itself widely liked, had shored up the economy. Gross Domestic Product (GDP) increased and considerable funding was made available for public services development as a consequence of this together with the widespread use of Private Finance Initiatives (PFI). Numbers of jobs increased during this period although, as mentioned above, many were unskilled or semi-skilled and low paid. Manufacturing was 20% of the UK economy in 1997 but a mere 12% in 2007. This decline was accelerated by the increase in the value of sterling between 1997 and 2001 thus making exports of manufactured goods less competitive. This overall economic success undoubtedly helped to secure the Labour election victories of 2001 and 2005. Construction, estate agency and property transactions increased from 12.6% to 16.2% of the economy in the ten years from 1997.[C11_18]

Considering the known influence of economic policies on electoral performance, it is surprising that interviewees did not place this higher up their policy priority rankings. That may be due to them not perceiving economic success primarily as an end in itself, but as a means to the end of increasing employment and growing public services. NL growth was secured through developing service industries rather than manufacturing industry and, above all, by turning the City into a major global financial centre. The means to secure City growth was laissez faire capitalist management of a market economy and "light touch" regulation of the banks and financial institutions. This had serious consequences after 2008.

In 2008 this economic strategy, combined with the global financial crisis, led to the UK financial crisis and subsequent bank bailout. Many interviewees considered that this method of operating (prior to 2008) amounted to economic mismanagement – the results of which should have been foreseen by the NL leadership. NL's other economic vice was to attempt a massive expansion of some public services without levying the level of taxation required to provide the necessary additional funding. This led to major funding shortfalls, some of which did not become apparent prior to the 2010 general election. The annual average increase in government spending in each of the years from 1999-2000 to 2007-8 was just over 16% compared with minus 5%, in each of the years of Tory government between 1979-80 and 1996-97.[C11-19] NL was terrified of the electoral effects of substantial increases in direct taxation and significant taxation of the wealthy. Throughout NL's reign, they usually avoided such taxation and lived according to the myth that it is possible to have improving public services underpinned by low taxes. This fable was disproved in 2010 when NL Chief Financial Secretary to the Treasury Liam Byrne MP announced that there was "no money left".

There follows comparison with records of earlier Labour governments on economic policy. At the end of the American Lend-Lease of 1945, a large loan was negotiated but was rapidly used up and a foreign exchange crisis followed. A programme to expand exports rapidly was introduced as a solution. There was heavy taxation on internal consumption and restrictions on overseas travel and imports to address the deficit. These measures contained the UK's economic problems prior to the start of the Marshall Plan for recovery.

Wilson also faced early insolvency problems and slowly rising unemployment. In response, he devalued the pound in 1967. This cured the weakness of sterling for some time and also provided an immediate boost to UK exports. Defence spending was cut by means of gradual withdrawal of British troops from East of Suez. The balance of payments deficit closed slowly but was well in the black by the 1970 general election.

Of the four occasions between 1945 and 1997 when the UK ran a budget surplus, Labour was in government for three of them. This should have been hammered home to Chancellor Osborne in 2015. The Labour Party consistently supported regional development policies from the 1930s though to 1994. Wilson introduced the Regional Employment Premium to bring jobs to the regions. Labour founded Regional Development Councils. However, regional economic policy was alien to NL. Despite contemporary doubts, Wilson's favourable renegotiation and use of a referendum to secure the UK's membership of the European Union did secure future exports and prosperity. There was a capital transfer tax and nationalisation of development land. The National Enterprise Board was set up to supervise the work of publicly owned companies. When the pound rode high Callaghan introduced selective employment tax to keep Britain's manufactures competitive.

The final denial of NL's commitment to the regions was signalled near the end of their term in early 2010, when GB decided not to intervene to prevent the closure of most of the remainder of Teesside's steel manufacturing industry in this area of very high unemployment (see Chapter 5).

The next most popular aim, 6th in ranked order, was: *"To win elections nationally and locally."* This aim, together with the 7th= aim concerning democracy; will be reviewed below following discussion of policy related aims.

Ranked 7th equal was: *"To deal with the environmental crisis, carbon emissions and environmental threats of urban development; these are the big issues of our times".*

Those MPs who identified this policy aim were critical about the extremely poor record of NL Government in this area. International agreements, in which the NL government participated, focused on offsetting UK carbon emissions against promised reductions,by poorer countries. There was no serious attempt to introduce a major carbon tax or carbon capture policy for the UK. There were half hearted policies on developing renewable energy sources. The domestic manufacture of most types of equipment to generate renewable energy, for example, wind turbines, virtually ceased. The plan was to rely increasingly on nuclear power and to build a new generation of nuclear power stations in Britain. There was even a large coal-fired power station being built in Kent when Labour left office. Virtually no thought was being given to the safe disposal of nuclear waste from new power plants. Another issue was that the country was becoming increasingly less self sufficient in food production. The large scale importation of food was greatly increasing the population's carbon footprint.

Alan Simpson MP proposed that green energy should be provided by re-empowered local authorities: as had happened in Britain during the nineteenth century. Above all, there was a serious lack of awareness among the population generally, but particularly within the political class, that we must green our energy production and lifestyle urgently. The alternative is facing intractable environmental problems in the near future. There is evidence that climate change is already with us, for example, the increase in temperature of our seas and the altering weather patterns following changes in the movements of the jet stream.

John Prescott attended the Kyoto Environment Summit, as Environment Secretary, in 1997. There he signed up to a 2012 target of cutting the UK's emission of greenhouse gasses by 12% of the level of our emissions in 1990; this was later increased to 20%. UK greenhouse gas emissions then fell by a meagre 3% per year during the NL period. When carbon emissions, caused by the manufacture of UK imports, were taken into account it was estimated that carbon emissions had risen 19% on the 1990 totals. The UK continued to send 75% of domestic rubbish to landfill sites; a higher proportion than most other EU countries. Toynbee and Walker summed up: "The politics of climate change were frustratingly 'not just yet'. Growth, jobs, freedom of the road and the fun of flying all took precedence."[C11_20]

Environmental protection polices did not feature strongly during Attlee, Wilson or Callaghan Governments, where the focus was on economic growth. However threats to the well-being of the planet were less well recognised then – reservations about nuclear power excepted.

7th=: *To promote equalities (of opportunity and outcome) and counter discrimination to benefit other frequently disadvantaged classes of people: women, racial and ethnic minorities, gay people and lesbians, minority religious groups and people with disabilities.*

Interviewees in this study were *less likely to identify, or prioritise, this aim than they were to call for a more equal society, including more equality of opportunity, in economic and social class terms.* Some critics of NL (such as Owen Jones) have suggested that NL emphasised the promotion and achievement of equalities relating to gender race, ethnicity, religion, disability and sexual orientation above the traditional Labour priority of working for social and economic equality.[C11_21]

Owen Jones argued that this approach was used to lower priority given to Labour's traditional promotion of working class interests and attacks on economic disadvantage or even to obscure them. However, some MPs, who praised concern for non economic equalities priorities here, *were* on the left (e.g. Lynne Jones and Roger Berry). Ken Livingstone was an assiduous promoter of such equalities at the Greater London Authority, as he had been earlier at the GLC. Several interviewees praised extended maternity and parental leave which conferred economic and social benefits to both women and men.

As discussed in Chapter 8, the much vaunted All Women Shortlists (AWS) were allegedly used by the Party machine to try to exclude credible non favoured male candidates, for example, John McDonnell in Hayes and Harlington in 1997 and Shahid Malik in Burnley in 2005 (where fear of the local BNP probably played a part) during parliamentary selections. Worthy as promotion of non economic equal opportunities is: it appears that the NL party machine sometimes had hidden agendas when promoting "other" equalities.

NL supported some legislation for the benefit of people with disabilities: often at the prompting of backbenchers such as Roger Berry. There was legislation during the 1990s to counter institutional racism. Several interviewees had received expressions of satisfaction from the Gay and Lesbian communities relating to NL's measures to enhance their rights. These included the welcome introduction of legal civil partnerships for gay and lesbian people in 2006. There were many measures that introduced improved rights of representation for women and members of ethnic minorities within the Party, for example, CLPs must send a woman delegate to Conference in alternate years.

The focus of Attlee governments was the successful promotion of social equality and improving the lot of working people. However Wilson governments introduced significant legislation to promote other equalities. There were Equal Opportunities and Equal Pay Acts largely championed by Barbara Castle. Gay sex between consenting adults was legalised, abortion law was liberalised and the death penalty for murder was abolished after campaigning by Labour MP Sydney Silverman. There was also a Chronically Sick and Disabled Persons Act promoting relevant interests that was championed by Labour's Alf Morris.

The above policy aims and priorities, and the order in which they were ranked, reflect closely the Party aims and values with which interviewees identified. Most indicate the desired aims of a priority policy programme. However it is interesting that two aims (6th and 7th equal) call respectively for:

6th prioritisation: "Winning elections nationally and locally and to keep the Conservatives out of power.

One of the few core aims of NL was to win elections with large majorities, especially nationally. Arguably it became their principal aim (see Chapter 2). To this end they transformed the Party into a different kind of organisation with a changed ideology, culture, aims and values (New Clause 4: Appendix 2). Labour became what Lilleker and Lees-Marshment (2005) classified as a "Market Oriented Party" (MOP).[C11_22] This was one in which the Party no longer formulated its policy democratically and then tried to persuade electors of its value. Instead focus groups of electors and right wing press proprietors were allowed to determine the policies put forward by the NL Leadership. Grass-roots Party members, and even Backbench MPs, were marginalised in the policy making process. Principles and values were reduced to vaguely worded platitudes by New Clause 4. Party members and MPs were expected to go out and sell the NL programme, handed down from on high, to the public. Initially, this programme helped to win the 1997 election with a landslide. However NL's majorities diminished steadily after that and the election of 2010 was lost badly. Further reported research by Professor John Curtice of Strathclyde University[C11_23], and other 1990s psephological data, indicated that a John Smith led Labour Party would probably have won power in 1997 without turning NL. Labour has to win future elections to fulfil its aims, but it also has to find ways of doing this without negating its core purpose and values. This issue is explored in the second section of this Chapter.

Labour won in 1945 on a popular democratic socialist mandate: to improve the lives of working people and to set up a welfare state after the privations of war. They lost between 1952 and 1964 because the Conservatives generally managed the economy effectively and stole some of Labour's political clothes by adopting moderate (Butskellite) principles and continuing to develop the welfare state. These Tories also had a better understanding of electoral dynamics than Labour and benefited from dubiously drawn constituency boundaries. Apart from the Heath interregnum from 1970-74, Labour ruled until 1979, often with small majorities. Generally Labour was able to demonstrate greater commitment to public services and to benefitting working people than were the Conservatives. They lost in 1970 partly because they reneged on some of the benefit increases they promised had in the late 60s. As with Kinnock subsequently, the author, who was then a candidate, believes they probably annoyed voters during the 1970 campaign with their arrogance about their prospects of winning. The 1979 election was lost partly because it was called six months too late after economic circumstances had deteriorated and industrial unrest caused public disquiet. Before 1979 democratic socialist Labour knew how to win, if sometimes by small margins, and how to rule in the interests of those it was supposed to represent.

It is significant that the goal of winning elections was given only sixth priority by interviewees overall. A few, including MPs Chris Mullin and John Grogan, acknowledged its essential nature.

7th equal was: *"To promote democracy and democratic institutions within the UK and throughout the world and to develop, and improve, democracy and democratic practice within the Labour Party."*

A major theme of this book is examining how NL damaged Party and Parliamentary democracy in the process of radically changing the nature of the Party and turning it into an election winning machine (MOP). The democratic socialist ideological blood of the party was watered down to the point of anaemia. Whilst pursuing more acceptable goals, such as expanding public services and securing economic prosperity, NL used the alien methods of privatisation and deregulating the financial markets. This abandonment of faith and principles had severely damaging "side" effects on the Party as an organisation, including precipitating the loss of almost two thirds of the individual members and several large trade union affiliates. It also sowed disillusion amongst those Parliamentarians that the NL hierarchy had not managed to hand pick by illicit means.

Mair,[C11-24] and the author's 2005 *Save the Labour Party* pamphlet,[C11-25] pointed out that, for a Party to be effective, and to have any credibility as a democratic organisation, it must have a mass membership. The more that Party wishes to be influential in politics, the more vital that membership is. Mair contended: "Warm bodies are important, and are not really substitutable." He adds, citing Pierre and Widfeldt, that "research demonstrates that parties need to maintain the image of being a mass Party as proof that they are seen as viable channels for political representation". Members also provide democratic legitimation for a Party. In addition, they campaign for a Party and mobilise voters as was evidenced in Seyd and Whiteley's[C11-26] comprehensive analysis of British Labour Party membership. Party members contribute significantly to Party incomes through membership subscriptions, donations and fundraising. Unsurprisingly, the NL Party was greatly in debt by 2010 and had to lay off many staff. As Mair[C11-27] and interviewee Lord S. pointed out, a Party also needs sufficient members to stand for election to local government bodies and to fill publicly appointed positions.

Research for the LabOUR Commission (2007)[C11-28] showed that many Party members felt marginalised and excluded from participation in NL's Party policy making process. As Chapter 7 demonstrates, many Party members saw these policy making processes as being unintelligible and undemocratic. By 2010 democratic participation in Conference and the National Policy Forum had become very difficult. There was interference by Party staff in Conference speech making and voting, whether for policy resolutions or Party rule changes and ballots for Party officers and Committees conducted at Conference. Members' influence in Parliamentary candidate selections and those for the European and devolved Parliaments was severely diminished. *The Party was no longer a democratically run organisation.* Consequently there was scant motivation for individuals to join or to remain in membership. However some improvements have been made since through the Refounding Labour[C11-29] initiative and diminution of trade union influence as a result of the Collins Report[C11-30] initiative and 2014 Special Conference (see Chapter 12).

Parliamentary democracy was limited for Backbench MPs, even before the advent of NL. The PLP was never truly a decision making body. During the NL era there were no votes taken at PLP meetings. The Leader attended PLP meetings occasionally to lecture backbenchers about loyalty to the leadership and promoting the Party. It was a top down monologue conducted as if through a loudspeaker. Several MPs described the leaders, especially TB, as "having a tin ear" for backbenchers' concerns. Dissident backbenchers who spoke up at PLP meetings were sometimes heckled or shouted down by their colleagues. MPs who voted against the whip, except occasionally, were usually excluded from the membership of Select Committees. These bodies need members who will challenge the power of the

Government when necessary. MPs were rarely promoted by TB if they were over 50, irrespective of talent and experience. The only sure route to promotion was allegedly to belong to the TB, GB or possibly JP's, gangs of supporters. MPs were instructed, on their pagers, what to say and do in minute detail. Those who voted against the whip repeatedly were threatened with de-selection from their constituency but this seldom actually occurred.

After the millennium this repression led to Labour's most rebellious Parliaments ever, despite NL's repressive rule of the Parliamentary Labour Party.[C11-31] Eventually the law of diminishing returns operated. The Party forfeited 4.5 million votes during Blair's premiership and lost the 2010 election by a large margin. In 2010 Labour's total percentage of the vote was barely lower than that obtained in the 1983 election during Foot's leadership.

Of course, there were policy achievements and three election victories during NL's 13 years of Government. However as Chapter 6, and summaries immediately above, demonstrate, NL did not make as effective a use of their time in office as did the Attlee and Wilson governments. To secure this limited achievement, NL inflicted enormous and traumatic pain on the Party on the Ground and the PLP. Party grass roots and Parliamentary democracy were all but destroyed. In addition, NL lost of millions of voters by 2010. NL drove a majority of the individual members out of the Party and many MPs to despair. In answer to the query "New Labour: was the gain worth the pain?" The answer is a resounding "No", with minor reservations. "

Part 2

VISIONS FOR THE FUTURE OF THE LABOUR PARTY

Finally, the 57 major stakeholders were asked to set out a vision for the future political and organisational direction of the Party that most of them had respected and served for many years. This reflects how interviewees perceived this direction as they saw it between 2009-2011 at the end of the last New Labour (NL) Government. Chapter 12 discusses similar issues as seen from a 2015 post general election perspective.

Contemporary reflections about Labour's defeat in the 2010 general election and implications of these for the Party's future

The election defeat of 2010 (pending in 2009 at the time of the majority of book interviews) and the supposed end of NL, as declared by new Leader Ed Miliband, marked a junction at which a review, with an eye to the future became necessary. However as things moved on through the febrile fad of Blue Labour and then to the proposed separation from the unions in 2014, the party seemed to be moving in dubious directions. It was vital to divine and design desirable and viable ideological and organisational futures for the Party. Interview material in this Chapter must be seen in its contemporary context (2008-11). A few interviewees declared nihilistic pessimism and most of these Cassandras were about to leave, or had left, the Party. Opinions of MPs and trade union leaders follow:

Senior backbencher M. said: "We must build up the Party again. Better policy comes from mass based collective decision making. That comes from collective common sense."

Alice Mahon MP contended: "The Party has to be reclaimed by members. We need someone in the leadership who does some radical thinking and has ideas. New Labour has lost their base as a movement."

The two latter views highlight the weakness of the Party on the ground at the time of the 2010 election and its diminishing support in the community. This decline was not only a threat to already impaired party democracy, but was a danger to what remained of the Party's democratic socialism. Lynne Jones MP said: "I'm not sure that I have a vision for the Labour Party's future. I can't give you any great hope for it. There have been many times when I've thought 'Why do I stay in the Party?' I would feel more comfortable in, say, the Green Party. If we had proportional representation, I probably would join a smaller party. I suppose you stay in the Labour Party, which is a broad church, because of our electoral system. I penned an article for the *House Magazine* in 2007 saying why I was resigning at the general election. I stated then that the Labour Party was the vehicle to bring about social justice. I'm not sure I feel that way any more. I don't think the Party can talk about democracy unless we practise what we preach. Clare Short said: "What matters is what happens after the probable (2010) general election defeat. If we get a new leader who carries on along the New Labour path it will get nowhere. *There will be new parties of the left as times get tougher."*

She lamented: "The spirit of the Party has gone, a lot of the membership has gone and the question is: will it ever come back? It may, it may. A period in opposition may bring people back to Labour – but it may not. *As NL fails I don't know whether the Labour Party can rebuild out of the ashes or has to create new fire in a new place."* Clare Short had left the Labour Party at the time of this interview.

On a more hopeful note, Lord S. said: "I am optimistic about the Party's future. At Party Conference this year (2009) I thought: "Here we are in a very difficult position. You and I remember the terrible days of the 1980s – and we got through those. But at Conference 2009 I was impressed by the numbers of young men and women. We are beginning to crack issues of inequality between men and women. These young people are much less bigoted than were their predecessors and this augurs well for the Party's future."

An uphill electoral struggle for Labour was anticipated following the 2010 election: John Cryer warned: "I think that the root of the problem that all political parties now face is that there's a growing sense in Britain that people have lost control of their own destiny. This is because people are in a position where they are losing status. People have lost pensions. They've lost their right to work. If they've got a family, they can't get a council house. There is a plethora of reasons."

Gordon Prentice said: "There's been too much mendacity and constant restatement about recent good policies, for example, on housing. People don't thank you for what you've done and we shouldn't expect them to. You've got to have a moving agenda. We must secure people's confidence for the next stage. It's a constant battle to retain confidence. Where we get things wrong, e.g. Foundation Hospitals, (which saw the unpopular closure of the Accident and Emergency Department in Burnley. That Department had served GP's constituency) that makes it more difficult to roll forward public confidence."

Senior Backbencher B. said: "If we want to win elections we've got to spell out what we stand for. Very often people don't remember what we've done and take it for granted. There *are* popular things we've done: the National Minimum wage, cold weather payments and free bus travel for pensioners. We should remind people of those."

These MPs highlighted public cynicism about Labour which was born of diminishing prosperity of the population, dishonest spin and failure to promote measures which helped working class people, driven by fear of alienating swing voters in the marginals. These factors undermined appreciation of UK democracy and posed a threat to it.

Some union views follow: Billy Hayes, General Secretary CWU, said: "We need to put together a progressive coalition, but the Party in opposition is not the same as being in government. That requires you to make difficult sometimes unpalatable decisions. *The main thing is to develop a progressive alliance and to re-energise the Party and get more people active in it. We're not going to be able to win the next general election until we've got an active Labour Party and it's prepared to go against the prevailing wisdom in order to set out a programme.* I am for analysing and watching opinion polls and social trends. But we need to have self confidence and to be a bit different. The one big change needed is to disprove the claim that: 'There's no difference between them (the parties)'. *As Wilson said: (although the term is no longer right to use) 'The Labour Party is a crusade or it is nothing'. What he was saying was 'The Labour Party is a vehicle for social change or it is nothing'. Apart from a small class of careerists, people join the Labour Party because they have some vision of a progressive society.*"

Liz Snape of Unison said: "People are not demanding. They just want to be treated with fairness and respect. This is a time to lay down our differences and work to get this Conservative led government out." Both union these leaders were optimistic in their assessment and wanted to rebuild the party.

The future strategic direction of the Labour Party

Questions must be asked about the future strategic direction of the Labour Party as a whole. NL was frequently criticised for a lack of strategic direction. This reflected the short term pragmatism adopted by Tony Blair (TB) and Gordon Brown (GB).

Some interviewees, such as MP Lynne Jones, questioned whether Labour had a future at all or whether we would be better to support and help to develop the Green Party instead. *The majority wanted the Party to return to its social democratic aims and values which would then shape progressive policies.* They also wanted the Party to be run more democratically in Parliament and in the country. A few, for instance Clare Short, wondered whether this is any longer feasible. Alan Simpson MP took the view that parliament itself is "past its sell-by date" and should be replaced by a more democratic institution (see below). *Constituency Secretaries, and most MPs, emphasised that Labour must continue to be able to win elections with workable majorities.* Therefore the Party needs good public and media relations. They stated that there also need to be measures to please the middle classes in marginal seats *as well* as policies to help the poor. This imperative could be changed by introduction of proportional representation.

A way of representing Constituency Secretary's strategic views: Constituency secretaries were asked to undertake an exercise that is sometimes given to students of organisational management. The purpose, in this context, was to get them to think about what sort of organisation the contemporary Labour Party was and how they would like it to be five years hence. This takes forward perceptions of MPs interviewed about what sort or organisation the Party had become under the NL Project. Secretaries were asked: "If the Labour Party were an animal what type of animal would it be now and what sort of animal would you like it to be in five year's time? Some secretaries, being unused to this type of exercise, did not complete it. However those replies that were received were illuminating and sometimes entertaining.

Secretary Bob saw the Party currently as resembling a rabbit, five years hence he would prefer it to be like an owl. Diane imaginatively likened the party currently to: "a fox frightened that the hunting ban is not only unenforceable but also about to be lifted." In five years time she foresaw it as being: "The same fox having had its worst fears totally realised."

Secretary John perceived the Party as being like an eel now! However he hoped that, in five years, it will resemble an otter. Quentin likened the current Party to a snake, but hoped that it would turn into a tiger. William currently saw a carthorse but hoped it would be transformed into a Labrador dog. An imaginative contribution from Irene likened the contemporary Party to Boxer the carthorse in Orwell's *Animal Farm*[C11_32]: "Unassertive, obsequious to the media, weary but well-meaning". She hoped that the future party will be "something fresher and more European like a beaver, building a sturdy dam for the future".

Yvonne saw a wounded lion at present but hoped for an Ox. Adele was the third secretary to liken the present Party to a carthorse but thought it would be more like a donkey in future. Fred compared the present Party to an elephant and hoped that, by 2014, it would be bee-like. Helen currently detected an ostrich but envisioned a wasp. Oliver saw a mouse now but preferred a racehorse for the future.

Nigel currently envisaged a giant panda (endangered?) but envisaged a plucked chicken in five years time! Una (an influential Party member) believed that currently we were "lions led by donkeys" alternatively a "herd of lemmings". For the future she would prefer a phoenix or a dove. Tom thought that the Party now compares to a sheep or pigeon and forecast that, in five years, it would be a dead sheep or ex-pigeon. Vince considered the contemporary Party to resemble a sloth but would prefer a panther.

There is little need to expand on contemporary diagnoses. Slimy, wriggling creatures and carthorses featured significantly suggesting deviousness and clumsiness respectively. The *Spitting Image* television programme, popular during the 1990s, portrayed Peter Mandelson as a writhing, hissing snake.

Some animals mentioned were wounded, scared or endangered – or a combination of these. The plucked chicken and the vanquished fox were depressing. Other animals selected were unrealistic, short sighted or unintelligent. Most of the negative images seemed to fit the contemporary Brown-led Party. In a Party that is run top down, blame must attach most readily to the Leaders.

Some aspirations for the future Party dwelt on speed and/or strength and sleekness (tiger, ox, panther, racehorse and Labrador). Others desired it to be hard working: bee, wasp, beaver, otter or wise owl. Una's wish for a phoenix or dove seems symbolic. A phoenix suggests the Party rising from its own ashes having burnt itself on a pyre. The dove probably signified internal peace which has often proved difficult to achieve.

Secretary Eric suggested: "We have to learn. Review must be as key a part of policy-making processes as planning and implementing policies are." The animal exercise proved quite illuminating although it had its limitations and ambiguities.

Overview of proposed future strategic policies

The first three elements of strategic policy direction relate to the Labour Party as an organisation, to its overall aims and values and its methods of operating at a strategic level. The remaining elements are major strategic policy areas that will determine policies in a variety of specific smaller operational areas.

Return to being a democratic socialist party

A common overarching theme was the aspiration for Labour to become a social democratic party again.

MP's visions: Clare Short said: "I'm a social democrat. I would like Labour to return to being a social democratic party. We should be more like the Scandinavian countries. They are much less unequal than any other countries. They have superb public services and efficient industries. They have some good environmental policies, such as phasing out fossil fuels. They stand up strongly for the United Nations and work for peace and international development. Green and social democratic traditions need to be grown and built. But we've deeply departed from them and moved heavily to the right, to where Macmillan was. *If we had the Macmillan government back now they would be left of where New Labour is.* Alternatively, when New Labour dies off in its own mess, we need a rebuilt social democratic party which, *in a changed electoral system*, would have a real chance to break through again."

Kelvin Hopkins believed: "We should try to create a more social democratic world. We need popular key actions on the national scene which would be a marker for the direction we intend to go in. We need to improve the quality of the Party's leadership. Under NL, the Leader could say: "I'm no longer accountable to you." A Wilson or Callaghan government included a range of views representing the whole PLP. It should be so in future."

He continued: "It is not only the Party, but also British democracy in general, that needs to establish pluralistic arrangements. We need a clear choice between a democratic socialist Labour Party with values and policies which are distinct from Conservative ones. What we have at the moment (2009) are three main parties that have coalesced into this neo-liberal model. So it's up to us to make our Party distinct from other parties and say: 'I don't necessarily want you to believe what I believe, but I want you to have the choice of supporting the Party that I believe in'."

Gordon Prentice said: "*For the future I'd like to see a place in the political firmament for a democratic socialist party. We don't have that at the moment.* I want to see re-invigorated democracy in the Labour Party. I wish to bring people into Party politics that have shunned it. Young people are now interested in politics, but not Party politics. When I speak to young people I engage their interest by saying: "You're more interested in sex and shopping than you are in politics." There's nervous laughter and then I say 'Well it needn't be like that', and talk about tuition fees and the environment: they feel strongly about those."

The decline of the Labour Party's membership was steep during the NL years. This loss was apparently of minimal concern to the NL Leadership, who did virtually nothing to retain or re-recruit members or motivate them by listening to their concerns or involving them meaningfully in policy making. In order to rebuild a democratic Party, more must be done to involve and satisfy grass-roots members.

Michael Meacher contended: "There were things wrong with the Labour Party in the 1970s and 1980s related to a past era. We now need a progressive and left Labour Party.

"We have been roundly defeated by the Blair machine. The good news is that machine lies broken. The economic system and the power structure associated with it are largely discredited. Pressures from outside must be strong and persistent."

Senior backbencher M. advocated: "I would like the Party to maintain a sense of radical transformation and purpose. The Labour Party needs to keep the tradition of challenging institutional inertia. *We need to maintain the instincts and values of a radical* Obama. You might say that he's brilliant. But I don't think he would have got there if he hadn't been preceded by Bush. The Americans felt that they'd been driven down so far by George Bush."

Austin Mitchell said: "The Labour Party is moving, despite the wishes of Brown, Mandelson and the Blairite species. The new direction is the only way of dealing with the recession. I think this creates a more understandable gap between the parties – more red water. It doesn't necessarily do us any good electorally. But it does us good with people who are alienated from us because we haven't been sufficiently radical and haven't delivered to the Party rank and file. We now need to move further left in a controlled fashion."

John McDonnell enthused: "The Labour Party will have a really exciting opportunity of demonstrating what socialism could mean in the twenty-first century. It's about saying to people that they determine their own destiny." Hopefully the Corbyn-led Labour Party will grasp this exciting opportunity.

NL's Third Way was in no way socialist. As Giddens pointed out, it differs from the established model of class politics and from concepts of capital and employed labour.[C11_33]

Billy Hayes, of the CWU, said: "The first thing is minimalist at the moment. It's to create a generally progressive alliance again and to ask the question: 'Why did Labour lose 5 million votes between 1997 and 2010?' There's some evidence that it was the result of falling living standards amongst working people."

Liz Snape, of Unison, said: "The Party needs a clear vision that it is a Labour Party; that it remembers what it was formed for; that is to look after the interests of ordinary working people. I hope that this is being restored now.

Len McCluskey, of Unite, said: "NL tried to take away the Party's working class values: solidarity, community spirit and helping people out – the values of the decent working class. The Party must return to these values which are part of democratic socialism."

Giddens[C11_34] proposed new roles for unions (to meet NL expectations). These were not compatible with democratic socialist thinking. McCluskey continued: "They need to promote employability – could negotiate links from workers to the wider community – and form private sector purchasing co-operatives".

A return to Labour's traditional aims and values: as adapted to the contemporary UK social and political environment

Visions of stakeholders for the Party's future emphasised aspirations for it to re-embrace many of its traditional values and aims. These focused on a serious commitment to create a more equal society and to redistribute wealth, power and privilege. There was prioritisation proposed for more equality of outcomes as well as equal opportunities for all. At the start of interviews, stakeholders were asked to identify their preferred aims and values for the Party (see Chapter 1). These often had more in common with the Party's traditional 1917 aims and values than they did with the NL version put forward in the constitution of 1995 (Appendix 2). Interviewees also discussed their aspirations for new Party aims and values for the future. MPs' views follow:

Jon Cruddas said: "If we return to the traditions of ethical socialism then I think there is a future for the Party. We've got to take the Party back to fundamentals relating to our identity .We're at the stage where you have to go back to first principles. You can't just amend policies. *You have to retrieve the essence of what it is to be a Labour Party. We've lost our language and our mission.*"

Colin Challen argued: *"*We need to spend time looking at our aims, and especially at recent history, in terms of where we've got." Linda Riordan said: "There's no love for the Tory Party. We need, above all, to listen to Party members, MPs and electors. We've got to get back to being *the* Labour Party and stand up for our values."

The above opinions endorse the need for Labour to re examine, re-shape and clarify its aims in the post NL era. This will involve redeveloping them in the context of redefined democratic socialist values which need to articulated and applied in the changed contemporary social and political environment.

Senior backbencher A. proposed: "We need to redefine our core values and ideas. This relates to what I did when I led the council in a large city local authority. Our Labour Group, and certainly our local Labour Party, knew what its values were and what it was trying to achieve. There didn't need to be a debate about it. The local public knew where I stood. There was no doubt anybody's mind, that we were about representing the whole city, but particularly the poor. We were also trying to build a modern city with modern services. *There is no perception in the Labour Party, any more, about what we stand for or of what our values and ideas are.* The MPs expenses stuff exemplifies that. We are: seen as a Party that represents social justice and the poor. That would require a certain ethos and set of values that we ought to live by. But we have a bunch of MPs (I don't exempt myself from this) who live a life that doesn't represent the values we claim to espouse. We need to think about how we should live our lives and how we express that."

A. continued: *"There's a huge job (to be done) on discourse and re-articulating our values in a modern setting. This should start with developing the state rather than the market and providing through public services, equity and social justice.* Labour lost five million votes between 1997 and 2005. These were mainly in social groups D and E, Muslims and progressive intellectuals. Public sector workers feel bruised by Private Finance Initiative (PFI) and privatisation policies. *No Party of the left can survive if the poor don't support them."*

As A. pointed out, Labour needs to return to unequivocally speaking up for and representing working class people. Under NL, measures to help the working class were often either hidden or played down. Fairness and electoral necessity demand that we represent the "squeezed middle" as well as, but *not instead* of, the working classes. What Labour should never do is represent the wealthy. It is also crucial that Labour MPs are seen to live reasonably modestly and not acquire and flaunt significant wealth.

Developing a Learning Organisation: learning from all aspects of Labour's past

In line with established principles of organisational learning, the Party needs to become a learning organisation. Such an organisation will learn from NL's and "Old" Labour's successes, as well as from their shortcomings. It will use this learning to improve its future performance.

"A Learning organisation is one which constantly reviews its past actions to identify what it has achieved and where it has failed. It then identifies what it has learnt from these outcomes that can usefully inform its future actions and endeavours. Lastly it puts this learning into practice." Reg Revans.[C11_35]

Many interviewees agreed that much can be learned from the essential ingredients of NL's election successes, particularly from its effective public and media relations. However, time showed that some of its controversial policies (e.g. bellicose foreign policies and failure to control the market) did not ultimately contribute to electoral success or to a better life for our society as a whole. More publicity should have been given to NL's measures to help the disadvantaged (see Chapters 2 and 5). Policies which proved egalitarian, popular and effective should be updated, emulated and developed. There was a price paid by the NL Party for turning Labour into an election-winning, "Market Oriented Party" in terms of Party and Parliamentary democracy (see Chapter 2).

Jon Cruddas feared that the Party might not learn from its mistakes during the NL era. He claimed: "The same sort of NL authoritarianism, the same lack of language, the same calculation would mean that our Party's trend continues to decline as it is doing now (2009). *Alternatively, we should say that this demands a different Labour Party so that we can analyse the future with reference to our own past and resurrect the traditions of our Labour movement to try to comprehend (our social and economic environment) and chart the future.* The danger is that we disregard our worst (2010) election disaster since 1910. In 1910 we were on the up and were prepared to defy Liberal Britain, the Liberals were doing badly."(The 2015 election result was even worse – see Chapter 12).

Colin Challen claimed: "The Party does not need to be re-vamped on US Democratic Party lines. We should go back to what was best about the Party (which has been a success as well as a failure) and see how that can be improved. The ideas that you have to get rid of Constituency Labour Parties (CLPs), or members, and that you have to re-invent something all the time are wrong. Ministers tended to go overboard – change for the sake of it. The Party doesn't need a complete radical overhaul. Sometimes it just needs improving. That's the way to keep people on board. *We need to ask ourselves again: 'What do we stand for?' and learn from the collected wisdom of the Party."*

Challen continued:"I recently had a letter published by the *Guardian* saying: 'We've got to recognise where we went wrong and admit it'. *Rather than arguing: 'a politician can never apologise'. That's in NL's genetic code. If they do apologise. it's: 'I'm sorry if I offended you' .but never: 'I made a mistake'. It's always surrounded by caveats and get-out clauses.* We need a really good truth and reconciliation approach to what NL did wrong. We should accept that our hubris got in the way and we boasted that we had ended boom and bust. It turned out that we'd only ended the Tory boom. *All these arrogant tendencies that have become part of our politician's make up have to be tackled so we can have a real clearance but not a bloodletting."*

Alan Simpson said: "There's going to have to be a root and branch re-organisation … How do I think that the Labour Party will deal with all the required changes? Well it will either die or they will be its wake-up call. This requires a different calibre of leadership and quality of vision and a different sense of courage that takes on the big vested interests of capital. Change will have to go from the grass roots upwards to central government."

Clare Short argued: "We need some continuity and building on Labour's more than 100 years of history. Whilst it is wise to counsel that the Party builds on NL's success, there were many failures, omissions and departures from long held principles. It seems right to recommend that the Party also acknowledges what went wrong under NL, apologises for these mistakes and promises to govern better in future."

Louise Ellman asserted: "We've had major achievements since 1997. But there's still a lot to do. We should be proud of our successes but must be sure we don't repeat our mistakes. *One of these mistakes was to negate the achievements of 'Old Labour' and not recognise them.* We must think about these and understand what can be learnt from both sets of achievements. This learning must be applied to the new situation in which we find ourselves. I feel strongly that, *in appealing to the middle classes, we have denied to working class people, what we have achieved for them. This was a great mistake. It was because we wanted to appeal to people in middle England. I don't think that most middle class people object to helping the poor.* There's a mood of defeatism around the Party now. We've got to re-energise ourselves again and once more become the Party of change."

Graham Stringer believed: "We should say: 'We had ten years of boom but house price inflation was supporting this'. We should have declared this publicly and prepared people for a possible downturn. *"*

John Grogan declared: "We're doing things now that are very encouraging. I wouldn't want us to go into opposition and completely dish our record or to write TB and GB out of our history, because much has been achieved. The policies that I'd like to see us develop in opposition are things we're in danger of forgetting, that are part of our social democratic and progressive ideals, for example, the public service ethos."

Katy Clark said: "I hope that the Labour Party re-connects with its roots. But I also hope that it takes the best of NL. I think we should keep some of the professionalism that went with NL. But we have to have a serious think about our orientation. *One of the big mistakes made by the NL Project was that its orientation was towards people who will never support the kinds of values that the Labour Party was created to deliver.*"

NL's election winning tactics and good media and public relations should be emulated (provided that the Party's values and principles are not abandoned in the process). That Blair and Mandelson made complacent statements about the super rich was indefensible and these should never be repeated.

Senior Backbencher B. stated: "One of the key things for the Labour movement is to understand why we lose general elections (and learning from and acting on that). After we lost the 1979 election, I said to my predecessor: "We got this pay policy wrong. I could have told you that from the views of my (union) members on the factory floor that they weren't happy. Sometimes there's a failure to listen. The Party's got to listen to people who (usually) vote for us."

Alan Simpson believed: "Defeat in the 2010 general election isn't inevitable, because I think we could rescue things if we were willing to do a radical re-configuration of our policies *now*. At this stage there isn't a deep rooted, desire (among electors) for the Conservatives. But there is cynicism about what Labour has come to represent."

Jon Cruddas said: "*We have to be prepared to think there's nothing inevitable about the Labour Party existing. In any period of major and profound social and economic change you see political realignments. I think there will be a major political realignment in the next few years the like of which I don't know – perhaps the re-emergence of a liberalism within the Labour Party; the New Labour/ Liberal agenda.* I think we'll see a rise of Fabianism and the development of a more scientific socialist response. We'll see a return to certain ethical traditions within the socialist wing which has always fought certain liberal traditions within the Labour Party itself. *That's where I will be hoping to contribute.*"

Graham Stringer said: "It will be a very different debate if we lose the general election. If we lose badly, the debate will be very fundamental: About what a centre left Party should be about. We will go through the constitutional debates and the local democracy debates."

He continued: "It is vital that comprehensive and objective reviews are done focusing on why Labour lost the 2010 election and what lessons should be learned from this. It is a fundamental question as to whether we will have the strength to stay together as a Party? *One side of it is the Campaign Group and the other – people who would like to ditch the trades unions and ally with the Liberal Democrats.*"

Cruddas and Stringer were clearly prophetic about the development of schools of thought and action attempting to drive the Party to right or left and the potential schism to which it could lead. This question was raised again after Jeremy Corbyn was elected Labour Leader because of the majority presence of Blairites in the PLP and the clear majority of democratic socialists now in the Party on the ground.

Then backbencher Jeremy Corbyn said: "We've got six months before the (2010) general election. At present the prospects don't look good for Labour. I notice that NL is now using the language of Nye Bevan. I wish they'd use his policies as well, at least his social policies! I hope that there will be some understanding that to make ourselves strong we need to make the Party strong. *We're losing a whole generation who do not feel that Labour is for them. It's a function of the Party to be proud of its history, proud of its roots and be prepared to campaign on them. There's an image that can get people in. At the end of the day it's the politics, the cause and the principles that matter.*"

It is now vital that comprehensive and objective reviews are done focusing on the reasons why Labour lost the 2015 election and what lessons should be learned from these.

Developing a strategic framework for future policies

Policies for promoting social equality and social mobility: realising Labour's core value and aim.

This was, predictably, a strong theme. Wilkinson and Pickett[C11_36] identified strong links between inequality, within societies, (including the UK) and the occurrence of health and social problems which Labour Governments usually want to address.

MPs' views: Graham Stringer argued: "When you try to address the *equality agenda* it's very difficult because Blair asks: "Why do you want to stop people earning ludicrous amounts of money?' It's an almost unanswerable question. But, if you can't answer that question, it's difficult to know what to do about equality issues. But you can certainly start by concentrating a lot harder at the bottom end of the policy agenda." This statement suggested that TB did not accept the need to create more equal society in Britain.

Frank Dobson said: "I would like the Party to get back to trying to reduce inequality, strive for far greater equality in our society and mesh this with a return to Keynesian economics. In pursing green policies we must ensure that frugality applies to the rich and that we don't penalise the poor."

Louise Ellman contended: "We must continue campaigning to bring more equality. It isn't possible to abolish poverty, but we must minimise it as much as possible. We need to embrace many levels of diversity in our multi-racial society. We should strive for prosperity for everyone. As the leadership feared at times, the middle classes probably felt afraid that Labour might tax them more heavily. That was never actually the case. We should be proud of what we've done to counter poverty. I believe in equality of opportunity and we should strive for equality of outcome. But I don't think that that can ever be achieved completely. We don't want to stifle people's ambitions."

Senior backbencher M. said: "Labour's history valued social justice and tried to develop policies to create a more equal society. We need to renew that commitment and pursue such policies more strongly in future. There was some progress under Blair in getting rid of inequalities in the UK but there will always be much more to do."

Christine McCafferty argued: "We need a future Labour Government that continues to have equality and equity as its fundamental basis. It should continue to strive to represent all the people, especially to defend the vulnerable and weak and to ensure that people who can't help themselves are the focus of strategic policy."

In furtherance of promoting equality in Britain, Toynbee and Walker, 2008, claimed: "Unless strong voices keep saying that public wellbeing depends on a redistributive government, the nihilists and privateers gain ground."[C11_37]

John Grogan called for "a review of the distribution of income and wealth in the UK."

Kelvin Hopkins wanted redistributive taxation. He said: "We need an immediate redistribution of income by raising taxes on the rich: make sure the wealthy pay more and pay their way. We need social justice and social equality."

It is often claimed that stopping tax avoidance and evasion is almost impossible and that the UK can do little to prevent abuses that are conducted in her offshore tax havens. Toynbee and Walker, 2008, quoting Lord Sainsbury's, then recent, review argued: "Countries have not lost their ability to regulate and tax their economies as the highly taxed but internationally competitive Nordic countries demonstrate."[C11_38]

Gordon Prentice emphasised the importance of equality issues and added: "But there is also the good life. The good life for people means supporting the arts and like things. It includes the right to roam. I think that's part of Labour's historic mission."

The gap between the richest and poorest in the UK increased under NL. In 2003·4 around 19,000 people had an annual income of over half a million pounds but two years later this number had grown by 34,000[43]. The Blairites were apparently still relaxed about the super rich!

Len McCluskey of Unite said: "Another main cause of inequality is the race to the bottom. Margaret Thatcher made it difficult for trade unions to organise in this situation and NL did nothing to put that right. It must be tackled by Labour in future."

Roger Berry contended: "I think we've got to be bolder about saying that, if the circumstances require it, people will have to pay more tax. Those who pretended that we can run Scandinavian levels of social welfare on American levels of taxation have never made sense. Before the 1997 election people who said that were regarded as being unhelpful and rocking the boat. In dealing with the global financial crisis and a big public sector deficit, it's not good enough for a Labour government to contemplate *only* reduction in public spending. The other side of the policy should be increasing taxation. Those with the biggest pockets should bear the burden."

CLP Secretary's views: Yvonne said: "The poorest members of society must be protected and inequality be reduced." John wanted Labour to: "Eliminate poverty and let everyone have an equal chance." Quentin said: "We should also take stronger measures to counter poverty."

Fiscal and welfare policies to achieve a more equal society are required. Fiscal policies underpin effective economic management but also play a significant role in determining the distribution of wealth in society, the viability of public services and, through redistribution, should help to deliver a more equal society.

Alice Mahon argued: "I don't think there is anything wrong with (progressive) taxation. They've moved a little on taxing the better off. I'm not keen on the use of VAT, as it's a heavy tax on the poor."

Kelvin Hopkins wanted redistributive taxation. He said: "We need an immediate redistribution of income by raising taxes on the rich and restoring the 10p rate of income tax as first steps."

Jeremy Corbyn said: "We have to boldly settle for universal benefits and taxation to pay for it, instead of going down the road of targeted means tested benefits which ultimately cost (the government) more."

Roger Berry believed: "Our society must be one in which public spending necessarily plays an important part. Taxation is a good thing if it creates greater equality and enables us to fund public spending. It's now clear that we cannot sustain appropriate levels of NHS, welfare and education provision without biting the bullet about taxation."

NL's record on progressive taxation was often poor. In the mid 1990s it cut capital gains tax from 40% to 10% and grudgingly raised it to 18% in 2009 after the crash. There was continuing reliance on the regressive Value Added Tax rather than increasing income tax on the better off (until Brown's eleventh hour).

Welfare benefits is a controversial area where ill informed, hostile opinion is frequently whipped up by the right wing press and then reflected in opinion polls. However a raft of benefits is necessary to alleviate both secondary and primary poverty. There is massive unemployment in areas where Thatcherite governments closed down former manufacturing and mining industries. There are many people who depend on benefits long term and would work if employment were available; particularly in the industrial wastelands. There are some who have got out of the habit of working and need retraining and re-motivating.[C11_39]

A minority of MPs took a hard line on benefit abuse, but most saw improved and universal benefits as one of the best ways of reducing poverty and providing a safety net for poor, chronically sick, elderly and disabled people.

Jeremy Corbyn supported: "The principle of universal benefits; because that's the type of society I want. People don't like the idea that all benefits should be means tested." John Cryer believed: "State pensions and pension rights must be strengthened."

Conversely, Graham Stringer declared: "I'm strong on welfare reform. I think that one of NL's failures has been being unable to find pathways for people out of chaotic lifestyles. Labour always shied away from this. It's a case of sticks and carrots and they're always keen on the carrots but less keen on the sticks. I share that emotion, but I don't think it will work for the future."

CLP Secretaries' views: Philip said: "We need fairer taxation, the 10p income tax rate was a good idea." William called for "more progressive taxation." Xenia added: "The rich should be taxed more". "Reform the tax system so that it is progressive," said Fred. Oliver also wanted "a more equitable tax system." Mike argued: "We should work for a fairer society through a revised tax structure."

Una demanded: "Restore out of work benefits, job seeker's allowance etc. to 1997 levels. Raise them substantially and then link further increases to earnings levels. The same should be applied to retirement pensions. Raise the national minimum wage. Bring in higher taxes for the rich if necessary." Tom said: "The incomes of the working class, but not the rich, should be improved."

Adopting a Green Political Strategy

In terms of respondent's policy priorities (see Chapter 1): there was strong support for development of a green policy agenda. Interviewees put forward their ideas for policies to be pursued by the next Labour Government. This, some correctly surmised, would follow a period of opposition rule after the coming election. Therefore they usually adopted a broadly strategic approach because it is difficult to develop viable operational policies long before they are due to be implemented.

Despite crocodile tears frequently being shed about the need for environmentally friendly policies, little was done to promote them by NL governments. Low priority was given to the development of renewable energy (for example, the only plant in the UK that manufacturing wind turbines was allowed to close).High priority was given to the development of a new generation of nuclear power stations. More land was to be freed up for residential and industrial development. The Green Party described the 2004 Planning and Compulsory Purchase Act as "The death of rural England".

MPs' views: Lynne Jones predicted: "We're facing disaster in my children's lifetimes if we don't face the issue of climate change. That is the number one fundamental issue. Someone must start putting the survival of the planet at the forefront of our political thinking."

Alan Simpson argued: "The resource crisis is inevitable. Peak oil is probably already here. Peak phosphate is not far away. That will have massive effects on agrichemicals. Issues about water supply and water management are going to become increasingly prevalent in the turbulence of climate change. We're in the dying days of dying energy resources." Senior backbencher M. said: "The new, and dominant, issue is climate change. To destroy the global environment would be to hit the poorest hardest."

The Labour Party needs to give urgent attention to developing a green political strategy, one that effectively addresses the threat of climate change and is prepared to revolutionise our strategy for energy generation and consumption. It needs to adopt policies for carbon capture and reduction of carbon emissions. We should not rely on carbon trading to pressurise poor countries to generate less carbon dioxide so that we may fail to reduce pollution or even pump more into the atmosphere ourselves.

NL Government did little to promote *green policies:* apart from participation in relevant international conferences and a half hearted commitment to small scale development of renewable energy. They also pressured local authorities to increase recycling of household waste.

Labour did not reduce the UK's dependence on carbon. Britain became even more dependent on energy supplies from overseas. In 2009 gas generated 45% of UK electricity and coal 32%. There was diminishing North Sea oil and gas production. Interviewees demonstrated a major concern for, and commitment to, green policies for the future.

More MPs' views follow: Alan Simpson said: "There is never going to be a return to the globalisation agenda of deregulated, global free-for-alls in trade on an ever rising tide of prosperity. The world will never go there again, partly because of the inevitability of resource crises. That's where we can make the shift into renewable energy systems. We can do that much faster than the government is proposing. Our level of ambition in the UK is pitifully low."

Simpson continued: "We need to make a new energy revolution akin to the one that began in the UK in 1817 when we set up our first energy company. We must use the same model. The revolution in the UK between 1817 and 1890 was driven by localities. We had municipal gas, electricity and water companies. Out of their profits these companies built parks, museums, libraries and swimming baths. They were funded by local government bonds where people put savings and pensions. In return they got their appropriate rate of interest *and* huge improvements in local infrastructure." Simpson's proposal to localise and municipalise energy supplies is imaginative and would involve a welcome re -empowerment of local government.

He continued: "We are reluctantly discussing 15% of our energy resources coming from renewable sources by 2020. *In reality at least a third of that isn't going to be met by ourselves.* It's going to be offset by paying the poor in other parts of the world to do the clean up for us. Germany is currently looking to delivering 100% of their energy from renewable sources by 2050. They, Scandinavia and parts of the US are driving ahead with the shift to renewables in a way that delivers jobs, energy security and ecological transformation. In order to make that transition, we have to shift power away from the big six energy companies."

Another positive example is Australia 2009-12 where, through Labor Government action, domestic users of solar energy were given rebates and surplus solar power manufactured by them was purchased back by energy companies.

Simpson continued: "They would not be consumers of any old energy for which they have to pay exorbitant sums. Transformation will be forced on us as our system breaks down. My optimism is that human ingenuity will drive that change in a way that Parliaments may not. Under this system food markets will probably return to more localised and regionalised systems. Governments will be forced to address questions of national food security without assuming that there are suppliers queuing up to sell us an abundance of food cheaper than we could produce it ourselves. During World War 2 public land was brought back into use for food cultivation. We were up to six times more productive in our cities than we were in the countryside."

Simpson asked: "Look at what's currently happening in Cuba. It's the only country on earth forced (by the end of the Soviet Union) into post oil agriculture. If you can't obtain agricultural chemicals then you have to go back to organic and traditional farming systems. In 2007 Cuba became self sufficient in organic food production. Last year they became a net exporter to others in their region. This illustrates that if we treat ourselves, and the planet, seriously we will start to ask ourselves what and how we put back into the earth rather than just what we take out? It *is* possible for us to live well and sustainably."

Linda Riordan asserted: "The environment is our biggest issue. That's something that people really care about, young people in particular."

The NL Government was not effective in dealing with greenhouse gas emissions which fell at about the same rate after 1997 as they had between 1990 and 1997.

Lynne Jones claimed: "I don't see the Labour Government as understanding environmental problems because we're still saying it's right that India and China should start reducing their carbon dioxide emissions. Our agreements with them are predicated on the fact that they have got to do that. We were the first industrialised nation. For the last 200 years, we've been chucking pollution into the atmosphere. Climate change will make certain parts of the world uninhabitable. We're going to have a huge refugee crisis. I'm sorry to be so pessimistic, but I sometimes wonder whether it's right to bring children into this world."

She continued: "I suppose that the political party who actually understand green issues, and go beyond setting targets for 2050, is the Green Party. Currently the Labour Party doesn't seem to have got it. They haven't realised that we have to start talking to people and to change our lifestyles completely now. We've got to start spending on making our homes energy efficient. We must invest in green technologies, export those to other countries and help them not to make the mistakes we've made."

Senior backbencher M. said: "Famine and floods are already with us, for example, recent floods in Bangladesh. The rich suffer less because they are able to create protection for themselves." Frank Dobson believed: "We must try to run a society which consumes less of the world's resources and is more frugal."

As these MPs lamented, there was an NL view that one way to make the world less polluted overall was to dump some of our responsibility for cleaning up on poorer countries, thus curtailing their economic growth whilst sustaining our own.

Colin Challen recalled: "I put forward a number of green policies. The most significant was probably the introduction of personal carbon allowances that I tried to introduce in a 2004 Private Member's Bill. Within two and a half hours David Miliband said that the Government would look at it. A Royal Society of Arts study concluded that it was ahead of its time. The government is seriously behind the times on this issue. This is progressive, redistributive policy. Rich people will have to pay a lot more for their carbon. Poorer people, who tend to use less, would get more credits. That would put money in their pockets and lead to many efficiencies. That's a market based mechanism too. I think we should elevate environment policy to a much higher status. *Some ministers see the environment as unimportant.*"

Chris Mullin argued: "We need to move to sustainable sources of energy. There must be a push on renewables. But that won't solve the problems. *There is a danger that the lights will go out in 15-20 years time if nothing is done. If we are to address climate change and ensure the survival of the planet we need to get a sustainable lifestyle as soon as possible or we will destroy the earth.*"

Lord S. said: "I was described by the *Independent* as: 'The first UK green politician to be on the front bench'. It's crucial to keep forestry in the public sector. It's only by setting a good example that you persuade others to agree with environmentally desirable policies. Climate change campaigns have provided a great fillip to this. But you've got to make sure that climate change policies don't cause the poorer people to suffer."

The above three Parliamentarians all had good green credentials and had thought seriously about how to develop environmentally friendly policies.

Linden argued: "If climate change is not tackled and adverse weather events become more frequent and severe, then the expenditure burden on governments in repairing the infrastructural and human damage would be enormous and difficult to fund."[C11_40]

CLP Secretaries' views: William cited "the environment" as the top policy priority area. Bob wanted priority given to "securing energy efficiency and environmentally friendly agriculture".

Keith said: "There must be a greater emphasis on environmental issues. This includes such things as food production, which may not matter too much at the moment. However, with global warming, they will become of paramount importance to future generations. We should remember that we are only tenants of this planet and we must leave it in a viable condition for our successors." Yvonne, Gary and Tom saw 'Tackling climate change' as being of the highest priority. Fred called for more investment in renewable energy.

All these secretaries stressed the need for urgent action without further equivocation. Linden admitted that we cannot be certain that we are heading for this nightmare but added: "when, in the past, have we demanded certainty before acting on a potential global threat?"[C11_41]

A new Alternative Economic Strategy: economic policy, industrial policy and policy on financial institutions

Most interviewees supported what they saw as a strong relationship between running a successful economy and providing high quality public services, promoting prosperity for all and winning elections. However, there was acknowledgement that the 2008 global financial crisis; the growth and economic expansion of the BRIC (Brazil, Russia, India, China) countries and the effects of that growth; and recognition that indefinite economic growth, even were it possible, would have severe environmental consequences. It was now clear that the old aspirations for economic growth and its benefits were no longer realistic.

MPs' opinions: Jon Cruddas proclaimed: "We are now in a period of epochal economic and social change which includes little or no economic growth. It depends how you see this. If you see it as an interregnum until we get back to normal, a triumph of neo liberalism – then more of the same is the solution. If, instead, you see this as a rupture between different periods of capitalist growth and stagnation and the end of an era associated with a particular form of economic dominance, namely, a semi liberal political economy. *Then that creates the need for a different type of social and economic project. If you think that it should be more of the same, 'steady as she goes'; the inevitability is that the Labour Party might die."*

John McDonnell said: "If we can democratise our economy and society, we can redistribute wealth and mobilise economic recovery to create equality and a more equal society. We must control the economy democratically at every level – including the banks and the financial sector. People must be given a say over the future of their workplace."

Senior backbencher A. argued: "Labour's flexible labour markets and the free movement of Labour, especially within the EU, have driven down wages. Employers opt out of good wage rates and so the locals have to accept lower wages. The NMW is set too low and needs raising. Rightly the social wage has increased through the welfare state, but private earned incomes have reduced relative to inflation. We need to revise and build a sound economy that is *not* based on the City."

The above MPs all saw the way forward as being a democratic socialist model of economic management. The NL approach of unfettered market economics was seen to be no longer fit for use by Labour administrations.

Michael Meacher adopted that theme: "A major disaster has been the economic collapse, the financial meltdown and the number of people who are hurt by this– losing their jobs, homes – and the colossal pressures on those struggling to retain their homes and jobs and make do in difficult and demanding times. I think that provides the driver for change. We have got to use those pressures."

Alan Simpson argued: "Now is the time in our evolution when it has never been more important for us to have a political take on current issues. There's a hanging on to the boat mentality. Many of those who are gripping on by their fingertips have this naïve belief that if we can just weather the current storm the seas will calm and we can get back on the voyage of the 'Free Enterprise' without realising that the 'Free Enterprise' sank! "We are not a poor country, but people who are continuing to put their money in to pension schemes are terrified. Their only choice at the moment is to throw their money into the speculative global economy which gambles their money away. It is taking people's pension contributions and pissing them up a wall which happens to be called Wall St. People are reaching a point at which they want to withdraw their savings from other people's right to speculate. That doesn't mean we're reluctant to have our money put into things that *will* deliver us security for the future."

Alice Mahon endorsed Cruddas' fears of the effects of continued adherence to neo liberalism. She regretted: "I'm disappointed with the finance white paper that the select committee has just criticised (July 2009). So there's going to be no change there. It's time we got our act together and put the bankers under some sort of decent regulation. They brought on the catastrophe. It's a pity that Gordon got sucked into neo liberal economics and can't get out of it."

Other respondents recommended a return to more traditional Labour economic strategies: Keynesian economic management; regulation of the markets; and, above all, stronger control; and, in some cases, outright ownership of the banks.

Frank Dobson thought: "We should go back the post war situation where the establishment and maintenance of full employment was a major national objective. If you look at the period when that sort of Keynesian approach was applied, in nearly all the western developed world, we had something approaching full employment. It was only when the neo-conservative/liberal lot started undermining Keynesian concepts that we started having high levels of unemployment and increasing inequality. I think we need to re-assert the merits of Keynesian economics and strive for Keynesian, and other post war, objectives."

Jeremy Corbyn said: "My future vision is that the leadership accepts that the financial crisis that we're in now is the endgame of the Milton Friedman economics of the 70s, 80s and 90s. It's the endgame of monetarism and marketisation. It's the endgame of global economic strategies based on the free market. I'm not sure that they will do that because, in nationalising the banks, they've put all the shares into a holding company and plan to sell them off in the near future. I'd like preparedness to boldly say that we want an economy that is based on needs and demands; not on profits, shares and greed in the market."

Roger Berry argued: "I strongly believe that GB has it right on the economy. The Tories are out of touch with the real situation. Labour has must say that we took the right action." Alan Simpson declared: "Markets are wonderful things, except for issues that are really important. Of course we can't run the economy without markets, nor should we try. But some markets are unsatisfactory. Now even some bankers describe half of their banking functions as 'casino activity'. Casino finance must be addressed. So must blind faith in markets and in the City. We've got have more scepticism than NL is prepared to have."

The case against NL's "hands off" economic management and continued reliance on unregulated capitalists was expanded in the testimonies below. However some sounded notes of caution:

Lord S. claimed: "We should not apologise for state intervention. If I were to be a bit critical of NL, it has perhaps given the impression that the market can solve all the problems. That's not true and we must get that message across. I think that the banking crisis has given us that opportunity, but I'm not convinced that we've rammed that home yet."

John Grogan said: "We need a slightly more critical approach to contemporary market capitalism. But I'm an equally strong believer in competition. We've been too uncritical of businesses like the energy companies. Our economic policy has probably reflected that."

Graham Stringer argued: "We need to move back to that part of the NL agenda which said: 'If you're going to make accommodations with the market, then you can't bail out 'the Meridens' – as was done in the 1970s or British Leyland – as in 2005. You have to let the market deal with it'. But the best way to support the economy is by investing in the infrastructure, transport (which has been a failure) and in the education infrastructure: which includes fast modern internet technology."

Chris Mullin forecast: "The country faces serious problems. *Any government will have to deal with a financial deficit. This was not caused by profligacy, as the Tories say, but has come from the global banking crisis.*"

Many respondents saw a crucial relationship between running a successful economy and providing high quality public services, promoting prosperity for all and winning elections. However, after the 2008 global financial crisis, it became clear that the old aspirations for economic growth and its benefits were no longer realistic.

Another perspective was offered by a trade union leader. Len McCluskey, of Unite the UK's largest (mainly industrial and private sector) union said: "The Labour leadership must support manufacturing industry which was under attack from both Tory and NL governments since 1979. We must invest in manufacturing in Britain. We must control predatory capitalists and get away from the society in which greed is rewarded. Otherwise our children will be worse off than our generation.

"We need a bold and radical industrial investment policy. We should have a publicly owned British Investment Bank to invest in industry and construction and start growth. We need 100,000 new homes – mainly social rented ones. Three million people currently need a decent home and we need to combine this factor with two others – taking the present 100,000 construction workers off the dole and using the current huge stockpiles of unused new construction materials. Labour must take the lead and Unite will help."

McCluskey continued: "When I was running for General Secretary (2011) I visited the Rolls Royce Factory in Goodwood and the Mini Factory in Cowley. Both are now owned by BMW. The Managing Directors are German. I asked one: 'What is the difference between the UK and Germany in your business?' He replied: *The UK doesn't take manufacturing seriously where Germany does*'. He explained that the problem in Britain was the supply chain. Parts and machinery are not made here and there are delays in delivery when it is needed. In Germany all parts are available locally. He gave the example of the huge robots used by BMW to build cars. These robots are German made. He would prefer these robots to be made in Britain and they and their parts to be made locally. This would provide high status, high wage jobs here. It would provide training and career opportunities for school leavers. *Unfortunately neither Conservative nor New Labour governments gave importance to manufacturing industry*."

CLP Secretaries' views reflected many opinions offered above. There was much support for continuation of the commendable aspects of NL's economic management, but with the addition of more regulatory systems. Philip said: 'We should continue with our good management of the economy. Quentin said: "We must prioritise and focus on the economy." William advised: "We should continue good economic management and also invest in manufacturing, innovation, research and development through a coherent industrial strategy." Oliver sought: "New regulatory frameworks for financial, employment and product markets." Yvonne called for a Labour Government to: "Get the economy working well." Fred demanded: "Reform of the economy." He also called for a strategy to create additional jobs. Vince argued: "We must aim to regulate the market for the benefit of the poorest in society and hold international conferences to pursue this cause. We must never again follow the philosophy 'Let the markets rule'."

A few secretaries reflected some MPs' preoccupations with the need to adopt Keynesian economic management and more effective regulation of the banks. Xenia thought: "The priority must be good management of the economy and effective control of the banks." Adele wanted them to "Get control of banking and the bankers". Fred requested "Reform of the economy." He also called for a strategy to create additional jobs. Colin wanted: "Neo-Keynesian economic policies with an identifiable element of redistribution of wealth." Keith said: "I see no reason why the Government should not reserve unto itself a veto on practices and senior appointments in the banking and financial services industries."

Bob was alone in mentioning meeting the challenges posed by the growth of the BRIC countries. He argued: "The next Labour Government will have to recreate a viable UK economy and come much more to terms with the rise of China, India etc. as centres of manufacturing and suppliers of labour-intensive service industries. There will not be massive extra resources and we shall have to come to terms with that. Irene insisted that: "We must ensure that the public services do not bear the brunt of dealing with the national debt."

A strategy for localism

In respect of *Local Government*: There was general agreement that NL had followed their Tory predecessors in pruning further the roles and powers of local government and that it was time to reverse these trends and to re-empower local authorities. The head of steam for greater devolution/independence for Wales and Scotland had not built up when interviews relating to this topic were undertaken (see Chapter 12).

M.P.'s opinions follow: Former councillor John Grogan said: "We need to get over New Labour's deep distrust of local government. That came partly from Blair and Brown being struck by the 'loony left' era. They never really valued local government. They always thought Whitehall civil servants were the only decent public servants. Our view of localism has been taken from Hazel Blears style focus groups. We need to let local councils decide more things. We set up quangos to make decisions. Local councils should be given more power, even if they don't always do what the Government wants. A reaction has already started against having too many targets in and too many supervisory bodies over local councils."

Opinions of another three former councillors follow: Kelvin Hopkins asserted: "We need stronger and more independent local government." Graham Stringer declared: "I'm very strong on decentralisation and democracy. One of the failures of the last 12 years has been the relationship with local government and local democracy. Central government now sees local government as an inefficient delivery system. They forget that there is a democratic element to it." Roger Berry stated: "Id like local authorities to be liberated so they can do rather more off their own bats."

TB and GB followed in the Thatcherite tradition of a top down, controlling central government. Nowhere was this more evident than in Local Government. There were twin fears of overspending and political initiatives that were not invented on sofas in central London.

Alan Simpson declared: "Local politicians must have courage to stand up to central government. The question is whether Labour is going to be up to meeting the vision and challenge of the need for different environmental and economic policies. It isn't difficult to do, but it can't be done by a little shift or nimble footwork. We need a fundamental shift in the way we plan our towns and cities. The infrastructures of public transport have to take precedence over the interest of private motorists. In ten years time we won't entertain planning permission for a building that doesn't generate its own energy or harvest its own rainwater and recycle it. Local politicians will need courage to stand up to builders who want to build for the past."

CLP Secretaries' opinions included Quentin's, he said: "Give more power back to local government." Oliver requested: "The revitalisation of local government in England."

Used appropriately, as in some of the imaginative schemes proposed by Alan Simpson, local authorities should be re-empowered and used to develop and implement polices better attuned to the needs and wishes of local people.

A strategy for public services and public enterprises

As Chapter 5 pointed out, many respondents were enthusiastic about NL's investment in public services, but less positive about the privatisation that usually accompanied it. They wanted the next Labour Government to develop public services further, but in a more rational and well planned manner, than during the NL era.

Colin Challen argued: "*New Labour has tended to change policies for the sake of it.* An example is PCTs (Primary Care Trusts). They were changed even though we'd not had a chance to see if they were working. We need to go back to previous models or we'll end up with huge unworkable organisations like regional police forces. It took ages to convince people, like Hazel Blears, that this was not the best policy."

Jeremy Corbyn believed: "We must stop lecturing people on public services and the threats that are implicit within them. I have spent most of my life on doorsteps defending the principle of comprehensive education; the principle of access to health services for all irrespective of their ability to pay – because that's the type of society I believe in."

John Cryer recommended: "We should have a massive social house building programme – which GB recently talked about. The number of new homes has to be in six figures (annually). The proposal that you increase the number of council homes being built from 2,000 per year to 4,000 is not good enough. Your average borough council has a waiting list of around 8,000 to 9,000 households. We should be building at least 150,000 council homes per year. Some of this could be done through housing associations, but most of it should be in the public sector."

John Grogan said: "We are now building council houses again in a very modest way. It's significant that Health Secretary Andy Burnham has recently said that the NHS is now the preferred provider of health services. These things prefigure the direction that we are going in."

Unfortunately the loss of the 2010 election and the arrival of the Coalition government meant that GB's social rented home building initiative was still born and stealthy privatisation of the NHS proceeded apace. The next Labour Government will need to rectify this situation quickly even if, due to financial constraints, that is through buying and reconditioning older dwellings.

Kelvin Hopkins proposed: "We should have free *long term care of the elderly.* Many people are forced to sell their homes to pay. It should be a public service paid for though taxation as the Royal Commission[C11-42] recommended. NL thought that it looked like socialism – a public service paid for out of taxation and free at the point of need. Going in that direction would have been anathema to Blair and Brown. We should bring all outsourced services in-house, re-nationalise the railways and abandon the Private Finance Initiative (PFI)."

Alice Mahon asserted: "*We've got to get these private companies out of the NHS.* The NHS urgently needs to be more democratically run. They abolished Community Health Councils which were wonderful little forums for getting people involved. All positions are appointed now and people like me never get appointed to public positions. Every appointee has got to be 'One of Us' (NL). We must work more closely with the unions (against privatisation), they know what's happening."

Backbencher B. said: "The NHS will never have all the money it needs, but we must make sure that people, in every part of the country, have equal access to health services. We also need policies that deal fairly with the elderly. Many fear losing their homes and their money if they, or their partner, has to be taken into care."

The above three contributors foresaw damage that an incoming right wing government would do: extending NHS privatisation and failing to make fairly financed and adequate provision for care of frail older people (see Chapter 13).

Alice Mahon said: "The vision for the future has got to be about things we all agree. This includes *free education*. I voted against bringing in (university) tuition fees, but you couldn't get people to see that it would get young people into thousands of pounds worth of debt. They've got to take fees out of education for the future."

Senior Backbencher B. stated: "We need to be spelling out what we're going to do about housing and how we're going to tackle problems in education. I know people who live in the poorest areas of my former constituency get the worst education. We are sentencing the next generation to disadvantage. In the constituency we now have a third generation of unemployed people. There are opportunities to get to university, even some grants for poorer students, but many are prevented. Our policies are stopping people from lower income brackets getting higher education. If their opportunities are limited because of family backgrounds and poverty then we must deal with that.

Gordon Prentice said: "We need to invest more in education. An example is computer suites for primary schools. We've had two new secondary schools built in Pendle. We've also had new health facilities built there. These programmes must continue. We need to reverse policies on foundation hospitals and university tuition fees which damaged the government badly."

The introduction of university tuition fees was bound to prove a regressive measure that would restrict the opportunities of young people from less advantaged backgrounds. It is a policy calculated to make access to education more unequal and should be scrapped by an incoming Labour government.

Alice Mahon avowed: "I believe in *public ownership*. We should start with the railways. I'm ashamed of our railways when I go to France and Italy and see what superb systems they've got."

CLP Secretaries were critical of some of the ways in which public services were managed by NL governments. These included under investment in infrastructure and educational measures to promote equality of opportunity, an end to the Private Finance Initiative (PFI) and desisting from making constant changes in the ways services are run. Many of these precepts probably stemmed from personal experiences as consumers.

Quentin said: "We should increase investment in *education and health* and take away the straitjackets put on staff. Fred proposed: "Reform education, stop nineteenth century style teaching and reform the health services so that they are more productive and responsive. Rebalance urban areas so that people have priority. Invest in public transport and in nuclear energy." Mike wanted: "More improvements in education including abolition of the remaining grammar schools. Nigel requested: "Better public education, health services and social reform." Una called for total abolition of the 11 plus exam.

William asked for: "*Public services* to be kept well financed and efficient. There should be more investment in public housing, public transport and other public infrastructures such as broadband." Adele called for: "The building of more public sector houses."

Helen argued: "Do away with PFI. Concentrate on trying to bring poorly performing schools and hospitals up to standard by ensuring that they *follow good practice rather than trying to change everything and creating chaos*. Some services need stability rather than ever changing policy initiatives. We should scrap the internal market in the NHS and use the money saved by having more initiatives to improve patient care. Bob proposed: "We need to deal with drugs and poor diet in the population. Above all, we need to find ways of making life fun and people happy."

Keith desired that Labour "Broaden the base of the public sector." Tom declared: "We should *protect public services and not destroy them. We need Socialism!*"

A strategy for foreign policy, peace and overseas development.

Foreign Policy, Peace and Overseas Development was given strong, and often critical, emphasis in policy evaluations (see Chapter 5). The harshest criticisms were reserved for TB's wars, uncritical participation in Bush's foreign adventures and continued development of the UK's nuclear arsenal. Interviewees sought a more peaceful future.

Backbench MPs' opinions: There was much disillusion about the domination of UK foreign policy by US interests during the NL era. Both TB and GB were fervent atlanticists. MPs speaking about this topic were keen to loosen the ties with Washington and become more independent of the USA in future. They wanted to avoid dubious foreign adventures.

Jeremy Corbyn believed: "Internationally we've got to admit the lies about Iraq. Maybe the (Chilcot) Inquiry will push us into that. We've got to recognise that the 'war on terror' is a ludicrous notion. The war in Afghanistan has already lasted for eight years (as at 2008), twice the length of world war two in Europe. There's no sign of it ending yet. The Ministry of Defence expect the UK to be there for another three decades. I don't think the public will stand for it much longer, we'll be forced to quit. It would be bad if a Tory government forced us out. You cannot pursue an international strategy based on the world vision of (GW) Bush. That creates a tension between west and east (the Muslim and poor world). There, people are starting to hate the UK because of these wars. It's time we understood that we're a small island off the edge of Europe. We could do much better than making nuclear weapons and going to war on behalf of Bush."

Gordon Prentice said: 'The Iraq war lost us millions of Labour supporters. We must not repeat the mistakes we made there." Linda Riordan proposed: "We need to end our involvement in the Afghan war. That's going to be New Labour's legacy if we're not careful. The Prime Minister gets up every Wednesday in the Commons and starts by reading out the names of those who've died. One of my constituents has lost a son, I understand because he didn't have the right equipment. How do I live with that as a politician? We'll never win in Afghanistan. History tells us that. The Russians couldn't win there."

Alice Mahon believed: "NATO has to be broken up. Its reason for existence has gone. I was sent as a representative from Parliament to NATO for 14 years. It's seeking new role for itself. What the hell is it doing in Afghanistan? It's the *North Atlantic* Treaty Organisation. This is about containing Russia as it tried to do in the days of the Soviet Union. The Russians are paranoid about their borders. They had 21 million dead in World War 2. We've encircled Russia. Why do we need anti missile defence in the Czech Republic? Presumably they're pointing at Iran."

She continued: "I make no bones about not wanting the Lisbon Treaty ratified. It's a disaster. We've given away far too many powers to the EU. The European Court of Justice is just business appointed judges who will bring down wages. I don't like that part of the Treaty which says that if human rights are not in the interests of the EU they have the right not to implement them. I'm not opposed to the EU itself. I think it's in the interests of all of us to work together to protect our borders and ourselves from forces that might want to harm us. *We should have a lot more independence in defence and foreign policy.* We need to work more closely with Europe in this area. They have a more civilizing influence. We must continue to address third world development. Clare Short was brilliant at the Department for Overseas Development (DFID) and GB is committed too."

Several MPs mentioned the link between our neo colonial wars, local poverty and security threats from poor countries. They also saw the intrinsic merit of NL's relatively generous aid to third world countries.

Frank Dobson stated: "We need to promote peace and prosperity abroad because, as various terrorist groups prove, in the inter related world we live in, if you have gross inequality then none of us will be safe. From a selfish viewpoint a more equal world will be a safer world for people living in Britain."

Gordon Prentice said: "Causes of terrorism in the world are poverty and illiteracy. If we had spent as much money on eliminating these as we did on nuclear weapons, we could have solved them. Backbencher B. declared: "I believe that GB's stance on third world poverty did a great deal of good. His policies should be continued."

Nuclear disarmament has always been an issue which evoked strong differing opinions in the Labour Party. It was also considered to be a reason for Labour loosing elections under Kinnock's leadership – despite the fact that he watered down his views before the 1992 election. TB, who was once a member of CND, expunged it from Labour's policy programme and, for most of the NL period, it was kept off the Party Conference agenda.

Senior Backbencher B. said: "We need to review the Trident weapons system. I'm basically a unilateralist, although I've generally been prepared to accept Party defence policy. Now public opinion has changed a lot. Financially we can't afford Trident. If we've got to cut, it should be Trident rather than other things. The PLP should be able to discuss Trident renewal properly and to vote on it."

Kelvin Hopkins said: "We're wasting £10 billion on a very dangerous weapon (Trident) because of political machismo. Internationally, we should start to withdraw from American led international military adventures. *We should begin to put ourselves in the way of being a peace-keeping country rather than a war-fighting country.* He continued: "We should abandon Trident now. It's an utter irrelevance and it's machismo on the part of NL who wants to show the world: 'We are not like the old socialists'." Senior backbencher M. said: "We must work to create a nuclear weapon free world. Democratic socialist parties, rather than parties of the right, are much more likely to achieve this."

Under NL the Government did not always support United Nations resolutions concerning war and peace, notably some of those disobeyed by Israel. It went to war in Iraq without the support of a further UN resolution thus arguably rendering the war illegal in international law. A future Labour Government should work more co-operatively with the UN.

Louise Ellman thought: "We must embrace *internationalist ideas*. I think we're in danger of becoming isolationists." Clare Short argued: "We need to strongly support he UN and its peace processes. Since Wilson's day we've had a better commitment to overseas development than the Tories. In the end development policy has to influence your foreign policy. You have to favour a world of international law, greater justice and equity: that needs to drive everything you do." Surprisingly, the incoming Coalition government maintained Labour's level of pledges of aid.

A Union Leaders' view from Billy Hayes was: "We should be more European and less American. We shouldn't cherish the nostrums of Trident and excessive military spending. We should be a Party of peace and socialism, equality, democracy and internationalism. The trades unions are an important part of that. "

Judging by the number of local Labour Party banners observed on the mammoth anti war March in 2003, many Party activists were opposed. Many joined the "Stop the War Campaign" and were active in CND.

CLP Secretary's views. Oliver called for Labour to "Reassess defence policy, including the future of the nuclear deterrent. Bob noted that money for public expenditure would be limited and added: "It will be a good time to tackle some big questions like nuclear disarmament." Diane called for one major change: "Scrapping the Trident replacement project." William also wanted Labour to "Scrap Trident in the near future". Quentin requested: "Policies to promote peace."

There were contradictory opinions about Afghanistan. Philip argued: "We should withdraw from Afghanistan very soon." Conversely William said: "If necessary, we should continue and increase our engagement in Afghanistan. Fred wanted Labour to "Finish the job in Afghanistan."

The straw poll of CLP Secretaries about NL policies (Chapter 5) also indicated that opinions about the legitimacy of the UK's involvement in the Afghan war were divided.

William, employed in international relations, wanted an enlightened internationalist policy. He envisioned a Labour Britain at the heart of Europe. He also wanted the UK to "support Turkish membership of the EU as long as it moves to full compliance with the 'Acquis Communautaire'." We should give our full support to the United Nations and to Obama (assuming that he continues on his present course). We ought to continue growing international aid, and pursuing human rights abroad (and in the UK)." He continued: "We should seek a two-state solution in the Middle East much more vigorously and be prepared to confront Israel openly." Fred wanted the UK to "join the Euro" (He might not have been as keen on this in 2015 as he was in 2009!).

The Labour movement in the UK has traditionally had a broad internationalist perspective and this should be retained and should inform future policy. We must always challenge UKIP on immigration issues rather than emulating them in the hope of electoral gain.

A strategy relating to trades unions and rights at work

TB attempted to divorce the Labour Party from the Unions. His decree nisi was taken forward by Ed Miliband in 2014 (see Chapter 13). TB's governments, and that of GB, failed to enact significant progressive workplace rights legislation. What Labour should have done, after 2010, was to mend fences with the unions and follow the example of the Australian Labor Party in repealing the anti labour laws of their right wing predecessors and developing a new raft of pro – employee measures.

John Cryer regretted: "People have lost their jobs in manufacturing. They might have a pension, but they're holding down two jobs because of the decline in wages linked to the decline in manufacturing. That's a section of society on which the Labour Party relies for votes. We should strengthen rights at work. People see that it is multinational companies who have disadvantaged and sacked British workers because they don't have the same trade union rights as workers in France, Germany and even Italy. There has to be compulsion, as in Australia (over the past 20 years), to force employers to contribute to proper, decent pensions."

Since 2010 the Coalition Government has introduced a contributory system of pensions for private sector employees but that should be reviewed and improved by an incoming Labour Government.

There were three vital messages for the future to Ed Miliband coming from these MPs:

Senior backbencher M. said: *"The trade union link is very important. Institutionally trade unions hold Labour movement values."*

Senior backbencher A. stated: "We need to go back to why the Labour Party came into existence. My analysis is that the price of labour, of what you earn, has gone down. The profits made by those who earn profits have gone up as a proportion of the division of spoils between capital and labour. So work has become more insecure. The Party came into existence because the trades unions realised that they could only get so far negotiating wages and conditions with their employers. After that it required Parliamentary action." Kelvin Hopkins said: "We must strengthen the unions. We should try to re-establish some of the trade union rights that the TUC supports and wants in a freedom of trade unions bill."

One *CLP Secretary* came up with an interesting proposal to enhance the Government's and public's valuation of the workforce. This would have provided evidence to support improvements in wages and conditions. Eric argued: "Labour should commission a report of equivalent status to the Beveridge Report to look into the possible advantages and drawbacks of moving to a system of human capital accounting. At present employers regard workers far more as costs than as assets. The labour market is a disgrace. The workers have been absolutely routed. I know this being a casual worker with no paid holidays, no pension scheme, no sick pay and no right of challenge to instant dismissal." Una demanded: "Raise the national minimum wage."

Strategies for other policy areas

Civil liberties: during policy evaluations (Chapter 5) there were several complaints about NL's cavalier attitude to civil liberties. Only one respondent mentioned this issue in his future vision.

Jeremy Corbyn contended: "We're increasingly moving into a society based on threats; on snooping; on observation and regulation. I think there is a view out there that is very angry with politicians of all classes and dislikes the surveillance society that we've moved into. We need to change it."

Prisons and the Justice System. This area has a high profile in the popular media. Under NL, the UK prison population exceeded the previous numbers of modern times. None of the MPs interviewed mentioned this policy area in any context.

Views of CLP Secretaries: William called for "Prison reform". Fred said: "Keep dealing with crime and disorder". Bob wanted "better criminal justice and, particularly, prison policies. There is a need to get the prison population right down."

Alison confined her prescription for future polices, saying: "I feel strongly about the appalling penal policies followed by one Home Secretary after another. In the UK 80,000 people are now (September 2009) in prison, twice as many as there should be. Many of these are mentally ill or drug addicts. Many are on remand for offences that do not carry a prison sentence. Numerous people are there for very minor offences. What are the costs and benefits of this? We should be prepared to stand up against the *Daily Mail* agenda and only imprison violent people (which should include violent partners). There are other ways of dealing with minor offenders – but only if government is prepared to put real money into this. Closing at least a couple of prisons would be a good start."

Here was a clear rejection of the lock up and leave policies adopted by a series of right wing Labour Home Secretaries who allocated few resources to rehabilitation. Between 1995 and 2009 the prison population in England and Wales grew by two thirds.[C9_43]

The Media: NL's courting of the media, as a response to earlier hostile coverage from many newspapers and TV channels, was a controversial aspect of its election winning strategy (see Chapter 2).

Secretary Eric said: "The government should regulate the press and broadcasting media. We have Rupert Murdoch who likes to think that he picks the British Government. The regulator should review businesses in this sector to test impartiality. It would have the power ultimately to impose a targeted tax. Perhaps, in the worst cases, it would be able to double the price of the offending newspaper. We should insist on one person, one vote, in both deed and spirit. Someone wealthy enough to own a newspaper should not be able to cast, in effect, one million votes. If Labour loses the next general election (2010) it will be because of the press. They should have no such power. They have it because Labour has been sleeping."

A strategy to reform the Party as an organisation

Promoting Party Democracy for grass-roots members.

The section above discussed the future of the Labour Party as a party committed to and promoting democratic socialism. However, that is not the same thing as having a party for democratic socialists that is democratically run – one that gives and upholds democratic rights for all its members.

As the LabOUR Commission Report (2007)[C11-44] clearly demonstrated, the NL Party was not democratically run. Rather it was a command and control organisation, in which the leadership deprived most members of the rights that they previously held and dictated to them, giving them little power in Party policy making or management.

By 2010 there was a commonly held view that the upper echelons of the Party needed to support an independent investigation (called by some a "Truth and Reconciliation Commission") into the disempowerment and disenfranchisement suffered by individual party members, members of trades unions, other affiliated organisations and by the Parliamentary Labour Party during the NL era. Perhaps, only in this way, can the hurts within the Party be healed and Labour's claim to be a democratic Party be restored. The need is still present in 2015, as comments made by some Senior Party members, during the 2015 Leadership election and afterwards, have demonstrated. (see Chapter 13).

Having a democratically run Party was widely seen by respondents as being central to the Labour Party's rightful social democratic aims and long established, pre NL, methods of operating. There was, therefore, a real desire for the Party to return to being a transparently and democratically run organisation.

Reforming the Party Culture: an end to 'top-downism'

Many Party staff should be retrained in democratic, ethical and transparent practices. New staff and candidates for public office need to be recruited on the basis of their commitment to Party democracy and democratic socialism and of their record of voluntary work for the Party. Lack of ideology and unquestioning subservience to the Secretariat should now be *disqualifying* factors.

Party members, as well as trades unions and members of other affiliated bodies, must be given a clear and major role in party policy-making and governance. There needs to be a more radical review and revision of Party rules to secure these ends –in addition to the "Refounding Labour changes of 2011.[C11_45]

MPs' views: Michael Meacher said: "However inspiring Labour MPs might be … they don't have much influence unless they carry, and are seen to carry, the support and enthusiasm of the Party rank and file. That's what gives them force and power within Parliament."

Jon Cruddas argued: "We need to have a plurality of ideas, opinions, identities and contributions within the Party that are respected and nurtured. We need a culture which is courteous and a dialogue within. *We need a leadership which actually wants to nurture all the different elements within the party and not just govern on behalf of one faction.* We need a culture, within the Party, which the Leaders themselves respect. That means a big *overhaul of the characteristics of the Party. Currently these are authoritarian, distrustful and almost gang-like. You can start to change by acknowledging the crisis of representation."*

Cruddas continued: *"The issue of democracy within the Party is a key proxy for our view about the wider society. That is: whether it's deliberative, open, discursive pluralistic, respectful, tolerant etc. or shrill, sour, authoritarian, top-down and Westminster-based. That's why debates on Party democracy are so important.* A lot of the problem is that we've become so emptied out as a democratic institution and a vehicle *for different traditions and ideas* that can percolate through to create policies … I don't know what will happen. I think that in any period of major and profound social and economic change you see political realignments."

Cruddas claimed: "It's a case of rebuilding different roles within the Party that keep it together the other side of an election (2010) and allow it to be re‑built as an integrated party. *If it is captured by different gangs, the tribalism will make it very difficult to cut out that poison which we have now. So it's important for all of us to develop an opportunity to establish a culture which is more cordial and respectful than we currently have in the Party, so that we can minimise the collateral damage and try to rebuild."*

Cruddas sounded a timely warning that a party which is undemocratically run on behalf of a minority of its members and supporters is heading for conflict and decline.

Senior Backbencher A. said: *"As the Party and the movement has atrophied at the behest of the Leadership, so the Leadership has become increasingly isolated and feels as though it is in a bunker. The structures of the Party need to be recalibrated so that the old federal character of the Labour Party is revived.* In that, the PLP was important but not absolutely dominant. It strikes me that *no radical government can survive for long unless, first of all, it renews its relationship with its Party and other supportive institutions such as the trades unions and the radical voluntary sector and then with the population as a whole.* A.'s recommendations should be followed as a priority if the Party is to be renewed and saved from oblivion.

Austin Mitchell considered: *"All UK parties have declined in recent years but ours has declined more rapidly. Part of the reason … is that members feel they are not listened to and are not believed to have anything worthwhile to say.* Our party has become a party managed from the top. Top down leadership has failed which means that the rank and file aren't getting the message."

Local Party Secretary's views: William argued: "There should be no more blind centralisation and control. Open up the Party and make it more transparent and accountable." Adele said: "It's OK as it is". Fred contended: 'We must stop being a control freak party." Diane asserted: "Grass-roots members should be heard and actually have influence."

Most secretaries wanted greater internal democracy now but others saw the issue as less urgent.

Reforming the Party Structures and Secretariat

Under NL, the Party, as an organisation, had been distorted and allegedly corrupted to secure the leadership's wishes and supposedly to make it more electable. It was no longer democratically run. This democratic deficit was especially great in the machine (administration) at national and regional levels.

What MPs said: Colin Challen, a former Party organiser, made useful suggestions for democratising the Party's structure. "I think that some of our Party's senior officers could be elected by the members. Why not have elected regional officers? They would have to be shortlisted by the Party centrally to exclude unsuitable people, for example a useless trade union officer that they want rid of. Members could vote for the General Secretary from a shortlist approved by the Leader. There has often been controversy over that."

He continued: "Staff should be chosen for their personal qualities – their experience of running an organisation and general election campaigns. This is very important at regional level. We need to have an effective, democratic regional structure."

Peter Kilfoyle (also a former Party officer) had a vision for the Party's organisation: "We should get back to what the Labour Party is supposed to be about. It needs to be run by experienced people, not just by young people who are not yet capable of achievement, have been led down the garden path by NL, and are unable to question things."

CLP Secretaries' thoughts on related issues and possible solutions: Fred said: "We should break up the current Party structure, create a federal structure instead and do more on the internet." Quentin wanted to: "Get rid of Party regional staff and regional offices. Instead, make County or Unitary Authority Parties the organisational centres."

Philip argued: "We should ban Branch Labour Parties (BLPs) based on a single electoral ward in urban areas. At present these branches are often so small as to be 'rotten'. They typically discourage new members with their attention to fairly trivial issues (e.g. local pavements and street lighting)."

Simon claimed: "Party membership fees are too high. I can afford to pay them, but I know people on low incomes who can't. There should be a basic fee with a top up to what people can afford." Vince argued: "Every election to all bodies within the Party should be by OMOV (One Member One Vote) ballot. MPs' should be recallable by their CLPs when the latter so desire. When we are in government Cabinet appointments should be vetted and accepted/rejected by panels of backbenchers."

One of the greatest sources of dissatisfaction, especially for CLP Secretaries, and as indicated in evidence given to the LabOUR Commission, was the virtual *exclusion of grass-roots members, and to a large extent MPs, from effective participation in the Party policy making process (this originated largely from Partnership in Power 1997).*[C11-46]

Christine McCafferty MP claimed: "Many Party members, even those very supportive of the government, feel exasperated and completely disenfranchised. We need a mechanism for empowering members again, for involving them in policy making and enabling them to participate at the level they want.

She continued: "The National Policy Forum (NPF) is useless. *If we are to stay in power, it is vital to allow people political participation.* We need to be able to see that policy drafts are going somewhere and not being lost in committees. Members often don't bother to go to meetings. We need to review how local meetings work."

Backbencher B. said: "In future, you've got to ensure that members have a say in policy-making. At Conference there'd be a very strong move against Trident. The views of the Party were totally ignored on Post Office privatisation."

Michel Meacher argued the Party needs to operate according to broad democratic principles. The Party membership neither need, nor desire, to dictate every detail to the Leadership. The relationship has to be co-operative and consultative. He continued: "We need a radically different view, not the government being mandated by the Party on every issue. It's about the general direction of the Party. We want you to carry through the kind of reforms that we're suggesting. It should be a relationship of give and take."

John Cryer regretted: "I would like to go back to the old style Party Conference, but that won't happen. It's unlikely that future leaders will go back to a truly transparent and accountable Conference. Voting on resolutions should never have gone (in 2007). It should come back (and did partly in 2010). At least the National Policy Forum (NPF) should be made more democratic and its franchise be widened (this democratisation was subsequently achieved at Conference 2009 against the leadership's wishes). Trade union representation on the NPF should be increased. The NPF should meet more frequently and regularly so there's more immediate accountability and transparency. They should report back regularly to the affiliates and hence the membership. That means more resources have to go into the NPF. The Party staff is stretched to the absolute limit now. People are doing three to four jobs each."

What CLP Secretaries thought: Fred said: 'We should open up the policy making process". Gary added: "We should allow CLPs to send policy motions direct to Annual Conference." Colin advocated: "Return to motions being debated and voted on by Conference. At least allow voting on the final NPF report to be taken in parts if that is so moved (see Chapter 7)." Tom said: "We need to abolish the NPF and (its regional versions as in Wales) and to restore the primacy of Conference."

Virtually all the above wanted to make Conference more responsive to members' policy aspirations. William argued: "There should be much stronger feed-in of policy from the regions to national policy development mechanisms. There should also be provision for members to vote regularly on national policy issues. We should use the power of web technology much more for this purpose; whilst not forgetting those members who are not online." Mike suggested: "Strengthen the National Executive Committee (NEC) and NPF structures."

Xenia and Nigel proposed extending regional and local opportunities for policy making. Regional policy making was removed from Regional Conferences by NL until after the 2010 election and GB's 2007 promise of a network of local policy forums was stillborn.

Xenia wanted the Party to "Use Regional Conferences as a sounding board." Keith said: "We should have regular Regional Labour Party meetings that discuss important issues of organisation and policy." Nigel proposed: "We should have local policy forums."

Improving the quality of Party leadership

This was a hot issue following almost 13 years of predominantly authoritarian, top down leadership under TB and GB.[C11_47]

MP's Views: Kelvin Hopkins reported: "Robin Cook said that one of the problems is that the leader is now elected by the mass party. That sounds democratic and looks good. But actually it's easier to control the mass membership through the media than it is to control the PLP." Cook suggested that when the leadership was no longer elected by the PLP it no longer had to pay any attention to them.

The failure of non NL candidates to make the ballot paper in the 2007 leadership election (as none could get the required 12% of the PLP vote) shows that MPs could not then be trusted to give the Party a choice of the variety of candidates that represent the shades of opinion within it. However subsequently non left MPs did give nominations to Diane Abbott then Jeremy Corbyn to facilitate a more representative field of candidates for Leader for use of the wider Party membership (see Chapter 13). Linda Riordan proposed: "After Gordon Brown we need a new leader *chosen by the whole Party.*" Further recent Australian Labor experience shows that a leadership change executed by a PLP alone can have damaging electoral and consequences within a Party (see Chapter 10*).

A CLP Secretary's view: Tom considered that: "We need to make the leadership subject to regular re-election and we should improve the autonomy of CLPs."

There is little doubt that the lack of accountability and poor calibre of NL leaders left MPs and grass-roots members crying out for better methods of electing and making them accountable.

Choosing Candidates to be Public Representatives

As was demonstrated in Chapter 8, a large measure of covert manipulation and alleged corruption had entered selection processes, especially for Westminster candidates. Not only was this ethically wrong, but it produced candidates who represented only a narrow sector of the total spectrum of opinion across the Party and who had limited work experience outside politics.

Backbenchers' views: Christine McCafferty recalled: "All Women Shortlists (AWS) were very successful in 1997 and 2001. Perhaps we now need to encourage candidates of both genders *and* from as wide a political background as possible. We do require more suitable and willing women. They have made a difference there and many policies now come about as a result of women lobbying for them, e.g. maternity pay; maternity and paternity leave; adoption leave; Sure Start; and early years education. These were previously not on the agenda because they were not accepted by most male MPs. Family friendly policies are vital for us to get elected."

CLP Secretaries' opinions: Only William favoured primaries for Parliamentary selections. A white male, he added: "Have all ethnic minority shortlists as well as all women shortlists."

Oliver argued: "We must choose our Parliamentary candidates carefully. We must select them for their personal integrity and common sense as well as for their ideology. We must be able to look to them to rebuild our support locally and nationally."

John called for "Removing from Regional Offices and the NEC the power/ability to impose, or otherwise interfere with, the selection of candidates."

Findings of this book have shown that room must be made for women of all shades of Labour persuasion, not just for NL protégées (see Chapter 8). Primaries for PPC s were tried on one occasion by the Conservatives and were such a failure that they were not tried again for a few years. These would be anti-democratic as they would deprive Party members and registered supporters of their rights and would open the door to Tories and other adversaries being selected.

Enhancing Parliamentary democracy

The quality of Parliamentary democracy has become strained (see Chapter 9). There was a widespread view that Party leaders must be more accountable to Parliament. They should abide by the conventions of the UK constitution and rules and customs of the Labour Party when making policy. This would entail a return to meaningful cabinet government with most important decisions being taken at Cabinet meetings and new policies announced on the floor of the Commons rather than at press conferences.

There should be a review of the role of Backbench MPs in policy making. Much could be learned from the Australian Parliamentary Party Room system where there are collective decisions and collective responsibility (see interview with Gary Gray MP Chapter 6). Backbench rebellions are unheard of in Australian Federal Government. This is largely because MPs and Senators have a sense of ownership of policies.

It was wrong that MPs, who voted against the Party whip, were covertly barred (under NL) from select committee membership as a punishment. This was irrespective of their expertise. Moreover the role of Select Committees is to hold Government to account and constructively critical members are needed. There must be a swift move towards an elected second chamber. Like the Australian Party Room, PLP meetings should have a powerful role in policy making. Whips and others should not be permitted to use PLP meetings to orchestrate the hounding of dissidents.

Michael Meacher said: "We must make MPs listen; *ideally without brutal de-selections. But we have to find ways of binding MPs as representatives of the people and of their parties.* They should no longer be instruments of the whips."

Senior Backbencher A. said: *"We need to make sure that when, and if, we are re-elected, the Leadership in particular, but the PLP as a whole, don't become the master of the machine. That is they become so dominant and pre-eminent that they can get their way even when the Party is horrified at what's been done in its name.* We need to rebuild all the institutions so that we have a different understanding of the nature of power and its relationship to others. But the question is: 'When you are in power are you ever going to give up the power of government to steam roller things through the Commons'?"

He continued: *"Instead of Parliament being used as a source of strength to the Government, they've seen it as a threat.* That's partly because of people like me who organise others. They should see us as partners, and listen to us, rather than treating us as potential threats and obstacles to what they want to achieve. If we wanted an executive with separation of powers (as they have in the USA and France) then we'd have a President or Prime Minister directly elected by the people. Parliament would be expected to stand in check. We've got a unitary system. It's very difficult if you're a backbencher who is part of the governing Party. There are many advantages of a Parliamentary system, but there are intrinsic problems. We need radical solutions (including much more time to debate bills)."

The above contributions highlight that there is potential for the PLP to modify the autocratic intentions of the Leadership but that they, in turn, must be responsive to the wishes of the public and the Party on the ground.

Kelvin Hopkins contended: *"The civil service should be de-politicised.* Following politicisation over the last 30 years, it should again have people with a range of opinions in it. The social democratic view has been selected out and been replaced by people taking a neo-liberal viewpoint. The House, as a whole, should elect the membership of select committees on a free vote instead of having them chosen by whips."

Colin Challen said: "It may not be a bad thing that we don't have Cabinet government any more, but how do you speak out in private? If you ring up the prime minister too many times to say that you're not very happy about things then you're out at the next reshuffle."

Lord S. said: "Currently Parliament isn't as strong as it should be. However we need more power to be given to Parliament. I applaud this new system that when major public appointments come in they should be confirmed by select committee. We need to explore, develop and extend this system even if though it's controversial now. Many other things could be done to strengthen Parliament at the expense of the Executive. Because, looking back after all these years, I sometimes feel that ministers can almost become civil servants rather than politicians."

John Cryer argued: "The Executive should be more accountable to the House of Commons. There's been too great a keenness to get news out to the media rather than making statements on the floor of the House. There need to be more policy announcements in the Commons. There should be greater adherence by the Government to Party policy as made at Conference, the NPF and in the election manifesto. These have often been ignored (by NL). We need to reverse the shift of power from Parliament to Whitehall that happened under Major. That continued under Blair and Brown. "

He continued: "To increase the accountability of the Leadership, we've got to change the way that Parliament works. Dating back to the Thatcher era, especially under Tory governments, backbenchers have increasingly become cyphers. Backbenchers must be given more power to introduce bills and prolong the debate on bills – even all night. If you have an early day motion with 40%–50% of MPs supporting it – then it should have a full day's debate. There should be detailed questioning allowed on the European Union (EU). Much of our legislation comes from there, but there's no detailed questioning of it in the House. There used to be an EU Question time in the Commons. The Tories got rid of that because things were getting too awkward."

Cryer added: "When it came to going to war, Blair set an interesting precedent. It was the first time that the UK Parliament was allowed to vote on the substantive issue. All previous UK parliamentary votes on going to war were on technicalities, so it allowed MPs off the hook because they could say: 'I'm not really voting on the issue'. Blair's handling of the Iraq vote injected a little accountability, but we need accountability on more issues than going to war."

He continued: "We need more powers for MPs to hold government to account. We should have a fair and transparent selection process for members of select committees. It's better than it used to be because these appointments are overseen by the Parliamentary Committee, the ruling body of the PLP. When there are sick and dying MPs, we shouldn't compel attendance of the sick and dying when we don't have to."

The above contributions by Lord S. and John Cryer suggest specific ways in which currently misused powers could be removed from the government and handed back to the PLP.

New MPs had tended to enter Parliament thinking that their main role would be policy making. They then found they had minimal direct involvement in this activity. Backbencher B. believed the Parliamentary system needs to be improved "so far as hours are concerned. That doesn't mean that I believe it can be a 9·5 job. The PLP should be able to discuss key policy issues more openly (see Chapter 9) and come to decisions or influence them.

Chris Mullin claimed: "The Tories have always been serious about power. Labour has never been. Parliamentary power can stop things happening but can't initiate. This should be changed. The influence of the policy making machine, in so far as it was ever listened to, has deteriorated. It needs redeveloping. Policy making was focused on Blair, *against his better judgement.*"

Louise Ellman said: "The problems under NL were due, not to too much government, but to too little. We've got to restore the importance of Parliament and the power of government. NL wanted young MPs, especially under Blair. Those promoted were *managerial* in approach. They had no ideology or ideals. This approach should be abandoned."

Roger Berry contended: "TB was ageist in choosing ministers. Younger ministers look better than older ones. Many older MPs, with very good track records, such as Louise Ellman, Graham Stringer and Jon Trickett never got senior ministries and often not even junior ones."

The above contributors detected a flawed Parliamentary policy making machine. Minsters, who potentially had a key role in policy making, were selected for their interest in managing (like quasi civil servants) rather than for their ideology or policy interests. The experience of older MPs was apparently not used for cosmetic and public relations reasons! A hidden agenda might be that some knew too much or had extensive experience of power elsewhere and so posed a threat to the leadership.

Gordon Prentice said: "I can tell so many stories about people (on Parliamentary committees) who should have been consulted over the Iraq inquiry and weren't. Things must not be run this way in future."

Senior Backbencher B. stated: "Turning to Parliamentary select committees, one of the failures of the Modernisation Committee (on which I sat) was that we made a government minister the chair! That meant that we couldn't discuss some issues, because, if the Government wasn't willing to support them, they got ruled out. Committees should be less rigidly controlled; except on key issues. B. continued: "We have to accept that not all good ideas come from the government side. When we examine draft legislation there should be more flexibility about detail and more positive debate instead of time wasting. Instead we had meaningless hours of filibustering. My longest, and most unconstructive, speech lasted four hours (on the instructions of the whips!)."

B. continued: "We should ensure that Parliamentary Committees are able to influence and draft legislation before it finally goes through the originating committee. Parliament should not have five one year terms but be a rolling Parliament. Instead of having a rigid timetable for debates there should be some flexibility. This would be better than having a push, after the summer recess, to get things completed before the state opening."

B. stated: "I want to see Parliament becoming more meaningful and more positive. I am considering writing to Tony Wright, Chair of the relevant select committee, about this. When I was a local council leader, the Labour group made collective decisions on rent and rates but after that councillors were able to speak freely on matters concerning their own wards. The Labour Leadership should learn from this and allow more freedom of speech in Parliament."

John Cryer said: "You could introduce far greater powers for select committees. These should have the sort of powers given to US Senate Committees. They can subpoena people whereas Commons Select Committees can't force people to appear before them."

Under NL, select committees had become increasingly powerless. For instance, they were prohibited from discussing important topics at the behest of the Leadership and could not force witnesses to appear before them. They should be re‑empowered and these and other democratic deficits be rectified.

Views of CLP Secretaries on required Parliamentary Reform: Quentin wanted to "Reform the electoral system and the Houses of Parliament. Reduce the numbers of MPs and the number of minsters to seven at Cabinet level." Fred desired "Reform of the voting system." William called for "Democratic reform (including proportional representation with the Alternative Vote) also for reform of the House of Lords and representation for overseas UK nationals who are not represented elsewhere."

Clearly TB's half hearted attempt at Lords reform has left seriously unfinished business which must be taken forward by the next Labour Government. After the Tories manipulated the PR referendum result in 2010, there is need to re‑examine that issue because the appropriate system would prove more democratic and deliver fairer results than first past the post as results of the 2015 election demonstrated.

This and preceding chapters have examined the record of New Labour Governments and have weighed their achievements against the price that was paid by the electorate and the Party in terms of policies and democracy in the country and the Labour Party. There were some gains, but more would have been made possible had NL made more effective use of their long and continuous period in office. Earlier Labour governments secured greater achievements, in democratic socialist terms in interspersed, and shorter, periods.

CHAPTER 12
2011 and what followed

"Old Labour forgot about the public. New Labour forgot about the Party. And by the time we had left office (in 2010), we had lost touch with both"
Ed Miliband addressing Labour's National Policy Forum, 2011

"Sadly for Party leaders, who are not also Prime Ministers, pretty much the only way the media are able to measure how well they are doing is to look at, and of course commission, opinion polls. This inevitably puts those leaders at a disadvantage"
Tim Bale, 2015, in *Five Year Mission the Labour Party under Ed Miliband*

In October 2014 the Author went to work in the Parliamentary by-election campaign at Heywood and Middleton where she had appeared on the candidate shortlist in the 1990s (see Chapter 8). Whilst working there she was invited to meet Ed Miliband who was campaigning there too. Having noted, with disgust, the way in which he was continually denigrated in the Tory press she half expected to see a diminutive and awkward man possibly lacking in social skills. Instead she and her fellow campaigners were greeted by a tall and elegant man who exuded warmth, charm and showed a real interest in all who he met. She thought "He should meet many more people and impress them: what a pity that it is not practical for him to meet millions of electors before May 2015!"

Chapter Contents
Brief discussion of the 2010 General Election and advent of the Coalition
Labour Leadership election 2011
Issues confronting the Opposition Leadership 2010-2015 The
restless Parliamentary Labour Party
Highlights of the Miliband Years
Opinion poll results and tribulations
Internal Party democracy; Refounding Labour; Blue Labour; Relationships with trades unions and the constitutional changes of 2014
The 2015 General Election
Coming of the Corbyn Leadership and enlargement of the Party on the ground

Introduction

The practical research for this book and the period that it principally aims to cover ended with the fall of the New Labour Government in 2011. However five years on, the loss of the 2015 general election by Labour, followed by Ed Miliband's resignation and the election of Jeremy Corbyn as Opposition Leader, it has become necessary to discuss the intervening period. This Chapter is, however, based on Library research and a contribution about Ed Miliband by one of his supporting MPs, former whip Graham Jones.

The 2010 General Election

The conduct of the 2007-2010 Brown (GB) led Labour Government is discussed in earlier Chapters. Ed Miliband was an advisor to Brown (GB) before he became an MP. Upon the retirement of Labour MP for Doncaster North (due to illness), Ed Miliband (EM) applied for this safe seat. For this he had to beat Michael Dugher: who, unlike EM, was local. Although heavily supported by some unions and some elements of the Labour hierarchy EM was able to convince the members that he was a battling outsider[C12_1] and was selected (the first non-miner ever to represent that seat although the author was the runner up at the previous Parliamentary selection there). In 2008 he was appointed Secretary of State for Energy and Climate Change, a Cabinet post which he held until the 2010 general election. Once in Parliament GB gave EM the task of developing the next general election manifesto (which officially is supposed to be developed by the Party's Policy Commissions and the National Policy Forum – see Chapter 7). In this he was supported by several others including former Mandelson advisor Patrick Diamond.

Meanwhile GB was losing the confidence of many Labour MPs, as is evidenced by the testimony of numerous backbenchers interviewed for earlier Chapters of this book (see Chapter 11). In early January 2010 Labour MPs circulated letter calling for a secret confidence vote on GB. The instigators were senior Blairite MPs. This was not supported by EM and no action was agreed. Meanwhile the development of the election manifesto continued and it acquired a strong emphasis on mutualism. On 6th April 2010, GB announced the general election and the manifesto was launched six days later. In view of the contemporary financial and fiscal situation: it contained a promise not to raise income tax, but there were no promises of substantial increases in public expenditure. There was a plan to halve the UK financial deficit by 2014. There were commitments to a global bank levy and a living wage of £7.60 per hour. Value Added Tax on essentials was to be frozen. Working family tax credits and nursery places were to be increased. Results of cancer tests were to be provided within a week. There was a promise to introduce the Alternative Vote system for elections starting with elections to a new second chamber of Parliament.

Labour did exceptionally badly in the 2010 election, securing only 29.7 % of the votes. The overall result led to no overall majority. This was Labour's worst result since its early days in 1918 when it won only 23.0%. However, Labour did do relatively well in Scotland (unlike its record in 2015) and secured its greatest improvement in the votes since 2005 in ten seats seven of which were in Scotland.[C12_2]. All but one of these Scottish seats were lost by Labour in 2015.

When the 2010 election produced no overall Parliamentary majority at Westminster, both Conservatives and Labour went into negotiations with the Liberal Democrats with a view to forming a Coalition. However the Liberals seemed less than enthusiastic from an early stage in the negotiations and many on the Labour side seemed to be hesitant (GB excepted). Meanwhile GB hung on to power initially refusing to resign. When he did go on May 11th, the Con-Lib coalition was virtually a fait accompli.

The 2015 General Election

This topic is discussed more fully in Chapter 3. In this Chapter, it is important to recall that Gordon Brown (GB) had been hoping to win the election and to stay on as Labour Prime Minister and Leader Indeed he did stay on for almost another two weeks until it became apparent that he had no hope of forming a coalition with the Liberal Democrats. Ed Miliband and his brother David were still Cabinet Ministers. Because of this situation, in which GB was still leader of the Labour Party, there could be no overt moves towards a Party leadership election. These could only commence after GB had resigned.

The Labour Leadership Election 2011

As the coalition negotiations were stalling, Ed Milband started to consider running for the Party Leadership and consulted one of GB's advisors and his friends MPs Hilary Benn and Peter Hain[C12-3] who encouraged him to stand. Later he received the support of Neil Kinnock. It was clear that his brother David would be running too and Alan Johnson, another potential contender, publicly agreed to support DM. It was also possible that Andy Burnham and Ed Balls would enter the lists. Although EM was said be worried about the personal ethics of standing against his brother, he felt justified because he considered David to be too managerial and technocratic.[C12-4] Subsequently, Ed Miliband frequently claimed that his main motivation was to ensure that the Party broke with New Labour (NL). This motivation became apparent to the democratic socialist left in the Party as the Leadership election approached. The Campaign for Labour Party Democracy, and its allies, decided to recommend their supporters to give Ed Miliband their second preference votes after giving first preference votes to the more left wing candidate Diane Abbott MP.

At the outset of the Leadership campaign the younger Miliband seemed poorly prepared compared with his brother who had been organising for months and was probably better funded. However, unlike Ed, it was difficult for David to repudiate the record of New Labour, as he had been such a prominent evangelist for it. Ed took care to distance himself from Peter Mandelson.

During the Leadership Campaign there were 56 hustings. All the four male candidates were white, in their 40s and graduates of Oxford or Cambridge. Diane Abbott was older, black and a woman. As the long campaign developed, it is probable that animosity developed between the brothers but both were discreet about this. Ed told his friends that he wanted to show the Party that there was a viable way to conduct politics that was not malicious, savage destructive or machine-like. Here, he clearly drew a distinction between his methods of operating and those of New Labour. A similar approach was taken by Jeremy Corbyn on assuming the Leadership. Those who encountered Ed like the author, found him pleasant and approachable. Ed wanted to avoid being seen as a negative Brownite.

There were suggestions that the Party machine was supporting David. Whilst their brief is to be neutral in Party elections they were frequently partisan in practice during the NL period (see Chapters 7 and 8).

If EM was to win he needed to secure a great deal of trade union support (DM would have the majority of MP electors). David was bound to have more difficulty in securing union support. Derek Simpson, Joint General Secretary of Unite was one of the first union leaders to support EM. By mid-July the leaders of the four biggest unions (Unite, GMB, CWU and Unison) had met in secret and agreed to work for EM's campaign and against DM who they saw as the NL standard bearer. EM had done much to convince the unions of his own suitability. However, Ed Balls, who also had hopes of their support, was disappointed. All the campaigns recognised the need to attract second preference votes . Patrick Hennessey[C12-5] wrote in the *Sunday Telegraph* that EM would not have beaten DM without second preference votes. Ed also successfully used the internet and social networking sites to enthuse and mobilise supporters and recruit volunteers, especially young ones, for his campaign. He also raised money in small donations, mainly through online appeals. In an appeal to voters near the end of the campaign EM wrote in a Fabian Society Essay: "*It is my rejection of New Labour nostalgia that makes me the modernising candidate in this election.*"

Results of the Leadership ballot were:

First round: Abbot 7.4%, Balls 11.8%, Burnham 8.7%, D. Miliband 37.8% and E. Miliband 34.3 %

By the fourth and final round it was: Others eliminated, D. Miliband 42.7% and E.Miliband 50.6%.

Ed Miliband had won a famous victory.

Issues confronting the Opposition Leadership May 2010 – May 2015

The Party staff had been asked to meet the new Leader immediately after the Leadership result was declared. However when EM went to greet them he found that they had all left early, apparently in protest at the result.[C12_6b] This was a gesture of contempt not only towards EM, but also to the majority of the electoral college who had democratically elected him. Their action tallied with discussions in Chapter 7 and 8 about the Party Secretariat's long established role as secret agents of the NL hierarchy and of their contempt for Party members' democratic rights.

Next came the task of forming the Shadow Cabinet. At this time it was elected by a ballot of the Labour MPs. The first 10 places went to MPs who had not supported EM's Leadership bid. Some supporters of EM, Sadiq Khan, Hilary Benn and John Denham were elected. Peter Hain and Diane Abbot came lower down the list and were co-opted. Ed decided to sack Nick Brown, probably in order to distance himself from GB, and supported Rosie Winterton, who was elected unopposed as Chief Whip. However, when the next Shadow Cabinet elections were due, EM changed the system, for the first time, so that he selected the members himself. This time he was able to choose to include Chuka Umunna and Rachel Reeves. This remains the system in operation to date.

In 2010 the UK's dire financial position had to be addressed speedily. Things were made far worse by the letter left by former Treasury Minister Liam Byrne to his Tory successor to the effect that there was "No money left" when Labour left office. This was used mercilessly by the Conservatives right up to, and including the 2015 general election campaign, in order to discredit Labour's financial competence. As is discussed in Chapter 5, there was failure in the latter Brown years to match taxation with social spending – and a pretence that the Government's social spending was being fully funded. This was a reaction to Labour's electoral problems in the early 1990s about being seen as a high taxing Party. The contemporary Labour Leadership made refuting the Tory's wilder claims about their past financial irresponsibility demonstrating Labour's current financial prudence in its policy planning a priority. The Party's Rebuttal Unit, set up under NL, was continued and employed in this refutation. However it was of little avail; it is much harder to demonstrate virtue by good words (when in Opposition) than by good deeds (when in power).

Shortly after the General Election came the referendum on changing Britain's voting system to the Alternative Vote (AV). This had been agreed by the Coalition Government as a sop to its Liberal Democrat Partners. There had been much debate and disagreement in the Labour party over proportional representation and over a long time. In the end it was decided not to take a Party line on the issue and to give MPs a free vote in the Commons about holding a referendum.

As indicated above, it is difficult for an opposition leader to demonstrate competence and ability to the media and the public when in Opposition. One of the only measures is opinion polls. These, along with local election results had to be closely and continuously studied by the Party's advisors. In the earlier years of EM's leadership Labour did reasonably well in opinion polls. For example in early March 2011 a ComRes poll showed Labour in the lead among unskilled and skilled manual workers and the lower middle class (often known as groups D2, D1 and C) (*Independent* 1/3/2011). However a subsequent ComRes Poll (*Independent* 26/9/11)[C12_7b] found that only 24% of voters considered EM to be a credible Prime Minister in waiting compared with 57 % who did not. At the end of April 2012 ICM reported Labour to have the support of 21% of voters; its best score since May 2003. However Cameron and Osborne were trusted to run the economy by 44% of voters compared with only 31% who favoured Miliband and Balls. An inspection by the author of Labour party canvass returns, in the marginal constituency where she lives, confirmed the ICM estimate of voting intentions tallied with contemporary canvass returns for then imminent local elections.

The next positive changes in polls came later in 2012. A mega poll by Lord Ashcroft[C12_8b] taken over the summer showed major improvements in Labour's scores. 43 % said that "Labour's heart was in the right place" compared with 24% for the Tories. 40% thought that Labour "stood for fairness". 53 % thought that Labour wanted to "help ordinary people get on in life"(53%:28%) and 44%:28% considered that Labour "stood for equal opportunity for all". After the One Nation speech at Conference in 2012 Ed Miliband's YouGov approval rating rose from minus 29 to minus 9. An Ashcroft poll in the following winter in marginal constituencies found that, although Labour was doing fairly well, it was weak in Southern and suburban seats. However, to win these seats, or even an overall majority, Labour would have to convert previous non-voters and some Conservatives.

After EM announced his intention to reform the Labour Party's internal voting system in 2013, his opinion poll ratings showed no improvement. In October 2013 EM's conference speech promised that Labour would freeze household energy bills. A ComRes poll[C12_9b] then found that 90% of Labour voters and 70% of Conservative voters supported this policy. However other news was no so good. At the same time, ComRes found that the majority of voters believed that the Tories were more likely than Labour to keep the economy growing and public expenditure down. However Labour was seen as being twice as likely as the Tories to keep prices down and more likely to ensure that their own families were better off. An Ipsos Mori poll around the same time found that EM's personal satisfaction ratings had improved greatly with Labour supporters and almost simultaneously YouGov found that Labour had increased its support among the section of the population described as the "Squeezed Middle".

By the autumn of 2014 the polls had deteriorated. Peter Kellner of YouGov found that, when asking Voters which way they would vote in an immediate general election, 2·4% of Labour supporters changed their minds when EM's name was included in the question. A ComRes survey in 40 marginals held at the end of September 2014 found that 59% said that EM put them off voting Labour: compared with 18 % who said he encouraged them to do so.[C12_10b]

Unlike opinion polls local election results do record actual support. However, they should still be appraised with caution because studies and canvass returns have shown that many people will vote on a personal, rather than a Party, basis for a respected candidate in a local election. However in a national contest, they are more likely to vote for a Party. It is also true that in a local election a single issue such as arguments for and against a new bypass or recycling plant may come to dominate the debate and squeeze out other issues and comprehensive local election manifestos.

The results of the 2012 local elections were respectable but not spectacular for Labour. Both Tories and Lib Dems had managed to hold on to some key authorities. Boris Johnson beat Ken Livingstone for the London Mayoralty. However Labour greatly improved its performance in elections to the London Assembly.

Seats being contested in local elections in 2013 had last been fought in 2009 at the nadir of the GB government's fortunes. Labour had polled 23% of the vote compared with the Conservatives' 38% and the Lib Dems' 28%. Opinion polls before the 2013 local elections suggested that Labour would take 350 seats but instead it achieved only 284 and won only two of the four county councils it had planned to take.

When it came to the local elections of 2014, the Labour Party was careful not to overstate its hopes and expectations a year before the general election. The Party forecast winning 200 seats but it actually won more than 300. However, as opposition parties usually do better a year before a general election than they do in that election, this was concerning. The Conservatives and Lib Dems did slightly better than their contemporary opinion poll performances predicted. UKIP won numerous seats in the West Midlands where Labour had hoped to win more. Labour performed exceptionally well in the London Boroughs. It also had considerable success in many Parliamentary target seat areas outside the capital. Another Ashcroft poll, conducted between local and European election results, found that half of UKIP's voters had voted Tory last time but only one in seven had voted Labour at the previous election. Next a mega poll of marginal seats showed that Labour had an average lead of 10 points which increased to 12 points when respondents were encouraged to think of their own constituency and its candidates. As yet there was little sign of the Tories' likelihood of winning the 2015 general election coming from local election results.

Unfortunately one of the downsides of EM's leadership was that poll after poll demonstrated that he never managed to convince the electors of his potential competence in managing the economy or his commitment to control immigration (in a humane and just way). The latter had become a high profile issue partly due to the growth in support for the United Kingdom Independence Party.

Highlights of the Miliband Years

Some of the main highlights of the Miliband years were his most effective Leader's speeches to Party Conference and other noteworthy speeches. At the Conference in Liverpool of 2011 he made a memorable speech analysing current business practices and classified businesses as being either "producers" or "predators". He used frank and populist language. It was a brave speech that did not go down well with many business people. However it included a telling blow for David Cameron when he said: "Only David Cameron could believe that you make ordinary families work harder by making them poorer and you make the rich work harder by making them richer". However Peter Oborne in the *Daily Telegraph*[C12_11b] described Ed's speech as "an intellectually ambitious and admirable contribution to the public debate".

One of his most noteworthy speeches in Parliament was his reply to the Conservative Budget in 2012. Describing the budget as an "Omnishambles". He focussed on the 5p cut in the top rate of tax: the 14,000 people in the UK who earned £1million a year or more would be richer by £40,000 per year. It was the government's own bankers' bonus[C12_12b]. EM continued: "Hands up in the cabinet if you get a benefit from the income tax cut (no one moved). Come on – one more chance … Well it's good news for him," he said pointing at Cameron "Now he can afford his own horse."[C12_13b]

One of EM's most memorable Conference speeches was his "One Nation" speech at Conference 2012. He defined "One Nation" as "a country where everyone has a stake", "where prosperity is fairly shared" and "where we have shared destiny, a sense of shared endeavour and a common life that we lead together". He added that Cameron and the Conservatives could no longer claim to represent One Nation because they had raised taxes on ordinary families, cut them for millionaires and divided the country between North and South and between public and private. One nation was about: "a country for all with everyone playing their part". Even Tony Blair congratulated him on this speech which was widely praised by others. However, the speech lacked much policy content.

In 2013 EM's Leader's speech included more policy content than its predecessor. In it, he confirmed Labour's unswerving commitment to the NHS and promised to repeal the Tory bedroom tax. He undertook to reduce business rates but to strengthen fines on businesses failing to pay the National Minimum Wage to drop the Tory cut in corporation tax and build 200,000 new homes annually through relaxing planning laws. But his main pledge was to freeze domestic gas an electricity prices for 20 months to re-set the market in favour of consumers. This pledge proved very popular with electors.

Sadly EM's last Leader's speech at Conference 2014 was uninspiring. Unlike previous speeches this time he found it difficult to speak without notes, tended to ramble. Worst of all, he accidentally omitted his intended discussion of how an incoming Labour Government would tackle the country's financial deficit and avoid accumulating deficits in future.

One of EM's triumphs, as Leader, was his handling of what came to be known as "Hackgate". On 5th July 2011, the *Guardian* reported allegations that the *News of the World* had hacked into the phone of murdered school girl Milly Dowler in 2002. Rebekah Brooks (a great friend of David Cameron) was then *News of the World*'s editor. Two months earlier EM had become the first Party Leader to demand an independent review of newspaper regulation and practices. Having consulted with his advisors EM (who had never approved of New Labour's close ties with Rupert Murdoch) decided that he had to attack News International on this issue.[C12_14b]

The Shadow Cabinet and EM's advisors were consulted, but many were nervous about attacking Murdoch. EM decided to call for Brooks' resignation, starting gently by asking her publicly to "consider her position". News International countered with threats to attack EM and Labour. At the following days Prime Minister's Questions, EM called for a public inquiry into phone hacking and attacked Cameron over his decision to appoint Andy Coulson, Murdoch's director of communications, as his advisor. EM was clearly speaking on behalf of the public, many considered it to be his best performance in the Commons since he became Leader. He called for a judge-led inquiry into News International. This was agreed by the Prime Minister a week later. EM then campaigned to prevent the proposed take over of BskyB by Murdoch's News Corporation. Labour tabled a commons motion calling for Murdoch to withdraw his bid for BskyB. On 15th July Brooks resigned apologising to her staff for her alleged wrongdoing and the *News of the World* was shut down. Murdoch also withdrew his bid for BskyB. In late July the Murdoch owned *Times* declared that "Ed Miliband has gone from zero to hero". The pattern of TB's alleged sycophancy towards Murdoch had been broken. EM's stand made him very popular with Party members and numerous polls showed that he had increased his public support.

Another of EM's achievements concerned the war in Syria where, in summer 2013, Bashar al Assad had been accused of bombing the civilian population with chemical weapons. The USA was keen to punish and deter him by engaging in missile, and possibly airborne, strikes. Cameron recalled Parliament seeking authority for the UK to join in. Although EM had publicly expressed regret for Britain's participation in the Iraq war it appeared that he was initially uncertain about attacking Syria. DC and EM met and Cameron left the meeting believing that Miliband would agree to Britain joining in the attack. EM then consulted with Shadow Cabinet colleagues and decided not to support this action until the UN Inspection Team, that was then in Syria, gave its report. Cameron was thus deprived of Parliamentary authorization for this action until after a general election.

Issues of Internal Labour Party Democracy

As Leader, Ed Miliband took a keen interest in issues of internal Party democracy. This partly stemmed from his experience of iron top down control of the Party on the ground exerted by both TB and GB (see Chapters 7 and 8). However, his experiences during his Leadership campaign had persuaded him that there were also problems relating to the roles of trades unions within the Party. His own credibility had been undermined by Blairites constantly bleating that he had won in the electoral college on trade union votes (this was proven).

"Refounding Labour" (RFL), 2011[C12_15b] was written by EM's friend and colleague Peter Hain. It addressed some general constitutional issues but specifically dealt with those linked to trade unions. First, it redefined the aims and purposes of the Labour Party in relation to TB's New Clause 4 of 1995 (see Appendix 2) . New Clause 4 indicated that the main purpose of the Party was to win elections. Refounding Labour stated that, in addition to winning all types of election, it was equally important for the Party to develop policies and also to work in such a way that communities were strengthened through collective action and were enabled to support and promote the election of local Labour representatives.

Specific measures relating to trade unions were introduced. Up until 2011, individual Labour Party members who also belonged to an affiliated trade union had two votes in Leadership elections: one as a party member and another as a union member. Refounding Labour enacted that all members/affiliates should have only one vote in Leadership elections.[C12_16b]

Some hoped that Refounding Labour would be used to build a bridge between Old Labour and New Labour members of the Party, but that did not happen.

EM also wanted to inject new life into the Party's policy making processes. The National Policy Forum (NPF) was a relatively powerless juggernaut despised by many grass-roots members and MPs (see Chapter 7). Many members wanted a fully re-empowered Conference. EM's compromise was to ask Jon Cruddas MP, one of the Party's most profound thinkers, to preside over a policy review distanced from the NPF.

In 2011 Jon Cruddas MP, Lord Glasman and other Labour intellectuals developed a set of theories and theoretical models which were intended to inform Labour thinking and policy development after New Labour (NL). These were referred to as "Blue Labour". This was a political theory involving reciprocity, mutualism and solidarity as an alternative to the post-1945 centralising tendency of the Party. It also rejected NL's uncritical view of the market economy and its destructive, depressing and doom laden neo-liberalism. Blue Labour theory suggests that Labour traditions such as concepts of equality and internationalism have held the Party back from identifying with the real concerns of many low paid workers about immigration. It favours community based solutions and mutualism rather than public ownership. It supports such policies as a community land trust and the living wage. So far these theories have not attained much traction in the Labour Party – old or new, but they still merit consideration.

Despite the changes in Labour's relationships with the trades unions in 2011 through Refounding Labour[C12_17b], the issue raised its head again. In the summer of 2013 the Parliamentary candidature of the seat of Falkirk West became available. It became the epicentre of a struggle between Unite the union (who wanted to secure the selection of more left candidates) and the Scottish New Labour protagonist MPs Douglas Alexander and Jim Murphy. Unite's favoured candidate was Karie Murphy, who was supported by its General Secretary Len McCluskey. An established scheme allowed trade unions to pay their members' subscriptions to the Labour Party in the first instance. It was alleged that Unite had used this scheme to sign up 100 of its members to the Falkirk West Labour Party. It was suggested that, in some cases, this was without the union member's knowledge or consent. In response to the latter allegations, the Party NEC put the Falkirk West Constituency Party into Special Measures. That meant that the NEC imposed a shortlist and only those local people in Party membership, prior to the sign up campaigns, could vote. The Conservatives used this incident denigrate the Labour Party.

Ed Miliband was angered and vowed to scrap the membership scheme that Unite had used to recruit new Labour members. He also declared an intention to review the Party's entire relationship with the trade unions because: "the integrity of my Party is at stake". Next, he proposed that trade unionists who wanted to join the Party should individually choose to be members rather than using the then contemporary system where they were collectively affiliated by their union because they were members of its affiliated political fund. In many unions the latter was automatic although that was not so in Unison. EM also announced that he had appointed former Party General Secretary Ray Collins to prepare a report. Union Leaders warned that this would have severe financial consequences for the Party.

Collins' investigation found[C12-18b] that Party rules had not been broken in Falkirk merely only "bent" and suspension on those involved was lifted. Meanwhile some larger unions announced that they were cutting their affiliated fees to Labour. Collins' terms of reference, relating to internal Party issues, were announced. He would be examining only how to deal with the issue of union members opting into Party membership. Although YouGov polls (on 09.09.2013), among the public and union members, showed a majority in favour of reform in both samples, Ed Miliband's personal poll ratings showed no improvement as a result of these actions. A special Party Conference was convened for Spring 2014 to consider Collins' recommendations[C12-19b] for a package which would reform Labour's relationships with the trade unions and also preserve one of the Party's major sources of income. At this Conference the Unions agreed that they would only affiliate to Labour those of their members who agreed to pay part of their political levy to the Party. Unions were given five years for gradual implementation of the system: which was to include existing as well as new members. People who opted in would become "affiliated supporters" and were eligible to vote in Leadership and London Mayoral elections, but not in parliamentary candidate selections. Their ballot papers were to be sent out directly by the Party but not by their union as previously. Unions retained their voting power on the NEC, NPF and at Conference, thus safeguarding their existing degree of influence on Party policy making.

The 2015 General election and months leading up to it

The Scottish Referendum on Independence was held in mid September 2014. It was a hard fought campaign. Labour had chosen to campaign within the cross party "Better Together Campaign" alongside the Conservatives and other Parties. This alliance was not well received by many Scots who, as long established voting patterns have shown, are mainly anti-Conservative and tend to lean leftwards. The situation was made worse because the Labour's Better Together team was led by prominent New Labour MPs Alistair Darling, Jim Murphy, Douglas Alexander and Blairite advisor John McTernan. There were issues about the London based Party seeking to dictate to the Scottish Party which valued its relative independence. Polls showed that the independence campaign might well win. The day was basically saved by proactive campaigning by Gordon Brown.

The result was: For Independence:44.70% . Against Independence: 55.3%.

The Scottish First Minister Alex Salmond demanded further devolution of powers to Scotland. Gordon Brown promised the next Labour Government would devolve greater specified powers to Scotland and set out a timetable which the Conservatives seemed to accept. However, on 19th September, Prime Minister Cameron announced a plan to prevent Scottish MPs at Westminster from voting on proposed legislation that affected only England and Wales (so-called "English Votes for English Laws"). This enraged the Nationalists and greatly increased their recruitment of members.

In early October 2014 came the Heywood and Middleton by-election in what was formerly a safe Labour seat. In the meantime UKIP had been increasing its support in opinion polls and local elections in deprived working class areas in the North of England. UKIP decided to offer a major challenge here and made much headway locally during the campaign. Labour's 6,000 majority in 2010 (when UKIP polled only 3% of the vote) was slashed to only 617. In the by-election Labour polled 41% of the vote to UKIP's 39%. This raised fears in Labour's ranks about what UKIP damage might do to Labour in the 2015 general election. Jon Cruddas MP did some research on the 2015 General election results which demonstrated that Labour lost 13 seats that it would otherwise have won due to the size of the UKIP vote locally.[C12-20b]

The General Election 2015

In the lead up to the general election, including early on polling day, Labour and the Conservatives were running neck and neck in most opinion polls. However, an exit poll[C12_21b] conducted by Professor John Curtice showed that Labour had fared far worse than earlier polls, during the campaign, had predicted. Labour gained only 10 seats from the Conservatives, 25% far fewer than had been expected. Labour even lost eight constituencies to the Tories. The percentage of votes predicted for other parties (UKIP 12.5%, Lib Dems 8% and Greens 4%) were within predicted margins of error. The Lib Dems held on to only eight of their 57 seats (26 of these were lost to the Tories). UKIP won 3.9 million votes and damaged Labour and the Tories equally. Substantial numbers of previous Labour voters changed to vote for the Tories. This was particularly marked in the Midlands.

Investigations are still ongoing but it is thought that many of these switchers were middle class families who were concerned about management of the economy and believed Cameron to be a more competent leader than Ed Miliband. Labour was tightly squeezed in Scotland by the Scottish Nationalists who won 40 out of 41 Labour held seats. The SNP polled only 50% of the vote. Labour also lost votes to the Greens and UKIP in England and Wales. Labour won a total of 232 seats. It gained 22 seats but lost 48. Labour polled 30.4% of the vote but the Conservatives polled 36.1%. Labour lost 26 seats.

It is difficult to know why the polls were so wrong. On BBC TV election programmes Professor Curtice spoke of the "shy Tories", a phenomenon first encountered in the 1992 General Election campaign. These electors included many previous Labour voters who did not like to admit to voting Conservative – perhaps because they might be seen as selfish or snobbish. Others lied to the pollster for unknown reasons. Others may have had a genuine change of mind on polling day.[C12_22b]

E. Miliband had had a reasonably good Campaign (but see MP Graham Jones' view below). He toured extensively, including Scotland. Near the end of the campaign he unveiled a large stone with Labour's election promises engraved on it. The media nicknamed this the "Edstone" and it received a mixed reception. Another feature of the Campaign was scaremongering by the Tories that Labour might form a coalition with the Scottish Nationalists and then agree to the scrapping of Trident. Miliband handed in his resignation as soon as the outcome of the general election was beyond doubt.

What about Ed?

Voltaire famously said: "I can deal with my enemies, but may God protect me from my friends". This quotation was particularly relevant for Ed Miliband as it continues to be for his successor Jeremy Corbyn. Through controlling the Parliamentary selections during the New Labour period (see Chapter 8) and the agency of Progress which continues to dominate them though its work which is heavily subsidised by Lord Sainsbury (see Progress website note) the Parliamentary Labour Party is still heavily New Labour. This never reflected the true composition of the Party's grass-roots membership, which was still about 45% Democratic socialist as YouGov polls for the LabOUR Commission 2007[C12_23b] demonstrated. As noted above, Ed Miliband tried to distance himself from New Labour. Further, he was rejected by many NL MPs because he had stood against his brother for the Leadership. However the New Labour faction dominated, and continues to dominate, the Parliamentary Labour Party and to confront the Leaders of other persuasions: EM and JC. The democratic socialist left in the Labour Party gave some support to EM. When the Leadership election was called in 2010 the Campaign for Labour Party Democracy asked its supporters to vote for Diane Abbot as first choice and to support EM as second choice. Then not to vote for any other candidate as they were considered unsuitable. Again, early in 2015 a discussion, within CLPD, produced consensus that they should continue to support EM as party Leader because the alternatives were worse!

Sadly for EM, his personal rating in the polls was often and undeservedly poor. From the outset his poll ratings were always lower than those of his Party. For example in an April 2011 IPSOS/Mori poll only 25% of the public said that he would make the most capable Prime Minister. With every adverse poll result the Blairite faction in the PLP renewed its attacks on his authority and credibility[C12_24b] which were echoed in the Tory press. There were the most vicious and unjustified attacks in the right wing tabloids (just as they had, for example, attacked Neil Kinnock before him). The distorted photograph of him eating a hamburger was a flagrant example. In order to set the record straight Graham Jones MP, who worked closely with EM has written an appreciation which appears below.

Assessment of Ed Miliband's Leadership by Graham Jones MP

Ed Miliband arrived into the Leader's office in 2010 handicapped by the delay in his succession and without the support of the majority of MPs. The applause that greeted him at his first PLP meeting did not extend to the elected Shadow Cabinet in private or in public.

A vacuum of hope had developed on the left of the Party, vacated by Blairites and Brownites which propelled the younger Miliband to victory amongst frustrated rank and file members and affiliates. In part his was helped by the overt tactics of sympathetic unions who emblazoned their endorsement all over their Leadership election literature and ballot paper envelopes. These unions were to be a drag anchor on people's perceptions of Ed Miliband on issues from funding to Falkirk.

The start of Ed Miliband's incumbency was the beginning of the end. This was because the Tories painted an unwanted portrait of some passé, left wing militant Red Ed. This was done through their patrons the tabloid press barons. His fumbling TV broadcasting style reinforced Tory propaganda about a man not up to the job. There were shackles that he was never able to free himself from. He was perceived as the "butcher" of his brother's career and was not to be trusted either.

The five years were also dogged by contradictions: a tough right wing economic strategy was lost in a slew of left wing welfare posturing. An inclusive and listening leader was reduced to a bunker filled with out of touch fawning wonks whose lasting epitaph was a laughable stone tombstone engraved with promises. A Red Ed reading a Blue Labour manual. In 2015 Labour had a manifesto for middle England (many of its policies were taken up by the Tories after the election). However, Labour's election strategy spoke only to the non-voting poor it threatened the wealthiest and said nothing to middle England. It spoke to young people but forgot to speak to the elderly. It spoke to people on benefits but did not speak too often to the many in work with their aspirations.

We had leader who himself reinforced these contradictions. He was able to present a coherent policy framework which did unite Labour MPs in Parliament. However his media and set piece performances were, too often mediocre at best, and divided the public. All this was encapsulated by a 2014 Conference speech in which he forgot to mention the deficit because his brilliance of memory, of just 12 months earlier, had abdicated. All the time Ed Miliband carried the full weight of responsibility with dignity and bravery; never cowering to his critics. He was an example of a man who brings in a new kind of politics. His was not the power of menace. His was not the power of menace but of someone who preferred the power of persuasion.

Behind that kindness was a Leader's office driven by indecision. It was severely lacking in emotional intelligence. Much of the "mea culpa" can be blamed on Ed's out of touch staff who were incapable of identifying what was electorally important or understanding Arcadia street realities. They were unable to connect to ordinary people other than through think tank papers. They were more consumed by Westminster gossip rather than by the real lives of single parents exploited by rogue landlords. The Leader was unable to reach out to another world beyond the Westminster wonk. He had so-called advisors who employed revolving door of unremembered slogans in re-launch after re-launch.

We had a leader who did not see that every welfare debate and every welfare comment was a dent in any economic credibility that remained with the Labour Party. That failed to tackle Tory messages attacking economic policy. We had a Chancellor who saw the detail but did not see that the economically incompetent Tories had had to abandon their Plan A. There was deafness of too many within the Labour Party to the issue of immigration and a public yearning for something meaningful beyond Westminster.

Ed Miliband came close to negating much of this but ultimately his failure to tackle the above issues and ferocious, registering Tory and SNP attacks meant that, in the final weeks of the election campaign, these resurgent issues collided in Labour's worst defeat for a long time. A good man was defeated by his own failings and his inability to ensure that those around him were up to the job.

Ed Miliband's project should and could have succeeded. The 2015 election manifesto spoke for Britain but alas the public were never presented with clarity of message, or substance."

Graham Jones has been Labour MP for Hyndburn, Lancashire since 2010. He was appointed as whip by Ed Miliband. Neither Blairite nor left-winger; he has been impressed by the writing of Jon Cruddas MP.

Labour's Leadership Election 2015

Because Ed Milband had resigned so rapidly, it was necessary to elect a New Leader in the relatively near future. Harriet Harman, the Deputy Leader stood in again for a second time and blotted her copy book by pressurising MPs to vote for a vicious package of Tory welfare cuts.

It will be recalled that "Refounding Labour" in 2011 and Labour's special Conference in Spring 2014 had created new categories of Party affiliate (trade union affiliated members and affiliated supporters) all of whom now had a full vote in the Leadership election. Party rules stated that in, order to be able to enter the member's ballot, a candidate must be an MP (or could be a peer) and they must receive nominations from 15% of their fellow MPs. Prior to 2010 this was only 12% but that was increased by Conference and re-endorsed by the Special Conference of Spring 2014. The problem originating from the New Labour years was that, due to the manipulation if Parliamentary candidate selections (see Chapter 8), fewer and fewer MPs were any degree to the left of New Labour. This made it very difficult to secure a range of Leadership candidates that included MPs on the Centre Left and Left of the Party. As mentioned earlier, in 2007 Michael Meacher and John McDonnell were unable to secure sufficient nominations to stand and Gordon Brown was crowned without facing an election. This was to the great dismay of many grass-roots Party members. In 2010 some non-left MPs "lent" a vote to Diane Abbott to enable her to stand in the Leadership election in order to broaden the choice for the benefit of the wider Party membership (45% of which have regularly polled as being left or centre left, for example, in NEC elections).In the 2015 Leadership election the left mantle was taken by Jeremy Corbyn. He too was "lent" votes by more right wing MPs, as Diane Abbott had been.

Jeremy Corbyn (JC) had long been an active campaigner and speaker who travelled all over the UK. He had frequently defied the whips and voted against the NL Leadership. They had reciprocated by keeping him off select Committees and out of other appointments, despite his tremendous knowledge about welfare policies, social housing and foreign policy (see Chapter 9). He had also been very active in working for the People's Assembly Against Austerity. As soon as nominations had closed, JC embarked on an extensive nationwide tour and found himself speaking to packed and enthusiastic public meetings. He also did a large number of hustings with the three other candidates, Andy Burnham, Yvette Cooper and Liz Kendall. The Labour Party electorate was rapidly swelled by JC's supporters. This was achieved primarily through internet based recruitment by his organisers. Polls of the Labour Party electorate showed Corbyn maintaining a good lead throughout the month-long postal election. The ballot was run on the basis of one member (or affiliated supporter/member, one vote (OMOV).

The outcome was that Corbyn took 59.5% of the total votes cast and even a majority among the full Party members. Andy Burnham, the runner up secured 19% of the vote, Yvette Cooper 17% ad Liz Kendall 4.5%. The total number of votes cast was 422,644. Jeremy Corbyn hailed his victory as a huge mandate for his anti-austerity programme and for a new democracy within the Labour Party. As noted above, there are still a large number of Blairites in the PLP. Most were the beneficiaries of the manipulated selections before 2010 (see Chapter 8). Some Blairites resigned from the shadow cabinet immediately after Jeremy Corbyn's victory. These included: Shadow Education Secretary Tristram Hunt, and Shadow Chancellor Chris Leslie who had been imposed on his Constituency by the NEC and had not been selected by a single vote of an ordinary local Party member (see Chapter 8).

Book Conclusion and Recommendations for the Contemporary Leadership of the Labour Party

A summary of the assessment of the book's main findings on these subjects appears at the end of Chapter 11.

What Future for the Labour Party?

At the end of the interviews (conducted between 2009 and 2011) the 57 main participants (Backbench MPs, Constituency Labour Party Secretaries and Trade Union leaders) were asked what future they saw for the Labour Party? In giving overviews many were quite pessimistic. The majority wanted the Party to return to being a progressive social democratic party with appropriate aims and values. Almost all believed that New Labour was past its sell by date. The Party should work for a radical transformation of our society. Labour needs to recreate a progressive alliance with the trade unions. The Party should embrace working class values and work to create a more equal society by redistributing wealth, power and privilege. Labour needs to re-examine and re-clarify its aims and values and rearticulate those values in a modern setting. The Party needs to rebuild its working class support. As Jeremy Corbyn has shown by example, Labour must connect with young people and also with members of ethnic minorities and women.

Labour needs to become a learning organisation which learns from all aspects of its past from error and successes. The Party must learn from the mistakes of the New Labour era and ensure that it does not replicate them.

The Party should develop a strategic framework within which to develop future policies. All policies must promote social justice and a more equal society. This would entail a living wage with support from those who cannot work through universal benefits. There must be progressive taxation with an emphasis on direct taxes. All policies should be planned with the aim of promoting a healthy and sustainable environment and minimising global warming. The Government should reduce its carbon footprint, perhaps by the allocation of personal carbon allowances. All energy manufacture should ideally be in the public sector (possibly run by local authorities, as in the past). It must be strictly regulated. Greenhouse gas emissions should be drastically cut and much greater use should be made of energy from renewable sources. These green measures are now needed urgently.

Neo-liberal economic policies must not continue. Light touch regulation (deployed by TB and GB's Governments) must end and the UK economy must be democratically controlled at every level. A sound economy, which is not so reliant on the City, must be re-built. There must be no more casino style financial management. The banks must be strictly regulated and, where possible retained, or taken back into public ownership. Some reduction of the public deficit will have to continue.

There must be redistribution of wealth through the tax and benefit systems but, above all, wage levels must be increased. The maintenance of full employment is vital. We should return to Keynesian methods of economic management (as the contemporary Australian Labor Government did). Investment, especially public investment, must be in projects which will deliver economic security and more jobs for the future. Public investment should be mainly in infrastructure especially building that for health and education services as it was under NL. However in future it should not be accompanied by the privatisation that NL introduced in tandem with its investments in infrastructure. The expensive Private Finance Initiative (PFI) for such capital building should be replaced by conventional public borrowing. Government investment in infrastructure should also be focused on developing transport and fast, modern internet technology. There should be government investment in manufacturing industry.

There were strong views that it was high time for local authorities be re-empowered, be given more devolved powers and be trusted more by central government. In particular, there was a desire for the redevelopment of local publicly owned public transport. Some wanted local authorities to take on the provision and management of the utility companies.

High priority was given to the successful development and management of the public services especially the NHS including its integration with social care ensuring equal access for all. Likewise for education. University tuition fees should be scrapped and Sure Start expanded. The highest priority should be given to building new social homes for rent as there has been an acute shortage in recent years and very few have been constructed. Serious consideration should be given to re-nationalising the railways which opinion polls demonstrate would be popular with the public.

Moving to foreign policy, some had strong views that we should apologise for our participation in the Iraq war and there was strong feeling the Britain went to war too often during the NL era. Most wanted to weaken our military ties with the USA and, especially, never to again ally with a right wing Republican US president. A few respondents wanted Britain to leave NATO or to see it broken up. Rather more wanted to review the updating of the Trident Missile system. Virtually all wanted to work for peace, for a nuclear weapon free world and to support, and co-operate with, the United Nations. Many also wished to improve European human rights policy.

Respondents wanted to strengthen the relationship between the trade unions and the Party and to work with them to improve the rights of people at work. There were calls to improve civil liberties in the UK and to improve prisons and the rights of prisoners.

In respect of Labour Party and Parliamentary democracy, stakeholders considered that there was much to be done. New Labour style top down Party management should cease. Grass-roots members should be given a much greater say in party management and policy making Jeremy Corbyn is already moving in these directions. Backbench MPs should be given a greater role in policy making within Parliament. Conference should be re-empowered and over-mighty members of the Party secretariat must understand that it is the party members and affiliated supporters (many in trade unions) who pay their salaries. They must be fully accountable to the Party on the ground and to the contemporary Leader in future. Future Leaders must also be held fully accountable to the Party. Economic, social and political planning for the future of Britain outside the European Community should now take place.

Jeremy Corbyn, Labour MPs and Party Members. affiliates and supporters now have a great deal to do to return the Labour Party to being an electable, democratically run, democratic socialist Party. Stakeholders contributing to this book have shown us the way ahead. It is expected, and hoped, that Labour will rise to this challenge.

Appendix 1
List of main participants interviewed in the research for this book

The 27 back bench MPs interviewed (listed in alphabetical order)

Name	Latest Constituenc	Served	Reason left
Roger Berry	Kingswood	1992-2010	defeated
Colin Challen	Morley and Outwood	2001-10	retired
Katy Clark	North Ayrshire and Arran	2005- 2015	defeated
Jeremy Corbyn	Islington North	1983-present	N/A
Jon Cruddas	Dagenham	2001-present	N/A
John Cryer	Hornchurch	1997-2005	defeated
John Cryer	Leyton and	2010 - present	N/A
Lord S. ++	former MP in Northern	1979-2001	went to Lords
Frank Dobson++	Holborn and St. Pancras	1983-2015	retired
Louise Ellman+	Liverpool	1997-	N/A
John Grogan	Selby (Yorks.)	1997-2010	defeated
Kelvin Hopkins +	Luton North	1997-present	N/A
Lynne Jones	Birmingham Selly Oak	1992-2010	retired
Peter Kilfoyle++	Liverpool Walton	1991-2010	retired
Senior backbencher	North West Region	1983- 2010	retired
Alice Mahon	Halifax (Yorks.)	1987 -2005	retired
Michael	Oldham	1970-2015	deceased
Christine McCaffer	Calder Valley	1997-2010	retired
John McDonnell	Hayes and Harlington	1991-present	N/A
Austin Mitchell	Great Grimsby	1983-2015	retired
Chris Mullin++	Sunderland South	1987-2010	retired
Senior Backbencher	North West	1983- 2005	retired
Gordon Prentice +	Pendle (Lancs.)	1992-2010	defeated
Linda Riordan	Halifax (Yorks.)	2005- 2015	retired
Clare Short ++	Birmingham Yardley	1983-2010	retired
Alan Simpson	Nottingham South	1992-2010	retired
Graham Stringer+	Manchester Blackley	1997-present	N/A
Senior backbencher	Blankshire	1996-present	N/A
Fifteen remained in the House of Commons and one in the House of Lords after May 2010 Nine retired voluntarily; none of those who retired was de-selected. Three were defeated in the 2010 general election and one, Katy Clark, in			
Key ++ = former minister + = former leader of a local authority			

Table 2 Constituency Labour Party (CLP) Secretaries interviewed

Code name	Gende	Region	Years in membership of Labour
Adele	F	Southern	35
Alison	F	Yorks./Humber	50
Bob	M	West Midlands	30
Colin	M	Eastern	35
Diane	F	Yorks./ Humber	30
Eric	M	North West	28
Fred	M	East Midlands	10
Gary	M	West Midlands	30
Helen	F	South West	14
Irene	F	North East	30
John	M	Southern	26
Keith	M	West Midlands	37
Lewis	M	West Midlands	39
Mike	M	Southern	10
Nigel	M	Eastern	15
Oliver	M	Southern	22
Philip	M	Wales	25
Quentin	M	Western	28
Roland	M	Scotland	36
Simon	M	London	12
Tom	M	Wales	29
Una	F	Southern	27
Vince	M	Western	38
William	M	International	10
Xenia	F	Eastern	36
Yvonne	F	North West	40
Zach	M	North West	29

Total= 27; Men = 18; Women = 9; Average Length of Labour Party membership =
Note: Names given to CLP secretaries are pseudonyms. This is because they answered questions in a personal capacity and not officially on behalf of their Constituency Party.

3. Former Party Staff Interviewed

David Gardner	Former Assistant General Secretary of the Labour Party (to 2001) and previously regional
Peter Killeen	Former Assistant Regional Organiser North West
'Malcolm'	Former Regional Organiser somewhere
'Ken'	Assistant Regional Organiser somewhere else north of Watford
'Ben'	former Local Organiser North West Region
Where only a first name is give it is a pseudonym	

4. Trades Union Leaders interviewed

Billy Hayes, General Secretary: Communication Workers Union

Len McCluskey, General Secretary, Unite the Union

Liz Snape, Assistant General Secretary, Unison

5. The 14 allegedly blacklisted/excluded parliamentary hopefuls interviewed

Mr. Jim d' Avila; Ms JR; Mr Mark James; Dr. Gaye Johnston (author); Mr Stan Jones; Ms. Anni Marjoram; Ms Teresa Pearce MP; Ms. Anne Pettifor; Ms Linda Riordan MP; Mr Mark Seddon; Ms. Christine Shawcroft; Ms J.C.; Ms. P.l.; and Ms. PW. Initials signify interviewees who wish to remain anonymous.

6. Several constituency delegates to Labour Party Annual Conference and relevant local Party members

(Mainly in 2009 when the author was also a constituency delegate) and local Party members involved in contentious selection processes for Parliamentary candidates.

Appendix 2
New Labour's New Clause 4

LABOUR PARTY CONSTITUTION 1995: NEW CLAUSE 4

Aims and values

1. The Labour Party is a democratic socialist Party. It believes that by the strength of our common endeavour we achieve more than we achieve alone, so as to create for each of us the means to realise our true potential and for all of us a community in which power, wealth and opportunity are in the hands of the many and not the few; where the rights we enjoy reflect the duties we owe and where we live together freely, in a spirit of solidarity, tolerance and respect.

2. To these ends we work for:

A A DYNAMIC ECONOMY, serving the public interest, in which the enterprise of the market and the rigour of competition are joined with the forces of partnership and co-operation to produce the wealth the nation needs and the opportunity for all to work and prosper with a thriving private sector and high quality public services where those undertakings essential to the common good are either owned by the public or accountable to them.

B A JUST SOCIETY, which judges its strength by the condition of the weak as much as the strong, provides security against fear, and justice at work: which nurtures families, promotes equality of opportunity, and delivers people from the tyranny of poverty, prejudice and the abuse of power.

C AN OPEN DEMOCRACY, in which government is held to account by the people, decisions are taken as far as practicable by the communities they affect and where fundamental human rights are guaranteed.

D A HEALTHY ENVIRONMENT, which we protect, enhance and hold in trust for future generations.

3. Labour is committed to the defence and security of the British people and to co-operating in European institutions, the United Nations, the Commonwealth and other international bodies to secure peace, freedom, democracy, economic security and environmental protection for all.

4. Labour shall work in pursuit of these aims with trade unions and co-operative societies and also with voluntary organisations, consumer groups and other representative bodies.

5. On the basis of these principles, Labour seeks the trust of the people to govern.

Glossary

Affiliates (Affiliated Organisations) affiliated to the Labour Party. They are trades unions and certain "socialist" societies (interest groups which have been associated with the Party for a considerable time).

Affiliated Party supporters and affiliated trade union supporters. New categories of Party supporters introduced in 2014.

AM Member of the Welsh or Greater London Assembly

AWS All women shortlists for Parliamentary candidate selections

BAME Black and Minority Ethnic (Party members/candidates) usually when in special Party sections or sections of shortlists e.g. for Parliamentary candidatures.

Campaign Group. A group of Left Labour MPs which also has a section for Grass Roots Party members.

Chartist A democratic socialist journal

CND Campaign for Nuclear Disarmament

CLP Constituency Labour Party.

CLPD Campaign for Labour Party Democracy. A long established national Organisation linked to the Labour Party and with members on the left and centre- left. All its members belong to the Labour Party. It focuses on improving Party democracy and Party rules but also takes policy positions.

The Co-operative Party. A sister Party of the Labour Party supported by the Co-operative movement. Some candidates run as 'Labour and Co-operative'.

CV Curriculum vitae. The personal, political and career profile of aspiring election candidates and job applicants.

CWU The Communication Workers Union representing postal and other communication workers

EC Executive Committee of the CLP

EM Eileen Mirfin Former Party Regional Organiser who investigated on behalf of the NEC

EPLP European Parliamentary Labour Party

Fabian Society. A think tank affiliated to the Labour Party

GB Gordon Brown

GC General (Management) Committee. Main the governing body of a CLP. Some CLPs now only hold open meetings instead.

GMB General Municipal and Boilermakers Union

Hustings The final meeting in the selection process where shortlisted Prospective Parliamentary Candidates (or candidates for other Party offices) speak and answer questions. Hustings/selection meetings are usually also held for local government candidates. At the conclusion of the hustings those who have not already cast postal votes (this currently means all postal votes) vote for their choice of candidate in an eliminating ballot.

JDA Jim D'Avila candidate for Parliamentary selection in Swindon North 1995

JP John Prescott

JS John Smith, Late Party Leader

Labour Briefing (the original) Democratic socialist journal.

Labour First a pressure group for grass roots Labour Party members holding New Labour views.

LDN Labour Democratic Network. Formerly Save the Labour Party (STLP) –see below

LRC Labour Representation Committee. An Organisation linked to the Labour Party, its Campaign Group and on its left wing. Many of its members are also Labour Party members. It focuses on developing a socialist policy programme.

LWAC Labour Women's Advisory Committee that campaigned during the 1990s for All Women short lists in candidate elections and for more women MPs.

"Meet and Greet". A mass membership meeting for Party members to meet aspiring candidates. It is held prior to initial nominations being made during in a selection process. Sometimes compared to speed dating; it permits small groups of Party members to meet many (but seldom all) of the hopefuls for three to five minutes each.

MEP Member of the European Parliament

MSP Member of the Scottish Parliament

MW Michael Wills, adviser to Gordon Brown, selected as candidate in Swindon North 1995 and became MP. He resigned as an MP in 2010.

NCC Labour Party National Constitutional Committee: responsible for disciplinary action and enforcement of Party rules.

NICE National Institute for Clinical Excellence(NHS)

NEC Labour Party National Executive Committee **NK**

Neil Kinnock

NL New Labour

NPF Labour Party National Policy Forum

NUM National Union of Mineworkers

OMOV One member, one vote election or selection. Every individual member of the Labour Party either nationally or in a given party unit (e.g. a CLP) has a vote. Some are postal votes others can be cast in person.

PC The Parliamentary Committee of Labour MPs: elected by themselves and representing their interests to the Leadership.

PK Peter Killeen: former Party Assistant Regional Organiser, North West Region.

PLP Parliamentary Labour Party

PM Prime Minister

PPC Prospective Parliamentary Candidate (they become simply 'Parliamentary Candidate' once the election is called).

Progress Group. A pressure group dedicated to preserving the ideas, ideals, methods of operation and functioning of New Labour within the Labour Party. It also supports aspiring Parliamentary candidates and MPs who share its ideals and ideas .Peter Mandelson is a prominent supporter and the group receives very substantial funding from Lord Sainsbury and others (Source: Progress Website).

PS Procedures Secretary: the lay party officer charged with the responsibility of running a parliamentary selection in a CLP.

STLP Save the Labour Party. National pressure group linked to the Labour Party. It campaigns solely for improvements in Party democracy. It was co-founded by the author in 2003. STLP changed its name to Labour Democratic Network (LDN) in November 2010.

SEA Socialist Educational Association-an interest group affiliated to the Labour Party

SHA Socialist Health Association-an interest group affiliated to the Labour Party.

SPAD Special Political Adviser (appointed not elected): usually to a minister or shadow minister.

TB Tony Blair

Tribune Group A Group of Centre Left Labour MPs killed off during in the early NL period.

Tribune A democratic socialist journal.

Unison The largest public sector union.

Unite The largest trade union representing transport, engineering and industrial workers.

USDAW Union of Shop, Distributive and Allied Workers (i.e. shop workers).

Ward Party (Branch) The most local unit of Labour Party membership based on residency in one or more local government wards.

Select Bibliography

Abse, Leo (1996); *The Man Behind the Smile*; *Tony Blair and the politics of perversion*; pub. London; Robson Books.

Australian Labor Party (2002); *Hawke-Wran Report on the Future of the Australian Labor Party*; pub. Canberra; AustralianLabor Party.

Bagheot, Walter; 1964 edition; ed. RHS Crossman; *The English Constitution*; pub London; C.A. Watts and Co.

Baker, C. (2004); *Membership Categorization and Interview Accounts* in D. Silverman (ed.) *Qualitative Research: Theory, Methods and Practice*; London; Sage.

Bale, Tim (2015); *Five Year Mission: the Labour Party under Ed Miliband*; pub. Oxford; Oxford University Press.

Barbour, R.S. and Kitzinger, J.(eds) (1999); *Developing Focus Group Research: politics, theory and practice*; pub. London; Sage

Beckett, Francis (2015) *ClemAttlee: Labour's Great Reformer* (second edition); pub. London; Haus Publishing.

Bevan, Aneurin (1978 edit.); *In Place of Fear*; pub. London; Quartet.

Blix, Hans (2005 edit.); *Disarming Iraq: the search for weapons of mass destruction*; pub. London; Bloomsbury.

Bower, Tom (2004);*Gordon Brown*; pub. London; HarperCollins.

Butler, P andCollins, N (2001); *Payment on Delivery – Recognising political service as marketing*; *European Journal of Marketing*; 35 (9-10) 1026-37.

Campbell, Alistair (2008); *The Blair Years: extracts from the Alastair Campbell diaries*; pub. London; Arrow Books.

Chalmers, Malcolm (1984); *Trident*; *Britain's Independent Nuclear Arms Race*; pub. London; Campaign for Nuclear Disarmament.

Chartist, various authors (2006) *Beyond Blair: Prospects for a new socialist left*; pub. London; Chartist Publications.

Cook, Robin (2003); *The Point of Departure*; pub. London; Simon and Schuster.

Cowley, Philip (2005); *The Rebels: How Blair mislaid his majority*; pub. London; Politicos.

Crouch, Colin (1998); *Fabian Ideas*; No 598; pub. London; The Fabian Society.

Cruddas, Jon (2011); *Democracy of the Dead*; in Glasman, M. Rutherford, J., Stears M. and White S.(eds) (2011) *Labour and the Politics of Paradox*; pub. London; Oxford London Seminars in conjunction with the Fabian Society, Compass and other similar societies.

Drower, George (1994); *Kinnock*; pub. South Woodham Ferrers, Essex; the Publishing Corporation.

Garrett, John (1992); *Does Parliament Work?*; pub. London; Victor Gollancz.

Giddens, Anthony (2000); *The Third Way and its Critics*; pub. London; Polity Press.

Glasman, Maurice (2011); *Labour as a radical tradition*; in Glasman, M. Rutherford, J., Stears M. and White S. (eds) (2011); *Labour and the Politics of Paradox*; pub. London; Oxford London Seminars in conjunction with the Fabian Society, Compass and other similar societies.

Gould, Philip (1999); *The Unfinished Revolution: How the Modernisers Saved the Labour Party*; pub. London;Abacus.

Handy, Charles (1999 edit.); *Understanding Organisations*; pub. London; Penguin Business.

Harris, John, (2005); *So now who do we vote for?*; pub. London; Faber and Faber.

Hasan, Mehdi and Macintyre, James (2011); Ed: The Milibands and the Making of a Labour Leader; pub. London; Biteback Publishing.

Jenkins, Simon (2007); *Thatcher and Sons: A Revolution in Three Acts*; pub. London; Allen Lane.

Johnston, Gaye (2005); *Does the Labour Party have a future without the Party on the ground?*; pub. Save the Labour Party; www.labourdemocratic network.org.

Jones, Mervyn (1994); *Michael Foot*; pub. London; Victor Gollancz.

Jones, Owen (2012 edit); *Chavs: The Demonization of the Working Class*; pub. London; Verso.

Kampfner, John (1998); *Robin Cook*; pub. London; Victor Gollancz.

Katz, R.S and Mair P.(eds.)(1994); *How Parties Organize: Change and Adaptation in Party Organisations in Western Democracies*; pub. London; Sage Publications.

Kilfoyle, Peter (2010); *Labour Pains: how the party I love lost its soul*; pub. London; Biteback Publishing.

Kinnock, Neil (1986); *Making Our Way*; pub. Oxford; Basil Blackwell.

Independent LabOUR Commission on Accountability, Party and Parliamentary Democracy (independent) (2007); *Renewal-a two-way process for the 21st Century*; www.labourcommission.org.uk; pub. London; The LabOUR Commission.

Labour Party (1997); *Partnership in Power*.

Labour Party (2007); *Renewing and Extending Party Democracy*.

Labour Party (2011); *Refounding Labour*.

Lanchester, John (2010); *Whoops! Why Everyone Owes Everyone and No One Can Pay*; pub. London; Penguin Books.

Lilleker, D.G. and Lees-Marshment, J. (2005); *Political Marketing: a comparative perspective*; pub. Manchester; Manchester University Press.

Loach, Ken, director (2013) film; *The Spirit of '45*; London; Film 4 /Channel 4 TV.

McDonnell, John (2007); *Another World is Possible: a manifesto for 21st Century Socialism*; pub. London; Labour Representation Committee.

McSmith, Andy (1994 edit.); *John Smith: A life, 1938-1994*; pub London; Mandarin.

Mair, Peter (1994); *Party Organisations from Civil Society to the State*; in Katz, R and Mair, P (eds.) *How Parties Organize: Change and Adaptation in Party Organisations in Western Democracies*; pub. London; Sage.

Megalogenis, George (2012); *The Australian Moment. How We Were Made for these Times*; pub. Camberwell, Victoria, Australia; Viking Australia.

Mowlam Mo (2002); *Momentum: the Struggle for Peace, Politics and the People*; pub. London; Hodder and Stoughton.

Mullin, Chris (2010); *A View from the Foothills*; pub. London; Profile Books.

Oborne, Peter (2007); *The Triumph of the Political Class*; pub. London; Simon and Schuster.

Ostrogorski, Moisei (1902); *Democracy and the Organisation of Political Parties*; pub. London; Macmillan.

Pelling, Henry (1976); *A Short History of the Labour Party*; (7th edition). pub. Macmillan; London and Basingstoke.

Perkins, Anne (2003); *Red Queen: the authorised biography of Barbara Castle*; pub. London; Pan Books.

Peters, Thomas J. and Waterman Robert H. (1982); *In Search of Excellence: Lessons from America's Best-Run Companies*; pub. New York; Harper & Row.

Pimlott, Ben (1993 edit.); *Harold Wilson*; pub. London; HarperCollins.

Prescott, John with Davies, Hunter (2008); *Prezza – My Story: Pulling no Punches*; pub. London; Headline.

Rawnsley, Andrew (2010); *The End of the Party: The Rise and Fall of New Labour*; pub. London; Viking.

Russell, Meg, (2005); *Building New Labour; the politics of Party Organisation*; pub. London; Palgrave Macmillan.

Seldon, Anthony (2004); B*lair*; pub. London; Free Press.

Seyd, P and Whiteley, P. (2002); *New Labour's Grassroots: the transformation of the Labour Party membership*; pub. Basingstoke and London; Macmillan.

Short, Clare MP (2004); *An Honourable Deception*; pub. London; Allen Lane.

Toynbee, Polly and Walker, David (2008); *Unjust Rewards: Exposing Greed and Inequality in Britain Today*; pub. London, Granta.

Toynbee, Polly and Walker, David (2010); *The Verdict: did Labour change Britain*; pub. London; Granta.

Winnett, Robert and Rayner, Gordon (2010 edition); *No Expenses Spared*; pub. London; Corgi Books.

Notes to chapters

Introduction

1. Report of the Independent LabOUR Commission on Accountability, Party and Parliamentary Democracy, 2007; pub. London; Labour Commission.

2. Handy Charles,1993 edition *Understanding Organisations*; pp.151-3, pub. London; Penguin.

3. Prescott, John with Davies, Hunter, 2008; *Prezza –My Story: Pulling No Punches*; p.193.

4. Lilleker, D.G. and Lees-Marshment, J, 2005, *Political Marketing: a comparative perspective*; pp7-11 pub. Manchester; Manchester University Press.

5. Jenkins, Simon, 2006/7; *Thatcher and Sons: a revolution in three acts*; p.59; pub. London; Allen Lane.

6. Drower, George; 1994; *Kinnock*; p.72, pub. South Woodham Ferrers; The Publishing Company.

7. Lilleker and Lees-Marshment; 2005; as above; p.18.

8. Drower, George; 1994; as above; p.91.

9. Jenkins, Simon; 2006/7 as above; p.201.

10. McSmith, Andy 1994; *John Smith: a life 1938-1994*; p.249; pub. London; Mandarin.

Notes to Chapter 1

1. Prescott, John, with Davies, Hunter; 2008; "*Prezza – My story: Pulling no punches*; p.198; pub. London; Headline.

2. Handy, Charles;1993 edit; *Understanding Organisations*; p.314; pub. London; Penguin.

3. Peters, T.J. and Waterman R.H.; 1982; *In search of Excellence: lessons from America's best run companies*; p.114; pub. New York, Harper and Row.

4. Drucker, P.F.; 1977; *Management*; pub. London; Pan Books.

5. Drucker, P.F.; 1977; as above p.15; pub. London; Pan Books.

6. Handy, Charles;1993 edit; *Understanding Organisations*; p.195; pub London; Penguin.

7. Labour Party; General Election Manifesto; 1964

8. Campbell, Alastair; 2008; *The Blair Years, extracts fromAlastair Campbell's Diaries*; p.78; pub. London; Arrow Books.

9. Interim Report of the Independent LabOUR Commission on Accountability, Party and Parliamentary Democracy; 2007; pub. London; Labour Commission.

10. AustralianLabor Party (ALP); 2002; *The Future of the Australian Labour Party* (Hawke-Rann Report); pub. Canberra, Australian Labour Party.

11. The Labour Party Constitution; 1917; pub. London; The Labour Party.

12. Abse, Leo, 1996, *The Man Behind the Smile: Tony Blair and the politics of perversion*; pp 62-63; pub. London; Robson Books.

13. Labour Party Annual Conference Report; 1959; pub. London; the Labour Party.

14. LadyGwendolen Cecil in the biography of her father quoted by Geoffrey Wheatcroft in *What is Labour for? We still do not know* in the *Guardian*; 29.07.2013.

15. Independent Labour Commission; 2007; as note 4 above.

16. Abse, Leo; as note 13 above pp 64-65.

17. The National Health Service; 2004; *An Organisation with a Memory*; pub. London Department of Health.

18. The Labour Party Constitution; 1917; pub. London; the Labour Party.

19. *Labour and the New Social Order*; 1918; pub. London; The Labour Party.

20. *Statement of Principles*; 1959, pub. London; The Labour Party.

21. Pimlott, Ben; 1993; *Harold Wilson*; p.264; pub. London; HarperCollins.

22. Gould, Phillip, 1999; *The Unfinished Revolution*;.p.212; pub. London; Abacus.

23. As immediately above; p.220.

24. Russell, Meg; 2005; *Building New Labour*; *the politics of party Organisation*; p.183; pub. London; Palgrave Macmillan.

25. Gould, P.; 1999; as note 23 p.220

26. Thompson, P. and Lucas B.;1998; *The Forward March of Modernisation*; *a history of the Labour Co-ordinating Committee*; pub. London; Labour Co-ordinating Committee.

27. Russell, Meg; 2005; as above pp.139-40.

28. Report of the Special Labour Party Conference; 1995; pub. London; The Labour Party.

29. Euan Ferguson; in *The Observer*; *the New Review*; 04.09.2011; p.17

30. As immediately above.

31. Australian Labor Party; 2002; as above.

32. Megalogenis, George; 2012; *The Australian Moment: how we were made for these times*; pub. Camberwell; Victoria; Australia.

33. McDonnell, John; MP; 2007; *Another World is Possible*; p.5; pub. London; Labour Representation Committee.

34. *The Economist*; 01 .02.2007.

35. Wilkinson, Richard and Pickett, Kate; 2010 edition; *The Spirit Level: why equality is better for everyone*; pp. 15-29; pub. London; Penguin.

36. As immediately above; p.20

37. Toynbee, Polly and Walker, David; 2010; *The Verdict: did Labour change Britain?* P.72; pub. London; Granta.

38. Lilleker, Darren and Lees-Marshment, Jennifer; 2005; *Political Marketing a comparative perspective*; p. 128; pub. Manchester; Manchester University Press.

39. Linden, Eugene; 2006; *The Winds of Change*; p.120; pub. New York; Simon and Schuster.

40. Joyce T; quoted in Linden, immediately above; p.149.

41. Wilkinson and Pickett; 2010; as above; p.23.

42. Glasman, Maurice; 2011; *Labour as a Radical Tradition*; in *The Politics of Paradox*; pub. London and Oxford Seminars in association with Compass, the Fabian Society and others.

43. Beveridge Report on the future of Health and Welfare Services; published 1940; HMSO.

44. The Labour Party; 1997; *Partnership in Power*; pub. London; The Labour Party.

Notes to Chapter 2

1. Gould, Philip, the late; 1999 edition; *The Unfinished Revolution: how the modernisers saved the Labour Party*; p.47; pub. London; Abacus.

2. Drower, George; 1994; "Kinnock" p.211 pub. South Woodham Ferrers, Essex; the Publishing Corporation.

3. Gould, P.; 1999; as above pp.55-6.

4. Lilleker D.G. and Marshment. J; 2005,*Political Marketing: a comparative perspective*; pp.9-11; pub. Manchester; Manchester University Press.

5. Gould, P.; 1999; as above p.57.

6. From a speech by Ed Miliband MP, Party Leader; given to the Labour National Policy Forum on 20/11/2010.

7. Quoted by Paul Routledge in the *Daily Mirror*; 20.08.2010; p.29.

8. Lilleker and Lees-Marshment; 2005; as above; p.5.

9. Harmel, R. and Janda; 1994; *An Integrated Theory of Party Change*; *Journal of Theoretical Politics*; 6(3) 259-287.

10. Laver, M.; 1994; *Private Desires: Political Action*; pub. London; Sage.

11. Lock, A. and Harris, P.; 1996; *Political Marketing: vive la difference*; *European Journal of Marketing*; 30 (10-11).

12. Lilleker and Lees-Marshment; 2005; as above p.5.

13. As immediately above; p.6.

14. As immediately above; p.8.

15. Drower; 1994; as above.

16. Lilleker and Lees-Marshment; as above pp.20-33.

17. Pledge card used in the 1997 general election campaign promoted by John Prescott MP.

18. Lilleker and Lees-Marshment; 2005; as note 16 above.

19. Handy, Charles; 1993 edition; *Understanding Organisations*; p.308; pub. London; Penguin.

20. Lilleker and Lees-Marshment; 2005; as above; p.10

21. YouGov Poll undertaken for the Independent LabOUR Commission on Accountability, Party and Parliamentary Democracy; June 2006.

22. Seyd, P. and Whiteley, P.; 2002; *New Labour's Grassroots: the transformation of the Labour Party membership*; pub. Basingstoke; Palgrave Macmillan.

23. Cowley, Philip; 2005; *The Rebels: how Blair lost his majority*; pp.106-128; pub. London; Politicos.

24. Report of the Independent Commission on the Voting System, chaired by Roy Jenkins; pub. London; 1998.

25. Lilleker and Lees-Marshment; 2005; as above; p.32.

26. As immediately above; p.33

27. Oborne, Peter; 2007; *The Triumph of the Political Class*; p.xvi; pub. London; Simon and Schuster.

28. Report of the Committee on State Funding of Political Parties, chaired by Sir Hayden Philips; 2010.

29. Mair, Peter; 1994; *Party Organisation from Civil Society to the State* ; p.15 in Katz R. and Mair

P. eds. *How Parties Organise: change and adaptation in party Organisations in Western Europe*; pub. London; Sage.

30. Johnston, Gaye; 2005; *Can the Labour Party Survive without the Party on the Ground?*; Pamphlet, pub. London/internet; Save the Labour Party .www.labourdemocraticnetwork.

31. Kenyon Peter; 2014; *Ten Years Wasted*; *Chartist*; May/June 2014.

32. Lilleker and Lees-Marshment; 2005; as above; pp. 29-30.

33. As immediately above; p.31.

34. Research done by the office of Ed Miliband MP; 2010.

35. Lilleker and Lees-Marshment; 2005; as above; p.32.

36. Roy Hattersley in an Endpiece article in the *Guardian*.

37. Gould, P.; 1999; as above; p.xviii.

38. Roy Hattersley in the *Guardian*; 09.09.2003.

39. Blair, Tony; speaking to Labour's National Executive Committee (NEC) at its June 1995 meeting.

40. Jenkins, Simon; 2007 *Thatcher and Sons*; p. 206 and pp. 214-5; pub. London; Allen Lane.

41. Campbell, Alastair; 2008, *The Blair Years: extracts fromAlastair Campbell's Diaries*; p. 455; pub. London; Arrow Books.

42. Harris, John in the *Guardian*; G.2; 19.07.2011; p.7.

43. Short, Clare; 2004; *An Honourable Deception*; p. 36; pub. London; Free Press.

44. Cohen, Nick; the *Observer*; 13.10.2013; p.41.

45. Campbell, Alastair; 2008; as above; p. xxvii.

46. Jenkins, Simon; 2007; as above p.248.

47. Chilcot Report into Britain's involvement in the Iraq war; published July 2016.

48. Blair, Tony; quoted in the *Daily Mail*; 30/06/1995.

49. Campbell, Alastair; 2008; as above p.281.

50. Article on front page of the *Sun*; general election day 1992.

51. Campbell, Alastair; 2008; p.281.

52. Jonathan Powell quoted in the *Guardian*; 19.07.2011; p.28.

53. Gould, P; 1999; as above; p. xxi.

54. DavidCameron says he has learned his lesson but has he?; Editorial, the *Observer*; 24.07.2011; p.32.

55. Bagehot, Walter; 1964 edition; ed. RHS Crossman; *The English Constitution*; p.153; pub. London; C.A. Watts and Co.

56. Gould, P.; 1999 as above; pp326-8.

57. Barbour, R.S. and Kitzinger, J. eds.; 1998; *Developing Focus Group Research: politics, theory and practice*;" pub. London; Sage.

58. Drower, G; 1994; as above; p.189.

59. Pelling, Henry; 1976; edit.; *A Short History of the Labour Party*; p.119; pub. Basingstoke; Macmillan.

60. Pimlott, Ben; 1994; *Harold Wilson*; pp. 193-6; pub. London; HarperCollins.

61. The Labour Party; 1997; *Partnership in Power*.

62. Jenkins, S.; 2007; as above; p. 213.

63. Gould, P.; 1999; as above p. xii.

64. Jenkins; 2007; as above; p. 236.

65. Tony Blair; interview with the *Observer* during Party Conference; 1995.

66. Abse, Leo; 1996; *The Man behind the Smile: Tony Blair and the Politics of Perversion*; p. 62; pub. London; Robson Books.

67. Giddens, Anthony; 2000; *The Third Way and its Critics*;" p.56; pub. London; Polity Press.

68. Tony Blair; interviewed on BBC *Andrew Marr Show*; 10.06.2012.

69. Jenkins, S.; 2007; as above; pp. 226‑7.

70. Bower, Tom; 2004;*Gordon Brown*; p.103; pub. London; HarperCollins.

71. Len McCluskey, General Secretary of Unite the union, in interview with Euan Ferguson in the *Observer: the New Review*; 04.09.2011.

72. Elliott, L. and Atkinson, D.; 2007; *Fantasy Island*; *waking up to the incredible economic, political and social illusions of the Blair legacy*; pp. viii‑ix; pub. London; Constable.

73. The late Bob Crow, General Secretary of the RMT Union, quoted in the *Daily Mirror*; 12.03.2014.

74. Seldon, Anthony; 2004 B*lair*; p. x; pub. London; Free Press.

75. McLuhan, Marshall; 1967; *The Medium is the Message*;" pub. London; Penguin.

76. Lilleker and Lees‑Marshment; 2005; as above; p. 36.

77. Gould, P.; 1999; as above; p. 182.

78. Report of the Independent LabOUR Commission on Accountability, Party and Parliamentary Democracy; 2007; (referred to below as The LabOUR Commission Report).

79. *The Dictionary of Politics*; 1993; p.130; pub. London; Penguin.

80. The LabOUR Commission Report; as above p. 11.

81. As immediately above; p. 11 and p. 16.

82. Oborne, Peter; 2007; as above; p. xv.

83. LabOUR Commission Report; pp. 30‑32.

84. Jenkins, S.; 2007; as above; p.214.

85. Campbell, A., 2008; as above; p. 673

86. Jenkins, S. 2007; as above; p. 248.

87. As immediately above; pp. 239

88. Crouch, Colin; 1998; *Fabian Ideas*, No 598; pub. London; the Fabian Society.

89. Letter from Lord Jeremy Beecham to the *Guardian*; 07.03.2014 p.37.

90. Seldon, A. B*lair*; as above; p. 123.

91. Miliband, Ed; research done by his private office; 2010.

92. Cook, Robin; 2003; *The Point of Departure*; p. 79 pub. London; Simon and Schuster.

93. Toynbee, P. and Walker, D.; 2010; as above; p.302.

94. Campbell, A.; 1993; Article in the Sunday Telegraph; 07.02.1993.

95. McSmith, Andy; 1994 *John Smith*; *a life*; p. 312; pub. London; Mandarin.

96. As immediately above; p. 334.

97. Seminar for backbench Labour MPs, given at the House of Commons by Professor John Curtice of Strathclyde University; 1997; as reported by Alan Simpson MP.

98. Lillleker and Lees-Marshment; 2005; as above; p. 6

Notes to Chapter 3

1. Lilleker D.G. and Lees-Marshment J.; 2005; *Political Marketing: a comparative perspective*; Chapter 1; pub. Manchester, Manchester University Press.

2. Report of the Independent Labour Commission on Accountability, Party and Parliamentary Democracy; 2007; pp. 2-3 pub. London; (referred to below as the LabOUR Commission Report).

3. Lilleker and Lees-Marshment; 2005; *Political Marketing: a comparative perspective*; pp. 7-8; pub. Manchester; Manchester University Press.

4. Lilleker and Lees-Marshment; 2005; as above; pp. 8-11.

5. Loach Ken, Director, Film: 2013 *The Spirit of 1945*; issued by Channel 4, BFI Films, Film 4 and Fly Film.

6. Beveridge Report (on the future of health and welfare services);1942; pub. HMSO.

7. McSmith, Andy; 1994; *John Smith: a life 1938-1994*; p. 332; pub. London; Mandarin.

8. Pelling, Henry; 1976; *A Short History of the Labour Party*; p. 129; pub. Basingstoke: Macmillan.

9. Lilleker and Lees-Marshment; 2005; as above; p. 7.

10. Pelling; 1976; as above; p. 129

11. Pelling; 1976; as above; p. 114.

12. Pimlott, Ben; 1993 edit.; *Harold Wilson*; pp. 193-6 and 200; pub. London; HarperCollins.

13. Pelling Henry; 1976; as above; p. 42.

14. Pelling, Henry; 1976; as above; p. 93.

15. Loach Ken; Film; 2013; as above.

16. Pelling, Henry; 1976 as above; p. 114.

17. Pelling,1976; as above; p. 157.

18. Pelling.1976; as above; p. 152.

19. Drower, George; 1994; *Kinnock*; p. 169; pub. South Woodham Ferrers; The Publishing Corporation.

20. Independent LabOUR Commission on Party and Parliamentary Democracy; 2007; p. 36.

21. Mair, Peter; 1994; *Party Organisations from civil society to the state*; p. 15; in eds. Katz R.S. and Mair, P. *How Parties Organise*; *change and adaptation in party Organisations in western democracies*; pub. London; Sage.

22. The Labour Party, 1997; *Partnership in Power*; pub. London; the Labour Party.

23. Pelling; as above; Appendix A.

24. The Labour Party, *Partnership in Power*; as above.

25. Source: the Labour Party National Executive Committee (NEC).

26. The *Guardian*; 01.05.2012; p.32.

27. Gould, Phillip; 1987; Report to Peter Mandelson.

28. Drower, G.; 1994; as above; p. 169.

29. Dower; as immediately above; p. 194.

30. The *Guardian*; 05.015.1993; p.12.

31. The *Independent*; 13.06.1992; p.15.

32. Rt. Hon. Jack Cunningham, interviewed by David Frost on TV AM *Frost on Sunday*; 31.05.1992.

33. Loach, Ken; film; 2013 as above.

34. Beckett, Francis, 2015; *ClemAttlee: Labour's Great Reformer*; pub. London, Haus Publishing.

35. As note 33.

36. Pelling, Henry; 1976; as above; p. 93.

37. Pimlott, Ben; 1993; as above; p. 265·6.

38. General Election Manifestos; February and October 1974; pub. London; the Labour Party.

39. Pelling; 1976; as above; p.160.

40. Rawnsley, Andrew; the *Observer: The New Review*; 14.10.2012; p.4.

41. Jones, Mervyn; 1994; *Michael Foot*; pp. 448·9; pub. London; Victor Gollancz.

42. Jones, M.; 1994; as immediately above; p.492.

43. Drower; 1994; as above; p.87.

44. Kinnock, Neil; interviewed on BBC TV news; 21.09.1983.

45. Drower; 1994; as above; p.94.

46. Labour Party Conference Report; 1988.

47. As immediately above.

48. MORI poll; 01.01.1989.

49. Drower, G.; 1994; as above; p.244.

50. Harris Poll; the *Observer*; 15.09.1991.

51. Opinion poll in the *Sunday Express*; 15.09.1991.

52. *The Times*; 16.9.1991; p.2.

53. Drower; 1994; as above; p.254.

54. *Daily Telegraph* 4.2.1989; p.18.

55. Drower; 1994; as above; p.267.

56. *The Independent*; Survey of voter opinion; 16.09.1991; p.9.

57. MORI opinion poll; October 1991.

58. *Guardian* /ICM opinion poll and *Times* MORI opinion poll; 01.04.1991.

59. *Sunday Mirror*; 18.05.2014.

60. McSmith, Andy; 1994; as above; p.267.

61. Jones, Mervyn; 1994; as above; p.492.

62. The Labour Party; Annual Conference Report 1985.

63. Jones, M.; 1994; as above; p.460.

64. Sykes, Patricia, 1988; *Losing from the Inside*; p.97; pub. London; Transaction Books.

65. *Sunday Times*; 15.2.1981; p.22.

66. Jones, M.; 1994; as above; p.463.

67. Pelling, 1976 ; as above; pp68·9.

68. As immediately above; pp108-11.

69. Jones, M.; 1994; as above; p.436.

70. Interview with Harry Tout, retired Party Organiser; 2009.

71. Beckett, Francis; 2015; as above; p.199.

72. Prescott, John and Davies, Hunter; 2008; *Prezza – My Story: pulling no punches*; p.198; pub. London; Headline.

73. Lilleker and Lees-Marshment; 2005; as above; p.10.

74. Labour Party Annual Report; 1957; p.181; pub. London; the Labour Party.

75. Pelling, Henry; as above; p.131.

76. Pimlott, Ben;1993; as above; p.348.

77. Pelling, Henry;1976; as above; pp 140-2.

78. As immediately above; pp 136-7.

79. The *Guardian*; 22.05.2012; Editorial: The Slow Return of Rage.

80. The Labour Party Manifesto; February 1974.

81. Perkins, Anne; 2003; *Red Queen: the Authorised Biography ofBarbara Castle*; pp.326-333 and 443; pub. London; Pan Books.

82. Jones, Mervyn;1994; as above; p.442.

83. Jones M.; 1994; as immediately above; p.471.

84. Jones, M.; as above; p.475.

85. Jones, M.; as above; p.511.

86. Drower, G.;1994; as above; p.109.

87. The Labour Party, 1986; *Freedom and Fairness*; pub. London; The Labour Party.

88. Labour Party Annual Conference Report; 1986.

89. Drower; 1994; as above; p.179.

90. Kinnock, Neil; *Making our Way*; 1986; p.v; pub. Oxford; Basil Blackwell.

91. *Hansard*; 17.02.1987.

92. Drower; 1994; as above; p.199.

93. As immediately above; p.209.

94. Labour Party Annual Conference Report; 1987.

95. Labour Shadow Communications Agency, 1987; *Labour and Britain in the 1990s*; pub. London; The Labour Party.

96. *Hansard*; 18.12.1991.

97. *Financial Times*; 21.04 1992.

98. Speech by John Smith MP, Labour Leader; TUC Conference; 07.09.1993.

99. Interview with John Smith by Michael Brunson; ITV News at Ten; 04.12.1992.

100. John Smith in R.H. Tawney Memorial Lecture *Reclaiming the Ground*; 20.03.1993.

101. Labour Annual Conference Report; 1993.

102. McSmith, Andy; 1994; as above; p.320.

103. Raynsford, Nick MP; *Fabian Review*, 104; 06.11.1992.

104. McSmith; 1994; as above; p.332.

105. Lilleker and Lees·Marshment; 2005; as above; p.9.

106. As immediately above; pp.9·11.

Notes to Chapter 4

1. The Labour Party, 1997; *Partnership in Power*; pub. London; the Labour Party.

2. Prescott, John with Davies, Hunter; 2008; *Prezza – My Story: pulling no punches*; pp. 192·3, pub. London; Headline.

3. The Commission on Funding of Political Parties in the UK, established 2008 reported 2010, Chair Sir Hayden Phillips.

4. As note 1.

5. The Labour Party; 2007; *Extending and Renewing Party Democracy*; pub. London; the Labour Party.

6. The Labour Party; 2010; TheCollins Report.

7. Pelling, Henry; 1976; *A Short History of the Labour Party*; p. 39 pub. London and Basingstoke; Macmillan.

8. Pelling; 1976; as immediately above.

9. Pelling; as above; Appendix A; p. 171.

10. The Labour Party; 1917; Annual Conference Report pub. London; the Labour Party.

11. Pelling; 1976; as above; pp. 53·54.

12. As immediately above; pp. 61·63.

13. Gilbert, Martin; 1976; *Winston Churchill*; as quoted in *Hansard*, Parliamentary Debates ser.5 ccccxiii, 94.

14. Pelling; 1976; as above; p. 68.

15. Allen, V. L.; *The Trades Unions and the Government*; 1960; p. 258.

16. Pelling; 1976; as above; p. 77.

17. Pelling; 1976; as above; p. 88.

18. *World News and Views*; xxvii; 1947; p. 463.

19. White Paper, *In Place of Strife*; 1969; pub. London; HMSO.

20. The Donovan Report; *Industrial Relations in Britain*; 1968; pub. London; HMSO.

21. Source: Office for National Statistics (ONS).

22. The Labour Party; 1971; Annual Conference Report; pub. London; the Labour Party.

23. Source: ONS.

24. Jenkins, Simon; 2007; *Thatcher and Sons A Revolution in Three Acts*; p. 19; pub. London; Allen Lane.

25. Thatcher, Margaret; 1993; *The Downing Street Years, 1979-1990*; p. 97·108; pub. London; Harper Perennial.

26. Jenkins, Simon; 2007; as above; p. 97.

27. Thatcher; 1993, as note 24; p. 272·6.

28. Jenkins, S.; 2007; as above; p. 97.

29. Rentoul, John; 2001; *TonyBlair*; pub. London; Little Brown.

30. Minkin, Lewis; 1995; *The Contentious Alliance*; pub. Manchester; Manchester University Press.

31. The Labour Party; *TheCollins Report*; 2014.

32. Extracts from interview of Dave Prentis, General Secretary of Unison, by Euan Ferguson; 4.9.11 the *Observer, The New Review*; p. 16.

33. Extracts from an interview of Len McCluskey, General Secretary of Unite by Euan Ferguson; 4.9.11; the *Observer, the New Review*; p. 16.

34. Extracts from interview of MaryBoustead, General Secretary, Association of Teachers and Lecturers, (not affiliated to the Labour Party) by Elizabeth Day; 4.9.11; the *Observer, The New Review*; p. 16.

35. As note 32.

36. Extracts from Interview of Brendan Barber, General Secretary of the TUC, by Elizabeth Day in the *Observer, The New Review*; 4.9.11; p. 16.

37. As immediately above.

38. Extracts from Interview of Bob Crow, General Secretary of the RMT (not affiliated to the Labour Party) by Euan Ferguson in the *Observer, The New Review*; 4.9.11; p. 15.

39. Jones, Owen; 2012 edition; *Chavs: The Demonization of the Working Class*; p. 220; pub. London; Verso.

40. Source: Website of the ProgressGroup.

41. The Labour Party; *Partnership in Power*; 1997.

42. Interim Report of the Independent LabOUR Commission on Accountability, Party and Parliamentary Democracy; 2007; labourdemocraticnetwork.org; p. 43 s.7.2.2.

43. Obituary for Bob Crow in the *Daily Mirror*; 2014.

44. Bob Crow; extract from Interview with Elizabeth Day in the *Observer, The New Review*; 4.9.11; p. 17.

45. Interview of Matt Wrack, General Secretary, Fire Brigades Union (not then affiliated to the Labour Party) by Elizabeth Day; *Observer, The New Review*; 4.9.11; p. 17.

46. *The Australian*; 6.3.12; p. 16.

47. As note 32.

48. As note 1.

49. Campbell, Alastair; 2008; *The Blair Years: The Alistair Campbell Diaries*; p.439.

50. The AustralianLabor Party (ALP) Hawke Rann Report *The Future of the Australian Labor Party*; 2002.

51. As immediately above; p. 4.

52. As immediately above; p. 17.

53. As immediately above.

54. As immediately above.

55. As above; p. 18.

Notes to Chapter 5

1. Independent LabOUR Commission on Accountability, Party and Parliamentary Democracy Interim Report 2007. Referred to below simply as "LabOUR Commission Report" www.labourcommission. org.uk or www.labourdemocraticnetwork.org or try http://bit.ly/w9vx10.

2. Toynbee, Polly and Walker, David; 2010 *The Verdict: did Labour really change Britain?*; p. 74; pub. London; Granta.

3. Radeep Ramesh in the *Guardian*; 20.04.2010.

4. Source: Office for National Statistics (ONS).

5. Jones, Owen; 2011; *Chavs: the demonisation of the working class*; pp. 185·9; pub. London; Verso.

6. As immediately above; p. 190.

7. Toynbee and Walker; 2010; as above; p. 72.

8. Lanchester, John, 2010; *Whoops! Why everyone owes everyone and no one can pay*; p. 192 pub. London; Penguin.

9. Jones, Owen; 2011; as above; p. 185.

10. Crosland, Anthony; 1956; *The Future of Socialism;* pub. London; Jonathan Cape.

11. Toynbee and Walker; 2010; as above; p. 72.

12. Berry, Roger and Hain, Peter; *Disability Rights* in *Commons Journal*; 1997·8 Vol 254 www.publications.parliament.uk.

13. The *Guardian*; 20.01.2010.

14. Toynbee and Walker; 2010; as above; p. 77.

15. Senior government economist Kate Barker interviewed on BBC Radio 4 Today programme; 08.08.2012.

16. Rawnsley, Andrew; 2010; *The End of the Party: the rise and fall of New Labour*; p. 485; pub. London; Viking.

17. Lanchester, John; 2010; as above; p. 216·7.

18. As immediately above; p. 201·2.

19. As immediately above; p. 14.

20. McDonnell John MP; 2007; *Another World is Possible*; p. 11; pub. London; Labour Representation Committee.

21. Keegan, William in the *Observer*; 16.05.2010.

22. Toynbee, Polly in the *Guardian*; 31.08.2010; p. 29.

23. Source: Office for National Statistics (ONS) .

24. BBC Newsnight poll of white working class opinion; 2008; see also Jones, Owen; 2011; as above; p. 248.

25. Peston, Robert; 2008; *Who runs Britain?*; pp. 10·12; pub. London; Hodder and Stoughton.

26. Source Office for National Statistics.

27. Barker, K.; 2004; *Report on Housing in the UK for H.M. Treasury*; pub. London; HM Treasury.

28. Toynbee and Walker; 2010; as above; p. 142.

29. Toynbee, Polly and Walker, David; 2008; *Unjust Rewards: Exposing Greed and Inequality in Britain Today*; p. 82; pub. London; Granta.

30. Jenkins, Simon; *Thatcher and Sons*; p. 205.

31. The *Guardian*; 3.12.2010; p. 27.

32. Lord William Beveridge; Chair of the Beveridge Committee on Social Insurance; 1942.

33. Professor Richard Titmuss.

34. Toynbee and Walker; 2010; as above; p. 226.

35. Beatty and Fothergill; *Incapacity Benfits in the UK*; pp 20-22 (cited byRoger Berry MP).

36. John McDonnell MP; 2007; as above; p. 16.

37. Blair,Tony; speech to theTUC; July 1995.

38. Prescott, John and Davies Hunter; 2008; *Prezza - My Story: Pulling No Punches*; p. 193 pub. London; Headline.

39. Rawnsley, A.; 2010; as above; p. 358.

40. Jones, Owen; 2011; as above; p. 248.

41. Toynbee and Walker; 2010; as above; pp 251-2.

42. Source: Department of Health.

43. Source: ONS.

44. Toynbee and Walker; 2010; as above; p.39.

45. As immediately above.

46. Rawnsley, Andrew; 2010; as above.

47. Polly Curtis in the *Guardian*; 3.12.2010; p. 11.

48. Toynbee and Walker; 2010; as above; p.91.

49. As immediately above; p. 92.

50. Source: As immediately above; pp. 64-66.

51. Short extract from interview of Alan Milburn MP, reported in Rawnsley; 2010; as above; p. 76.

52. Source: An interview of one ofGordon Brown's aides in 2009.

53. Department of Health; www.dfh.gov.uk; 2004.

54. Information provided by Unison; 2011.

55. Harris, John; 2005; *Who do we vote for now?*; pp. 105-7; pub. London Faber and Faber.

56. Jenkins, Simon; 2007; as above; p. 336.

57. McDonnell, J.; 2007; pp. 58-60.

58. Jenkins. S; as above; p. 60.

59. Jenkins, S.; 2006; as immediately above.

60. Toynbee and Walker; 2010; p. 286-7.

61. As immediately above.

62. Cook, Robin; 2003 *The Point of Departure*; p. 271; pub. London; Simon and Schuster.

63. McDonnell, John; 2007; as above; p. 48.

64. Cowley, Philip; 2005; *The Rebels: how Blair mislaid his majority*; p. 106; pub. London; Politicos.

65. Cook, Robin, 2003; as above; pp 134-197.

66. Hutton Inquiry relating to circumstances surrounding the Iraq war.

67. Cook, Robin; 2003; as above; p. 206.Chilcot Report, pub HM Government 2016.

68. As immediately above.

69. McDonnell, J.; 2007; asabove.

70. Cowley, Philip; 2005; as above; pp. 106-7.

71. Cook, Robin; as above; p. 197.

72. Keegan, John; *The Iraq War*; 2004; p. 125; pub. St. Helens, Lancashire; Ted Smart.

73. Pilger, John in the *Guardian G2*; 10.12.2010; p. 7.

74. According to Andrew Rawnsley; 2010; p. 53.

75. Toynbee and Walker; 2010; pp. 282-3.

76. Mowlam, Mo; 2002; *Momentum:the struggle for peace, politics and people*; pp. 206-7; pub. London; Hodder and Stoughton.

77. As immediately above; pp. 222-3 .

78. Alastair Campbell; Diaries; 2008; p. 297.

79. Toynbee and Walker; 2010; pp. 283-4.

80. Cook, Robin; 2003; as above; p. 34.

81. Winnett, Robert and Rayner, Gordon; 2010 edition; No Expenses Spared; p. 93; pub. London; Corgi Books.

82. As immediately above; p. 250.

83. Toynbee and Walker; 2010; p. 252.

84. Jones, Owen; 2011; as above; p. 256.

85. YouGov poll, 2006; for LabOUR Commission Report; 2007.

Notes to Chapter 6

1. Wilkinson, Richard and Pickett, Kate; 2010; *The Spirit Level: Why Equality is Better for Everyone*; pp. 18-21; pub. London; Penguin.

2. Pelling, Henry; 1976 edit.; *A Short History of the Labour Party*; pp. 35-36; pub. London and Basingstoke; Macmillan.

3. Pelling, H.; 1976; as above; p. 27.

4. Pelling as immediately above; p. 58.

5. Pelling; as above; p. 27.

6. Pelling; as above; p. 42.

7. Pelling; as above; p. 92.

8. Martin, Kingsley; 1953; *Harold Laski*; p. 161.

9. Labour Party Conference Report; 1942.

10. Labour Party Manifesto; 1945.

11. Beveridge Report on Social Security, Health and Welfare; 1942; pub. London; HMSO.

12. Government White Paper on Employment; 1944.

13. Peter Hennessy, quoted in Beckett, Francis; 2015; *Clement Attlee: Labour's Great Reformer*; p. 259; pub. London; Haus Publishing.

14. Clement Attlee, speech; in Beckett, Francis; 2015 as immediately above; p. 188.

15. Aneurin Bevan; speech in Parliament about the NHS.

16. National Health Service Act; 1946.

17. *Hansard*; 05.07.1948.

18. Beckett, Francis; 2015; *Clement Attlee: Labour's Great Reformer*; p. 254 pub London; Haus

Publishing.

19. As immediately above.

20. As immediately above; p. 265.

21. As immediately above.

22. Pelling, Henry; 1976; as above; pp. 100-101.

23. As immediately above; p. 98.

24. Source: Office for National Statistics (ONS).

25. Pelling; 1976; as above; pp. 101,142 and 159.

26. Pelling; as above; pp. 100-101.

27. Pelling as immediately above; p. 99.

28. As immediately above.

29. Beckett, Francis; as above; pp 282-90.

30. As immediately above; rear jacket cover.

31. Pimlott, Ben; 1992; *Harold Wilson*; p. 264; pub. London; HarperCollins.

32. Crossman, Richard, *Sunday Pictorial*; 17.02.1963.

33. Callaghan, James; 1980; *Time and Chance*; p. 178.

34. As immediately above; pp. 167-8.

35. The National Plan; 1965; pub. London; HMSO.

36. Pimlott, Ben; as immediately above; p. 360.

37. Labour Party; General Election Manifesto February; 1974.

38. Pimlott; 1992; as above; p. 602.

39. As immediately above; p. 357-8.

40. As immediately above; p. 602.

41. White Paper; *In Place of Strife*; 1969.

42. Pimlott; 1992; as above; pp528-9.

43. Pimlott; 1992; As immediately above; pp. 358-9.

44. Jones, Mervyn; 1994; *Michael Foot*; p. 401; pub. London; Victor Gollancz.

45. Trade Union and Labour Relations Act; 1974.

46. Employment Protection Act; 1976.

47. Jones, M.; as above; p. 367.

48. Perkins, Anne; 2003; *Red Queen: the biography of Barbara Castle*; pp. 374-80; pub. London; Pan.

49. Jones, M.; as above; p. 420.

50. Sexual Offences Act, 1967.

51. Abortion Act, 1967.

52. Chronically Sick and Disabled Persons Act, 1970.

53. Perkins; 2003; as above; pp. 333 and 443.

54. Townsend, Peter; 1970; *Poverty*; pub. London; Penguin.

55. Source: ONS.

56. Pimlott; 1992; as above; p. 512.

57. As immediately above; p. 625.

58. As immediately above; p. 393.

59. As immediately above; pp. 457-67.

60. As immediately above; pp. 727-8.

61. As immediately above; p. 393.

62. As immediately above.

63. Wilson, Harold; 1953; The *War on World Poverty: an Appeal to the Conscience of Mankind*; pub. London; Gollancz.

64. Wilson, Harold; 1953; *Two Out of Three: The Problem of World Poverty*; Peace Aims Pamphlet No. 57; pub. London; National Peace Council.

65. Labour Party; General Election Manifesto 1970.

66. Chalmers, M.; 1984; *Trident: Britain's Independent Nuclear Arms Race*; pub. London; CND.

67. Jenkins, Simon; 2006; *Thatcher and Sons*; 1986; p. 66; pub. London; Allen Lane.

68. Jones, Mervyn; as above; pp. 436-7.

69. Ken Livingstone speaking on BBC Radio 4 Today programme; 08.05.2012.

70. Frank Field MP; interviewed in the *Guardian*; 03.12.2010.

71. Report of the Royal Commission on the Long Term Care of the Elderly; 1999; pub. HMSO.

72. Toynbee and Walker; 2010; *The Verdict: did Labour change Britain?*; p. 130; pub. London; Granta.

73. As note 71.

74. Toynbee and Walker; 2010; p. 230.

75. As immediately above; pp. 17 and 30.

76. Source; Office for National Statistics.

77. Pelling; as above; p. 78.

78. White Paper; *Better Services for the Mentally Ill*; 1975; pub. HMSO.

79. Department of Health; Mental Health Service Frameworks; 1999-2000.

80. Jenkins, Simon; 2006; *Thatcher and Sons*; p. 126; pub. Penguin.

81. Barker, Kate; 2004; Report to HM Treasury on the availability of Housing in the UK.

82. Toynbee and Walker; as above; p. 138.

83. Jenkins, S.; 2006; as above; p. 105.

84. Research by Prof. Allyson Pollock for Unison.

85. Harris, John; 2005; *So who do we vote for now?*; pp. 106-118; pub. Faber and Faber.

86. Independent LabOUR Commission on Accountability, Party and Parliamentary Democracy; 2007; p. 15.

87. Toynbee and Walker; as above; p. 274.

88. Cook, Robin; 2003; *The Point of Departure*; p. 76; pub. London; Simon and Schuster.

89. AustralianLabor Party; 2002; Hawke Rann Report on the Future of the Australian Labor Party.

90. Johnston, Gaye; 2009; *Lessons from Down Under*; *Chartist*, 147, No 239 July/August 2009; p. 19.

91. Toynbee and Walker; 2010; as above; p. 303.

Notes To Chapter 7

1. *Renewal: a two-way process for the 21st Century*; Interim Report of the Independent LabOUR Commission on Accountability, Party and Parliamentary Democracy; 2007 www.labourcommission. org.uk referred to subsequently in notes as the LabOUR Commission Report.

2. As immediately above; pp. 6-7.

3. Mair; 1994; *Party Organisations: from Civil Society to the State*; p. 4; in Katz R.S and Mair (eds.); *How Parties Organise: Change and Adaptation in Party Organisations in Western Democracies*; p. 9 London: Sage.

4. See Minkin, Lewis; 1980 edition; *The Labour Party Conference*; p. 12; Manchester; Manchester University Press.

5. LabOUR Commission Report; as above.

6. Gould Phillip, 1999, *The Unfinished Revolution*; pp. 240-241; pub. London; Abacus.

7. As note 1; p. 11.

8. As note 1; p. 51.

9. LabOUR Commission Report; 2007; as above; Appendix A.

10. Gould, P; 1999; as above; p. 242.

11. Jones, Mervyn; 1994; *Michael Foot*; p. 447; pub. London; Victor Gollancz.

12. Interview with Peter Willsman, former Labour NEC member; November 2010.

13. The Labour Party; Report of Special Conference 1988.

14. Russell, Meg; 2005; *Building New Labour: the politics of Party Organisation*; p. 7 pub. London; Palgrave Macmillan.

15. Alderman, K. and Carter, N.; *The Labour Leadership and Deputy Leadership Elections of 1994*; *Parliamentary Affairs* 48 (3); p. 452.

16. LabOUR Commission Report; as above; p. 17; S.3.2.

17. Responses from the author's questionnaire to 27 Constituency Labour Party Secretaries from England, Scotland and Wales; October 2009.

18. LabOUR Commission Report; as above; p. 28.

19. YouGov opinion polls undertaken for LabOUR Commission; 2007.

20. LabOUR Commission Report; as above; p. 39.

21. Russell; 2005; as above; p. 37.

22. The Labour Party; 1997; *Partnership in Power*; (PiP).

23. Golding, John; 2003; *Hammer of the Left*; p. 34; London; Politicos.

24. Seyd, Patrick; 1987; *The Rise and Fall of the Labour Left*; Basingstoke; Macmillan.

25. Russell, Meg; 2005; as note 14; p. 289.

26. The Labour Party; *Partnership in Power*; as note 23.

27. As immediately above.

28. Russell, Meg; 2005; as above; p. 289.

29. Price, Lance; 2005; *The Spin Doctor's Diary: inside Number 10 with New Labour*; p. 31; pub. London; Hodder and Stoughton.

30. Russell, Meg; 2005; as above; pp149-50.

31. The Labour Party; *Partnership in Power*; 1997 as above.

32. As immediately above.

33. Information from Peter Willsman as note 12.

34. Russell, Meg; 2005; as above; pp148-9.

35. The Labour Party Rules, 2009; Clause X1.

36. Russell; 2005; as above.

37. As immediately above.

38. The Labour Party; 2007; *Renewing and Extending Party Democracy*.

39. Underhill, Reg; 1975, *How the Labour Party Works*; p. iiix.

40. The Labour Party; 1985; *Report of Annual Conference*; Speech by Ron Hayward, General Secretary.

41. Pimlott, Ben; 1992; *Harold Wilson*; pp. 391-3; pub. London; HarperCollins.

42. The Labour Party; *Partnership in Power*; 1997; as above.

43. Russell, Meg; 2005; p.47.

44. Seyd and Whiteley; 1992; *Labour's Grass Roots: the politics of Party membership*; p. 72; pub. Oxford; Oxford University Press.

45. Minkin, Lewis; 1992; *The Contentious Alliance: Trades unions and the Labour Party*; p. 98; pub. Edinburgh; Edinburgh University Press.

46. The Labour Party; *Renewing and Extending Party Democracy*; 2007.

47. LabOUR Commission Report, 2007, as above, pp.14-15.

48. As immediately above p.14.

49. Interview with Liz Snape, Assistant General Secretary, UNISON.

50. The Labour Party; *Annual Conference Report 2010*

51. As immediately above

52. As immediately above.

53. The Labour Party; *Refounding Labour*; 2011

54. YouGov polls undertaken for the LabOUR Commission, 2006/7 as above.

55. Report of focus groups conducted by Professor Stuart Weir in 2006 for the Labour Commission; see Appendix A in LabOUR Commission Report.

56. Angela Eagle MP; Introduction to the LabOUR Commission Report; 2007; p.5.

57. LabOUR Commission Report (as above) p.5.

58. LabOUR Commission Report; 2007; p.28 as above.

59. As immediately above.

60. YouGov polls for LabOUR Commission as above.

61. *The Big Conversation*; public consultation by the Labour Party; 2003.

62. YouGov; Polls for the LabOUR Commission; 2007

63. Gould Philip; *The Unfinished Revolution* p.628; 1999; pub. London: Little Brown

64. *Partnership in Power*; 1997; as above

65. Interview with "Brenda" former CLP delegate to Annual Conference; September 2010.

66. Text of a flyer circulated anonymously to CLP Conference delegates by Party Regional staff at

Conference 2009.

67. Research by the Campaign for Labour Party Democracy.

68. Extract from *Campaign Briefing*; Circulated to Conference Delegates; 29.09.2009.

Notes to Chapter 8

1. Harris, John Memo to Labour: please think about how it looks – talk of a stitch up in candidate selection adds to a sense the party is out of touch; *Guardian*; 15.04.2009; p. 31.

2. Russell, Meg; 2005; *Building New Labour: the politics of Party Organisation*; p. 34; pub. London; Palgrave Macmillan.

3. King, Anthony; A cutback in MPs will make the Commons even more feeble; *Observer* 14. 11.10; p. 6.

4. Hattersley, Roy; Endpiece; *Guardian*; 13.5.2007; p.24.

5. Who's Who?; 2009; Entries about contemporary Labour Ministers.

6. Labour Party Rules; 1994-2008; pub. London; The Labour Party; see www.labour.org.uk.

7. Mills, James; Comment Is Free; Guardian; 13.6.10.

8. Smith Institute; 2010; *Guide to the 2010 General Election*; pub. London; Smith Institute.

9. Labour Party Rules for the selection of candidates for the Scottish Parliament, Welsh and London assemblies in force up to 1999.

10. Labour Party rules for the selection of Prospective Parliamentary candidates 1945-1992.

11. Russell, Meg; 2005; as above; pp 44-45.

12. Straw poll added to qualitative survey (by the author) responded to by 27 Constituency Labour Party Secretaries (from England, Scotland and Wales) in September 2009.

13. Labour Party Rules 2001.

14. Information provided by Labour Party members in the North West Region.

15. Information from members of the Labour Party National Executive Committee (NEC).

16. *Tribune*; 16.04.2010.

17. Labour Party rules; 2006.

18. Labour Party rules; 1994.

19. Labour Party rules; 2004.

20. *Tribune*; 16.10.2009.

21. *Tribune* 17.04.2009.

22. Saner, Ermine; I signed it. Then the man said: 'Have you met Georgia? She's very nice'; *Guardian*; 18.04.2009; p. 13.

23. Saner, Ermine; I signed it. Then the man said: 'Have you met Georgia? She's very nice'; *Guardian*; 18.04.2009; p. 13.

24. *Tribune*; 17.04.2009.

25. UK Employment Tribunal judgement on equal opportunities in employment; 1995.

26. The Labour Party Annual Conference Report; 1988.

27. Information given to the author by the partner of a minister in 1998.

28. *Tribune*; 17.04.2009.

29. Source: author's friends in Stoke Central Constituency Labour Party.

30. Tribune; 17.04.2010.

31. Rainsborough, Thomas; *Rage against the Machine*; *Red Pepper*; 10.04.2009.

32. *Labour Briefing*; January 2010; p. 19.

33. *Tribune*; 9.04. 2010 and 16.04.2010.

34. Report from Peter Killeen, former Chair West Derby Constituency Labour Party to Labour's NEC on Parliamentary Selection Process in that Constituency; 2007.

35. Interim report of the independent LabOUR Commission on Accountability, Party and Parliamentary Democracy, 2007; p. 52; www.labourcommission.org.uk and www labourdemocratic network.org or http://bit.ly/w9vx10.

36. Report to the Labour Party NEC from senior Party officer Eileen Murfin on the Parliamentary candidate selection in Swindon North; 1995.

37. Quotation from Jon Cruddas MP, given in an interview and reported in the *Observer*; 28.10.2010.

38. Source: Campaign for Labour Party Democracy.

39. Fashion Photo shoot with Caroline Flint MP; *Observer Magazine*; May 2010.

40. Report of the LabOUR Commission; 2007; as above; Report of Focus Groups with Labour Party members led by Professor Stuart Weir; Appendix A.

41. Individual reports from Labour Party members in merging constituencies.

42. As note 41.

43. As note 41.

44. Patricia – is the pseudonym for an applicant to become a Prospective Labour Parliamentary candidate during the New Labour era.

45. Julia, same role as Patricia.

46. Mary, same role as Patricia.

47. Beckett, Francis; 2000; *ClemAttlee: a biography*; p. 25; pub. London; Politicos.

48. Russell, Meg; 2005; as above; pp. 68-71.

49. Wring, D., Baker, D. and Seawright, D.; 2000; *Panelism in action: Labour's 1999 European Parliamentary Candidate selections*; *Political Quarterly* 31(3): pp. 300-11.

50. Russell, Meg; 2005; as above; pp 72-3.

51. Bradbury, J., Bennie, L. and Denver, D.; 2000; *Candidate selection, devolution and modernization: the selection of Labour Party candidates in the 1999 Scottish Parliament and Welsh Assembly elections*; *British Elections and Parties Review 10*; pp. 151-72.

52. Russell, Meg; 2005; as above; p. 76.

53. LabOUR Commission Report; 2007; YouGov Opinion poll; as note 37.

54. Source: Campaign for Labour Party Democracy.

Notes to Chapter 9

1   Cowley, Philip 2005; *The Rebels: How Blair mislaid his majority*; pp. 263-73; pub. London Politicos.

2   Cowley; 2005; as above; pp. 106-9.

3   Cowley; 2005; as above; p. 3.

4   Garrett; 1992; as above; p. 29.

5   Mitchell, Austin MP; in *The Parliamentarian*; January 1985 edition.

6   Garrett; 1992; as above; p. 16, 2005; as above; p. 16.

7   Cowley; 2005; as above; p. 3.

8   Oborne, Peter; 2007; *The Triumph of the Political Class*; pp. xiv-xvi; pub. London; Simon and Schuster.

9   McDonnell, John; *Another World is possible*; 2007; pub. Labour Representation Committee.

10   Report of the LabOUR Commission on Accountability, Party and Parliamentary Democracy 2007; p. 10; pub. London, LabOUR Commission.

11   Oborne, P; 2007; as above; p. 12.

12   Mullin, Chris; 2010; *A View from the Foothills: the diaries of Chris Mullin*; p. 69; pub. London; Profile Books.

13   Oborne; 2007; as above; p. 12.

14   Cowley; 2005; as above; p. 253.

15   Cowley; 2005; as above; p. 77.

16   The Labour Party, 2011; *Refounding Labour*; pub. London; the Labour Party.

17   Labour Party Rules since 1993.

18   Rawnsley, Andrew; 2010; *The End of the Party: the Rise and Fall of New Labour*; p. 253; pub. London; Penguin.

19   Seldon, Anthony; 2004; *Blair*; p. 437; pub. London; Free Press.

20   Jenkins, Simon; 2007; *Thatcher and Sons*; pp. 237-8; pub. London; Allen Lane.

21   Seldon, Anthony; 2004; *The Blair Effect*; p. 23; pub. London; Free Press.

22   Jenkins, Simon; 2007; *Thatcher and Sons*; as above; p. 254.

23   Jenkins, Simon; as immediately above; p. 266.

24   Mullin, Chris; as above; p. 7.

25   Bagehot, Walter; 1964 edition; *The English Constitution*; pp. 85-100; pub. London; C.A. Watts and Co.

26   Campbell, Alastair; 2008; *The Blair Years: extracts from Alastair Campbell's Diaries*; p. 279; pub. London; Arrow Books.

27   Cowley; 2005; as above; pp. 8-9 and 79-100.

28   Mullin, Chris; 2010; p.73.

29   Cowley; as above; p. 106.

30   As immediately above; p. 134.

31   Bagehot,W.; as above; pp 134-6.

32   Cook, Robin, 2003; *The Point of Departure*; p. 280; pub. London; Simon and Schuster.

33   Politics Professor X; in conversation with the author in 1998.

34   Winnett, Robert and Rayner, Gordon; 2009 edition; *No Expenses Spared*; p. 244; pub. London; Corgi Books.

35   Reported in the *Daily Telegraph*; May 2009.

36   Ostragorski, Mosei; 1902; *Democracy and the Organisation of Political Parties*; pub. London; Macmillan. Quoted by John MacDonnell MP in interview.

Notes to Chapter 10

1   Garrett, John; 1992' *Does Parliament Work?*; pp. 29-30; pub. London; Victor Gollancz.

2   Lilleker, D and Lees-Marshment, J.; 2005; *Political Marketing: a comparative perspective*; p. 8; pub. Manchester; Manchester University Press.

3   The Independent LabOUR Commission on Accountability, Party and Parliamentary Democracy, 2007; pp. 35-37 (abbreviated below as LabOUR Commission); pub. Labour Commission.

4   Source: Campaign for Labour Party Democracy.

5   Price, Lance; 2005; *The Spin Doctor's Diary: inside Number 10 with New Labour*; p. 33; pub. London; Hodder and Stoughton.

6   Tony Blair quoted on BBC TV *Newsnight*.

7   YouGov Opinion poll; 2006; conducted for the LabOUR Commission – as note 2.

8   As note 7.

9   Pelling, Henry; 1976 edition *A Short History of the Labour Party*; pp. 1-33; pub. Macmillan; London and Basingstoke.

10 The Labour Party Constitution; 1918.

11 Pelling; 1976; as above; pp 53-54.

12 As immediately above; pp 48-50.

13 Labour Party Rules; 2014.

14 Pelling; as above; p. 84.

15. The *Guardian*; 11.05.2010.

16. Attlee, Clement; 1954; *As it Happened*; p. 156; pub. London; Heinemann, Weidenfeld and Nicholson.

17. Harris, Kenneth; 1982, *Attlee*.

18. Pelling, Henry; as above; pp. 53-4.

19. Pimlott, Ben; 1993 edition; *Harold Wilson*; p. 252 pub. London; HarperCollins.

20. Interview with Clare Short MP 2009.

21. Jones, Mervyn, 1994; *Michael Foot*; p. 441; pub. London; Victor Gollancz.

22. The *Guardian*; 10.09.1981.

23. The Labour Party; 2007; *Extending and Renewing Party Democracy*.

24. The Labour Party; 1997; *Partnership in Power*.

25. Jones, M.; 1994; as above; p. 458.

26. As immediately above; p. 462.

27. Williams, GL and Williams Alan L.; 1989 *Labour's Decline and the Social Democrat's Fall*; p. 114; pub. Macmillan; London and Basingstoke.

28. LabOUR Commission Report; 2007; as above; p. 17.

29. Jones, M.; 1994; as above; pp. 468-9.

30. *Tribune*; 12.06.1981.

31. Russell, Meg; 2005; *Building New Labour: the politics of Party Organisation*; p. 135; pub. London; Palgrave Macmillan.

32. Jones, M.; as above; p. 506.

33. The *Guardian*; 10.07.1981.

34. Russell, Meg; as above; p. 137.

35. *Partnership in Power*, 1997; as above.

36. Russell, M.; as above; pp 138-9.

37. Drower, George, 1994; *Kinnock*; p. 219; pub. South Woodham Ferrers: the Publishing Corporation.

38. Conversation between the author and Tom (later Lord) Sawyer in 1986.

39. Labour Party Annual Conference Report; 1987.

40. Drower, G., 1994; as above; p. 229.

41. As immediately above; p. 212.

42. As immediately above; p. 215.

43. Lilleker and Lees-Marshment; 2005; as above; p. 9.

44. *Partnership in Power*; as above.

45. LabOUR Commission; 2007; as above; p. 36.

46. TheCampaign Group; 1988; *Agenda for Change: a Campaign for socialism programme*.

47. The Labour Party Annual Conference Report; 1997.

48. McSmith, Andy; 1994; *John Smith; a life 1938-1994*; p. 264; pub. London; Mandarin.

49. Interview with Clare Short MP.

50. John Smith; interviewed on BBC TV *On the Record*; 5.7.1992.

51. McSmith; 1994; as above; p. 269.

52. As immediately above; pp. 329-30.

53. Sir Hayden Phillips chaired the Committee on the State Funding of Political Parties.

54. TonyBlair; from a speech at Labour Party Conference; 1995.

55. Angela Eagle MP; in LabOUR Commission Report 2007; as above; p. 3.

56. Russell, Meg; 2005; as above; pp. 139-142.

57. *Renewing and Extending Party Democracy*; The Labour Party; 2007.

58. A General Election was rumoured in 2007, but GB failed to call it.

59. YouGov poll for Labour Commission (see above); held 2006.

60. LabOUR Commission Report 2007; p. 4; see above.

61. AustralianLabor Party; 2002; Hawke-Wran Report on the Future of the Australian Labor Party.

62. Hawke-Wran Report; as immediately above; p. 11.

63. As immediately above; p. 35.

64. *Partnership in Power*, The Labour Party; 2007.

65. Hawke-Wran Report; as above; p. 37.

66. As immediately above; p. 38.

67. As immediately above; p. 41.

68. As immediately above; p. 44.

69. As immediately above; p. 43.

70. As note 65.

71.   Attlee, Clement, 1954; *As It Happened*; p. 156; pub. Heinemann, Weidenfeld and Nicholson.

72.   Cowley, Philip; 2005; as above; p. 3.

73.   Pimlott, Ben; 1992, *Harold Wilson*; pp. 262-3; pub. London; HarperCollins.

74.   Pelling, Henry; as above; p. 139.

75.   Pimlott, Ben; 1992; as note 73.

76.   Jones, Mervyn; 1994, *Michael Foot*; p. 364; pub. London; Victor Gollancz.

77.   As immediately above; p. 398.

78.   Jones, M.; 1994; as above; p. 500.

79.   Labour Party Annual Conference Report; 1979.

80.   *London Labour Briefing*; May 1981 edition.

81.   Jones, 1994; p. 502.

82.   McSmith, Andy; 1994; *John Smith: a life 1938-1994*; p. 129; pub. London; Mandarin.

83.   Garrett, John; 1992; as above; p. 167.

84.   As immediately above; p. 168.

85.   As immediately above; p. 16.

86.   As immediately above; p. 149.

87.   Cowley; 2005; as above; p. 59.

88.   As immediately above.

89.   Garrett, John; as above; p. 149.

90.   Cowley, Philip; 2005; as above; pp. 26-27.

91.   Prescott, John and Davies Hunter; *Prezza – My Story: pulling no punches*; pp. 301-18.

92.   Swift, Jonathan; *Gulliver's Travels*; Book 1, Lilliput.

93.   Australian Labor Party; 2002; Hawke-Wran Report; as above; p. 31.

94.   As immediately above; pp. 22-24.

95.   As immediately above; p. 32.

96.   As immediately above; p. 41.

Notes to Chapter 11

1.   Wilkinson, Richard and Pickett, Kate; 2010; *The Spirit Level. Why equality is better for everyone*; pp. 43-45; pub. London; Penguin.

2.   As above; p. 159.

3.   Jones, Owen; 2012; *Chavs. The demonization of the working class*; p. 260; pub. London; Verso.

4.   Polly Toynbee in the *Guardian*; 27.07.11; p. 29.

5.   Toynbee, Polly and Walker, David; 2010; *The Verdict: did Labour change Britain?*; p. 297; pub. London; Granta.

6.   Source: Office for National Statistics (ONS).

7.   Toynbee and Walker; 2010; as above; p. 78.

8.   Jones, Owen; as above; p. 230.

9.   Source: pressure group Defend Council Housing.

10. Rawnsley, Andrew; 2010; *The End of the Party: the rise and fall of New Labour*; p. 358; pub. London; Penguin.

11. Jones, Owen; as above; p. 266.

12. Prescott, John with Davies, Hunter; 2008; *Prezza – My Story; pulling no punches*; p. 193; pub. London; Headline.

13. Campbell, Alastair; 2008; *The Blair Years; extracts from the Alastair Campbell Diaries*; p. 58.

14. Jones, Owen; as above; p. 257.

15. Toynbee and Walker; 2010; as above; p. 287.

16. Jenkins, Simon; 2007; *Thatcher and Sons*; p. 247; pub. London; Allen Lane.

17. As immediately above; p. 248.

18. Source: ONS.

19. As immediately above.

20. Toynbee and Walker; 2010; as above; p. 239.

21. Jones, Owen; as above; p. 255.

22. Lilleker, Darren and Lees-Marshment, Jennifer; 2005; *Political Marketing: a comparative perspective*; p. 11; pub. Manchester; Manchester University Press.

23. Research by Prof John Curtice at a seminar for MPs; as reported by Alan Simpson MP.

24. Mair, Peter; 1994; *Party Organisations from Civil Society to the State*; in Katz, R and Mair, P (eds.) *How Parties Organise: change and adaptation in party Organisations in western democracies*; p. 15; pub. London; Sage.

25. Johnston, Gaye, 2005; *Can the Labour Party Survive without the Party on the Ground?;* pub. On internet by Save the Labour Party/Labour Democratic Network.

26. Seyd, P. and Whiteley, P; 2002; *New Labour's Grass Roots: the transformation of the Labour Party's membership*; pub. Basingstoke and London; Macmillan.

27. Mair, Peter; as note 27.

28. Research for the Independent LabOUR Commission on Accountability, Party and Parliamentary Democracy, Appendix A, and YouGov poll; 2007; pub. London; LabOUR Commission.

29. *Refounding Labour*; 2011; pub. London; the Labour Party.

30. The Labour Party; *The Collins Report*; 2013.

31. Cowley, Philip; 2005; *The Rebels: How Blair mislaid his majority*; p. 137-139; pub. London; Politicos.

32. Orwell, George; 1951 edition; *Animal Farm*; p. 17; pub. London; Penguin.

33. Giddens, Anthony; *The Third Way and its critics*; p. 41; pub. London; Polity Press.

34. As immediately above.

35. Revans, Reg; Paper on *Action Learning*; 1988; p. 1; pub. University of Salford.

36. Wilkinson and Pickett; as above; p. 12.

37. Toynbee and Walker; *Unjust Rewards*; 2008; as above; pp. 204-5.

38. As immediately above; p. 203.

39. As immediately above; p. 3.

40. Linden, Eugene; 2006; *Winds of Change*; pp. 226-7; pub. New York; Simon and Schuster.

41. As immediately above; p. 269.

42. Report of the Royal Commission on the Long Term Care of Older People; 1999; pub. HMSO.

43. Toynbee and Walker; 2010; as above; p. 178.

44. LabOUR Commission Report, 2007; as above; pp. 35-36.

45. Refounding Labour; 2011; as above.

46. The Labour Party; *Partnership in Power*; 1997.

47. The LabOUR Commission Report; 2007; p. 6 as above.

48. As immediately above; p. 42.

Notes to Chapter 12

1. Hasan, Mehdi and Macintyre, James; 2012; *Ed, the Milibands and the making of a Labour leader*; p. 114; pub. London; Biteback Publishing.

2. As immediately above; pp. 117-8.

3. Private information given to Hasan and Macintyre; 2012, as above.

4. As note 3, p399.

5. Patrick Hennesey in the *Sunday Telegraph* during the Labour Leadership election campaign.

6. Hasan and Macintyre; 2012, as above, p239.

7. ComRes opinion polls; March 2011.

8. Lord Ashcroft mega poll, 2012.

9. Comres poll of marginal constituencies; October 2013.

10. Comres poll ,as immediately above, but taken in September 2014.

11. *Daily Telegraph*; 03.09.2011.

12. Quoted in Bale, Tim; *Five Year Mission: the Labour Party under Ed Miliband*, p.101; 2014; pub. Oxford; Oxford University Press.

13. The *Guardian*; 05.07.2010.

14. Hasan and Macintyre; 2012; as above; p. 303.

15. The Labour Party; *Refounding Labour*; 2011; pub. The Labour Party; London.

16. As immediately above.

17. As immediately above.

18. The Labour Party; TheCollins Report; 2013; pub. The Labour Party; London.

19. As immediately above.

20. The *Daily Mirror*; 15.10.2015.

21. Results of an exit poll for the 2015 general election conducted for BBC TV by Professor John Curtice of Strathclyde University.

22. The *Guardian*; 09.05. 2015; pp. 3-5.

23. Report of the Independent LabOUR Commission on Accountability, Party and Parliamentary Democracy; 2007; pp. 45-8; pub. London: LabOUR Commission.

24. Hasan and Macintyre; as above; p. 266.

Index

Please note: every Chapter is divided into sections: each of which cover the subjects indicated at the head of the Chapter. Therefore there should be less need to use this index.

A

Abbott, Diane MP 220, 254, 390, 399, 400, 409, 412
Academy Schools 154, 348
Affordabilty of public services (1940s) 191
Afghanistan war 159, 161, 180, 182, 183, 210, 350, 380, 381
Ahern, Bertie 162
Alexander, Douglas MP 405, 407
Ali, Tariq 59
Allaun, Frank MP 334
Alternative Vote 36, 208, 343, 394, 397, 400
Amos, Lady Valerie 308
Armstrong, Hilary MP 300
Ashdown, Lord Paddy 103, 335
Ashton, Lady Catherine 308
Attlee, Clement MP 23, 74–76, 79–82, 88, 93, 102, 111–112, 134, 143, 158, 184, 186, 191–194, 203–204, 207, 210, 215, 225, 275, 310, 319–321, 332, 337–341

B

Balls, Ed MP 86, 254, 290, 299, 399
Balogh, Lord Thomas 321
Barber, Brendan 117
Barker, Kate 321
Beckett, Margaret MP 71, 99, 117, 300, 326
Benn, Hilary MP 399–400
Benn, Tony MP 3, 84, 283, 286, 322–324
Berry, Roger MP 25, 27, 29, 32, 35, 49, 51, 61, 80, 134, 136, 139, 142, 144, 149, 160, 203, 205, 210, 221, 232, 238, 241, 292, 298, 301, 305, 352, 353, 369, 375, 377, 393, 417
Bevan, Aneurin MP 47, 84, 93, 131, 190–191, 283, 320, 323, 332, 333, 367
Bevanites 332
Beveridge, Lord William 38, 144
Beveridge Report 76, 144, 188–189, 192, 383
Bevin, Ernest MP 111–112, 188, 192, 206, 320, 338, 349
Blaenau Gwent, parliamentary constituency 268
Blair, Tony MP 6, 10, 14–16, 20, 33, 39, 41, 44, 50–56, 58, 65–68, 71–72, 81–82, 107, 109, 114, 118, 135, 136, 138, 140, 143, 144, 147, 153, 155–162, 176–177, 185, 198, 200, 211, 213, 220, 222, 229, 235, 257, 267–268, 271, 283–284, 290–292, 295, 297–298, 300, 316, 327, 333, 339, 347–348, 350, 355, 359, 362, 366, 368, 377–378, 393, 403
Blears, Hazel MP 86, 299, 377, 378
Boustead, Mary, General Secretary, Association of Teachers and Lecturers 116
Boyce, Max, comedian 85
Brezhnev, Leonid, President USSR 96
BRIC countries 374, 376
Brittan, Lord Leon 3, 275
Brown, George MP 193, 320, 333
Brown, Gordon MP 14, 49, 64, 102, 104, 134, 136, 139, 155, 213, 220, 255, 258, 267, 280, 320, 359, 390, 398, 407, 412
Brown, Nick MP 279, 280, 287, 292, 400
Bryant, Chris MP 243
Burma 191, 350
Burnham, Andy MP 254, 290, 378, 399, 412
Butler Inquiry, Iraq war 53, 68
Butler, Lord R A 'Rab' 188, 348
Byers, Stephen MP 121, 123
Byrne, Liam MP 127, 152, 351, 400

C

Cable, Vince MP 134

Callaghan, James MP 13, 44, 76, 80, 82–83, 92, 95, 96, 102, 106, 112, 114, 139, 158, 163, 185, 186, 193–194, 196, 197, 199–200, 203, 204, 206–207, 210, 215, 220, 226, 320, 322, 333, 337, 338, 349, 351, 352, 362

Cameron, David MP 80, 104, 165, 400, 403–404, 407, 408

Campaign for Democratic Socialism 112, 320

Campaign for Labour Party Democracy 220, 224, 238, 250, 273, 321–322, 324, 327, 409

Campaign Group 68, 236, 275, 286, 293, 295, 325, 332, 367

Campbell, Alastair 50, 52–55, 71, 107, 112, 121, 162, 217, 320, 348

Canavan, Dennis MP 86, 277

Castle, Barbara MP 3, 83, 84, 113, 195, 197, 333, 353

Catering Wages Act 188

Cecil, Lady Gwendolen 21

Chagos Islanders, resettlement of 198

Challen, Colin MP 28, 29, 32, 34, 35, 36, 52, 60, 134, 136, 144, 156, 168, 184, 233, 286, 304, 314, 334, 364, 365, 373, 378, 388, 392, 417

Chevaline, Polaris nuclear warheads 95, 334

Chiffley, Ben, Australian Prime Minister 16

Chilcot Report 39, 53, 160, 380

Chile, 1974 coup 198

Churchill, Winston MP 111

Citrine, Lord 111

Civil Rights and Liberties (UK) 131, 148, 174, 211

Clark, Katy MP 27, 31, 50, 52, 135, 136, 138, 142, 143, 146, 149, 151, 155, 156, 158, 159, 165, 205, 206, 208, 280, 284, 298, 305, 366, 417

Clinton, Bill 162, 349

Coalition Government (UK) 112, 115, 117, 124, 139, 143, 158, 168, 208, 319, 320, 378, 381, 383, 395, 397, 400

Collins Commission (Labour Party, 2013) 109, 115, 354

Communication Workers Union (CWU) 24, 27, 59, 107, 109, 111, 117, 120, 122, 123, 127, 358, 363, 399, 420

Communist Party (UK) 65, 112, 319–320

Compass, Labour Party pressure group 245, 319

Construction industry (UK) 350

Cook, Robin MP 69, 71, 130, 159–161, 164, 211, 238, 284, 286, 298, 300, 306, 308, 316, 323, 390

Co-operative Party 263, 265, 319

Cooper, Yvette MP 254, 412

Corbyn, Jeremy MP 9, 15, 18, 28, 31, 33, 34, 36, 57, 137, 138, 141, 142, 149, 153, 156, 158, 159, 161, 163, 203–205, 210, 220, 233, 241, 245, 254, 279, 284, 291–293, 300, 334, 337, 347–348, 363, 367, 369–370, 375, 378, 380, 384, 390, 395–396, 399, 409, 412–416, 417

Corston, Jean MP 286

Cousins, Frank, Transport and General Workers Union leader 112, 320

Crime and Civil Liberties Policies 148

Crossman, Richard MP 94, 193, 332

Crow, Bob, trade union leader 61, 118, 123

Cruddas, Jon MP 11, 20, 25, 28, 32, 34, 49, 59, 127, 134, 136, 142, 144, 146, 152, 158, 163, 185, 203, 204, 206–207, 221, 233, 239, 244, 262, 267, 284, 295, 315, 364–367, 374, 386, 405, 407, 411, 417

Cryer, John MP 27, 32, 33, 52, 133, 142, 146, 152, 155, 159, 165, 203, 208, 241, 242, 245, 262, 281, 282, 301, 302, 349, 357, 370, 378, 389, 393, 394, 417

Cunningham, Jack MP 81

Currie, Edwina MP 97

Curtice, Professor John 353, 408

D

Darling, Alistair MP 119, 319, 407

Darlington by-election 1983 83, 96

D'Avila, Jim, selection process 266, 267

Day, Sir Robin 85

Democracy (Labour Party) 9–16, 362
  policies to promote 208

Democratic centralism 65

Denham, John MP 400

De Piero, Gloria MP 255, 258, 268
Deputy Leadership election, Labour Party, 1984 88
Developing Countries, UK aid to 94, 158, 177, 180, 181–183, 198, 206, 215, 304, 349, 380–382
Devolution and Constitutional Reform 36, 95, 117, 131, 163, 169, 180, 199, 205–206, 216, 333–334, 339, 377, 407
Dewar, Donald MP 163
Disraeli, Benjamin MP 21
Dobson, Frank MP 21, 27, 32, 34, 69, 142, 150–156, 167, 183, 201–202, 205, 211, 234, 284, 298, 307, 338, 349, 368, 372, 375, 380, 417
Doncaster North, Parliamentary Constituency 104, 397
Donnelly, Desmond MP 194
Donovan Commission on Trade Unions 113, 349
Douglas-Home, Lord Alec 94
Durham Miners' Gala 87, 123, 147

E

East Coast Main Line 210
Economic policy, Labour up to 1979 33, 92, 93, 94, 95, 96, 189, 191, 193, 194, 195, 196, 197
Economic policy, New Labour 6, 38, 40, 61, 62, 117, 118, 133, 134, 135, 136, 137, 143, 171, 181, 203, 347, 350, 375, 376, 405, 414, 423
Eden, Anthony MP 92
Education policy, Labour up to 1979 188, 215, 347
Education policy, New Labour 155, 175, 203, 284, 347, 379, 415
Electoral College, Labour Party 13, 87, 334
Ellman, Louise MP 25, 31, 52, 69, 99, 133, 143, 153, 202, 232, 239, 242, 255, 263, 290, 295, 300, 302, 310, 366, 368, 381, 393, 417
Employment, UK, increased levels 133–134
Environment, Labour Party policies after 1997 351
Environment, Labour Party policies up to 1979 352
Equalities legislation, up ro 1979 196, 353
Equalities policies, non-economic 36, 117, 149, 187, 196, 205, 346, 352–353
Equality of opportunity 25–28, 38, 346, 352, 368, 379, 423
Equal Pay legislation 31, 196, 353
European Union 39, 163, 204–205, 351, 393

F

Fabian Society 22, 110, 133, 220, 399
Falkirk, Labour Party parliamentary candidate selection, 2013 121, 129, 277, 405–406, 410
Falklands war, 1982 13, 63, 90, 96, 105, 159, 199
Faulkner, Lord Charles 308
Fire Brigades Union 109, 124, 129, 323
Flint, Caroline MP 86, 254, 268, 299
Follett, Barbara MP 84, 268
Foot, Michael MP 13, 83, 86, 95, 196, 233, 272, 321, 323–324, 332
Foreign and defence policy, Attlee Government 191
Foreign and defence policy, New Labour 11, 39, 59, 62, 158, 159, 177, 193, 216, 380
Foundation Hospitals 154, 168, 209, 215, 226, 284, 358, 379
Freedom of Information Act 163, 205
Frost, David 98
Fulham by-election 78, 80

G

Gaitskell, Hugh MP 20, 23, 80, 82, 112, 191, 193, 316, 320, 333
Gardner David, former assistant general secretary, Labour Party 228, 231, 259, 267, 277, 419
Gay and Lesbian Rights 29, 36, 90, 149, 196, 205, 352, 353
General Election results, 1992-2015 103–104
Gibson, Dr. Ian MP 291–293, 322
Glasman, Maurice Lord 38, 405
GMB, formerly General, Municipal and Boilermakers Union 122, 220, 399
Gould, Bryan MP 14, 71, 326
Gould, Georgia, daughter of Philip 273
Gould, Lord Philip 16, 24, 44, 55, 56, 58, 65, 74, 76, 80, 85, 218, 238, 257, 273

Grass Roots Alliance 223, 250, 278, 318, 327

Grass Roots Umbrella Network 327

Gray, Gary. Australian Federal Labor MP and Minister 9, 20, 212, 329, 342–343, 392

Greater London, government of 90, 163, 255, 277, 352

Greenberg, Stanley, US pollster 56

Greenham Common Peace Camp 97

Green Party, UK 357, 359, 371–372

Green policies, Germany 372

Green, Sir Philip, former owner BHS 140

Grogan, John MP 28, 31, 36, 50, 134, 138, 142, 149, 152, 156, 163, 168, 205–206, 234, 242, 247, 263, 286, 292, 304–307, 337, 354, 366, 368, 375, 377–378, 417

H

Hain, Peter MP 136, 400, 405

Hardie, Keir MP 110, 184, 187

Harman, Harriet MP 221, 412

Harold Macmillan 92

Hart, Judith MP 333

Hattersley, Roy MP 45, 49, 50, 87, 254, 276, 345

Hayes, Billy, former Communication Workers Union general secretary 26–27, 59, 107, 109, 115, 117, 122–127, 328, 358, 363, 381, 420

Hayward, Ron, Labour Party General Secretary 78, 87, 225, 334

Healey, Denis MP 87–88, 95, 97, 194, 197, 321–323

Health, welfare services and social security, 1945–76 190, 196

Health, welfare services and social security, 1997–2010 202–205 Heffer, Eric MP 324–326, 333

Henderson, Arthur MP 22, 77

Hewitt, Patricia MP 153

Heywood and Middleton by-election, 2014 276, 395, 407

Hill, David 81

Hoey, Kate MP 165

Hopkins, Kelvin MP 28, 33, 35, 37, 46, 62, 65, 72, 135, 138–139, 142, 144, 154, 159, 163, 165, 206, 224, 234, 242, 263, 267, 268, 277, 283, 362, 368–369, 377–378, 381, 383, 390, 392, 417

House of Lords 101, 163–164, 181, 206, 211, 264, 268, 279, 287–288, 291, 299, 303, 308, 308–309, 322, 335, 337, 339, 394, 417

Housing, social rented 17, 27, 33, 141, 172, 191, 207, 215, 284, 310, 347–348, 412

Howells, Kim MP 290, 298 Hughes, Simon MP 90

Hunt, Lord Philip 286

Hunt, Tristram MP 255, 258, 412

Hussein, Saddam 160–161, 180, 181

Hutton Inquiry, Iraq war 53, 68, 160

Hutton, John MP 130, 152

Hydrogen bomb 93

I

Independent Labour Party (ILP) 88, 110–111, 187, 319

India 137, 191, 212, 372, 374, 376

In Place of Strife, white paper, 1969 195, 349

International Monetary Fund loan 83, 194

International Organisations, UK support for 204

International relations and peace policies
  Before New Labour 35, 96, 198
  Under New Labour 11, 37, 39, 132, 158–165, 349, 350, 380

Iraq war 11, 53, 59, 71, 78, 102, 117, 140, 159–161, 182, 183, 198, 206, 210–211, 212, 222, 243, 271–272, 292–293, 297, 302, 305–306, 317, 336, 339, 350, 380, 404, 415

Israel-Arab war 193

J

James, Mark 272

James Purnell 258

Jenkins, Roy MP 87–88, 333
Jennifer's Ear, election broadcast fiasco
100 Johnson, Alan MP 152, 399
Jones, Dr. Lynn MP 15, 27, 31, 47, 49, 52, 54, 60, 66, 144, 149–150, 154, 165, 203, 205, 208–209, 242, 248–251, 287, 291, 305, 307, 339, 352, 357, 359, 371–372, 417
Jones, Graham MP 396, 408–411
Jones, Jack 113, 195

K

Karzai, Hamid, President of Afghanistan 161
Kaufman, Gerald MP 84
Khan, Sadiq 118, 400
Kilfoyle, Peter MP 26, 34, 50, 52, 62, 65, 78, 87, 136, 151, 159, 184, 210, 233, 242, 287, 388, 417
Killeen, Peter 229, 260–261, 419
Kinetic, privatised 210
King, Mervyn 137
Kinnock, Glenys 97
Kinnock, Neil MP 13, 19, 35, 44, 54–55, 66, 86, 92, 96, 103, 196, 220, 323–325, 335, 399, 409
Korean War 76, 93, 192, 210, 350
Korean war, controversial in Labout Party 192, 210

L

Labor Party, Australian 9, 16, 20, 23, 29, 67, 89, 108, 124, 128, 184, 212–214, 304, 307, 315, 316, 317, 329, 330, 341–343, 349, 372, 383, 390, 414
Labour Party
  Aims and values 22–30. *See also* Chapters 1 and 11
  Annual Conference 10, 13–14, 22, 24, 67, 79, 81, 88, 112, 115, 131, 194, 217–218, 223–226, 244–245, 251, 255, 312, 315–316, 318–319, 321, 323, 325, 334, 357, 381, 389, 403, 406
  Charter of Party members' rights 67 History.
  See Chapters 3, 6 and 10
  Leadership issues 82–86
  Liberal Party, coalitions with 22, 77, 195, 319
  Local policy forums 65, 225
  National Constitutional Committee 224, 273
  National Council of Labour, run as by TUC 111, 187, 319
  National Executive Committee 10, 13, 15, 20, 23–24, 57, 65–66, 77–85, 87, 110–111, 121, 217, 223–225, 227, 229, 237, 240, 242, 249, 251–258, 268, 271–278, 284, 312, 318–327, 330, 332, 337, 389, 391, 405–406, 412
    Organisation Sub-Committee 57, 78, 220, 223, 266, 323
  National Policy Forum 17, 45, 65, 125, 127, 154, 217–218, 223–224, 241, 246, 249, 284, 321–322, 354, 388–389, 395, 397, 405
  New Labour
    Changes to Party "democracy" 13–15, 44, 109, 225–226, 327
    Determination of European, Scottish, Welsh and London Assembly candidates 253 Development
    of longstanding core policies 202–204
    Manipulation of PPC selection 251. *See* Chapter 8
    Marginalisation of grass-roots members 24, 65, 218–219, 238–245, 275
    Membership decline under 208
    Methods of operating 44–57
    New Clause 4 10, 16–20, 24, 38, 40, 64, 109, 125, 208, 318, 327, 353, 405. *See* Appendix 2
    Non-economic equalities policies 205
    Party staff, major changes to 228–232
    Policies on poverty in UK 38, 136, 142, 143–145
    Policy failures of Governments 207–211
    Policy record 9–12. *See* Chapter 5
    Talent of parliamentarians squandered 289–296
    Third Way ideology 58, 62, 119, 363
  OMOV, one member one vote 13, 14, 24, 218, 220–225, 238, 249, 255–256, 259, 271, 272, 277–278, 318, 324, 324–328, 388, 412
  Policy commissions 17, 65, 127, 223–225, 242, 245, 324, 397 Joint
  policy commission 223
  Record of pre-1979 Governments 22
  Rules and Organisation. *See* Chapters 7 and 8 Truth

and reconciliation commission, need for 385
Lend-Lease, American 351
Livingstone, Ken MP 200, 205, 237, 324, 352, 401

M

Maastricht Treaty 99, 101
MacDonald, Ramsay MP 77, 88, 111, 121, 187, 332, 338
Macmillan, Harold MP 92
Macmurray, Prof. John, influence on Tony Blair 62
Mahon, Alice MP 27, 33, 34, 50, 52, 61, 86, 138, 143, 146, 151, 153, 161, 202, 209, 235, 243, 244, 248, 262, 265, 286, 292, 298, 303, 337, 357, 369, 374, 378, 379, 380, 417
Major, John MP 13, 29, 85, 92, 103, 105, 114, 184
Malik, Shahid MP 352
Mandelson, Peter MP 6, 14, 21, 32, 44, 51, 60, 65, 76, 80, 81, 84, 85, 117–119, 136, 137, 142, 238, 253, 258, 302, 315, 319, 320, 324, 327, 359, 363, 366, 397, 399
Manpower Services Commission 194
Manufacturing, policies for 19, 97, 118, 133, 210, 211, 346, 350, 351, 369, 371, 375–376, 414
Marjoram, Anni 275
Market Oriented Party 44–49, 75–81, 90–91, 97, 353, 354
Marshall Plan 189, 192, 206, 347, 351
Martin, Michael MP, Speaker of the House and expenses scnadal 165
McCafferty, Christine MP 29, 52, 54, 60, 148, 149, 151, 156, 159, 162, 165, 203, 205, 208, 210, 211, 243, 293, 303, 304, 310, 334, 368, 388, 391, 417
McCluskey, Len 26, 34, 58, 61, 109, 115, 118, 121–123, 127, 129, 227, 363, 369, 375, 405, 420
McDonnell, John MP 26–28, 31, 41, 66, 135, 138, 146, 155, 156, 159, 160, 209, 234, 242, 244, 262, 264, 268, 285, 298, 300, 315, 352, 363, 374, 412, 417
McNulty, Tony MP 293
McTernan, John 407
Meacher, Michael MP 6, 25, 28, 31, 36, 41, 50, 62, 65, 72, 137, 138, 140, 142, 143, 146, 148, 149, 152, 153, 159, 217, 230, 234, 241, 244, 255, 263, 280, 283, 292, 295, 300, 303, 313, 338, 362, 374, 386, 389, 392, 412, 417
Mid-Staffordshire by-election 99
Mikardo, Ian MP 333
Milburn, Alan MP 65, 152–154, 319
Miliband, David MP 238, 254, 289–290, 373, 398, 399
Miliband, Ed MP 18, 45, 49, 51, 69, 86, 102, 104, 118, 123, 220, 254, 276, 304, 327, 357, 383, 395, 395–401, 405–411
Militant Tendency 13, 66, 81, 83, 87, 105, 251, 323
Millennium Dome 298
Minimum wage, national 31, 99, 100, 172, 180, 182, 346, 370, 383
Mitchell, Austin, MP 15, 27, 31, 33, 34, 60, 72, 135, 136, 138, 140, 141, 143, 146, 153, 163, 202, 204, 207, 253, 255, 282, 304, 336, 337, 363, 386, 417
Monks, John, TUC general secretary 121
Monmouth by-election, 1991 99
Morgan, Rhodri MP 237
Morris, Alf MP 196, 334, 353
Morrison, Herbert MP 60, 189, 320, 332
Mountbatten, Lord Louis 191
Mowlam, Mo MP 162, 198, 284
Mullin, Chris MP 34–35, 50, 54, 55, 58, 69, 138, 142, 145, 148, 149, 159, 162, 163, 165, 205–206, 211, 233, 244, 279, 280, 286, 289, 292, 293, 297, 304, 306, 338, 354, 373, 375, 393, 417
Munich Agreement 93
Murfin, Eileen 265–266
Murphy, Jim MP 405, 407

N

Napolitano, Joe, US adviser to Neil Kinnock 56
National Air Traffic Services, privatisation of 155, 248, 306
National Enterprise Board 95, 193, 194, 210, 215, 351
National Government, 1940–45 77, 191, 319
National plan, in 1964 general election manifesto 19, 193
National Union of Mineworkers 276
National Union of Public Employees (NUPE) 123, 220

NATO (North Atlantic Treaty Organisation) 97, 192, 350, 380, 415
NHS, introduction of charges 190, 191
Nigerian (Biafran) civil war, 1967 – 1970 193
Northern Ireland, peace settlement 11, 117, 162–163, 169, 177, 183, 197–198, 206, 215, 349
Nuclear weapons policies, UK, recent 162, 180, 182, 207, 380, 381
Nursery Places, UK, additional, recent 397

O

Oddy, Christine MEP 277
Olympic Torch events, 2012, model for ideal society 118
Omnishambles, Ed Miliband on 2012 budget 403
One Nation speech, Ed Miliband 401, 403
Organization for Economic Co-Operation and Development (OECD) 139, 158 Osborne,
George MP 187, 351, 400
Osborne Judgement (1909) 351 Owen,
Bill, 'Compo' actor 96 Owen, David MP
87

P

Pakistan 191
Palestine 159, 162, 191
Parliamentary candidates, selection of 3, 13, 17, 48, 228, 293, 327, 341, 354, 412. *See* Chapter 8
Parliamentary democracy 9, 332, 341. *See* Chapter 9
Parliamentary Labour Party
  'Gangs' within 295–296
  Rebellions over imited role in policy making 302–307
Parliament, media coverage of 338
Patient choice 153, 175, 202, 209, 215
Pearce, Teresa MP 248, 273
Peston, Robert 140
Pettifor, Ann 273 Phillips, Sir
Hayden 109
Phone hacking scandal 80, 404 Pike, Peter
MP 300
Polaris, re-arming of 199, 338. *See* Chapter 6
Poll tax 82, 99
Prentice, Gordon MP 26, 27, 32, 61, 65, 86, 139, 149, 155, 159, 205, 221, 235, 243, 267, 280, 283, 284, 290, 295, 298–300,
        337–339, 358, 362, 368, 379, 380, 381, 394, 417
Prentice, Reg MP 197
Prentis, Dave, Unison General Secretary 59, 115, 117, 125, 227
Prescott, John 217
Prescott, John MP 21, 86, 100, 109, 146, 217, 249, 295, 326, 348, 352
Price, Lance, former Labour Party communications director 223 Prices and
incomes policy, 1975–6 194, 196
Prisons, in the justice system 384
Private Finance Initiative 60, 140, 150–157, 176, 180, 190, 196, 202–203, 209, 311, 348, 350, 364, 378–379, 414
Privatisations, electricity and gas 114 Product
Oriented Party 46, 76, 80, 106
Proportional Representation, Jenkins Commission on 47, 318
Public ownership 19, 27, 33, 40, 76, 112, 153, 176, 186, 187, 189, 194, 210, 236, 241, 303, 320, 347, 379, 405, 414
Public Sector Borrowing Requirement 209 Public
services
  New Labour, investment in 150–153, 175 Record of
  earlier Labour Governments 347–349
Public trust, loss of 165–455, 208
Purnell. James MP 258, 290

R

Rank and File Mobilising Committee 322
Rather, Dan, CBS news anchor 161 Raynsford,
Nick MP 101

Reagan, Ronald, US President 96–98, 138, 159

Reeves, Rachel MP 400

Refounding Labour 231, 386, 395, 405, 412

Regional development policy 342, 351

Reid, John MP 65, 107, 279, 300, 319, 338

Rhodesia, unilateral declaration of independence 198 Rights, human and related policies 149, 423

Riordan, Linda MP 27, 53, 68, 144, 150, 154, 155, 160, 168, 203, 209, 236, 244, 248, 262, 265, 272, 286, 291, 293, 298, 299, 301, 337, 364, 372, 380, 390, 417, 421

RMT, trade union 61, 109, 118

Rogers, Bill MP 87

Rose, Ron, playwright 276

Rothermere, Lord, media owner 55

Rudd, Kevin, Australian Labor leader 89, 212–214, 341

Rwanda 117

S

Saatchi and Saatchi 95

Sales Oriented Party 46, 76, 80, 82, 90, 106 Salmond, Alex MP 407

Save the Labour Party, pressure group 3, 48, 208, 327, 354

Sawyer, Lord Tom 98, 232, 325

Scanlon, Hugh 113

Scargill, Arthur 96

Scotland, independence referendum 95, 163, 199

Scottish National Party 84, 102, 104, 140, 162, 235, 408, 410

Scottish Parliament 277, 335

SDLP (Social Democratic and Labour Party, N. Ireland) 162

Seddon, Mark 272, 278, 421

Short, Clare MP 27–28, 34–36, 51, 56, 66, 84, 136, 142, 148, 152, 158, 160, 162–163, 165, 185–186, 203, 206, 208, 211, 230, 232, 236, 244, 264, 284, 286, 290, 291, 293, 295, 297, 300, 325, 337, 345, 357, 359, 362, 366, 380, 381, 417

Silkin, John MP 323

Simpson, Alan MP 27, 33–34, 46, 51, 71, 135, 140–142, 144, 155, 157, 160, 203, 209, 236, 244, 255, 262, 285, 293, 303–304, 313, 335, 337–339, 352, 359, 365–366, 371–372, 374–375, 377, 399, 417

Sinn Fein 162

Skinner, Dennis MP 308

Smith, John MP 6, 14–15, 51, 56–57, 59, 71–72, 76, 83–84, 86, 91, 99–101, 163, 220, 244, 255, 273, 275, 295, 325–326, 334, 335, 339, 353

  R.H. Tawney Lecture (1993) 100

Snape Liz, Assistant General Secretary of Unison 27, 34, 59, 114–115, 117, 120, 122–123, 125, 127, 224–225, 227, 358, 363, 420

Social Democratic Party (SDP) 13, 72, 81, 87–88, 96–98, 322

Social mobility 346–348

SPAD (Special Political Adviser) 126, 260, 276

State funding of political parties 48, 109, 121–122

Straw, Jack Lord 149, 202

Stringer, Graham MP 28, 31, 49, 60, 62, 68, 83, 134, 137, 142, 144, 151, 155, 165, 185, 203, 205, 208, 233, 238, 239, 241, 245, 262, 284, 288–289, 292, 299, 301, 306, 366, 366–368, 370, 375, 377, 393, 417

Sure Start (education project) 117, 122, 151, 172, 180–182, 202, 346, 391, 415

Swan, Wayne, Labor Treasurer of Australia 124

Swindon North, candidate selection 265–267

T

Tatchell, Peter 90, 323, 335 Taverne, Dick MP 321

Teesside, steel works 108, 130, 351

TGWU (Transport and General Wotkers Union) 84, 112–113, 122, 146, 195, 320

Thatcher, Margaret MP 17, 98, 118, 184, 369 Todd, Ron, trade union leader 84

Trade Disputes Act (1927) 111

Trades Union Congress (TUC) 80, 96, 100, 110–113, 120–121, 129, 187, 195, 319, 319–321, 332, 349, 383
Trades unions
   Ballots of members, compulsory 113–114, 121, 349
   Industrial relations, 1966–1979 194–196
   Political education 120
   Relationship with Labout Party and Governments 120–127. *See* Chapter 4
   Workers' rights 118–119, 173
Trades unions, Australian 118, 128–129
Tribune Group 196, 295, 332–333
Trickett, Jon MP 319, 393
Trident, nuclear weapons system 162, 177, 182, 207, 226, 325, 381, 388, 408, 415 Turner,
Lord Adair, Chair of Pensions Commission, 2002-4 144

U

UKIP (United Kingdom Independence Party) 140, 163, 235, 382, 402, 407–408 Umunna,
Chuka MP 400
Underhill, Reg, Labour Party National Agent 225 Unemployment,
trends in 13, 94–95, 112, 114, 347, 351, 375
Unison, Trades union 27, 34, 59, 109, 114–115, 117, 122–123, 126, 156, 224–225, 358, 363, 399, 406, 420
Unite, Trades union 26, 34, 58, 61, 109, 115, 118, 122, 122–123, 227, 363, 369, 375–376, 399, 405–406, 420
USDAW (Union of Shop, Distributive and Allied Workers) 220 Ussher,
Kitty MP 254

V

Varley, Eric MP 333
VAT (Value Added Tax) 60, 139, 197, 304, 347, 369
Vietnam, war 198, 210, 225, 350
Voluntaryism, civilian war work policy 112, 188

W

Wales, National Assembly for 163, 237, 255, 277, 334, 335
Wareing, Bob MP 260, 291 Watson, Tom
MP 221
Wealth, redistribution of 19, 25, 32, 58, 133, 145, 368–369, 376, 414 Westland
Helicopters, political crisis 96
Whitelaw, William MP 162 Williams,
Shirley MP 87, 322
Willsman, Peter 4, 224, 248
Wilson, Harold MP 3, 19, 75–77, 82, 94, 112, 184, 185, 193, 197–198, 220, 225, 243, 275, 320, 333
   Assessment of Governments' records 200, 207, 215–216, 353
   International debt, commitment to issue 198
   Vietnam   war   policy   198
Winterton, Rosie MP 400 Women's
suffrage 187
Working family tax credits 180, 397
World War, First 77, 90, 187 Wyatt,
Woodrow MP 194

Those who are, or have been, MPs are indicated as MP.

Printed in Great Britain
by Amazon